D1738651

THE ROOTS OF AMERICAN
INDIVIDUALISM

The Roots of American Individualism

POLITICAL MYTH IN THE AGE OF JACKSON

ALEX ZAKARAS

PRINCETON UNIVERSITY PRESS

PRINCETON & OXFORD

Published by Princeton University Press
41 William Street, Princeton, New Jersey 08540
99 Banbury Road, Oxford OX2 6JX

press.princeton.edu

All Rights Reserved

ISBN: 978-0-691-22631-6
ISBN (e-book): 978-0-691-22630-9

British Library Cataloging-in-Publication Data is available

Editorial: Rob Tempio and Chloe Coy
Production Editorial: Jenny Wolkowicki
Jacket design: Karl Spurzem
Production: Erin Suydam
Publicity: James Schneider and Carmen Jimenez

Jacket image: Winslow Homer - Woodcutter 1891. Artefact / Alamy Stock Photo

This book has been composed in Arno

Printed on acid-free paper. ∞

Printed in the United States of America

10 9 8 7 6 5 4 3 2 1

For Tess

CONTENTS

ACKNOWLEDGMENTS

IN THE EIGHT YEARS it took me to write this book, I benefited immensely from the help and generosity of others. I had four terrific undergraduate research assistants, each of whom contributed valuable evidence and detail to the manuscript: Sophia Billias, Brendan Hersey, Carrie Madden, and Audrey Oliver.

My colleagues and my department at the University of Vermont have been consistently supportive and encouraging. I want to thank Bob Taylor and Patrick Neal in particular, who helped me think through all stages of this project and who read and commented on drafts of each and every chapter. Amani Whitfield offered me very helpful advice and feedback on many different parts of the manuscript. Melanie Gustafson gave me incisive comments on chapter 10 and pointed me toward relevant literatures.

I received funding from the University of Vermont's Humanities Center, whose support in 2019–20 allowed me to make valuable progress on the manuscript in its later stages. I also benefited from a generous grant from the Louis Rakin Foundation, which enabled me to organize a manuscript workshop in 2019. I'm grateful to the Yale Department of Political Science and to Steven Smith in particular for hosting me during my sabbatical in 2013–14.

A number of scholars beyond UVM read part or all of the manuscript, and I learned a great deal from their comments and suggestions. I want to thank Joshua Lynn most of all for his sustained and detailed comments on the entire manuscript. Josh was exceptionally generous with his time—and his considerable expertise—over the last several years. Along with Amani and Josh, Harry Watson, Jason Frank, and Timothy Breen also participated in my manuscript workshop in the summer of 2019, and each gave me excellent feedback and advice—I am very grateful to all three. Many others have read and commented on chapters of the manuscript over the years, including Will Barndt, Eric Beerbohm, Josh Cherniss, Yiftah Elazar, Bryan Garsten, Lisa Gilson, Michael

Lienesch, Luke Mayville, Susan McWilliams, Danilo Petranovich, Jim Read, Jeff Sklansky, Steven Smith, and Jack Turner.

I am deeply grateful to the librarians at the University of Vermont's Howe Library, who provided substantial help and support throughout this project. I am especially indebted to Lisa Brooks and Sarah Paige, who tracked down countless obscure sources for me.

Special thanks, also, to Rob Tempio at Princeton University Press, who believed in this book and helped me bring it to fruition, and to the press's anonymous reviewers, whose thoughtful comments helped me improve and reshape the book in important ways.

Portions of chapter 7 were previously published in Alex Zakaras, "Nature, Religion, and the Market in Jacksonian Political Thought," *Journal of the Early Republic* 39, no. 1 (2019): 123–133, and appear courtesy of the Society for Historians of the Early American Republic and the University of Pennsylvania Press.

This book reflects the influence of a great many teachers who have influenced my thinking over the years and inspired my love for the history of ideas. In particular: Tom Goepel, Joel Greifinger, Pratap Mehta, Tyler Roberts, Louis Miller, Philip Fisher, Seyla Benhabib, Jonathan Allen, George Kateb, Stephen Macedo, Jeff Stout, Philip Pettit, Charles Taylor, and both my parents, who are gifted and passionate teachers in their own right.

Finally, I would be nowhere without the love and support of my family: my wife, Tess, and daughter, Charlotte, my parents, and my brother Michael. Every day, they remind me of what's really important. They also contributed significantly to the book itself: Mom's trained editorial eye helped me figure out the book's structure and draw out its main storylines; countless conversations with Dad pushed me to sharpen and refine my ideas; Tess lovingly protected my research time, even through the pandemic's stresses, and her astute questions and insights helped me improve the book in many ways.

1

Introduction

THE FREE INDIVIDUAL has long dominated the American political imagination. To this day, we often envision the sovereign individual standing proudly against an array of encroaching forces: big government, big corporations, intolerant majorities. In one leading version of this drama, these antagonists threaten our rights. They want to control our bodies or our sexuality, take away our guns, invade our property and our privacy, or push us to violate our conscience. Victory, in such struggles, is imagined as a defense of individual dignity and freedom against unwanted intrusion.

Another prominent variation pits individual merit and effort against unearned privilege. As a culture, we lionize the entrepreneur whose initiative and talent bring new value into the world and the modest self-starter who rises, through tireless effort, from poverty to the middle class. We celebrate these figures because of what they have individually accomplished, and we resent those who would lay claim to their hard-earned rewards. In the popular imagination, these claimants come in many guises: they include overzealous regulators imposing their own visions of the common good, wealthy oligarchs using political influence to absorb more than their rightful share, and the poor pressing collectively for state benefits. All are commonly presented as potential threats to the meritocratic order of American society, which is supposed to leave individuals free to make their own way.

We also imagine a perpetual social and political struggle against personal dependence. Our most treasured marker of independence is property: we celebrate home owners, small farmers, and small business owners—all masters of their own private domains—as archetypes of self-reliance. On the other hand, we are embarrassed by young adults who live with their parents, by welfare recipients, by unpaid debts, and by old age itself and the many forms of dependence it augurs. Our debates over social policy are often framed around encouraging people to "stand on their own two feet."

These narratives are more prominent on the political right than the left, but their prevalence there has long tilted the balance of public opinion. Surveys have shown that unlike our counterparts in Europe, Americans would rather enjoy the freedom "to pursue . . . life's goals without interference from the state" than see their government take "an active role in society so as to guarantee that no one is in need." These political views are reinforced by a scaffolding of other, related convictions. Americans are far more likely, for example, to reject the view that personal success is "determined by forces outside our control" and to affirm that people can rise out of poverty on their own.[1] Many American Christians, meanwhile, believe the Bible teaches that "God helps those who help themselves."[2] Such notions have broad ramifications for the shape of American public policy, from health care and social welfare to taxation to speech and gun rights. They contribute to a libertarian tilt that distinguishes the United States from most other affluent democracies.

Even the center-left bears their mark. Leading Democratic politicians often speak of boundless opportunities and unparalleled personal freedom as the birthrights of all Americans. They may warn that these opportunities have lately been imperiled by corporate greed, stagnant wages, and yawning inequalities. They may denounce the long-standing racism and patriarchy that have curtailed many Americans' freedoms. But they, too, exalt the autonomous, upwardly mobile individual earning his or her place in a meritocratic society.

How and why did these tendencies rise to dominance in America? How and why, in other words, did so many Americans come to think in these terms about their politics and society? In addressing these questions, this book advances three main arguments. First, it shows that these ideas took hold in the Jacksonian Era (1820–50). Historians of political thought tend to see Jacksonian America as a fairly barren landscape, sandwiched between the epochal events of the founding and the Civil War. This book contends, instead, that it should be regarded as a seminal time—in some ways *the* seminal time—in forming the popular political narratives that continue to permeate our political life. Second, rather than treating American individualism as a single dogma or creed, this book presents it as a set of three overlapping myths, each containing its own idea of personal freedom and its own distinctive story of American exceptionalism. These myths have served as potent sources of shared meaning and identity, and their variety and flexibility help explain why they have appealed to so many different constituencies over time. Third, this book argues that American individualism harbors profoundly utopian aspirations that still influence our politics today. Historians have often described it as a fundamentally *practical* outlook, a preoccupation with moneymaking combined with a visceral intolerance of authority. In fact, the power of individualist rhetoric has derived, time and again, from long-standing utopian dreams embedded within. Let us consider each of these arguments in more detail.

The rise of individualism in Jacksonian America was precipitated by two great changes that convulsed Americans' lives and reshaped the way they thought about their society and politics. One of these was the advent of mass democracy. In the decades following Thomas Jefferson's election to the presidency in 1800, popular participation in state and federal elections rose dramatically and property qualifications for white male voters fell away. Modern political parties took shape, led by a new class of professional politicians, and rolled out campaigns designed to mobilize a mass electorate. As all white men came to feel entitled to a political voice, they shattered the deferential tone that had ruled American political life throughout the eighteenth century. *Democracy*, a term that had aroused suspicion among the nation's founders, became their political watchword.[3]

These same years also brought transformative economic change, fostered by a combination of new technologies, ambitious infrastructure projects, cheap and expanding credit, and booming demand for domestic products and services. Their cumulative effect was to link America's local and regional economies into an integrated system that reshaped the lives of millions of producers—both free and enslaved—who formed its backbone. In the North, small farmers produced surpluses designed for sale to distant markets and calibrated their decisions to the market's price signals. They sold more goods for cash, which they could then use to buy the consumer products—from fabrics and hats to furniture and musical instruments—that flooded into the American inland on canal barges, steamboats, and rail cars. Their economic lives were less and less governed by the interpersonal bonds that had anchored local economies for generations, and increasingly structured by impersonal competition and contract. Americans were becoming aware that they belonged to an economic *system* whose impersonal laws and norms affected everyone, for good or ill.[4] In the South, these same forces accelerated cotton production for the global market and intensified the domestic slave trade, forcing a million Black men, women, and children further west into the southern heartland.[5]

These transformations changed the way white Americans thought about themselves and their country: between 1820 and 1850, both democracy and the market were woven into the very idea of America. Increasingly, these were the institutions that Americans invoked to illustrate their society's remarkable progress and to demonstrate its superiority. The United States, they argued, was the only democracy in the world, an egalitarian political beacon that others were destined to follow. It was also, they alleged, home to a uniquely free, dynamic, and meritocratic market economy in which people reaped the rewards of their own work without unwanted political interference. Together, these two generalizations underwrote the widely shared conviction that Americans enjoyed liberties unknown and even unimagined in other parts of the world.

These changes also shifted the way Americans understood their freedoms. In an affluent and fluid society exploding with opportunity for young whites, freedom was increasingly understood as a feature of private life: it was associated more and more with the individual's control over his own work, his private enjoyment of rights against government, his ability to rise through the social ranks through effort and discipline. Many began to see the burgeoning market economy as freedom's natural domain. Moreover, in a far-flung, decentralized society long suspicious of government control, democracy was often imagined as a way of curtailing the power of political elites while empowering ordinary people to defend their rights. Both were increasingly seen as means of shielding the sovereign individual from unwanted interference.

Although these individualistic tendencies originated much earlier, the Jacksonian Era saw them coalesce into a set of powerful political myths that would shape American political thought and rhetoric for generations to come. If the founding was the formative period for America's constitutional structure, Jacksonian America—the so-called "Era of the Common Man"—was the crucible for American political myth.[6] Beginning in the 1820s, a new class of political entrepreneurs successfully reformulated the founders' patrician political ideas for a more democratic age; in doing so, they infused them with the free-market optimism that had only gradually penetrated American consciousness in the early decades of the nineteenth century. The vast expansion of print culture that brought cheap newspapers into so many American homes ensured that these new ideas circulated widely to a mass electorate.[7]

As this book traces the sources of these intellectual shifts, it focuses substantially on the Jacksonian Democrats. In recent decades, Andrew Jackson and his political party have fallen out of favor, and for good reason. They built American democracy on a foundation of racial hierarchy and Native American genocide. They weaponized white supremacy as a populist, political cause in ways that still infect our politics today. But their intellectual legacy does not end there: through their wide-ranging attitudes about the economy, the role of government, and the nature of democratic politics, they bequeathed a broad and varied set of political ideas. They were the period's most successful conceptual innovators and political myth-makers, and this book therefore pays particular attention to the ways in which Jacksonian Democrats interpreted the political ideas of the founding generation and reformulated them for a mass electorate.[8]

The book's second main argument is that American individualism has been expressed and transmitted, across nearly two hundred years, by three powerful political myths: the myth of the independent proprietor, the myth of the rights-bearer, and the myth of the self-made man. Each is best understood as an idealized story about *what America is*. Each assured its audience that America was, above all, an exceptional land of liberty, in which both people and institutions—and even the land itself—were uniquely suited for expansive personal freedom. Each offered a slightly different vision of both the free individual and the dangers that threatened to fetter him, and each drew on a different combination of intellectual traditions.[9]

Over the next ten chapters, we explore how each of these myths shaped American political debates and the ideas that animated them. The myths were not *owned* by any one side in the controversies that roiled Jacksonian politics—rather, they came to define a shared terrain on which anyone hoping for a broad audience was constrained to argue. They coursed through the political rhetoric of conservatives and reformers alike, and they even infused the self-consciously radical perspectives of abolitionists and early feminists. Their dominance ensured that all sides were competing to position themselves as the true defenders of individual liberty.

In discussing these myths, we pay particular attention to the themes of inclusion and exclusion. All three myths were variously used to fix the boundary between insiders and outsiders, between *us* and *them*. They defined a deeply felt sense of national identity and purpose, which set Americans apart, in their own eyes, from the Old World. They also shaped the content of both whiteness and masculinity: as historians have firmly established, individualist ideas were repeatedly used to construct archetypes of white male character and identity against which subordinate groups were defined and contrasted. White men insisted that women and people of color lacked the innate characteristics required to thrive as autonomous persons in a free society and a rugged, competitive economy. They were therefore destined for subordination—or, in the case of Native Americans, for extinction. In this way, paradoxically, individualist ideas underwrote an expansionist politics of white male supremacy, premised on innate group superiority, that was anything but individualistic.

At the same time, those pressing for greater inclusion turned to the same myths to challenge racial and gender hierarchies. Abolitionists and feminists decried what they saw as a caste society that awarded privileges to white men regardless of their individual merits or attributes. Feminists insisted that women were amply qualified for independent property ownership and entitled to live autonomous lives. Abolitionists, meanwhile, deployed an inclusive ideal of individual rights to highlight both America's hypocrisy and its unrealized moral potential. Both mobilized America's individualist myths to try to relocate the boundary between citizens and subordinates and promote a more inclusive vision of the American nation. In the ensuing chapters, then, we explore how American individualism has been harnessed to both expand and contract the boundaries of moral and political community.

Finally, this book argues that America's individualistic myths have often conveyed a utopian vision of American society. All three have described America as the site of an emergent, harmonious order in which people are rewarded for hard work, self-discipline, and personal virtue. All three have also attributed this meritocratic order to God or nature. According to these myths, the United States is unique in escaping the profane and "artificial" hierarchies of the Old World. It is a nation in which autonomous individuals, directed by the hand of a benevolent God, produce their own fair and prosperous equilibria, so long as government lets them flourish unimpeded.

Although these utopian ideas have taken several different forms, they have found most consistent expression in the idea of the free market, which was widely popularized in the Jacksonian Era and which has deeply shaped the terms of American political debate ever since. For so many Americans, the inchoate sense that the market embodied a natural and providential order essentially removed it from the list of threats to human freedom. To suffer losses, defeats, or constraints because of the spontaneous agency of the market was a kind of misfortune, not a kind of oppression. On the other hand, to suffer setbacks at the hands of government regulators was to be deprived of liberty; it was a call to arms. This fundamental asymmetry, firmly grounded in utopian assumptions, has had profound implications for the trajectory of political ideas into the twentieth century and beyond.

There is nothing new, of course, in the suggestion that free-market ideology in America is laced with utopian dreams. This book helps us understand how these dreams were born and how they acquired such a hold on the American imagination. It helps us excavate the origins of the ideological patterns that still hold so many of us in thrall. It shows, among other things, how they were facilitated by important transformations in American political and religious thought in the first half of the nineteenth century.

It should be clear, by now, that this book does not strictly withhold judgment of its subject matter. While parts 1 through 3 are devoted to a careful exploration of individualist ideas in the Jacksonian Era, part 4 offers a critical evaluation of the period's intellectual legacies. In so doing, it draws attention to both the pathologies and potentials of American individualism. The pathologies lie mostly in its exclusivity, its latent utopianism, and its nationalist triumphalism, all of which have helped rationalize or conceal exploitation and injustice. Its potentials, on the other hand, lie in the dissenting countercurrents that have opened paths for greater equality and inclusion.

In the mid-twentieth century, an influential group of historians argued that American political culture has been thoroughly individualistic since the Revolution, if not earlier. They argued, for example, that the Declaration of Independence and the catalog of rights enshrined in state and federal constitutions already placed the individual at the center of the political universe. They suggested that the framers' unapologetic commercialism, reflected for example in the *Federalist Papers* and the thriving export economies of the eastern seaboard, foreshadowed the nation's headlong embrace of competitive capitalism. They also pointed to several features of white male society in eighteenth-century America, including its wide-open economic opportunities, its cultural and religious fragmentation, and the relative absence of feudal or aristocratic institutions, as fertile ground for individualist assumptions. They maintained that American individualism—some preferred the term "liberalism"[10]—formed a fundamental consensus or creed that has defined and limited American political thought throughout the nation's history.[11]

Six decades of sustained scholarly criticism have exposed this argument's shortcomings. In the 1960s, historians began challenging the "consensus" interpretation of American history by drawing attention to the powerful, anti-individualist narratives that still coursed through sermons, pamphlets, and speeches in late eighteenth-century America. They pointed, for example, to the ubiquitous Protestant drama of the sinful self whose unruly appetites and natural selfishness need constraining by the virtuous community. Or they highlighted an even older, neoclassical story that presents individual ambition and self-interest as the leading threats to a free and stable republic. Both of these commonplace variants featured a central struggle between the corrupt or anarchic individual and a harmonious social order overseen by both church and state. Some of these revisionist historians also emphasized the vast powers that state and local governments routinely claimed over Americans' private lives well into the nineteenth century.[12]

In subsequent decades, intellectual historians broadened these criticisms by highlighting the diversity of American political ideas in the nineteenth and twentieth centuries too. They showed, for example, how the Protestant "politics of sin" has continually shaped mainstream American politics. From the antebellum Temperance movement to the Reagan-era War on Drugs and mass incarceration, political movements seeking moral reform and control have used the American state(s) to invade private life and restrict individual liberty.[13] Historians have also spent the last forty years unearthing the powerful white supremacist and patriarchal ideas that have both influenced and circumscribed American individualism throughout the country's history. The systematic marginalization and oppression of women and people of color over the last two centuries reflect powerful and resiliently collectivist features of the national *ethos*. Each of these countertraditions—and others, including the social gospel that flourished in the late nineteenth century and helped shape the Progressive movement—has competed and intermingled with liberal individualism to create a far more complex and varied intellectual landscape than the midcentury historians allowed.[14]

This book does not attempt to resuscitate the consensus interpretation of American political or intellectual history. Rather, it suggests a different way of approaching the phenomenon that interested the consensus historians: the long-standing, preponderant influence of individualist ideas in American politics. It suggests that we approach this influence not by positing the existence of a timeless American creed but by studying three potent national myths that coalesced at a particular period in American history, that emerged gradually out of prior patterns of thought, and that shifted and adapted over time as they were appropriated by different political groups and applied to different policy controversies. It explores how these myths sometimes conflicted with one another, and how they interacted with—and sometimes infiltrated and intermingled with—the competing, anti-individualistic currents of thought that have also shaped American political culture since its inception. In pursuing this more modest strategy, it reaffirms some of the valuable insights of the midcentury historians without exaggerating their explanatory reach.

Several further clarifications are worth offering about what this book *is not*. It does not attempt a complete history of American political thought in the Jacksonian Era. It has little to say, for example, about the overtly aristocratic proslavery ideas that emanated from the deep South during this period; it does not explore the important constitutional debates over states' rights and the limits of federal authority; nor does it study the political ideas of utopian socialists or Transcendentalists. These exclusions are not arbitrary or accidental. They are guided by two broad criteria: first, since this book's subject is American individualism, its main goal is to explore those intellectual strains that have contributed directly to it. Second, with the exception of chapter 3, the ensuing chapters focus on *popular* currents of thought—that is, on political ideas that were widely shared. This is not a book mainly about intellectuals: the stories explored here are drawn largely from popular sources, including newspapers, public speeches, sermons, and magazines.[15] They are also drawn, as much as possible, from representative sources: that is, from sources that either circulated widely or that reflected widespread ideological patterns. Since political parties were the dominant institutions shaping popular political ideas in the Jacksonian Era, they receive a great deal of attention throughout the book. Time and again, we look to partisan newspapers, election pamphlets, and political speeches to understand the dominant narratives that shaped the political outlooks of millions of voters, forged partisan identities, and brought citizens to the polls in record numbers.

The list of political myths explored in this book is not meant to be exhaustive. In fact, the three myths detailed here form part of a broader constellation of national myths that has shaped the American self-image across the centuries, including the democratic myth of Americans as a uniquely self-governing people, the Protestant myth of America as a community of saints dedicated to the moral and spiritual regeneration of humankind, and the ethnoracial myth of America as a white or Anglo-Saxon nation carrying the seeds of liberty in its ancestral heritage.[16] This book maintains, however, that the individualist myths have occupied a dominant place in this constellation. Their dominance is evident not only in their ubiquitous appearance in American political rhetoric but also in the way they have influenced the content of these other, competing national stories. Over the course of the next ten chapters, we explore how individualistic ideas have shaped the prevailing conceptions of democracy (chapters 4 and 5) and race (chapters 4, 6, and 11), and how they have also suffused the idea of America as a Godly nation (chapters 7, 8, and 9).

Since this is a book about political myth, it is necessarily about idealization and misrepresentation. The individualist myths studied here have consistently described American society as a collection of autonomous and enterprising individuals making their own way in the world. In doing so, they have under-emphasized the many forms of community that have in fact structured and enveloped so many American lives. They have sidelined families, kinship groups and ethnocultural identities, rich traditions of local and communal self-governance, as well as the churches, clans, unions, and fraternal groups to which Americans have consistently turned for fellowship, solidarity, and iden-tity. In presenting stylized representations of the American nation and its poli-tics, the myths have downplayed local diversity and variability.[17] They have also continually deemphasized the role of state and federal governments in shaping American society and its economy. This book explores the powerful influence that these fictionalized narratives have exerted over American poli-tics; it does not take them at face value.

Although political myth is the book's main subject matter, it is not *only* about political myth. It is also about the intellectual traditions out of which America's individualist myths were constructed. They were not invented out of whole cloth: popular political myths invariably borrow values, concepts, and narrative elements that already resonate widely among the national popu-lation. Over the course of the book, we explore how the three individualist myths absorbed ideas from a neoclassical republican tradition that circulated widely among transatlantic elites; from Protestant theology and its anti-authoritarian popularizations in the early nineteenth century; from the radical, egalitarian political culture that had long flourished among urban artisans in both England and its colonies; and from Scottish Enlightenment ideas that had reshaped the American view of God and human society alike. We trace the ways in which these and other diverse intellectual currents were combined and reworked into popular political narratives that were then deployed to shape public opinion and win elections. We pay close attention, in other words, to the intellectual contexts that allowed these particular myths to be-come popular and powerful.

This book does not present individualism as a uniquely American phenom-enon. Comparable patterns of ideas can be found in Australian and Canadian political culture, for example (although they are somewhat less prominent there). Moreover, the ensuing chapters detail how American individualism has been shaped by transnational currents of thought, including British economic ideas, which were simplified, sacralized, and repurposed for the American electorate during the Jacksonian Era. While this book does highlight the differences between American and European political cultures in the nineteenth century, and while it explores the particularity of American individualism in some detail, nowhere does it suggest that the United States is somehow categorically distinct from other human societies.

Finally, this book is about ideas, and as such it offers only partial explanations of American political history and development. While it does assume that ideas exert some independent influence on political behavior, it certainly does not assume that they *determine* behavior. In fact, as the following chapters repeatedly suggest, ideas are influenced by—and interact with—a host of other factors, including geography and demography, economic and technological forces, the dynamics of class and party formation, and other cultural and political institutions. Together, these factors shape political behavior and, subsequently, the course of political history.[18] It follows that the content of American political ideas, and the myths in which they are encoded, tells only part of the story of why American politics developed the way it has.

2

Foundational Myths

There is no way to give us an understanding of any society, including our own, except through the stock of stories which constitute its initial dramatic resources. Mythology, in its original sense, is at the heart of things.

—ALASDAIR MACINTYRE[1]

THE TERM "MYTH" is often used to connote falsehood. To describe a political claim or story as a *myth*, in this sense, is to mark it as untrue or fabricated. In this book, "myth" has a different meaning: broadly speaking, a political myth is a widely accepted story that is used to make sense of political events and experiences.[2] Such myths can be true or false; they typically weave together elements of both. They are defined above all by the function they serve: they offer simple storylines that reduce the chaos and complexity of political life to familiar patterns. They do this, typically, by staging moral dramas and projecting them onto political and historical events.[3] Although their explicit subject matter may lie in the distant past, political myths remain myths only so long as they give meaning to the present.[4]

In the modern world, the most powerful political myths are those that describe the origins and character of the nation itself, or *foundational myths*. Foundational myths construct a glorified image of a national people and present it as a worthy object of devotion and sacrifice. They tell a story of national origins that illustrates its people's basic values or character traits. These include economic and religious virtues, political values, imagined ethnic or racial traits, idealized cultural attributes, and more. Such qualities are typically highlighted through a contrast with some threatening other—some antagonist or rival, or some source of pollution or decay against which struggle was and is necessary. Because such struggle requires leadership, foundational myths also tend to offer an account of political authority; that is, they explain who speaks for the nation collectively, who its natural or appropriate leaders are.[5]

Such myths answer to a range of political and psychological needs. Politically, they serve as centripetal forces holding the national community together under an established institutional order. As Western nation-states consolidated in the late eighteenth and nineteenth centuries, they faced the immense political challenge of creating new forms of collective identity, of fusing often diverse and far-flung groups with competing cultural, ethnic, and religious attachments into a cohesive national *people*. They also faced the ongoing challenge of holding this people together through the economic turbulence and growing inequality of the industrial age. Foundational myths helped weaken these sources of conflict and fracture by subsuming potentially disruptive forms of group identity—including class and religious identity—into a unified national solidarity. In doing so, they also encouraged the habits of compliance and cooperation required by all stable nation-states.[6] They were deployed, first of all, by the political and economic elites who aspired to unify and govern these emerging political communities.

Foundational myths derive their power and resilience, however, from another source: they also answer to deeply felt psychological needs, notably the need to live in a meaningful world.[7] The modern state and the economy it regulates exert tremendous, structuring power over individual lives, yet their inner workings can seem mysterious and arbitrary. Like the cosmos itself, they often appear indifferent to the rhythms and travails of ordinary life. Myths help dispel this indifference. They not only render the political world intelligible, they also present it as an unfolding drama, with clear moral stakes, in which their believers are called to play a role. Political myths *orient* people, in other words, in a field of friends and enemies, heroes and villains, and invite them to take action in pursuit of imagined triumphs. Like sacred myths, they help human beings feel at home in the world.[8]

Myth could not possibly serve these functions without shaping political thought and belief.[9] In conjuring up a people with a certain imagined history and character, foundational myths explain which political commitments *belong* to them and which are alien. In doing so, they make believers receptive to certain kinds of political argument while skeptical of others. Even more fundamentally, these myths shape the way their adherents perceive the landscape of politics itself. In dramatizing the national people's epic struggle with antagonistic peoples or forces, foundational myths define the dominant storylines that help people make sense of both triumphs and setbacks. They bring certain actors to the fore even as they conceal or ignore others. In these ways, they structure a nation's political consciousness and render themselves relatively impervious to rational argument.

Land of Liberty: Myth-Making in the Early Republic

The need for a set of unifying myths was urgently felt in the young American republic. In the decades between the Revolution and the Civil War, political elites struggled to articulate the terms of a shared American nationality. They were well aware of the obstacles they faced: until recently, Americans had proudly identified as British subjects, inheritors of a unique slate of English liberties; they were also divided by state and regional loyalties that were often stronger than their allegiance to the nation.[10] In many places, moreover, the population was a patchwork of immigrant groups separated by cultural, religious, and ethnic differences.[11] For these reasons and others, the Constitution's framers had worried that interstate conflict and other centrifugal pressures might yet rip the United States apart. Famously, the Constitution's opening words—"We the people of the United States"—reflected a self-conscious attempt to construct or imagine a unified national public and relocate sovereign authority in its will, rather than in the separate states. The framers were struggling to tell a cohesive story of national unity, and this struggle only intensified in the ensuing decades, as national elites tried to defuse the recurrent sectional crises that threatened to permanently divide North from South.[12]

The dominant myths they deployed to meet these challenges told a story of liberation and rebirth. In countless Fourth of July orations, sermons, newspaper editorials, and campaign speeches, Americans were told that their nation was born out of an epochal struggle for liberty. It was much larger than a battle between the British crown and its restive colonies; it was a struggle between the Old World and the New. The Old World stood for oppression and hierarchy, which arose out of long-standing corruption and decadence. Its once-promising ideals had grown frail and tarnished through centuries of misrule. The New World, on the other hand, held out a once-in-history opportunity for Western civilization to shed its accumulated infirmities, to rise again in the strength and purity of its youth, and to set out on a new, free trajectory.

This narrative of rebirth appeared in several different forms, as the restoration of a truer Christianity, of a long-lost Saxon freedom, or of the republican ideals of Greek and Roman antiquity. It was almost always clothed in religious significance: the West had squandered its God-given opportunity to realize freedom on earth, and the New World was its (only) second chance. It was here, in America, that human freedom would either reach its zenith or wither and die. "We cannot admit the thought, that this country is to be only a repetition of the old world," wrote William Ellery Channing, a leading Unitarian preacher and theologian, in 1830. "We delight to believe that God, in the fulness of time, has brought a new continent to light, in order that the human mind should move here with a new freedom, should frame new social institutions, should explore new paths, and reap new harvests."[13] His view was typical: over and over, Americans celebrated their country as the land of the free, the refuge for the oppressed, the place where people could—at long last—lay claim to the liberties that were their natural birthright.[14] Over and over, they presented it as an exceptional nation, not just different than any other place on earth but destined to lead or redeem humankind.

If governing elites often deployed this mythology for their own purposes, however, it also escaped their control.[15] In the wide-open, decentralized media environment of the early American republic, a broad range of dissenting politicians, factions, and movements laid claim to it for themselves. These included workingmen's advocates condemning wage labor as a violation of American freedom; Anti-Masons assailing Freemasonry as a secretive, aristocratic cabal that stood deeply at odds with America's republican principles; free-soil activists decrying the expanding reach of slavery in national politics; and evangelical reformers lamenting drunkenness, Sabbath-breaking, and unrepentant materialism as fundamental threats to free society. All accused governing elites of endangering or betraying America's exceptional freedom; all positioned themselves as its natural defenders. In the most radical instances—in certain abolitionist circles, for example—America's foundational myths were inverted and thrown back against the American Constitution itself as challenges to its very legitimacy.[16]

These foundational myths are best understood, therefore, as offering a shared grammar of political argument and counterargument, a reservoir of key values, symbols, and imagery that anyone bidding for power and influence had to harness. They supplied the key symbolic and narrative tools that could, if skillfully wielded, reshape public opinion and mobilize the electorate. And yet their versatility was not limitless. Even as they generated diverse and contested interpretations, they also constrained the range of plausible alternatives. They provided avenues for challenge to the status quo and at the same time limited the range of political goals and strategies that reformers could embrace without alienating their political audiences.[17]

Three Visions of Individual Freedom

Three foundational myths were especially prominent in the political rhetoric of Jacksonian America. Each offered a variation of the narrative of liberation and rebirth, premised on a sharp contrast with the Old World. Each featured its own mythic hero: the independent proprietor, the rights-bearer, and the self-made man. These three figures, endlessly acclaimed in Jacksonian political life and letters, displayed three subtly different visions of the free individual and three corresponding, idealized portraits of the American nation and its people.[18]

THE INDEPENDENT PROPRIETOR. The first myth described white American society as the province of independent men who controlled their own livelihoods: they owned the land they cultivated or the small business they operated. They did not depend on the patronage or good favor of some powerful landlord or master. They were their own men, and in this sense they were free. The Old World, by contrast, was seen as a site of dependence, exemplified by the feudal serf who worked at his lord's discretion or the desperate factory worker toiling under his boss's thumb, without any meaningful control over his own labor. Such economic subservience was widely described, in Jacksonian America, as a form of "slavery."

In the dominant, agrarian version of this myth, it was *land* that set America apart from Europe: with its vast western "wilderness" promising a nearly endless supply of fertile soil to cultivate, the American continent could house millions of small farmers and nourish the distinctive political values that came naturally to them.[19] It told the story of so many European immigrants who were reborn in America when they took possession of their own farms. Freed from dependence, they could speak their own mind and think for themselves. They could embrace a natural skepticism of authority. They could also gather as social equals to deliberate about public affairs. In all of these ways, they were well suited for democracy: it was *because* they were independent, many Americans believed, that they were capable of self-government.

THE RIGHTS-BEARER. The second myth imagined that Americans were united by a shared desire to secure their natural rights against political oppression. It told of a land originally peopled by exiles fleeing religious persecution, who came to America to live, work, and worship in peace. Their most iconic rights, therefore, were the rights of religious conscience and association, though these were joined by many others, including rights to free expression, property ownership, and fair legal procedures. Like the first myth, this one was fundamentally about freedom: it told the story of a long-awaited human emancipation from bondage.[20] What distinguished Americans, as a people, from the rest of the world was their ardent and uncompromising devotion to liberty, which had been transmitted through the generations, from the earliest Puritan exiles. But the ideal of liberty presented here was slightly different: it was freedom from political and ecclesiastical oppression, not mainly from economic dependence.

Like the first myth, this one too derived much of its power from a sharp contrast between the New World and the Old. It described human history as a nearly unbroken litany of political oppressions: except for a few brilliant but ephemeral exceptions, human beings had always stood at the mercy of their rulers, who could use up and destroy their lives at their pleasure. America alone, it claimed, had broken this long-standing pattern. The American founders, distilling the libertarian folkways of colonial life, had installed individual rights as the highest purpose of government. The myth of the rights-bearer held up the Declaration of Independence, with its assertion that governments were created to secure certain self-evident rights, as a decisive affirmation of this new reality. So long as Americans remained true to their defining convictions, then, their government could remain something new under the sun: a mere tool in service of the sovereign individual, a guarantor and enforcer of his natural freedoms.

THE SELF-MADE MAN. The third myth imagined America as a pure meritocracy. Like the other two, it began with a vivid contrast: whereas all other societies were marked by sharp caste hierarchies that defined, from birth, who and what every individual could be, no such hierarchies existed in America—certainly not for white men. Instead, the myth taught that American society was fluid and classless, and everyone had to earn their place in it through personal effort and achievement. In the United States, hard work, ingenuity, and perseverance were rewarded, while laziness, indiscipline, and wastefulness were punished. Those who failed to get ahead therefore had no one but themselves to blame. On the other hand, those who succeeded earned that special, highly individualized form of esteem owed to the person who makes his own luck.

This myth was partly about justice: it imagined America as a uniquely *just* society, for it gave individuals what they deserved, no more and no less. But it was also, of course, about the individual's freedom to be who he wanted to be, to leave his humble beginnings behind and make something of himself. It told of a land settled by enterprising migrants eager for an opportunity to make their own way in the world, to leave behind the strict social and economic limits of the Old World and rise as far as their effort and talent would take them. In the figure of the self-made man, then, this myth offered a third vision of individual freedom: the freedom to fashion one's own life and identity, to be the "architect of one's own fortunes."[21]

These three mythic figures were never wholly separate. The small proprietor owed his independence partly to property rights, which secured his dominion over his own private patch of earth; he was therefore simultaneously a rights-bearer. Property ownership, meanwhile, was celebrated as a path to social mobility: cheap land in the West, especially, was thought to provide pathways to the middle class for so many poor white immigrants and wage workers. In this sense, the mythic small proprietor was also a self-made man, rising to respectability through hard work, initiative, and courage. The rights-bearer and the self-made man converged, too: rights were often held up as shields that prevented governments or economic elites from foreclosing the opportunities that would allow ordinary people to shape their own lives. Finally, all three mythic protagonists were almost always imagined to be white Protestant men, and all three of these ideals of freedom were routinely understood to be the prerogatives of this privileged group.

These three myths are best understood, therefore, as offering three different *versions* of the sovereign individual who dominated the American imagination during the Jacksonian Era. Each myth foregrounded different aspects of his character and circumstances. Together, they lent the ideal of American freedom a richness and flexibility that helped make it truly ubiquitous in the period's political rhetoric. As political leaders, editors, and activists tried to align themselves with the cause of liberty, they constantly invoked one or more of the myths. They argued, for example, that predatory bankers and land speculators were victimizing small farmers and destroying their dream of independent proprietorship. They argued that tariffs, in driving up prices and unfairly subsidizing industrialists, were violating the natural or God-given rights of so many farmers and consumers. They argued that slavery was teaching white Americans to despise manual labor, and so short-circuiting the incentives to work hard and get ahead that encouraged self-made men. In these contexts and so many more, they labored to position themselves as champions of America's exceptional freedom and show that their opponents were betraying it. They channeled the myths, and the myths shaped the content of their political appeals.

Specifically, these three foundational myths framed political debates in sharply individualistic terms. They did so, first, by asserting the moral and political priority of relatively *private* conceptions of individual freedom. Each located freedom largely within the domain of private choice, ownership, and control, and each uncoupled it from stringent civic or social obligations. Throughout eighteenth-century America, the idea of freedom had carried many competing connotations and meanings.[22] Some of them had linked freedom closely to an ideal of collective self-government that depended on citizens' willingness to be active and self-sacrificing members of the body politic. In the foundational myths that circulated through Jacksonian America, however, these civic connotations had moved into the background. This key shift, which we will explore over the course of the book, coincided with the rise of market society and the popular new economic ideas that accompanied it. As the economic connotations of freedom grew more prominent, the idea of freedom itself was steadily privatized.[23]

Second, all three myths imagined white society as a collection of free and equal individuals, each in control of his own fate. As a number of European observers noticed, Americans tended to imagine not just their government but also their society itself as an association of individuals drawn together by common interests and values and united by contractual agreements. Whereas Europeans generally saw their societies as groupings of social "ranks" or classes bound together in traditional patterns of mutual dependence and obligation, Americans saw things differently.[24] In fact, white Americans in the Jacksonian Era often described the uniqueness of their own society in exactly these terms: in America, they declared, individuals stood apart from inherited group identity or status; they were their own selves, free to go their own way. The idea of America as a nation of immigrants, who chose to emigrate here and to submit themselves to its authority, only reinforced this narrative: in America, the people itself, and not just the constitution or government, could be imagined as an artifact of consent.

One of the inferences that seemed to follow naturally from this conception of American society was that individuals were responsible for who and what they became—or failed to become. In the Old World, individuals were *acted on*; their lives were shaped by deeply entrenched patterns of hierarchy, oppression, and exploitation. In America, where no such obstacles were presumed to exist, *individuals* were the actors. Each would chart his own course through the world. Much more than their European counterparts, observed French political theorist Alexis de Tocqueville, Americans commonly believed "that their fate lies entirely in their own hands."[25] Although this idea found clearest expression in the myth of the self-made man, it was amply evident in the other myths, too. Both the independent proprietor and the rights-bearer were defined, above all, by their expansive freedom to make their own choices, define their own commitments, follow their own consciences.

This, then, is what "individualism" means in this book: the idea that America *is and ought to be (a) a polity devoted to the expansion of private liberty and (b) a meritocratic society in which individuals are responsible for their own fates.*[26] One of the distinctive features of American individualism, so understood, is that it has functioned simultaneously as a moral ideal and a description of American society. As we explore in the coming chapters, Americans—especially the white men who have dominated the country's political discourse—have tended to believe that their individualistic values are already (mostly) realized in America. Time and again, they have framed their political conflicts around the need to protect these values from corruption or external threat.

Inclusive and Exclusive Individualism

In the politics of Jacksonian America, all three myths combined egalitarian principles with sharply hierarchical assumptions. As historians have often pointed out, their *explicit* language was often universal rather than parochial: rather than emphasizing shared ethnicity, language, cultural traditions, or even a particular homeland, these myths commonly celebrated shared opportunities and ideals. Moreover, many politicians and journalists presented these ideals not as the exclusive inheritance of a particular culture or people but as universal principles whose spread epitomized the moral and material progress of the human race.[27]

The apparent inclusiveness of the myths arose, most of all, from their treatment of social class. As we have seen, Americans often defined themselves against Europe; and in the American mind, nothing represented the Old World so much as rigid class hierarchy.[28] In its own way, each of the three foundational myths announced that such hierarchy was alien to American life. Personal independence, for example, was imagined to be open to any white man who came to own property.[29] From colonial times onward, Americans also firmly believed that even the poorest European immigrant could, through hard work and frugal self-discipline, accumulate wealth and ascend into the property-owning middle class. Meanwhile, the idea of natural rights was commonly understood as a repudiation of the aristocratic and authoritarian pretensions of European elites (and their American imitators). It affirmed that rich and poor alike were entitled to the same legal and political consideration. When Americans reached—as they so often did—for universal language to describe their national way of life, they often meant just this: American opportunities and ideals were available to white men of all social classes, no matter how humble their beginnings.

When our focus shifts from class to other forms of hierarchy, however, America's individualist myths look far less inclusive. In fact, American national identity has always carried strong ethnoracial, gendered, and religious overtones that excluded many groups from its supposedly universal promise. Throughout the Jacksonian period, Native Americans were cheated, dehumanized, and killed to make room for expanding white society. Irish Catholic immigrants were denigrated and denied economic opportunities. Women were held in legal and economic subjection and denied a political voice. Moreover, the prosperity and the very identity of white America was propped up by the forced labor of millions of Black slaves. Time and again, European observers were struck by this fundamental hypocrisy of American life: here was a society that ardently and continually affirmed a broad set of egalitarian ideals and at the same time blithely perpetrated some of the world's harshest forms of oppression and exploitation.

In fact, many white Americans celebrated these exclusions explicitly: as elites in Jacksonian America competed to find ways of maintaining a unified *people* in the face of growing sectional divisions, they also reached for bluntly exclusive narratives that emphasized racial, ethnic, and religious superiority. The explosive debates over slavery and African American citizenship that erupted in 1819 and culminated in the Missouri Compromise, for example, followed by the emergence of an organized and radical abolitionist movement in the early 1830s, created new opportunities for political entrepreneurs to use race as a way of mobilizing allegiance. Denouncing antislavery activists as radicals and racial perverts, and playing to white fears of racial mixing, political entrepreneurs in the Democratic Party constructed an ideal of America as a pristine "white republic" premised on the moral, economic, and intellectual superiority of the white or Anglo-Saxon "race." Others appealed instead to a generalized "Protestant Americanism," which they asserted against the emerging threat of immigrant Catholicism and the supposed atheism and secular radicalism of labor activists and other social critics.[30] In their eyes, America was a redeemer nation destined to realize a specifically Protestant vision of freedom and moral virtue.

Those who deployed these exclusive narratives often wove them together with the foundational myths. In fact, they commonly used these myths to define the political meaning of whiteness, "Anglo-Saxonism," or Protestant Americanism. Those who imagined America as a white or Anglo-Saxon republic, for example, insisted that only whites (or Anglo-Saxons) were suited for the several forms of freedom championed in their foundational myths. Only whites could be responsible and virtuous proprietors. Only whites were entitled to the full slate of civil and political rights that Americans claimed as their birthright. Only whites were capable enough to negotiate the demands of a free, competitive economy without sinking into abject "degradation"— only whites, in other words, could be self-made men. Drawing on a blossoming pseudoscientific literature on race and catering to the intense economic desire for Black bodies and Native American lands, white Americans thus erected racial boundaries to restrict access to their individualist ideals.

In doing so, they used these ideals to construct their own racial identity.[31] Historian David Brion Davis spells out the symbiotic relationship between individualism and white supremacy with unusual clarity and insight:

> A dialectical and historical connection developed between American slavery and American freedom, between the belief in an inferior, servile race and the vision of classless opportunity. Blacks represented and sometimes absorbed the finitude, imperfections, sensuality, self-mockery, and depravity of human nature, thereby amplifying the opposite qualities in the white race. And this parasitic relationship came to be driven by the special nature of the American "mission" and dream of overcoming the limits and boundaries of past history.[32]

The racialized idea of the rational, enterprising, and autonomous self, in other words, reassured white Americans that they were uniquely suited to meet the unprecedented challenges and opportunities offered up in their land of liberty, and that America's exceptional destiny belonged to them. In a society in which traditional identity markers—including class and heredity—were relatively weak, the need for such reassurance was widely felt. Racial pride helped soothe a pervasive status anxiety.[33] Nowhere was this dynamic clearer than among recent European immigrants, many of whom quickly learned to find their footing in a fluid and unfamiliar society by embracing their whiteness, accented by triumphantly individualistic traits, as a crucial badge of belonging.[34] In these several ways, then, the narratives of racial exclusion were used to *reinforce*, not to displace, the dominant, individualist myths.

In fact, these exclusions reveal an essential doubleness at the heart of all three myths: each defined the American people in two different ways, using two different kinds of contrast. The first of these contrasts defined Americans against the hierarchy and corruption of the Old World (and, much later, against the radicalism and tyranny of Soviet communism).[35] This version was relatively inclusive: anyone fleeing oppression and hierarchy elsewhere could, in principle, come to America to enjoy their natural liberty. The un-American "other" was defined largely in political terms, as an accretion of unjust, oppressive traditions that anyone could, in principle, escape.[36] The second contrast was exclusive: it described America's freedoms as the distinctive inheritance of a people delineated by racial, ethnic, or religious boundaries. Here, the "other" was defined by ascriptive identity-markers that characterized whole categories of people as impure or inferior, and therefore as dangers to American society.[37] The hysterical fear of racial "amalgamation" that motivated northern race riots throughout the Jacksonian Era epitomizes this exclusivist tendency.

It is tempting to say that the foundational myths were inclusive when it comes to class and exclusive when it comes to race, gender, and religion, but this solution is too tidy, for it conceals a fundamental tension that has unsettled American national identity from the beginning. In fact, the American Revolution and its aftermath, in its sustained assault on European inequality and aristocracy, gave rise to a powerful set of egalitarian ideals whose inner logic was inclusive. As abolitionists understood, meritocracy promised equal treatment to anyone with talent and ability. The doctrine of natural rights promised equal treatment to all who could show evidence of their common humanity. Although these ideals were originally conceived as part of a struggle against social and economic hierarchy, their inclusive logic constantly threatened to spill over into other political contexts, and they were routinely appropriated by Americans fighting for greater racial, gender, and religious equality. Throughout American history, these inclusive ideals have comprised what some historians have called a "civic" version of American national identity, which has competed with an "ethnoracial" alternative.[38] They told competing stories—inclusive and exclusive—about who America's individualist ideals were *for*.

These stories have competed and intermingled over time as marginalized groups have fought for inclusion and dominant groups have fought to retain or augment their privileges.[39] In the Jacksonian Era, those pushing inclusive visions of American national identity included defenders of Cherokee rights against expropriation, advocates for women's rights, and of course abolitionists defending racially inclusive conceptions of citizenship. Others promoted inclusive and exclusive visions simultaneously. Mainstream Democrats, for example, welcomed Mormons and the Irish into the American fold as equals even as they moved to consign people of color to permanent inferiority. If the long-standing argument over the meaning of personal freedom has defined one key axis of political dispute in America, this conflict over who has access to America's liberties has defined another.

To argue that individualist myths dominated American political life in the Jacksonian Era, then, is not to deny the salience or power of collective identity. In fact, these myths sought to express *what it meant* to be an American: even as they celebrated the free individual, they also defined a widely shared sense of national identity and "mission." As we explore over the course of this book, many of the dominant stories told by competing political parties and movements in the Age of Jackson were about the betrayal and corruption of America's exceptional purpose. They identified and vilified some corrupting "other" who was undermining American freedom and called on *true Americans* to rise up in its defense. In this way, America's individualist myths were used to define and reinforce a variety of collective identities, from nationality to partisan and ethnoracial identities, each of which strove to position itself as the authentic embodiment of Americanness.[40]

Enabling Conditions

Political myths remain powerful only as long as their adherents identify with them. These myths must therefore speak to their audience's lived experience or risk fading into oblivion. Politicians and ideologists in Jacksonian America understood this, and they formulated the three foundational myths to "fit" certain defining features of American society. First among these was a long-standing political culture centered, even in the colonial years, on the value of freedom.

The several successive waves of British subjects who settled in North America in the eighteenth century had already considered themselves exceptional people, possessed of liberties that existed nowhere else in the world. Even the poorest men among them laid claim to the mantle of the "free-born Englishman" who, unlike his counterparts on the European continent, enjoyed a broad slate of rights and liberties.[41] Immigrants from different parts of Britain, emigrating at different times and in the midst of different historical pressures and crises, brought with them varying ideas of freedom, ranging from the "ordered liberty" of the New England Puritans to the fiercely individualistic backcountry freedom of the Scotch-Irish.[42] They shared a tendency, however, to place *liberty* itself at the center of their public discourses and self-conceptions. The Revolution had shifted the locus of liberty, in the American imagination, from Britain to the United States and given rise to a potent narrative of national exceptionalism. The war years had also encouraged Americans to identify freedom with collective self-determination sustained by shared sacrifice. By the 1820s and 1830s, however, as this discourse of freedom was reformulated for generations born after the Revolution, it increasingly foregrounded private conceptions of freedom.

This shift was accelerated by three unusual characteristics of antebellum white society, which combined to make Americans receptive to individualistic political narratives: its abundant economic opportunities, its social and geographic mobility, and its pervasive religious voluntarism. First, compared to their counterparts in Europe, white Americans greeted the vast expansion of the market economy in the first half of the nineteenth century from a position of relative privilege. The apparently endless supply of cheap land, combined with free-flowing credit, a steady stream of useful new agricultural technologies, and the relative scarcity of labor, allowed for the expansion of a broad middle class of land-owning small farmers, especially in the North and West.[43] Unlike so many European peasants and farmworkers, American farmers tended to own their land; they could also move west and buy inexpensive, larger plots to accommodate their growing families. With fairly abundant acreage, they could support themselves with their own farm produce, which afforded them some protection from the market's fluctuations even as it allowed them to earn income from their marketable surpluses.[44] Because labor was relatively scarce, landless farmworkers commanded fairly high wages—compared to their counterparts in Europe—which allowed them to accumulate savings and become land owners themselves.[45] In short, many white Americans, a great majority of whom lived in rural areas and worked the land, were well positioned to take advantage of the opportunities that the burgeoning market economy had to offer.

These privileges must be seen from another perspective, too: much of the suffering that economic liberalization inflicted on European peasants and farmworkers was displaced, in antebellum America, onto Native Americans

whose lands were seized and Black slaves whose labor fueled the unprecedented cotton boom in the South. As a result, the white electorate was insulated from the harshest inequalities that were felt in America during its transition to a market economy. This pattern of racial supremacy and territorial
conquest allowed white American society to postpone for another two generations the acute social problems that were precipitated, in Europe, by the swell-
ing numbers of landless white laborers who felt excluded from the benefits of
economic modernization.[46] In America, even those farmers who felt threatened by economic development—such as upland southerners who clung to
traditional, premarket ways of life—often confronted it from a position of
privilege: many were small proprietors who exercised broad control over their
own economic lives and who were also conscious of their membership in a
privileged racial caste.

These economic conditions were fertile ground for the free-market optimism that came into circulation in Jacksonian America. Although the prevailing ideas of the market were diverse and often inchoate, the general idea of a
self-regulating and fundamentally beneficent economy, which could flourish
with little government intervention, achieved a widespread popularity that it
enjoyed nowhere else in the world. While the field of "political economy"
developed a reputation as a harsh and dismal science in England, for example,
it was received very differently in the United States. Americans on both sides
of the political aisle believed that, if it was not corrupted by malign political
forces, their unique economy would bring them prosperity, meritocratic justice, and relative equality.[47] Even those who railed against injustice or rising
inequality tended to treat these as temporary or "artificial" distortions of the
American norm.[48] As we will see, this view, inflected as it often was with millennial religious hope, was profoundly significant for the course of American
political thought.

Mobility was another distinguishing feature of American society. Between
the Revolution and the Civil War, several different patterns of mobility disrupted settled ways of life, opened up wide fields of opportunity for white
Americans, and weakened communal forms of identity. The most important
was surely the tremendous westward geographic mobility that was constantly
uprooting families and communities and pushing them into new and unknown territory. In the first two decades of the nineteenth century, the population living west of the Appalachian Mountains grew from around three hundred
thousand to over two million. Explosive population growth, combined with the
opening of vast new territories to settlers, pushed Americans westward. Those

who moved once often moved again: in the early nineteenth century, only 30 percent of those living in an average western community were likely to be there a decade later.[49] "It is astonishing," wrote one Scottish observer in the late 1840s, "how readily . . . an American makes up his mind to try his fortunes elsewhere, . . . no matter how remote, or how different in climate and other circumstances from what he has been accustomed to."[50]

The social effects of such mobility were profound. The social hierarchies, and the stabilizing institutions of church and state, weakened and largely disappeared as settlers moved further west. With the exception of small clusters of family or neighbors who moved together, new communities presented themselves as motley collections of strangers. Mobility leveled social distinctions, disrupted stable groups, and left to individuals—especially white male heads of household—the task of defining their own social position anew.[51] These effects were plainly visible to the migrants themselves, including Timothy Flint, a Yankee who had resettled in the Ohio Valley. "Everything shifts under your eye," he reflected ruefully. "The present occupants sell, pack, depart. Strangers replace them. Before they have gained the confidence of their neighbors, they hear of a better place, pack up, and follow their precursors. This circumstance adds to the instability of connexions."[52] Migration, writes historian George Pierson, "was an almost irresistible Disintegrator or Atomizer."[53]

Economic mobility was also disruptive. Although American society was never the pure meritocracy that its defenders championed, white men enjoyed an unusually wide field of economic opportunities.[54] The scarcity of labor led to relatively high wages, which allowed workers to save and accumulate capital of their own. The widespread availability of cheap land, and relatively low rents, allowed landless farmworkers to become proprietors in their own right—and even small-scale land speculators—after some years of saving.[55] The proliferation of new towns and cities, especially in the North, created tremendous demand for merchants, shopkeepers, lawyers, doctors, and other professionals.[56] Ambitious young men leapt into these professions after only the briefest, informal apprenticeships, and they built careers by trial and error. Mobility worked downward, too: debt and bankruptcy were commonplace, even among the relatively affluent. During economic contractions, banks failed and disappeared, business ventures collapsed, and speculations went awry and plunged even wealthy land owners into debt.[57]

If geographical mobility disrupted communities and undermined local and regional identities, economic mobility undermined class identity and solidarity. European observers invariably commented on the relative absence of durable social classes among white Americans—and they were astounded that American society could hold together in their absence.[58] In America, they observed, there was no landed nobility to speak of, and there was no distinct class of peasants. Among white Americans, wrote English critic Harriet Martineau, "there is no class of hereditary rich or poor. Few are very wealthy; few are poor; and every man has a fair chance of being rich."[59] As a result, Martineau and others observed, most white Americans did not identify with a particular social class. Americans, wrote French engineer and economist Michel Chevalier, were far more likely to identify with a profession than a social class. But even these identifications were often fleeting, because Americans thought nothing of jumping from one line of work to another. The only constant was the universal expectation that, through hard work, prudence, and ingenuity, any white man could "make his fortune."[60] Economic mobility, writes historian Joyce Appleby, "eroded expectations of enduring status and scrambled the social codes inherited from a Europeanized colonial world."[61]

Finally, the tenor of evangelical Protestantism in America, which had lately been convulsed by the revivalist fervor of the Second Great Awakening, also contributed to the popularity of individualistic myths. Its contribution is more complicated, however, because evangelicals often denounced and resisted the individualistic tendencies in American life. Revivalist preachers assailed the sinful excesses of the unrestrained individual and exhorted their audiences to embrace strict moral rules, even a kind of worldly asceticism. Church members commonly forswore drinking and gambling and other playful diversions, as well as certain luxuries and material indulgences. They were taught that subduing and overcoming earthly desires, and acknowledging the evanescence of worldly goods and pleasures, were preconditions for fully embracing Christ. Popular revivalists also promoted an ethic of benevolence and love against what they saw as the selfish tendencies of the age.[62]

Moreover, in a fluid and unstable social and economic world, religious community was a source of stability, solidarity, and restraint. It was an antidote to the loneliness of the frontier and the diffusive forces that drew countless families west, away from their families and childhood homes. Amid the "flux and disintegration" of a society convulsed by rapid economic change and westward migration, writes one historian of religion, "new certainties, new communities, new social networks, and new patterns of living were needed."[63] Evangelical Christianity offered all of these things. In homes, barns, rustic schoolhouses, makeshift churches, and clearings in the woods, its faithful would gather and bare their souls to one another, jointly scrutinize their individual motives and behavior, and join in celebratory rituals. In all of the major evangelical denominations, lay church members also exercised a great deal of responsibility for the organization and maintenance of their local churches. Through its formal meetings, rituals, and governance practices—and through the informal relationships that grew out of them—evangelical Christianity created and sustained unusually intimate forms of community. In these ways, as historians and contemporary observers alike have argued, the evangelical churches functioned as counterweights to the individualistic tendencies of antebellum American life.[64]

And yet, popular religion in Jacksonian America also displayed several sharply individualistic characteristics. For instance, it continually asserted the primacy of individual judgment and conscience against condescending elites and the ecclesiastical traditions that legitimized them. As evangelical revivalism swept through the United States in the early decades of the nineteenth century, its advocates radicalized the Lutheran idea of a priesthood of all believers. Far more successfully than their counterparts in Europe, these preachers urged their audiences to reject the authority of "learned" and "literary" ministers and consult scripture themselves. They held that the Bible was a simple book accessible to all, and that God spoke directly to individuals through prophetic dreams and visions. They taught their faithful to heed their own intuitions, which gave them access to timeless moral and spiritual truths. Such attitudes underwrote a wide-ranging suspicion of institutional authority that colored Americans' response not just to the educated clergy but also to doctors, lawyers, and politicians.[65]

These tendencies were amplified by countless sermons and conversion narratives that foregrounded the virtuous individual's struggle against corrupt social pressure. Over and over, American audiences heard the stories of pious young men who rejected the authority of their fathers, who forfeited lucrative careers and endured the ridicule of their worldly peers, who literally took to the woods in trembling solitude to search for answers and fortify themselves for the transformative act of *choosing* God. Channeling the growing Arminian[66] conviction that salvation lay within the individual's control, these narratives dramatized the anguish and triumph of the autonomous agent who, through a prodigious act of will, wrenched himself free from conventional society and pledged allegiance to the almighty.[67] "Revivalist conversion," writes historian Mark Noll, "was the religious analogue to Lockean individualism. It signaled the freeing of individuals from tradition, family, and inherited authority, even as it allowed believers to take in hand the commerce of their own souls."[68]

Whether out of conviction or necessity, revivalist evangelicals came to see their churches as voluntary communities of believers that stood in constant competition for members with rival groups. Church members routinely switched from one denomination to another and commonly attended sermons by rival preachers bidding for their allegiance and jousting for theological supremacy. They saw themselves as free agents choosing among competing slates of spiritual offerings. Historians of religion have often commented on the importance of such voluntaristic ideas: they made churches as fragile and fissiparous as many other forms of American community; they democratized preachers' authority and lent their teachings a pragmatic and anti-intellectual cast; they also underscored the need to fashion one's own individual identity in a fluid and diverse society.[69]

This combination of affluence, mobility, and religious voluntarism made fertile ground for the three foundational myths. Together, these factors weakened Americans' identification with community, social class, and the institutional authority of the church, and encouraged them to construct their political arguments and grievances, instead, around the ideal of individual freedom. Strikingly, this tendency was evident even among rural traditionalists who mistrusted economic modernization. Holding forth in nostalgic tones, they celebrated the simple and virtuous life of the independent farmer whose livelihood and domestic authority were under threat by the ambition and greed of bankers, speculators, and the corrupt politicians who did their bidding. Or they accused wealthy bankers and middlemen of accumulating *unearned* wealth by stripping America's hardworking producers of the fruits of their labor, and so violating their natural rights. They imagined both the modern state and the expanding market, in other words, as encroachments on the sovereign individual.

These individualistic languages of political reaction underscore another important difference between Europe and America. In nineteenth-century Europe, individualist ideas—both political and economic—were met by powerful, collectivist countertraditions. The first of these was grounded in the conservative authority of the church; the second was premised on the emerging solidarity of the working classes. Both taught that meaningful human freedom had to be secured *against* a harsh and anarchic market, and that this could only be accomplished by turning to the state—and often also the church—as a source of order, security, or redistributive equality.[70] As historians and political scientists have often observed, such ideas have always had a weaker hold on the American political mind.[71] The codification of individualist myths in the Jacksonian period, and the circumstances that lent them plausibility, help us understand the roots of this divergence more clearly.

PART I

The Independent
Proprietor

THE MYTH of the independent proprietor played a seminal role in American political thought and rhetoric from colonial times through the end of the nineteenth century and beyond. It served several different purposes. First of all, it told a story of national distinction: America, it said, offered uniquely fertile soil for human liberty. With its immense reserve of western land and its intolerance for titled nobility, America nourished a society of independent white proprietors who were both uniquely free and uniquely capable of self-government.

The myth also conveyed the meaning of personal freedom. In the life of the independent proprietor, freedom meant control over one's own work and home and a corresponding capacity for unbiased judgment and uncowed self-assertion. It encouraged, as one historian puts it, "a jealous regard for personal autonomy," "a hearty confidence in the individual['s] . . . ability to manage his own affairs," and a mistrust of any and all claims to authority, especially government's.[1] It made American men acutely sensitive to the encroachment of new forms of power that threatened to erode their control over their own economic and domestic lives.

This way of understanding both American uniqueness and American freedom shaped the political thought and rhetoric of the Jacksonian Era. It played an especially prominent role for Jacksonian Democrats, who used it to justify Andrew Jackson's insurgency against the political establishment and to channel voters' anxieties about economic change. The myth offered a master narrative that helped voters make sense of leading policy controversies. In the political struggles over banking and the currency, the tariff, land policy,

33

territorial expansion, and slavery, they were invited to see and resist threats to their personal independence. They learned that these threats arose from the ambition and greed of American elites and from the insubordination of "inferior" races, both of which threatened the property and status of small white proprietors. More fundamentally, voters were invited to see political power itself as a source of metastasizing dependence that had to be contained.

To bring this Jacksonian iteration of the myth into focus, however, we must understand how it had changed. Like many political myths, this one was woven out of ideological materials inherited from earlier times. The ideal of personal independence had come to colonial America from England as part of a neoclassical republican tradition that celebrated land ownership as a precondition of civic virtue. At first, it was not an especially individualistic notion. It formed part of a worldview that emphasized unity and harmony within a hierarchical body politic, the importance of civic duty, and disruptive danger of private interest.[2] But it changed over time to accommodate the conditions of American life: by the Age of Jackson, it conveyed an image of white society that was at once more egalitarian, more amenable to the market economy, and more thoroughly racialized. These changes, in turn, gave rise to new ideas about the purpose of government and the nature of democratic politics. In place of the founders' qualified optimism about the fate of the American republic, the Democrats substituted an increasingly utopian political faith centered on expansive personal freedom and the unconquerable integrity of the autonomous small proprietor.

The next three chapters explore these shifts and their far-reaching intellectual consequences. Historians have long associated the rise of American individualism with the gradual eclipse of the republican ideas that still ran strong among the founding generation.[3] Part 1 retells the story of this transformation through the lens of a single, powerful ideal: personal independence. It shows that important elements of the republican worldview continued to figure centrally in the American self-conception in Jacksonian America. It also shows how they changed over time and came to express an individualistic vision of white society and its politics. In doing so, it also reveals that many of the founders' political ideas were rejected and superseded just a few decades after they reigned supreme.

3

Republican Origins

Dependence begets subservience and venality, suffocates the germ of virtue, and prepares fit tools for the designs of ambition.

—THOMAS JEFFERSON, 1785[1]

WHEN THOMAS JEFFERSON drafted these lines in the early 1780s, he was contrasting the small farmers of his native Virginia to the urban laborers of Europe. In Europe, he observed, virtually all of the arable land was already owned, and so many landless men had no choice but to move to the cities and sell their labor in large urban "work-shops" where they manufactured consumer goods. In Jefferson's eyes, this was an ominous trend, a symptom of Europe's moral and political decline. America, on the other hand, with its "immensity of land," drew its working men to the soil, and would do so for many generations. This fact was very important to Jefferson; it allowed him to hope that manufacturing would stay in Europe and that America would remain, as long as possible, an agrarian republic.[2]

The moral foundation of Jefferson's agrarian vision was the ideal of personal independence. Unlike the European factory hand, the American farmer owned and worked his own land. He controlled the source of his own livelihood. In this fundamental economic sense, he was beholden to no one. By contrast, the laborer owed his wage and his job to someone else, and so he stood in his employer's power. Jefferson believed that this relationship of economic dependence was corrupting. It made men subservient and untrustworthy; it made them less likely to think and act for themselves; it made them "tools" to be used and manipulated by the wealthy and ambitious. Tenants who leased their farms from landlords could also be described in this light: "To live in that dependent way," said one North Carolina congressman in 1796, "has a tendency to vitiate and debase their minds, instead of making them free, enlightened, and independent."[3]

The ideal of personal independence and the mythology that encased it were vastly important in eighteenth- and nineteenth-century American thought. It is no exaggeration to say that the two great values of the American Revolution—liberty and equality—cannot be fully understood without reference to it. When Americans commented on the remarkable equality of their new society, for example, they meant not mainly the relatively equal distribution of wealth or property but rather the absence of hierarchical ties of dependence.[4] In America, they saw few tenants and no hordes of landless, urban wage workers. Instead, they saw independent farmers and artisans—men who owned their own land or shop, or could reasonably aspire to do so, and who therefore controlled their own economic lives. The very structure of European society, with its fixed and unequal "orders" of people linked together in an ascending hierarchy—the lower ranks dependent on the higher—had been shattered. For Americans and their European admirers alike, personal independence formed the centerpiece of a story of American exceptionalism: it set America apart from the Old World and made it fertile ground for republican government. On both sides of the Atlantic, personal independence was deeply woven into the idealized image of America.[5]

To understand this image more fully, we must begin by looking in some detail at the neoclassical republican ideas out of which it was fashioned. In particular, we must observe a bifurcation in the republican idea of independence that has received relatively little attention from intellectual historians. Originally, it was applied to two different figures, with two different levels of social and political status: the small farmer who worked his own land without debts or other corrupting entanglements, and the leisured, patrician landholder whose freedom from (most forms of) labor allowed him to prepare for the responsibilities of political leadership. As these ideas were carried across the Atlantic and applied to American society, this distinction began to erode, setting in motion a series of intellectual shifts whose implications were still being felt in the Jacksonian Era.[6]

The Neoclassical Republican Tradition

The republican tradition, stretching back through the Italian Renaissance to Greek and Roman antiquity, was one of several intellectual currents that shaped the political thought of the American founders. Eighteenth-century

Americans absorbed this tradition mainly from English philosophers, politicians, and social critics who, beginning in the seventeenth century, had begun drawing on republican ideas to justify their demands for political reform and revolution.

Over the course of the eighteenth century, republican ideas came to permeate English political thought, in both Great Britain and its far-flung American colonies. Just about everyone—from radical to conservative—laid claim to them in some form.[7] Still, beneath the disagreement and semantic confusion, the outlines of a distinctive political theory can be found. Broadly speaking, republicanism was a theory of free government—that is, of government controlled by free citizens. Free governments, or republics, were distinguished by the rule of law; the election of public officials; a limited, property-holding electorate; and extensive civic duties. Republics were thought to be more fragile and demanding than other forms of government. In a republic, no single person or group would be powerful enough to subdue everyone else and maintain order through force or fear.[8] Instead, peace and cohesion would depend on consent and collaboration among a free people.[9]

In the classical republican imagination, such collaboration would always be difficult to sustain: it was vulnerable to the competing ambitions, jealousies, and interests of individuals or rival groups. Collaboration would devolve easily into factional conflict, which led either to instability and chaos or—when one group succeeded in imposing its will on the others—to tyranny. To survive, republics would have to draw on two important resources. First, they would need a well-designed constitution that maintained a delicate balance of power between competing groups. Second, and more fundamentally, they would need citizens who were willing to subordinate their own private interests and factional loyalties to the public good. This devotion to the public good formed the heart of the republican ideal of civic virtue.[10]

Cultivating and sustaining civic virtue was the cornerstone of the republican political project, and it was a broad and ambitious goal. Virtue was not simply a matter of education, narrowly understood. Republicans believed that virtue could survive only under the right social, economic, and political conditions. Too much inequality, for example, would destroy it—no matter how carefully citizens had been educated—by fraying the bonds of civic solidarity and creating permanent class divisions. So would too much affluence or luxury, which would lure citizens away from public life, or even too much economic specialization, which would narrow their horizons and leave them unfit for public service. Professional armies were also dangerous, partly because they stripped ordinary citizens of the martial virtues they would need to protect their own freedom.[11] Imagining the preconditions of civic virtue, therefore, meant imagining a whole society, and with it an economy and a political constitution, calibrated to nurture certain forms of civic character. This was the republican philosophical project in a nutshell, and in seventeenth-century England, the ideal of propertied independence came to play an important role in it.[12]

Virtue, writes historian J. G. A. Pocock, "required an individual so independent of other men and their social structures that his dedication to the *res publica* could be wholly autonomous. It must be autonomous if he were not to be another man's creature, and so a source of illegitimate private, instead of public, power."[13] This last line cuts to the heart of English republican thought. From its point of view, legitimate public power arose through the deliberation and judgment of free citizens, each of whom served as an independent arbiter of the public interest. Economic dependence threatened to undermine this kind of power completely: anyone who depended on a social superior for his livelihood stood *under that superior's influence*. When push came to shove, the dependent would be unable to speak or act freely without risking his own livelihood. He would be a bought man, so to speak, subservient to another. Subservience of this kind was considered appropriate to the household—to the relationship between man and wife, master and servant—but it had no place in the public sphere. As soon as subservience pervaded the public sphere, the republic—the *res publica*—was transformed into the private domain of tyrants or oligarchs.

To be fully independent, one had to be an economically self-sufficient head of household. In the paradigmatic instance, the independent man was a land owner who earned his livelihood from his own property. In this, he depended only on members of his household who were under his power: his wife, children, and his servants or tenants.[14] He was therefore free from the control of others, and he exercised governing control over his own private estate.[15] Economic conditions held a special importance in this picture. They shaped social and political relations;[16] they also shaped individual character: economic dependents were politically suspect not just because they would not speak their mind but because their very capacity for autonomous judgment and impartiality—and therefore, virtue—was compromised by their subservience. In fact, the term "independence" often had a double meaning: it referred not only to a condition of economic self-control but also to an ideal of character enabled by and appropriate to that condition. Meanwhile, property was understood not only as a form of wealth; more fundamentally, it was a means of securing economic independence and the social and civic status that accompanied it. "All men are animated by the passion of acquiring and defending property," wrote the influential English journalists John Trenchard and Thomas Gordon, "because property is the best support of that independency, so passionately desired by all men."[17] Many republican writers throughout the seventeenth and eighteenth centuries argued that a wide diffusion of landed property would lay the foundation for a virtuous public.[18]

It should be clear that this proud, self-assertive ideal was thoroughly gendered: independence was reserved for men alone. In republican thought, the polity consisted of households, each with an independent man at their head: in this political model, writes historian Matthew McCormack, "the male household head controls, protects, dominates and represents the other members of the household, who are all dependent upon him."[19] Women, who were believed to be fundamentally passionate creatures incapable of sober self-direction, were consigned, like slaves and children, to the status of dependents. For them to aspire to independence was unseemly and unnatural. In fact, dependence itself was consistently feminized: for a man to be dependent was to be emasculated, to lack strength and virility. In the republican imagination, public virtue and masculinity were inseparably linked.[20]

Two Tiers of Independence

Independence, then, was a complicated and contested ideal that cut across the public and private divide, and historians are still uncovering the full range of its meanings. But English republicans *located* personal independence in two different places on the social hierarchy—one "lower" and one "higher"—that corresponded to different levels of political status and agency. On the lower end of the political spectrum, independence demarcated the boundary of full citizenship: only independent persons were considered fit to hold political rights (notably the right to vote).[21] On the higher end, leisured independence rendered men eligible for membership in the leadership class—the class of trained elites whose responsibility it was to hold important public offices.[22]

Let us begin with the lower, or plebian, version. As we have seen, only independent persons were thought to be in full control of themselves—their livelihoods, their homes, but also their minds and their very "identities." "In a sense," writes McCormack, "the 'dependent' were not held to be subjects at all—they were the objects of political action rather than its originators."[23] Independence, then, defined a lower threshold below which persons could not be expected to act freely and with integrity. When English republicans insisted that "the people" should be enfranchised, therefore, they meant only a particular subset of the population. They excluded not just women but servants, tenants, "day laborers," and any recipient of charity; they sometimes excluded merchants and artisans too.[24]

Who exactly counted as independent enough to qualify for full citizenship was a matter of continual debate and revision over the course of the eighteenth century.[25] Even so, many working men in England believed that the threshold was within their reach. Historian Daniel Vickers, who argues that independence is best understood as a matter of degree, writes that "some small measure of economic independence was generally within plausible reach, and working Englishmen considered the pursuit or protection of this status to be a central organizing principle of economic life." For men who worked with their hands, it meant "possessing the means of self-employment"—owning land or a small shop.[26] The language of independence was also appropriated by artisans, for example, who laid claim to it in virtue of their membership in a trade, which allowed them to be economically self-supporting and, in some English boroughs, also qualified them for the vote.[27]

This "lower" expression of independence was commonplace in the American colonies too. In 1776, for example, James Iredell argued that only independent men should be granted the vote, since only they would be "free from influence, and have some knowledge of the great consequence of their trust."[28] In the same year, John Adams wrote, "Is it not . . . true that men in general, in every society, who are wholly destitute of property, are . . . too dependent on other men to have a will of their own?"[29] In keeping with these ideas, all thirteen of the original American states maintained some sort of property qualification for the vote.[30] In America, however, unlike in England, property was plentiful and easily acquired, and most white men cleared the threshold. Even in the South, which had historically been more unequal than New England, egalitarian pressures were opening up citizenship to a wider group of people. Edmund Morgan's landmark study of colonial Virginia shows that these more egalitarian strains blossomed there over the course of the eighteenth century, just as chattel slavery was taking hold. As social and economic elites felt the need to build solidarity with poor whites against the growing population of Black slaves, they appealed to a republican ideal of propertied independence to extend political rights to small farmers.[31] In this new, more inclusive vision of the colonial polity, "the yeoman farmer, standing foursquare on his own plot of land, gun in hand and virtue in his heart," became "the ideal citizen of a republic."[32]

At the higher end of the social and political scale, on the other hand, independence underwrote a patrician ideal of character that was associated with political leadership.[33] English gentlemen owned landed estates from which they derived enough rent to sustain a comfortable livelihood; they could therefore afford to turn their interests to public affairs. Freed from the need to struggle for their living—freed, in most cases, from the need to work—they could cultivate impartiality and a breadth of knowledge that would prepare them for political leadership. With the benefit of a classical education, moreover, they could learn to bring their selfish passions under the governance of reason, to disdain luxury and personal ambition, and to become true "guardian[s] of public liberty."[34] Independence applied, paradigmatically, to these gentlemen of "standing and property" who prepared themselves to serve in Parliament. And so writers paid homage to independence in the self-help books and rhetoric manuals of the leisured classes—as well as in private diaries and memoirs—well into the nineteenth century. It described not only an economic condition but also a way of speaking and comporting oneself in public, and more broadly, a way of handling political responsibility.[35]

This "higher" republican ideal of leisured independence held a powerful appeal for the upper classes in colonial America. Though colonial society was far less stratified than England, American elites still saw themselves as the peers of the British gentry, inhabiting a similar social world.[36] What is more, the very insecurity of their social position pushed them to strive all the harder for the outward appearance of European gentility. Taking stock of the "lace ruffles, silk stockings" and "elaborate houses" that the colonial gentry used to set themselves apart from their social inferiors, historian Gordon Wood speaks to the ideals that underlay the finery: colonial elites were straining to live up to "the classical characteristic of being free and independent." The gentleman's distinctive social identity, he writes, "came from being independent in a world of dependencies, learned in a world only partially literate, and leisured in a world of laborers."[37]

What, then, was the relationship, in the republican mind, between these higher, leisured paragons of independence and the lower farmers and artisans who barely cleared the threshold of full citizenship? Broadly speaking, it was the relationship between political leaders and the enfranchised public that chose them and then deferred to their authority (so long as they did not abuse it).[38] Even the republican philosophers who rejected hereditary political privileges believed that leaders would occupy a higher social class and possess distinctive political virtues. James Harrington, one of the seminal figures in the

English republican tradition, imagined a natural aristocracy distinguished not only by talent but also by property ownership, classical education, and leisure.[39] These leisured elites would be elected by the propertied public but would enjoy broad discretion while holding office—their independence would be manifest in their handling of political responsibility with integrity and honor.[40] Summarizing colonial perceptions of the great Virginia planters who stood out as paragons of this "higher" independence, historian T. H. Breen writes that they "stood above the scramble after power and wealth and thus seemed ideally suited to provide leadership for the small planters."[41]

Meanwhile, the "lower" independence of the modest freeholder was required in the moment of election itself, when citizens would have to declare their vote publicly, sometimes in the teeth of hostile, raucous crowds.[42] In these decisive moments, citizens were asked to use their own judgment to discern the virtue and talent of the natural aristocrat, who would faithfully guard their liberties, and stand up for him.[43] In this spirit, the Philadelphia pamphleteer "Constant Truman," writing in 1735 to artisans who qualified for the vote, urged them to "come unanimously to the Election, and there to give your Votes as becomes honest Men, without Fear or Favour, but according to your Conscience and the best Understanding you are Masters of." If the city's humble freeholders allowed themselves to be intimidated or overawed by "great Men," he warned, their liberty would be forfeit, and they would soon be no better than "Slaves" and "Beasts of Burden."[44] These humbler, propertied citizens were also expected to serve in militias and juries and to hold other local offices.[45]

The republican preoccupation with independence—both high and low—helps explain several widely held political attitudes in Revolutionary America. It explains the hatred of lavish royal courts, which used public money to bestow patronage, creating a powerful class of dependents who spread corruption and lived like leeches on the body politic.[46] It explains the mistrust of the unpropertied poor, whose economic need made them dependent and vulnerable to cheap bribery by tyrants and demagogues.[47] It also explains the suspicion of political parties, which seemed, by their very nature, to promote factional instability and erode independent political judgment. Finally, it explains the pervasive concern about corruption, among both officeholders and the people at large, which was often associated with the spread of luxury and economic dependence. These attitudes reveal, moreover, that the class of economic dependents who might be presumed unfit for politics was broad and economically diverse: it included not just women, servants, and the poor but also courtiers, financiers, and military officers drawing generous salaries from the state.[48] Republican ideas could be invoked in service of both hierarchical and egalitarian political agendas.

By the middle of the eighteenth century, however, the classical republican tradition was under pressure. The rapid expansion of commerce in the Atlantic world seemed, to many observers, to threaten the very foundations of republican society and politics.[49] Viscount Bolingbroke, one of John Adams's favorite philosophers, summed up the problem succinctly: "What expectation can be entertained of raising a disinterested public spirit among men who have no other principle than that of private interest, who are individuals rather than fellow-citizens, who prey on one another, and are, in a state of civil society, much like to Hobbes's men in his supposed state of nature?"[50] Simply put, commerce, which was dominated by the pursuit of private self-interest, and which involved extensive relationships of dependence on others, threatened to extinguish civic virtue.[51] Critics such as Bolingbroke associated the rise of modern commercial societies with the spread of extravagance, indebtedness, and avarice, which in turn produced servility: people seemed willing to do anything, including abasing themselves at the feet of the wealthy and powerful, in the frantic scramble for money.[52] Republicans had traditionally seen landed property as a means of standing apart from the struggle for economic advancement that defined market relations. Now, the civic character that such property nourished seemed to be under threat.

Defenders of modern commerce, on the other hand, argued that many of the lessons of antiquity had outlived their usefulness. They argued that Western civilization had passed into a new historical stage—a commercial stage—in which republican freedom would have to be secured in other ways than through the austere, self-sacrificial virtue of the ancients.[53] Some argued that commerce engendered its own "softer" set of social virtues—including "frugality, economy, moderation," and "order"—that could bind modern individuals and societies together peacefully.[54] Others argued that commercial prosperity itself restrained the arbitrary power of political rulers: it made kings reliant on an economy that flourished only if they managed it with restraint, and on merchants and investors who could move their capital elsewhere if political conditions turned inhospitable.[55] Over the course of this debate, which stretched across the eighteenth century and into the nineteenth, defenders of modern commerce—including Charles de Montesquieu, Adam Smith, and David Hume—blended republican ideas with principles that we now recognize as liberal.[56] The linchpin of this gradual shift was the idea that a free society could be sustained not by citizens' disinterested civic virtue but by their prudent self-interest.

The idea of landed independence, however, fit more comfortably on the other side of the contest, with those who were skeptical of the rise of commercial modernity. In fact, it belonged to a republican tradition that was, in several ways, anti-individualistic. Republicans often emphasized civic duty and denigrated private interests; they tended to imagine society as a community or "body" devoted to shared, public purposes and sustained by citizens' shared devotion to a common good. Still, a great deal can be understood about the rise of individualism in America by studying the persistence and transformation—one might say, the *individualization*—of the idea of independence in American thought. For it survived and thrived in America well into the nineteenth century, despite the destruction of many of the other underpinnings of republican philosophy, despite the coming of market society and the rise of mass political parties, and despite the repudiation of aristocratic leisure. Americans exalted and mythologized this "traditional figure, the virtuous yeoman freeholder," writes historian John Murrin, "into an ideal detached from its older, more organic social and civic context."[57]

Plebian Independence: Farmers and Artisans in Jeffersonian Lore

Both tiers of personal independence—the lower, plebian tier and the higher, patrician tier—persisted in American political thought after the Revolution and into the early decades of the nineteenth century. The plebian tier was especially central to the emerging national mythology of the virtuous yeoman: in America, after all, land was cheap and abundant, and hereditary aristocracy was virtually absent. Independence seemed to be the natural condition of the American farmer. In a pamphlet that was widely circulated in America in the 1780s, the English radical Richard Price praised Americans as "an independent and hardy YEOMANRY, all nearly on a level—trained to arms,—instructed in their rights—clothed in home-spun—of simple manners—strangers to luxury—drawing plenty from the ground—and that plenty, gathered easily by the hand of industry." In its youth and virtue, wrote Price, America seemed to herald a new dawn of the republican freedom of "Greece and Rome," after an "intermediate period of thick darkness."[58]

Price's descriptions were not just fanciful idealizations. Whereas only one-fifth of adult men in England owned land, two-thirds of all adult white

American men were land owners—and of the remaining one-third, many were either recent immigrants or young men waiting to inherit land or move west.[59] "From Georgia to New York," writes historian Joyce Appleby, "a hinterland ran westward that gave the new American nation what no other people had ever possessed: the material base for a citizenry of independent, industrious property holders."[60] These material facts were tremendously important in shaping American society. In England, society could plausibly be imagined as a hierarchy of different social "orders" bound together by ties of patronage and dependence, with land owners commanding the political fealty of their economic dependents. In America, where such ties did exist at all, they were shallower and more brittle. Starved of funds, colonial governors had little patronage to dispense.[61] And with cheap land available, the stable relationship between landlord and tenant, which had formed the "heart of monarchical society," could not be widely sustained.[62]

Both before and after the Revolution, Americans used these facts to tell a potent story of American exceptionalism: America's unique economic and geographical conditions, they argued, laid a foundation for republican virtue that simply could not exist on the overcrowded European continent. As we have seen, Jefferson himself was one of the most influential purveyors of this American mythology. He famously insisted that "those who labor in the earth are the chosen people of God, . . . whose breasts He has made His peculiar deposit for substantial and genuine virtue." "Corruption of morals in the mass of cultivators," he continued,

> is a phenomenon of which no age nor nation has furnished an example. [Corruption] is the mark set on those, who not looking . . . to their own soil and industry, as does the husbandman, for their subsistence, depend for it on casualties and caprice of customers.[63]

This last line highlights a tension in Jefferson's own thinking. Even as he promoted transatlantic free trade, he also worried that commerce would eventually corrupt the American republic. Farmers who traded their surplus to pay for imported manufactured goods could preserve their virtuous independence, but those who derived their livelihoods mainly from trade crossed a crucial moral threshold. They became more thoroughly dependent on the "casualties and caprice of customers." Would such people be willing to take controversial opinions—to speak their mind plainly, with an eye to preserving the public good—even at the risk of alienating their clients? Jefferson had his doubts.[64] Like the dependent wage laborers of European city slums, merchants would lose their capacity for uncorrupted political judgment and action.

Many of Jefferson's contemporaries shared these concerns.[65] In 1803, for example, Alan Magruder, a Kentucky-born lawyer who would later serve as a U.S. senator from Louisiana, celebrated the Louisiana Purchase because it would open wide tracts of land for the independent farmer and so preserve the youth and virtue of the American republic. "There is a dignity and independence of manner," he wrote, "that belongs to the rustic life . . . that bids defiance to tyranny and which does not patiently yield to the seductions of luxury." Even as he insisted that farmers must have access to international markets to trade their surplus, Magruder drew a sharp line between farmers and the "commercial body" of the nation, which he described as "venal," "avaricious," and "dependent."[66] Because the merchant's livelihood rendered him thoroughly dependent on his clients, his judgment was inevitably tainted by private interest. The Pennsylvania gentleman-farmer George Logan, meanwhile, argued that the yeoman farmer's patriotic devotion to the common good derived from his aloofness—and his geographical remoteness—from the corrupt schemes of ambitious politicians and speculators.[67] With his own livelihood under his control, the independent farmer was immune to these temptations. His stake in the land, moreover, gave the farmer a long-term interest in the success of the political community. Unlike the "stockjobber"[68] and the "speculator"—figures universally reviled in agrarian rhetoric, whose property was fluid and volatile—farmers were invested for the long term; their overriding interest was in peace, security, and liberty, and with it a stable, incremental prosperity.[69]

While conservatives continued to invoke the ideal of personal independence to restrict voting rights, Jefferson, Logan, and other agrarian democrats saw it as more inclusive and egalitarian.[70] In a draft of the 1776 Virginia constitution, for example, Jefferson had proposed that all adult white men be guaranteed at least fifty acres of land. This policy would lay the foundation, he believed, for a virtuous, democratic republic. Meanwhile, the French immigrant J. Hector St. John de Crevecoeur celebrated the fact that any "German boor" with a little credit could buy his own land in America and experience a social and political rebirth: "From nothing to start into being; from a servant to the rank of a master; from being the slave of some despotic prince, to become a free man, invested with lands, to which every municipal blessing is annexed! What a change indeed!" Land ownership, he thought, not only conferred instant civic standing but also brought crucial changes in personal character. "The instant I enter on my own land," he wrote, "the bright idea of property, of exclusive right, of independence exalt my mind."[71] In these more inclusive agrarian visions, independence formed part of an egalitarian political ideal that was made possible, in America, by the availability of land. Historian Merrill Peterson describes this as the great "anomaly of American politics": in its inception in America, "the democratic tradition was the tradition of landed property."[72]

The small farmers mythologized in Jeffersonian lore were, of course, white men, and their independence was increasingly premised on the subordination of people of color. The land that the federal government sold to white settlers had been expropriated from Native American populations by force and fraud, and a racialized ideal of independent proprietorship was consistently invoked to justify these takings. As land hunger grew, white Americans increasingly argued that the natural inferiority of other races left them incapable of the distinctive virtues associated with independent proprietorship. In this sense, the Jeffersonian vision of an "empire of liberty" stretching westward and peopled by yeoman farmers was also a colonial vision of an expanding white population that would, in time, permanently overrun and dispossess other peoples. We explore these white supremacist ideas, which reached a fever pitch in the Jacksonian Era, in more detail in chapters 3 and 6.[73]

Land-hungry farmers were not the only ones, however, to lay claim to this plebian mantle of independence and industrious virtue. Shopkeepers, small-scale merchants, and artisan producers in various trades could claim that, like their freeholder counterparts in the country, they did not depend on the patronage or favor of any master. They operated their own businesses; they controlled the conditions of their own economic lives.[74] Unlike Jefferson, these merchants and artisans expressed little concern about commerce's supposedly corrupting effects on character (though they often warned of the corrupting effects of luxury and "opulence"). For them, writes historian John Brewer, "operating in an open market, free from the constraints, whims, and fancies of a patron, might well be the way of securing independence, of exchanging the personal capricious control of clientage" for the more "impersonal and egalitarian" relations of contract and exchange. Commerce, from this point of view, enacted reciprocal relationships between free and equal people liberated from dependence on powerful patrons. It offered nothing less than a new paradigm for social relations in egalitarian, republican societies, and a way of contesting the boundaries of republican citizenship and virtue.[75]

In America—especially in the eastern cities—these currents of thought nurtured a distinctive variety of urban, artisan republicanism. In the late eighteenth and early nineteenth centuries, American industrialization lagged behind Britain's: a great deal of urban production was still carried out on a small scale, by master craftsmen and the journeymen working for them in small urban shops. These artisans—bookbinders, tanners, tailors, shipwrights, shoemakers, and so forth—laid claim to the Jeffersonian ideal of independence to carve out a place for themselves in American society and distinguish themselves from the dependent poor.[76] Unlike their counterparts in Britain, declared Tristam Burges in an 1800 speech to the Providence Association of Mechanics and Manufacturers, American artisans were no "pitiful hirelings of the wealthy." Their independence, he continued, gave them both the time to educate themselves and the discretion to form their own political judgments. They were their own men, and stood ready to rise up virtuously in defense of American liberty whenever it was threatened.[77]

If the myth of the independent proprietor projected a distinctive set of *political* virtues onto the farmer and artisan, it also invested him with the industrious self-discipline celebrated by Protestant religion.[78] One of the farmer's cardinal virtues, repeated time and again by those who mythologized the American yeoman, was *industry*: whereas the stockjobber and speculator were idle connivers, farmers were patiently industrious. Their industry arose from the felicitous combination of land ownership and trade: industrious farmers who owned property could sell their surplus crops and so improve their condition.[79] Surpluses would pay for higher living standards, for capital improvements on the farm, and eventually for more land.[80] "Without commerce to yield a market to the products of agriculture," wrote Magruder, "that agriculture would languish, and the mass of society be thrown into a state of listless indolence and dissipation."[81] In a commercial society, on the other hand, land ownership became a source of moral discipline, for it provided a strong incentive to work.[82]

The Protestant virtues of industry and frugality would also help the yeoman resist the temptations that presented themselves in an increasingly affluent world. The farmer's hard work and patience served as a corrective, for example, to the speculative enthusiasms—and with them ruinous personal debt—that swept through America in the decades after the Revolution. "The moderate and sure income of husbandry," wrote Jefferson, "begets permanent improvement, quiet life, and orderly conduct both public and private."[83] Meanwhile, John Taylor of Caroline, perhaps the leading philosopher of Jeffersonian democracy, lamented the defections from agriculture by those "seduced by the temptations of wealth."[84] Markets could unleash turbulent passions just as easily as they could promote discipline and steady self-improvement; in the figure of the yeoman farmer, the pursuit of wealth was regulated by the steady rhythms of nature: the seasons, the land's capacity, the labor-intensiveness of improvements. The yeoman was a model of moderation and self-control in a world unsettled by economic upheaval. This convergence of republican virtue and the Protestant work ethic made the plebian archetype of independence more resilient and durable than it might otherwise have been. It also weakened its patrician counterpart, which connoted leisure rather than diligent labor.

Patrician Independence and Natural Aristocracy

If the farmer and artisan embodied the plebian ideal of independence, the wealthy southern planter stood for its higher, patrician analogue. Colonial elites in the North and South alike had aspired to a leisured independence that could underwrite a life of public leadership. Aspiring gentlemen went to great lengths to conform to the classical ideal, including distancing themselves from the semblance of commercial activity, which might connote base or self-interested motives, buying landed estates, and obsessing over the refinements of gentlemanly culture.[85] Meanwhile, candidates for office were expected to avoid any direct appeal to the electorate, for such appeals would reveal a "self-interest and sordid avarice" unbecoming of independent gentlemen.[86] This ideal of leisured, landed public men always fit better in the South, where plantation slavery supported a class of wealthy land-owning elites—indeed, it survived there until the Civil War.[87] For southern elites, the republican language of agrarian independence and virtue suggested itself naturally as a way of justifying their political power and standing and distinguishing themselves from northern capitalists.[88]

When Benjamin Watkins Leigh rose to defend the political privileges of slaveholding planters at the Virginia constitutional convention of 1829, he drew liberally from this patrician tradition. Leigh asked the assembled delegates whether "those who are obliged to depend on their daily labour for daily subsistence, can, or do enter into political affairs?" "They never do," he declared, "—never will—never can."[89] While his barbs were intended for propertyless "day-labourers," they were poorly received by small farmers throughout the state, for they seemed to cast manual labor itself into disrepute.[90] Even more telling, however, was Leigh's own striving for the leisured independence of the European nobility: "Educated myself to a profession," he admitted, "which *in this country* has been supposed to fit the mind for the duties of the Statesman,

I have yet never had occasion to turn my mind to any general question of politics, without feeling the effect of professional habits to narrow and contract the mind."[91] Trained as a lawyer, Leigh felt a tension between his professional interests and persona and the ideal of disinterested statesmanship to which he aspired—an ideal that could be sustained only by extensive property holdings.

In the relatively egalitarian circumstances of white male society in the American colonies, however, this patrician ideal of independence had always been vulnerable. After the Revolution, it came under attack at the hands of Jeffersonian agrarians, among others. Jefferson was adamant in attacking the "patrician order" that was sustained by privilege and wealth. In its place, he envisioned a "natural aristocracy" of talent and virtue.[92] In the preamble to his 1779 Bill for the More General Diffusion of Knowledge, for example, Jefferson had explained one of the main purposes of his proposed educational reforms: he believed that "those persons, whom nature hath endowed with genius and virtue, should be rendered by liberal education worthy to receive, and able to guard the sacred deposit of the rights and liberties of their fellow citizens." Like Taylor, he believed that virtue and talent were widely distributed through the different classes of society. He insisted, therefore, that the talented and virtuous should be promoted "without regard to wealth, birth or other accidental condition or circumstance."[93] In his republican ideal, there still existed a leadership class distinguished by its excellence and classical training from the rest of society; but it was a class open to talent.

Still, both Jefferson and Taylor imagined these virtuous leaders to be independent land owners. Landed independence was especially important, in their view, to counteract the growing power of a new breed of modern elites who threatened to corrupt the young republic. These were men who clustered around the centers of power, lived off government largesse, and secured special economic privileges from government. They were wealthy beneficiaries of exclusive corporate charters, ministers and army officers with generous salaries, but most of all the bankers and "stockjobbers" who funded government debt or secured exclusive rights to print currency. These modern power brokers had proliferated in Britain, and Jefferson and Taylor were determined to prevent their ascendancy in America. Instead, they wanted a landed, agrarian elite that would be "uncorrupted by stock-jobbing, by a view of office, or by odious personal vices; taking care to combine talents with this genuine character."[94]

These convictions reflected the influence of a strain of eighteenth-century English republicanism that historians have called Country ideology, which had been highly influential among the Revolutionary generation in America. At its heart lay a concern about the explosive growth of executive power and its subversion of the hallowed balance of the English constitution.[95] Beginning in the 1690s, the English government had begun to finance its ambitious foreign wars through debt, had established the Bank of England to manage its interest payments, and had laid new taxes that required a substantial expansion of the state bureaucracy. Great chartered corporations had also arisen to oversee commerce and imperial expansion, and with them a new class of wealthy merchants and financiers. From the Country perspective, these new elites, who possessed none of the independence of landed proprietors, presented a profound threat to English liberties, for they enhanced royal power without providing any salutary check on it.[96] Jefferson and Taylor agreed: in their eyes, this was precisely the kind of corrupt aristocracy that Alexander Hamilton and the Federalists—and later, the nationalist wing of the Republican Party—were trying to introduce in America. Widespread *dependence* was one of its leading characteristics.[97]

To avoid such corruption, the young American republic needed not only virtuous and independent leaders but also an electorate dominated by vigilant small proprietors who would choose them and hold them in check. James Madison had once suggested that the republican electorate was wise enough, at least, to "select men of virtue and wisdom" for office.[98] Jefferson, too, believed that yeomen would recognize and defer to superior talent; but he also thought that they would keep careful watch over their leaders. In fact, the political virtues he attributed to the yeomen were typically negative or defensive: they should be *jealous* of their rights, ever *vigilant* about plots to subvert their liberties, and willing "to resist, by arms when necessary, every encroachment, real or imagined."[99] As we have seen, plebian independence was integral to this story: according to the myth, the small proprietor was incorruptible and always disposed to form his own judgments. Unaccustomed to servitude in any form, he would fiercely resist any encroachment on his liberty. "The glorification of the yeoman," writes Morgan, "served paradoxically as the central ideological tenet of deferential politics" in which independent farmers were meant to rally behind the natural aristocracy against the corrupting forces that threatened them.[100]

In most of the young nation, this deferential politics would not survive for long: the Revolution had unleashed a powerful tide of political egalitarianism that would, by the Jacksonian Era, discredit the idea of a natural aristocracy among white men and compel American elites to reimagine their political life in terms that were both more democratic and more individualistic.[101] During the debates around the ratification of the U.S. Constitution, for example, a number of Anti-Federalists had gone much farther than Jefferson and rejected the premise that political leaders should be *superior*—in their talent, training, or virtue—to their constituents. Instead, they argued that the legislature ought to serve as a mirror of society: political representatives should reflect the same backgrounds and characteristics as their constituents, so that they could speak for them faithfully.[102] "The farmer, merchant, mecanick [*sic*], and other various orders of people," wrote the Anti-Federalist essayist Brutus, "ought to be represented according to their respective weight and numbers," so that legislators would be "intimately acquainted with the wants" of the people.[103] Brutus and other radical Anti-Federalists insisted that the independent yeoman and artisan possessed all the knowledge and virtue they needed to govern themselves—they had no need for a classically trained or leisured leadership class.[104] Any talk of natural aristocracy, they suggested, was a ploy to preserve the political privileges of social and economic elites.

After Jefferson's election to the presidency in 1800, the more radical wing of his political coalition embraced and expanded this egalitarian perspective. Philadelphia journalist and politician William Duane, for example, was one of its most ardent promoters. Duane was one of the most widely read editors in Jeffersonian America, and viewed from one angle, his writing mirrors the agrarian republicanism of Jefferson and Taylor: he railed against government patronage; he criticized funded government debt and the "adventurer[s]" and "speculator[s]" who profited from it; he warned against increasing tax burdens on farmers, which endangered their independence to pay for the lavish lifestyles of a new, parasitic nobility.[105] Like Jefferson and Taylor, he also appealed to Americans to avoid, at all costs, the British model of government, which he thought Federalists were determined to re-create in America, for it would convert American farmers and mechanics from freemen into "slaves."[106]

But rather than contrasting the corruption of this new, financial and bureaucratic nobility to the virtue of an independent leadership class, he relocated political virtue entirely into the hands of America's humble producers—those who lived off their own labor—which Duane estimated at "seventeen-twentieths of our population."[107] It was these producers, he argued, whose toil and innovation had made modern society possible in the first place.[108] It was they—and they alone—who contributed every day to the public good without seeking special favors from anyone. They were the "*useful members* of society," which he contrasted to "idle" and "profligate" elites who were constantly trying to profit from other people's industry. Moreover, it was their capacity to subsist on their own labor that gave farmers and mechanics a claim to independence. "Tell [the Federalists] you are entitled to independence as well as themselves," Duane urged. "Ask, in *your minds*, who are they in America, with so many hundreds of millions of acres of lands, that can best do without *each other—farmers and mechanics*—or *merchants?*"[109] In the same breath, he lampooned the self-important British aristocrats who felt their station entitled them to be released from the "dull pursuits of civil life": they were leeches who contributed nothing to society.[110]

In Duane's satirical attacks on British and American elites, the classical idea of the leisured and independent gentleman, freed from the demands of labor so that he could turn his attention to public affairs, was turned on its head. Incapable of sustaining himself by his own labor, he became just another species of predatory dependent. Duane was drawing together the plebian strains of his republican inheritance with the producerist egalitarianism that had long flourished among Philadelphia's artisans, which was itself inflected with an egalitarian strain of evangelical Protestantism. This heady combination foreshadowed the populist, democratic rhetoric that would become orthodox among Jacksonian Democrats.

4

Jacksonian Independence

What possible mode could you adopt so well calculated to develope all that is great and noble in the character of a people, as that of making every citizen of the country a freeholder[1]—the lord of the soil on which he lives?

—REP. ALBERT GALLITON HARRISON, 1838[2]

ALTHOUGH THE MYTH of the independent proprietor remained central to American political thought and rhetoric in the Age of Jackson, its content had changed. By the 1820s, with the exception of the deep South, the patrician ideal of a leisured, public-spirited gentry had all but vanished from American political rhetoric. All that remained was the plebian independence of the yeoman and artisan. As it had for farmers and artisans in the late eighteenth century, independence in the Jacksonian Era stood for social status: to be independent was to be a full citizen in a social world that viewed dependence as a mark of social inferiority and economic failure. But it was now a single, undifferentiated status to which all white men believed themselves entitled, and Jacksonian Democrats used it to underwrite a robustly egalitarian, democratic vision of white male society. In their hands, the myth of the independent proprietor fueled a populist politics that took aim at the unfair privileges of the rich and powerful and the government largesse that ostensibly enabled them.[3]

The myth also channeled these populist energies into a defense of expansive personal freedom and property ownership. The villains, in Democratic Party rhetoric, were powerful elites who threatened to encroach on the small proprietor's domain: bankers who held the power to recall their loans on short notice and sow panic among the cash-strapped farmers; factory owners whose new production methods stripped workers of the skills they would need to achieve ownership and self-mastery; speculators who bought up huge tracts of land and evicted settlers trying to gain a small foothold.[4] Each, in their own way, eroded farmers' and artisans' control over their property and working lives and made them feel like tenants or wage workers. Against this background, independence had come to describe a condition of private autonomy in which small proprietors retained control over their own work, including the extent of their exposure to market forces.[5]

As we explore over the next two chapters, Jacksonian Democrats also blamed government for accelerating the erosion of personal independence. Legislatures granted special charters to bankers, including the powerful Second Bank of the United States, which empowered them to manipulate the economy to their benefit. They imposed tariffs to protect and enrich domestic factory owners. They cut deals with wealthy, well-connected speculators, who then turned to the courts to secure their holdings against poor settlers. Thus the first mass, egalitarian movement to make itself felt in American politics saw itself defending private liberty against the state. It was a movement that harbored no socialist or revolutionary dreams and spoke not for a dispossessed laboring class but for small white proprietors (and would-be proprietors) who already enjoyed full democratic citizenship and looked forward to sharing in the wealth and opportunity brought by expanding markets.[6] Many subsequent generations of Americans frustrated with growing economic inequality would find themselves following in the same ideological grooves.

Even as the Democratic Party enlisted white male proprietors in a fight to protect their property and freedom from predatory elites, it also simultaneously invited them to assert their superiority over people of color and women. The white farmer's independence was premised on the availability of cheap land, and land hunger led to the violent expropriation and mass murder of Native American tribes, which Democrats increasingly justified through racist dehumanization. At the same time, a rising tide of racism, which represented African Americans as "servile" and dependent by nature, was used to roll back their civil and political rights even as these expanded for whites. Finally, white men also invoked a gendered ideal of independence to assert and defend their patriarchal domination over their households and resist expansions of women's rights. In these several ways, the increasingly populist, individualistic ideals inscribed in the myth of the independent proprietor were formulated, ever more explicitly, as the prerogatives of the white male. This too would prove to be a durable legacy.

The Revolt against "Aristocracy"

When Andrew Jackson ran for president in 1824, he presented himself as the consummate political outsider.[7] Born to Scotch-Irish immigrants and raised in the Carolina backcountry, he had learned to practice law and dabbled in politics on the Tennessee frontier, and then won national fame as a military commander in the War of 1812. Leading a band of volunteers from Tennessee and Kentucky, Jackson had defeated a far larger and better-trained British army in the Battle of New Orleans, salving a national pride that had been badly bruised by a string of embarrassing defeats. He had then achieved further military exploits in fighting the Seminoles and helping annex Spanish Florida, and he went on to serve a brief term in the U.S. Senate.

Despite his popularity as a war hero, Jackson's political rivals in 1824 dismissed him as an unseasoned upstart. Since Jefferson's election in 1800, national politics had been dominated by the Republican Party, whose leaders had handpicked first James Madison and then James Monroe as the next presidents. Absent a clear successor to Monroe, several candidates with long-established political careers stepped forward to compete for the presidency. These included John Quincy Adams, son of the elder John Adams; Henry Clay, speaker of the House of Representatives; and William Crawford, who served as secretary of the treasury under both Madison and Monroe. Jackson stunned the field by winning a plurality of electoral college votes, but fell well short of the majority needed to claim outright victory. As required by the Constitution, the election was then thrown to the House of Representatives, where Clay used his influence to deliver the presidency to Adams. Adams then appointed Clay as his secretary of state. The exchange was swiftly and widely denounced as a "corrupt bargain" and an affront to the august standards of republican political morality. Jackson condemned Clay as the "Judas of the West" (Clay was from Kentucky) and set his sights on 1828.[8] Adams, meanwhile, proved an unpopular and politically maladroit president who left himself vulnerable to challenge.

Meanwhile, broader shifts in the electorate tilted in Jackson's favor. The decade following Jackson's defeat of the British army in 1815 had seen a substantial widening of the franchise. Property qualifications had been eliminated in several older states, and new states with more inclusive constitutions had joined the union.[9] The same period also saw a shift in the way presidential electors were chosen: by 1828, only South Carolina and Delaware left the choice to their state legislatures; everywhere else, they were elected directly by voters.[10] Jackson's allies mobilized these new voters by spreading dense networks of organizing committees and partisan newspapers across the country and created—for the first time in American history—a mass electorate on a national scale.[11] Their campaign message was perfectly adapted to this new political reality: they presented Jackson as a pure embodiment of the will of the people who would reclaim their rightful power from a corrupt Washington establishment. In the same breath, they derided Adams as an effete snob and a cosmopolitan who stood profoundly out of touch with the lives of ordinary Americans.

Jackson's decisive victory in 1828 brought a reorientation of American party politics. His ascendancy finally fractured the long-standing Republican coalition and brought the Democratic Party into being. His opponents, led chiefly by Clay, eventually coalesced into the Whig Party in 1834, thereby inaugurating the Second Party System, which would last just two decades. It would take Democrats several years to fully find their political identity, but when they did, it reflected key elements of Jackson's carefully crafted political persona: Democrats claimed to speak for ordinary people against the "aristocrats" who had long dominated American politics. They claimed to represent the economic interests of America's small farmers against bankers, industrialists, and land speculators.[12] They also claimed to embody the rights of plain white folk against the "inferior" races that resisted their hegemony.

As they crafted this political message, Democrats relied heavily on the myth of the independent proprietor, which they repurposed into a vehicle for populist protest. Time and again in pamphlets, public speeches, and editorials, they spoke of unsettling changes sweeping the land: the cherished independence of ordinary Americans was being undermined by a rising class of elites who had amassed special economic privileges and powers and used them to gain control of the national economy. Soon, they warned, America's proud yeomen and artisans would be reduced to "the dependents of a few capitalists" and mere "serfs upon the soil of which their fathers were the lords."[13] These appeals formed part of an immensely successful rhetorical strategy that Democrats deployed to channel Americans' anxieties about economic and social change. Its appeal was strengthened by the ominous idea—ubiquitous in Democratic Party rhetoric—that that America's exceptionalism was itself under threat: the erosion of independence would tun the United States into Europe, with its hordes of landless poor dominated by a small class of aristocrats, and eviscerate America's redemptive moral potential.[14]

Where, then, did the main threats to personal independence lie? First of all, the economic panic and contraction of 1819—the country's first serious economic depression—had exposed the enormous power that *banks* held over the lives of ordinary people. Many farmers, especially in the West, had bought their farms from government land offices on installment plans, and they needed money to make their payments. When the sudden recession threw countless local banks into crisis, their notes depreciated wildly. Land offices stopped accepting many local banknotes altogether. Even with a sound currency, falling prices for wheat and other staples would have made it difficult for farmers to meet their obligations, but what money they did receive was of no use. Waves of foreclosures swept through the western states. Meanwhile, as banks desperately recalled their loans to preserve their solvency, scores of small-scale entrepreneurs and business owners operating on credit in towns and cities throughout the United States were thrown into bankruptcy.[15]

Banks were widely blamed for these painful upheavals, and the broad discretion that they exercised over economic life came under heightened scrutiny. Banks could not only choose their borrowers but also recall their loans selectively. They could shield favored clients, who were typically wealthy entrepreneurs, and when the banks' own reserves were depleted, they could protect themselves from insolvency by suspending payments in gold or silver coin (or "specie"). Small proprietors discovered, to their alarm, that they depended on what seemed to them the arbitrary will of a new caste of elites who now controlled the flow of currency and credit to the whole country. John Branch, the populist governor of North Carolina, fumed that banks could avoid repaying their own debts, even while their small borrowers were "degraded and stripped even to the last cow that gives sustenance to his family, to meet the demands of his creditors."[16] Meanwhile, employers could legally pay workers' wages in banknotes even when these notes had depreciated severely, so the pain spread to wage earners, too.

To William Allen, a Democratic senator from Ohio, the entire banking system came to seem profoundly aristocratic: by granting a small, privileged class monopoly control over the currency and exposing ordinary Americans to its unpredictable fluctuations, it "bereave[s] a vast proportion of our citizens of that independence of spirit and purpose indispensable to the support of freedom."[17] In this context, indebtedness itself came to seem like a dangerous form of dependence. The Democratic *New York Evening Post*, for instance, lamented that once a farmer has been persuaded to take out loans against his land—for improvements, or for "finery"—"his house, outhouses, fences, and fields of clover . . . [are] only a shadow, for the occupant is a tenant at will." The bank was now the de facto proprietor, and the farmer could no longer "look out on his fields of grain and grass with the calm, satisfied consciousness of independence."[18] In eroding the farmer's independence, debt also reintroduced profound inequalities to American society. "Individual debts," the Democrats warned, ". . . are productive of a condition of dependence destructive of equality among men."[19] Their political opponents might extol credit and a plentiful paper currency as sources of economic growth and shared prosperity; in fact, said the Democrats, they were dividing American society into unequal classes: the creditors and their dependent borrowers.

The fight against the Second Bank of the United States that erupted in the early 1830s and came to dominate the politics of the period tapped this deep vein of anxiety and frustration over the growing power of the new financial elite. The Bank was a corporation owned by private shareholders, yet it served a number of vital public functions: it collected federal tax receipts, loaned money to the federal government, and paid its bills; in making and recalling loans to smaller state banks throughout the country, it also exercised considerable control over the national currency.[20] Democrats came to see this hybrid public-private entity as the embodiment of everything they feared: the consolidation of vast powers in the hands of a new, financial aristocracy.[21] Jackson's controversial decision to veto the Bank's rechartering in 1832 set off a national furor and sharpened partisan identities for the ensuing two decades.

Speaking to fellow Democrats in Pittsburgh, Judge Shaler warned that the Bank of the United States had extended its aristocratic tentacles across the entire economy: "The mercantile community became its debtors. The manufacturers permitted themselves to be dependent on its will. Trade, commerce, exchanges, the rise and depression of property, . . . every thing in the commercial and manufacturing cities, depended on its sovereign will."[22] The Bank represented a new, organized "*moneyed power*" that was quickly and efficiently reducing the entire American population to a condition of economic dependence. Who would stand up to it politically, he asked, once its economic power was complete?[23] Meanwhile, Thomas Hart Benton, the powerful Democratic senator from Missouri, inveighed against the Bank as the centerpiece of a "moneyed oligarchy." Among his many worries were its broad real estate hold-ings, which effectively made it a landed aristocrat of old and a master to count-less tenants. "Republics want freeholders," he declared, "not landlords and tenants."[24]

Alongside banks, factories—and the intensified division of labor they augured—stood out as emerging threats to personal independence. As new markets opened up for eastern artisans, they faced pressure to expand, and enterprising master artisans, with the help of merchant-capitalist investors, began to devise new, cheaper methods of production that relied more heavily on unskilled labor.[25] Increasingly, capital-intensive factory production drove a wedge between ownership and labor, which had been united in the figure of the master artisan. Journeymen, who had once expected to attain indepen-dence at the end of a fixed term, found themselves stuck in these new, larger urban shops, deprived of the opportunity to acquire the necessary skills and capital, working indefinitely for lower wages.[26] Even in rural areas, artisans were increasingly exposed to competition from large, urban shops that pro-duced goods much more cheaply. To many artisans, the dream of indepen-dence, of becoming something other than a dependent wage laborer, seemed to be evaporating.[27]

The working-class political rhetoric of the period reflects these anxieties. Seth Luther, a Rhode Island carpenter and early labor organizer, pilloried the cotton mills of the Northeast as unrepublican, "aristocratical" institutions that reduced workers to a condition of total dependence and were therefore unfit for freemen.[28] Silas Wright, who served as Democratic governor of New York, argued that factory workers suffered from a "peculiar dependence, unknown to any other classes of laborers in our country." He accused capitalists of hold-ing tremendous power "over the living, the comforts and independence of the manufacturing laborer" and he blamed special privileges granted manufactur-ers by law for forcing workers into "these dependent situations."[29] Factory workers, lamented the *Washington Globe*[30] in 1842, had sunk to the level of "wretched slaves" whose masters formed a new and dangerous aristocracy.[31] In an address to workingmen reprinted in the *New England Artisan*, one speaker declared that the factory would render workers "wholly dependent upon a few employers, and forever crush that spirit of independence which is the only safeguard of freedom."[32]

Part of the problem lay in the "de-skilling" of artisan labor: unlike ap-prentices in preindustrial workshops, who would eventually master their craft and set out on their own, laborers who worked in factories or urban manufactories[33] were more often confined to simpler, repetitive tasks that would never amount to skilled trade.[34] Lacking the skills they needed to strike out on their own, they might then remain wage workers indefinitely, dependent on their bosses for their daily bread, working in "closely supervised," regimented workplaces.[35] For many workingmen, this condition of perpetual wage work was inherently demeaning; they called it "wage slavery" (or "wages slavery"). One labor spokesman explained, for example, that urban workingmen "do not complain of wages slavery *solely* on account of the poverty it occasions." "They oppose it," he insisted, "because it holds the laboring classes in a state of abject dependence on capitalists, not only for the bread it is their right to eat and the work it is their duty to do, but for the continuation of their lives, and the preservation of their morals."[36]

Like banks, which were created by special legislative charters, factories were widely seen as creations of the state. After the War of 1812, the federal government had imposed stiff tariffs on manufactured goods to protect the young domestic industries that had sprung up during the conflict with Britain. These protective tariffs grew through the late 1820s and eventually angered not only farmers and planters, who felt they suffered unfair retribution from their trading partners abroad, but also urban workers who saw them as subsidies for rich capitalists.[37] The *Western Review* argued that protective tariffs were part of a conspiracy to "destroy the independence of the laboring people of the republic." These tariffs, the *Review* argued, were designed to speed America's transition to a manufacturing economy, which would accelerate the division of labor and reduce American workers to the poverty and misery of their counterparts in Britain.[38] The *Globe*, meanwhile, urged its readers to remember that while tariffs were supposed to protect domestic workers, they did not protect "the healthy mechanic or artisan, who works for himself at his own shop." Instead they tended to create a workforce dependent on "the discretion of a penurious master."[39]

This anxiety over the growing dependence of America's small producers could also be found, finally, in the debates over land policy—and the policy of "preemption" in particular—in the 1830s.[40] Preemption allowed squatters on federal lands to buy the farmland they occupied and cultivated for the minimum government price of $1.25 per acre before anyone else was allowed to bid for it. Opponents, including the Whig leader Henry Clay, insisted that it was a giveaway to scofflaws. Supporters, on the other hand, argued that it enabled poor farmers to achieve the independence they so desired. On the Senate floor in January 1838, William Fulton of Arkansas spoke of the "enterprising spirit which made [the settler] risk so much in pursuit of independence," and worried that it would be snatched away if lands were sold at auction to wealthy speculators.[41] Clement Comer Clay of Alabama urged his colleagues to "extend the favor of the Government so far as to give to every industrious poor farmer of the old states, who was not a freeholder, the opportunity of becoming so." After all, he argued, these were the pioneers whose "enterprise and perseverance" had made civilization possible.[42]

From the mainstream Democratic point of view, the main culprits were the "bands" of wealthy speculators who bought up huge tracts of western lands and waited to resell them at a profit once local development had increased their value. Defenders of preemption in the Senate, many of whom represented the newer states, worried that these speculators would become landed aristocrats in the European style who would turn America's proud settlers into tenants. Robert Walker of Mississippi argued, for example, that large auction sales to speculators

> will certainly introduce into the new States the system of landlord and tenant, by which the occupant will not be the owner of the soil he cultivates, but the tributary of some absentee landlord, who will, in the shape of an annual rent, reap nearly all the profits of the labor of the cultivator. It will establish a relation of abject dependence, on the one hand, and tyrannical power on the other.[43]

Lucious Lyon of Michigan added that the accumulation of vast tracts of land in speculators' hands would ensure that the poor farmer of the East had no place to go, forcing him to remain "the tenant of some wealthy landlord" and to "place his children in a manufactory."[44] In this way, preemption was presented as an antidote to dependence in the East and West alike. Walker made this explicit: the preemption bill, he said, "encourages agriculture, that mother of freemen, that nurse of virtue, liberty, and independence."[45]

By the 1840s, cheap lands in the West had become a kind of Democratic panacea. Not only would it give white farmers an opportunity to own a farm of their own; not only would it provide a kind of safety valve for urban wage workers who yearned to escape their bondage; but it might also raise wages for those workers who stayed behind. A special edition of the *Globe* during the election of 1840 defended preemption in these terms:

> The laborer or mechanic suffering from low wages or a want of employment, or finding himself degraded by a state of dependence, may, under the

policy of these laws, not only emancipate himself at once, but secure independence and comfort to his children. And the greater the number thus withdrawn from labor in the old States, the higher will be the wages, and the less the dependence of those who remain.[46]

Cheap land in the West would siphon off excess labor from the eastern cities, reducing labor competition and raising wages. In a similar vein, Col. Benjamin Faneuil Hunt argued that the availability of land in the West was a precondition of freedom for the working man: "A man may work for himself, if another does not offer him enough. He is free to make his bargain, as a boundless and virgin soil invites him to manly toil . . . [and] the delights of an independent home."[47] The openness of the "virgin" West meant that the American worker was not captive to employers offering low wages; his horizons were so much broader than the poor "wretches" who worked in English factories.[48] The land reform agenda, which found such broad resonance among Democrats in the 1830s and 1840s, was eventually taken up by the Republican Party in the late 1850s, and it resulted in the passage of the Homestead Act of 1862.

Because Jacksonian Democrats criticized "capitalists" and lamented growing economic consolidation, some historians have presented them as nostalgic defenders of pre-market, subsistence culture. In this interpretation of antebellum politics, the rhetoric of personal independence was the rallying cry of rural communities anxious to insulate themselves from economic modernization and to preserve their relative isolation from the wider world.[49] Although this view captures the attitudes of some isolated subsistence farmers in such areas as the southern highlands, it fundamentally misdescribes the broader political landscape of the Jacksonian Era.[50]

In fact, orators and journalists on both sides of the political aisle celebrated spectacular growth of the American economy, which seemed to be opening up unprecedented opportunities for working people and sowing the seeds of a great and prosperous new nation. "Our commerce has flourished by its own inherent vigor," crowed Massachusetts Democrat Robert Rantoul Jr., and "gathered the spoils of every clime." He went on to praise the growth of America's "great cities," and the canals and railways that linked them to the country's interior and delivered a widely shared prosperity.[51] In fact, few editorialists or politicians could be found who did not welcome these transformations as a form of divinely sanctioned progress.[52] By the time the Whig Party coalesced to oppose the Jacksonian Democrats in the early 1830s, the broad economic disagreements between them were not about *whether* to embrace market society—this question had been mostly settled. It was, rather, about what *kind* of market society to embrace.

As they sought to articulate a clear economic vision, Democrats used the idea of personal independence to define the kind of hybrid economy they wanted. Broadly speaking, they embraced what political theorist C. B. MacPherson has called "simple market society": a society in which "the production and distribution of goods and services is regulated by the market but in which labor itself is not a market commodity." In such a society, workers retain ownership of their land or their shop and work for themselves—they "retain the control of their own energies and skills."[53] As we explore in chapters 6 and 7, Democrats consistently praised markets themselves for bringing prosperity and economic opportunity to the country's small proprietors. On the other hand, they criticized the powerful economic institutions—such as large banks and corporations and factories—commonly associated with the rise of a "mature" capitalist economy.[54] They saw these as aristocratic devices that threatened to distort the operation of healthy markets in favor of the wealthy, and in so doing to reduce small proprietors to a condition of dependence.[55] Jacksonian Democrats, in other words, saw an alternative path to national progress and prosperity—a path that also preserved the exceptionalism of America's small-producer-led economy.

The Privatization of Republican Ideas

The gradual disappearance of the patrician ideal of independence in the United States coincided with a privatization of republican ideas that had begun in the eighteenth century. This privatization is evident in the changing content of two other concepts that were integral to the myth of the independent proprietor: landed property and civic virtue. In English republican thought, land was not understood as a commodity; rather, it was meant to be a stable possession passed down through generations of the same family. If the purpose of property ownership was to ensure a balanced distribution of power in the republic, it was important that property be stable—indeed, it was *security in property* that guaranteed the landholders' independence, and hence their liberty.[56] In this context, property ownership was understood as a form of heritable dominion: its owner was allotted the responsibility of ruling this domain, and this responsibility would be passed down through generations.[57] Ownership of landed property was thought to create a permanent stake in the community;

it signified long-standing attachment. It was contrasted to the more fungible forms of property—stocks and credit, for example—which could be "withdrawn at pleasure."[58] Landholders who could expect their children and grandchildren to inherit and live on the same plot of land could therefore be expected to have the long-term interests of the community at heart—the permanence of their landed interest was one of the wellsprings of their civic virtue. Property, as Pocock puts it, "anchored the individual in the structure of power and virtue."[59]

These ideas were never as widely held in America as in Britain. Colonial Americans chafed at what they perceived to be feudal restrictions on property, which they associated with hereditary aristocracy.[60] After the Revolution, their resistance had only intensified. Jefferson himself had attacked the law and custom of primogeniture: if property were divided among a family's sons, he argued, then families would not be able to preserve their dominance across many generations. The law of entail, which prevented owners from dividing or selling their estates, was also attacked and dismantled.[61] Jefferson pushed for a view of ownership as "absolute dominion," which he associated with a pre-feudal Saxon past.[62] The prominent Federalist Noah Webster, meanwhile, argued that "an equality of property, with a necessity of alienation, constantly operating to destroy combinations of powerful families, is the very soul of a republic."[63] Alienation—which simply meant the right to sell or transfer property to another—was widely linked to equality and meritocracy: it meant that any man could, in principle, acquire as much property as his hard work and talent allowed.

The tendency to regard land as a commodity only intensified in the Jacksonian Era: loosening the legal restrictions on land owners was one of the central concerns of American property lawyers during the antebellum period.[64] Restrictions on owners' use of their land were attacked as vestiges of a corrupt and aristocratic age, and even as speculation in land was often condemned, the idea of land as marketable property was identified with personal freedom. In practice, moreover, land was being bought and sold constantly, as low prices enabled farmers to buy land, make improvements, and then resell it at a profit, taking their families further west. The idea of land as a permanent stake in the community had all but lost its relevance.[65] Far from anchoring the individual in a particular community and in a network of reciprocal duties, this emerging, market-compatible view of property ownership delineated a private sphere in which the individual was free from interference—including interference by government—and largely free from specifically defined obligation to others.

The social status that independence afforded was uncoupled from the civic "personality" of the neoclassical republican tradition.[66]

Parallel changes also gradually redefined the republican idea of virtue, lending greater importance to private character traits. We saw, in chapter 3, that the Jeffersonians had associated plebian independence with private, Protestant virtues—notably industry, frugality, and moderation—alongside the more traditional, civic virtues that had dominated the republican tradition.[67] This same combination was already evident earlier, on both sides of the debates around the American founding. The Vermont and Pennsylvania constitutions, for example, insisted that "frequent recurrence to fundamental principles, and a firm adherence to justice, moderation, temperance, industry, and frugality are absolutely necessary to preserve the blessings of liberty and keep a government free."[68] Meanwhile, Federalists and Anti-Federalists alike traced the crisis that they saw in American republicanism to the rise of luxury and avarice and the decline of "industry and frugality" among the people. According to one intellectual historian, "noncivic" conceptions of virtue circulated in the 1780s with "formulaic frequency."[69]

Benjamin Franklin, whose *Autobiography* remains one of the great manifestos of American individualism, epitomized this merger of republican and Protestant virtues. First published in 1791, it saw twenty-two editions republished between 1794 and 1828. Its influence was felt especially among the "producing classes" to whom the Jacksonian Democrats appealed. Among the virtues that Franklin famously celebrated, industry and frugality were arguably the most important. These were the virtues most directly responsible, wrote Franklin, for maintaining his personal independence, and keeping him "free from Debt, which exposes Man to Confinement and a Species of Slavery to his Creditors."[70] Moreover, all thirteen of the virtues he names were *private* in the sense that they were presented as a recipe for personal success, wealth, and happiness, not mainly for public, political goals. Virtue, for him, was closely associated with the prudent pursuit of individual interest.[71]

It would be a mistake, however, to describe Franklin's idea of virtue as egoistic. Time and again, Franklin presents industry and frugality not only as a "Means of procuring Wealth" but also as a precondition of moral probity: honesty and justice, he writes, always come easier to a man of independent means.[72] Franklin's own later career, of course, exemplified a devotion to the public good, as he emphasizes at length in the third part of the *Autobiography*. Indeed, his *Autobiography* can be read as a sustained effort to reconcile the prudent pursuit of self-interest with moral and political virtue. For Franklin, these were all mutually supporting elements of the good life—a good life available to anyone, no matter how humble his beginnings. Hard work, careful saving, and simple habits all enabled Americans to attain a measure of wealth; to be free of the corrupting influence of poverty and lavish luxury alike, both of which brought dependence; to build a sound reputation; to be happy and free from obligation to others; and eventually to devote energy to public projects. The main ethical challenge, in achieving such a life, was not the conquest of self-interest in the name of the public good, as the classical republican tradition would have described it. Instead, it was the conquest of sloth and indiscipline in the service of purposive activity that served both self and society.[73]

The elevation of private virtues such as industry, frugality, and prudence had coincided, over the course of the eighteenth century with a reassessment of the idea of self-interest itself. "At the beginning of the period," writes historian Daniel Walker Howe, "self-interest had generally been considered one of the passions," which needed to be strictly contained through rational self-discipline. "By the end," however, philosophers and theologians "had definitely promoted it to the rank of a rational faculty."[74] They had done this, in part, by breaking it in two: "self-indulgence," or short-term self-interest, was still a dangerous impulse, but long-term, "enlightened self-interest" was not.[75] Indeed, enlightened self-interest could be a source of self-discipline and an enemy of both idleness and impulsive self-gratification. As such, it was not only a source of individual happiness and fulfillment but also a way of motivating individuals to contribute productively to society.[76]

By the Jacksonian Era, Franklin's virtues, and the motivational power of enlightened self-interest, had become fully incorporated into the ideal of republican citizenship. "The manly virtues of the republican citizen," writes one historian, overstating his case somewhat, "were practically narrowed down to the hard work, saving, and reinvestment that were supposed to be the best means for individual success and for the economic progress of the country."[77] It would be more accurate to say that these economic virtues were *merged* into the older idea of civic integrity and devotion. "It is the correct understanding of his own true interests," wrote Rantoul Jr., "that makes one man happily virtuous." Hard work, frugality, and honesty would lead to propertied independence, which in turn would enable the individual to resist corrupting influences and stand for "light and conviction."[78] The individual's own interests and happiness would coincide, therefore, with the good of the community.

Writing about the ambiguities of "virtue" during the Revolutionary period, Gordon Wood observes that while "classical virtue had flowed from the citizen's participation in politics, . . . modern virtue flowed from the citizen's participation in society," specifically in productive economic activity.[79] In the political thinking of Jacksonian Democrats, this "producerist" ideal—which we saw in the writings of radical Jeffersonian William Duane—achieved a decisive victory. Time and again, we find the Democrats linking the farmer's or the artisan's virtue to his status as an independent *producer*. Time and again, we find them casting suspicion on politics as such as a source of moral corruption, not virtue. This shift can be traced, once again, to Jacksonian egalitarianism. The Democratic electorate in the Age of Jackson was composed of small farmers, artisans, and laborers who spent the vast majority of their time engaged in economic activity. To celebrate them as the paragons of republican virtue—while erasing their patrician counterparts or denigrating them as aristocrats—was to shift the meaning of the term, to foreground the dignity and value of economic life over political life.[80]

In fact, the yeoman and artisan of antebellum America were the perfect transitional figures, standing at the confluence of republican and liberal capitalist ideals: as independent proprietors, they escaped the vices of dependence; at the same time, they were producers and creators of wealth contributing to an increasingly global market economy. "As long as the market actor could plausibly be associated with the classical image of the free-holding citizen," writes political theorist Eric MacGilvray, "then these two conceptions of freedom could be used almost interchangeably: The right to free exchange on which a market economy depends could be treated as a corollary of the right to the secure ownership of property on which republican freedom had always rested."[81] The Jacksonian Democrats' ideology flourished just before this fortuitous confluence began to collapse, and this timing accounts for its tremendous optimism about the compatibility of market freedom and political freedom. We will explore this optimism, its political implications, and its lasting imprint on American political ideas in more detail in later chapters.

The Salience of Race

Originally, the republican ideal of independence had told a story of distinction. It told of privileged classes of property owners whose character and virtue made them uniquely suited for political agency and responsibility. The poor, by contrast, were marked as politically untrustworthy. Their economic dependence left them vulnerable to manipulation and capture by wealthy patrons or demagogues. Their lack of a long-term, propertied "stake" in

society, meanwhile, made them a potentially radical and irresponsible political force.

As Jacksonian Democrats assailed this long-standing exclusion as a relic of
European aristocracy, they faced the challenge of explaining why even the
poorest whites were fit for self-government. Increasingly, they turned to race
to supply this explanation: the Jacksonian mythology of independence told of
the men of a privileged race who, by virtue of their ethnic and cultural inheritance, were uniquely suited to hold political power and destined to own and
command the North American continent.[82] Thomas Roderick Dew, whose
full-throated, 1832 defense of slavery marked a turning point in southern opinion, made this explicit: in Virginia, he wrote, "color alone is . . . the badge of
distinction, the true mark of aristocracy, and all who are white are equal in
spite of the variety of occupation."[83] In this way, white supremacy became part
of the very premise of the yeoman republic: Native and African Americans
were the degraded classes in contrast to which whites could affirm their civic
status.[84]

The mythology of the enterprising, courageous, and peaceful white settler,
whose civilizing labors were obstructed by the "savage" recalcitrance of the
Native Americans, was one key vehicle for this racialization of personal independence. In some ways, of course, the popular caricature of Native Americans
epitomized independence. They were often portrayed as fiercely resistant to
authority, stubborn to a fault, comfortable in solitude, resilient and self-
supporting. And yet, in the white imagination, such independence seemed
fatally disconnected from any kind of improvement or *progress*. Countless
whites claimed that even with ample leisure time, Native Americans showed
no interest in cultivating their minds, morals, or manners. They accused indigenous Americans of showing no inclination to work—certainly not to the
agricultural work that "improved" and civilized the American landscape. They
routinely perpetuated the racist stereotype of Native Americans as childlike
and irrational: their minds, wrote Lewis Cass, who served as Andrew Jackson's
secretary of war, were unusually susceptible to "wild and debasing supersti-
tions." Despite the strenuous efforts expended by white missionaries and educators, he continued, the Native American seemed incapable of rational self-
control: "reckless of consequences, he is the child of impulse. Unrestrained by
moral considerations, whatever his passions prompt he does."[85] In short, wrote
another commentator, his "rude independence" never bore any of the intellectual, moral, and civic fruits that would qualify him for citizenship in a
republic.[86]

By the 1830s and 1840s, the prevailing explanation for this supposed deficit was racial. After suggesting that there seemed to be "some insurmountable obstacle in the habits or temperament of the Indians" that barred them from improvement, Cass got more specific: those few who had "acquired property" and come to appreciate republican institutions, he claimed, were *"half-breeds"* whose white blood had opened the gates of civilization.[87] Cass's view reflected an important shift in the American understanding of racial difference. Whereas the founding generation had still believed, for the most part, that racial differences had environmental causes, this view had gradually crumbled in the face of a rising pseudoscientific discourse of innate racial hierarchy.[88] Drawing on the emerging pseudoscience of phrenology, American intellectuals lent credibility to the crudest racial invective. Speaking at the annual meeting of the Boston Society of Natural History, for example, the prominent physician and natural scientist Samuel Morton argued that Native Americans formed part of a separate race whose moral and intellectual inferiority was empirically demonstrable. Citing extensive ethnographic observations as well as an analysis of skull size, he claimed that they were violent, duplicitous, and amoral by nature. He also insisted that they were cognitively impaired: "their minds seize with avidity on simple truths," and they showed no "predilection for the arts or sciences."[89]

These racist ideas were absorbed into the myth of the independent proprietor and became part of the justification of westward expansion. Discussing the settlement of the Oregon Territory in 1845, for example, Rep. Alexander Duncan, a Democrat from Ohio, declared that American institutions were designed for "our Anglo-Saxon-American race," which would "thrive and prosper" under their aegis. He seemed to view this as a fairly inclusive category, encompassing both the "Russian serf" and the "Ottoman's slave," both of whom, when transported to America, "become a freeman, with a soul as responsible as that of the master from which he has fled."[90] The Native Americans, however, were different. They were not fit for such freedom, he declared; instead, they were "made for a state of nature." Senator Benton drew a similar contrast when justifying the killing and displacement of the Florida Seminoles: hardy and virtuous white proprietors were the bearers of civilization; the field could be cleared for their labors only by vanquishing the intractable "savages" who stood in their way.[91]

Such arguments shed more light on the conceptual transformation of personal independence in Jacksonian America. No longer a vehicle for excluding poor whites, independence had morphed into both an *entitlement* owed equally to all (hardworking) white men and the key to unlocking their moral and civic potential. The commonplace image of the degraded and ignorant English factory worker showed that neither whiteness nor even Anglo-Saxon blood was enough to produce virtuous citizens. But give this "hardy race" of men ownership of their own plot of land, and they blossomed into autonomous, hardworking, responsible individuals of independent mind and spirit, bringing free civilization in their wake.[92] This reformulated ideal was simultaneously inclusive and egalitarian for white men—including the European immigrants whom the federal government deliberately recruited to settle western outposts—and harshly exclusive of people of color.[93] Within the myth of the independent proprietor, then, class hierarchy had morphed into racial hierarchy; full citizenship, in this newly democratic nation, had become a prerogative of whiteness.[94]

Independence and white supremacy were linked in other ways, too: if a racialized myth of the independent proprietor was used to *justify* expansionist violence, the political economy of small proprietorship helped motivate it. In fact, land hunger was endemic to smallholder society. As families grew and sons aspired to become independent proprietors in their own right, they needed more land to claim. "The basic drive to procure enough land and productive equipment," writes historian Daniel Vickers, "to ensure, at the very least, that nobody in one's family would have to depend on others for work" was both "socially divisive" within communities and violently expansionist without.[95] Over and over, white settlers' desire for land fueled expansionist policies, from Jackson's forced removal of tens of thousands of Creeks and Cherokees from their ancestral lands to the recurring Seminole Wars. It also drove the federal government's strategic use of land policy to overwhelm native groups with large inflows of settlers.[96] Jackson owed his electoral success, in no small part, to his willingness to force the southeastern tribes off of their land, which made him virtually unassailable throughout the southern states.[97]

The fact that propertied independence required constant territorial expansion was no mystery to Americans at the time. As we saw in chapter 2, Jefferson himself had understood it clearly; so did Alexander Duncan. Had the American nation been confined to its original thirteen states, he argued, it would consist of "hundreds of rich monopolists, capitalists and landlords, and millions of slaves, beggars, and paupers." Population growth and geographical confinement would by then have reproduced "European" patterns of inequality and dependence. He contrasted this unhappy vision with the American West as he now saw it, teeming with more than ten millions of happy and independent beings, who eat and sleep and work at the mandate of no master, who cringe at the frown of no *superior*; but eat the bread of their cheerful labor which God blesses; drink the pure water that gushes from their own fountains; who walk erect, and carry within them a soul responsible to their-fellow men while here, and responsible to their God hereafter; who carry in their manly countenance the image of their Maker.[98]

White land hunger is transformed, here, into a noble prerequisite of republican liberty. In fact, Duncan was hardly alone in presenting territorial expansion as an obligation to both present and future generations of whites. This was part of the idea of Manifest Destiny, which many Democrats enthusiastically promoted: as the American population grew and as more Europeans fled their oppressive circumstances to find independence and freedom, they would need land to occupy. Was this not, after all, the destiny that God had ordained for North America?[99]

As legal historian Aziz Rana has documented, both the ideal of independent proprietorship and the fervent desire for territorial expansion formed part of a "settler colonial" mentality that had defined the American political project from its earliest days. Rana lists its four key components: first, the view that "economic independence [was] the ethical basis of free citizenship"; second, a commitment to conquest so as to acquire the territory necessary for widespread land ownership; third, an exclusive idea of republican citizenship which held that many people were unfit for "the benefits of economic independence"; and fourth, a desire to recruit and welcome white immigrants in order to populate newly conquered territories.[100] As Rana points out, Americans often labored to conceal this violent, colonial feature of their society even from themselves: "the vision of indigenous territory as empty land was part and parcel of settler efforts to transform themselves into 'natives' and to escape the very category of colonialism."[101] This tendency is abundantly evident in the debates over the Oregon Territory in the 1840s, for example, in which Democratic politicians repeatedly contrasted the benign and peaceful spread of American liberty to brutal British colonialism all around the world.[102] The myth of the independent proprietor and its idealized image of the peaceful and industrious white settler contributed to this obfuscation.

Native American leaders and activists saw these obfuscations for what they were, and they vigorously contested the narrative of the peaceful yeoman spreading civilization in his wake. They told instead of unscrupulous white invaders who coveted their land and took it by force and fraud, in violation of their own treaty obligations and in contravention of every conceivable principle of justice and international law. They told of Cherokee farmers and small proprietors brutalized and forced from their homes, their land, crops, and livestock stolen with impunity.[103] Such outrages, wrote Cherokee activist John Ridge, revealed the United States to be a predatory colonial power, activated by the "inglorious doctrine, that *'force is right,'*" and hiding its naked self-interest under the veneer of a racist paternalism that declared—in the face of overwhelming evidence—that Native Americans were incapable of "civilized" life.[104]

If Native Americans were thought to exemplify a primitive independence that showed no capacity for improvement, African Americans were commonly depicted as servile and dependent by nature. Speaking at the Michigan constitutional convention of 1850, one Mr. Britain reflected on the "dependence, subserviency, and meniality of the great body" of "colored persons" everywhere. They had been slaves in Africa, he argued, subject to the iron rule of petty princes and chieftains. Set them free and they would hardly know what to do with themselves, for they were "incapable of self-government."[105] Others invoked precisely the language that had once been used to justify excluding propertyless whites: Blacks, they argued, were ignorant and easily manipulated by "designing" men with political ambitions. Lacking the cultivated independence to form their own judgments, they were easily whipped up into a "dangerous" force.[106] Such representations were reinforced by the minstrel shows that became immensely popular in the 1820s and commonly portrayed Black slaves as infantile, contented, and easily deceived.[107]

These ubiquitous representations of African Americans as servile and "degraded" were integral to the gradual disenfranchisement of free Blacks in the northern and western states. As white voting rights expanded in the early decades of the nineteenth century, Black voting rights contracted. Several states—including New Jersey, Maryland, and Connecticut—which had extended voting rights to Blacks after the Revolution stripped or limited them by 1820. New York, Pennsylvania, and North Carolina followed suit shortly thereafter, and every new state that joined the union after 1819 prohibited Blacks from voting.[108] Those who justified such contractions at the state constitutional conventions that ratified them often invoked the crudest racial stereotypes.

In fact, such stereotypes were integral to the construction of *whiteness* as a collective identity. As European immigrants from different cultures and backgrounds struggled to assert their membership in their new country, their whiteness became an important badge of belonging. In America, writes historian David Roediger, workers of diverse European backgrounds "were becoming *white workers* who identified their freedom and their dignity in work as being suited to those who were 'not slaves' or 'not negurs.'"[109] If blackness stood for meekness and childlike dependence, whiteness embodied the industriousness, rationality, and fierce spirit of independence that were required for both progress and self-government. Many white workers therefore resisted racial mixing of any kind, for it threatened to blur this crucial boundary. Defenders of the violent 1834 race riots in Columbia, Pennsylvania, for example, wrote of a plot "to break down the distinctive barrier between the colors that the poor whites may gradually sink into the degraded condition of the Negroes—that, like them, they may be slaves and tools."[110] To raise the economic, social, or political condition of Blacks was to threaten this "distinctive barrier" that preserved that status and privilege of the independent white freeman. In fact, many poor whites in Jacksonian America came to imagine their whiteness itself as a form of *property*, much like artisans sometimes defined their skill as a kind of property that set them apart from the underclass and marked them as stakeholders in the republican polity.[111]

Slavery, which was now more expansive and profitable than ever, propelled this resurgent white racism. In fact, the Jacksonian Era marked the high point of what historians have called "second slavery" in the United States. By the 1820s, the sugar production, powered by slave labor, that had driven economic expansion in the Atlantic world had begun to stagnate, and it was replaced by another staple commodity: cotton. The invention of the cotton gin, the seizure of Native American lands in the fertile southern plains, and the rise of industrial textile production in Britain combined to create a tremendously profitable new business. At its heart lay the forced labor of over a million Black slaves. To meet the skyrocketing global demand for machine-woven textiles, Americans financed and created vast new forced labor camps and filled them by buying up slaves from their eastern masters, separating them from their families, and marching them—chained and at the point of a whip—hundreds of miles into the fertile cotton belt. As cotton produced tremendous wealth for the South and North alike, chattel slavery insinuated itself ever more deeply into the American economy.[112]

As we have seen, Americans had long understood slavery as the antithesis of personal independence. This polarity showed up constantly in their political rhetoric: factory workers were being reduced to *slaves*; debtors had become *slaves*; planters who paid tariffs to subsidize northern industry were becoming *slaves*. The first meaning given for the term "freeman" in the 1828 edition of Webster's dictionary is: "One who enjoys liberty, or who is not subject to the will of another; one not a slave or vassal."[113] This focal contrast had always played an important conceptual role in republican thought, going back to its classical origins. But by the Jacksonian Era, at the height of the global cotton boom, it had become clearly racialized: it was Black slaves, specifically, who epitomized the subjugation and dependence from which white republicans took flight.[114] We explore the ideological significance of slavery in more detail in chapters 6 and 8.

"Dependent and Defenceless": Gender and the Family

The myth of the independent proprietor also served, finally, as an ideological vehicle for American patriarchy. As we saw in chapter 2, the republican ideal of propertied independence had always been gendered: it connoted masculine virility, self-assertion, and self-control. In the republican imagination, it had long been linked to military valor: freeholding men were also citizen-soldiers who took up arms to defend their freedoms. Dependence, by contrast, was consistently feminized. "Wives and unmarried daughters," writes historian Rowland Berthoff, "like servants and slaves, had been dependents both in classical republican theory and in ordinary experience." In nineteenth-century America, he continues, "womankind in general was often lumped together in phrases like 'frail, lovely and dependent.'"[115] A man who lost his independence was thought to be emasculated, reduced to something like a woman's condition.[116]

In antebellum America, these assumptions were deeply inscribed into family life and family law. When a woman married, she lost the ability to hold property in her own name. All of her possessions, including any wages she earned, passed to her husband.[117] For married women, independent proprietorship was therefore literally unattainable. In fact, American family law was still largely governed by the archaic common law ideal of "coverture," which stipulated that a married woman's legal and civic identity was subsumed into her husband's. In the words of the influential English jurist William Blackstone, "the very being or legal existence of the woman is suspended during the marriage, or at least is incorporated and consolidated into that of the husband; under whose wing, protection and cover, she performs everything."[118] According to this view, the woman could have no interest, and no publicly significant voice, separate from her husband's. This legal fusion of the husband and wife was, of course, explicitly hierarchical: the wife occupied an inferior and subservient role, strictly subject to her husband's authority.[119]

A woman's dependent position in the family marked her as unworthy of full citizenship in the republican polity. As we have seen over the last several chapters, the myth of the independent proprietor forged a powerful connection between property ownership and civic competence and virtue. Addressing the Massachusetts constitutional convention of 1853, one Mr. Simonds spelled out its implications for women bluntly:

> I find that mankind, in common with all created intelligences, are divided into two principal classes, the independent and the dependent. My idea of sovereignty . . . is, that those rightfully possess it, who stand in the relation of independent in the community, and not that of dependent. I necessarily come to the conclusion, then, that the female portion of the community are in this condition of dependence, that they never can, and never ought, rightfully, to be considered as possessing sovereign power.[120]

Simonds was expressing a commonly held view, according to which women were grouped with children in a category of second-class citizens whose dependence disqualified them from political rights.[121] "As inhabitants of the state," writes historian Linda Kerber, "women were merely residents. Only men were members of the commonwealth."[122] In fact, as voting rights were gradually extended to all white men, and as class distinctions therefore became irrelevant to the allocation of full citizenship, both race and gender gained importance as markers of citizenship's boundaries.[123] To be a full citizen was to possess the particular virtues and capacities of the white male.

Beginning in the 1830s, however, the nature and scope of women's dependence became a matter of public controversy. Critics of the common law began to argue that its strictly hierarchical view of the family was a relic of feudal oppression. Many states began to consider legal reforms that would, at least, enable married women to own property.[124] At the Indiana constitutional convention of 1850, for example, radical Democrat Robert Dale Owen took up the mantle of women's property rights. Extending familiar republican categories to marriage, he argued that women's inability to hold property subjected them to a form of total and degrading dependence that corrupted both their characters and their husbands'. There was great danger, he warned, that the husband's absolute dominion would give rise "in coarse and overbearing natures, to tyranny, and . . . in timid and yielding natures, to abject fear." Under these circumstances, how could the home be a source of civic virtue? How could such women mold their sons into virtuous citizens? "From [a] source so base and low," he asked, "can any thing good or noble spring?"[125]

The answers he (and fellow reformers) received exposed and clarified the gendered assumptions encoded in the ideal of personal independence. The most common anxiety, expressed over and over in antebellum constitutional conventions, was that women's property ownership would corrupt the marital union itself, replacing blissful harmony with rivalry and discord. Responding directly to Owen, Mr. Rariden argued that reformers would rupture the "unity of interest" that lent marriage its "charm and strength"; in its place, they would leave only "discord and alienation."[126] Mr. Haddon went further: "A wife with a separate estate secured to her independent disposal and management," he complained, "might rival her husband in trade, or become the partner of his rival—adverse and opposing interests would be likely to grow out of such relations." Even the potential for such competition, he predicted, would bring the "utter destruction of the sentiments which they should entertain towards each other, and to the utter destruction of true felicity in married life."[127] Others foresaw escalating "dissention and strife" in families, as the bonds of love and selfless submission were replaced by shrewd calculations and bargaining over "interest."[128]

As historian Norma Basch has suggested, such responses reveal a fundamental anxiety about the scope of individualism itself. To empower women to own property—to thus reimagine marriage as a contractual relationship between property-owning individuals—seemed a step too far to most American men.[129] Speakers on both sides of the issue imagined American society to be divided into separate spheres: the harsh, manly, competitive world of politics and the market; and the peaceful, nurturing domain of domestic life. The first was egalitarian, individualistic, and conflictual; the second hierarchical, communal, and harmonious.[130] To imagine collapsing this boundary and subsuming the family into the rugged male world was to imagine a kind of dystopia—a world of discrete individuals in endless and exhausting rivalry. "I look upon woman as being fitted for another sphere," said Mr. Bascom.

> I look upon her, not as being designed to mingle with us in the busy scenes of life, to participate in its toils, its struggles, and its cares, but to be placed within our homes, to be by our firesides after our daily toil is finished, to welcome us with her smiles, and receive us with that affectionate greeting which alone can make a happy home. This is the position—this the place for which she is adapted.[131]

Woman's distinctive role was to complement and offset the harsh individualism of man's domain, and this meant preserving her social and moral difference, which was premised on her dependence. It was, "in a great measure, that very dependence," said Rariden, "which promotes and cultivates in the female those endearing qualities" that constituted her distinctive virtues. Dependence nourished women's "devotional and self sacrificing spirit," he added, and made them "ready to offer up all [their] hopes upon the shrine of a husband's wishes."[132]

Those who, like early feminists Sarah Grimke and Elizabeth Cady Stanton, argued that it was unjust and suffocating to confine women to such subordinate positions and shape them into sweet supplicants, were ultimately met with appeals to nature. The popular women's writer Lydia Sigourney, for example, argued that women were naturally suited to their dependent role, for it was dependence that elicited their distinctive virtues. "The duty of submission," she insisted, "imposed both by the nature of our station and the ordinances of God, disposes to that humility, which is the essence of piety." It also accentuated their trusting and selfless dispositions.[133] In a similar vein, Catharine Beecher, an influential writer and educator, insisted that woman's excellence of character depended on her "retaining her place as dependent and defenceless, and making no claims, and maintaining no right but what are the gifts of honour, rectitude and love." God had made woman different than man and blessed her with different modes of influence, which her dependence only enhanced: a wife's reliance on her husband gave her powerful incentive to shape his character for the better; to do so, she would strive to be "so cultivated and refined in intellect, that her taste and judgment will be respected; so benevolent in feeling and action; that her motives will be reverenced."[134] In fact, Beecher argued, women's natural reliance on private suasion and example made them, on balance, morally superior to men.[135] She also maintained that their loving and conciliatory nature left them a crucial (though indirect) role in American politics: as wives, mothers, educators, and writers, they could mediate conflicts and soften the factionalism and rancorous "party-spirit" that seemed to be tearing the nation apart.[136]

Not all reflections on women's nature were so charitable. Alongside this exalted image of woman as a creature governed by pristine, selfless emotion was another, darker impression of libidinous wives whose unruly appetites made them incapable of rational self-control.[137] Reflecting on the history of married women's property rights in ancient Rome and modern France, Mr. Nave (also of Indiana) linked them to "infidelity" and "debauchery." To make women independent of their husbands, he thought, would loosen the bonds of marital control and court sexual anarchy. "It is the feeling that there is one on whom she can rely, one to whom she can look up, one to whom she can give her heart, her all," Nave insisted, "that alone controls the female portion of the community."[138] Nave's comments reflected the long-standing tendency to portray women as seductresses who threatened male self-control as soon as they escaped their subordinate sphere. In Jacksonian America, women who dared speak publicly as advocates for political reform—such as Frances Wright, Sarah Grimke, and her sister Angelina Grimke—were routinely condemned as harlots sowing social disorder.[139]

The upshot of these various appeals to nature was an urgent warning: to assimilate women to the category of the independent proprietor would produce either a grotesque and unnatural spectacle of gender inversion or a destruction of women's natures, either of which would bring grave social consequences. Mr. Badger fretted, for example, that married women's property rights would "reverse that declaration of the Most High," who had directed wives to obey their husbands. Instead, it would tend to "make the woman the ruler over the man."[140] Mr. Clark, on the other hand, cautioned that "you could not give to [woman] the power which a man has, and which he exercises in the affairs of State and of trade, for if you could, she would then cease to be woman." Her nature would be corrupted, her virtue degraded—she would become something monstrous.[141] Speaking in a similar vein to the California convention in 1849, Mr. Botts declared that "this doctrine of woman's rights, is the doctrine of those mental hermaphrodites, Abby Folsom, [Frances] Wright, and the rest of that tribe."[142] In entering the public sphere, these aberrant women had, in effect, immolated their own feminine selves.

As American women walked the long road to suffrage, which was finally guaranteed to them by the Nineteenth Amendment in 1919, the gendered mythology of personal independence remained an important obstacle. Addressing the New York legislature in 1854, Stanton reserved her sharpest criticism for the assumption that personal independence was something that women neither yearned nor were suited for. The belief that women were naturally suited to the "degradation of living by the will of another, the mere dependent on his caprice," she argued, was the very wellspring of male prejudice, for it convinced them that legal and political inferiority ultimately did women no harm.[143]

In the political rhetoric of Jacksonian Democrats, the myth of the independent proprietor was harnessed by a privileged class—white men—who presented themselves as standard-bearers for political and economic equality. As we have seen, this egalitarianism was not simply an affectation: the eclipse of its patrician variation had brought the plebian archetype of the independent farmer and artisan to the fore and turned it into a weapon against economic inequality. This same shift had also bound personal independence more closely to the everyday, Protestant virtues of industry and frugality and deemphasized the civic virtues of neoclassical republicanism. But it had also deepened the myth's exclusivity: as the white male electorate sought to justify its own power and status, it sharpened the boundaries that excluded both women and people of color from full citizenship. We turn next to the ways in which these changes reshaped the American understanding of both democracy and the state itself.

5

Democracy

[Factory workers] hold their livelihood at the pleasure of their employers, and most vote according to their will; they become mere dependents, and lose that spirit which should be possessed by every American citizen.

—SENATOR FELIX GRUNDY, 1832[1]

EVEN AS IT shed many of its republican connotations, the ideal of personal independence played a vital role in the Jacksonian Democrats' theory of democratic politics. It was at once a defense against the irrationality of the mob and a bulwark against tyrants and demagogues. In fact, their political optimism rested, in large part, on the conviction that Americans were different than virtually any other *people* in history: they possessed not just equal rights and liberties but also the independence necessary to defend them. In this sense too, the Democrats leaned heavily on the agrarian myth that they had inherited from Thomas Jefferson and John Taylor of Caroline.[2]

The disappearance of the "higher," patrician ideal of leisured independence, however, brought with it a revision of the Jeffersonian view of politics. Jefferson, along with Madison and other leading lights of the founding generation, had imagined a class of virtuous elites—men who were classically educated and trained for political leadership—who would govern at the sufferance of the broader public. These elites were necessary, they believed, partly because of the nature of politics itself: it was a complex and delicate art requiring no small measure of education and practical wisdom.[3] Most Jacksonians rejected this view of politics decisively. Riding a wave of egalitarian sentiment, they redescribed politics as a relatively simple affair requiring only common sense and personal integrity. The great aim of politics, they argued, was the protection of equal, universal rights against the power and privileges of elites. For this work, the simple virtue of the yeoman, which was manifest in his defensive vigilance against the ambition of the rich and powerful, was sufficient. The wisdom, training, and book learning of Jefferson's "natural aristocracy" had become superfluous.

This shift marks the rise of a deeply influential strain of American antipolitics. Jacksonian Democrats came, increasingly, to view the *constructive* uses of political power with suspicion.[4] In their eyes, politics was no longer the Promethean activity of creating and maintaining order out of anarchy. Instead, it was the more modest business of shielding the independent individual from unwanted encroachment. Alongside this anemic conception of politics arose, in the figure of Jackson himself, an enduring American archetype: the political outsider, the humble man of the people, riding to Washington to do battle against the excesses of the political class, to shield American liberties from the outrages of big government.

The Democratic Public

As we saw in chapter 4, Jacksonian Democrats constantly warned that Americans were being reduced from freeholders to tenants and slaves. This warning captured an acute anxiety, felt among farmers and artisans, about the erosion of their social status. It also reflected a specifically political concern about the health and survival of the republic. Like Jefferson and Taylor, many Jacksonians doubted that a republic—much less a *democratic* republic—could survive amid widespread economic dependence. To see why, we must look more closely at the Jacksonian understanding of democracy itself.

For many Democrats, the advent of democracy in America marked a decisive break, not just with Europe but with the entire political history of the human race. As they saw it, Americans were the first in the world to recognize that the "right of every man to a voice, and an equal voice, in the government over him, is a natural and innate right," an "immediate gift of God," which did not depend on any "accident of birth, or [on] the possession of property."[5] Early in his 1841 book *Democracy*, Democratic theorist George Camp expresses wonder at the deficiency of all inherited political theories, and adds that "it may be confidently asserted that *a connected and philosophical exposition of the peculiar theory of democratic government has never yet been written.*"[6] From his vantage point, the political thinking of all previous ages had been vitiated by assumptions of inequality that were obviously false; he felt that he was stepping into uncharted territory. Meanwhile, the *Democratic Review* urged its readers to treat "the scenes of antiquity" as nothing more than "lessons of avoidance," and to move confidently into the "untrodden space" of a democratic future.[7] Such attitudes marked a sharp break from the thinking of the American founders, steeped as it was in the lessons of the Roman republic. Indeed, in the retelling of some Jacksonians, even the glorious Roman republic was reduced in retrospect to a "grinding despotism" in which "privileged orders" ruled at the expense of the many, who toiled in "hereditary, intolerable, hopeless servitude."[8]

The Democrats' confidence arose, fundamentally, from a potent story of American exceptionalism. They were convinced that democracy would succeed in America because they thought the American *public* was unlike any other in history. The trait that most distinguished white American men from their European counterparts was propertied independence. Along with their access to education, Americans' independence would enable them to answer two ubiquitous criticisms of democracy: first, that it would devolve into anarchy, the fickle rule of a turbulent mob; second, that it would slide into tyranny as the people fell under the influence of ambitious demagogues who appealed to their passions. These were the concerns that democracy's critics had gleaned from the example of classical Athens, and they had been reinvigorated by the implosion of the French Revolution and the ensuing rise of Napoleon Bonaparte. Democrats believed that America had been saved from such dangers only by a distinctive "intelligence and virtue in the mass of the people"; and this virtue was always linked to the mythology of independence.[9]

Consider, first, the danger of mob rule. Democrats often contrasted the orderly, rational public of America with the turbulent, irrational multitudes of Europe. Rather than denying or ignoring the image of the licentious and anarchic mob, Democrats simply quarantined it in the Old World. Robert Rantoul Jr., for example, declared that "we have no such hordes of unprincipled and abandoned wretches as are to be met with in the corrupt cities of the Old World." The American public, he explained, is a property-owning public, which therefore has a strong interest in order and the rule of law.[10] Meanwhile, "A Yeoman," writing for the *Globe* in 1837, addressed head-on the notion that the democratic people were "volatile" and "capricious," with "arbitrary and ever-changing behests." This "common" mistake arose, he argued, from simple confusion: the "educated" and "industrious" citizens of America were worlds removed from "the ignorant mob, the inflammable populace, the dependent plebians of the ancient Republics." America simply could not be compared to the "fierce democracie" of Athens, nor could its freedoms be easily trans-planted to countries whose people did not possess the "sober" virtue and in-dependent spirit of the American public.[11]

At the same time, reformers and labor activists warned that the advent of factory production would render American workers uneducated and depen-dent, which would then make them turbulent and irrational. The long hours and grinding conditions of the factory left workers "buried in ignorance," with neither the "moral dignity, nor intellectual nor organic strength to resist the seductions of his appetite."[12] Wages were so low that workers could barely live, and had neither the time nor the resources to educate themselves or their children; they were sinking fast to the degraded level of the European la-borer.[13] More specifically, the constant toil of the factory led to the "immola-tion of the whole higher nature": workers were reduced to "animals" who could not be expected to govern themselves, whose passions would be unre-strained by reason.[14] Democrats warned that workers who were reduced to brutes straining for the barest subsistence could not be expected to form a rational, orderly public. Rather than blame laborers' degradation on their own "licentiousness"—an old republican (and Puritan) trope—they reached in-stead for structural economic explanations.

In articulating these concerns, the Jacksonians drew from Jefferson, among others. In America, he had argued, "every one, by his property, or by his satis-factory situation, is interested in the support of law and order." Americans were therefore suited for freedom and self-government in a way that the "canaille[15] of the cities of Europe" were not. In the hands of the European masses, Jef-ferson had warned, American freedoms would "be instantly perverted to the demolition and destruction of everything public and private." This fundamen-tal difference in the economic condition of the people explained why the French Revolution had failed where the American succeeded: "it has failed . . . because the mobs of the cities, the instrument used for its accomplishment, debased by ignorance, poverty, and vice, could not be restrained to rational action."[16] The French Revolution's collapse and the persistence of monarchy throughout Europe only intensified the American feeling that, in the short term anyway, they alone were capable of orderly self-government.

For most Democrats, though, these concerns about the anarchic irrational-ity of the mob were far less important than the second potential source of democratic failure: the gradual eclipse of liberty through the advent of aristoc-racy or tyranny. We have already seen that Democrats worried about the rise of a new, commercial and industrial aristocracy that was consolidating power and undermining the American republic. The political theory that they had inherited from Jefferson, Taylor, and others of their generation predisposed them to focus on this threat.[17] In fact, Democrats commonly asserted that almost all previously existing societies had been sites of oppression in which the few conspired to dominate the many. "In every human society," observed Senator William Allen, "there is an effort continually tending to confer on one part the height of power and happiness, and to reduce the other to the extreme of weakness and misery."[18] Amos Kendall, a close advisor to Andrew Jackson and one of the architects of Democratic policy, argued, in fact, that "*Nobility Systems*" had insinuated themselves in "all civilized as well as barbarous countries," by which "the few are enabled to live upon the labor of the many."[19] Human history seemed to them to offer an uninterrupted spectacle of oppression and domination.[20] It was not uncommon for Fourth of July orations to begin by canvassing the catalog of tyrannies and abuses that had enveloped the entire inhabited world until 1776.[21]

The vehicle for domination, in their view, was invariably government. Elites conspired to use the power of government to confer special privileges on themselves, which enabled them to exploit the rest of the people. They made themselves kings and lords, and excluded the common people from political power.[22] "The object of government among nations," said one speaker at a Northampton Workingmen's convention in 1834, "has ever been opposed to an equal enjoyment of natural rights, and the mass of people have always been reduced to labor for the support of a few, no better than themselves."[23] As we will explore in chapter 6, this emphasis on economic exploitation was commonplace: Jacksonians believed that elites had *always* used the power of government to extract labor from the many and that this illegitimate extraction had formed the material basis of history's leisure classes. This was one of the fundamental historical narratives that structured their understanding of the political world. "Power," declared the masthead of Jackson's first party newspaper, the *United States Telegraph*, "is always stealing from the many to the few."[24] Government therefore presented itself mainly as a danger to liberty—a danger to be carefully contained.[25] Democrats tended to see politics itself as an endless war between liberty and power.[26]

This point cannot be emphasized enough. From the Democratic point of view, *the* challenge of sustaining a free republic was restraining political power. Aristocracy was, to them, a fundamentally political term: it described a class of people who used the law—and behind it, the coercive power of the state— to confer privileges on themselves.[27] A writer for the *New York Evening Post*, signing his name *"Anti-Privilege,"* defines a nobleman simply as one who has been granted "civil rights" or "civil privileges" by government, which are "denied to the mass of the community."[28] These legally conferred privileges—whether hereditary titles or exclusive bank charters—enabled them to dominate and exploit the majority. Though governments ostensibly existed for the equal protection of the many, they were invariably corrupted and used to advance the private designs of the powerful.[29] Indeed, this is precisely what corruption meant: the usurpation of public power for private or factional ends.

Democrats explained this pervasive tendency toward corruption by appealing to the structure of men's characters. "Man in power," warned one Democratic orator, "is very unlike man out of power. Condition works great changes in character."[30] Specifically, proximity to power inflamed men's "ambition" and threw their character out of balance; their appetite for power became insatiable. Only the strongest characters could withstand these corrupting effects; only the strongest could preserve the preeminence of reason and the common good over selfish passion. To most Jacksonians, it seemed foolish to pin their hopes on the extraordinary self-restraint of political leaders. "The most dangerous tendency of the age," wrote George Bancroft, one of the leading lights of the Democratic Party in New England, "is to corruption in the administration of the government. Men in power of whatever character, naturally love to extend their patronage."[31] This view had deep republican roots: it had been an article of faith among the English Country ideologists who had influenced Jefferson and Taylor;[32] it ran strong among the Anti-Federalists; and it was fully inherited by Jacksonian Democrats.[33]

As historian Daniel Walker Howe explains, the prevailing ideal of personal character was informed by a "faculty psychology" that "conceived of human nature as consisting of a hierarchically arranged series of powers or faculties: the 'mechanical' (reflexes over which there was no conscious control), the 'animal' (instinctive desires and emotions), and the 'rational' (prudence and conscience)." The rational power was meant to regulate the rest and bring them into a harmonious balance. But it was also the weakest, and its admonitions were often overrun by the urgent demands of the lower faculties. As we will see, the Whigs worried most about the anarchic and disordering passions that roiled the uncultivated character of the democratic majority. The Democrats, on the other hand, told an opposite story: in their view, it was cultivated elites whose character was typically thrown out of balance by their proximity to power. It was their inflamed pride and ambition that posed the greatest threat to the American constitutional order.[34]

Another variation of the same story described the lust for domination as a natural by-product of concentrated wealth. Encased in their opulent surroundings, the wealthy found it easy to imagine their own superiority and to feel themselves entitled to political dominion. Senator Allen, for example, traced the threat of political corruption to the "pride of wealth" that morphed so easily into the "desire for political ascendancy."[35] Wealth might also simply inflame its holder's "avarice" and "cupidity": Andrew Jackson spoke constantly of the "moneyed interest" whose desire to protect and enlarge its wealth stoked its craving for limitless power. The influential political journalist William Leggett, meanwhile, pointed to "insatiate ambition of wealth" as the primary source of American corruption, and the "CONCENTRATED MONEY POWER" as the "sly, selfish, grasping and insatiable tyrant" who posed the most urgent danger to American liberty.[36]

Restraining ambitious men who craved political power, then, was one of the most urgent aims of any democratic government; in fact, it would be no exaggeration to say that the Democrats understood democracy itself, in large part, as a strategy for limiting political power.[37] Following Jefferson and Taylor, they insisted on a strict construction of the Constitution. If politicians and judges enjoyed broad discretion in interpreting constitutional clauses, the Constitution would cease to function as an effective check on political power. Democrats also defended states' rights against the consolidated might of federal government, and they placed individual rights, understood as checks against government excess, at the very center of their political theory. Moreover, they pushed for shorter terms in office and shorter legislative sessions, for an elected judiciary, for popular referendums on important policy questions, and even for constituents' right of instruction[38]—all to keep public officials on a short tether. They found themselves in the paradoxical position of trying to fetter the very democratic majorities that they had worked to enfranchise.[39] But it was not the majority that they wanted to limit; it was the exercise of political power by its political representatives.[40]

Democrats knew, however, that the institutional checks they had devised could be circumvented by determined aristocrats and tyrants. "Principles, and written compacts, and obligations and oaths," said Samuel Young, "are but feeble barriers against the aggressive encroachments of cupidity and ambition."[41] Their own theory predicted that elites would strain against constitutional limits and look to extend their power wherever they could. Against this tendency, the safeguard of last resort was the people. It is "the people alone who can provide against [the] danger" of expanding power.[42] In an encomium to North Carolina senator Nathaniel Macon, the *Democratic Review* praised his view that "a tendency to usurpation and corruption was the nature of all human institutions; and the only palliative, a frequent recurrence to the fundamental and absolute authority of the popular voice."[43] The people had a fundamental role to play in this theory, and it was a conservative, defensive role. The people had to prevent ambitious elites from subverting republican freedom; they had to stand up for their rights and defend constitutional limits on power.[44]

Like Jefferson, Democrats described good citizens as *jealous* of their liberties; indeed, they often praised this particular form of jealousy as the pinnacle of civic virtue. Writing in the *Boston Quarterly Review*, Orestes Brownson described the good democrat as "one who is jealous of power, and always interprets all doubtful questions so as to increase the power of the people, rather than of the government."[45] The people, others warned, should remain ever "jealous of their rights."[46] Or again, in the words of Jackson himself, they should be "uncorrupted and incorruptible, and continue watchful and jealous of their rights."[47] In fact, this jealousy forms the heart of the Jacksonian account of civic character: citizens should be proud of their own liberty, autonomous and irascible, deeply skeptical of the motives of politicians, and unwilling to defer to pompous elites. They should bow only before the authority of the Constitution itself, and the laws it authorized, for these were imagined as embodiments of the sovereign people.

It is precisely at this point in the story that the myth of the independent proprietor becomes salient. To many Democrats, it seemed obvious that only an independent people could successfully play the role to which Jacksonian theory appointed them. William Gouge, who helped shape the Democratic Party's economic policy, argued that "farmers and mechanics" were the only people independent enough to resist the growing political power of the banks. "The mercantile classes," he wrote, "are so entangled in the meshes of the Banks that they cannot yield much assistance."[48] Editors, too, he warned, were typically beholden to the financial interests that subsidized their newspapers. Others worried, similarly, that the profusion of "dependent borrowers" would make it difficult to oppose the growing power of banking elites. They urged their fellow citizens to elect "independent" representatives, such as farmers who derived their sustenance from their own hard work.[49] Senator Allen argued that banks were silently spreading their patronage so as to create huge "dependent interests" to counteract the democratic power of the majority.[50]

Senator Thomas Hart Benton put it most bluntly when he predicted that the Bank of the United States, with its growing real estate holdings, would soon be able to "turn . . . out tenants to vote."[51]

If bankers were gradually amassing political fiefdoms, governed by relations of patronage and dependence, manufacturers and other capitalists were not far behind. In Kendall's eyes, manufacturers were steadily breaking the political will of "the independent mechanic interest": "already we have heard," he writes, "of their male operatives carted to the polls to vote the will of their masters."[52] Others told stories of intimidation by factory owners when their employees tried to present themselves for political office.[53] Simply put, factory workers—"operatives," as they were often called—were cowed by their economic dependence. For Jacksonian Democrats, as for many republicans before them, subservience translated readily from the economic to the political domain: people who worked "at the pleasure" of others, who depended on them for their livelihoods, would simply find it difficult to stand up to their political influence.[54] Or—even worse—their dependence might corrupt their very capacity to think freely: "The laborer is dependent for his house, which he cannot own; for his daily food, which he is compelled to take at the enormous prices of the forestallers and hucksters; and, O saddest of all, he is dependent for his thinking."[55] Either way, laborers would prove unable to serve the basic function that the democratic public *had to* serve in the Jacksonian political imagination: containing political power within its proper bounds.

For other Jacksonian writers, it was crowded city life itself that seemed to breed dependence. "In the city," writes the *Democratic Review*, "men move in masses." "They catch the current opinion of the hour from their class," or from the press, which makes "flaming appeals to their passions, their interests, or their vanity." Acutely conscious of the fine-grained social hierarchies of urban life and thoroughly dependent on the opinion of others, city dwellers became absorbed by "artificial" fashions and fads. Such conditions could only be injurious "to all true independence and elevation of character—to all mental freedom and fearlessness." In the cities, people would be easier prey for ambitious demagogues. In contrast, the yeoman farmer, working in relative isolation, managing his own affairs, and pursuing a more "independent course of life," had time and space enough to form his own ideas.[56] Others echoed this view that farmers lived far from the plague of urban vice.[57] Agriculture, in promoting independence, "both in spirit and condition," insulated yeomen from the "contagion of corrupt example."[58] By the 1840s, the Transcendentalists had appropriated some of these themes; they would come to see mass society, and the conformity it demanded, as a danger to the independent mind and character. Indeed, Thoreau's *Walden* can be read as an experiment in personal independence, with scrupulous attention to its economic preconditions.[59]

Of course, independence was not the only source of the yeoman's political virtue. First, most Americans during this period took for granted that Christian faith was an indispensable precondition of civic virtue for all citizens, propertied or not.[60] Second, the yeoman lived closer to nature, which, in the Jacksonian imagination, was a wellspring of moral courage and physical vitality.[61] On the farm and the frontier, "every thing around him is large, open, free, unartificial, and his mind insensibly . . . takes a corresponding tone." Under these more natural circumstances, he would gravitate to the "broad principles of natural right" on which democracy was founded.[62] In an 1831 address, William Foster Otis instructed the "Young Men of Boston" to look, for inspiration, to the "new-created West. There the fountains are uncorrupted. There civilization meets nature unimpaired. There we can behold how the young armed American grapples with the wilderness, and thence we can return and imagine how our fathers lived."[63] The idea of the *natural*—as against the artificial—served a powerful symbolic function in Jacksonian rhetoric, which we will explore more fully in chapter 7.[64] For now, it is simply worth noting its association with the yeoman's independence: nature "preserved man in the condition of self-reliance" by keeping him distant from the "false corruptions" of urban centers.[65]

As it had in the neoclassical republican tradition, then, the Jacksonian ideal of personal independence underwrote civic virtue. Propertied independence would allow American citizens to resist the corrupting onslaught of both political power and economic modernization and stand fast for the public good. As it had in its earlier, Jeffersonian incarnation, the Jacksonian myth of the independent proprietor was also tinged with nostalgia. For Jefferson and others of his generation, it had harkened back to a mythic Saxon past, before the Norman invasion of England in 1066, before corrupt feudal hierarchies were imported from the European continent, when Englishmen had lived simple and self-sufficient lives on the land.[66] The Jacksonian Democrats, in turn, transposed this nostalgia onto the American founding. They promised a return to the simplicity and virtue of the first years of the republic, which had since been corrupted by ambitious, aristocratic elites. In doing so, they mythologized late eighteenth-century America as an egalitarian democratic society sustained by the plain virtue and common sense of so many ordinary people.

The Simplicity of Politics

For some Democrats—especially those who had begun to absorb Romantic ideas—the independence and virtue of the American electorate granted it privileged access to moral and political Truth. People who made decisions in a mass might be swayed by illicit appeals to passion or cowed by the mob, said Bancroft, but if public opinion represented an aggregation of so many independent decisions, it would be clearsighted and unbiased. People possess "an instinct of liberty; a natural perception of the loveliness and beauty of freedom," and unless that instinct was clouded by conditions inimical to free thought, it would surely prevail.[67] Democrats therefore distinguished between two versions of the public—a mob on the one hand, and an aggregation of independent individuals on the other. Public opinion—a term that was first widely used in Jacksonian rhetoric—would be *true* only if it reflected the "nobler mental freedom" of so many independent souls.[68]

Others made more modest claims on behalf of the independent public and sought to ground even its civic virtues in prudent self-interest. Independent men, they argued, would not hesitate to stand up, uncowed, for their own interests.[69] Jacksonian audiences were constantly being exhorted to stand up for what was *theirs*—their rights and opportunities, their liberties, their social status—before it was too late. Some Democrats thought, moreover, that this confluence of virtue and interest lent strength and stability to democratic institutions. After all, if democracy made extravagant demands of ordinary people—if it required extraordinary knowledge or altruism—its prospects would be dim. Taylor had warned that the virtue of the people was too brittle and unevenly distributed to anchor free institutions; instead, he thought that even a people lacking civic virtue might, under the right institutions, protect liberty simply in self-defense, provided they were empowered to keep watch over their governors.[70] Similarly, Camp took pains to argue that democracy required no special feats of popular virtue, and that even a self-interested people could be expected to defend mutually beneficial rules and institutions.[71]

Jackson himself embraced this view when he contrasted the naked ambition of the "moneyed interest" to the modest self-interest of the "great body of the people," which led them to not only work hard and save but also treat others with decency and respect: "If they have no higher or better motives to govern them," he declared, "they will at least perceive that their own interest requires them to be just to others, as they hope to receive justice at their hands." Since they had no reasonable expectation of special privileges or monopoly, small proprietors were led by their own interest to "love liberty and desire nothing but equal rights and equal laws," for these were the conditions under which they would thrive.[72] In the same vein, the *Democratic Review* praised the "unambitious laborer" who "is content to be useful, without craving to be admired, or in any way distinguished." Though he may not be "gifted in the power of reasoning," his own modest self-interest embodied a simple but unimpeachable rationality that led him to affirm liberty and equality and abhor the "demon of aristocracy."[73]

For many Jacksonians, then, the genius of democracy lay in empowering the very people whose liberty had always, historically, been assailed—the laboring multitude—to protect themselves. The right of suffrage, which the Jacksonians proclaimed to be natural, was their means of self-defense.[74] In fact, some wanted to imagine democracy as a "self-regulating" system—much like the market itself—that contained the means of its own correction.[75] As long as the people were independent, unhabituated to any form of political or economic subservience, they would stand as a permanent, corrective counterpoise to the avarice and ambition of elites. The virtue required for such correction would be akin to an instinct of self-preservation: it would arise naturally, as long as land was plentiful and widely distributed. And the near-infinite stretches of western territory would guarantee it for generations to come.

The replacement of virtue with interest as the dominant political motive in American thought is often traced back to the Federalists in the late 1780s, who had grown disillusioned with America's democratic experiments after the Revolution. In Federalist No. 10, for example, James Madison had famously argued that self-interested factions were an inevitable feature of political life in any free society. "The latent causes of faction," he had argued, "are thus sown in the nature of man," and could usually be attributed to competing economic interests. Madison believed, however, that only a large, representative republic could temper the effects of such divisions. First, a well-designed scheme of representation could ensure the election of virtuous leaders who would serve as "proper guardians of the public weal." Second, modern republics would be so large, and contain so many different factions and interests, that none would easily monopolize political power.[76]

The Jacksonian Democrats rejected both of these Madisonian arguments.[77] First, as we have seen, they rejected the supposition that elections should or could empower impartial elites whose wisdom and virtue would transcend factional strife; in fact, they believed the opposite: with few exceptions, elites were more likely than ordinary people to pursue private and factional interests.[78] On the other hand, the public's interest in preserving its own liberty would be less tainted by faction: here was an interest so broad and widely shared that it might simply *coincide* with the public good. Second, the Jacksonians denied that America's territorial expanse hindered factional tyranny. Their central narrative warned of the emergence of a moneyed interest, national in scope, with tentacles in every state. A small minority of Democrats had also begun describing the power of slaveholders and their northern financiers— or the "slave power"—in similar terms.[79]

The Democrats' answer to the problem of factional interests was therefore different than Madison's. As we explore in chapter 7, Democrats hoped to exclude factional strife from politics by keeping government strictly limited and preventing it from allocating wealth and economic opportunities. While they agreed with Madison that economic interests were the most important source of faction, they believed that competition over economic goods could be rigorously excluded from the public sphere by a government that did little more than enforce basic rights. To ensure that government remained, in this sense, strictly limited, was the people's main democratic responsibility. As long as they fulfilled it, government could run itself—and the American republic could remain free and just—without heroic feats of virtue. To see how Jacksonian Democrats came to this view, it is useful to return again to Jefferson and the republican antecedents of Jacksonian democracy.

The Jeffersonians, too, had believed that the principal threat to liberty would come from corrupt, ambitious elites—notably Alexander Hamilton and his acolytes. Drawing partly on Country ideology, Jefferson had maintained that power corrupted the human character, and that such corruption would inevitably threaten republican liberty. He warned, as political theorist Jean Yarbrough puts it, of "the venal and ordinary desires of nearly all elected officials to increase their power and advance their private interests at the expense of a complacent and distracted majority."[80] John Taylor, meanwhile, had argued that political power was, in its very nature, aggressive and expansive.[81] Both were therefore preoccupied with the limitation and dispersal of power. "Concentrating all cares and powers into one body," wrote Jefferson, was the surest way to obliterate liberty.[82] The dispersal of political power to state and local government and the strict interpretation and enforcement of constitutional limits were centerpieces of their political vision. After the Jeffersonians swept into power in 1800, they reshaped the American state in ways previously unknown to the modern political world: they deliberately shrank the size of government, reduced taxes and federal debt, canceled diplomatic missions to all but three countries, dismantled the military, and promoted free trade as vigorously as their anemic foreign policy apparatus would allow. The Jeffersonians, writes Gordon Wood, aspired to "create a general government that could rule without the traditional attributes of power."[83]

Like Jacksonian theories of democracy, Jefferson's political theory relied heavily on the independent people to keep vigilant watch over ambitious elites. Jefferson had believed, however, that the people's vigilance would be complemented by the positive responsibilities of a leadership class. Jefferson's account of classically educated "natural aristocrats" was embedded in a classical understanding of politics as a fragile and demanding practice that called for considerable practical wisdom and virtue. In 1779, for example, Jefferson had written that the coming of republican government in America would call for "extraordinary abilities," and that American universities would have to impart the necessary "science and virtue" to the "future guardians of the rights and liberties of their country."[84] The people, who were not thus trained, were meant to impose strict limits on the political power of the leadership class, but within these boundaries, they were meant to defer to the virtue and judgment of the *aristoi*.[85] "That form of government is best," he famously wrote to John Adams in 1813, "which provides the most effectually for a pure selection of these natural aristoi into the offices of government."[86] The hierarchical structure of the classical republican polity—with its different social orders—had been flattened, but not all the way.

As we saw briefly in chapter 3, the role of the "natural aristocracy" had been a key point of contention in the debates around the ratification of the Constitution. Federalists, reacting to what they perceived to be the disorderly chaos of state politics after the Revolution, had wanted to restore political power to men of talent and distinction—men who would naturally command the respect and obedience of the people.[87] Anti-Federalists therefore accused them of conspiring to create an aristocratic government: in removing power from state legislatures, which were broadly representative of ordinary people, and relocating it to a distant capital, where a small number of powerful officials would control the fate of the whole American territory, Federalists were empowering the "wealthy and ambitious" few at the expense of everyone else.[88]

The Anti-Federalists lost the argument over the Constitution, but in the Age of Jackson, their anti-aristocratic version of democratic representation took its revenge. Over a generation later, the Jacksonian Democrats finally decapitated the Jeffersonian body politic—in theory, at least, if not in practice. There was no room, any longer, for the idea of a natural aristocracy. In the struggle to expand suffrage in the early decades of the nineteenth century, Democrats had rejected the argument that politics was a domain that required the special virtues of a trained elite.[89] By the late 1820s, this view of politics seemed, to them, unacceptably elitist. Democrats argued for an equal right to hold political office, and they tended to receive any candidate's claim to superior talent and training with suspicion. They argued that important legislative questions should be settled by popular referendum. They extended their suspicion to the judiciary as well as the legislatures: judges, they argued, ought to be ordinary people making commonsense judgments, not experts invoking arcane legal doctrine that the people could not understand.[90] Governor John Barry of Michigan insisted that "plain men of sound heads and honest hearts are found adequate to the highest and most responsible duties of government."[91] These plain men were still expected to govern with a disinterested regard for the public good, but they needed no special talent or training to do so. Indeed, since Jacksonians insisted on the right of instruction, they could maintain that elected office required no special capacity for judgment or wisdom: representatives became vehicles for public opinion. The responsibilities of public office, as Andrew Jackson himself put it, were "so plain and simple that men of intelligence may readily qualify themselves for their performance."[92]

This Jacksonian anti-elitism forced a reconceptualization of politics itself. Rather than insisting that the people were capable of mastering the wisdom and expertise that had once been the purview of the trained political elite, Democrats simply denied that any such expertise was necessary. They rejected the idea of politics as a complex and delicate practice. They therefore rejected as politically irrelevant—if not outright corrupting—the speculations of "academicians" such as John Quincy Adams.[93] They argued that politics, rightly understood, was a simple affair that required only the faithful application of natural principles, or of intuitive common sense. Those who argued otherwise were the very people who had fought to restrict suffrage; they were perpetuating an ancient myth—the myth of *arcane complexity*—whose purpose had always been to rationalize the people's exclusion from power.[94] Democracy, as the Jacksonian Democrats understood it, exploded this myth, for it embodied the epochal discovery that legislators need only "sit down at the feet of Nature, as simple disciples," and enact its laws—nothing more.[95] These basic natural laws—these "few brief, self-evident axioms"—were equally evident, moreover, to the people and their representatives.[96]

In this view of politics, the irascible, negative virtues embodied in the Democratic myth of the independent proprietor were the only ones necessary. While Democrats called on the public to be active and engaged in political life, its main responsibility was to ensure that its representatives were faithfully implementing common sense or natural law—law that any independent individual could apprehend—and not using government to enrich themselves or their friends.[97] As historian Brian Balogh has argued, this new adaptation of republican thought preserved republican *vigilance* but discarded republican *governance*.[98] In this new, democratic political mythology, the people's voice was pristine and virtuous because it was depoliticized: it was seen not mainly as a vehicle for political power but merely as a check on it. It could therefore remain untainted by power's inevitable corruption. The Jeffersonian ideal of independence, like the classical republican ideal before it, was split: for ordinary yeomen, independence motivated a defensive vigilance; for a leisured leadership class, it required a more demanding, rigorously disinterested character, as well as the talent and training appropriate to political leadership. While this split persisted in the political thinking of many Whigs, Democrats overwhelmingly rejected it.

When John Henry Eaton sang Jackson's praises in his influential campaign propaganda, the *Letters of Wyoming*, he argued that Jackson, as an outsider to Washington and to the intrigues of federal politics, embodied the rugged independence of a modest farmer who left his plow only reluctantly for the halls of power. Jackson was "a private citizen, committed to no party, pledged to no system, allied to no intrigue, free of all prejudice, but coming directly from the people, and bearing with him an intimate acquaintance with their feelings, wishes, and wants." To the cunning elites, schooled in European manners, who conspired against American liberty, Eaton warned that Jackson's natural "discernment" would "unriddle your schemes, and his independent honest demeanor will put them to shame." Here was the Democratic vision of leadership: a man who perfectly embodied the honesty and simple virtue of the people themselves, a self-made man who owed his reputation to no one but himself, a man untainted by aristocratic European ideas and book learning, who would stand for common sense against the corrupt refinements of the "*leading men*."[99] Jackson was the first president to run as an outsider; the first to hail from the Western frontier; the first who was born in poverty, to a family with no pedigree. His success defined a new model for the American statesman—a model that remains powerful to this day.

Of course, Jackson was also a wealthy slaveholder. In fact, he kept over a hundred slaves at just one of his several properties, the Hermitage—which placed him in an exclusive southern elite. Historians who have studied the political leadership of the Democratic Party in the Age of Jackson have concluded that there were few, if any, substantial social or economic differences between them and the Whig leaders. All tended to be men of high social standing. "Ohio Jacksonians," writes one historian, "like their opponents, included 'large proportions of merchants, manufacturers, bankers, business men and professionals.' . . . The leaders of both parties in Mississippi had an affinity for slaves, banks, and speculation."[100] The rhetoric of egalitarian inclusion was, in this respect, misleading: for the most part, we do not find the "common man" occupying positions of political leadership in Democratic Party politics. What we find, instead, is a shift in the way American elites justified their political power: elites learned that they had to present themselves as plain men of the people, men of modest origins and humble common sense. With this shift, we witness the birth of a long-running American dishonesty: the dishonesty of oligarchy clothed in the mantle of democracy. Jacksonian democracy had broadened political inclusion for white men at the bottom of the political scale, much less at the top.[101]

It is worth pointing out, moreover, that this Jacksonian dishonesty advanced the interests of slaveholders in particular. In assimilating planters to the mythology of the virtuous "lords of the soil," it helped shield them from the egalitarian thrust of Democratic Party politics. "The tradition of Jefferson and of the Democratic Party," writes historian John Ashworth, "was one that obscured the social power of the slaveholder, by merging him with the farmer, even as it ignored the plight of the slave."[102] When John Taylor had sung the praises of the "agricultural class" and extolled agriculture as the "guardian of liberty," he had illustrated this merger perfectly.[103] From his vantage point, the virtues and the independence of the land owner and the agriculturalist belonged alike to the humble yeoman and the wealthy, slaveholding planter. The real divisions, Democrats insisted, were between these landed interests and the bankers and industrialists who besieged their independent way of life. To make this story plausible—to refashion the planter into a farmer who worked the land—the slave had to disappear from view entirely. And indeed, the Jacksonian Democrats did their best to keep slavery out of the nation's political conversation. Their efforts were epitomized by the infamous "gag rule," which forbade Congress from reading or discussing any of the antislavery petitions that poured in from constituents between 1836 and 1844.

The Democratic confidence that politics was a simple affair governed by self-evident principles must be seen, finally, in a religious context. Many of the evangelicals whose populist egalitarianism attracted them to the Democratic Party—including many Methodists, who by 1830 were the largest denomination in America—were deeply suspicious of a Calvinist ministry that they accused of trying to monopolize state power.[104] Over the first three decades of the nineteenth century, for example, itinerant Methodist ministers—most of whom had little or no formal education—had unleashed a torrent of criticism directed at the Calvinist clerical establishment and its presumption that its learned ministers could dictate theological doctrine to the masses. These dissenters taught that divine inspiration could come to people of all ranks and classes, but especially to the humble—to "a plowman, a tailor, a carpenter, or a shoemaker."[105] They often reminded their audiences that Christ himself had been the son of a carpenter, and the Apostles poor and uneducated.[106]

Such attacks rested on the fundamental assumption that life's most important truths were simple and plainly accessible to anyone who sought them earnestly. In matters of the spirit, as in moral and political matters, there was simply no need for the tutelage of experts.[107] This assumption lent broad support to the Democrats' view of politics. If the clerical establishment was a caste of fraudulent elites who had an interest in propagating the view that God's word was complicated and decipherable only with proper training, the pretensions of the educated political class could easily be cast in a similar light.[108] For many evangelicals, as for Democrats more generally, this seemed a progressive and emancipatory doctrine, a fulfillment of the epochal democratic assault on aristocracy. It was the convergence of this Protestant celebration of private conscience with the democratic exaltation of the ordinary voter's judgment, writes historian William McLoughlin, that "eventually produced the anti-institutional individualism which dominated American life in the nineteenth century."[109]

The "Spirit of Party"

In one important area of their emerging theory of politics, Democrats found themselves at odds with the myth of the independent proprietor. By the late 1830s, under the guidance of Martin Van Buren, they had built the first professionalized, mass political party in history. They had created a nationwide network of party committees, "reaching up from the ward and the township level to the quadrennial national convention," and including not just nominating committees to select candidates but "central committees, poll committees, and various auxiliary organizations."[110] Political activity continued almost year-round, with local committees gathering to approve nominations, draft public resolutions, and organize political processions.[111] Alongside this broad popular mobilization, a new class of professional political organizers arose to replace the older, more informal leadership of coastal elites.

As we noted in chapter 3, the republican tradition had regarded parties as *factions* advancing their own partial interests over and against the public good—and the American founders had agreed. The Democrats' attempts to achieve party discipline therefore met stiff resistance in some parts of the country, especially those parts of the South and West that had not yet experienced meaningful two-party competition.[112] Controversies erupted, for example, around the use of party conventions to select nominees for office. Many voters—from radical to conservative—bridled at the suggestion that they ought to endorse the candidate chosen by a party convention. One Illinois citizen, expressing a view that was still pervasive there in 1819, insisted that "every citizen who appreciates his consequence, as an *equal* member of this sole and august nation of freemen, will independently judge and act for himself, ... uninfluenced by caucuses, nominations, or delegations." He condemned political parties as "machines in the hands of the designing, the wealthy, and the vicious" that aimed to manipulate public opinion.[113] He favored the practice of self-nomination, which prevailed at the time in Illinois politics: candidates for office would simply announce themselves through local newspapers, and voters would judge them on their merits, free of any party identification.[114]

Similar controversies—in Illinois and elsewhere—intensified in the 1820s and 1830s and soon became a matter of partisan debate nationwide. By 1836, many Whigs framed the presidential election as a referendum on the issue of popular sovereignty itself, and whether "a Convention of office holders, self-elected and irresponsible, shall dictate to a free people. ... in a word, whether Martin Van Buren shall be forced upon the American People, whether they will or not."[115] They also assailed Jackson for trying to "dictate to the People who they should choose as his successor."[116] Such language was integral to the Whig self-conception for many years. "[Whigs] think for themselves and act upon their own judgments," wrote the *Cincinnati Gazette*, "and in so doing they cannot become or remain part or parcel of an administration that requires implicit subservience to all its behests from all admitted into the pale of its supporters." Democrats, by contrast, seemed content to be "led by the nose, subjected to the collar, or put under the whip."[117]

In fact, Whigs used the myth of the independent proprietor to develop a powerful critique of Democratic party building. The Democratic Party, they argued, had achieved popularity by cultivating a wide network of political dependents. Whigs accused Jackson of doling out federal offices to loyal partisans and bribing members of the press.[118] More fundamentally, they accused Democrats of practicing a style of politics—premised on fealty to "King" Andrew Jackson—that corrupted the people themselves. Jackson's henchmen formed "an army of mercenary dependents, spread over the whole country, in its cities, its villages, and even its hidden vallies [*sic*], infecting the whole community with the taint of their opinions and their servility."[119] If everyone hoping for public office came to believe that abject subordination to party was the main requirement, Whigs argued, the character and independence of virtually all politically active citizens would be endangered.[120] "Thus men must be kept in the party, and faithful to its usages, decisions, and nominations," wrote Calvin Colton, editor of the *True Whig* and ardent promoter of Henry Clay, "*not by attachment to its principles and measures, but through fear*, that, if they assert their independence, they will lose their share of *the spoils*."[121]

All in all, Whigs painted a dark picture of Jacksonian politics. It was a top-down, populist politics in which self-aggrandizing political elites and their bribed henchmen manipulated the public—especially the poor and disaffected—and deliberately inflamed its passions.[122] The "*genius*" of the Democratic Party, wrote Colton, "is *obsequiousness and servility* in the masses, and *despotism* in the leaders. It is utterly *hostile* to true democracy, and a suitable foundation, on which to erect a *despotic throne*."[123] There was no room in this picture for personal independence. The Democratic Party, then, represented democracy in name only; in fact, it stood for populist tyranny. The qualities it rewarded in its faithful were obedience and servility—qualities unbecoming to free men.[124] The passion it stoked was envy, which it would satiate by assaulting rich men's property. Here, in the Whig view, lay the greatest threat to the Jeffersonian vision of a republic of virtuous, independent proprietors.[125]

Democrats responded forcefully to these attacks, mobilizing one strain of their republican mythology against another. The real danger, they argued, was that wealthy aristocrats would thwart the will of the people by dividing their allegiance and exploiting their lack of organization. In an open letter to fellow "Democratic Republicans of Illinois," for example, a young Stephen Douglas warned that the people "may rely too much safety upon the purity and integrity of their motives and thereby fail to act with sufficient concert and energy." Douglas was defending statewide nominating conventions, which alone could "embody and give effect to the popular will; to maintain [the people's] ascendancy, to unite their efforts."[126] Opponents of party conventions and party discipline, wrote the *Chicago Democrat*, were merely "aristocrats" who would profit by "sowing dissention in the party."[127] Douglas also insisted—somewhat disingenuously—that conventions were "free and voluntary," "spontaneously gotten up and disinterestedly conducted."[128] Their verdict was none other than the voice of the people itself.

Looking back at the origins of American parties, Martin Van Buren himself argued that, in the absence of party organization, the country's politics had been "overrun with personal factions" vying for power. Such disorder and division among the people, he argued, benefited only ambitious elites. In fact, he maintained that this was the aristocracy's only hope of attaining power in a truly democratic republic: they had to ensure that their "opponents were divided amongst several" candidates.[129] In his eyes—and the eyes of most Democrats—the decisive illustration of this truth was the infamous "corrupt bargain" of 1824. To Van Buren, this setback had proved that party organization and discipline were indispensable correlates of popular sovereignty: without them, the people would remain vulnerable to the machinations of the aristocracy.[130] Whenever the Democratic Party "had been wise enough to employ the caucus or convention system," he wrote, "and to use in good faith the influence it is capable of imparting to the popular cause," they had emerged victorious.[131]

Once again, it is worth noting the contrast between the Democrats' political theory and the political vision of the *Federalist Papers*. In Federalist No. 10, Madison had described mobilized popular majorities as *factions* that threatened to overrun the rights and interests of minorities. He had hoped that, in a large and diverse republic, such factions would have trouble coalescing at all. The Democrats turned this theory, which was still embraced by many Whigs, on its head. For Van Buren, the function of political parties was precisely to create and sustain nationwide, mobilized majorities that could act with a unified purpose. Furthermore, he saw the august halls of Congress, to which Madison had turned as a last resort against factional aggression, as the very epicenter of aristocratic corruption. It was there, after all, that the "corrupt bargain" had been executed, and it was there that personal ambition and intrigue might once again wrest power from the people.[132]

Interestingly, even as Democrats insisted that party discipline involved no serious "sacrifice of principle or independence," they also argued that citizens had a moral duty to subordinate their own preferences to the party's for the good of the country: "Would it be better that they should endanger the public happiness or the public liberty, than give up some favorite scheme of policy"? Citizens were free, of course, to express their preferences fully during the nominations process; but afterward, they were obliged to accept the party's "compromise of views" rather than hold stubbornly to their own. "They might discover too late," warned the assembled members of the Baltimore Democratic convention, "that they had sacrificed the best of causes to that pride of opinion, which is not satisfied with success, but with nothing short of attaining it in its own way."[133] In such admonitions, the jealous independence of judgment commonly celebrated in Democratic rhetoric became a form of selfishness that impeded the formation of a democratic will.

———

The Jacksonian ideal of personal independence, which played such a prominent role in Democratic Party rhetoric, had come a long way from its aristocratic English roots. By the 1820s, it was noticeably inflected with the egalitarian currents of thought that had come to fruition among some Anti-Federalists and among the radical artisan activists of the 1790s.[134] Jacksonian Democrats addressed and represented a mass public and a conception of independence that included, in principle, all white men. Whereas the ideal of independence had earlier demarcated a class boundary among white men that defined the threshold of full citizenship, it had ceased to serve this function for Democrats. When they acknowledged the existence of a class of dependent white men, they did so to call attention to a grievous anomaly in American life, a corrosion of American exceptionalism. The proper response was not to exclude these dependents from the franchise but to correct the problem at its source and restore the promise of propertied independence to all white men who were willing to work for it.

In several ways, this newly egalitarian myth reflected sharply individualistic values and assumptions. Most importantly, it celebrated a predominately private vision of personal liberty. As the ideal of independence gradually disembedded itself from older republican assumptions, as it abandoned Jefferson's natural aristocracy and its strenuous ethic of civic devotion, it focused ever more on private life. It celebrated the autonomous man's control over his own work and household and the absence of constraints or obligations that might impinge on it. It underwrote a politics whose stated aim was to prevent government from meddling in the affairs of the sovereign individual.

The myth also imagined white American society as a collection of enterprising agents responsible for their own fates. This tendency was accentuated not just by the expansion of the market but also by the West. In the sprawling debates over land policy and Manifest Destiny, those who favored cheap land and military expansion continually mythologized the intrepid settler who picked up his stakes and ventured west, braving all manner of danger, clearing the land with his own hands, making his own fate through hard work, prudent self-discipline, and masculine bravado. This restless figure, whose labor literally created human civilization, was routinely held up as a paragon of independence. As the plebian ideal of independence was transposed from the pastoral English countryside to the rugged American West, its meaning changed: the settler came to represent a dynamic and fluid society created and re-created through individual initiative and effort.[135]

At a time when a broad swath of the white male electorate owned their own farm or shop—or could reasonably aspire to—this individualistic myth often advanced an egalitarian agenda. Jacksonian Democrats deployed these political ideas to shield white proprietors from predatory lending and cash-poor farmers from onerous taxes. They used it to democratize state and local governments and win greater accountability from elected officials. They also invoked it to try to shield artisans' livelihoods from the capitalist transformations that were reducing them to long-term wage laborers. And since they tended to believe that wealthy bankers, speculators, and industrialists owed their riches to corrupt government favoritism, their antigovernment rhetoric often underwrote a broad attack on concentrated economic power (with the conspicuous exception of plantation slaveholding).

At the same time, this individualistic vision was also profoundly and violently exclusive. In England, the myth of Saxon independence had been formulated for an ethnically homogeneous society riven by sharp class hierarchy. In nineteenth-century America, it was repurposed to suit an ethnically and racially diverse society marked by growing white male equality but an intensifying racial caste system. Increasingly, people of color were described as constitutionally incapable of the personal independence required by both democracy and civilized society. Increasingly, the rugged, self-reliant virtues associated with independence were encoded in the very idea of whiteness. In this way, the myth of the independent proprietor also expressed a collectivist vision of white male supremacy that justified aggressive territorial expansion, slavery, and patriarchal domination. Membership in the individualistic society idealized in the myth was the privilege of white men who sat atop racial and gender hierarchies in which personal status was determined, above all, by heritable group identity.

Finally, as they repurposed the myth of the independent proprietor to mobilize a mass electorate, Jacksonian Democrats painted a strikingly utopian picture of American democracy. They sang the praises of the modest yeoman and artisan, whose property ownership alone seemed to engender personal integrity and unbiased judgment. They insisted that such everyday virtues were sufficient for the business of governing, which was merely a matter of resisting corruption and overseeing self-evident natural laws. They therefore viewed much of what their governments did with suspicion. All of these ideas were inscribed, furthermore, into an exceptionalist vision of the American nation, which stood increasingly apart, in the Democratic imagination, from the course of human history. This heady ideological cocktail, which virtually all of the founders would have rejected, would change the terms of American political discourse.[136]

PART II

The Rights-Bearer

AMERICAN INDIVIDUALISM'S DOMINANT political language, since the late eighteenth century, has been the language of rights. The Declaration of Independence famously asserted that all men were "endowed by their Creator with certain unalienable rights," which served as the foundation of all legitimate government. Many of the state constitutions framed in the first half of the nineteenth century repeated this language with only slight variations. The Ohio Constitution of 1802, for example, declared "that all men are born equally free and independent, and have certain natural, inherent and unalienable rights." Included in its list were life, liberty, property, and "happiness and safety." It insisted, furthermore, that "every free republican government" was "founded on their sole authority, and organized for the great purpose of protecting their rights and liberties, and securing their independence."[1] This fundamental conviction that government existed, first of all, to serve individuals by protecting their rights permeated the political rhetoric of Jacksonian America.

In the Jacksonian imagination, protecting rights meant shielding individuals from unwanted interference. State constitutions declared that individuals possessed the right to worship, to speak, to assemble, and to hold property without obstruction. They had a right to bodily security and rights against arbitrary arrest and detention. They had the right to bear arms and the right not to have soldiers quartered in their houses. Jacksonian Democrats drew on this language constantly: in articulating the natural rights of individuals, writes historian Rush Welter, Jacksonians were typically "cataloguing the things they would not permit governments to do to themselves."[2] Rights delimited the boundaries within which the sovereign individual was supposed to reign, supreme and unmolested.[3]

These convictions shaped the powerful American myth of the rights-bearer, which held that Americans were uniquely free to make their own choices, to pursue their own happiness, and to reap the rewards of their own productivity, without intrusion. Here, according to this narrative, lay the most fundamental American promise: the promise of release from the shackles of oppression that fettered the individual in the Old World. Rights, enshrined in constitutional documents throughout the United States and extended equally to all white men, were the guarantees that were supposed to make this promise real.

This pervasive myth ensured that political debates, across a wide range of important policy areas, resolved themselves into disputes over personal freedom. Democrats in particular invoked it to defend the separation of church and state and assert the rights of individual conscience and religious liberty. They mobilized it to denounce temperance laws as paternalistic invasions of American freedom, and also to press for expansive freedom of expression against both formal and informal censorship. They reimagined suffrage as a natural right and harnessed the myth of the rights-bearer to defend it against property qualifications and nativist restrictions. Rather than trying to discuss all of these different controversies, however, the next three chapters focus on the two contexts that held the greatest significance for the development of American individualism: the economic debates that so often dominated Jacksonian politics and the rising controversy over slavery.

Chapters 6 and 7 revisit the economic debates over banking and currency, tariffs, industrialization, and land explored in part 1. But they approach these debates from a different angle: rather than highlighting the motif of the independent proprietor, they focus instead on the rhetoric of rights. They show that editors and politicians, especially on the Democratic side of the aisle, *also* presented these controversies as dramatic contests between oppressive power and the natural rights of the individual. In these various debates, Democrats accused the wealthy of violating the property rights of American producers by divesting them—often with the government's help—of the hard-earned fruits of their labor. In their rhetoric, the problem of economic inequality was recast into the ubiquitous idiom of private liberty.

Chapter 7 focuses specifically on the popularization of free-market ideas. As they cast around for ways of imagining a society of rights-bearing individuals insulated from discretionary power, many Jacksonian Democrats embraced the utopian idea of a natural, self-regulating market. They came to believe that America's national genius lay in its willingness to cast off the "artificial" hierarchies of the Old World and inaugurate a new, providential order defined by natural rights and market freedoms. In such a society, they argued, individuals would choose and compete freely, and rewards would flow naturally to the most deserving. Pampered elites would be stripped of their special privileges, while hardworking small producers accumulated wealth enough for a comfortable living. In a fluid and relatively affluent society of small white producers, an egalitarianism founded on the dignity of *labor* came to underwrite a sharply individualistic vision of economic competition and private desert.

Although the Democrats' rhetoric of rights was inclusive and egalitarian in some respects, it was sharply exclusive in others. The paradigmatic rights-bearer was white and male, and those who shared neither of these privileged traits found their rights tenuous if not entirely nonexistent. While chapter 6 explores these exclusions, chapter 8 considers how abolitionists harnessed the myth of the rights-bearer to challenge them. Abolitionists recognized, in the ideal of natural rights, the kernel of an egalitarian critique whose scope could not easily be contained. To identify America with natural or God-given rights was to associate it with a mythic pre-political past, stripped of conventional hierarchies. From this vantage point, a great many social and political inequalities—including patriarchy and white supremacy—could be made to seem unnatural and illegitimate.[4] And so they used the foundational myth of the rights-bearer to reach for an inclusive politics of human rights. In the long term, abolitionist ideas would influence virtually all subsequent egalitarian movements in America, and they would reshape both the discourse of rights and the meaning of American individualism.

Finally, all three ensuing chapters shift our attention from republican ideas to a different set of intellectual traditions. The myth of the rights-bearer drew from a wide range of sources: from Calvinist theology and the long-standing Protestant struggles for religious toleration, from widespread popularizations of John Locke's philosophy, and from the Scottish Enlightenment. As they made use of these traditions, of course, political myth-makers in Jacksonian America also repurposed them to suit a fluid, democratic society increasingly defined by market relations. Like part 1, then, part 2 shows how ideas that originated largely in Great Britain were absorbed and reinterpreted in the United States and how they came, by the Age of Jackson, to express an individualistic view of white society.

6

Producers' Rights

The use of society, is to secure the fruits of his own industry and talents to each associator. Its abuse consists in artifice or force, for transferring those fruits from some partners to others.

—JOHN TAYLOR OF CAROLINE, 1813[1]

AS THEY CONDEMNED rising economic inequality, Jacksonian Democrats made use of several different political languages. In part 1, we saw that they harnessed republican ideas to denounce bankers, speculators, and wealthy manufacturers as domineering aristocrats who threatened the proud independence of America's small proprietors. At the same time—often in the very same speeches and editorials—they invoked the complementary language of natural rights. They presented these same aristocrats as opportunistic leeches who, rather than working for themselves, *stole* from America's hardworking producers, abrogating their property rights.

This alarming story drew moral urgency from the myth of the rights-bearer. America was meant to be a haven where all white men enjoyed their natural rights on equal terms. Property, in particular, lay at the heart of this egalitarian promise: whereas Old World producers were habitually robbed of most of what they made, Americans were supposed to *own* the full value of their work.[2] Democrats insisted, however, that unscrupulous elites were polluting this wellspring of American exceptionalism. Rich land speculators were swooping in, after settlers had cleared and cultivated the land, to steal the proceeds of their work. Manufacturers were securing protective tariffs that drove up the prices of consumer goods and so, in effect, robbed workers of the fruits of their effort. Bankers were manipulating credit and currency in ways that defrauded hardworking farmers of their earnings. Democrats warned that these assaults had rendered producers' property rights insecure.

Like the myth of the independent proprietor, the myth of the rights-bearer infused these wide-ranging economic debates with individualistic assumptions. It conjured up an image of American society as an aggregation of free individuals pursuing their own interests and happiness. It suggested that *work* itself was strictly an expression of individual effort and skill. It maintained that producers were entitled to what they earned through their own personal exertion and ingenuity—no more and no less—and that *interfering with this meritocratic order* was the very definition of economic injustice. In Democratic rhetoric, then, the fight for economic equality became a fight to shield private property rights from interference so that America's producers could work and compete to the best of their abilities.

These powerful ideas also shaped the intensifying controversies over race and gender in Jacksonian America. As they justified the expropriation of Native Americans, the enslavement of African Americans, and the subordination of women, white men invoked the sanctity of their own rights *as producers*. They insisted that these excluded groups were incapable of working conscientiously without coercion or managing their earnings responsibly. Property rights, they concluded, were owed only to those who were naturally equipped to make productive use of them. At the same time, excluded groups—including women and Black abolitionists—harnessed the same myth to condemn both patriarchy and white supremacy as forms of caste privilege that violated the meritocratic tenets of the American creed. In all of these ways, rights became focal points in the wide-ranging debates over equality and inequality.

To bring these ideas into clearer focus, we must begin by exploring their intellectual origins. We must look, in particular, at the labor theory of property, which came to America through both Protestant theology and John Locke's influential political writings.[3] The theory dominated American thinking about economic justice in the Jacksonian Era, and it thoroughly shaped the popular conception of property rights. It therefore formed an essential component of the myth of the rights-bearer.[4]

The Labor Theory of Property

The labor theory of property holds that all legitimate title to property comes, originally, from individual labor. In his *Second Treatise of Government*, John Locke had famously argued that individuals in the state of nature acquired property by mixing their labor—which they owned—with nature.[5] When they gathered apples in the forest, when they cultivated a small plot of land and reaped its harvest, their labor converted a small share of unowned nature into personal property. Locke argued, moreover, that such labor gave rise to an entitlement: individuals had a *right* to the fruits of their own labor.[6] Securing this right was, in his view, one of the fundamental purposes of any legitimate government. It followed that depriving another of the fruits of his labor, without his consent, was a violation of natural right.

The full significance of the labor theory of property emerges only in the context of several other background beliefs. By the early nineteenth century, almost all Americans rejected the idea that leisure was a mark of nobility or distinction. This rejection marked the culmination of an epochal revaluation of human labor. From classical antiquity onward, writes political theorist Judith Shklar, "it had been almost universally believed that physical work defiles us, that those who labor are impure."[7] Americans, by contrast, constantly praised hard work—including physical labor—and the related virtues of frugality, economy, and prudence. As we saw in part 1, they associated these virtues with republican citizenship and projected them onto the idealized image of the yeoman farmer. In fact, the American preoccupation with work led genteel European visitors to complain that Americans thought of nothing else, which left them little leisure to cultivate the more refined aspects of the human character. Americans were "a very grave people," wrote Captain Basil Hall in 1829, ". . . woefully ignorant of the difficult art of being gracefully idle."[8]

The American revaluation of labor had two important intellectual sources. The first came from the nascent Enlightenment "science" of political economy. The idea that *growth* was the natural trajectory of commercial economies had emerged only in the second half of the eighteenth century, in response to decades of unprecedented economic expansion and prosperity in the Atlantic world. By then, political economists had found reason to hope that their societies might permanently escape the cycles of stagnation and poverty that had afflicted the Western world for over a thousand years.[9] This hope rested on the promise of human labor. As Adam Smith made clear on the opening page of his *Wealth of Nations*, the growing prosperity of Western societies was due wholly to improvements "in the productive powers of labour."[10] In this context, work could no longer be seen merely as profane, if necessary, drudgery. Work was the engine of human progress. "Those who marveled at the world's new productivity," writes historian Joyce Appleby, "were enhancing the worth of labor—what ordinary men and women did." In the writings of

Enlightenment political economists and their admirers, *homo faber*—man the producer—had emerged as an agent in world history.[11]

The second, older source was Calvinist theology. Sociologist Max Weber famously drew attention to the dignity and importance that labor assumed in seventeenth-century Puritan thought. Work had become a divine commandment, issued to all classes of society. Diligent labor, and even profit and material affluence, was celebrated as evidence of individual saintliness.[12] Puritans praised labor as a way of overcoming idleness and the vices that arose inevitably from it.[13] It also helped ward off the habit of luxurious consumption, which made people irrationally self-indulgent. In both of these senses, the discipline of work was seen as a precondition of social harmony: it made people less self-centered and enabled them to find their own productive place in the divinely ordered creation.[14]

Both of these sources lent moral support to the labor theory of property. If labor was dignified and godly, then so too was the laborer himself, and his natural entitlement to the fruits of his own toil seemed a just and appropriate recognition of his worth. This idea had long flourished among artisans who regarded their own productive contributions to society as a badge of dignity and status.[15] In America, where small producers composed a majority of the white male population, it blossomed into a powerful moral consensus. In fact, in a fluid society mostly bereft of leisured aristocrats, *work* was fast becoming the centerpiece of American status and identity among rich and poor alike. "An utterly new understanding of the individual and society was emerging," writes historian Isaac Kramnick. "Ascription, the assignment to some preordained rank in life, came more and more to be replaced by achievement as the major definer of personal identity." And achievement was defined, increasingly, as a function of work.[16] Those who drew their living from the labor of others had no legitimate place in this emerging conception of society—they were thieves who assaulted the liberty and dignity of their fellow men against the wishes of God himself.[17]

The labor theory of property, along with the labor theory of *value* from which it drew support, was pervasive in Revolutionary America.[18] It provided one of the conceptual lenses through which Americans could see the uniqueness of their own society. "Never before has the experiment been so effectually tried," wrote Congregationalist minister Ezra Stiles in 1783, "of every man's reaping the fruits of his labor, and feeling his share in the aggregate system of power."[19] "The American is a new man," wrote J. Hector St. John de Crevecoeur, a man liberated from the "involuntary idleness, servile dependence," and "penury" of the Old World: "Here the rewards of his industry follow with equal steps the progress of his labour."[20] This was just another way of saying that America was founded on a rejection of aristocracy. If aristocrats were an unproductive class who appropriated the labor of others, then the refusal to countenance such appropriations meant the rejection, in principle, of aristocracy.

This formulation of American uniqueness continued throughout the antebellum period, and was repeated by Americans and foreign visitors alike. "This is the first time since the origin of society," wrote French engineer and economist Michel Chevalier, "that the people have fairly enjoyed the fruits of their labours, and have shown themselves worthy of the prerogatives of manhood. Glorious result!"[21] Indeed, throughout this period, Americans contrasted their own society to Europe in these terms: Europe was still in the grips of a political economy of aristocracy,[22] where one class secured its living by stealing what belonged rightfully to another. In America, by contrast, workers "are permitted to work for their own benefit, to work for *property*, at such occupations as are useful to themselves, and thus to enjoy the produce of their labours."[23] In an anonymous "Address to Working Men" in 1840, "A Mechanic" observed that European laborers could not be compared to their American counterparts because "their labor belongs to the lords of the soil."[24] Here lay, in this author's view, the decisive difference between Europe and America.[25]

In the Jacksonian Era, this Lockean story of American exceptionalism found support on both sides of the political aisle: Whigs too paid hearty tribute to it. America, wrote Whig congressman Nathan Appleton, was "a great novel experiment in politics and civilization": unlike anywhere else, labor had "the assurance of enjoying its own fruits."[26] What distinguished the Democrats' view from the Whigs' was simply this: whereas the Whigs felt that the labor theory of property was, by and large, upheld in the United States, the Democrats believed that it was being systematically violated. They believed that a new class of unproductive aristocrats had arisen in America. For Jacksonian Democrats, then, the labor theory of property was both a means of celebrating the uniqueness of American life and a means of excoriating those who were betraying it. It thus became, for them, the foundation of an egalitarian critique of the emerging economic order: its critical edge, which had once mainly pointed outward at Europe, was now also turned inward at their own society.

This egalitarian turn had its own intellectual and political history, which reached back all the way to the English Civil War. Before Locke immortalized it, the Puritan Levellers had used the labor theory of property to justify their attacks on the English aristocracy. In the words of one historian, the Levellers embraced the "fundamental principle that a man was entitled to the fruit of his own labour; that he had a right of property in it and that to take it away from him was theft."[27] They drew on the labor theory of property to condemn excise taxes, tithes, merchants who used their leverage to extract goods at low prices, and other forms of appropriation they saw as unjust. "What then are your rustling silks and velvets, and your glittering gold and silver laces?" asked Leveller leader John Lilburne. "Are they not the sweat of our brows, and the wants of our backs and bellies?"[28] Another Leveller pamphlet condemned such appropriation as a direct violation of the biblical command, "*In the sweat of thy face thou shalt eat bread.*" "By *Thou* is meant all mankind," the author chided, "none exempted."[29] Though it was mostly dormant for many decades after the restoration of the English monarchy in 1660, this strain of "producerist" egalitarianism would survive in artisan communities on both sides of the Atlantic before erupting again in the late eighteenth century.[30]

Its resurgence marks an important feature of American political thought in the early republic. It can be found, for example, in the writings of Massachusetts farmer and tavern keeper William Manning, who condemned the "pride and ostentation" of the wealthy merchants and lawyers who lived on the backs of America's hardworking producers.[31] "No person can possess property without laboring," he insisted, "unless he gets it by force or craft, fraud or fortune, out of the earnings of others."[32] Manning's views exemplified a strain of artisan producerism that celebrated the self-discipline, hard work, and modest property and respectability of the small producer against both the greed and luxurious excess of the rich and the supposed indolence of the poor.[33] This egalitarian narrative can also be found in the writings of several French Enlightenment thinkers whose works made their way across the Atlantic in the late eighteenth century and helped shape American opinion.[34]

These disparate intellectual currents coursed through Tom Paine's writings. In his explosive and widely influential *Rights of Man*, for example, Paine had placed the theft of labor at the very origin of politics: government was "a continual system of war and extortion," which appropriated and consumed "more than one fourth of the labour of mankind."[35] The "object" of revolutions, he added, was to free civilization from this exploitative system and secure property rights to producers.[36] Jefferson himself had argued, moreover, that the "first principle of association" was "the *guarantee* to every one of a free exercise of his industry, and the fruits acquired by it."[37] As we saw briefly in chapter 3,

Jeffersonian radicals such as William Duane used this conceptual framework to press more ambitious attacks on American inequality. The virtuous producing classes, he wrote, constantly fell victim to the privileged leeches who absorbed an ever greater share of their productivity and who represented the pervasive tendency of "*lazy luxury* to enslave the men of industry who acquire their bread by labor."[38]

Who exactly counted as an "aristocrat," however, remained a matter of evolving disagreement and controversy. French Enlightenment thinkers, for example, tended to denounce oppressive European governments, idle landed nobles, and rapacious clerical elites in the name of economic liberalization.[39] Manning's list of culprits was far broader and included wealthy American merchants and speculators as well as professionals—lawyers and bankers—who "get a living without bodily labor."[40] Paine himself was torn between his attraction to laissez-faire principles and the view, widespread among Philadelphia's working classes in the late 1770s, that wealthy grain exporters driving up the price of bread were *taking* from the poor.[41] This variety illustrates the flexibility and indeterminacy of this narrative of producers' rights. In an economic world in flux, it could be deployed against both older and newer forms of wealth; it could therefore be used both to endorse and to resist the emerging liberal economic order.[42]

Producers' Rights in Jacksonian America

This same egalitarian narrative—and these same tensions and ambiguities—laced through the political rhetoric of Jacksonian Democrats. They routinely identified their own constituents as the "producing classes" and accused their political opponents of catering instead to an unproductive aristocracy. To the editors of the *Indiana Democrat*, for example, this seemed like *the* great political divide in the United States: while Andrew Jackson had the support of "the real bone and sinew of the country," his opponents were simply "*those persons who think themselves privileged* TO LIVE ON THE LABOR OF OTHERS."[43] Like Paine, Democrats also imagined human history as a story of continual encroachment by elites on the rights of humble producers.[44]

In fact, Democrats described the habitual theft of labor as part of a broader story of "equal rights" betrayed. Following Locke, they held that the *purpose* of all legitimate governments was to protect the natural rights of individuals. The American Constitution was authoritative, in their eyes, because it codified and guarded these natural rights.[45] They therefore rejected the view, commonly defended by Whigs, that individuals forfeited some or all of their natural rights when they left the state of nature for civilized society. In what became a popular talking point, Democrats denounced the Whig doctrine that human societies were founded on a "compact" or "contract" through which individuals gave up their natural rights in exchange for a charter of social rights and liberties.[46] Following Jefferson, Democrats insisted that this premise was simply a cover for exploitation and injustice, for this historical *charter* might well sanction any number of abuses and special privileges. In England, for example, outright theft of labor was sanctioned by "royal charter," which "supersedes the decrees of justice and the laws of nature."[47]

Against these historically sanctioned injustices, Jacksonian Democrats asserted the individual's timeless right to the fruits of his labor. In all times and places, declared Robert Rantoul Jr., producers possessed the same natural rights: "*we have a* RIGHT *to all our* FACULTIES *of whatever name or nature— bodily, mental, moral—and the products of their exercise.*" From the Lockean premise of self-ownership, he derived the individual's property right to the fruits of his labor. Each individual worker, he argued, had the right to obtain "the highest price [he] can fairly obtain" for the use of his own talent and skill. And no one else had any legitimate claim to these earnings: they were his to dispose of as he saw fit, so long as he did not "invade the rights of any other person."[48] "The right of property, then, secures to every man the just fruits of his own labor," concurred the *Democratic Review* emphatically, and "it forbids every one from appropriating to himself the fruits of the labor of another."[49]

As we have seen, this prohibition underwrote a particular story of American exceptionalism, which the Jacksonian Democrats gladly perpetuated: they continually hailed the United States as the world's only true refuge for producers' rights. "If equal rights and a fair field be continued," declared one Democratic election pamphlet, "we, and our children, and our children's children to the latest generation, will enjoy the fruits of their labor, and rear up their descendants in respectability and independence."[50] European laws and institutions, on the other hand, had been deliberately designed "to transfer the property of the many to the few."[51] Democrats constantly accused Whigs of working to re-create such European schemes in America and to vitiate the natural rights on which the country had been founded.[52]

In fact, Democrats applied this broad narrative of producers' rights to virtually all of the major economic controversies of the day.[53] In the recurrent debates over land policy in the West, for example, the Democrats described speculators as an unproductive class trying to "enrich themselves by preying on the industrious cultivator," by taking the proceeds of his hard labor.[54]

The settler, on the other hand, was part of the productive class that made civilization itself possible through the "sweat of his brow": he cleared the land and made it suitable for cultivation, only to be dispossessed by the idle speculator.[55] Congressman John Galbraith of Pennsylvania concurred: "Speculators produce nothing," he said. "They are the drones of the bee-hive, which live and fatten upon the labor of others."[56] The *Northampton Democrat* argued, moreover, that free access to western lands was the key to enabling working men to claim the fruits of their own labor, for the landless laborer "does not receive, and cannot command, only about one-fourth or one-third of the products of his labor."[57]

The same rhetorical pattern laced through the debates over tariffs. Willie Mangum, senator from North Carolina, argued that protective tariffs reflected "the interest of monopolists, of capitalists—of all those who consume more of the fruits of the earth, than they produce by the sweat of their brow."[58] These tariffs, he maintained, were a means of transferring the proceeds of Americans' hard work to manufacturers: it inflated the price of consumer goods, and the profit was pocketed by capitalists.[59] John Taylor of Caroline had made the same argument in his 1821 treatise, *Tyranny Unmasked*: that the tariff was a means of appropriating the fruits of agricultural labor—which in his view included the "labor" of the slaveholding planter—and moving it illicitly into the manufacturer's pocket.[60] Mississippi congressman John Claiborne raised the stakes even further by accusing wealthy manufacturers of being fundamentally *unproductive*: "What is your tariff system," he charged, "but a daring outrage on the principle of equality, . . . a shameful plan to enrich the non-producers at the expense of those who produce?"[61] A decade later, Amos Kendall agreed that the tariff was but a "modern device to cheat the *workers* into the support of the *idlers*, and sustain unnatural and unjust distinctions in society, taking the place of the direct plunderings, the vassalage, the tithes and other contrivances of ancient times, now too well understood to be tolerated by the laboring millions."[62] The tariff, in other words, was no less than a systematic theft of American farmers' property and a grievous violation of their rights.

But it was the controversies over banking that especially brought this populist rendering of the labor theory of property to the fore. William Gouge, whose *Short History of Paper Money and Banking* circulated widely among Democratic readers and policymakers, grounded his attack on the banks in man's natural right "to the whole product of his labor."[63] He observed that banks had won the privilege of printing paper notes, and so of lending and profiting from far more money than they actually held in their vaults— imaginary money, in essence. Since wealth could not simply be created out of thin air, it was clear to him that banks were in fact seizing a portion of the community's productivity through legally sanctioned fraud. John Galbraith concurred: bankers were merely "those who have thus transferred to them the products of the labors of others," and that lending money did not involve the "production of any thing by labor."[64]

These were among the arguments that drew more radical Democrats to hard money—gold and silver coin—whose worth, they believed, more accurately reflected the value of the labor exchanged for it. It is worth remembering that the United States had no government-issued paper currency at the time. The paper notes that exchanged hands were printed by competing banks and distributed in the form of interest-bearing loans. Their value on the street depended on each particular bank's reputation, which could change overnight. To many Democrats, this system came to seem like a corrupt scheme designed to deprive working men of the full value of their labor.[65] Until Americans were defrauded by "paper promises" and "paper banks," wrote the New York Evening Post, "every man's labour was his own, and every man enjoyed the fruits of his labour, without the deduction of a per-centage, to support the splendours of his master." In this author's view, bankers were no more than "legalized usurpers of the fruits of toil," who brazenly violated the worker's "personal rights."[66] Many Democrats did not go so far, however: they directed their ire not at banking or paper currency as such but rather at the discretion that wealthy elites exercised, by means of their ownership and operation of private banks, over the economy.[67]

For some Democrats, moreover, banks merely highlighted a broader set of problems that were endemic to the corporate form. In 1845, for example, the Ohio Statesman attacked "the countless plans and schemes of associated wealth, by acts of incorporation, under the deceptive garb of public utility, for filching and plundering the producing classes of their well-earned gains." From the Statesman's point of view, most corporations were little more than legislative tricks designed to confer unfair advantages on wealthy investors. "So cunningly devised are these schemes of private gain," the author continued, "that their operations are scarcely seen or felt, being so mystified and professing so loudly to benefit the working class, as to lull them into the belief that they are necessary to their very existence."[68] Investors claimed to need these privileges to do publicly valuable work; Democrats argued, instead, that they used them to siphon away the proceeds of other people's labor.

It must be pointed out, however, that many Democratic politicians—the very politicians who could be heard fulminating against bankers, speculators, and other "aristocrats"—were themselves deeply involved in banking and land speculation, and so fit their own descriptions of an unproductive aristocratic class. Many, including Jackson himself, were plantation owners and slaveholders whose wealth was taken, in the most literal sense, from the labor of others. Many were very rich by the standards of their time and had made their money in speculative windfalls rather than through patient accumulation.[69] Such men had been drawn to the Jacksonian banner because they were frustrated by their exclusion from the spoils of political power, or because they felt that their own towns or regions were not sharing equally in the economic benefits of modernization and growth. These elites, writes historian Randolph Roth of Democratic leaders in Vermont, "still wanted railroads, banks, factories, and colleges in their neighborhoods"; and they often privately "conceded that they could attract investment only with guarantees of liability limits" for corporations and with tariff protections.[70]

Here we confront one of the most resilient problems facing populist democratic movements everywhere: the problem of representative leadership. Democratic activists naturally looked to men of reputation to help them win elections. These men came to understand that they could win popularity and power by embracing a stridently populist economic message and denouncing privileged elites. They understood that they had to be perceived, in both their speeches and their legislative record, as populist reformers. But in the North and South alike, they often had a strong personal interest in frustrating the egalitarian political aims that they publicly proclaimed. Wealthy Democratic leaders, writes Roth, often worked behind the scenes to moderate their party's policy objectives, to prevent the party from turning into a genuinely "progressive insurgency."[71] America's two-party system further exacerbated this tendency. As it competed to attract the broadest possible slice of the white electorate, the Democratic Party had strong incentive both to absorb the political energies of workingmen's groups and to blunt their radicalism.[72] Its particular version of the myth of the rights-bearer, which foregrounded the sanctity of private property rights, facilitated this effort.

Labor's (Market) Value

The labor theory of property formed the centerpiece of the antebellum American idea of economic justice. For Whigs and Democrats alike, a just society was a society in which white producers reaped the fruits of their own labor, in which there existed no class that lived on the backs of other white men.[73] Yet this abstract consensus masked fundamental disagreements about the nature and value of *productive labor*. As they staked out a position in these controversies, Democrats increasingly yoked the idea of labor itself to the market and to a vision of autonomous, rights-bearing individuals competing for its rewards.

In the Jacksonian Era, America disagreed, first of all, over who counted as a producer. On one end of the spectrum, urban labor activists insisted that only those who worked with their hands counted as producers; in their view, only farmers, artisans, and factory workers were members of the "producing classes."[74] Here is Theophilus Fisk, for example, addressing the mechanics of Boston:

> But the monopolists, the professional men, the men of wealth, THEY labor, it is said, as well as the farmer and the mechanic. They do labor to be sure— but IT IS LABORING TO COLLECT THAT WHICH OTHERS HAVE EARNED. The Lawyer's "may it please your honor" never made the pot boil. The Presidents' and Cashiers' printed paper rags covered with false promises to pay, never crowned the hill with the ripening sheaf, nor made the valley smile. The lazy drone by sticking a quill behind his ear, never yet felled the boundless forest.[75]

The banker and the lawyer might spend long hours in their offices working, but this did not make them *producers* in Fisk's eyes—for they produced nothing but fraudulent schemes to skim wealth from others; they created no real wealth themselves. More moderate, mainstream Democrats tended to cast their net wider to include shopkeepers, clerks, small-scale merchants, professionals of various kinds, slaveholding planters, and even government officials.[76] Whigs, on the other hand, tended to define the class of producers as broadly as possible: they included virtually anyone who was employed.[77] The stakes in this disagreement were high, for anyone who stood outside the producing class was presumed to be stealing from others and was therefore tarred with the brush of aristocracy.

Americans also disagreed about how to *measure* the fruits of individual labor. In a semi-subsistence economy, the labor theory of property was relatively easy to apply: farmers produced most of their own goods from start to finish, and sold or bartered only a limited quantity of their produce for what they considered a fair return. What exactly they produced was clear; and short of theft or fraud, taxation was the only obvious means by which they might be deprived of the fruits of their labor.[78] But in a society increasingly enmeshed in market relations, increasingly reliant on credit and on a paper currency of fluctuating value, and with increasingly complex supply chains, the theory's application became more difficult, and the means of illegitimate extraction seemed to multiply.[79] Did the price farmers received for their goods reflect the full value of their labor, or were various middlemen conspiring to deprive them of some portion of it?[80] Did the journeyman's wage reflect the true value of his labor? How could the value of anyone's labor be ascertained?[81]

For some artisans and workingmen's activists in the northeastern cities, the answers to these questions pointed away from individualism. They blamed market competition for disrupting traditional patterns of craft production, driving down wages, and thereby *robbing* skilled producers of the fruits of their labor. Baltimore's artisans, writes historian William Sutton, tended to embrace a strain of producerist ideas "which defended the rights of industrious and temperate workers to the fruits of their labor and advocated opposition to market practices that would inevitably serve, in the popular idiom, to 'grind the faces of the poor.'"[82] These ideas mingled with early currents of socialism, which had gained a wide audience among the English working classes and underwrote an emergent class consciousness.[83] In New York, Philadelphia, and Baltimore, workers experimented with different forms of organization— from unions to producers' cooperatives—designed to secure them, collectively, the earnings they deserved.[84]

Outside of America's few cities, among a largely rural, property-owning electorate awash in the mythologies of individual freedom, these collectivist ideas held limited appeal. As they tailored their egalitarian message to these voters, mainstream Democrats turned instead to the individualistic logic of the market to arbitrate labor's value. Surveying the many strategies that elites had used throughout human history to extract wealth from the producing classes, the *Western Review* insisted, for example, that free trade alone would allow the producer to "enjoy the fruits of his own well-directed industry."[85] Many Democrats agreed: they saw the market as an impartial system that rewarded labor and protected property rights from the grasping hands of unproductive elites. Adam Smith's vision of free trade, wrote the *Democratic Review* in a similar vein, was destined "to enable [man] more completely to realize all the fruits of his industry."[86]

It followed that any attempt to redirect the flow of wealth through legislation amounted to a violation of producers' rights. Protective tariffs, in this sense, *stole* from some people to give to others. For Amos Kendall, this was no different, in principle, than outright theft by "*Pirates*" or "*Highwaymen*."[87] The *Southern Literary Messenger* describes the situation in these terms: one man "goes industriously to work on a farm; the other says, I will work at nothing but manufactures, and by this work I cannot live unless the farmer gives me a third or a half of his earnings."[88] Instead of finding a productive line of work, the manufacturer demanded that the state subsidize his unprofitable career. And the government, in effect, *took* this subsidy from the farmer through import duties, which drove up the price he paid for consumer goods. This whole argument supposes that the fruits of individual labor are simply his "earnings"—that is, whatever the market, undistorted by tariffs, would pay him for his work.[89] Kendall made this clear when he argued that only unfettered "exchanges of products or manufactures" between individuals would yield, to each party, "the entire fruits of his own labor."[90] In forcing the farmer to pay more than market value for his necessities, tariffs deprived him of the true value of his work.

Indeed, this language of *theft* and *takings* was common in Democrats' broadsides against tariffs and bankers: anytime the law redirected the flow of wealth from its "natural" channels, it stole from America's hardworking producers. Or, to restate the point slightly: any alteration by law of the market price of goods or labor was a violation of natural rights. The *New York Evening Post* argued, for example, that bank charters enabled financial elites to reap far more than market value—or *"exchangeable value"*—for their services, by enabling them to print "spurious" paper rags and pass them off as real money. This was simply legalized theft. Exchangeable value, the *Post* maintained, was the true measure of labor's worth, but only so long as it was not distorted by fraud, monopoly, or other legislative interference.[91] To shield the economy from such takings was, for many Democrats, among the fundamental responsibilities of legitimate government. Free markets, then, imagined as systems of perfectly free exchange, were the only way for individuals to retain their natural right to the fruits of their labor.[92]

Some free traders reformulated this Lockean right to make it more explicitly favorable to market competition. "It is the unquestionable right of every individual," proclaimed a report produced by a Philadelphia free trade convention, "to apply his labor and capital in the mode which he may conceive best calculated to promote his own interest."[93] From this perspective, it seemed clear that tariffs and other restrictions on trade were violations of individual rights and betrayals of the legitimate function of free government. "For what purpose were Constitutions framed, and laws enacted," demanded the State Rights and Free Trade Association, "but to enable every citizen to use his labour honestly to the best advantage . . . and be protected in so doing equally with every other citizen?"[94]

As the preceding paragraphs should suggest, the "producing classes" mythologized in Democratic rhetoric were not a social or economic *class* in any conventional sense of the term. They were imagined, rather, as an aggregation of enterprising individuals, of various backgrounds and trades, laying claim to the fruits of their private exertions. Prominent among them were the solitary settler who, "by his own labor and industry, opened his farm and built his cabin, to retain possession, and enjoy the fruits of his toil and enterprise," the "industrious and enterprising" small farmer hauling his surplus to market, and the slaveholding planter whose income depended on international commodity prices.[95] From the Democrats' points of view, the moral logic that unified these disparate producers was meritocratic: on a rugged frontier and in a competitive economy, white men were entitled to precisely as much as their effort and talent would earn them. Democrats had absorbed an egalitarian, producerist language whose leading edge could point in more radical directions and tethered it to the market.

Many Democrats remained convinced, however, that this meritocratic vision would yield broadly egalitarian results for white men. They believed this not only because they presumed that white American men were roughly equal in their capacities but also because they thought that productive labor's rewards were incremental.[96] "The planter, the farmer, the mechanic, and the laborer," wrote President Jackson in his Farewell Address, "all know that their success depends upon their own industry and economy, and that they must not expect to become suddenly rich by the fruits of their toil."[97] Families could become wealthy over time, through a lifetime of labor and frugal saving, but sudden windfalls were suspect. "Large fortunes," declared Congressman John Bell of Tennessee, were typically "made up of the fruits of the labor and capital of others, won from them by cunning, imposition, and fraud."[98] Marcus Morton, the Democratic governor of Massachusetts, therefore felt confident that "the most effectual guaranty against that gross inequality of social condition" was simply to secure "to everyone the fruits of his own industry, with an equal division of intestate property among heirs."[99] Surveying a largely rural economy still dominated by small producers, Democrats believed that their economic individualism was a broadly egalitarian doctrine.[100]

Producers' Rights and White Male Supremacy

Like the myth of the independent proprietor, the myth of the rights-bearer was used simultaneously in service of equality and subordination. Even as they asserted producers' rights against bankers, wealthy speculators, and other capitalists, Jacksonian Democrats were also recasting these rights as the exclusive privileges of white men. In their rhetoric, the labor theory of property was closely intermingled not just with a narrative of national exceptionalism but also with a theory of racial hierarchy. Here too, they stood at the leading edge of ideological change.

Over and over, Democrats used the labor theory of property to justify the expulsion and extermination of Native Americans, both of which were high on the list of party priorities. They often described Native Americans as pre-agricultural savages who did not *labor* to improve the earth and who therefore possessed no legitimate title to their ancestral lands.[101] "There can be no doubt," wrote Lewis Cass, ". . . that the Creator intended the earth should be reclaimed from a state of nature and cultivated; that . . . a tribe of wandering hunters . . . have a very imperfect possession of the country over which they roam."[102] Congressman James Wayne of Georgia, meanwhile, quoted the Swiss philosopher Emer de Vattel on the floor of the House: "Those people, like the ancient Germans and modern Tartars, who, having fertile countries, disdain to cultivate the earth, and choose rather to live by rapine, . . . deserve to be exterminated as savage and pernicious beasts."[103] He grudgingly conceded that such people might possess "usufructory" claims to the game they killed or the fish they caught, but he insisted that they had no legitimate property right to the soil, and hence no right to exclude the western settler. To some Democrats, this failure carried moral and religious significance, for it suggested that the Native Americans had fallen from God's grace. After all, God had commanded that humans earn their bread by toil. For Wayne (as for Vattel), this implied "an obligation to cultivate the soil"; it also implied private land ownership. The indigenous people of North America were, in short, "not in the condition which God intended his creatures to be."[104]

These were not new arguments, nor were they original to Vattel. In fact, they came straight from Locke, who had used them to develop a novel justification of colonial settlement. Legitimate title to land had traditionally been accorded on the basis of first occupancy, but Locke had reformulated its legal and moral foundation with the American continent in mind.[105] "As much Land as Man Tills, Plants, Improves, Cultivates and can use the Product of," wrote Locke in the *Second Treatise*, "so much is his Property. He by his Labour does, as it were, inclose [*sic*] it from the Common."[106] When Locke wrote these lines, he was almost certainly thinking of America. He had been directly involved in drafting a new constitution for the fledging colony of Carolina, and the crucial fifth chapter of the *Second Treatise*, concerning property, is littered with references to Native Americans.[107] He pointedly contrasted the tilled and

enclosed land of the industrious cultivator to the "wild woods and uncultivated waste of *America*."[108] During the Revolutionary period, New England's
Puritan preachers had used these ideas repeatedly to justify the dispossession
of Native Americans. Prominent jurists adopted it, too. Hugh Henry Brackenridge, a Jeffersonian Democrat who served on the Supreme Court of Pennsylvania, argued, for example, that "the aborigines of this continent can . . . have
but small pretence to a soil which they have never cultivated. The most they
can with justice claim, is a right to those spots of ground where their wigwams
have been planted."[109]

Jefferson himself had written that "cultivation or industry appear to me the
only just criterion of property."[110] But whereas he had believed that Native
Americans could assimilate to Western civilization, learn to "live by industry"
on the land, and so become rights-bearers themselves, many defenders of Jackson's purges argued that they were incapable of the discipline of labor.[111] Native
Americans were now described as an infantile race "clinging with a death grasp"
to their primitive ways of life, impervious to change.[112] Like untutored children,
they were governed by "passion" and "sloth," and by a fierce attachment to their
own personal freedom, which they would never willingly relinquish. Democrats and Whigs alike used these racist assumptions to argue that Native Americans were unsuited by nature for the rigors of a civilization whose energy derived from labor, and that they were therefore destined for extinction.[113] "Their
Constitution has barbarism distinctly stamped upon it," said Georgia congressman Richard Wilde, by which he meant specifically that "the Indian cannot
work."[114] As we saw in chapter 4, these views were buttressed by a burgeoning
pseudoscientific literature that claimed to demonstrate that people of color
were constitutionally inferior.[115] At the turn of the century, educated Americans had, by and large, shared the Enlightenment view that all human beings
belonged to a single race, that all were equally capable of improvement, and that
observable differences between them were mainly environmental. Over the
course of the Jacksonian Era, this view was eclipsed by a new, "scientific" racism
that drew sharp distinctions between the races.[116]

The canonical renditions of the labor theory of property began with the
state of nature—a condition of shared ownership of land as yet unimproved
by human labor—and told of the human ascent into civilization. From Locke
through Jefferson, Native Americans had always been used to exemplify this
primitive state. In Jacksonian eyes, they were consigned there forever: here
was a savage "race" unfortunate enough to lack the perfectibility that had enabled whites to lift themselves out of nature into civilized life. "The Indian is

hewn out of rock," wrote contemporary historian Francis Parkman. "You can rarely change the form without destruction of the substance. Races of inferior energy have possessed a power of expansion and assimilation to which he is a stranger; and it is this fixed and rigid quality which has proved his ruin."[117] To such a people, the basic distributive principle that each was entitled to the fruits of his own labor could provide neither security against western encroachment nor hope for affluence and progress.[118]

Native American writers and activists condemned these racist arguments in the strongest terms and drew attention to their evident hypocrisy. In their "Memorial and Protest of the Cherokee Nation," for example, Cherokee leaders argued that it was systematic white violence against them, legitimized by the policy of forced expulsion, that was driving them from their settled, agricultural state into a "savage life" without land, security, or traditional community. Far from an agent of "civilization," the United States—and the state of Georgia in particular—had become a source of lawlessness and barbarism.[119] In making this case, moreover, the authors emphasized the *labor* that Cherokees had invested in their land. They spoke of the fields of corn, the apple and peach orchards, the mills and brick homes and other "extensive improvements" that were being despoiled by white intruders and thieves. Their rights were being destroyed, they argued—and all the fruits of their labor taken—to satiate white land hunger, animated by "the sordid impulses of avarice." In vain they demanded that "the individual rights of the Cherokee citizens, in their possessions and claims, should be amply secured," and that "as freemen, they should be left at liberty to stay or remove where they please."[120]

Chattel slavery also contributed immeasurably to the racialization of property rights in America. Enslavement was, after all, one of the dominant metaphors of Jacksonian social criticism, and it was deeply linked to the labor theory of property. "The very essence of slavery," wrote one labor activist, "is in being compelled to labour, while the proceeds of that labour is taken and enjoyed by another."[121] As we have seen, Democrats routinely accused their political opponents of treating white workers in precisely this way. Factory laborers, they argued, were simply slaves by another name: their labor was *taken* by their employers, and instead of being housed and fed, as the Black slave was by his southern master, they were paid a wage barely adequate to sustain them.[122] Farmers, meanwhile, became "slaves" when the proceeds of their toil were siphoned away by various legislative tricks, including bank charters and paper money, tariffs, and expropriation by land speculators. "Give those who DO NOT WORK license to increase at will the burdens of those

WHO DO," thundered one Democratic speaker in 1840, "either through the banks or the Government, and you make yourselves and your posterity their slaves."[123]

Such arguments should, of course, have led the Democrats to oppose chattel slavery on principle. The "second slavery" that flourished in the Jacksonian South was an extraordinarily brutal, systematic, and unrelenting system of forced labor. As slaveholders strove to maximize their yields and minimize their costs, they developed a highly refined combination of surveillance and torture calculated to wring every last drop of productivity from the bodies of their enslaved workforce. Under the "pushing system," slaves were expected to meet ever-escalating quotas, and violently beaten if they failed. They were pitted against each other to see who could work fastest and brutalized if they fell behind. "Every modern method of torture was used at one time or another," writes historian Edward Baptist, including "sexual humiliation, mutilation, electric shocks, solitary confinement in 'stress positions,' burning, even waterboarding."[124] Their effects can be seen in the ubiquitous newspaper ads offering rewards for the capture of escaped slaves, which often listed their scars and deformities in lurid detail. Historians have now shown that such "innovation in violence" led to vast productivity gains on the cotton fields in the decades leading up to the Civil War. And the "fruits" of this productivity were monopolized, of course, by plantation owners, who became "the richest class of white people in the United States, and perhaps the world."[125]

It is difficult to imagine an economic system more profoundly incompatible with the labor theory of property. Early critics of slavery had, in fact, invoked this very theory to condemn slaveholders as aristocrats who forcibly extracted and stole labor from others.[126] Crevecoeur, for example, had lamented the unnatural spectacle of an idle elite living luxuriously "without labour, without fatigue," while slaves toiled "without any prospect of ever reaping for themselves."[127] For most Jacksonian Democrats, however, this logic foundered on the self-serving premise of Black racial inferiority. They denied that Black laborers were entitled to the fruits of their labor, for this was a privilege they reserved for whites. The "black race," they insisted, was unfit for individual rights because of its inferior intelligence and deficient moral character.[128]

James Paulding's 1836 book, *Slavery in the United States*, is illustrative. A prominent Democrat close to Martin Van Buren, he argued that Blacks were naturally unfit for economic freedom. They were cursed with an "innate lazy apathy which forms a part of the very constitution of the African race" and made them unresponsive to ordinary economic incentives. They were also entirely "divested of [the] divine attribute of progressive improvement," which had been so liberally bestowed on whites. He described Africa as a whole as a region of "desert sterility, of savage beasts and savage men" who had lived in uninterrupted degradation until Europeans had landed on their shores. Set free from the salutary compulsion of slavery and endowed with equal rights, Paulding predicted, Blacks would sink into oblivion: they would perish "amid the frosts of winter, like grasshoppers which have wasted their summer in idleness."[129] To treat them as free citizens entitled to the fruits of their own labor, he maintained, was therefore a form of cruelty. Others likened free Blacks to "locusts" who, unable or unwilling to work for themselves, would "consume the fruits of industry and labours of our [white] citizens."[130] They agreed that the uplifting logic of the labor theory of property was simply inapplicable.

Such racist exclusions were often woven into the fabric of Jacksonian egalitarianism. For many Democrats, to deny whites the fruits of their own labor was *to treat them as though they were Black*—that is, as though they were members of an inferior race, an underclass unfit for freedom. Claiborne, for example, condemned northern factories for rendering white men and women "more servile than a southern slave."[131] In fact, Democrats often accused northern industrialists of treating their (white) workers *worse* than southern planters treated their slaves. Such mistreatment, they argued, was a profound insult to the dignity of free white workers—a dignity grounded not just in their worth as individuals but in their membership in a privileged race.[132] The term "white slavery," which was widely used by the Democratic press in the 1830s and 1840s, captures this sense of racial indignation: while its moral outrage was sometimes directed at slavery as such, it was also used to condemn the reduction of whites to a status properly reserved for Blacks.[133] In this way, white racism lent moral energy to Jacksonian egalitarianism.

Beginning in the 1830s, a small minority of Democrats began to insist that slavery *was* in fact a violation of producers' rights.[134] "The cotton bale and the bank note," said the dissident Ohio senator Thomas Morris, ". . . have at last met and embraced each other, both looking to the same object—to live upon the unrequited labor of others." The "slave power," in Morris's view, was an aristocratic force akin to the power of banking elites, both of which thrived on the exploitation of labor.[135] Theodore Sedgwick Jr., a prominent Massachusetts Democrat, opposed slavery on similar grounds, arguing that the southern planters formed an unproductive aristocracy for whom labor itself had become tainted with servility and disgrace. For him and other Democrats who would later join the Free Soil Movement, slavery seemed to be a corruption of the American vision of a free society—a society in which individuals lived as equal rights-bearers on the fruits of their own toil. Slavery was a reincarnation of European-style aristocracy and labor exploitation, and as such it had no place in the free world.[136]

Even those Democrats who opposed southern slavery, however, typically rejected abolitionist appeals: why were northern elites—who themselves probably practiced "white slavery" or "wage slavery" in their workshops—so fixated on the plight of Black slaves in the South? "There are many among us," wrote the *Northampton Democrat* in 1847, "who talk loud and long of the 'unrequited toil' of the black slave who is compelled to labor from fear of the lash." But these same critics "have nothing to say in behalf of those whose toil brings them a much smaller recompense in proportion to the labor, when it is done from fear of starvation and other evils more serious than the driver's whip."[137] In the *Democrat's* view, white factory workers retained an even smaller share of the fruits of their toil than did the southern slave, who was at least housed and cared for in old age.[138] To focus political energy on Black slavery, then, was to distract attention from the even deeper exploitation suffered by the white working class—and it was a distraction that served the interest of the "pious" northern capitalist.

It was the abolitionists themselves who finally harnessed the labor theory as part of a racially inclusive vision of equal rights. Slavery, wrote Frederick Douglass, could be justified only through a grotesque inversion of the theory: the slave could "own nothing, possess nothing, acquire nothing, but what must belong to another. To eat the fruit of his own toil, to clothe his person with the work of his own hands, is considered stealing." To him, slave owners were in fact that most egregious example of an illegitimate aristocracy, living "in idleness" on the labor of others, which they extorted through brutal violence.[139] The *Voice of Freedom* concurred: tapping a vein of biblical argument that ran back to the Levellers, it condemned the slaveholder as a rebel against God, "eating *his* bread in the sweat of other people's faces."[140] The only just response to such moral outrages, abolitionists insisted, was the immediate abolition of slavery and the affirmation of equal rights for African Americans in the South and North alike. Many also condemned widespread northern prejudice for maintaining a "caste" society that foreclosed economic opportunities to free Blacks and thus denied them the fruits of their labor. We explore these ideas more fully in chapter 8.

Finally, women in the antebellum United States—married women in particular—enjoyed little claim to the fruits of their labor. With few exceptions, married women's lives were tremendously labor-intensive. On the farm, they raised the (often numerous) children, cooked the food, cleaned the house, and washed, ironed, and mended the clothes. They also produced a wide range of goods that their families needed to survive: they tended the chickens and collected eggs, fed and milked the cows, churned butter, made cheese, and raised vegetable gardens.[141] Even middle-class women in rural areas not only sewed but also made their own fabrics: they washed and cleaned the fibers, "spun, and wove the wool and flax, making the blankets, fulled cloth, and linen."[142] They also made "pickles, cider, dried fruit, soap, candles, and nearly every other thing that made the difference between a hovel and a home."[143]

Wives also did many kinds of work outside the home. Poorer women carried farm produce to town and sold it in the streets and markets; they did paid housework in other households; they "worked as cooks and laundresses for railroad construction crews." They shopped for household necessities or, to minimize household expenses, they scavenged for food, used clothes, discarded household tools, and firewood.[144] Early industrialization also brought women, increasingly, into various kinds of wage work, producing garments, shoes, and textiles, among other mass-produced goods. But the fruits of their labor—paid or unpaid—belonged to their husbands. The premise of self-ownership that lay at the heart of the labor theory of property was thus widely understood as not only a white right but also a male right. "The husband owned, not only the value of his own labor time," writes historian Jeanne Boydston, "but the value of his wife's as well."[145]

As we saw in chapter 4, the idealized view of family life that pervaded antebellum literature was premised on a strict separation of the intimate domestic sphere from the market, where men worked for wages or profit. The home was presented as a refuge, a place of "sweet repose for his weary limbs, of calm and sunshine amid the lowering storm."[146] In keeping with this romantic ideal, women's domestic work was often described not as a form of labor but as a kind of delightful leisure.[147] The cheerful, orderly home, writes Boydston, became an "emanation of Woman's nature," or an effusion of her love and natural affection. Child-rearing, of course, was paradigmatic. In these ways, the idea of labor itself (not just ownership) was gendered: it was the province of the male breadwinner.[148]

Early feminist advocates asserting women's right to control their own labor thus confronted several layers of ideological barrier, which they fought by asserting both the reality and the equal dignity of women's work. Across many different cultures and civilizations, argued Sarah Grimke in her pathbreaking *Letters on the Equality of the Sexes* (1838), women were in fact exploited laborers whose toil subsidized the leisure of others: "she performs the labor, while man enjoys what are termed the pleasures of life." Grimke went on to describe the systematic devaluation of women's work in America, even in the formal economy: "In those employments which are peculiar to women," she wrote, "their time is estimated at only half the value of that of men."[149] In her view, this devaluation arose from a patriarchal culture that treated women not as rights-bearers but as instruments to be used in service of male desire.[150] In arguing for married women's property rights, meanwhile, Robert Dale Owen simply universalized the time-honored Lockean principle that the law should "secure to her, that, to which every human being has an inherent right, the ownership of the produce of her own labor."[151]

It should be clear by now that the labor theory of property, as well as the natural rights it justified, was flexible and fraught with ambiguity.[152] Factory workers, farmers, merchants, plantation owners, abolitionists, feminists—all could use it to advance their own cause.[153] As we have seen, there was broad disagreement about who counted as a producer, what counted as productive labor, and who was entitled to rights in the first place. In the sprawling and well-organized Democratic Party press, however, the prevailing view was that producers' rights belonged exclusively to white men and that these rights were best institutionalized through the market.

In fact, the free market would become, alongside white supremacy, one of the Democrats' defining ideological commitments. Through their influence, it would become inseparable from the myth of the rights-bearer and, more fundamentally, from the idea of American freedom. To understand its growing significance and popularity, we must take a fuller view of the market as it appeared in Democratic rhetoric: we must try to see it not only as an embodiment of producers' rights but also as a reflection of natural law and a source of divinely appointed harmony. As they searched for a source of cohesion that could hold an expanding, modernizing, and increasingly divided nation together without vastly extending the government's power, Democrats embraced a strain of free-market ideology laced with utopian religious hope.

7

The Free Market

Leave property to seek its own channels, . . . and the natural course of things will direct its transmission to those who have earned it by their industry and frugality.

—GEORGE CAMP, 1841[1]

IN THE SPRAWLING economic debates that took center stage in the Jacksonian Era, both Democrats and Whigs celebrated the market[2] as an agent of moral and material progress. Democrats in particular came to see it not only as an embodiment of American freedom and a guarantor of individual rights but also as an egalitarian system that promised to tear down the "artificial" privileges of the emerging financial and industrial elite. In their writings and speeches, Democrats converted free-market individualism into both a discourse of national exceptionalism and a language of popular protest. In doing so, they shifted the trajectory of American political ideas: no single ideological achievement has contributed more decisively to the triumph and resilience of individualism in the United States.

As we saw in the previous chapter, Democrats popularized the free market partly by associating it with producers' rights: shielded from legislative interference, they argued, the market would guarantee that small producers reaped the full fruits of their labor. Democrats justified this promise, increasingly, by invoking a utopian vision of the market as a domain of *natural* and harmonious abundance that stood apart from government. Time and again, they contrasted two visions of society: in the first, social order was sustained by coercive political power, which oppressed the many to benefit the few; in the second, it was upheld by natural laws whose benign and egalitarian constraints protected everyone's rights equally and delivered widely shared prosperity. Among these were the economic laws of the market which, like the laws of gravity, constrained and directed human action without impinging on their freedom.

This powerful argument drew on an idealized, Newtonian[3] conception of nature that carried explicit religious overtones. Democrats imagined nature as a harmonious system whose intricate design reflected God's wisdom, and they assimilated the market to it. Its laws therefore seemed to reflect God's benevolent intentions for human societies, and for America in particular: it was here, in this New World, that human society would finally shed the artificial hierarchies of Europe and realize the natural and peaceful freedom that God had intended. This religious nationalism, which shaped American economic thinking throughout the nineteenth century, invested free-market ideas with considerable authority.

The Democrats' free-market rhetoric also drew strength from its adaptability. When they contrasted it with European aristocracy, the free market connoted meritocracy, opportunity, and economic growth. It represented the triumph of progress and divine reason over backward forms of hierarchy and prejudice. On the other hand, when Democrats contrasted it with the industrial economy that had emerged in Britain and parts of the American Northeast, the market connoted simplicity, decentralization, and virtue. Specifically, they invoked free trade to criticize government support for the modernizing projects that might disproportionately enrich commercial and industrial elites and endanger small producers' control over their own lives. This more conservative narrative, centered on the market's impartiality and on its tendency to promote virtuous character, was perfectly tailored for farmers and artisans who felt anxious about the disruptive effects of economic modernization.

Before we can explore the several complementary ways in which Democrats popularized free-market ideas, we must begin with the long-term intellectual shifts that set the stage for them. Most important, in this context, was the Scottish Enlightenment, whose influence had pervaded American popular ideas, both secular and spiritual, in the young republic's early decades and imbued them with a worldly optimism.

The Advent of Natural Society

Over the course of the eighteenth century, optimistic new ideas of human nature and society began to displace long-standing Calvinist orthodoxies. These new ideas, which shaped the thinking of Thomas Jefferson and Tom

Paine, suggested that people could live together peacefully and cooperatively, and enjoy relative economic equality, with little interference from the state. They expressed an optimism drawn from Scottish Enlightenment philosophy and Newtonian science, both of which would continue to shape American political thought in the Jacksonian Era.

In the late eighteenth century, however, these new ideas still faced considerable resistance. Federalists tended to believe that human beings were impulsive, unruly, and prone to violence when they faced adversity. Absent the strong arm of the state, they argued, society would devolve into chaos.[4] "Nothing but Force, and Power and Strength," wrote John Adams to Jefferson, could restrain human appetites and passions enough to maintain social order.[5] Such pessimism was reflected, for example, in their view of the proper role of the military in public affairs. Alexander Hamilton had argued that "government can never [be] said to be established until some signal display, has manifested its power of military coercion."[6] Like Adams, Hamilton firmly believed that force—or at least, the credible threat thereof—was the only means of maintaining social order.[7] These ideas, which had been reinforced by their perception of rising social unrest and anarchy under the Articles of Confederation, underwrote the Federalists' support for a stronger federal government in 1787–88.[8]

At the same time, the conservative New England clergy taught that any successful government had to "make provision for curbing the lusts, and bounding the riotous appetites of men."[9] They believed that state coercion was necessary to enforce public morals and protect society from radicalism and social unrest.[10] Such views reflected their pessimistic assessment of human character, which they inherited both from Calvinist theology and from certain strains of republican thought. Both traditions suggested that men harbored unruly passions that could be checked only by strenuous discipline and virtue.[11] "The mass of men are neither wise nor good," wrote John Jay, one of the authors of the *Federalist Papers*, "and the virtue, like the other resources of the country, can only be drawn to a point and exerted by strong circumstances ably managed, or a strong government ably administered."[12]

The leading challenge to these orthodoxies had come from Scotland. Scottish Enlightenment philosophers—including Francis Hutcheson, Lord Kames, David Hume, and Adam Smith—had argued that human motivation was relatively orderly, driven by predictable passions and interests.[13] Among these was a natural sociability that drew people into peaceful association, as well as the ubiquitous human "desire of bettering our condition." This desire, wrote Adam Smith, "though generally calm and dispassionate, comes with us from the womb, and never leaves us till we go into the grave."[14] Smith and others argued that, by and large, people could be counted on to pursue their own interests, and that this common, rational pursuit would lead them to cooperate—and also to compete productively—with one another. This view of human motivation posed a direct challenge to the older notion that people were capricious and unruly unless subjected to the ordering force of government.[15]

If human behavior was at once sociable and broadly predictable, then society itself could be conceived as a law-governed system subject to rules—much like the physical universe itself.[16] "The concept of innate sociability," writes historian Yehoshua Arieli, "transferred the Newtonian image of the system of nature to society and created a social universe out of the motivations and drives of men."[17] Human sociability and benevolence would preserve "order and harmony" in society, said Boston minister Jonathan Mayhew in 1749, "just as the regular motions and harmony of the heavenly bodies depend upon their mutual gravitation towards each other."[18] These optimistic new ideas of social order—summed up in the idea of "society" as a discrete entity, worthy of study and governed by its own laws—marked a powerful conceptual innovation.[19] Anarchy was no longer the only imagined alternative to state control.[20]

Jefferson had been deeply influenced by this philosophical revolution.[21] So too had Tom Paine, whose *Rights of Man* helped popularize it in America. A "great part of that order which reigns among mankind," he wrote, "is not the effect of government." Indeed, Paine argued that society had "existed prior to government" and would continue to exist even if government were abolished. Society was bound together not by coercion but by "mutual dependence and reciprocal interest." "Nature" had made human beings sociable, and had endowed them with "natural wants greater than [their] individual powers." They were therefore drawn, naturally and inevitably, into society. Society, moreover, was orderly and predictable, and subject to natural laws. "If we consider what the principles are that first condense men into society, and what the motives that regulate their mutual intercourse," wrote Paine, man "is more a creature of consistency than he is aware." Among the natural laws that spontaneously directed the workings of human societies were the laws "of trade and commerce."[22]

These optimistic Newtonian ideas were later absorbed by many Jacksonian Democrats. As we saw in chapter 5, Democratic politicians and editors often argued that government's most important function—to some, its sole legitimate function—was to codify and implement natural laws and protect the rights associated with them. John O'Sullivan, for example, declared that "the same hand was the Author of the moral, as of the physical world"; both were governed by "the same fundamental principles of spontaneous action and self-regulation." In his view, therefore, human societies needed only imitate "the perfect self-government of the physical universe, being written in letters of light on every page of the great bible of Nature."[23] Others likened the laws binding society together to "the laws of light, heat and gravitation"—all were manifestations of the Creator's benevolent genius.[24] Democratic senator William Rives of Virginia declared that "Adam Smith had done for the science of political economy what Bacon and Newton had done for physical science, and Sydney and Locke for the science of government."[25]

Once society was thus reconceptualized as a quasi-autonomous system subject to orderly laws, the function of government could be fundamentally revised. Its role in maintaining social cohesion could be vastly curtailed: it could focus strictly on protecting natural rights.[26] Indeed, the limitation of government could come to seem like a way of liberating "natural society," and the rights that inhered in it, from artificial constraint. Government regulation, by contrast, could come to seem like *unnatural* interference in the otherwise smooth functioning of a law-governed system.[27] This was precisely what Paine had argued. "How often is the natural propensity to society disturbed or destroyed," he lamented, "by the operations of government!" "Government is no farther necessary," he continued, "than to supply the few cases to which society and civilization are not conveniently competent."[28]

The Jacksonian mythology of the rights-bearing individual belonged to this optimistic, Newtonian vision of the world. When seventeenth-century Puritans had invoked the idea of natural rights, they referred to a set of immunities derived from the Ten Commandments and therefore grounded in biblical revelation. These were moral restraints imposed by God on a sinful humanity.[29] By the time Paine and Jefferson defended natural rights as the foundations of all legitimate government, they had crossed a vast conceptual Rubicon. For them, natural rights were derived from basic human wants and needs, which could be ascertained through empirical inquiry: all human beings wanted security and liberty; all craved happiness (and its inverse, the avoidance of suffering); all yearned for property as a means to these ends. Natural rights, wrote Paine, consisted of "all those rights of acting as an individual for his own comfort and happiness, which are not injurious to the natural rights of others."[30] Governments were needed to secure these rights; beyond that, it had merely to leave individuals alone to engage, on equal terms, in their voluntary pursuits.[31]

The rise of this voluntaristic idea of natural society, which was routinely used to construct an idealized image of the United States, marked a watershed in the progress of American individualism. Drawing on their Puritan heritage, the Federalists had tended to imagine society in corporate terms, as a collection of interlocking groups or "orders," arranged hierarchically, each serving a distinctive function. The metaphor of the "body politic" expressed this idea perfectly. In 1808, for instance, the Boston clergyman Jedidiah Morse had declared that "there must be rulers and subjects, masters and servants, rich and poor. The human body is not perfect without all its members, some of which are more honourable than others; so it is with the body politic."[32] Only in working together under the direction of the "head"—which was comprised of the educated upper strata of society—could the different parts of the body politic form one cohesive society. "The cement of this political system," writes historian David Hackett Fischer, "was the deferential spirit of eighteenth-century Anglo-American society, in which the 'multitude' were trained from birth to 'submit to that subordination necessary in the free'est [sic] states.'"[33] As we saw in chapter 3, this corporate, hierarchical conception of society was part of the legacy of English republicanism.[34]

By the dawn of the Jacksonian Era, this organic and hierarchical conception of society was in full retreat. Americans on both sides of the political aisle—but especially Democrats—had reimagined American society as a voluntary association of autonomous individuals, each endowed with natural rights, bound together by mutual interest, contract, and natural sociability, and subject to the spontaneous, harmonizing influence of natural law.[35] Indeed, this egalitarian reimagining had made the free-market, small-government ideal held by many Jacksonian Democrats a conceptual possibility. A young journalist for the *Brooklyn Eagle* named Walt Whitman put it this way: "In each modern nation there is a class who wish to deal liberally with humanity, to treat it in confidence, and give it a chance of expanding, through the measured freedom of its own nature and impulses." Opposing this class was another "who look upon men as things *to be governed*—as having evil ways which cannot be checked better than by law."[36] This latter class, he thought, was invariably the champion of big, restraining government and the enemy of both free markets and human progress.

Although this ideal of a natural and self-regulating market drew support from Americans' long-standing resistance to centralized political power, it also shifted the way this resistance was articulated. When the Anti-Federalists had criticized the new Constitution for consolidating power in the federal government, they had done so in the name of smaller political units—states and local communities whose autonomy they thought worth preserving. In smaller polities, they had argued, citizens would be able to watch over their elected officials more closely and prevent the rise of an insular and imperious aristocracy. They had worried that the new federal government would behave less like a republican government and more like a seat of imperial power, commanding its far-flung territories from a distance. The idea of a self-regulating social order was different in that it was fundamentally apolitical. Free-market enthusiasts proposed to limit the size and scope not just of federal government but of *all* government, and they did so in the name of an idea of a spontaneous economic and moral order unspoiled by political power and its inevitable corruption.[37] Both of these strains of anti-statism survived and flourished in American political thought, but the individualist variant became the dominant one.

Its rise to prominence in Jacksonian America marked an important intellectual breach between America and Europe, where the French Revolution had produced a strong, anti-individualist reaction. For Europeans across the political spectrum, from conservative to radical, this backlash was animated by an acute anxiety about the disintegration of social order and the rise of an egoistic anarchy in its place. Influential European liberals, from Alexis de Tocqueville and Germaine de Stael to a young John Stuart Mill and Giuseppe Mazzini, all worried that their societies were increasingly "atomistic," riven by the rise of individual self-interest and the decline of social affections and solidarity; meanwhile, socialist radicals from Saint-Simon to Pierre Leroux and Romantic anti-liberals such as Friedrich Schleiermacher also condemned the rise of "individualism" in post-Revolutionary Europe and looked to the state to provide the new sources of solidarity that would replace older, traditional bonds of church and caste.[38] The French Revolution's chaotic aftermath, as well as the deep class divisions inherited from feudal society, had left European reformers much less confident about the emergence, out of the ruins of traditionalism, of a naturally harmonious social order. By and large, they turned to the state to engineer a new, modern society. This fundamental difference in perspective explains a great deal of the divergence between American and European thought in the nineteenth century and beyond.

Nature's Economy: The Influence of Natural Religion

"Nature" was a protean and contested concept in Jacksonian Democratic thought. For some, appeals to nature formed part of a broadly conservative response to the new economic powers and institutions that were transforming American life—the bank, the corporation, the factory—and to the urban centers in which their wealth was concentrated.[39] Natural, in this context, meant pastoral. It expressed nostalgia for simpler times and the idealized virtue of settlers and backwoodsmen against the vanities and luxuries of eastern elites. The yeoman, in this sense, lived a natural life on the soil, free from the "artificial" temptations and distractions of urban life. Others, however, used the idea of nature to express a progressive political vision grounded in Enlightenment principles. Like their more nostalgic counterparts, they identified nature with formal equality and meritocracy and contrasted it to *privilege* or aristocracy. But to them, a "natural" economy was a commercial economy brought in line with the laws of God and reason and tethered to an ideal of moral and material progress. This more optimistic, Enlightenment conception of nature suffused the writings and speeches of the more "progressive" wing of the Democratic Party.[40]

For these Democrats, the idea of natural society was largely an economic idea. If society was formed to meet the "mutual and reciprocal interest" of its members, the laws that held it together were economic laws—the laws of the market, which ordered its patterns of voluntary exchange.[41] Like Paine, Democrats tended to describe these laws as natural. When they were disturbed by legislative "interference," the resulting allocation of wealth became *artificial*. Congressman John Bell, for example, criticized concentrations of wealth brought about "by artificial means, by law, by protection, bounties or premiums."[42] Others complained about the aristocrats who were "invited by artificial laws to withdraw from the walks of industry" and become a "burden upon those who remain."[43] Protective tariffs were everywhere described as "artificial" devices that enabled wealthy manufacturers to enrich themselves on the backs of the many.[44] Meanwhile, the great Democratic enemy, the Bank of the United States, was often described as a monstrous deviation from natural principles.[45]

"Nature," then, served as an important moral criterion for Democrats, and it applied especially to the allocation of wealth and property. In *Tyranny Unmasked*, John Taylor of Caroline had demanded whether "the feudal, the hierarchical, the banking, the funding, the lottery, and the protecting-duty modes of accumulating wealth in a few hands" were "all forged in nature's work-house?"[46] The answer, to him, was obvious: these were artificial contrivances, and as such they were presumptively unjust. We find the same rhetorical pattern in one of Andrew Jackson's most famous presidential messages:

> In the full enjoyment of the gifts of Heaven and the fruits of superior indus-try, economy, and virtue, every man is equally entitled to protection by law; but when the laws undertake to add to these natural and just advantages artificial distinctions, to grant titles, gratuities, and exclusive privileges, to make the rich richer and the potent more powerful, the humble members of society—the farmers, mechanics, and laborers—who have neither the time nor the means of securing like favors to themselves, have a right to complain of the injustice of their Government.[47]

Injustice is here imagined as an intrusion of artificial privileges into a natural, meritocratic order. In that natural order, structured by voluntary production and exchange among free and independent individuals, everyone reaped the fruits of their own labor. The market, then, emerged for Democrats as the embodiment of nature itself.[48]

This vastly significant intellectual move cannot be understood without exploring the idea of natural religion, which was another powerful legacy of the Scottish Enlightenment. Scottish ideas had a broad reach in America: they shaped not only the thinking of religious skeptics such as Jefferson and Paine but also the fundamental tenets of Protestant theology. Starting in the mid-eighteenth century, American theology had absorbed the lessons of Scottish common sense philosophy, which had begun to displace Calvinist pessimism about the human mind. Whereas orthodox Calvinists had doubted the human mind's capacity to *know* without the help of divine revelation, this new Scottish philosophy taught that human intuition and observation could yield accurate knowledge about both God and the world he had created.[49] This Enlightenment confidence was well suited to an American society marked by economic growth, scientific discovery, and technological innovation.

The idea that God could be known through reflection on human consciousness and experience was the keystone of natural religion. Francis Wayland, for example, whose *Elements of Moral Science* was widely read and assigned in American colleges, argued that there were two ways for human beings to know their moral duties. The first was revealed religion, or the study of God's word as revealed in scripture. The second was "natural religion," or rational inquiry into the structure and design of the natural world.[50] Wayland, like so many

Americans in the Jacksonian Era, believed that the universe over which God presided was an orderly system governed by natural laws carefully designed to advance his moral purposes.[51] These laws included not just the laws of physics and chemistry but also the empirical laws of the human mind and the moral laws that governed human relations. "Both the natural and the moral worlds," writes historian D. H. Meyer, "were considered to be law-bound systems, legislated by God according to the law of His own being (not by an arbitrary act of will), and superintended by God to establish his glory and effect the ultimate redemption of mankind."[52] The study of these laws, through empirical science or simply through the methodical application of reason, could therefore help reveal God's intentions and expectations for humanity.[53]

Natural religion taught that moral laws, in particular, could be derived from a study of human nature. "The principles of duty and obligation," said Presbyterian luminary John Witherspoon, "must be drawn from the nature of man. That is to say, if we can discover how his Maker formed him, or for what he intended him, that certainly is what it ought to be."[54] And one of natural religion's key "discoveries" was that human beings were meant to be happy. All humans, wrote Wayland, exhibit the "general power of being pleased or pained"—which he also called "sensitiveness," or "the power of being made happy." The very existence of this power, he inferred, must be "an indication of the will of our Creator": in creating the human capacity for happiness, and in surrounding us with objects "precisely adapted to these capacities," God had revealed that human happiness was part of his plan.[55] So fundamental was this premise that Meyer describes natural religion itself as "a method of ethical reasoning premised on the belief that God wills the happiness of mankind, and that what promotes human happiness must conform to God's will and, therefore, be right."[56] The idea that human happiness was among God's highest objectives, and that it should therefore be a leading aim of all social and political organization, was one of the most enduring legacies of Scottish philosophy in America, and we find it repeated both by scions of the eastern religious establishment and by the fiery frontier evangelicals who challenged them.[57]

A number of the most influential academic economists in the Jacksonian Era—or "political economists," as they were then known—conceived of their fledgling science as a subset of natural religion.[58] If moral philosophy asked how individuals could promote human happiness through their private actions, political economy asked how societies could promote it through public policy. Political economy, wrote Rev. John McVickar, a professor at Columbia University, "is to states what religion is to individuals, the 'preacher of righteousness.'" "What religion reproves as wrong," he continued, "Political Economy rejects as inexpedient—what religion condemns as contrary to duty and virtue, Political Economy proves to be equally opposed to the peace, good order, and permanent prosperity of the community."[59] Political economy, in other words, was nothing other than an inquiry into God's own intentions with respect to the structure of human societies. American political economists claimed to have discovered *natural* economic laws that, if faithfully implemented, would maximize human happiness and in so doing bring their society into harmony with divine will.[60]

It is worth noting that Adam Smith, who was widely revered by American political economists as the founder of their discipline, had not held this view. Although he did associate markets with "natural" liberty, he was also a notorious religious skeptic.[61] Early American political economists—many of whom were ordained ministers—subtly reworked Smith's teachings to fit their own religious convictions. "Steeped as the[se] clerical economists were in the natural theology of their day," writes historian Stewart Davenport, "which told them that all of nature was the work of the benevolent creator, they rather easily inserted God back into Smith's [economic] mechanism, where he fit comfortably as its designer and possibly its sustainer."[62] They also criticized or downplayed Smith's English successors, Thomas Malthus and David Ricardo, whose far more pessimistic economic visions were less amenable to this kind of reformulation.[63] This fusion of economics with natural religion would shape the course of American political economy throughout the nineteenth century. As late as 1880, an English writer commenting on the distinctiveness of American political economy pointed to "the conspicuousness of the theological element," as well as its unrelenting optimism.[64]

Crucially for the course of American political ideas, the fundamental assumptions linking natural religion and economic order were not confined to academic economists. In fact, they spilled over into the political rhetoric of the time, especially on the Democratic side. The most ubiquitous defense of the market economy, for example, rested on the premise that God had implanted in human beings a natural desire to "improve their condition." Democrats and Whigs alike often appealed to this desire in explaining why America's economy was superior to all others. Only the American economy, they argued, enabled individuals to improve themselves according to their own effort and ability. In this sense, the American economy *fit* uniquely with human nature: in rewarding individual productivity, in leaving individuals free to apply their labor and dispose of their property as they saw fit, it gave free range to their ambition to improve their lot. This ambition, in turn, benefited everyone and lifted society from barbarism to civilization.[65] In virtually all other countries, by contrast, whole strata of society were confined by the artificial barriers of class, guild, or inherited title—and everyone suffered as a result.[66]

Although Americans pointedly rejected such "artificial" inequalities, they accepted *natural* inequalities as perfectly legitimate. In fact, Democrats and Whigs alike often pointed out that diversity was one of the governing principles of the natural world. In human beings, it was manifest in different levels of natural talent and ability, which helped justify the division of economic labor: different people were naturally suited for different kinds of work. It also militated against any form of durable aristocracy among white men, because aristocratic distinctions did not reflect real or *natural* differences in individual ability or character. One Democratic speaker argued, for example, that God had made some "superior to others in physical and mental power," and that in a free society, as individuals made use of their God-given talents, these differences would naturally give rise to social and economic inequalities. Such inequalities were the "necessary offspring of God's laws" and ought not be interfered with. On the other hand, any inequality that arose because of legal privilege bore no relation to God's own distribution of talents and abilities; it created artificial rather than natural distinctions among men.[67] Political economist Thomas Cooper concurred, and he therefore counseled against fighting "the laws of nature, which assign universally, a greater share of the good things in life, to superior ability, energy, knowledge, and persevering industry."[68]

Just as God had given men different talents and abilities, so too had he distributed distinct advantages and disadvantages to different regions of the earth, and to different states and nations. "The universal freedom of action which [free trade] allows," wrote the members of a national Free Trade Convention in 1831, "tends most thoroughly to develope [*sic*] the moral and physical energies of each nation, and to apply them to those objects to which they are best adapted." On the other hand, "the nation which resorts to a restrictive policy, legislates to her own disadvantage by interfering with the natural & most profitable employment of capital."[69] Like individuals, then, nations had unique natural capacities to develop, and free trade was the mechanism that would help them do so. Democratic free traders often wrote of the trade's "natural channels"—that is, of the channels dictated by the principle of comparative advantage, unhampered by restrictive trade policy. America's advantage, in their eyes, lay in agriculture, in the fertility and expanse of its lands. For the time being anyway, agriculture was its natural form of production.

God had not only created natural diversity, then, but he had also framed it with a set of laws that made it useful and bountiful to humankind. These were the laws of free competition and trade. Competition would unlock the diverse abilities of human individuals, producing efficient results; trade would enable all of the disparate regions of the earth to share in one another's natural wealth, bringing a peaceful prosperity to all. If only human government stayed out of the way and released trade from artificial fetters, Providence would do its work.[70] Responding to Henry Clay on the Senate floor, Robert Hayne, the fiery free trader from South Carolina, extolled the bountiful prosperity that God himself had written into the natural design of the cosmos:

> Sir, as there is a religion, so I believe there is a politics of nature. Cast your eyes over this various earth—see its surface diversified with hills and valleys, rocks, and fertile fields. Notice its different productions—its infinite varieties of soil and climate. See the mighty rivers winding their way to the very mountain's base, and thence guiding man to the vast ocean, dividing, yet connecting nations. Can any man who considers these things with the eye of a philosopher, not read the design of the great Creator (written legibly in his works) that his children should be drawn together in a free commercial intercourse, and mutual exchanges of various gifts with which a bountiful Providence has blessed them?[71]

This providential design required only a small measure of human cooperation: people had to refrain from legislating any "vile system of artificial stimulants" that would subvert the spontaneous operation of nature.[72] Of course, given the equally natural human tendency to grasp for money and power by securing special economic privileges, this was no simple matter. But its achievement was vital, Democrats argued, in preserving the exceptionalism of their young nation.

Because the market embodied the Creator's own intelligent design, which brought the natural diversity of the world into a fruitful harmony, any attempt to redirect or improve it was hubristic, if not heretical. "The earth, the sun, and countless systems wheeling through universal space," wrote Robert Walker, secretary of the treasury in the Polk administration,

> move onward in perfect order and beauty, but even the harmony of the spheres would be disturbed, if the legislation of man could interfere and arrest the laws of nature. The natural laws which control trade between nations, and regulate the relation between capital and profits on the one hand,

and wages and labor on the other, are perfect and harmonious, and the laws of man, which would effect a change, are always injurious.[73]

Democrats sometimes used such language to tell a story of providential inevitability: try as they might, human legislatures could only delay, but never destroy, the ascendant natural logic of the market.[74] At other times, however, they used it to warn against the overweening conceit of those who would substitute artificial laws for the order of nature. "A Merchant" writing in to the *New York Evening Post* warned ironically of the Whig desire to replace "the natural laws of trade, which are of God's own enacting," with a "grand regulator" who could correct their "deficient natural sagacity."[75] Another Democratic speaker described protectionism as an attempt "to attain that by artificial means which is clearly opposed to Divine policy."[76] Thus did economic regulation come to seem like supreme arrogance—the arrogance of those who mistook themselves for gods.[77]

These ideas drew support from the writings of English free trader Richard Cobden, whose agitation against the British Corn Laws in the 1830s and 1840s attracted an international following and influenced American opinion, especially in the North.[78] Cobden believed that free trade, unfettered by protectionist barriers, would bring global interdependence, the end of war, and the advent of a universal prosperity. In his view, tariffs were a profoundly "unnatural" distortion of God's emancipatory plan for the world. The Corn Laws, which imposed heavy tariffs on imported grain, were but one flagrant example of a "law which interferes with the wisdom of the Divine providence, and substitutes the law of wicked men for the law of nature."[79] Cobden's writings nourished a northern strain of free-trade economic thinking that blended with antislavery opinion and contributed to the emerging celebration of "free labor."[80]

For Cobden, as for the Democrats who celebrated free trade, the idea of a natural economy was deeply aligned with natural rights. Like Jefferson and Paine before them, Jacksonian Democrats commonly derived both natural rights and natural economic laws from the precepts of natural religion: both were features of a moral world designed according to rational principles, which could be discovered through careful analysis of human beings' God-given capacities. Rights described the basic protections that individuals needed to navigate this world freely and unfold their native faculties and talents. "The preservation of man's equal rights," wrote William Leggett, "is the be-all and end-all of the natural system of government." The great principle of equal rights, he continued, is "in the political world, what gravitation is in the physical—a regulating principle, which, left to itself, harmoniously arranges the various parts of the stupendous whole, equalizes their movements, and reduces all things to the most perfect organization."[81] For Leggett, the laws of the free market formed an integral part of this natural architecture.[82]

Some readers may resist the notion that Jacksonian Democrats were deeply influenced by religious assumptions, partly because historians have sometimes presented them as an essentially *secular* party.[83] This interpretation is defensible, however, only if we understand "secular" as a comparative term. It is true that Democrats typically opposed the use of state power to advance sectarian goals—such as forbidding mail deliveries on the Sabbath or discriminating against Catholics. Compared to the Whigs, they were also less likely to frame American politics in the language of sin and redemption. But they were not religious skeptics, nor did they exclude overtly religious premises from their political arguments. Indeed, the moralized conception of natural law that appears so often in their rhetoric would have seemed incomprehensible to most Americans—Democrat or Whig—if stripped of its theological underpinnings.[84]

In their political rhetoric, then, the Democrats tended to embrace economic laissez-faire. This did not mean, however, that they opposed all government regulation of the economy. In their ongoing struggle to limit bankers' power over the domestic economy, Democratic administrations pushed to forbid commercial banks from issuing small currency notes; they pushed for the creation of a publicly owned "People's Bank" and later an independent Treasury to handle federal money; they pushed to curtail speculative bubbles by, for instance, requiring that all lands purchased from the government be paid for with hard currency. And indeed, "hard money" itself is best understood as an attempt to extend public control over the currency and the economy by limiting private banks' discretion.[85] In fact, many Whig commentators of the period castigated the Democrats for "governing too much," especially in their efforts to regulate banks and the currency.[86]

Democrats responded by insisting that government intervention was sometimes required to *defend* the natural economic order against the artificial privileges or combinations that were distorting it. "A good deal of positive government may yet be wanted," O'Sullivan conceded, "to undo the manifold mischiefs of past mis-government."[87] Democrats strained to justify even the ten-hour workday in these terms. Governor Marcus Morton of Massachusetts argued, for example, that poverty, geographical dispersal, difficulty organizing, and lack of education made workingmen vulnerable to the economic power of elites, who sometimes took advantage of this power to compel workers to work longer days than they wanted, and for lower pay than was reasonable, and so to extract more than their share of the "fruits" of the workingman's labor. But he blamed this outcome not on market forces themselves but rather on the "cupidity" and "ambition" of those rich men who abused their economic power. It was this unnatural abuse, in his view, that justified legislation limiting the workday to ten hours in certain professions.[88]

In the end, whether or not their legislative agenda can be fully reconciled with their rhetoric, Democrats succeeded in popularizing a new way of understanding the relationship between political and economic life. "The clearest test of the power of the laissez-faire ethos," writes historian Daniel Rodgers about nineteenth-century America, "lay not in the statute-book exceptions but in the realm of conviction—in the rendering of public economic action as an 'intervention' in the realm of 'natural' economic law and economic 'freedom.'"[89] It was the Jacksonian Democrats who turned this conviction into a popular American creed.

Market Freedoms

The idea that markets embodied human freedom was a centerpiece of Democrats' economic rhetoric, and it too drew strength from their fusion of economics with natural religion. Democrats repeatedly presented the market as a domain of orderly abundance that bore little trace of *coercion*. This utopian view was facilitated, in turn, by the conviction that markets were natural and "spontaneous," effusions of divine intelligence rather than human law.

As we have already explored, economic laws appeared natural because, like physical laws, they seemed to work without human intervention. Out of chaos, they fashioned an order that was not, it seemed, the work of human planning. "Spontaneous" was the term that Democrats typically used to describe such order. And in their eyes, the opposite of spontaneity was force—the coercive force of laws that imposed their own order on human affairs. We often find Democrats arguing, for example, that protective tariffs *forced* trade out of its natural channels. "In those countries where the whole system of things is artificial," said Rantoul Jr., ". . . injudicious and mischievous laws *force* enterprise and industry from the most productive occupations."[90] Another Democrat argued, meanwhile, that "legislative interference in favor of any particular pursuit of industry, necessarily *forces* capital and labour from one occupation to another."[91] It was through such coercive intervention that humans rendered their economies artificial rather than natural.[92]

If spontaneity stood opposed to force, it was easily identified with freedom. Uncoerced by economic regulation, *trade* itself was thought to be free, and so were the individuals who engaged in it. Exposed only to market competition, people's fates would be determined by their own "individual enterprise & intelligence," rather than the "guardianship and control of governmental action."[93] They would be "free" to move "from one employment to another."[94] Economic regulation, on the other hand, was "repugnant to the spirit of the age, which sets strongly in favor of unrestrained freedom of individual action."[95] The domain of "free competition and association" was a field of "VOLUNTARY" human action, whereas government intervention was a source of coercive constraint.[96] Since market competition was so strongly identified with individual freedom, any legislative intervention in the market would necessarily appear as an attack on human liberty.

The association of markets with individual freedom may seem obvious to twenty-first-century readers, but in fact, there is an important conceptual puzzle to be solved here. It is true, of course, that markets decentralize economic decision making: decisions as to how and what to produce are left to individuals and firms responding to market pressures, rather than to government directives. But these market pressures surely do *constrain* individual choice, sometimes severely. The German American economist Friedrich List saw this clearly enough: while free traders asserted that the protective tariff *forced* capital into certain "employments," he wrote, "it may be replied that the want of it compels men to invest [their capital] in commerce or agriculture, without any other choice."[97] Free markets, he might well have said, do not necessarily make free men.

In fact, Democratic free traders acknowledged as much: they conceded, for example, that without tariff protection, many Americans who wished to make a career in manufacturing would likely find this economic path barred to them—market conditions would prevent them from making a living in this way. Just as tariffs would *direct* human productivity, making some avenues more profitable and others less, so too would market forces. More broadly, Democrats conceded that competition and technological change could drive down wages and drive workers out of their jobs and even their occupations: they could impose harsh constraints on the range of alternatives available to particular workers and investors.[98]

Why, then, did the market's constraints not count as barriers to individual freedom? Why were people exposed to the rigors of market competition imagined to be perfectly free?[99] Part of the answer came down to aggregate productivity: free traders believed that a loosely regulated market would create more prosperity, and so more economic opportunities for people overall.[100] But this was only part of the answer. For American promoters of free trade, the fact that tariffs were humanly imposed and therefore "artificial," while markets were "natural," seemed deeply significant. If economic laws were indeed akin to "those which keep the planets in their orbits," then it seemed frivolous to treat them as limitations of human liberty in the first place.[101] In this view, economic laws were no more limiting to human liberty than the law of gravity. Hypothetically speaking, of course, we might imagine being freed from the laws of physics, but no one could reasonably claim any moral or political *entitlement* to this kind of "artificial" freedom. In the same way, no one could possess any plausible entitlement to be free of nature's economic laws or the constraints they imposed on individual action.

More fundamentally, if the order of nature was thought to reflect God's will, then the escape from its benign constraints was not a form of freedom to which humans should legitimately aspire. "The moral and the physical world," said John Larue, speaking to the Louisiana Democratic Association in 1846,

> are alike regulated by the great Author of all, and it would be as wise for puny man to attempt to change the direction of the wind or check the falling of the rain, . . . as to endeavor to divert the course of human industry from its natural channels, in order to reap greater profit from his coal mine or his cotton mill.

Larue knew, of course, that humans *could* redirect the course of human industry if they chose—in fact, he went on to chastise protectionists for doing just that. He also knew that the "protected classes" *could* reap greater profits from such redirection. What he meant, then, was that such redirections were perverse. If economic laws were manifestations of divine wisdom, designed for the benefit of all, then the struggle to be released from the market's constraints was both illegitimate and ultimately damaging to everyone. Freedom—the only kind of freedom worth aspiring to—was a condition to be realized entirely within these benign constraints, not by escaping or subverting them. Human industry should be left "as free as the air of heaven," subject like the air itself only to the beneficent laws of nature.[102]

Indeed, this is what some Democrats understood by "freedom" in the first place: the condition of being constrained only by nature's law, nothing more.[103] "Let all international exchanges of products move as freely in their orbits, as the heavenly bodies in their spheres," wrote Walker.[104] His choice of metaphor is revealing. What makes the planets free, in this view, is the fact that the laws that constrain and direct them, no matter how inflexibly, are natural laws, God's own laws. Freedom is imagined, here, as submission to natural constraints. We find this same tendency in O'Sullivan's rhetoric: "Afford but the single nucleus of a system of administration of justice between man and man," he writes,

> and, under the sure operation of [the voluntary principle], the floating atoms will distribute and combine themselves, as we see in the beautiful natural process of crystallization, into a far more perfect and harmonious result than if government, with its "fostering hand," undertake to disturb, under the plea of directing, the process.[105]

Here again, the freedom of human individuals in market society is likened to the movement of natural bodies, directed by physical laws. If the laws of trade, like the laws of physics, were natural and therefore godly, it followed that submission to them could never render anyone *unfree*. "Freedom of trade," proclaimed the *Western Review* in an especially telling formulation, "is the true interest of man, because it leaves him free to pursue the course which nature dictates to him."[106] In this way, the market was thoroughly assimilated to that greatest of American values, liberty.[107]

Although this may seem like a somewhat obscure point, it has had vast implications for the way many nineteenth-century Americans made sense of their lives, especially their economic hardships. It framed a fundamental asymmetry between the market and the state: the one was an impartial domain of divinely appointed order, in which rights-bearing individuals stood perfectly free from coercive constraint; the other was a source of forcible interference in people's economic lives. Economic setbacks suffered at the hands of the market, then, could be chalked up to bad luck, but never to *oppression*.[108] Limits and regulations imposed by the state, by contrast, seemed a direct and immediate threat to personal liberty. This sharp disparity embedded itself in Americans' tacit assumptions about politics and survives to this day.[109]

In Jacksonian America, it was further reinforced by republican ideas. In chapter 3, we saw that eighteenth-century artisans turned to the market, with its myriad impersonal transactions, as a source of liberation from dependence on powerful patrons. Democrats advanced a version of the same argument: if government was responsible for directing the flow of wealth in society, then all would be dependent on it, and it could become a capricious and arbitrary master. "Government may at pleasure elevate one class and depress another," warned Leggett, and ". . . all thus become the mere puppets of legislative cobbling and tinkering, instead of independent citizens, relying on their own resources for their prosperity." In this way, he continued, government "assumes the functions which belong alone to an overruling Providence."[110] The government's arbitrary power, and the dependence that it inflicted on those who suffered it, was an artifact of its *will*: it was a powerful agent that could deliberately hold people under its thumb. By contrast, markets, considered as natural systems, reflected no particular agent's will—or if they did, they embodied divine will, which could never be arbitrary. Like the laws of physics, the market's laws were possessed of a kind of moral innocence: they could never subject people to arbitrary control, they could never turn them into *dependents*. To the extent that freedom was understood as the absence of arbitrary power, it could not therefore be endangered by markets, no matter how capricious their workings might seem.[111]

Critics of both inequality and economic volatility therefore worked hard to assign their causes to particular agents—be they monopolists, speculators, privileged corporations, or government—rather than to the market itself, so that they could appear to be assaults on individual liberty. The Democrats' war against the Second Bank of the United States embodied this tendency: here was a "great controlling institution" whose discretionary control over the economy could be blamed for virtually all economic ills.[112] The Bank filled an important rhetorical and theoretical need: it enabled Democrats to preserve the ideal of a *free* and natural market whose beneficent effects were being distorted by a cabal of aristocrats. This was one of the reasons for the Bank's disproportionate prominence in the economic debates of the period.

Artificial Inequalities

The growing popularity of free-market ideas in Jacksonian America rested, also, on the conviction that markets were broadly egalitarian. As we began to explore in the previous chapter, Democrats expected that free competition among small producers would deliver widely shared opportunity and wealth. In fact, they often attributed the vast inequalities of Europe to the *artificial* character of its political and economic institutions.[113] "It is only when the natural order of society is disturbed," wrote President Van Buren to a constituent, ". . . that the wages of labor become inadequate." "Left to itself, and free from the blighting influence of partial legislation, monopolies, congregated wealth, and interested combinations, the compensation of labor" would always be generous enough to "provide comfortably" for the worker and his family, and to save enough to meet the "wants of advanced age."[114] Rantoul Jr. shared this optimism: absent "artificial" economic conditions, anyone could, through hard work, earn enough to "place him in an independent affluence."[115]

It is easy to dismiss such proclamations of economic faith as the dishonest rationalizations of wealthy Democratic elites. In some cases, they were. But for many others, the faith ran deep and seemed to draw support from the material facts: in an expanding economy of small producers, with a vast surplus of available land, it seemed reasonable to anticipate that expanding markets would bring greater economic equality. In such circumstances, wrote Senator William Allen, "the natural disparity in the capacities, energies, and dispositions of men, unaided by political discriminations, [is] insufficient to destroy that equality of conditions so essential to the safety of each, and to the common happiness of all."[116] If only it could be protected from the distorting influence of irresponsible banks, monopolistic corporations, and unequal laws, the market itself would prevent serious inequality—or so it seemed to many of the Democratic faithful.[117]

Evidence of this expectation can be found throughout the Democratic ranks, even among labor activists, who commonly attributed American inequality to "artificial" legislative interference.[118] Levi Slamm, for example, speaking at a workingmen's meeting in New York, blamed "special bank charters" and the "system of monopoly and restriction" for the plight of the American worker. Against these malign forces, he invoked the "principle of equal protection to all and favors to none—or, equal rights and free trade."[119] Meanwhile, Ely Moore, who served as president of the National Trade Union, commented on "this strange and unnatural inequality" caused by "partial, special and unequal laws."[120] In his view, these laws distorted a natural economy that would otherwise have yielded greater equality for working men. Many of the leaders of the early labor movement, writes historian Edward Pessen, were "ardent believers in natural laws and natural rights" who attributed poverty and inequality to "artificial social institutions" that frustrated "nature's benevolent designs for man."[121] Most were therefore opposed to any deliberate government redistribution of property or wealth.[122]

Leggett, whose dogged assaults on monopoly and elite privilege in the New York press won him admiration among many working-class activists, embodied this frame of mind.[123] "In as far as inequality of human condition is the result of natural causes," he wrote, "it affords no just topic of complaint." Only when it is brought about by "the intermeddling of legislation" did it present a moral problem.[124] And Leggett attributed the majority of American inequality to such corrupt interference, which distorted an egalitarian natural order. He therefore warned against "that folly which would substitute the laws of men for those of nature, and wholly change the irreversible order of causes and effects."[125] The "natural system of government," he insisted, was one that confined itself to enforcing equal rights and protecting free trade. Only in this way could the working men of America get their due.[126]

We saw in the previous chapter that some labor leaders and freethinkers rejected these individualistic assumptions altogether and gravitated instead toward socialist critiques of the emerging capitalist economy. One of the deepest challenges to the Democrats' faith in a natural and egalitarian market society, however, came from another source entirely: from Thomas Malthus's theory of population and David Ricardo's law of rent. Malthus had argued that the rate of population growth naturally exceeds the growth in food supply, and that starvation and misery were nature's way of keeping population under control. He also believed that the suffering of the lower classes was a necessary inducement to work, and that any effort to improve the condition of the poor through legislation was bound to prove futile. Here is radical Democrat Stephen Simpson's assessment of Malthus's ideas:

> In the midst of plenty, avarice, power, ambition, extortion—all start up to monopolize the bounties of nature, and create a famine to seven eighths of mankind, in order that the remaining fraction may riot in gluttony, and luxuriate in excess. And the famine thus caused by the diabolical passions of man, is attempted to be ascribed to nature; whilst the pampered scribes of voluptuous nobility coolly sit down, and under the pretence of philosophy, affect to calculate that nature has not provided subsistence for her children.

To Simpson and his peers, Malthus's argument represented the ultimate perversion of the order of nature, which was "ever harmonious in her plans—ever beneficent in her economy."[127] Nothing could be more galling than the idea that nature herself—the very standard to which they turned for deliverance from oppression and hierarchy—had ordained the suffering and poverty of the working class. Malthusian pessimism was far less influential in antebellum America than it was in Britain, where anxiety about population pressures preoccupied even liberal optimists such as John Stuart Mill.

The Market's Virtues

If the Democrats' idea of the free market expressed a deeply optimistic, Enlightenment view of American society, it also bore strong traces of the more nostalgic, republican and Protestant ideas that we explored in earlier chapters. In fact, Democrats sometimes presented free trade as part of a vision of republican equality, simplicity, and virtue that hearkened back to the Revolutionary years. This versatility in tone and mood, too, is critical to understanding how the Jacksonian Democrats turned the free market into a populist rallying cry.

The market's most important moral feature, in this context, was its supposed *impartiality*. In defending free trade, Democrats routinely appealed to the principle of "equal laws and equal rights," which they saw as a part of the very foundation of republican government in America.[128] When they described the "genius" of American political institutions, for example, Democrats often singled out the absence of *privilege* or *exclusive privilege* of any kind. "The guiding spirit of our American institutions," according to an 1832 pamphlet on free trade, "is equality of rights without exclusive privilege, equality of burdens without distinction, by laws equally enacted and administered: no preference of one section over another, of one class over another, . . . of one citizen over another."[129] Such language was commonplace; the Fourth of July addresses of the period are littered with proud appeals to America's system of "equal laws."[130] As we saw in chapter 5, Democrats saw aristocracy as a creation of law: it was sustained through special legal privileges conferred by government. In their eyes, a republic—or indeed a *democracy*—was a political community in which no such privileges divided white men from one another.

When they looked at American politics, however, Democrats saw evidence of special favors everywhere. In antebellum state legislatures, public funding and economic opportunities were often allocated on an ad hoc basis.[131] The modern administrative state had not yet come into existence, and lawmakers spent much of their time adjudicating local conflicts and conferring benefits on particular persons and groups.[132] As states ramped up public support for infrastructure and economic development, they set off a scramble for legislative favors. Corporate charters, which had to be specially conferred by legislatures and often granted lucrative and exclusive economic privileges to the grantees, seemed an especially visible case in point. At a workingmen's meeting in the District of Columbia, one Democratic speaker argued that these exclusive charters made bankers, for example, a "PRIVILEGED ORDER" established "in direct violation of the principle of equal laws, which professedly forms the basis of our institutions."[133]

Democrats warned repeatedly that such favoritism corrupted Americans' virtue. The *Democratic Review* made this case over the course of a number of articles: as soon as political elites found that they could use unequal laws to dole out special favors, the very nature of a nation's political life changed. Ambitious politicians could then enlist "one portion of the people to plunder another, and they increase their mercenary corps by every unequal law which confers on some favored class a peculiar privilege."[134] Politics became a "low strife for doles and rewards, obtained by trampling on the equal rights of the people." And this, in turn, encouraged the worst forms of individual character: "it quenches the sentiment of patriotism; excites a feverish thirst for sudden wealth; provokes a spirit of wild and dishonest speculation; allures industry from its accustomed field of useful occupation; pampers the harmful appetites of luxury," and more.[135] It could also inflame sectional strife as different regions competed for the spoils of government patronage. "Once disturb the equilibrium which equal laws maintain in a society," warned the author, "and its institutions, if popular in their form, decline from that moment."[136]

It is significant that Democrats often used the term "monopoly" to describe the unequal laws that wreaked these corrupting effects. George Bancroft insisted, for example, that "democracy demands equal laws for the general good; hence democracy tolerates no monopolies."[137] Like other Democrats, he used the term "monopoly" loosely: it described any economic regulation, corporate charter, or tax that tended to restrict competition.[138] Democrats used it to describe corporations chartered to build turnpikes or run ferries, whose charter shielded them from competition; bank charters, which gave their recipients the exclusive privilege of printing paper money; tariffs, which protected domestic manufacturers from foreign competition; and more. When Jackson famously vetoed the recharter of the Second Bank of the United States, he described it as a "monopoly," because it was the sole federally incorporated bank, and as such it enjoyed unique legal advantages. He insisted that the government restrain itself to providing "equal protection" rather than monopolistic privilege.[139] "Monopoly," writes one historian, "came to represent to the Jacksonian all those forces seeking to rob him of his freedom";[140] it was the "demiurge of evil inequality."[141]

The opposite of monopoly, of course, was competition—and if monopoly bred vice, Democrats argued that market competition taught virtue. The bitter debates over tariffs brought this tendency to light clearly. Protective tariffs were repeatedly denounced as a form of corrosive monopoly granted to northern manufacturers at the expense of the broader public.[142] In place of the market's natural impartiality, tariffs tended to pit the different regions of the country against each other in a zero-sum struggle for legislative favor. Democrats often maintained that the market's wholesome competition, by contrast, promoted *honest industry*. If only government refrained from interfering with it and let its impartial laws guide economic behavior, the market would encourage people to be productive rather than to seek political favors. It would also replace the "feverish thirst for sudden wealth" with patient and determined labor, which would then nurture frugality and tend to cure Americans of their "harmful appetites of luxury" and even their "intemperance."[143] Time and again, Democrats maintained that market competition promoted old-fashioned Protestant virtue.

They made similar arguments about banking. Addressing a meeting of Vermont Democrats in 1839, Edward Barber denounced the "paper money systems" that had lately come to dominate the American economy, and the "spirit of monopoly" they embodied, as sources of rampant vice. Under their influence, "the desire to become suddenly rich seizes upon all classes" and opens the door to "scheming, cunning and fraud, . . . and a rage for display and luxury." "All the solid virtues of life are cast in to shade," he continued, "by the showy and magnificent." He contrasted this corrupt system to a purer and more egalitarian alternative, founded on "individual enterprise, and competition."[144] Such arguments were commonplace among Democrats. Col. Benjamin Faneuil Hunt of South Carolina declared that "paper" banks were defrauding honest Americans of their earnings and so degrading and demoralizing labor itself. But supply the American worker with a stable currency and leave him "free to make his bargain," and he would labor virtuously in his calling.[145]

As they linked market competition with both Protestant and republican virtue, Democrats were echoing an eighteenth-century tradition of thought that long preceded Adam Smith. In a widely influential series of essays written in the 1720s, English Country ideologists John Trenchard and Thomas Gordon associated "unequal Laws" with the corruption of government and the servility and "slavish flattery" of those who scrambled for favors from the powerful rather than trying to succeed on their own merits.[146] Under these circumstances, they wrote, men's energies would be directed to procuring "monopolies, exclusive companies, liberties of pre-emption, etc.," rather than to advancing honest trade.[147] Free trade, by contrast, would ensure that men worked honestly and prudently for their wealth and distinction. "In fine," they concluded, "monopolies are equally dangerous in trade, in politicks, in religion: A free trade, a free government, and a free liberty of conscience, are the rights and the blessings of mankind."[148] Such arguments, which fused republican, liberal, and Protestant ideas in defense of an expanding commercial society, had also been advanced by eighteenth-century English radicals such as Richard Price, Joseph Priestly, and James Burgh. They were eventually absorbed by John Taylor of Caroline, among other Americans, whose denunciations of banking and paper currency seethed with indignation over "monopoly" and exclusive privilege.[149]

The transition between republicanism and liberalism is often described as a shift in the way social cohesion was imagined and explained—a shift from virtue to self-interest. But Democrats did not celebrate self-interest as such. After all, the speculators and bankers competing for legislative patronage were driven by self-interest. Their kind of predatory egoism, which contributed nothing to society, was condemned as *avarice*.[150] On the other hand, Democrats lauded the prudent self-interest of the honest farmer or merchant who sought no special privileges, who contributed to the overall productivity and "happiness" of the community. Self-interest, then, could be a harmonizing force, but only when expressed through productive activity; and this in turn depended on a market society governed by equal laws, in which citizens enjoyed equal rights.

In such a society, self-interest did not replace virtue as a source of social cohesion; it *reinforced* virtue. Citizens trying to better their condition would find themselves encouraged to be honest, industrious, moderate, and temperate, for these were the virtues that yielded success in a market society.[151] As we saw in chapter 4, this argument marked the culmination of a long-term ethical shift that gradually redefined the relationship between virtue and self-interest. In the seventeenth-century republican tradition of James Harrington and Algernon Sidney, the very linchpin of virtue was the ability to transcend or suppress private interest in order to become an impartial defender of the public good. Conceptually, private interest and the common good were close to antonyms: to pursue one was to sacrifice the other. The common good, moreover, was identified mainly with the preservation of republican liberty, which meant protecting the rule of law and the delicate constitutional balance that held both tyranny and anarchy at bay. Over the course of the eighteenth century, as Western societies began to attain levels of prosperity unseen in human history, the idea of economic growth suggested itself ever more insistently as an alternative conception of the common good. The more economic growth and prosperity came to define the common good, the more virtue came to be identified with economic productivity, and the more it came to seem compatible with self-interest.[152] So long as he did not violate the rights of others, the productive individual was simultaneously improving his own condition and doing his part to advance the prosperity of society.

In the Jacksonian Era, however, this new, liberal perspective was still deeply enmeshed with republican and Protestant ideas. As we have seen, Democrats saw a direct relationship between prudent self-interest and the preservation of republican liberty. In their eyes, the self-interest of the honest tradesman or farmer was a form of human striving that did not threaten to corrupt the polity and undermine liberty, for it did not seek any special political privileges. Here, then, is one of the reasons why Americans in the Age of Jackson could believe that self-regarding virtues such as industry, frugality, and economy might offer credible alternatives to the more traditional, civic virtues of the classical republican tradition: they provided an alternative way of protecting liberty from human ambition. Rather than keep such ambition in check by inculcating a demanding and disinterested civic virtue, the market opened up safe, alternative channels for it. It ensured that individual self-interest assumed a politically benign form.[153]

The idea that the market promotes both private and public virtue touches on one of the central paradoxes of Democratic thought, captured here by historian Marvin Meyers:

> The movement which helped to clear the path for laissez-faire capitalism and its culture in America, . . . held nevertheless in [its] political conscience an ideal of a chaste republican order, resisting the seductions of risk and novelty, greed and extravagance, rapid motion and complex dealings.[154]

As we have explored over the course of this chapter, Democrats sometimes appealed to the market as a defense against certain aspects of economic modernity—the modernity embodied in the emerging system of finance, the advent of large, commercial corporations, and the growth of domestic industry. They fought for an alternative economic order of small producers and independent farmers that they associated with republican virtue and simplicity.

But it was a resolutely commercial order, a market order. "Far better would it have been for all concerned," proclaimed one partisan pamphlet, commenting on the profusion of speculation in land, fueled by banks, "had trade been left to its old-fashioned, honest and legitimate course."[155] Free trade, here, becomes the stuff of nostalgia, referring to an age as yet uncorrupted by modern finance and industry.

This particular vision of market freedom fit comfortably with both the myth of the independent proprietor and the labor theory of property. All three converged on a common vision of society: the free and natural economy was simultaneously an economy of independent men who controlled the conditions of their work and jealously guarded their autonomy. Moreover, the virtues of industry, frugality, and prudence, so often associated with the independent smallholder, were simultaneously projected onto the small producers who met society's needs while reaping the fruits of their labor. Finally, all of these overlapping political narratives singled out aristocracy as the enemy. In Jacksonian America, both republican and liberal strains of thought were bound together, as historian James Huston puts it, by "the common enemy of aristocracy," which stood accused of capturing government and using it to violate producers' rights, eviscerating their independence *and* subverting the natural order of society.[156] It followed that government "intervention" in economic life tended to seem both oppressive and ungodly. This powerful confluence of ideas helps explain why free-market ideas in America have remained so popular, even among rural and disaffected constituencies who have so often suffered from their effects.

8

Rights against Slavery

In no country has so much been said about rights, as in this; and it is also said,
that in no other country, have rights been more outraged and trampled on.

—CITIZENS OF MEDINA COUNTY, OHIO, 1836[1]

WHEN THEODORE PARKER rose to address the antislavery gathering in
Abington, Massachusetts, on July 5, 1852, he summoned the rhetoric so often
deployed in Independence Day orations.[2] The American Revolution, he declared, had marked a turning point in human history and inaugurated a new
and final "epoch" in the unfolding progress of human liberty, whose inception
he traced back to the birth of Christ. This climactic stage of human history,
Parker explained, would be dominated by "the American Idea," which proclaimed that "all men have natural rights to life, liberty, and the pursuit of
happiness." As Parker interpreted it, this same Idea also held "that all men are
equal in their natural rights; that these rights can only be alienated by the possessor thereof; and that it is the undeniable function of government to preserve
their rights to each and all."[3]

In these few sentences, Parker summarized the Lockean creed that had
laced through American ideas since the early eighteenth century and shaped
the Declaration of Independence. Like so many of his fellow abolitionists,
Parker argued that the United States had betrayed this creed profoundly: he
saw not just slavery but also rampant racial prejudice as evidence of a fundamental hypocrisy at the heart of American life. At the same time, he was hope-
ful for their imminent disappearance. "It would not be historical," he continued, "to expect a nation to realize its own Idea at once."[4] There was still time
for Americans to bring their actions in line with their ideals, but they had to

act swiftly and purposefully, for divine judgment could not be indefinitely deferred.

Parker's oration was typical: throughout the 1830s and 1840s, abolitionists had constantly invoked the myth of the rights-bearer to both praise and criticize the American nation.[5] Like mainstream Democrats, they lauded the Jeffersonian ideal of natural rights and presented it as a glorious American inheritance. Like Democrats, they often saw American politics as a great drama in which the sovereign individual faced off against an ascendant aristocracy conspiring to strip him of his rights. From this shared foundation, however, abolitionists moved in sharply different political directions. Their focus on slavery and racial discrimination led them to highlight a broader slate of rights than Democrats typically did. Moreover, while Democrats tended to identify equal rights with both democracy and the market, abolitionists were more conflicted. In their eyes, the "slaveocracy" drew strength both from the widespread prejudices of the democratic public and from the insatiable profit-seeking unleashed by the market revolution. Their struggle to vindicate equal rights was therefore a struggle to contain the moral pathologies endemic to both of these defining American institutions, and it would eventually lead them to embrace a more muscular federal government than Jacksonian Democrats could accept.

Abolitionists also fused their urgent appeals to natural rights with an evangelical reform impulse that ran much stronger in the Whig Party.[6] Unbound by the egalitarian teachings of Christ, they argued, both democracy and the market would give rise to predatory assaults on minority rights. In fact, as Parker's oration suggests, abolitionists saw the very idea of equal natural rights—or "human rights," as they began calling them—as an embodiment of Christian ideals whose modern origins lay in the Protestant Reformation and the struggles for religious liberty in colonial America.[7] The first step, then, toward abolishing slavery and overcoming racial prejudice was to restore the pure spirit of the gospels to a nation that had grown corrupt, materialistic, and immoral. Specifically, they drew on Christian moral principles to encourage an egalitarian empathy with the oppressed, an acute sense of personal responsibility for injustice, and a habit of organized civic action. In this way, they embedded the myth of the rights-bearer in a tradition of grassroots activism whose legacy extends into the twentieth-century struggles for women's suffrage and civil rights. Their writings illustrate the breadth and malleability of rights discourse in Jacksonian America, and they shed further light on the diverse Protestant roots of American individualism.

Like both of the major political parties that defined the American political landscape, the abolitionist movement was ideologically diverse. It drew support from both disaffected Democrats and renegade Whigs, from establishment businessmen and labor activists, and from a wide variety of Protestant denominations and sects.[8] By the late 1830s, the movement itself had splintered into several factions whose members disagreed over both strategy and principle.[9] Unlike the major parties, abolitionism was also an interracial coalition, which made its ideas that much more varied: Black abolitionists brought their own distinctive experiences and perspectives to the fight against slavery, which led to disagreements with their white allies.[10] In generalizing about the political thought of American abolitionism, therefore, we must look for intellectual and rhetorical patterns that cut across many, if not all, of these divisions.[11] The ubiquitous language of natural or human rights defines one such pattern: for abolitionists of many different backgrounds, it served to translate the moral teachings of the gospels into political claims that resonated powerfully in the political climate of Jacksonian America.

Slavery and American Exceptionalism

The idea that the United States was exceptional for its commitment to human liberty laced through abolitionist writings as a tragic irony. "Equal rights, liberty—Oh! whither, whither are ye fled?" lamented one abolitionist correspondent. "Do Americans boast a country free? a land of liberty? Truly, with two and a half millions of human beings in chains and ignorance, and dirt and rags."[12] In their speeches and proclamations, in their constitutions and other official documents, Americans constantly proclaimed their unique devotion to equal rights and universal freedom. For abolitionists, slavery rendered these proclamations abhorrent: how could a people who held millions in bondage claim to be a beacon of liberty for the world?[13]

If anything, they argued, America was exceptional for its unparalleled oppression and moral depravity. "Go where you may, search where you will, roam through all the monarchies and despotisms of the old world," thundered Frederick Douglass, ". . . and you will say with me, that, for revolting barbarity and shameless hypocrisy, America reigns without a rival."[14] This was true not only because of the unprecedented cruelty of American chattel slavery but also because American slaves lived in such close proximity to freedom.[15] "The sting of oppression," wrote David Lee Child, "acquires a new venom in an atmosphere of freedom. The condition of slaves in the United States of America, consists of two component parts, the labor of Sisyphus and the torment of Tantalus."[16] To live as a slave in a society formally dedicated to universal human liberty, moreover, was to suffer an especially harsh form of degradation: it was to be treated as subhuman. Where else in the world, abolitionists asked, could naked, dehumanizing oppression be found on such a scale? "There has been tyranny and oppression and cruelty," said Nathaniel Rogers in an 1837 address, "but never such a wanton, insulting, mocking, annihilating slavery as ours."[17]

In fact, abolitionists constantly tried to embarrass their audiences by dramatizing the chasm that separated America's exceptionalist ideals from its harsh reality. They compared the United States to the Egypt of Exodus, in which the Israelites had labored as slaves—inverting the image of America as the promised land.[18] They also reversed the contrast, so central to the American self-conception in this period, between American freedom and European oppression. They described the United States as a "caste" society and imagined the despots of Europe taking eager lessons from southern "Lynch laws."[19] They pointedly lauded Britain—which had abolished slavery in 1833—as the world's leading agent of moral progress. Describing his flight from southern slavery, William Wells Brown recalled his dreams of "Victoria's domain" north of the border, which beckoned as the land of the free. Here was "an American citizen," he observed caustically, "fleeing from a Democratic, Republican, Christian government, to receive protection under the monarchy of Great Britain."[20] So much for the idea of America as refuge for the world's oppressed.

And yet, for all their scathing denunciations of American hypocrisy, abolitionists rarely rejected the mythology of American freedom altogether. Instead, they tried to harness its moral power in the fight against slavery. "The American revolution was incomplete," wrote Elizur Wright, a leading abolitionist, in 1833. "While this nation held up its declaration of independence— its noble bill of human rights, before an admiring world, in one hand; it mortified the friends of humanity, by oppressing the poor and defenceless with the other."[21] The goal, for Wright and so many of his peers, was to complete the "noble" project announced in the Declaration. The path to exceptionalism still lay open, in other words, if only Americans would abolish slavery and extend their freedoms equally to all. "This nation can never rise with strength to follow the beck of Providence, and to fulfil its high mission in the cause of human liberty," wrote the *Reflector and Watchman* in 1848, "until it shall be pervaded by a juster sentiment of liberty itself."[22] Above all, this meant recognizing that slavery could have no place in a free society.

Abolitionists often argued that the American founders, swept up in the heady idealism of the Revolutionary era, had come closer to this recognition than their descendants in the Age of Jackson. "Oh my country!" lamented William Ellery Channing, "hailed once as the asylum of the oppressed, once consecrated to liberty, once a name pronounced with tears of joy and hope! now a by-word among the nations, the scorn of the very subjects of despotism! How art thou fallen, morning star of freedom!"[23] Citing Jefferson's misgivings and George Washington's posthumous liberation of his slaves, abolitionists argued that the founders had seen their own ideals as part of an unfinished moral project that included the eventual abolition of slavery.[24] But no longer: the spread and intensification of southern slavery in the early nineteenth century, along with the rollback of Black voting rights and the growing racial violence in the North, offered striking evidence of America's moral decline. Channeling the rhetorical power of the Puritan jeremiad, they exhorted their fellow countrymen to recommit themselves to their own principles, whose original promise had been corrupted by apathy, greed, and bigotry. Abolitionism would finally prevail, argued one speaker, "by erecting again the Standard of our fathers, with which they secured the admiration and sympathy of the whole civilized world."[25]

For obvious reasons, Black abolitionists tended to hold more ambivalent views of the founding. Speaking at a Black freedom celebration on July 5, 1832, Rev. David Nickens reminded his audience that they were not there to celebrate American independence—for that would "betray in us a want of sound understanding." In his eyes, the United States was a nation born in sin, where the "descendants of Africa" had from the very beginning been brutally excluded from the promise of equal liberty.[26] At the same time, many Black abolitionists positioned themselves as the true inheritors and interpreters of America's redemptive "first principles."[27] Even as they reinterpreted American history to place slavery at its very center, they also tended to present the Black journey from bondage to freedom as the key to fulfilling America's providential meaning. In convention speeches and freedom celebrations, Black speakers presented African Americans as the true champions of American ideals, whose pursuit and attainment of equality would at last transmute America itself from the Egypt of Exodus to the promised land of freedom.[28]

For almost all abolitionists—Black and white alike—the Declaration of Independence stood out as *the* foundational articulation of these ideals.[29] No passage was so frequently cited in abolitionist writings and speeches as the Declaration's assertion that "all men are created equal" and "endowed by their

Creator with certain unalienable Rights." "On this endurable basis of human rights," said one abolitionist speaker, "has been reared the proud superstructure of the American Republic. And is not the banner of such a government the refuge of the oppressed of all nations?"[30] Others declared it *the* "principle from which [the United States] broke allegiance with her fatherland: 'All are born *free and equal*; endowed by their Creator with *life and liberty, inalienable rights.'*"[31] For most abolitionists, then, America seemed exceptional in two very different ways: first, because of its formal dedication to universal human rights, and second, because of its shocking betrayal of this very standard. In invoking the myth of the rights-bearer, they invoked what they hoped to be the true and exceptional meaning of America, which they asserted against its fallen reality.

Natural Rights and Protestant Dissent

Although the Declaration of Independence offered abolitionists a powerful source of moral authority, they ultimately found it insufficient. In the North and South alike, most Americans read the Declaration through the lens of white supremacy: its rights, they believed, were for whites, not for those "degraded" races who could not possibly make responsible use of them.[32] Some slaveholders went so far as to condemn the Declaration explicitly and dismiss its universalist language as a meaningless rhetorical flourish.[33] Even more troubling to abolitionists was the fact that so many American churches fell in line with the "slave power."[34] Prominent ministers in both the North and South spoke of slavery's scriptural foundations; others looked the other way to avoid offending and dividing their congregations. Those who did criticize slavery typically endorsed the American Colonization Society's racist agenda of deporting freed Blacks to Africa. Moreover, northern churches practiced widespread racial discrimination in their own seminaries and congregations.[35] Abolitionists saw such racism as evidence of a profound corruption of Christianity, and they turned to the Bible to vindicate the promise of equal rights.[36]

In chapters 6 and 7, we traced the roots of American rights discourse back to the labor theory of property and the optimistic naturalism of the Scottish Enlightenment. As abolitionists combed through scripture to justify and universalize the principles of the Declaration, they drew instead on a tradition of anti-authoritarian ideas that had long coursed through American Protestantism. This Protestant tradition, too, could claim John Locke as one of its intellectual patrons. When the colonial clergy had rallied in defense of the

American Revolution, for example, they too had frequently appealed to a Lockean view of government: "Thanks be to God," preached Congregationalist minister Samuel Langdon in 1775, "that he has given us, as men, natural rights, independent on all human laws whatever." When a government violated these rights, he continued, its subjects could rightly "put an end to it and set up another."[37] Langdon and his peers had justified this revolutionary stance through appeal to scripture, from the decalogue to the teachings of St. Paul. The fulcrum, for many of them, lay in their revisionist reading of Romans 13, in which Paul had declared that "the powers that be are ordained of God," and that "whosoever therefore resisteth the power, resisteth the ordinance of God." Drawing on a tradition of Protestant dissent extending back to the midsixteenth century, they maintained that Paul had urged submission *only* to rulers who governed justly and with proper regard for their subjects' natural rights and liberties.[38]

The Protestant clergy might well have retreated from these Lockean arguments, however, if not for another, older political conflict that unfolded from the seventeenth century onward: the struggle for religious toleration and, eventually, disestablishment. In fact, the 1790s had brought a substantial reorientation of clerical opinion in America. The French Revolution, whose radicalism and anticlericalism appalled much of the American Protestant establishment, led them to draw back from the Lockean premises of the 1760s and 1770s. Unnerved by the spread of radical ideas and the erosion of deference to both political and ecclesiastical authority in the young republic, many turned to England as a model and to the hierarchical conservatism of the Federalist party as a shield against incipient social disorder. The publication of Tom Paine's heretical *Age of Reason* in 1794–95 helped consolidate the clerical view that political radicalism, centered on the idea of the universal "rights of man," posed a fundamental threat to both social stability and Christian orthodoxy.[39]

It is deeply significant, then, that just as the clerical establishment was pivoting toward Federalist conservatism, its political and intellectual influence was on the wane. The most potent challenge to its authority came from a rising evangelical movement whose leaders took Jefferson's side in the fateful election of 1800. These evangelicals, who had suffered persecution in many American colonies throughout most of the eighteenth century and were therefore deeply suspicious of the alliance of church and state, increasingly spoke the language of natural rights to delineate the proper limits of government authority.[40] They appealed specifically to the rights of individual conscience as a justification for limited government.[41] They derived this and other rights, moreover, not just from reason and "Nature's God" but from the text of the Bible and presented them as the unfolding of a distinctively Christian, scriptural understanding of a just and well-ordered community. These evangelicals—most of all the Methodists and Baptists—were unusually influential in the United States, where the clerical establishment was relatively weak and fragmented.[42] Their numbers exploded in the early decades of the nineteenth century, and their biblical arguments, which reinvigorated the myth of the rights-bearer among American Protestants, form an important part of the story of American individualism.

Throughout the colonial period, religious dissenters had clamored for greater religious tolerance against the established churches.[43] Beginning with Roger Williams's storied revolt against the standing order of the Massachusetts Bay Colony, they pressed their claims in different moral and theological languages. One recurrent theme, however, was the Lutheran idea of dual jurisdictions, which was grounded in the scriptural injunction to "render . . . unto Caesar the things that are Caesar's, and unto God the things that are God's."[44] This edict was widely understood to delineate two separate spheres of authority: the secular and the spiritual. American religious dissenters interpreted it, increasingly, to mean that government could not legitimately regulate matters of the soul. Williams himself had declared that "the *Lawes* of the *Civill Magistrates* government extends no further then over the *body* or *goods*, and to that which is *externall*: for over the *soule God* will not suffer any man to *rule*: onely he *himselfe* will rule there."[45] To extend secular authority over matters of the soul, he taught, was to violate divine edict and encroach on a domain that the almighty had reserved for himself. Over the course of the eighteenth century, Williams's intellectual descendants harnessed this argument to oppose the persecution of evangelicals and Quakers, and eventually for an end to religious establishment altogether.[46]

As this struggle unfolded, religious dissenters reached increasingly for the individualist, Lockean language of rights to describe the appropriate political recognition of this jurisdictional divide.[47] In an influential 1767 pamphlet, for example, the Massachusetts dissenter Ebenezer Frothingham had argued that "no Man, whether Saint, Priest, or civil Ruler, can stand between the great and terrible God, at the Judgment Day, to plead off his Neighbour from the Execution of strict Justice." From this he inferred a "Right of private Judgment, or Liberty of Conscience, in Matters of Religion." In forming beliefs and judgments about spiritual matters, he argued, individuals should answer to no one but

God. Here, as in Locke's famous *Letter Concerning Toleration*, the idea of a distinct, spiritual jurisdiction was intensely personalized: "Jesus Christ challenges the sole Right of Conscience, yea, the whole human Soul, with all its Powers and Faculties, to be intirely [*sic*] at his Dispose."[48] This argument became commonplace among New England Baptists, for example, who by 1760 were describing the rights of individual conscience as "natural" and "inalienable."[49]

This intellectual legacy ran strong among the evangelicals who flocked to Jefferson's banner in 1800 and beyond. In the early decades of the nineteenth century, evangelicals widely embraced a Jeffersonian language of natural, individual rights when they celebrated the uniqueness of American freedom.[50] The Baptist preacher and activist John Leland, for example, detailed individual rights "so inalienable in their nature that they *cannot* be surrendered," and placed these at the core of his theory of government. "Of this description," he continued, "are the *rights of conscience and private judgment*."[51] For him, the recognition of such rights in America marked the liberation of Christianity from the corrupting influence of the state. Meanwhile, "Crazy" Lorenzo Dow, an influential Methodist preacher who held revivalist meetings all across the country, taught that the purpose of "all political associations" was simply "the preservation of the natural and imprescriptible rights of man; and these rights are liberty, property, security, and resistance of oppression."[52] He also cited freedom of conscience and "private judgment," which were to him the linchpin of religious freedom. Both he and Leland saw this Lockean vision of government as the only one suitable for creatures intended by God to be "free and independent" agents.[53]

It is important to see that such appeals were not part of a secular vision of either government or society. Unlike Madison and Jefferson, who joined forces with them in the fight against established religion, evangelicals were fighting to purify and renew American Christianity.[54] For them, these Lockean arguments were fully compatible, first, with the widely shared belief that political leaders should be godly men, and that American law and political deliberations should be deeply informed by Christian principles. They were also compatible with an aggressively expansionist vision of evangelical Christianity. Evangelicals rightly believed that once established religious groups were stripped of state subsidies, they would quickly lose ground to their evangelical challengers. In their view, disestablishment was one step on the path to the total Christianization of America and the triumph of true religion over all obstacles. It is highly significant, however, that the fight against established religion led evangelicals to harness popular Lockean principles to their own advantage, and to foreground a political narrative that pitted the organized power of the state against the freedom and integrity of individual conscience.

This key narrative shaped the thinking of abolitionists who, starting in the early 1830s, called for an immediate and unconditional end to American slavery. For many of these abolitionists, the idea of America as a polity uniquely committed to the protection of natural rights formed part of Protestant vision of a purified Christian nation whose principled devotion to individual liberty would hasten the end of days.[55] Like the dissenters before them, they told a story of an unholy power, emanating from government and the privileged elites who controlled it, that was destroying the natural rights ordained by God himself. And like the dissenters, they tended to ground these rights in appeals to scripture. In their telling, the American myth of the rights-bearer marked the culmination of an ancient narrative, with its origins in the book of Exodus, which told of an unfolding sphere of personal liberty on earth.

Abolitionists commonly grounded their idea of natural rights, for example, in the idea that human beings were created in the image of God. "*In the image of God made he men,*" declared Rev. Samuel Crothers, paraphrasing Genesis 5:1. "He who makes merchandise of man, makes merchandise of the image of his Maker." It was this divine likeness, Crothers reasoned, that entitled him to a range of "inalienable" rights over his own person.[56] To treat God's own image as mere property—or to treat it as a mere beast of burden—was a form of desecration. Speaking to a gathering of free Blacks in Philadelphia, William Whipper agreed: "If there be those who doubt that we are made in the image of God, and are endowed with those attributes which the Deity has given to man," he declared, "we will exhibit them our 'hands and side.'" From this he inferred an "inalienable right" to liberty, which was the birthright of all human beings.[57] For him, natural rights described the measure of respect owed to a creature created in the likeness of God.

Among the key attributes borne by God's image were freedom and responsibility. God had made humans free to make their own choices, to choose virtue over vice and his own will over Satan's. God made man "a moral and accountable agent," wrote the Congregationalist pastor Amos Phelps, and thus gave him a distinctive place in the great "scale of being." To recognize the "inalienable rights" of all human beings, he argued, was to acknowledge their proper place, as free and responsible agents, in the divine order. Slavery, on the other hand, dragged them down to a lower order of being: in treating humans like brutes "to be governed by physical force," it "makes a rupture in God's order of existences."[58] Without rights, wrote another leading abolitionist, no man could be properly "accountable to [his] Maker"—for he was unable to make his own choices.[59] Whereas earlier defenders of religious toleration had asserted God's exclusive sovereignty over individual conscience, Phelps, William Lloyd Garrison, and other leading abolitionists broadened the sphere of divine prerogative considerably. Created as free beings in the image of God, they argued, all humans were entitled to pursue happiness on their own terms, to educate themselves, to marry and raise families, to reap the fruits of their labor. To deny them the natural rights that secured these freedoms was to usurp God's authority.[60]

Others presented equal rights as correlates of the moral equality announced in the New Testament. "As God has created all men equal," declared the Rhode Island Anti-Slavery Convention, "as he equally regards them, and as he commands them equally to regard each other, we hold it demonstrably certain that he regards them all as possessing equal rights."[61] The scriptural passages most commonly cited to underwrite this egalitarian posture included Acts 10:34, which describes God as "no respecter of persons" (in the sense that he shows no partiality to any), and Acts 17:26, which announced that God "hath made of one blood all nations of men for to dwell on all the face of the earth." Abolitionists maintained that equal rights were the appropriate moral and political embodiment of the fact of human equality, which was an essential feature of divine creation: all persons were equally objects of God's love and forgiveness. Slavery, in enthroning some as gods among men and reducing others to property, subverted the egalitarian essence of Christianity.

Still others derived rights from the golden rule or the Christian duty of brotherly love. Rev. William Brisbane, for example, argued that God "evidently gave the [golden rule] for the purpose of securing to every man his right to 'life, liberty and the pursuit of happiness.'"[62] To strip another innocent man of his rights was an especially egregious violation of God's fundamental moral law. In a similar vein, one contributor to the *Quarterly Anti-Slavery Magazine* asked "how can it be right to deprive fellow men of what they feel in their own persons to be the most sacred rights of humanity—to degrade men to the condition of brutes? How is it conformable to Christian precept, to do unto men what they would not for worlds should be done [*sic*] unto themselves?"[63] The influential editor and activist William Goodell, meanwhile, described God's fundamental law as requiring "every man to regard every other man as his equal, and love him as he loves his own soul." For him, this demanded above all that they appreciate "the solemnity of man's inalienable rights."[64]

Rights, here, are presented as a fundamental token of the reciprocity and love that all others are owed as a matter of Christian duty.

Abolitionists often combined several of these arguments in the same few paragraphs. In its "Declaration of Sentiment," for example, the Ohio Anti-Slavery Society declared slavery a grievous sin against God: in stripping slaves of their rights, it converted persons into things and God's image into "merchandize"; it also contravened both the "law of love" and the "golden rule." "What is that but a sin," its authors continued,

> which sinks to the level of brutes, beings ranked and registered by God a little lower than the angels . . .—breaks open the sanctuary of human rights, and makes its sacred things common plunder—driving to the shambles Jehovah's image, herded with four-footed beasts and creeping things, and bartering for vile dust the purchase of a Redeemer's blood, and the living members of his body?

To reduce people to "mere instruments" to be used by others for their pleasure and profit, the authors argued, was to impugn the dignity that God had invested in all human beings, and to denigrate Christ's own sacrifice, which was offered for all humans alike. They went on to demand that slave owners immediately "stop robbing [slaves] of inalienable rights which they have never forfeited."[65] In all of these different arguments, abolitionists invested the individual with a fundamental moral dignity and worth, derived from the revealed word of God and embodied in the idea of natural rights, which served as shields against oppression and intrusion.[66]

These rights gave rise, moreover, not just to moral duties but also to political obligations. They formed part of a distinctly liberal theory of politics, which ran from Locke through the Revolutionary clergy and the evangelical dissenters who had aligned themselves with Jefferson. "The true glory and interest of a nation," wrote the Quaker abolitionist John Greenleaf Whittier, "consist in the secure and free exercise on the part of each individual of his natural rights, the humblest as well as the proudest. And never—never can that glory be permanent, nor that interest real, which is purchased by the violation or the surrender of those rights."[67] Like so many of his peers, Whittier presented individual rights as the highest aim of all legitimate government: any goal that stood in conflict with such rights had to give way.[68] "The grand object of law," wrote leading abolitionist Theodore Weld, "is to *protect men's natural rights*, but instead of protecting the natural rights of the slaves, it gives slaveholders license to wrest them from the weak by violence, protects them in holding their plunder, and *kills* the rightful owner if he attempt to recover it."[69] For them, the laws establishing and protecting slavery were the very antithesis of legitimate power, for they annihilated all of the slave's natural rights.[70]

In fact, abolitionists commonly presented individual rights not just as the highest goal of government but also as a strict constraint on legitimate state action. "The rights of personal liberty, of property, of conscience, and of the pursuit of happiness were all inherent, immutable, and eternal," declared the American Anti-Slavery Society. "They were based on the nature of our being, and were the rich endowments of our Creator."[71] With Locke and Jefferson, they held that the natural rights were pre-political and could not be bargained or contracted away—nor could any state legitimately abrogate them. These rights formed the foundation of their withering criticism of American government. Abolitionists constantly drew attention to—and quoted from— southern statute books, which denied all rights to the slave and legalized the most egregious forms of abuse and exploitation. They continually highlighted the federal government's manifold complicity in these injustices. They also condemned the many forms of racist discrimination that were either allowed or mandated by state law throughout the North. In destroying the natural rights of millions of Americans, they argued, state and federal governments alike had betrayed the divine logic of the Declaration and become agents of oppression on a par with the most despotic states on earth.[72] "If governments must be instituted among men," insisted Brisbane, "it is for the protection of the individual's liberty, and not for its restraint. It is to prevent his abuse of it, to the injury of others, but never to limit it. This is God's prerogative, not man's."[73]

In this sense, the abolitionist theory of politics ran closer to the Jacksonian Democrats than the Whigs. Although abolitionists pilloried Democrats for their white supremacist assumptions, they ultimately sought to universalize the Democrats' promise of "equal rights" and ground it in divine revelation. This was true not only of those elements of the movement—such as the Liberty Party—which appealed explicitly to the Democrats' slogans and positioned themselves as the "true friends of Equal Rights."[74] It was true also of the Garrisonian faction which, like the Democrats, tended to see American politics as a struggle between the sovereign, rights-bearing individual and the encroaching power of a government controlled by a cabal of wealthy and self-interested elites.

It is important not to exaggerate the liberal or individualistic tendencies of abolitionist political thought. In condemning slavery and racial discrimination, abolitionists drew on three principal moral languages: the Lockean language of natural rights, the republican language of arbitrary power, and the confessional language of sin and repentance.[75] This third language, in particular, often pulled in a different direction than the first. Evangelical abolitionists commonly argued, for example, that the slave owner's absolute power inflamed a wide range of sins, including greed, cruelty, ungodly pride, and adultery.[76] Meanwhile, his idleness gave rise to a thirst for useless luxury and a disdain for the discipline of labor. Slaves, on the other hand, were consigned by oppressive law to live in adultery and selfish ignorance. Slavery, in other words, loosened the moral bonds of community by dividing it into antagonistic castes and by stoking aberrant desires at all levels of society.[77] In fact, many devout abolitionists saw their crusade against slavery as part of a comprehensive Christian response to the epidemic of egoism and worldly lust that they saw sweeping across the country along with the market revolution.[78]

In their battle against licentiousness and moral corruption, moreover, religious reformers in Jacksonian America repeatedly enlisted the coercive power of the state. They pressured public officials to prohibit mail deliveries on the Sabbath and to criminalize the consumption and sale of alcohol.[79] They expected state and local governments to police a wide range of private behavior, including gambling and sexual promiscuity. Many leading abolitionists were involved in these campaigns, especially the temperance movement. It seemed evident to them that individual rights did not extend to conduct forbidden by scripture: people had the right to act in accordance with the moral law, no more. True liberty, many abolitionists believed—as opposed to corrupt "license"—extended only to the (wide) range of human behavior that did not violate divine command. A government that failed to draw the distinction, in their view, was a government that failed to meet one of its cardinal obligations.[80]

The prominence of natural rights in abolitionist rhetoric, then, shows not that abolitionism—still less evangelical Protestantism—was uniformly liberal or individualistic.[81] It shows, rather, that *some* powerful strains of Protestant thought lent support to the myth of the rights-bearer. It also shows that the Lockean theory of politics, with private liberty as its centerpiece, rested on two overlapping intellectual traditions. Whereas most Jacksonian Democrats—along with more secular abolitionists—drew on an Enlightenment tradition that ran through Jefferson and Paine, most abolitionists placed themselves in a Protestant lineage that extended back through the American founders to Roger Williams, Luther, and Paul.[82] This second tradition was itself shaped by Enlightenment values and assumptions that had, over time, been absorbed into American Protestantism. But it also drew on a rich, transatlantic tradition of religious dissent that found its origins in the Reformation.[83] In a society that was increasingly devout—owing largely to the explosive influence of the Second Great Awakening—this convergence was profoundly important.

In fact, this second Lockean tradition touched not only abolitionists but also the wider circle of northern Protestants who, while they continued to see abolitionists as dangerous radicals, were also increasingly critical of American slavery. They too tended to see slavery as a violation of natural rights and a subversion of the cherished myth of the rights-bearer.[84] "What flagrant injustice," said Rev. Samuel Cozzens, "what cruel oppression is this—to presume to hold in bondage human beings, like ourselves born free and equal; who like ourselves possess the same inalienable rights."[85] For them, as for the abolitionists they criticized, natural rights delimited a space of personal freedom, ordained by God, within which individuals could act and worship as free and responsible agents. In the late 1840s and 1850s, with the rise of the Free Soil Movement, these more moderate Protestants joined abolitionists in a broadening antislavery coalition whose ideas laid some of the foundations of the emerging Republican Party's ideology.[86]

Slavery's Widening Assault on Individual Rights

Time and again, abolitionists presented slavery as an assault on the natural rights of the individual. Whereas Protestant dissenters had focused largely on the rights of conscience and religious exercise, abolitionists cast their rhetorical net far wider. They began with the rights of the enslaved, including their rights to security and free movement, property, conscience, and marriage, and their rights to seek remedies at court—all of which slavery entirely destroyed. But this was only the beginning: they also described a widening arc of rights violations that marred the lives of free Blacks and northern whites, whose rights of speech, petition, and even basic security were increasingly jeopardized by angry proslavery mobs. Slavery, they argued, involved a comprehensive subversion of individual rights, for Blacks and whites alike, and a fundamental betrayal of the promise of American liberty.

In fact, many abolitionists *defined* slavery as a total annihilation of individual rights. "Slavery in America reduces a *man* to a *thing*, a 'chattel personal,'" wrote leading abolitionist Angelina Grimke, and "*robs him* of *all* his rights as a *human being.*"[87] "The slave," Douglass concurred, "is a human being, divested of all rights—reduced to the level of a brute—a mere 'chattel' in the eye of the law."[88] To be a "brute" or "chattel" was precisely to be some*thing* that possessed no rights under the law—something that could be disposed of at will. Of course, since slavery was legal under southern state law, it violated no statutory rights there. The rights at issue were *natural* or human rights: American slavery rested on the insidious assertion that Black slaves possessed no such rights in the first place. Slavery, wrote James Brown, "supposes that there is no man to oppress, no rights to encroach, no domestic ties to rend."[89] Nothing could be more antithetical, in abolitionists' eyes, to the moral universalism of the Declaration.

The most fundamental right destroyed by slavery was the right of self-ownership. "The foundation of all rights," declared one abolitionist address, "the right of personal independence and self-ownership, by which every human being is invested with the free use and disposal of his own body and his own soul, is denied to the slave."[90] Self-ownership, as abolitionists understood it, encompassed a cluster of liberty rights, including freedom of movement, freedom from assault and rape, freedom of thought, and the freedom to form intimate relationships.[91] A person who owned or controlled herself, in this sense, was a person who could move freely through the world and exercise a fundamental measure of control over her own body and mind. On the other hand, a person who was *owned* by another was thereby stripped of her very humanity and all of its concomitant rights. "Slaveholders talk of treating men well," wrote Weld, "and yet not only rob them of all they get, and as fast as they get it, but rob them of *themselves*, also; their very hands and feet, all their muscles, and limbs, and senses, their bodies and minds."[92] Affirming a moral premise that stretched back as far as the English Civil War, abolitionists argued that self-ownership was a natural entitlement of all human beings and that there could therefore be no natural right to hold other persons as property.[93]

As historians have often pointed out, abolitionists saw self-ownership as the foundation of economic freedom: people who owned themselves could not be forced to work without consent, nor could they be forcibly deprived of the fruits of their labor. "The right to enjoy liberty is inalienable," declared the American Anti-Slavery Society, "to invade it, is to usurp the prerogative of Jehovah. Every man has a right to his own body—to the products of his own labor—to the protection of law—and to the common advantages of society."[94] To own oneself, according to the familiar Lockean fable, was to own the basic instruments of labor: after all, people created value by applying their bodies and minds to productive work. The ownership of those basic instruments, then, conferred just title to the fruits of their productivity. It was the basis of property rights. Under slavery, wrote Lydia Child, "MAN can own *no* property, and is daily plundered of the fruits of his toil. Says God, 'The laborer is worthy of his hire:' says the slaveholder, '*I* will yoke him with the brutes, and he shall *toil for* ME.'"[95] From this point of view, slavery was a system of brutal, organized theft—"the robbery of the labor of a whole life"—driven by a lust for profit.[96]

To many abolitionists, however, the rights of conscience and religion seemed even more fundamental than economic rights. Slaveholders possessed the legal authority, in many southern states, to deny their slaves access to the Bible, to religious instruction of any kind, and even to basic literacy that such instruction presupposed.[97] The slave "cannot learn what God requires of him and cannot improve the capacity for serving God; and in the next place he cannot carry out the convictions of his own conscience as to the service he owes, unless those convictions accord with his master's judgment." Such a condition, Brisbane continued, was wholly incompatible with the "rights of conscience and of private judgment."[98] These rights, in turn, were foundational to the very possibility of Christian salvation: without them, slaves could be kept in eternal "darkness."[99] Abolitionists argued, moreover, that such outrages were not just cruel aberrations; rather, they were necessary to slavery's survival, for the light of divine revelation would inevitably "excite dissatisfaction in [slaves'] minds" and stoke a yearning for freedom.[100]

Abolitionists also emphasized slavery's destruction of the rights of marriage and family. Their newspapers dramatized devastating scenes of families being sold separately on the auction block; they reprinted ads from southern newspapers advertising the sale of family members, "together, or SEPARATELY, to suit purchasers."[101] Even the harshest despotisms in the world, observed one Kentucky abolitionist, recognize the "*right of marriage.*" American slavery, by contrast, "denies *all rights,*" including those intimate rights without which the (traditional) human family could not exist.[102] This particular denial struck abolitionists as an astonishing form of cruelty and a stark impediment to God's law: "slavery wholly forbids the *right* and practice of marriage to the slaves," said Charles Olcott, "and compels them as it were, to break the law of God, by living in unlawful and frequently promiscuous concubinage."[103] In routinely breaking up families, slavery also made it impossible to fulfill the obligations of filial piety and parental love and nurture so clearly demanded by scripture.

These abominations were compounded by the slave's utter lack of due process rights, including the right of habeas corpus, the right to bring legal charges at law, and the right to a trial by jury. Without these, the slave had no effective recourse against the most brutal and invasive violations. The slave, wrote Parker, "cannot bring an action against the oppressor in his own name—for, as a THING, he has no Rights." This left slaves entirely at the mercy of their masters, with "no legal right of self-defence against . . . assault and battery" or any other form of "brutal violation."[104] What few legal protections they were nominally afforded were therefore meaningless in practice. Abolitionists often cited these facts as evidence of the unique depravity of American slavery: in ancient Greece and Rome, as in biblical Judea, they pointed out, slaves were not entirely stripped of legal standing. They had recourse to the law to protect them; they were thus recognized as members of the human community.[105]

In drawing attention to the slave's profound and manifold vulnerability, abolitionists helped shift and expand the American discourse of rights. As legal historian Elizabeth Clark has argued, they drew attention to rights of "bodily integrity" and private self-control that were not typically enumerated in constitutional documents; they also foregrounded sexual violence against women as an especially egregious rights violation.[106] They envisioned rights not just as limitations on state action but as shields against private domination. In all of these ways, they made rights at once more expansive and more inclusive: whereas the dominant myth had always pictured the rights-bearer as a white, property-owning man, abolitionists recentered the myth around the figure of the suffering (and often female) slave. In so doing, they helped convert the language of rights into a vehicle for broad and radical protest against existing power relations, which spilled over not only into the early struggles for women's rights and suffrage but also into a broader humanitarian movement that denounced capital punishment; violence and cruelty in schools, prisons, and mental hospitals; and marital abuse.[107]

When they shifted their attention from slaves to free Blacks, abolitionists also called out a litany of injustices, which they also commonly framed as violations of natural or human rights. Free Blacks in the northern states were "borne down by the weight of innumerable persecutions," observed James Forten Jr., and "nearly stripped of their [natural] rights."[108] They were frozen out of virtually all skilled professions and public offices; their children were denied access to public schools; they were consigned to separate sections of churches, trains, and ferries; they were subject to mob violence with little hope of legal redress. In several northwestern states, discriminatory "black laws," deliberately designed to deter Black settlers, added further indignities and inequalities. In condemning these injustices, abolitionists decried "the anomaly of that political ethicks [*sic*] which makes a distinction between man and man, when its foundation is 'that all men are born equal,' and possess in common 'unalienable rights.'"[109] Pervasive racial discrimination, they argued, had eroded and destroyed so many of Black citizens' essential rights and liberties.

The American Colonization Society (ACS), which proposed to deny Black Americans even the right to reside in their own country, came in for especially sharp criticism. Because it was so influential, many abolitionists saw it as one of the leading sources of racial prejudice in America. Its members and supporters included some of the most powerful men in the country, including James Madison, Henry Clay, and Daniel Webster. The ACS taught that Blacks had no place in America because racial conflict, driven largely by white prejudice, would forever prevent them from thriving and bar them from civil and political equality.[110] Their best chance lay in Africa, it insisted, where they could found new, Christian commonwealths and also bring the word of God to heathen lands.[111] To Elizur Wright, such views represented an appalling revision of the foundation of American rights: "If their right to a residence here, and to all the sympathies and aids which their condition demands, is abridged by their blackness, then ours depends upon our whiteness—that is to say, our boasted, inalienable, indefeasible rights, lie skin-deep."[112] To ground rights in racial physiognomy was to render them brittle and arbitrary; it was also to transform them into instruments of oppression.

Abolitionists argued, furthermore, that free Blacks lacked even the fundamental right of self-ownership, which was jeopardized by the kidnappings that haunted Black citizens in northern cities. In New York, for example, Black abolitionists repeatedly petitioned for the right to a trial by jury for those accused of being fugitive slaves. They described a climate of pervasive fear, in which a single judge's verdict could condemn a free person to slavery, and they presented "the sacred right of trial by Jury" as a fundamental safeguard without which no liberty could be secure.[113] No white American, they argued, would consent to have any property, no matter how trivial, seized without it. And yet free Blacks' most essential property right—their right to their own selves—hung by a thread.[114] "If we are arrested on suspicion of having stolen our own bodies, and run away with them," said Forten Jr., "so few are the advocates we have at the Bar of Justice, that the pleadings of humanity are silenced, and we too frequently consigned to hopeless bondage."[115] As abolitionists often pointed out, this insecurity was amplified by the high price that Black bodies fetched on the southern market, which made kidnapping a lucrative business.[116]

Abolitionists also protested the rollback of Black voting rights throughout the North and pressed for an equal right to suffrage.[117] Speaking at a public meeting of the "Colored Young Men of the City of New York," Peter Simons lamented that "the rights of God and nature [are] violated, by divesting us of that ineffable endowment, our rights of suffrage, (which is estimated the highest endowment, by all republican governments)."[118] At the same time, abolitionists pilloried Democrats who argued for an "inalienable" right to suffrage but still found reason to exclude Blacks. The *Liberator*, for example, attacked the "pseudo champions of free suffrage" in Rhode Island, "who are bawling for equal rights at the top of their lungs" but who simultaneously proposed to exclude Blacks from the vote in their 1841 draft constitution.[119] Citing Jefferson, abolitionists defended self-government as a natural right, which was not only a token of respect owed to all men as moral equals but also a crucial political safeguard for virtually all other rights and liberties.[120]

Over the course of the 1830s, abolitionists broadened their appeal even further and began to frame slavery as a threat to the rights of *all* Americans. The rise of "immediatist" abolitionism in the early 1830s, which demanded an immediate and unqualified end to slavery, had coincided with Nat Turner's rebellion, the most violent slave uprising in American history. Slavery's allies had responded forcefully. Antislavery speech was harshly suppressed in the South, and abolitionist publishers and speakers in the North were subject to escalating violence at the hands of racist mobs. Bowing to southern pressure, Congress passed the infamous "gag rule," which automatically tabled any and all antislavery petitions without allowing them to be read on the House floor. This crackdown, which was unpopular with many northern voters, created new opportunities for abolitionists to present slavery as a threat to white Americans. The murder of abolitionist printer Elijah Lovejoy by a proslavery mob in November 1837 was a galvanizing moment. "Lovejoy has fallen a victim to the violence of a band of armed ruffians," lamented the *Emancipator*, "fallen nobly too, in defence of those inalienable rights which were given to him by God, and guarantied [*sic*] to him by the Constitution. Rights as precious to you and me, and to every other American citizen as they were to him."[121] At issue here were the rights of free expression and conscience: who could claim to live in a free society if citizens could be killed with impunity for speaking their minds? America had fallen a long way, warned the Cincinnati-based *Philanthropist*, since "our fathers dared to speak, and . . . the press was unshackled, and when men held rights by the tenure of law." In the abolitionists' eyes, Lovejoy's murder sent a clear message: when it came to voices critical of slavery, it was "*silence or death.*"[122]

Starting in the late 1830s, abolitionist newspapers began reporting countless examples of lawless assaults on abolitionists, on civil rights activists, and even on hapless travelers to southern states who happened to be carrying an antislavery letter or pamphlet. "A northern citizen cannot cross the Potomac, without subjecting himself to all the liabilities of 'Lynch Law,'" wrote the *Colored American*, citing several well-known recent victims by name. "He knows not how soon he may be tared [*sic*] and feathered, rode upon a rail, or cowskinned."[123] Even women were not exempt: in a popular pamphlet, Mrs. M. B. Davis, who had recently traveled to the South to visit old friends, reported she had been warned to keep quiet for her own safety. "Be assured no one is safe here," a local newspaper editor had cautioned her, "who is known to be an abolitionist, whatever their standing, circumstances or sex."[124] For abolitionists and a growing number of northern sympathizers, such outrages showed that slaveholders and their allies would go to any lengths to defend their cherished "property," including the wholesale destruction of white citizens' rights to security, speech, and political voice.[125]

In the abolitionists' eyes, this widening arc of rights violations dramatized a fundamental antagonism at the heart of American life. On one side lay the cause of freedom, as embodied in the Declaration of Independence and its doctrine of universal rights. On the other lay slavery, whose very existence was a standing affront to these ideals. Slavery assaulted the Declaration's legacy directly by denying and destroying the slave's natural rights, as well as indirectly by fomenting lawless violence and intimidation and eroding the very meaning of rights among the American public.[126] It also lay at the root of racial prejudice: as long as millions of Black slaves were held as property, abolitionists argued, there could be no hope that free Blacks would ever escape the stigma of racial inferiority. To vindicate the myth of the rights-bearer—in the North and South alike—America had no choice but to eradicate slavery altogether. The question, said the Monroe County Anti-Slavery Society, "is nothing less than liberty for the slave, or slavery for the free? The contest will not cease."[127]

The Sources of Injustice

To eradicate slavery and extend equal civil and political rights to free Blacks was no simple matter. If some abolitionists had initially entertained high hopes for the swift moral conversion of the country, their optimism faded quickly.

By the mid-1830s, as they confronted a rising tide of violence, ridicule, and repression—and as white abolitionists struggled to confront their own racial prejudices—abolitionists acknowledged that the sources of racial injustice were deep and resilient.[128] Two stood out to them in particular: greed and entrenched racism—or as Angelina Grimke put it, the *"bonds of interest"* and the *"cords of caste."*[129] In elaborating these key impediments to equal rights, abolitionists offered a sharply different diagnosis than their counterparts in the Democratic mainstream.

Abolitionists commonly listed greed as slavery's strongest sustaining motive. "The whole system of forcing our fellow men thus to toil," wrote the *Pennsylvania Freeman*, "is a system of injustice and robbery, aggravated by a cruelty which the iron heart of covetousness alone is capable of inflicting."[130] Only the unlimited appetite for wealth, this author argued, could so thoroughly dull the moral sense. Abolitionists constantly described slaveholders as lusting after luxuries, worshipping "almighty dollars," or simply *"actuated by the love of gain."*[131] Nor were these acquisitive passions confined to slaveholders themselves: the northern bankers, merchants, and industrialists who also profited handsomely from slavery—"whose narrow souls . . . seem unable to move in a wider circle than the circumference of a guinea"—were equally liable to its corrupting effects.[132] Next on the list, for some abolitionists, were northern consumers who seemed unable to deprive themselves of cheap goods produced with slave labor: "Their own hands, it is true," wrote Quaker abolitionist Elizabeth Chandler, "do not wield the blood-extorting lash, or rivet the fetter, but they know that is done by others, in order to afford at the cheapest rate, the luxuries which they neither will resign, nor make one exertion to obtain from the hands of freemen."[133] Runaway greed, she argued, ramifying through the economies of both southern and northern states, made it especially difficult for Americans to wean themselves from slavery.[134]

Although they sometimes described such greed as an extraordinary and irrational passion, abolitionists also saw how thoroughly it had been normalized by the market economy. "I am informed by credible persons," wrote David Lee Child, "that the slave traders take just so much care of their merchandize, in its passage from market to market, as is necessary for its *preservation*, and *no more*. Whatever they can economize in this respect, is clear gain, added to the difference of value in different markets."[135] Historians have lately debated whether we should see slaveholders as akin to premodern patriarchs who governed their fiefdoms like feudal estates, or modern businessmen who functioned—and saw themselves—as part of an expanding, global market economy.[136] The latter view was decidedly more prevalent among American abolitionists. Some argued, in fact, that the formal abolition of the transatlantic slave trade in 1808 had been the key catalyst: "It converted the entire 'chivalry' of the old dominion," wrote the newspaper *Human Rights*, "into negro-breeders, watching the man-market, and noting the daily fluctuations of the price-current of human flesh."[137] Time and again, abolitionists presented slavery as a profitable business subject to market discipline.[138]

Abolitionists often appealed to market incentives, for example, to explain some of the acute moral pathologies of the slave economy. Families were routinely separated, they argued, simply because it was more profitable to offer slaves separately, to suit the diverse needs of the buyers. They also described slave "breeding" as a profit-making enterprise, subject to familiar economic pressures and incentives. Quoting an English observer, Amos Phelps noted that male slaves were forced into marriage and compelled to have "*many* wives" so that the master could "*increase his stock* . . . and in the same way married females are often *obliged* to receive more husbands than one, as the planter may order."[139] Even rape, they argued, had become a profitable business. George Bourne, for example, described a "*girl-market*" where young virgins were "sold expressly for concubinage and the manufacture of light colored slaves," who would fetch a higher price at auction.[140] To expose the grim apotheosis of this profit-maximizing logic, abolitionists repeatedly described slaveholders who got rich by "breeding" and selling their own mixed-race children. In such passages, the cold, calculating egoism of the market invades every crevice of human life, ruptures the most intimate human bonds, and converts everything into a salable commodity.[141]

In February 1848, the *North Star* ran a short satirical piece titled "The Way to Wealth in the Model Republic." It was a mock advice column promising a sure path to riches. After advising its readers to speculate in railroad and government stock and lend money at interest, the author suggested that they "buy a NEGRO—an article of commerce in this land of 'inalienable rights,' which some 'fanatics,' in the height of their credulity, are so unreasonable as to call a MAN, with thoughts, and feelings, and affections, like other men." The slave should be worked "from early dawn to the latest sun," to wring every last drop of productive labor from his captive body. The profits could then be reinvested in southern land and more slaves, along with other necessary tools of the trade: "chains, and whips, and thumbscrews." If properly handled and exploited, he explained, slaves would yield huge profits and offer the surest path to wealth and distinction. "Breed for the market. SELL YOUR OWN OFFSPRING, with pigs, and horses, and cattle. And you will be wealthy and perhaps a senator."[142]

Here again, slavery is described as an example—the most egregious possible—of the profit motive run amok. What do you get, abolitionists asked, when you elevate the thirst for profits to the supreme, governing principle in society?[143] The answer was slavery. Wherever it was profitable, market incentives would give elites powerful reasons to dispense with wages and turn laborers into personal property, to minimize labor costs. Abolitionists often emphasized how cheap and convenient it was to keep a slave barely clothed and fed rather than deal with the expense of a free labor force.[144] Parker, for example, quoted one southerner boasting about slavery's economic advantages: "You own [the slave's] labor, can regulate it, work it many or few hours in the day, accelerate it, stimulate it, control it, avoid turnouts and combinations, and pay no wages."[145] When slaveholders pilloried the exploitative tendencies of northern capitalism and presented slavery as a humane alternative (in which laborers were fed and cared for from birth to death), abolitionists had a ready answer: their supposed paternalism was merely a veil that they used to conceal their naked greed. In fact, abolitionists often argued that slaveholders had their designs on the northern economy too, where they would think nothing of enslaving white workers if it made them money.[146] Untethered from moral restraints, the profit motive trampled even the most fundamental human rights.

Of course, Democrats too had condemned *avarice* as a source of injustice and a threat to equal rights. They too had shown how greed pushed elites to extract wealth ruthlessly from other people's labor. But whereas Democrats associated such greed with a fairly small class of conniving aristocrats—and whereas they had typically excluded slaveholders from their ranks— abolitionists saw it ramifying through the entire national economy. They found it not only among plantation slaveholders and their acolytes but among northern merchants and financiers and textile manufacturers, and among consumers everywhere. "Practically speaking," wrote Henry David Thoreau, the main opponents to antislavery reform "are not a hundred thousand politicians at the South, but a hundred thousand merchants and farmers here [in Massachusetts], who are more interested in commerce and agriculture than they are in humanity."[147] Many abolitionists agreed. In Democratic rhetoric, the excessive greed that brooked no moral restraints seemed a perversion of the pristine moral logic of the market; in abolitionist writing, it often seemed like an endemic threat.

Several prominent historians have argued that abolitionism helped justify the emerging capitalist economy. Abolitionists, they argue, came to identify economic freedom largely with freedom of contract: if the slave was unfree because his labor was *forced*, the wage laborer, by contrast, was free because his labor contract was voluntary.[148] The ideological success of this individualist perspective, they argue, helped justify the structural inequality and exploitation of the emerging industrial economy. While there is important truth in this insight, the preceding paragraphs suggest a more complicated picture. If many abolitionists saw slavery itself as an expression of the market's logic, if they believed that capitalism harbored within it voraciously immoral and "unnatural" tendencies that had to be carefully bounded by moral and political restraints, then we must proceed cautiously. In fact, the idea of free labor that abolitionists promoted was a complex and contested ideal shot through with Christian moral assumptions; to them, it stood *opposed*, in important ways, to the unfettered capitalism of the slave economy.[149]

Although abolitionists commonly acknowledged that slavery was profitable to both slaveholders and the northern elites who did business with them, they also insisted that slavery was a net economic loser for the South and for the country. Slavery, they argued, had blighted the southern economy, mainly because it demoralized and drove out free laborers, who were more productive than slaves.[150] Viewed from a strictly economic perspective, then, slavery enriched a minority at the expense of the majority. Indeed, when abolitionists railed against the "slaveocracy" for capturing the government to advance its own sinister objectives, they often presented it as an undemocratic force. Wealthy slaveholders, they maintained, exercised a power vastly disproportionate to their numbers. This disproportion was amplified by the federal Constitution, whose three-fifths clause granted extra representation to southern states, and by some southern state constitutions, which granted unequal power to plantation elites. The fight against slavery was sometimes presented, then, as a fight against an undemocratic minority and the aberrant institutions that empowered it.[151]

But abolitionists ultimately knew better than to argue that either slavery or racial discrimination was strictly the work of a determined minority. In fact, they often highlighted the culpability of the democratic public at large. "Majorities *rule*," wrote the *American Anti-Slavery Almanac*. "The free states have always had the majority in Congress—consequently the *power* and *responsibility*. How have we used this power?" The author then cataloged a long list of injustices, including the slave trade that flourished unhampered in the District of Columbia, the fugitive slave law, the widespread denial of civil rights and economic opportunities to free Blacks, and the abrogation of speech rights.

"Hundreds of other outrages upon the rights, persons, and property of abolitionists have been committed," he continued, "many of them at noon-day—
the officers of the law quietly looking on, governors, judges, mayors, aldermen,
members of Congress, and attorneys general, *conniving*, and in some instances
openly aiding and *leading*."[152] In other words, the racist mobs that attacked
abolitionists, disrupted their meetings, and torched their meetinghouses operated with the tacit consent of the government and the broader public from
which it drew its legitimacy.

Theodore Weld made a similar point in his influential book, *Slavery as It Is*.
Responding to the argument that public opinion might shield slaves from the
worst abuses, Weld argued that "it was public opinion that *made man a slave*.
In a republican government the people make the laws, and those laws are
merely public opinion *in legal forms*. We repeat it,—public opinion made them
slaves, and keeps them slaves."[153] Weld was referring especially to southern
opinion, which underwrote oppressive southern state law. So was Judge
William Claggett of New Hampshire when he wrote that "under our form of
government, our laws are but an emanation of the popular will."[154] For them,
slavery therefore pointed to the pathologies of democratic politics itself, trace-
able ultimately to the moral corruption of the sovereign people.[155] Far from
offering a corrective to slaveholders' iniquity, it was the corrupt "opinion" of
the southern public, Weld continued, that had "robbed [the slave] of his right
to his own body, of his right to improve his mind, of his right to read the Bible,
of his right to worship God according to his conscience."[156]

Why, then, did the white majority, which did not profit directly from slavery and whose own labor was devalued by it, refuse to turn against it? The
answer, abolitionists argued, was racial prejudice, which offered its own distinctive psychological benefits. Abolitionists constantly named prejudice as
the intractable obstacle that left the white majority unresponsive to their appeals. Prejudice, wrote Lydia Child, was promoted by "all our books, newspapers, almanacs and periodicals," which "represent the colored race as an inferior and degraded class, who never could be made good and useful citizens."[157]
If greed was the passion that motivated those who profited most directly from
slave labor, "pride" was the sinful passion that sustained such widespread racial
slander. Reflecting on racial discrimination and exclusion in northern
churches, the *Liberator* condemned the "wicked distinctions in society which
germinate in the pride of the human heart."[158] The pride in question was white
racial pride, which was mortified and affronted by the suggestion of Black
equality.

While some abolitionists were confident that the progress and "improvement" of the free Black population would gradually erode the foundation of such pride, others were less sanguine. Writing for the *North Star*, Douglass pointed out that *color* itself was not the root of racism: whites had no objection to Blacks so long as they kept to subordinate roles, where they could remain objects of "amusement" and ridicule.[159] In this role, they were integral to white "vanity" and "pride": looking down on them, whites of all social classes could regard themselves as members of a privileged caste, uniquely qualified for political and economic freedom. It was the aspiration to racial equality that provoked hatred and violence, for it affronted the racialized identity that lay deeply embedded in the mythologies of American exceptionalism. If Blacks were equal to whites, then there was nothing special or distinguished about whiteness—or the vaunted Anglo-Saxon bloodlines—after all; and here lay the most intractable psychological obstacle to racial equality.[160] At any sign of Black progress or improvement, wrote Black Congregationalist minister Hosea Easton, "an unrelenting hatred arises in the mind which is inhabited by that foul fiend, prejudice; and the possessor of it will never be satisfied, until those indications are destroyed."[161] He worried that Black progress, which challenged the racial caste system and threatened white racial identity, was simply intolerable to most white Americans.

Other abolitionists thought that racism reflected a visceral—and thrilling—lust for domination. In a passage reprinted in the *National Anti-Slavery Standard*, Ralph Waldo Emerson noted that, "besides the covetousness, there is a bitterer element, the love of power, the voluptuousness of having a human being in absolute control."[162] While Emerson was describing the psychology of slaveholding, others extended his diagnosis to racial prejudice and violence in the North. "It is a comfort to the lowest and most degraded of the whites," wrote the *Liberator*, "to feel that there is a class of society which they can despise and trample. In the States which make the loudest pretensions to Democracy and regard for popular rights, the popular right of insulting and injuring the colored people with impunity is one of the most prized of all."[163] The experience of brutalizing and dehumanizing others, this author argued, was a source of gratification to many whites and a prerogative jealously guarded by the sovereign majority.[164] Whether they described it as an outgrowth of pride or lust, abolitionists consistently denounced racial prejudice as "sinful in the sight of God."[165]

In confronting widespread racism in America, abolitionists faced a familiar democratic problem: the tyranny of the majority over a vulnerable minority.

"They who are for trampling on the rights of the minority, in order to benefit the majority," wrote Garrison, "are to be registered as the monsters of their race."[166] But to him and his allies, the problem presented itself in a new light, because the conventional safeguards against such tyranny had failed Black Americans completely. The framers of both federal and state constitutions had often worried, of course, that covetous and irrational majorities would trample on the rights of minorities. In response, they designed a number of formal bulwarks: they enumerated specific individual rights and embedded them in the text of their constitutions; they created independent judiciaries to oversee and protect these rights; and they designed checks and balances to forestall the majority's ability to act rashly. But none of these safeguards had shielded Black Americans from the worst forms of oppression: the white majority had simply written them out—both formally and informally—of the protective ambit of their institutions.

As they searched for answers, then, to both profit-driven exploitation and majority tyranny, abolitionists found themselves looking beyond the formal constitutionalism of the founders. Even enfranchising Black voters would, in most places, give them a small share of the electorate's voting power, which could easily be overridden at the polls. Abolitionists understood that they had to strive, instead, to transform the moral culture of the white majority.[167] They had to cultivate a culture of democratic inclusion by both challenging racism and indiscriminate profiteering and inducing sympathetic white voters to take action against racial violence and injustice. Only then, they believed, could the universal rights announced in the Declaration be realized. Abolitionists offered a theory of rights, in other words, that revealed them to be more fragile than liberal constitutionalists supposed, and also more dependent on what Alexis de Tocqueville called social "mores."[168]

Realizing Rights

How could abolitionists hope to achieve such a transformation? How could the "bonds of interest" and the "cords of caste" be severed and the promise of the Declaration vindicated? Although abolitionists disagreed deeply over the best strategies to pursue, they agreed broadly on a number of "intermediate" objectives. First, Americans had to be convinced to empathize, deeply and responsibly, with the experiences of enslavement and racial discrimination. Second, they had to see and acknowledge their own personal complicity in these injustices. Finally, they had to be presented with clear courses of action, so that their dawning moral horror could be harnessed to effect change. For abolitionists, all three goals were inseparably linked to the moral lessons of the gospels.

For most abolitionists, the only way to conquer both inveterate selfishness and deeply entrenched prejudice was through the moral teachings and example of Christ. Like so many other abolitionist papers and pamphlets, for example, the *Liberator* appealed to "the moral efficacy of the gospel in elevating the human character—in subduing prejudice—in expanding the heart—in levelling the distinctions of pride and vain-glory."[169] To abolitionists, the gospels offered more than just an assertion of human equality; they also offered an extended lesson in its moral psychology. Christ and his apostles had modeled a Christian identity grounded in love for others as equals and shared humility before God. In so doing, they challenged the nearly universal human tendency to draw self-respect from group distinction. The "cords of caste," as abolitionists often emphasized, were powerful and pervasive. To sustain a truly egalitarian sense of self, to neutralize the feelings of collective superiority that were so enticing to the human ego, required heightened self-awareness and spiritual discipline. For abolitionists, this discipline comprised the heart of Christian ethical practice.

Essential to this practice was the active cultivation of empathy for the oppressed. Abolitionists often referenced the passage in Paul's Epistle to the Hebrews, where he instructed them to "remember them that are in bonds, as bound with them; and them which suffer adversity, as being yourselves also in the body."[170] So much of abolitionist rhetoric was calculated to awaken an acute emotional response to the victims of both slavery and prejudice. Over and over, they described—often in graphic detail—the torture and maiming of slaves for trifling offenses. The dwelled at length on the shocking scenes that unfolded around the auction block, where human beings were callously appraised and sold, where families were separated forever. With the help of fugitive slaves' firsthand accounts, they dramatized not only the suffocating surveillance and cruelty of slave drivers but also the despair and hopelessness born of northern racial prejudice. They demanded that their audiences imagine themselves, as best they could, in these oppressive circumstances. Describing a family being sold separately at auction, Elizabeth Chandler asked her readers to "picture to yourself what would be the agony of your feelings, was your infant about to be severed from your arms, forever, to '*suit*' the *convenience* of some cruel barbarian."[171] Likewise, the New Hampshire Baptist preacher Enoch Mack asked his audience to put themselves, as best they could, in the slave's place:

The enslaver has seized you—secured you as his property—soul and body—to sell you—work you—whip you—torture you just as he lists, be he humane—cruel—infidel or villain! So, also, of your wife—your children—your parents—brothers—sisters. He sets you up at auction. You stand upon the platform in the marketplace—the bidders come around and feel your joints—examine well your limbs—and shake your frame to see if you are put together well and likely to be a bargain.[172]

Such passages were intended first of all to humanize slaves, to pierce through the racism that allowed white audiences to excuse or look away from such appalling scenes. How would you respond, abolitionists asked, if the victim were white? What if she were your own friend or relative? And what if it was happening to you?

Black abolitionists made similar demands of white audiences. "We entreat you to make our case your own," wrote a coalition of Black activists in Philadelphia of the rash of kidnappings in the North, "—imagine your own wives and children to be trembling at the approach of every stranger, lest their husbands and fathers should be dragged into a slavery worse than Algerine—worse than death!"[173] To willingly empathize with such terror was to acknowledge the sufferers' humanity, and thus to acknowledge them as worthy objects of moral and political concern.[174] Speaking to the New York State Anti-Slavery Society about the effects of racial prejudice, Rev. Theodore Wright made a similar plea. Invoking the spirit of the gospels, he asked his white audience to imagine what it would be like to live in a climate of racial animus that blanketed everything, from schools to workplaces to churches, "like an atmosphere . . . withering all our hopes." He asked that they imagine what it was like for Black parents to look at their son, to contemplate his sorrowful future in a country filled with racial hatred, and "to wish he had never been born."[175] Meanwhile, the autobiographies of fugitive slaves, which began circulating widely in the 1840s, invited their readers at every turn to see and feel American bondage and prejudice as their authors did.[176]

A number of historians and literary critics have condemned the abolitionist appeals to empathy, especially when elicited through graphic displays of human suffering.[177] Empathy can be condescending when it is untethered from egalitarian commitment; it can be complacent when used merely to affirm the fellow-sufferer's moral bona fides; it can also devolve into gratuitous voyeurism.[178] But empathy is also, as Black and white abolitionists alike understood, indispensable to the pursuit of moral and political equality. The fundamental question at issue was: *who is entitled to human rights?* The best way to affirm a racially inclusive view of rights, abolitionists believed, was to show that human beings of all races were, in every morally relevant sense, the same. They harbored the same hopes and ambitions, they felt the same emotional attachments and the same anguish at their destruction, they burned with the same indignation when summarily deprived of opportunity and freedom. To demonstrate this essential likeness was to demonstrate that the denial of rights to Black Americans was wholly arbitrary, an exercise of nakedly despotic power. Abolitionists typically deployed empathy, in other words, in service of a particular, egalitarian objective: the extension of natural or human rights to all men on equal terms.[179]

They also cautioned repeatedly against morally complacent sentimentalism. "You tell me," wrote a woman contributing anonymously to the *Genius of Universal Emancipation*, "that you cannot encounter the trouble and inconvenience of doing any thing further than occasionally indulging in a pathetic lamentation over the sufferings of the poor slaves." She then reminded her readers that such lamentations were often heard from the lips of slaveholders themselves, who "will repeat over as feelingly as yourself, the set phrases of regret for the existence of the system" even as they brutalized their slaves.[180] In fact, abolitionists insisted that genuine, morally responsible empathy with victims of injustice *had to* motivate remedial action—and so their appeals to empathy were typically paired with specific exhortations to act.[181] Abolitionist societies organized petition drives, boycotts of consumer products touched by slavery, vigilance committees to help fugitives, political campaigns to protest civil rights violations, countless public lectures and publications designed to help shift public opinion, and a great deal more.[182] Although the movement was divided, as of the late 1830s, over the most appropriate means to employ, all agreed that urgent action was morally required. Drawing on an evangelical culture that successfully underwrote a broad range of reform movements in antebellum America, abolitionists of all stripes enlisted empathy to impress this obligation on their audiences.

The abolitionist appeal to empathy was amplified by their claim that northern citizens were personally complicit in perpetuating both slavery and racial discrimination. This argument was directed especially to those who acknowledged the injustice of slavery and/or racial inequality but denied their own responsibility for it. Abolitionists argued, for example, that citizens who lent support to either of the mainstream political parties were in effect supporting slavery (since both parties promised not to interfere with it). They argued that worshippers who belonged to mainstream churches—or churches that practiced discrimination—were actively contributing to the evisceration of Christian principles. They argued that those who consumed products—including sugar and cotton—made with slave labor were subsidizing slavery and helping make it profitable. Even before the passage of the strengthened fugitive slave law of 1850, they argued that northern states were complicit when they allowed escaped slaves to be captured and shipped south, or simply when they enforced discriminatory statutes within their own borders. By virtue of their own actions and affiliations, they argued, northerners contributed palpably to racial injustice.

One broad version of this argument touched on the meaning of democracy itself: in a democratic political community, where sovereign power was widely dispersed among the general electorate, responsibility followed. "It may be urged that New-England has no participation in Slavery, and is not responsible for its wickedness," wrote the *Emancipator*.

> Why are we thus willing to believe a lie? New-England not responsible! Bound by the United States Constitution to protect the slave-holder in his sins, and yet not responsible! Joining hands with crime—covenanting with oppression—leaguing with pollution, and yet not responsible! Palliating the Evil—hiding the Evil—voting for the Evil, do we not participate in it?[183]

New Englanders lived under a Constitution that not only sanctioned slavery but demanded (via the fugitive slave clause) that they help slaveholders control their slaves. This Constitution drew its authority and legitimacy from popular consent, which meant that responsibility for its injustice flowed directly to the citizens of New England. Moreover, New Englanders could vote, and they were responsible for how they used (or failed to use) their political power. If they cast their ballots for candidates or parties that compromised with slavery, downplayed its moral significance, or just looked the other way, they were culpable. "We have all sinned together," insisted Unitarian radical Charles Follen: when the national government adopted a policy favorable to slavery, its unjust actions enmeshed all American citizens.[184] With such ubiquitous claims, abolitionists were trying to tear down the imagined barrier that had allowed northerners, starting around the time of the Missouri Compromise, to believe that the South was separate from America itself, a kind of self-contained anomaly whose moral horrors did not taint the national project.[185]

This ethic of democratic complicity resonated with the evangelical commitment to take responsibility not just for one's own sins but also for the sins of others. "In the word of God it is written," wrote the *Pennsylvania Freeman*, "'Thou shalt not suffer sin to remain upon thy brother'—'Have no fellowship with the unfruitful works of darkness but rather reprove them.'"[186] From this point of view, apathy and silence in the face of injustice were themselves violations of moral duty to God, for they expressed a tacit acquiescence to sin. "Every one does countenance and authorize [slavery]," wrote the *National Enquirer*, "who suffers any opportunity of expressing his deep abhorrence of its manifold abominations to pass by unimproved."[187] The scriptural duty to oppose and eradicate sin, these writers argued, established a moral baseline against which all Christians should be judged. To fall short of that standard was, in effect, to choose sin over righteousness.[188] Of course, this aggressive moral posture also motivated a reformist zeal that called for social control of "deviant" behavior, from drinking alcohol to doing business on the Sabbath or exercising a measure of sexual freedom.

Paradoxically, this emphasis on moral complicity also reveals further dimensions of the abolitionists' individualism. Many abolitionists, writes historian Aileen Kraditor, felt that "the guilt of slaveowning and the obligation to repent were individual, not collective, responsibilities."[189] The Protestant image of the free individual standing alone before God, answerable to him directly and completely, was a powerful and recurrent trope in abolitionist writing. Like the fire-breathing preachers who stoked the flames of religious revival, they urged each individual in their audiences "to separate themselves entirely from sin" and avoid "all compromising connections with evil in any shape or form."[190] This was true especially of the Garrisonians, many of whom refused even to vote out of concern that political engagement would compromise their moral integrity as individuals and weaken the moral power of their message. They saw American society as a collection of so many individuals, each separately responsible to their own conscience.

It is important to add, however, that even this highly individualized conception of responsibility often motivated political action. Even the Garrisonians did not call for individual withdrawal from society; rather, they took for granted that humans were social beings who would always be enmeshed in communal institutions and bonds.[191] The only way to escape personal complicity, most abolitionists argued, was ultimately to cleanse the community itself of injustice, through moral exhortation or political action or both. Although they located moral responsibility in individuals and described slaveholding as a (personal) *sin*, they also routinely described both slavery and racism as structural problems, with deep political and economic roots, that could be defeated only through coordinated action.[192] Moreover, they thought carefully (and disagreed endlessly) about the likely effects of different forms of activism, from consumer boycotts to "vote scattering" and other strategies.[193] Most did not see their protests as merely symbolic gestures intended to cleanse their own moral consciences.[194]

For abolitionists, then, individualizing responsibility was—at least partly— a way of responding to collective apathy: they believed that northerners had to be convinced to stop laying blame elsewhere and join the fight. In their discussions of personal complicity, as in their appeals to empathy, abolitionists worried about moral complacency. "Why are so many [good people] inactive?" asked the *Freeman*. "*They do not see, they do not feel that their exertions are required.*"[195] To prevent guilt from devolving into self-pity, Americans would have to be shown how and where to act.[196] For the anti-Garrisonian wing of the movement that formed its own rival organizations in the late 1830s, this increasingly meant political engagement. They organized mass petition campaigns, formed their own political party, and organized to defeat discriminatory policies in northern states. Their newspapers printed how-to articles designed to instruct their faithful in the details of successful grassroots mobilization.[197] For the Garrisonian wing, on the other hand, action meant "moral suasion": they published and circulated countless antislavery tracts and newspapers, blanketed the North with itinerant lecturers, staged acts of civil disobedience to protest racial discrimination, worked tirelessly to convert church leaders to their cause, and more. They also modeled inclusion in their own organizations: Garrison welcomed both women and Black abolitionists and routinely featured them as speakers and writers.[198] With Garrison's support, female antislavery societies did a great deal of the work of abolitionist organizing: they raised funds, sold subscriptions to abolitionist newspapers and periodicals, circulated petitions, and helped finance the underground railroad.[199] Together, these different groups of abolitionists laid the foundation for the mass, democratic antislavery movement that helped bring Lincoln to power in 1860.[200]

The necessity of action brings one final layer of abolitionist individualism into focus. Abolitionists expected that those who acted publicly against slavery and racism would suffer serious social consequences. They would lose the esteem of friends and colleagues; they would lose jobs or customers. They would be condemned as dangerous radicals. In the face of such withering pressure, many would learn to keep their convictions to themselves.[201] To do otherwise would require unusual courage and self-trust. Committed abolitionists would have to trust their own judgments despite widespread censure and draw strength and confidence from their own righteousness in the face of disdain, ostracism, and ridicule. Most pleasing to God, wrote the *Weekly Advocate*, "is that man, who firmly convinced that the sentiments which he defends, are founded in immutable truth, adheres to them with a tenacity which nothing can relax . . . fearlessly bidding defiance to the malevolent shafts of ignorance or prejudice—resolutely buffeting the tide which is raised to overwhelm him."[202] Emerson's word for this posture was self-reliance; others have called it fanaticism.[203] Either way, abolitionists drew such self-assurance, in part, from an evangelical culture that consistently assailed the authority of clerical elites and church traditions and exalted the authenticity of individual experience, feeling, and judgment.[204] Here too, we find clear lines of confluence between American individualism and evangelical Protestantism.[205]

In his landmark *Appeal to the Colored Citizens of the World* (1829), the Boston shopkeeper David Walker had issued a bitter plea to white Americans. "See your declaration, Americans!!!" he implored. "Do you understand your own language? Hear your language, proclaimed to the world, July 4th, 1776—'We hold these truths to be self evident—that ALL MEN ARE CREATED EQUAL!! that they *are endowed by their Creator with certain unalienable rights.*'"[206] Walker's plea spoke to the central challenge that abolitionists confronted as they tried to mobilize moral outrage and action among northern whites: how could they be persuaded to live by their own stated ideals? It was futile, abolitionists saw, to hope that formal institutions would force them to do so. Individual rights would never be real for racial minorities, they believed, until the democratic majority itself took responsibility for their protection. Rights depended, ultimately, on a culture of democratic inclusion and on a widely diffused habit of taking responsibility for injustice. The first could be sustained only by a willingness to hear and empathize with marginalized communities and confront patterns of exclusion and dehumanization. The second could be achieved only if white northerners learned to recognize their own—and their neighbors'—complicity in injustice and took decisive remedial action.

Once public opinion had shifted in their favor, however, many abolitionists did not hesitate to call for muscular state action against injustice. The Thirteenth, Fourteenth, and Fifteenth Amendments, which vastly extended the scope of federal power and made it, in effect, the guardian of individual rights against states and local communities, received their enthusiastic support. In fact, many abolitionists pressed for a far more dramatic, federally enforced restructuring of postwar southern society, including the confiscation and re-distribution of plantation lands to freedmen.[207] Although moral suasion was their preferred strategy, many also saw that the project of universalizing and protecting rights would ultimately mean imposing legal uniformity in the teeth of local resistance, and that it therefore stood at odds with the long-standing localism and decentralization of American politics.

Like the Jacksonian Democrats, they often justified federal action as a de-fensive step required to protect free individuals from "unnatural" exploitation and assault (of which slavery was the epitome). But because these distortions were so deeply embedded in local culture and economic life, and because they were perpetrated not just by a small class of elites but by a much larger class of whites for whom the prospect of Black citizenship was anathema, the defen-sive idea of a federal government protecting rights from assault morphed, for many of them, into an ambitious vision of federal intervention in state and local life. This idea of a federal government as an agent of emancipation cen-tered on defending and extending the rights of the most vulnerable has, of course, shaped the American left from the Civil War through the civil rights and feminist movements to the twenty-first-century push for "health care as a human right."

———

The myth of the rights-bearer drew together a cluster of related beliefs. First came the moral and religious idea that "all men" possessed, on equal terms, a dignity and inviolability that others were bound to respect.[208] Second came the political conviction that any legitimate government had to enshrine this dignity in its fundamental law, by enumerating and pledging to defend a slate of individual rights. This political conviction was typically accompanied by a third, social idea: that so long as they were undistorted by oppression and exploitation, human societies were best understood as associations of rights-bearing individuals who interacted freely and equally for mutual advantage. Society's fundamental "building blocks," so to speak, were free persons "un-tangled . . . from the myriad associations of class, church, guild, and place."[209] This idea of society was sometimes linked to a Lockean myth of origins, which held that both societies and legitimate governments were formed when so many rights-bearing agents came together voluntarily, in a state of nature, for their mutual benefit.

This cluster of beliefs—moral, political, and social—forms the core of the liberal tradition in Western political thought, and the foundational myth of the rights-bearer inscribed them into the idea of America.[210] Indeed, as political theorist Louis Hartz pointed out, Americans commonly read their own history through this Lockean lens: they imagined white society as a collection of individuals who, in the crucible of their Atlantic crossings, were stripped of the trappings of European identity and reborn simply as rights-bearing persons.[211] They imagined their state and federal governments, too, as artifacts of consent that came into being when so many sovereign individuals willingly accepted their terms.

As we have seen over the last three chapters, these liberal ideas could be used to serve a wide range of political purposes. In some contexts, the myth's promise of *equal* rights made it an effective vehicle for egalitarian protest. Democrats invoked the rights of small producers to attack government subsidies for the wealthy and emerging concentrations of economic power, and to decry both political and economic inequalities within white society. Under the banner of equal rights, they also opposed discrimination against European immigrants and pressed for greater religious toleration for white minority groups. Abolitionists pushed much further: they harnessed and expanded the liberal ideals of the Declaration of Independence to articulate an inclusive politics of human rights that extended to all men and, for a number of abolitionists, to women too. They demanded not just emancipation but civil and political rights; they denounced not just slavery but also racial discrimination and northern apathy in the face of appalling injustice.

This more radical egalitarian posture was also evident at the 1848 Seneca Falls Convention, which launched the movement for women's suffrage. "We hold these truths to be self-evident," its participants declared, "that all men and women are created equal, that they are endowed by their creator with certain inalienable rights, that among these are life, liberty, and the pursuit of happiness." They invoked these rights as remedies against a wide range of abuses, including women's legal subordination to their husbands; their forfeiture of property in marriage; their exclusion from colleges, seminaries, and most forms of "profitable employment"; and their taxation without representation. In all of these ways and many others, they argued, men had "endeavored . . . to destroy her confidence in her own powers, to lessen her self-respect, and to make her willing to lead a dependent and abject life." To the small group of women assembled at this epochal convention, equal rights meant not just full equality under the law and "immediate admission into all the rights and privileges" of citizenship but also an affirmation of their standing as autonomous persons entitled to direct the course of their own lives.[212]

Even as the myth of the rights-bearer channeled a wide range of egalitarian yearnings, however, white men in Jacksonian America also used it aggressively to curtail challenges to their power and privilege. They often did so by expanding the scope of their own rights. Women's labor was subsumed into the expansive ambit of male possession. Slaveholders claimed ownership rights over Black bodies and deployed free-market ideas strategically to cripple the federal government's power to interfere with the booming business of slavery. Settlers and expansionists invoked the priority of their own property and security rights as they laid claim to western lands and obliterated Native American and Mexican American communities. White men bridled at the prospect of interference with what they saw as their God-given entitlement to command their subordinates and keep them in their place. Thus was a strident, antigovernmental politics of individual freedom deployed to reinforce broad—and manifestly illiberal—assertions of group privilege.[213]

Throughout the Jacksonian Era, many Democrats reconciled this glaring tension by erasing women and people of color from their political rhetoric altogether: they transmuted the exclusive rights of white men into the equal rights of the abstract individual. This erasure allowed them to present themselves as path-breaking egalitarian reformers doing battle with all manner of unjust hierarchies, and their country as a universal beacon of liberty. This posture began to change after 1848: as the Democratic Party morphed into an embattled proslavery coalition dominated by its southern members, its white supremacy grew more explicit and its mythology of rights more overtly conservative. Party spokesmen now argued that the principal enemies of equal rights were not rapacious aristocrats but political radicals working to extend rights to the naturally unfit and undeserving. Democrats steadily "transferred their animus," writes historian Joshua Lynn, "from the Whiggish Money Power to a new tyranny—fanatical reformers who craved centralized state power to inflict moral reforms on otherwise autonomous white men." In this way, the cause of equal rights for white men, asserted against the overbearing power of federal government, became a conservative American cause—a form of "indigenous American conservatism" that runs strong to this day.[214]

Finally, American liberalism in the Jacksonian Era also absorbed a set of utopian assumptions that would shape its trajectory for generations to come. As we have seen, Democrats grafted the Lockean idea of natural rights onto an idealized notion of *natural* society, governed by harmonious economic laws that would deliver prosperity, relative equality, and—as long as government did not interfere—untrammeled freedom. In a devout country whose optimistic Protestant faithful embraced scientific and material progress, Democrats successfully positioned the market as an emanation of divine intelligence. In a vast and expanding country whose "laboring classes" included millions of property-owning farmers, they offered up a vision of commercial prosperity that would preserve the small proprietor's way of life: it would simultaneously strip unproductive elites of their privileges, keep government power in check, and hold the horrors of British industrialization at bay. It would expand white Americans' access to both markets and land while leaving their autonomy and independence intact. It would ensure that wealth still depended on productive labor, and so perpetuate the everyday virtues that, in their eyes, helped make America exceptional.

It is remarkable that the main alternative to this idealized national self-image, in the political mythology of Jacksonian America, was *also* fundamentally market-oriented and individualistic. As Whigs struggled to compete with the Democrats on the national stage, they developed their own mythic story of American freedom. Its organizing concept was the self-made man.

PART III

The Self-Made Man

LIKE THE TWO other foundational myths we have explored, the American myth of the self-made man long preceded the Age of Jackson. Throughout the eighteenth century, Americans described their society as a place where poor and low-born Europeans could transform themselves through effort and discipline. In his short 1784 essay, "Information to Those Who Would Remove to America," Ben Franklin described the upward arc that hardworking white immigrants might reasonably expect their American lives to follow. "If they are poor," he wrote, "they begin first as Servants or Journeymen; and if they are sober, industrious, and frugal, they soon become Masters, establish themselves in Business, marry, raise Families, and become respectable Citizens."[1] The idea that individuals would be rewarded in proportion to their personal effort and merit, not their inherited identity or caste, was part of the transatlantic myth of America well before the Revolution.[2]

The anti-aristocratic thrust of the Revolution only reinforced this national self-image, as did the opening and settlement of the trans-Appalachian West.[3] In the popular mind, the West stood for new beginnings and almost limitless opportunity. Its vast territories offered the promise of land ownership and the status it conveyed; its burgeoning towns created opportunities for tradesmen and aspiring professionals.[4] The West reinforced an impression of American society in constant motion, full of people restlessly seeking new and better lives. In the mythology of the age, writes historian Robert Wiebe, each of these strivers was typically imagined "alone, a sovereign atom in a sea of alternatives."[5]

As we saw in part 1, the ideal of the independent proprietor contained elements of this myth. It offered a promise of advancement and respectability to white tenants, immigrants, and workers, no matter how modest their beginnings. In Jacksonian America, this promise was often expressed through the narrative of the settler moving west, acquiring and clearing land, and securing hard-won independence for himself and his family. In his 1818 epic poem, *The Backwoodsman*, for example, James K. Paulding had lionized the "meanest farmer's boy" who, desperate to own "the land he plows" and escape dependency, sets off for the untamed West:

> And hence it comes, he leaves his friends and home,
> Mid distant wilds and dangers drear to roam,
> To seek a competence, or find a grave,
> Rather than live a hireling or a slave.

This farmer's boy epitomized an essentially agrarian (and artisanal) ideal of self-making defined by the rise from dependence to independence through effort and will. Though he left home, he yearned to re-create familiar patterns of life under more auspicious circumstances, where the soil was "unexhausted" and good land was available for "almost naught," and where his husbandry would be more "nobly repaid."[6]

Increasingly, this more moderate ideal of self-making competed with another, more ambitious and more avowedly capitalist alternative.[7] Reviewing almost two hundred autobiographies of men born between 1765 and 1804, historian Joyce Appleby documented the emergence of a new set of ideals centered on the young man not just leaving home but breaking with patriarchal authority and parental expectations, navigating a fluid and "unformed social environment," and fashioning a life and career of his own choosing. In so many of these narratives, writes Appleby, "the opportunity to quit the family farm is presented as a deliverance" that opens up a wide field for individual agency.[8] These autobiographers celebrated education and virtuous self-discipline as the keys that unlocked vast opportunities in a new economic landscape. They presented the successes they achieved, moreover, as their own.[9]

This new, modern myth of the self-made man was harnessed, especially, by the Whig Party and its spokesmen.[10] While Democrats emphasized the liberating effects of economic independence, Whigs often advanced an alternative view of freedom as self-creation.[11] In the uniquely dynamic and classless American economy, they argued, white men could become anyone they wanted: they could rise from poverty to wealth, from ignorance to educated refinement; they could change jobs and vocations at will.[12] Their identity itself could be a matter of deliberate choice and effort.[13] In Whig rhetoric, the yeoman farmer standing proudly astride his plot of land was gradually displaced by the self-made man whose upward, autonomous trajectory mirrored the rise of the modern, prosperous American nation. This powerful ideal shaped American politics in ways that would survive long after the Whig Party itself had vanished from the scene.

Like the myth of the rights-bearer, the myth of the self-made man was infused with a progressive optimism that found its origins in the Scottish Enlightenment. Its emergence in Whig Party rhetoric was also facilitated, however, by two important shifts that occurred largely within American intellectual culture. The first was a transformation and liberalization of conservative thought as it competed for adherents in the mass, democratic politics of the Jacksonian Era and yoked its fortunes ever more tightly to an emerging capitalist economy. The second was a sharp erosion of Calvinist orthodoxies fueled by the optimistic popular messages of the Second Great Awakening. Together, these shifts underwrote an alternative politics of personal freedom that could thrive on an ideological terrain largely defined by Democrats.

9

Freedom in the
Conservative Mind

Labor is the master here; it is the great capitalist; the embryo millionaire; and
he who can stand up, in the bloom and vigor of ripening manhood, pure in
heart, and determined to prosper, though he has not a penny in the world,
may . . . behold a large estate within his reach.

—CALVIN COLTON, 1844[1]

IN THE MYTH of the self-made man, Whigs found their answer to Jacksonian
Democrats' admonitions about a rising American aristocracy. In a classless
society in which white men could be anything they wanted, there could be no
such thing as aristocracy. There could be no need, either, for economic reforms
designed to curtail its supposed privileges. In fact, Whigs deployed this myth
as part of a self-consciously conservative political agenda: despite their celebration of human perfectibility and economic progress, Whigs typically presented themselves as guardians of an economic and constitutional order that
was under siege by Democratic radicals.

This conservative posture harbored its own version of American exceptionalism. In America, Whigs insisted, there could be no serious economic *conflict*.
In a dynamic, capitalist economy awash in credit and opportunity, all hardworking Americans—rich and poor—would rise together. Moreover, while
the industrious poor became rich, the idle rich fell quickly into poverty, and
this double mobility guaranteed that wealth found its way into the hands of
those who deserved it. Whigs therefore insisted that the class divisions that
still sundered the Old World had no real basis in the New. At the heart of this

idealized image of America lay the premise of individual responsibility: those who failed to advance and prosper in these uniquely propitious American circumstances had only themselves to blame.[2]

While Democrats used individualistic ideas to defend a simple market society in which small producers owned their own land or shop and worked for themselves, Whigs deployed them in service of a more "mature" and diversified capitalist economy powered by plentiful credit, domestic manufacturing, and well-remunerated wage labor. In their eyes, moreover, government was a key partner in fostering economic growth and development. It imposed tariffs to shield American manufacturing from unfair foreign competition, invested in the education of the American workforce, and subsidized infrastructure projects that multiplied economic opportunities. It also promoted the moral and religious reforms that enabled individual discipline and responsibility. As long as it avoided any deliberate redistribution of wealth from rich to poor, they argued, an active government could help preserve and expand individual freedom. In Whig political thought, then, we find a version of American individualism far more reconciled to the constructive use of state power and less beholden to utopian ideas of a natural and apolitical market.

But Whig thought harbored its own utopia: for many Whigs, this faith in human progress was deeply linked to a religiously inspired belief in the perfectibility of the individual. The Second Great Awakening had popularized the conviction that sin and holiness were matters of individual choice and that individuals therefore held their spiritual fates in their own hands. While many Whigs still believed, as their Calvinist inheritance had taught them, that human nature was unruly and recalcitrant, they were increasingly confident that its sinful tendencies could be overcome through self-cultivation and discipline. In their view, this moral reformation of the individual could then unlock a tremendous renovation of American society and hasten it ever closer to its millennial destiny. This worldly confidence, in turn, infused Whig thought—and American conservatism itself—with a forward-looking optimism and a growing confidence in the autonomous agency of the enlightened individual.

The contrast between Whig and Democratic rhetoric should not be overstated. When the Whig Party mobilized to oppose Andrew Jackson in the early 1830s, its spokesmen often operated on the Democrats' conceptual plane. They extolled the independence and virtue of America's yeoman farmers, for instance, and argued it was the Democrats' reckless economic policies that endangered their way of life. They appealed to the labor theory of property and insisted that only their economic agenda, with its promise of stable credit, expanding infrastructure, and a growing domestic market, would ensure that all Americans reaped the fruits of their labor. In many cases, they accepted the fundamental values and narratives that structured the Democrats' rhetoric but worked to bend their arc in a different political direction. This chapter focuses, however, on several deeper differences between Whig and Democratic rhetoric, which would have long-term implications for the shape of American political thought.

Finally, it is also important not to exaggerate the Whigs' ideological consistency. The Whig Party—like the Democratic Party—drew together a diverse coalition, which included conservative eastern businessmen and financiers; rural, egalitarian evangelicals and Anti-Masons; middling western farmers and entrepreneurs on the rise; and aristocratic southern planters.[3] Even more than the Democrats, Whigs had to labor to hold together diverse interests and ideological strains. From the beginning, they were torn between a more conservative, paternalist wing that had much in common with New England Federalism and a more progressive and self-consciously democratic wing laboring to cast off any association with it. The best we can do, then, is pay attention to the core ideas and stories that surfaced regularly across several decades of Whig rhetoric and explore their contribution to the rise of American individualism.

Whig Conservatism

Although Whigs were economic innovators who embraced a broadly capitalist vision of American society, they considered themselves conservatives, and they drew self-consciously from the rich vein of Anglo-American conservatism that had nourished the Federalist Party before them. In several ways, this conservative tradition led them to reject the individualistic ideas championed by Jacksonian Democrats. Unlike Democrats, for example, many Whigs saw American society as an organic whole that evolved over time; many also grounded the legitimacy of American government not in the natural rights of individuals but in long-standing political tradition. To understand the Whigs' distinctive contribution to American individualism, we must begin by exploring this conservative inheritance and observing how they repurposed it to advance their own ideal of private liberty.

The Whigs' conservatism can be seen, first of all, in the way they mocked their rivals as radicals, reckless experimenters, and dreamers enamored of hopelessly utopian visions of politics and society. Democratic opinion-makers,

wrote New York Whig David Francis Bacon, were "sickly dandified philosophers, of a variety of accent never before congregated out of Babel"; their theories amounted to "a ballooning flight through the airy and windy regions of
philosophical speculation and experiment, under the guidance of political
economists."[4] Other Whigs accused the Democrats of languishing in the
"metaphysical age, during which they fashion in their minds abstract creations,
to whose agency they refer the various changes that are going on in the world";
with the Democrats, "theory is everything; while facts, instead of being 'stubborn things,' are accounted as nothing."[5]

The Democrats' penchant for abstract speculation might have been harm-
less if confined to "Academic groves"; in politics, the Whigs argued, it was
dangerous. They often compared the Democrats to the French revolutionaries
who had used "golden visions" of expansive natural rights and social equality
to incite the mob against all established order and to turn the poor against the
rich.[6] The *Daily Ohio State Journal* promised, for example, that a Democratic
defeat at the polls in 1844 would liberate the country from the "disorders
which Jacobin ignorance and leveling demagogueism [sic] have entailed upon"
it.[7] The "Jacobinical philosophy" of the Democrats, wrote another Whig essayist, amounted to a reckless assault on existing customs and institutions, an
attempt to remake society around completely untested, speculative principles.[8] Specifically, they accused the Democrats of conspiring to bring about a
perfect "equality of condition" by attacking the property of the rich.[9] The predictable result, in America as in France, would be chaos and violence as well
as economic contraction and poverty. "There is scarcely any dangerously radical opinion, any specious, delusive theory, on social, political, or moral points,"
wrote the *Whig Review*, "which does not, in some part of the country, find its
peculiar aliment and growth among the elements of that party."[10]

By contrast, Whigs presented themselves as "in all things essentially conservative." They fought to preserve the Constitution and the "permanent prosperity of the country" against all "reckless innovations and experiments."[11]
They lamented the "disorganizing" tendencies in American life and the rapid
rate of social change, which tended to make people defiant of authority and
settled tradition and enamored of whatever seductive ideas their demagogues
were peddling.[12] Time and again, they presented themselves as the guardians
of America's "venerated institutions," to which Democratic radicals were laying waste. They also described themselves as sober empiricists, and they celebrated their resistance to "every experiment of a reckless [Democratic]
party."[13] "For all of their innovations in economic policy," writes Daniel Walker

Howe, the preeminent historian of Whig political ideas, "the Whigs usually thought of themselves as conservatives, as custodians of an identifiable political and cultural heritage."[14]

The Whigs' conservatism had a number of important implications for their view of society and politics. For instance, it underwrote a distinctive interpretation of the American Revolution. For many Whigs—as for their Federalist predecessors—the American Revolution had been a fundamentally conservative event: Americans had fought to protect their existing liberties against the novel and oppressive policies of the British crown.[15] They had "fought . . . not for the acquisition of new privileges, but for the preservation of old ones; not for the abstract doctrine of the equality of the human race, but for the maintenance of their charters, and of the right, which they had inherited from their fathers, of being taxed only by their own representatives."[16] Likewise, Whigs argued that the revolutionaries' *ideas* had been drawn from their own historical experience; not from abstract philosophy. "The Declaration was *a mere recapitulation of fundamental principles of civil liberty*," insisted one Whig writer, "which were quite as well understood and cherished, and the practical blessings flowing from which were as fully enjoyed, at that day as now."[17] Compared to the French Revolution, wrote a correspondent to the *National Intelligencer*, "ours can scarcely be called a revolution."[18]

The Whig view of the Revolution reveals a fundamentally conservative idea of political authority. From the Whig perspective, the Revolution had derived its legitimacy not from abstract principles of natural right but rather from long-established traditions of liberty. Their idea of authority was at once conservative and pragmatic. American colonial institutions developed legitimate authority over time because they *worked*: they enabled their subjects to lead free and prosperous lives. They worked because they were well adapted to the American character; they were well suited—in a way abstract principles never could be— to the people who lived under them. This was true partly because they had evolved through centuries of trial and error in both England and America. American liberties, wrote one Whig commentator, "*had so long been held as to seem part of their mental and moral constitution*."[19] The American colonists had owed their freedom and prosperity, then, to the "ancient forms and privileges" they had inherited from England, and it was those very privileges that had justified their rebellion.[20] When the British crown had trampled these forms and privileges, it had vitiated its own legitimate authority by cutting off its source.

Implicit in this view of authority lies an idea of society as a *political* entity with a particular history and identity stretching across time.[21] Many Whigs recoiled at the idea of human society as a mere "aggregation of individuals" unified by convenience or reciprocal exchange.[22] Drawing on Irish statesman and philosopher Edmund Burke, they argued that societies were historical entities with distinctive characters. As such, they could be vastly different from one another.[23] A constitution that worked in one place, for example, might prove disastrous in another. Societies were also political entities, in the sense that the particular character, customs, and habits of the people were shaped, from the very beginning, by their political institutions.[24] Unlike Democrats, Whigs tended to reject the notion that "society" could be conceptualized apart from government. "There has been no society, no aggregation of men on the earth—History does not inform us of any," declared Whig congressman Daniel Barnard, "so rude and savage, as to have been without some sort of organization, some sort of rule and government. All have had their laws, and some authority by which those laws are enforced."[25] The idea that government should merely protect the natural order that obtained in pre-political society seemed, from this point of view, like sheer nonsense. If order was ever achieved in human affairs, it was the work of government. When Whigs reached for scientific metaphors to describe human society, they often turned to biology, not Newtonian physics: they described society as a political organism—a body politic, with a government at its head—that matured and developed over time.[26]

For this reason, many Whigs rejected the notion that their government's legitimacy rested on natural rights. Natural rights, they argued, were forfeited the moment people entered political society and were replaced by social and political rights. "The moment he enters into society," wrote Whig propagandist Calvin Colton, his "system of natural rights, is abridged, while other rights are multiplied; and if the state of society is good, his newly-acquired rights are more valuable."[27] The rights that Americans possessed derived from social compacts—in this case the state and federal constitutions—not from philosophical abstractions. Like many of his conservative Whig colleagues, Colton worried that natural rights were so vague and "indefinite" that they could be used to justify any and all forms of resistance and rebellion.[28] Indeed, Whigs taunted Democrats about the potentially radical implications of their appeals to natural rights: "If the right of suffrage is a 'natural right,'" said Indiana congressman Caleb Blood Smith, "let me ask my colleague by what means he arrives at the conclusion that nature has conferred this right upon the white population alone?"[29] Time and again, we find the Whigs emphasizing the indeterminacy of natural rights: who knew what supposedly natural rights the next crop of radicals would dredge up? Grounding the authority of government on natural rights was like building a fortress on shifting sands: neither would last long.

By the late 1840s, The Whig coalition would begin to founder over precisely this issue. By then, many northern Whigs had come to see slavery as an evil that had to be urgently contained, if not eradicated. When they explained why, they reached increasingly for the language of natural rights.[30] In a famous 1850 speech, William H. Seward, one of the acknowledged leaders of the northern Whig Party, denounced slavery as an affront to "the security of natural rights, the diffusion of knowledge, and the freedom of industry." "Slavery," he maintained, "is incompatible with all of these; and, just in proportion to the extent that it prevails and controls in any republican state, just to that extent it subverts the principle of democracy, and converts the state into an aristocracy or a despotism." Seward insisted that there was a "higher law than the Constitution," which limited the authority of all governments.[31] Such language, which was denounced by Henry Clay and other more conservative Whig leaders, helped open a deep rift in the party and drive southern Whigs into the Democratic ranks, paving the way for the collapse of the Second Party System. "Who are they," Clay demanded, "that venture to tell us what is divine and what is natural law? Where are their credentials of prophecy?"[32]

By the time Abraham Lincoln emerged as a leading figure in the new Republican Party in the late 1850s, natural rights were the moral centerpiece of his rejection of slavery. Lincoln denied that Blacks and whites were social and political equals, but he maintained that Blacks enjoyed certain natural rights, which any legitimate government was obliged to protect. In an extended criticism of the Supreme Court's decision in *Dred Scott v. Sandford*, Lincoln argued that "in some respect [a Black woman] certainly is not my equal; but in her natural right to eat the bread she earns with her own hands without asking leave of any one else, she is my equal, and the equal of all others."[33] This right, he insisted, had been clearly affirmed in the Declaration of Independence, with its guarantee of "certain inalienable rights, among which are life, liberty, and the pursuit of happiness."[34]

In several ways, then, mainstream Whig political thought rejected the individualistic premises widely held by Democrats. Drawing on Burke and Federalist conservatism, they saw American society as a unique cultural and political project, extending across time, linking the generations together, shaped by its religion and its Constitution and the habits of life that had evolved under them. It was these forces—and not *nature*—that enabled American individuals to enjoy unprecedented freedom to shape their own lives. They also rejected the Democratic view that government drew its authority strictly from its capacity to protect individuals' natural rights. One of the most fundamental functions of government, in their view, was to nurture the growth and progress of American society, understood as a corporate entity; the rights supposedly enjoyed in an imagined state of nature were largely irrelevant to this goal. For in the Whig view, the liberties worth caring about—the liberties actually experienced and enjoyed by Americans—were the delicate fruits of human law and civilization, not the remnants of some pre-political idyll.

And yet, despite these overtly collectivist elements, Whig political thought contributed powerfully to the evolution of American individualism. When it came time to describe the particular values that were embodied in the great, shared project of American civilization, Whigs emphasized meritocracy and personal freedom. In fact, many Whigs argued that American society was unique in the world in enabling individuals to become the architects of their own lives, without arbitrary restrictions. In America, they argued, all talk of hereditary social class had become obsolete, and individuals were uniquely responsible for their social and economic fortunes. These were the conceptual building blocks of the rising myth of the self-made man.

The Harmony of Classes

As we saw in chapters 4 and 6, the Democrats constantly drew attention to the widening class divisions in American society. They told a story of rising inequality featuring a new class of American aristocrats who conspired against the independence of the farmer and artisan, or who stole from the pockets of America's humble producing classes. The Whigs strongly rejected these stories and worked hard to replace them with a less conflictual narrative of shared prosperity and progress. The Whig response had two key features, each of which was designed to undercut the central thrust of the Democratic push for egalitarian reform: first, they posited a fundamental harmony between economic classes; second, they emphasized the increasing economic mobility of the individual and linked it closely to America's expanding, credit-driven economy. Both proved to be important contributions to American individualism.

In the Whig descriptions of the American economy, all people—rich and poor—rose and fell together; their economic interests were closely united.

"We frequently hear such expressions as 'Capital against Labor,' the Capitalists vs. the Operatives," complained the *Lawrence Courier*, "as though there is a natural antagonism between the two. Such expressions are calculated to mislead and deceive, and to create a misunderstanding between those classes whose interests really lie in the same direction."[35] Instead, Whigs argued that prosperity for the rich—be they merchants or bankers or industrialists—inevitably brought economic benefits to the rest of society. Merchants enabled small farmers to reach wider markets and brought them cheap consumer goods; bankers ensured a steady stream of credit for small entrepreneurs. Industrialists, meanwhile, not only created jobs but also opened up a "home market" for America's limitless agricultural produce. "Think you that none but rich capitalists profit by those stupendous establishments?" asked Congressman Caleb Cushing, defending the factories and mills of New England. He pointed to the "5730 persons employed in the cotton mills of Lowell," and the "4100 cords of wood, and 500,000 bushels of charcoal, which are annually consumed by eight of the manufacturing companies in that town."[36] When wealthy manufacturers succeeded, so too did farmers and laborers.[37] "Far distant be the day," said Whig titan Daniel Webster, "when the people of New England shall be deceived by the specious fallacy, that there are different and opposing interests in our community; that what is useful to one, is hurtful to the rest; that there is one interest for the rich, and another interest for the poor; that capital is the enemy of labor, or labor the foe of capital."[38] Such proclamations were ubiquitous in Whig rhetoric.

Not only did all social classes rise and fall together, their members belonged to professions that were mutually dependent and complementary. The work of each profession, said Edward Everett, a leading Whig politician and orator, was indispensable to the others. The telescope, for example, was made possible by the mathematician and the scientist but also "the brass-founder" and the "glass-polisher"; moreover, its glass had to be produced in factories, powered by furnaces, fueled by wood and coal. "We cannot take up any one of *these* trades," he declared, "without immediately finding that it connects itself with numerous others." All formed "links of the same chain, every one of which is essential to its strength." Everett therefore insisted that every man with an honest profession was "entitled to the good fellowship of each and every other member of the community"—what benefited one would invariably benefit all.[39] Whigs insisted that agricultural, manufacturing, and commercial interest were "closely entwined and enlaced together." "Their interests," wrote political economist

Alonzo Potter, "consequently, are identical; and any attempt to advance that of one at the expense of the others, must be equally prejudicial to all."[40]

For Whigs, the harmony of classes was not a truism that applied to all societies; in their eyes, it was a unique feature of America's free economy. The "odium" cast on capitalists, said Everett, was a relic of bygone times, when property was accumulated through violence, fraud, and hereditary privilege. "The roots of [this] opinion run deep into the past," to the Old World and its legacy of feudal aristocracy. American society, by contrast, offered "no basis for a prejudice of this kind against capital." In America, all wealth "may be traced back to industry and frugality."[41] Whig industrialist Nathan Appleton concurred: in Europe, labor was "always and everywhere degraded"; in America, it was the only path to success.[42] Here, according to this foundational myth, was one of America's defining accomplishments: wealth could be accumulated only through hard work and ingenuity, which benefited everyone. "In this country," declared one anonymous Whig pamphlet, "all the large fortunes have been accumulated by industry and integrity."[43] In this sense, America was completely unlike the "Old World," where the rich "live by devouring the poor": on this side of the Atlantic, the rich were necessarily "public benefactors."[44]

As we saw in chapter 6, Whigs denied that American society could be divided into a class of producers and a class of wealthy, unproductive parasites. "Away with the miserable jargon of the political economists," wrote Massachusetts state representative Harrison Colby, "who write so complacently about the producing and non-producing classes." In America, such divisions had "no foundation in nature or in experience. Whitney, whose cotton-gin doubled the value of every acre of land in the South, raised more cotton with his head than any other man ever raised with his hands."[45] Whig orators commonly warned, therefore, against dismissing certain classes as unproductive "drones." Any "well-organized" and prosperous community depended on the hard work of "the learned professions, lawyers, doctors, divines, the merchants, tradesmen, factors, and transporters."[46] In America, wrote Appleton, everyone labored: "Occupation, labor, is the natural lot of all. The eloquent advocate, the learned divine, the able writer, the successful merchant, manufacturer, or agriculturist, are allotted the highest places in society. These places are only obtained through an active and successful industry."[47] The only exceptions that Whigs allowed were the indolent poor who squandered their productive potential.

In America, then, virtually everyone contributed to a shared prosperity. Whigs imagined American society as a harmonious system that worked to everyone's benefit, bound together by industry, commerce, and credit:

> Hark to the voice of life and business which sounds along the [railroad] lines! While we speak, one of them is shooting onward to the illimitable west, and all are uniting with the other kindred enterprises, to form one harmonious and prosperous whole, in which town and country, agriculture and manufactures, labor and capital, art and nature—wrought and compacted into one grand system—are constantly gathering and diffusing, concentrating and radiating the economical, the social, the moral blessings of a liberal and diffusive commerce.[48]

Whereas Democrats had envisioned American society as a natural system that needed protecting against the interference of corrupt elites, Whigs celebrated an advanced and "civilized" social order in which elites played an important role. In their eyes, businessmen, bankers, and industrialists, as well as the state itself—the very source of social and economic order—formed integral parts of the social whole. Without them, it would collapse into either poverty or anarchy.

In this optimistic Whig vision, even corporations, which the Democrats assailed as bastions of elite privilege, became agents of social harmony. "The joint stock companies of the North, as I understand them," said Henry Clay in one of his seminal speeches, "are nothing more than associations, sometimes of hundreds, by means of which the small earnings of many are brought into a common stock." "Nothing can be more essentially democratic," he continued, "or better devised to counterpoise the influence of individual wealth."[49] Others insisted that the stockholders of America's banks were mainly "the mechanic, the solitary female, the minor child, the public institution of charity," or "widows and orphans," as well as "sailors and laborers."[50] In the Whig view, corporations enabled small investors to share in the economy's growth and bound their interests together with the rich. Without corporations, not only would the economy be deprived of valuable capital to fuel its "diffusive" prosperity, but the gains would flow mainly to wealthy individual investors.

This Whig narrative of social harmony had a very important political upshot, which they constantly emphasized: persistent poverty and economic hardship in America had no *structural* cause. There was no class of people in America getting rich at the expense of the working class or exploiting their labor. Time and again, Whig speakers warned against populist demagogues who conjured up imaginary class divisions where none existed, who fanned the flames of envy among the idle and dissolute poor. In some cases, they fully inverted the Democratic story of labor exploitation that we explored in chapter 6: it was the *rich* who were being victimized by a grasping, profligate class, whipped up by Democratic politicians who resented their success and coveted the hard-earned fruits of their labor.[51] Because the American economy was fundamentally fair and inclusive, Whigs insisted, such resentments were wholly illegitimate—they were but symptoms of "envious indolence and disappointed ambition."[52] Those who failed to succeed in America had only their own personal shortcomings to blame.

Architects of Their Own Fortunes

Even more important, in the long term, than this story of social harmony was the Whig narrative of economic mobility. The ideal of social harmony suffered from one important rhetorical weakness, for it seemed to presuppose the reality of social class. The rich might be allied with the poor, but the narrative of harmony suggested that they still formed a distinct stratum of society. As such, they were vulnerable to the Democratic charge of aristocracy. After all, why should the wealthy enjoy superior social status, privileged access to political power, and conspicuous luxuries that were out of reach for most Americans? To attack the charge of aristocracy more directly, the Whigs turned to a story of economic mobility designed to show that there was no stable *class* of wealthy people in America at all: before long, the poor became rich and the rich poor.[53] In doing so, they wrote meritocratic assumptions, and with them an expansive and increasingly private conception of individual freedom, into the very foundation of American conservatism.

"Aristocracy in America!" exclaimed Senator Richard Bayard. "Where are its elements, where its means and appliances?" In this country, he continued, "the wheel of fortune is perpetually revolving; . . . the poor man of to day becomes the rich man of to morrow [*sic*]."[54] The idea of aristocracy, Whigs argued, connoted a permanent class who owed their wealth to durable or heritable privileges. In America, they insisted, there was no such thing. The rich had risen through their own effort and ingenuity; they were simply successful laborers. "Will those political quacks and imposters," demanded a Whig pamphleteer in 1840, "have the impudence to pretend that Stephen Girard, in passing from the obscure state of a poor boy to the enviable condition of a 'millionaire,' by his own industry and economy, was at the same time necessarily transformed into an *aristocrat* or an 'enemy to the cause of democracy?'"[55] Another pamphlet suggested that America's "independent Farmer" was, in truth, the only American aristocrat, for his wealth and status derived from "landed possessions." America's rich were far less secure, and could therefore hardly be counted as a *class* at all: "He who is rich to-day, may be poor tomorrow."[56]

In fact, one of the most ubiquitous claims in the whole body of Whig political rhetoric was that wealth in America never stayed in one family for more than a few generations. "The most huge masses of wealth ever rolled up in this country," declared Congregationalist minister Hubbard Winslow, "are melted away and dispersed in a thousand directions within two or three generations."[57] "Scarcely ever," wrote Colton, "does [wealth] remain in the same line to the third generation."[58] "No overgrown fortune," wrote another pamphleteer, "has ever descended three generations—they are constantly revolving."[59] Whigs continually drew attention, in other words, to the *downward* mobility of America's elites. If the sons and grandsons of successful men were not themselves industrious and frugal, their wealth would quickly dissipate. "Through improvidence and vice," Potter observed, "the children of the opulent are perpetually descending from their elevation, to learn, in the school of poverty, the necessity of diligence and prudence."[60] The ranks of the wealthy were constantly churning, then, as feckless sons fell into poverty; America's rich were not a stable or continuous class at all. "To speak of a clan of men thus constituted as an aristocracy," wrote Colby, "is as sound and sensible philosophy as to point to the insects of summer as emblems of eternity."[61]

No sooner had wealthy heirs fallen from prosperity than their places were taken by enterprising workers on the rise. "The poorest boy," wrote Massachusetts correspondent John Aiken, "if he be industrious and frugal, when attained to manhood, may be found a man of substance, and, in his old age, a man of wealth." In fact, he continued, "almost every free laborer has begun to be a capitalist as soon as he has begun to labor."[62] In America, upward mobility was no distant dream; it was a constant reality. Many of those who "are laborers to-day," said Webster, "will be capitalists to-morrow. A career of usefulness and enterprise is before them."[63] Versions of this story had circulated in America, of course, since the days of Ben Franklin, but the Whigs emphasized it over and over and made it a central feature of their political and economic theory. The Whigs, we might say, codified a profoundly important American myth: the myth of limitless upward mobility, and of class boundaries so fluid and porous as to undermine the very existence of class itself.[64]

Along with this myth came a distinctive idea of individual freedom. In America, Whigs insisted, white men could become whoever and whatever they wanted; they could shape and reshape their lives to suit their own ambitions and ideals. "On this soil," said New York preacher and educator Nathan Beman, "every man, under God, may build his own fortunes, and mark out and fill up his own earthly destiny."[65] "Ours is a country," wrote Colton, "where men start from an humble origin, and from small beginnings rise gradually in the world, as the reward of merit and industry, and where they can attain to the most elevated positions, or acquire a large amount of wealth, according to the pursuits they elect for themselves."[66] As we have seen, the Democratic ideal of freedom emphasized economic independence and ownership of the means of production; it emphasized control over the daily conditions of one's own economic life, including the right to trade and transact business without government interference. The Whig ideal was subtly different. Whigs typically projected the ideal of freedom over the entire arc of a man's life: over time, he could rise through the ranks; he could attain status and wealth. He could create and re-create himself. Successful men in America, wrote Colby, "are self-made men—the architects of their own fortune."[67]

As they told this story of ascent from rags to riches, then, Whigs reformulated the meaning of economic freedom.[68] For them, workers were free to the extent that they could change jobs and careers without impediment. "No laws exist here, directly or indirectly," wrote Potter, "confining men to a particular occupation or place, excluding any citizen from any branch he may at any time think proper to pursue. Industry is in every respect free and unfettered: every species of trade, commerce, and professions and manufacture being equally open to all without requiring any regular apprenticeship, admission, or license."[69] "The man who enjoys perfect freedom," wrote Henry Carey, another influential Whig political economist, "has entire control over his own actions. He may change his place of residence and his mode of employment at will."[70] Although Whigs did sometimes invoke the ideal of economic independence, they did so less consistently and with less conviction than Democrats did. It was less integral to their economic vision. While both sides celebrated the dignity of *free labor*, then, they advanced different understandings of the freedom that lay at its heart.

In some cases, Whigs attacked the older ideal of the independent yeoman directly. "[The farmer] is now too nearly an isolated being," wrote Horace Greeley, founder and editor of the influential *New York Tribune*, in 1850. "His world is a narrow circle of material objects he calls *his own*, within which he is an autocrat, though out of it little more than a cipher." Too often, he continued, the cultivation of the earth was little more than "a mindless, repugnant drudgery," and he "a boor or a clod." The isolated farmer needed the "expanding influences of general society" that would give "larger scope to his aspiration and a wider field for the infinite capacities of man's nature." The glorious ideal of independence is here reduced to a combination of stultifying isolation and petty despotism. The remedy, thought Greeley, could be found in the application of technology and modern techniques of industrial production to the farm, so that the farmer himself would become a "master and manager of steam," just like the owner of a modern factory. The application of science and technology to all domains of human production would open up a wide variety of careers for talented, educated young men. Until then, they would continue to flee the farm, "they care not whither, to escape the insupportable exertions of a life of toil which has ceased to bear due relations to or satisfy the wants of their enkindled souls." And who could blame them? They wanted to be free to shape their own lives, to "choose a pursuit and a sphere of life-long effort" commensurate to their intelligence and ambition.[71]

At the heart of this ideal of freedom lay the premise—both exciting and unsettling—of boundless human desire. Everett commented, for example, on this "curious provision of nature" that distinguished us from the beasts: "in proportion as our bare natural wants are satisfied, artificial wants, or civilized wants, show themselves. And in the very highest state of improvement, it requires as constant an exertion to satisfy the new wants, which grow out of the habits and tastes of civilized life."[72] Men, in other words, were never satisfied with their lot; they always wanted more. It was precisely this limitless desire that drove them to rise through the ranks, and that drove societies upward from savagery to civilized refinement.[73] "The universal impulse is forward," said Jonathan Wainwright in a sermon on inequality, "and if it produces some evils in exciting ambition, envyings, jealousies, dishonesty and strife, it calls into existence a thousandfold more blessings in the bright and varied intelligencies [sic], the hardy ennobling virtues, the dauntless and persevering energies of our nature."[74] America's growing economy liberated these energies from the fetters of poverty and stagnation and gave people the freedom to change their social and economic condition. The modest independence of the Jeffersonian yeoman sitting contentedly under his fig tree—a ubiquitous image in early American letters—would no longer suffice. New desires would soon unsettle his earthly paradise and set him striving for more; and as long he pursued them prudently and within moral limits, everyone would benefit.[75]

Young Whigs such as Abraham Lincoln embraced this new ideal of freedom wholeheartedly. Born into rural poverty, Lincoln had wanted nothing more than to leave his narrow, rural world behind and remake himself completely. His yearnings were widely shared: surveying the surviving autobiographies of Americans who lived during this period, historian Joyce Appleby attests to the ubiquity of this desire to escape simple farm life and get ahead. Having launched careers in commerce, journalism, the ministry, or the law, many young men were thrilled to have left behind "a life of hard work on the farm, [with] no hope or prospect of an education."[76] "Such a desire to make oneself over, widespread in nineteenth-century America," writes Howe, "would help to explain why the culture of Whiggery appealed to so many people outside the confines of what we would regard as the bourgeoisie proper."[77] The Whig economic vision promised limitless opportunity in an affluent and modernizing world. As president, Lincoln would later identify such opportunity closely with the promise of American freedom: "nowhere in the world is presented a government of so much liberty and equality. To the humblest and poorest among us are held out the highest privileges and positions."[78] The Whig answer to the Democrats' independent yeoman, lord of the soil, was the self-made man rising through the social ranks.[79]

The Whigs' talk of millionaires and boundless desire should not obscure the fact, however, that the social mobility they imagined was usually far more modest. For the most part, they envisioned poor wage workers rising into the middle class and channeling their burgeoning desires into the growing consumer economy. In fact, as the expanding market and new techniques of mass production brought a vast array of new consumer goods to inland communities, white Americans were spending an increasing share of their incomes on the comforts and adornments of middle-class life: they added parlors and libraries to their houses; they bought sofas and rocking chairs, fashionable clothes, dinnerware, musical instruments, and other symbols of the "refinement" after which they strove. In a fluid and mobile society in which people interacted more and more with strangers, these markers of gentility helped Americans lay claim to social status and respectability.[80] They also reinforced the Whig narrative of mobility, for as historian Richard Bushman puts it, they "offered the hope that anyone, however poor or however undignified their work, could become middle-class by disciplining themselves and adopting a few outward forms of genteel living."[81]

Personal Responsibility

Crucially, the Whigs' faith in economic mobility, like their view of social harmony, allowed them to maintain that wealth and poverty were a matter of individual choice, effort, and discipline. Those who worked hard and saved rose in the ranks; those who squandered their time and money languished in poverty. The term "meritocracy," which dates from the twentieth century, contains a certain ambiguity, as between systems that reward native talent and those that reward virtuous effort. The Whigs very clearly favored the latter: in their descriptions of the American economy, the virtues needed to succeed—including industry, frugality, temperance, initiative, and punctuality—were available to everyone, no matter how naturally gifted. "All property, among us," wrote Colton, "tends to the hands of those who work and wait for it. They are as sure to get it, as the sun is to rise and set." "It is impossible," he continued, "to keep money and property out of the hands of those who work for it, who are industrious and enterprising. They *earn* it, and they *get* it."[82] Of course, this egalitarian view of economic opportunity suggests that the successful individual deserves full credit for his achievements—for they cannot be ascribed even to the unearned advantage of superior natural talent. In America, unlike anywhere else in the world, the individual was in full command of his own economic destiny. With this command came full responsibility.

When the leading Unitarian luminary and moralist, William Ellery Channing, delivered his *Lectures on the Elevation of the Laboring Portion of the Community*, this was his teaching, too: American workers were responsible for their own spiritual and material condition in life. Although he acknowledged that many laborers languished in poverty, he attributed this fact mainly to intemperance, "Sloth," and the "want of strict Economy." He was especially concerned that the laboring classes were absorbing the "artificial wants and diseased tastes" of the upper classes, which led them to "waste their earnings on indulgences which may be spared," leaving them with "no resource for a dark day, and . . . always trembling on the brink of pauperism."[83] Channing presented this as an optimistic message: in America, there were no barriers to the elevation of the laboring classes—no "irresistible obstacles." They needed only "the Will" to improve.[84] This emphasis on the individual's responsibility for his own moral and mental cultivation—and with it his economic success—was a ubiquitous theme in Whig social criticism.

While Channing was fairly delicate in chiding his working-class audience, others put the point more starkly. Addressing itself to the "grumblers" in

America who complained about inequality, the *Philadelphia North American*, a leading Whig newspaper, was very clear about the sources of the problem:

> Fickle dispositions, irregular performance of duty, improvidence, waste, contempt of small beginnings, marriages without a cent saved, and without prospects of better fortune,—to say nothing of positive idleness and vice, may safely be pronounced the real cause of nearly all the destitution and discontent to be found in such a country, and under such a form of government as that of the United States.[85]

The author compared the situation of American workers to laborers in England and every other "monarchical country," where "honesty, thrift, industry avail nothing to keep multitudes from a poor house."[86] Workers in these other places, he argued, might have legitimate grounds for complaint; American workers disappointed with their lot had no one but themselves to blame.

These arguments were often deployed to undermine both labor activism and Democratic criticisms of economic privilege. "How often do we see in this country," asked Mississippi congressman Sargent Smith Prentiss, "that the employer of to-day is the laborer of tomorrow, and the laborer, the employer." "When such is the evidence," he added, "how dare any man rise up and address himself to the passions of different classes of the community and declare there is a distinction between them."[87] Aiken, too, argued that any attempt to raise the condition of America's poor through political reform was indecent, because America was a land "where an open and equal field is given to all under equal laws, so that the poorest boy that blows the blacksmith's bellows may become a member of Congress, or the Governor of a State, or it may be the President of the United States."[88] In Europe, he argued, political solutions might be necessary; in America, the only appropriate response to economic hardship was hard work and self-improvement.

Whigs preached their doctrine of individual self-improvement, therefore, to the working classes in particular. The *Bangor Whig*, for example, criticized the mechanics of New York for organizing to try to ensure that their own members were elected and appointed to political office. It was all well and good for mechanics to associate "for the improvement of each other," so that they could jointly "labor vigorously in the work of self-cultivation."[89] If they did so, many of them would succeed and thrive. But to try to improve their situation through political action was illegitimate—it was an expression of envy or jealousy. Indeed, any attempt to correct inequality through collective action—though union activism, for example—was both unjust and probably fruitless.

"In order to rise," wrote Potter, the worker "ought to aim, first of all, at the exaltation each of his own individual character. To give real and permanent improvement to a class, while the individuals who compose it are degenerating, must be a vain attempt."[90] Any American who wanted to improve his station in life, according to another Whig writer, need only "cultivate his mind" and "improve his higher faculties."[91]

It would be easy to dismiss these arguments as cynical rationalizations of inequality, but there is every reason to believe that these views were deeply and sincerely held. Like Democrats, Whigs linked their economic arguments to a story of American exceptionalism suffused with religious meaning. If America had finally realized a long-awaited, meritocratic order—an order that embodied the divine principle that hard work be rewarded and idleness punished—then it was important to fight hard against any attempt to subvert it.[92] The sermons of Whig evangelical ministers were full of warnings about the incipient "insubordination" of the American people, fueled by radical agitators who sought wholesale transformations of American society. Among the sins that these agitators promoted, warned Lyman Beecher, was an acute "jealousy of the higher orders of society," which glowed "like the ceaseless burning of heated iron" and inspired calls for the redistribution of property. Beecher worried that such jealousies—roused by the "infidel trumpet-call" of atheistic reformers—would "undermine the faith and moral principle of the nation."[93]

Likewise, the Whig plea for self-cultivation and self-improvement was part of a sincerely felt religious passion to transform and uplift the nation, one person at a time. Many leading Whigs were tireless advocates of social reform, and many threw themselves into the organized movements to promote temperance, observance of the Sabbath, prison reform, public and religious education, and antislavery, among other causes. Whig preachers responded to economic crisis with calls to personal austerity and morality. If only individuals could resist the temptation of reckless speculation and debt and tame the passion of avarice, then the economy would surely be restored to its benign harmony and prosperity.[94] The wealthy were not spared in these economic jeremiads: if the poor were guilty of indolence and profligacy, the rich were guilty of reckless luxury, debauchery, and runaway selfishness. The New York–based *Commercial Advertiser* summarized the prevailing Whig view when it insisted that social relations could not be restored to harmony without a "genuine reformation of character and conduct" on the individual level. Its authors pleaded for widespread Bible study and personal self-improvement, not political activism, in response to the growing tensions between labor and capital.[95]

This, then, was the deepest layer of Whig individualism: the persistent tendency to treat social and economic problems as failures of individual character and will. Although they conceded that economic hardship in America was sometimes the result of "singular misfortune," Whigs were determined to resist any suggestion that it arose from structural features of the American economy. The evangelical energy that animated Whig reform movements prevented this tendency from being merely complacent. Whig reformers believed that they were responsible not only for their own characters and souls but also for the characters and souls of those around them.[96] They therefore felt compelled to use all of the tools at their disposal—the vast popular press, organized reform societies, and even the law itself—to help people improve themselves. But their deeply felt responsibility to reform the dissolute poor did nothing, in their judgment, to lessen the poor man's responsibility for himself, nor did it give this poor man in particular any just claim to public assistance. Citizens could rightly expect their government to promote policies that would enhance the general prosperity, but the poor as a group had no special claim to its attention. The right response to economic hardship was simply hard work and self-improvement.

It is worth noting, finally, that although Whigs were the leading expositors of this version of individualism, they were not its only defenders. Over the course of the 1830s, moderate Democrats increasingly frustrated with what they perceived to be the party's growing anti-bank radicalism began distancing themselves from the Van Buren administration and finding their own political voice. Through their leading newspaper, *The Madisonian*, they criticized the president's economic policies using the very language that Whigs commonly employed. Like the Whigs, these more conservative Democrats praised the banking system for promoting prosperity and upward mobility and facilitating individual freedom.[97] The myth of the self-made man, like the other two foundational myths we have explored, was not monopolized by any single party or group.

State-Sponsored Capitalism

Whigs made it clear that personal freedom, as they imagined it, depended on a growing consumer economy fueled by credit, powered at least partly by wage labor, and buoyed by widespread educational opportunity. Like Democrats, they saw the free market as an integral piece of their economic vision. Unlike Democrats, however, they were far less inclined to see the market as a *natural* institution: they tended to see it, instead, as a political creation that depended on active government stewardship. In Whig political thought, then, we glimpse an alternative to the antigovernmental individualism of Jacksonian Democrats: for Whigs, both state and federal governments were essential partners in creating the vibrant capitalist economy that would facilitate individual mobility and freedom.

The Whig conception of personal mobility depended, first of all, on widespread access to credit, guaranteed by a stable and well-regulated banking system. Credit, according to an anonymous Whig essayist, is what "raises the small dealer and the humble beginner to the extensive merchant and the man of wealth."[98] When a young man with no inheritance started his career, he had few options, and it might take him a long time to save enough money to launch his own venture. But the "credit system" helped him get a start in life, and when he succeeded, wrote Colton, he was "a made man, and made by credit; a blessing to himself, to his family, to society." Without the banker's helping hand, he "would have been doomed to remain where he was."[99] This last phrase is revealing: to *stay put*, for Colton, was the very mark of unfreedom. To be free was to have the opportunity to rise, to change one's condition in life. And for that, the young man needed credit and a dynamic, expanding economy. "Every young man whose fortune is yet to be made by his industry can have no hope of success through any other means," according to a speech printed in the *Albany Evening Journal*, "than the credit which his character may enable him to obtain."[100] It followed that the Democratic attacks on banking were nothing less than an assault on freedom itself.

Whigs singled out credit, moreover, as a source of both Christian and civic virtue. To extend a loan to a young farmer or entrepreneur was to express confidence in him and to spread around the blessings of wealth rather than hoard it unproductively. Credit was a way for successful men to extend a helping hand to "my brother, or other relative, or the friend who is dear to me, or the industrious poor citizen who I may think deserves encouragement."[101] It was also a way of rewarding the integrity and good character of those who had little else to their name but good reputations.[102] The Democrats' attacks on banking and credit, along with their hard money austerity, amounted to "a quenching of the spirit of noble and generous confidence; it is cramping the expansive powers of sound public morality."[103] In celebrating credit, the Whigs were in effect praising a form of economic patronage and dependence, albeit a temporary one. Since debt facilitated upward mobility, however, it posed no grave threat to their conception of freedom.[104] In sharp contrast to the Democrats, then, who worried about economic dependence and who often described free-flowing credit as a source of temptation toward speculation and excess, the Whigs often presented it as a source of mutual trust, integrity, and liberty.[105]

Whigs also looked far more favorably on wage labor than Democrats did. An expanding industrial economy needed an industrial workforce, and as long as wages were high enough to enable workers to save and get ahead, the Whigs saw no problem with it. "It is through high wages," explained Maryland politician John Pendleton Kennedy, "that we make the laboring man a partner in the gains of the rich." High wages, he continued, not only afforded him "a full remuneration for his toil" but also "time for mental and moral improvement, by which he shall be progressively lifted up into a higher scale of social respectability and usefulness."[106] Whigs saw high wages, like easy credit, as one of the hallmarks of the American economy and one of the key guarantors of mobility. "It is peculiar to our Country," said Massachusetts governor John Davis, "that all who have the ability to labor and the disposition to be industrious" could find "such ample remuneration either in wages or some other form" as to "attain to all the comforts . . . which reasonable wealth will command." This was true, he insisted, even for "he who enters the world, as most of us do, with no capital but his hands."[107]

When Jefferson had become president in 1800, only 12 percent of the American labor force worked for wages; by 1860, the figure had reached 40 percent.[108] By then, although America was still an overwhelmingly rural country, the amount of industrial production in America was second only to Great Britain.[109] Whig thought reflected this changing economic reality. Rather than pillorying wage labor as a form of economic dependence, as the Democrats often did, the Whigs saw it as an inevitable part of a dynamic and diversifying economy. The crucial contrast, for them, was not between the independent farmer (or artisan) and the dependent wage laborer but rather between the high and low rewards for individual productivity. In a stagnant economy, both farmers and wage laborers would find their avenues for self-improvement closed, for their revenues would be meager. In a thriving economy, by contrast, any economic dependence would prove temporary and would therefore present no serious obstacle to individual freedom.

This argument was central to the Whig defense of their economic program, including high tariffs to shore up American wages against foreign competition and robust investment in domestic infrastructure to help farmers bring their goods to market at a profit.[110] Time and again, Whigs argued that free trade across international borders would force American workers into competition with the "degraded vassalage" or the "dependent pauper population" of Europe, and thereby reduce their wages to a pittance.[111] The question, said John Clayton at a Whig convention in Delaware, was "whether we shall sink the mass of the laboring freemen of this country, who now gain their bread by the sweat of their brows, to the level of the European paupers."[112] Because wages were so low in Europe, Whigs insisted, manufacturers there had an unfair advantage over their American competitors. "Free trade," wrote the editor of the *Jonesborough Whig*, would invite a "ruinous, one-sided traffick." "England is overrun with manufactures," he continued, "and she abounds with hundreds of thousands of naked and perishing men, women and children, who are glad to find employment for a mere livelihood."[113] Without the protective shield of the tariff, the American worker could only sink to the same level. The Whigs therefore decried "this leveling free trade system," which would strip the American worker of both his mobility and his independence.[114] This was by far their most common justification of economic "protection."

But the Whigs also went further: to answer the Democratic argument that free trade was benign and natural, the Whigs responded that *international* free trade was, in fact, an artifact of British colonial power. Free trade, said Henry Clay, "is, in effect, the British colonial system," designed to render Americans "subservient to the pride, and the pomp, and the power" of Great Britain.[115] The British, he argued, pursued a deliberate policy of flooding foreign markets with cheap manufactured goods to drive competitors out of business and ensure that America would remain a provincial agricultural supplier of raw materials for its industrial juggernaut, dependent on its manufactured exports. The obvious purpose of the British cries of "*Free Trade*," wrote one Whig critic, was "to reduce us to colonial vassalage, in which we should not have power to make even a hobnail."[116] The origins of this system, they argued, could be found in British colonial policy in the eighteenth century, which had imposed punitive sanctions on American manufacturers.[117] Far from embodying any providential design, then, the global free market had been invented by British elites to secure their economic dominance. "Shall we continue to be made 'hewers of wood and drawers of water,'" one southern Whig demanded, "by European despotism?"[118]

Other Whigs argued that free trade across international borders was absurd simply because other countries would never cease to impose tariffs on American goods. To lower tariffs at home amounted to unilateral disarmament. America would find itself then in the "situation of two hostile cities, the one strongly walled and defended at every point, the other entirely exposed, and destitute of defence."[119] Here again they accused Democrats of indulging in theoretical abstractions that proved ruinous in practice. "FREE TRADE," declared Congressman Alexander Stuart, "is predicated upon a notion of what men and nations ought to be, instead of what they are! Like the wild conceit of the perfectibility of man, it seizes upon the minds of its votaries, and causes them to lose sight of the existing state of things in the contemplation of some dim visions of futurity."[120] Since states could be counted on to advance their own interests against their economic competitors, "universal" free trade was simply a foolish and self-destructive notion.

At home, though, the situation was different. When it came to "internal commerce," some Whigs used the same laissez-faire language as the Democrats. The "True doctrine of American democracy," Colton insisted, is "DON'T GOVERN US TOO MUCH. Another version of this same sentiment is—*Let the people alone*."[121] In fact, he argued that the Democrats violated their own principles when they sought to regulate the banks and the currency. "No Government ever went into trade, in money or any thing else," he continued, "without injury to the rights of citizens; or with gain to itself, except in the augmentation of its power, which is always its object."[122] Potter, meanwhile, described the law of supply and demand (as applied to the labor market) as one of the "inviolable and resistless laws of nature, which are nothing less than laws of God."[123] In conspiring to limit the supply of labor, he argued, labor unions were violating natural law, and in so doing damaging the whole American economy, themselves included.

Such language was not as common, however, on the Whig side of the political aisle. On the whole, although the Whigs emphasized the harmony of America's social classes, they were less inclined to treat the market itself as a source of such order. They worried, for instance, that market relations were sustained by individual self-interest, which would not always align with morality or justice. "We all know," wrote Greeley, "that the general if not universal rule is to buy cheap, hire cheap, and regard Necessity rather than abstract Justice in business transactions, and I do not suppose that Manufacturing employers are better in this respect than other men."[124] The results were often damaging to the laborer. They saw that people's economic interests often came into conflict, not just with one another but also with the "general welfare of society." "The interests of individuals, and the general interests," wrote the *Southern Literary Messenger*, "so far from always harmonizing, are frequently in direct hostility. Men might derive great profits from some occupations which would be dangerous to the peace, morals or health of the community." "The maxim of *let us alone*," the author continued, ". . . is altogether inapplicable to a law-governed community."[125] It represented an abdication of the duty to legislate for the general good.

Instead, many Whigs treated the harmony of classes as a *political* accomplishment. The fact that classes stood in harmony in America was not caused by nature alone but also by an enlightened constitutional order that promoted opportunity and mobility, and by intelligent laws that harnessed people's self-interest—including, notably, the interest of the rich—to the general good. Economic order was a political creation. In fact, the Whigs saw the state as a principal engine of social, economic, and moral progress. The state created the conditions under which progress in all of these domains could take place; and this required a good deal more than simply protecting citizens' equal rights. "Running through Whig political appeals," writes historian Daniel Walker Howe, "was the concept of consciously arranged order. This was characteristic of their reliance on government planning rather than the invisible forces of the marketplace."[126] Such order was the product not only of wise legislation but also of the prudent managerial influence of wealthy elites, exercised through such institutions as the Bank of the United States.

For many years, the centerpiece of the Whigs' legislative agenda was Henry Clay's "American System," which combined tariff protection for American industry, a national bank to regulate the currency, and federal investment in infrastructure projects around the country to facilitate internal commerce. Reflecting on the sources of American prosperity in 1832 (and comparing it to the recession of the early 1820s), Clay observed that "this transformation of the condition of the country from gloom and distress to brightness and prosperity, has been mainly the work of American legislation," first of all the tariff, which enabled American industry to flourish.[127] Colton argued that American prosperity depended on the "fostering care" that the government extended to "moneyed capital" in particular. It was a fundamental "duty of the Government," he maintained, to encourage and protect investment in the domestic economy—to ensure that capital remained secure and productive. With government's helping hand, capital would be put to work in service of a general prosperity, including higher wages for the working class.[128]

In the wake of the economic panic and contraction of 1837 (which lasted into the 1840s), Whigs directly attacked the Democratic idea that the world was "governed too much." They argued that the federal government had an active role to play in facilitating economic recovery: it had to regulate the currency more effectively; to facilitate credit; to encourage industry; and to invest in roads, bridges, canals, and railroads.[129] "What is this government," demanded Congressman Richard Fletcher, "that spurns the people, and bids them hold their tongues, and not be running to the government with impertinent petitions?"[130] In times of economic distress, the idea of laissez-faire amounted to callous abandonment of the people and a failure to exercise a salutary, directing influence over the economy. Americans should elect "men who will watch over their interests, provide for their wants, regulate their commerce, protect their labor, and carry out those great ends of common defense and general welfare, for which the Constitution was at first created."[131] In the Whig view, Americans needed "the beneficent, protective influences of government, by which alone they can rise, and raise their co-evals with them."[132]

The most incisive statement of this view came from Whig political economist Willard Phillips. To him, the economic doctrine of "*let-us-alone*," with its implication that a natural system of free trade could flourish to everyone's benefit without legislative intervention, was pure nonsense. Government is constantly and inevitably involved, he argued, in the promotion of "useful industry." Everything from defining and securing property rights to building roads and canals, prohibiting child labor, regulating fisheries, coining money, building lighthouses, maintaining public schools, and a great deal more had direct implications for the country's economic productivity. The government could not possibly leave the economy alone, because the economy itself was a political creation. To suppose otherwise was to imagine that the economy itself is "a sort of live mechanism, each living part being adapted and impelled by its nature, to perform its functions in the best possible manner, provided you never mend or regulate it." But this was a piece of utopian fancy as preposterous as anything "the Saint-Simonians, the Fourierites, the Communists, [or] the Amazons" had ever conceived. If the economy was ever to function as a harmonious system uniting the different classes of society, it would be because of prudent legislative design.[133]

Finally, the Whig defense of education also reflected the relationship, in Whig thinking, between personal mobility and public investment. If Whigs commonly saw public education as a corrective to the political irrationality of the mob, they also saw it as a guarantor of social and economic mobility.[134] In reviewing the differences between America and England, Whigs often cited American education as a decisive influence. "The universal diffusion of education," wrote Appleton, "places our mechanics higher in the scale of intelligence than the same class has ever stood in any country. They have the elements of character which enable them to rise to any position in society."[135] In this sense, then, they understood mobility as a *product* of deliberate public intervention in human affairs. By funding an equitable public education for all, the government could prevent the hardening of class boundaries. "Universal education is the great agrarian agent," said Seward, "the leveller we must use to prevent wealth and power from building up aristocratic institutions, and dividing society into unequal classes."[136]

The Whig Millennium

Like Democrats, Whigs overwhelmingly rejected Malthusian pessimism.[137] The corrupt Old World might well be beset by insoluble economic problems, but in America, the arc of history bent upward. For many Whigs, this confidence was deeply inflected with religious faith: although they believed that progress would result from "consciously arranged" economic order, they also believed that it would be guided by the hand of God. They saw God's agency in the benign religious and political restraints that shaped American society, preserved it from anarchy and conflict, and guided it toward a beatific end state. Indeed, the Whig mythology of the self-made man cannot be understood without reference to the evangelical conviction that both individuals and human societies were capable of almost limitless perfection, and that America was the historical site of this transformation and uplift.

The foundation of this optimistic faith lay in shifting theological attitudes. The Second Great Awakening marked the culmination of a half century of escalating assaults on the Calvinist idea of predestination, which had taught that individuals had no control over their own salvation. In its place, evangelicals of many different denominations had begun teaching the Arminian doctrine that Christ had died not just to redeem the elect but for all sinners, and that salvation therefore lay within everyone's reach. With this newfound power came tremendous personal responsibility, which was dramatized over and over in evangelical sermons. The immensely influential Presbyterian evangelist Charles Grandison Finney explained that sin itself was a voluntary condition, a choice to turn away from God. Its renunciation required a change or renovation of the heart, which "consists in changing the controlling preference of the mind in regard to the *end* of pursuit," from self-gratification to God's own glory. This change, he taught, lay entirely within the individual's power. Those who refused did so out of their own "obstinacy," not out of any inexorable or predestined proclivity.[138]

To Finney and many other evangelists, this voluntaristic doctrine suggested that human beings were perfectible: through personal effort, they could cleanse themselves of sin *in this world* and live strictly holy lives. Orthodox Calvinism had taught that human nature was indelibly tainted with sin and that people could hope, at best, only to mitigate its influence through strict discipline. To Finney, such pessimism was simply an excuse for half-hearted moral and spiritual effort.[139] In sermons delivered throughout the country, he and other evangelical preachers offered up spiritual rebirth in Christ as an opportunity for personal uplift and wholesale renewal. And such renewal suggested the realistic possibility of ambitious social transformation. "In philosophical terms," writes historian William McLoughlin, "it meant that if immediate conversion is available by an act of the human will, then, through God's miraculous grace, all things are possible: human nature is open to total renovation in the twinkling of an eye and so, then, is the nature of society."[140]

Touched by this optimistic faith, many exuberant Whigs wrote progress into the very nature of man. They constantly cited the human impulse to "improve his condition," which was naturally and universally felt, and which had both moral and material overtones. Whig congressman Daniel Barnard insisted, for example, that human beings were self-evidently *designed* for constant improvement and perfectibility. Human history itself was a constant demonstration of this great truth: "the sum of wisdom, virtue and happiness in human life . . . for all the great epochs of [man's] time on the earth, will be found to have been greatly on the increase."[141] Barnard fervently expected that America was to be the leading edge of this "moral renovation, reform, and progress" in his time.[142] America's great accomplishment would be to make the perfectibility of the human mind and character—which was in previous epochs reserved for "a few bright names" such as Virgil and Cicero—accessible to all. This, he argued, was to be the highest stage of human civilization, when the whole "race" would be "exalted, made reasonable, and virtuous, and happy."[143]

It is striking to find such affirmations of human progress and perfectibility among inheritors of Calvinist pessimism about human nature, and among a group of Americans who worried constantly about the corruption and irrationality of the democratic electorate. In order to make sense of this peculiar combination, it helps to remember that the intellectual sources of Whig optimism lay as much in millennial Protestantism as in Enlightenment rationalism. Americans had long nurtured a faith in the thousand years of peace and justice—the so-called millennium—prophesied in the book of Revelation and associated with the second coming of Christ.[144] The most widespread version of this faith in nineteenth-century America was *post-millennial*: it held that Christ's return would mark the *end* of the millennium, which would itself be brought about partly through human progress.[145] The coming of the millennium—which many Americans thought imminent—was to be a story of human redemption and transformation from sin to holiness in this world. The most important harbinger of this imminent redemption, for most devout observers, was not affluence or technological improvement but the unprecedented religious revival that swept the country during this period, in which they saw the "glorious and unceasing effusions of the Holy Spirit."[146]

For the post-millennialist faithful in America, the ascending path of progress was more perilous and uncertain than it was for their secular, Enlightenment counterparts who envisioned a steady triumph of science and reason over prejudice and irrationality.[147] American evangelicals tended to believe that human nature was sinful until it was purified by the transformative effects of religious conversion and the "regeneration" it brought.[148] And even then, until the regenerative process was complete, people could lapse back into their sinful ways. Even as they expressed triumphal optimism about the imminent end of history, then, they also worried that Americans might yet stray from the path that God had laid before them. Evangelical preachers often warned, for example, that rampant materialism and love of luxury, as well as the growing influence of Roman Catholicism in America with the influx of Irish and German immigrants, were subverting the moral progress of the nation.[149] Unless Americans did their part by laboring strenuously to resist these and other sources of corruption, they cautioned, the millennium might be "interminably deferred" and the wrath of God unleashed.[150] Sermons were commonly divided between exuberant proclamations of the coming millennium and stark warnings of growing immorality, with graphic images of apocalyptic chaos reminiscent of the book of Revelations.[151]

It is difficult for secular readers today to appreciate the depth and intensity of this millennial hope, fear, and faith. "Far back in the world's rude infancy," wrote the eminently respectable *North American Review*, ". . . there were written predictions of a golden age to come, when the love of God should be the all-pervading principle, when men should learn war no more, when the waste places of humanity should rejoice, and the wilderness blossom." As he wrote these words in the fall of 1846, the author believed that he was witnessing "the faint dawn" of this new era, which was to be the final stage of human history:

"this last stage of progress, this final era of humanity, yet remains," he predicted, "—the era when there shall be recognized no form of greatness apart from moral goodness."[152] To attain this final stage, Americans would still have to make great sacrifices; mainly, they would have to purify their own characters more rigorously than any people in history had yet done.[153] But this widespread purification now seemed, for the first time in the history of any human society, within reach.

The influential Presbyterian revivalist (and committed Whig) Lyman Beecher told of a sweeping and permanent "renovation of the world," which would "bring down the mountains, and exalt the valleys," and "send liberty and equality to all the dwellings of men." The "monopoly of the soil" by kings and nobles, which had for millennia shackled human energies, would be destroyed once and for all. Democracy would spread across the world and elevate humankind both morally and intellectually. And finally, conscience would be set free from centuries of oppression, and people everywhere permitted to "read the Bible, and judge for themselves" what it taught. In this great drama of human redemption, America would of course play the leading role. The recent progress of religious revivals had reassured him that America was indeed to be the "almoner of [God's] mercy to the world"—the great example that other peoples would look to for inspiration.[154] Still, even as he affirmed this confidence in sweeping rhetoric, he gave alarmist reports of the aggressive spread of radicalism and "political atheism" throughout the country, which was instigating the "most fearful paroxysms of infuriated depravity," and he beseeched his audiences to redouble their efforts to resist the temptations of sin and social disorder.[155]

For most American Protestants, the story of human progress and redemption was inseparable from the political and economic fate of the United States. In America, with its unique blend of political freedom and religious devotion, God had laid out a path for human redemption in this world—a path that led away from the decadence and immorality of the Old World and toward a higher state of civilization defined by not only peace and justice but also prosperity, scientific and technological advancement, and ever-increasing freedom.[156] The nineteenth century, writes historian Perry Miller, saw the emergence of "a form of romantic patriotism" in which spiritual and political ideals were deeply interwoven.[157] "With her free government, her extended coasts, her vast commercial connections, her indomitable Anglo-Saxon spirit," crowed Rev. Lucien Berry, America was destined to achieve "the highest point of social perfectability [sic], that can be reached in this world." It would then become "the fountain head of moral and intellectual power—elected to this destiny—to be the great leader and abetter of social progress throughout the world."[158]

The evangelical fervor of the Second Great Awakening, which coursed through American society during the Jacksonian Era, is sometimes imagined as a reaction against modernization and secular rationality. In fact, its post-millennial fervor often made it self-consciously progressive. For Americans across the political spectrum, it was the relentless optimism of this religious revival, combined with the tremendous material and technological progress they were witnessing in the first several decades of the nineteenth century, that allowed them to decisively reject the older, republican view of political history as a recurring cycle of rise and fall. "With the invocation of Providence," writes Howe, "the evangelicals escaped the constraints of [this pessimistic] tradition and opened the way to a vision of unbounded progress for America."[159] America would not follow "the fate of lost republics," said Gardiner Spring, an influential Presbyterian pastor. Instead, it would remain the "habitation of justice and mountain of holiness" indefinitely.[160]

Although evangelicals in both parties embraced this progressive, utopian vision of the American future, the Whig version was especially unusual because of the way it married frank utopianism with political conservatism. Whig evangelicals such as Beecher and Spring argued, in effect, that progress toward the millennium had to be defended against radicals and "disorganizers," with their dangerous dreams of remaking society along speculative, "atheistical" or "agrarian" lines. Spring, for example, issued stern warnings about the political "insubordination" that had become "one of the traits of the American character." He cited, among other disorganizing influences, "the clamour about the rights of man, as paramount to all constitutions and compacts." Such influences were among the leading obstacles, he thought, to the coming of the end of history, the "predicted period of Zion's glory."[161] Whereas the coming of the millennium would, in other parts of the world, require violent and dramatic "overturnings," in America it would not. In America, where the institutional structure was fundamentally just and harmonious, the remaining work of human improvement would involve no political upheaval. It was mainly the work of moral suasion and personal self-improvement, carried out by organized reform societies and revival movements as well as by devout and educated individuals everywhere, and facilitated by the benign and progressive influence of government.[162] Politically, therefore, the function of the clergy was to inspire "obedience to law, respect for magistracy, and the maintenance of civil government" against the "anarchical principles of self-styled reformers."[163]

As explored in chapter 8, the most explosive challenge to this conservative millennialism came from within the ranks of northern evangelicals themselves. Antislavery agitators increasingly saw slavery as a deep moral stain on the nation. By midcentury, many northern evangelicals had come to believe that the millennium could not begin until slavery had been abolished in America. "From the Northern point of view," writes historian Curtis Johnson, "the Antichrist now appeared in the form of the slave-power conspiracy."[164] For them, it was becoming apparent that dramatic political changes would in fact be needed to usher America into the last days. Many southern postmillennialists, on the other hand, imagined that slavery would remain as part of the coming utopia. They imagined their slaves, all converted to Christianity, working happily and voluntarily at their daily tasks.[165]

The Whig ideal of progress or "improvement" always operated across two parallel domains: the national and the personal. The progress of American society would be mirrored by a comparable progress of the individual. But the moral centerpiece of this reciprocal process was the renovation of individual character. All of the outward trappings of civilization—the economic, scientific, technological, and artistic advances—were ultimately means to the improvement and redemption of the individual person. With the progress of human society, writes Carey,

> man passes gradually from a state of slavery to that of perfect freedom, exercising full and uncontrolled power over his own actions and thoughts, over the employment of his time, and over the proceeds of his labour, while abstaining from interference with the exercise of similar rights by his neighbours.[166]

Whigs expected such freedom to reach its apotheosis in America, and as we have seen, they argued that its institutional preconditions were mostly in place. Freedom of conscience, which gave oxygen to the flames of religious revival, enabled each individual to find his own path to God and embrace Him voluntarily. The diffusion of knowledge and education—through common schools, libraries, and the popular press—allowed him to cultivate his mind and character. And America's unique, meritocratic economy enabled him to chart his own course in society. All that remained was for individuals to seize these epochal opportunities, to take command of their own destinies, and to become fully free. This was the teaching of Channing's influential 1838 address, "Self-Culture." "In this country," wrote Channing, "the mass of the people are distinguished by possessing means of improvement, of self-culture," possessed nowhere else in the world. They needed only to be "roused" to the activity of self-cultivation.[167]

What exactly this activity should look like was a matter of enduring controversy. In this chapter, we have been emphasizing its economic dimensions, which were often foregrounded in Whig political rhetoric: the pursuit of wealth and professional success and the virtues that enabled it. These virtues included not only industry and frugality but also a comprehensive ideal of self-discipline embodied in the Victorian culture of politeness and respectability.[168] Whigs believed that such character was a necessary precondition of modern freedom. In a wide-open society increasingly untethered from traditional roles and norms, temptations multiplied just as surely as opportunities. To avoid dissipating their energies and losing themselves to vice and idleness, individuals would need to be more disciplined, more self-directed, than ever. In fact, the 1830s and 1840s saw a profusion of etiquette manuals pertaining to virtually all aspects of social and private life, from bathing and grooming to "the accoutrements and deportment of both domestic and formal dining" and "the proper conduct of shopping, business, and social exchanges."[169] As a rule, these manuals taught the importance of self-control: the mastery of emotions and appetites and the construction of a carefully curated, polite persona. At the same time, they urged Americans to surround themselves with the visible trappings of middle-class respectability, thereby inflaming new desires for consumer goods.[170]

For more devout Whigs, of course, the myth of the self-made man always had a strong spiritual dimension too. As many historians have pointed out, the evangelical call for personal awakening and reform stood in a complicated relationship with the enterprising self-determination of the aspiring capitalist. On the one hand, as historian John Wigger puts it, Arminianism "offered ordinary Americans the opportunity to seize control of their own spiritual destiny in much the same way that many were striving to determine their social and economic destinies."[171] Like the meritocratic economy mythologized by Whig politicians, it offered them the opportunity to become self-made men, architects of their own fortunes. On the other hand, evangelicals routinely taught that the man who elevated the gratification of his appetites to "the supreme end of pursuit" declared nothing less than "enmity against God."[172]

Evangelicals commonly excoriated Americans' preoccupation with luxury and material comfort instead of spiritual regeneration. Although Whigs constantly proclaimed that moral and material advancement went hand in hand, and although they insisted that enlightened self-interest would lead men to subordinate secular gains to spiritual rewards, this unresolved tension continued to unsettle their ideal of the self-made man.

———

Like the other two myths we have explored, the myth of the self-made man has shaped the American political imagination for over two hundred years. Generation after generation have used it to conjure up an image of their country as the land of opportunity where individuals can get ahead through their own effort and virtue and become whoever and whatever they want. As we have seen, this myth is premised on a distinctive idea of personal freedom—freedom as the boundless opportunity for self-creation and self-improvement.

Surveying American society in the 1830s, Alexis de Tocqueville linked this idea of freedom to the economic and geographic mobility that constantly disrupted the ties that bound both generations and social classes together. In America's fluid society, he wrote, "new families are constantly springing up from nothing, while others fall, and those who remain change their appearance." Whereas Europeans learned who they were from family traditions and vocations passed down through the generations, no such continuities existed in America. "The fabric of time," he wrote, "is forever being ripped, and the vestiges of the generations disappear. People easily forget those who went before them and have no idea of those who will come after."[173] Isolated from their past and uncertain of their family's future, Americans also lacked the stable class identity that provided their European counterparts with solidarity and a sense of belonging.[174] In America, he wrote, white men were not born into social identities; they had to invent them.

Tocqueville noted several effects of this social and generational rupture. On the one hand, it opened up wide horizons of possibility and unleashed tremendous energy. Americans tended to believe that they could be whoever and whatever they wanted. Unhampered by inherited identities and blessed by material abundance, they chafed against any and all limitations and constantly strove to get ahead. They were inveterate optimists, he thought, both about their own individual potential and about humanity's potential for improvement and progress: Americans believed in an almost limitless human "perfectibility," and this belief underwrote a restless energy. The American individual, he wrote, was "always searching, falling, picking himself up again, often disappointed, never discouraged," always marching "indefatigably on" toward his goals.[175]

This very breadth of possibility also gave rise, however, to an unmistakable anxiety: Americans were haunted by a persistent worry that they were missing out or making the wrong choices. This worry, he wrote, "fills him with anxieties, fears, and regrets and keeps his soul in a state of constant trepidation that impels him again and again to change plans and places." And so Americans were constantly on the move, settling in one place and then another, trying out one line of work and then another. "In the United States," he wrote, "a man carefully builds a home to live in when he is old and sells it before the roof is laid. He plants a garden and rents it out just as he is about to savor its fruits." This restlessness cast a shadow, Tocqueville thought, over many American lives: although they lived in "the happiest circumstances to be found anywhere in the world," few seemed satisfied with their lot. Like many European observers, Tocqueville was struck by how hard Americans worked, always pursuing some new objective, and how little time they reserved for leisure and contemplation. He also noticed that Americans channeled most of their restless energy into the pursuit of wealth: in an egalitarian society without any other widely recognized marks of success and distinction, material well-being had become the lodestar.[176]

As we have seen, this fascination with worldly success was plainly evident in Whig political rhetoric. When they defended banks, factory production, corporate consolidation, and public investment in infrastructure, Whig politicians and their inheritors in the postwar Republican Party presented them as foundations of economic mobility and personal freedom. They celebrated the restless drive for worldly success as the foundation of human progress and civilization. It is striking that these very Whigs were the ones who first popularized and adopted the term "conservative" in American political discourse.[177] In fact, Whig political thought reveals the paradoxical character of political conservatism in the United States, whose dominant mood has rarely been nostalgic or traditionalist. As historians have often pointed out, American conservatives have typically labored to "conserve" their own distinctive vision of American progress from the reformers who would, in their view, dash it to pieces. More precisely, Americans identifying as conservative have consistently yoked their ideological fortunes to corporate capitalism, the single force that has done more than any other to shatter and displace traditional American ways of life.[178] Under its influence, the traditionalist temperament in America has always flirted with dreams of success and self-creation that stand at odds, in their very nature, with the constraints of time-honored convention. We return to these themes in the next chapter.

No treatment of self-making in Jacksonian America would be complete, finally, without acknowledging its more radical implications. If Whigs deployed the myth of the self-made man for broadly conservative purposes, others imbued it with more subversive meanings. Transcendentalists and abolitionists, for example, repurposed it as a call for civil disobedience. The truest self-made men, they argued, were those who heeded their own conscience and took action against injustice even in the face of ostracism and violence. Former slaves, meanwhile, reappropriated and subverted the myth in their increasingly popular memoirs and autobiographies. Frederick Douglass's 1845 *Narrative* of liberation, for example, detailed his own ingenuity and relentless determination in resisting the dehumanizing effects of chattel slavery. For him and other fugitives, it was the flight from slavery to freedom— and the tremendous courage and resourcefulness it required—more even than the ascent from poverty to wealth, that defined the trajectory of the self-made man. Douglass's *Narrative* remains the single most powerful homage to self-making in American letters.

Meanwhile, feminists used the myth to condemn patriarchal control and insist that women, too, were entitled to direct the course of their own lives. In her pioneering 1845 treatise, *Woman in the Nineteenth Century*, Margaret Fuller detailed the many ways in which women were denied the privilege of self-making. From their mothers and fathers, from their peers and schoolteachers, and from the instructional literature of the age, they imbibed a suffocating and superficial ideal of femininity. They learned to shape themselves to the contours of male desire: to be pretty, compliant, nurturing, agreeable. They learned that "nothing is so much to be dreaded for a woman as originality of thought or character."[179] The American woman, wrote Fuller, perceives from an early age that America's limitless opportunities are not for her but for the men she raises, nurtures, and serves. She therefore learns to "stifle such aspirations [to happiness, to originality] within her secret heart, and fit herself, as well as she can, for a life of resignations and consolations." Meanwhile, those rare women who did—by fortuitous miracle or sheer force of will—reject such constraints and heed their own ambitions, found themselves despised and alienated. There was no place for them.[180]

Even as she condemned the American mythology of self-making for its gendered exclusions, Fuller—like many American feminists after her—moved to reappropriate it and assert its relevance to women. "The world at large," she wrote, "is readier to let Woman learn and manifest the capacities of her nature than it ever was before, and here [in America] is a less encumbered field and freer air than anywhere else."[181] Women too, she insisted, were entitled to direct the course of their own lives and avail themselves of America's expansive opportunities. Anticipating twentieth-century feminist perspectives, Fuller cautioned that women did not simply want access to the *male* dream of success and self-creation, for this too was structured by gendered assumptions. Conceived in contrast to the feminine "sphere," the male idea of freedom was itself limited to certain domains of life, certain virtues, certain modes of feeling and expression. In their flight from effeminacy, men too held a diminished sense of human possibility. Fuller maintained that all human beings contain both "masculine" and "feminine" potentials, and that the highest form of reflective self-creation would develop and interweave both in varying combinations.[182] For men and women alike, she thought, such striving would be political as much as personal, for they would have to confront and overturn the immense weight of patriarchal tradition and the forms of identity it valorized.

In fact, this *critical* idea of self-making, which seeks not mainly success within an inherited framework of norms but reflective struggle against them, had deep roots in Jacksonian America. In 1841, Fuller's mentor and friend Ralph Waldo Emerson published his famous essay "Self-Reliance," which remains one of the iconic celebrations of American individualism.[183] Four years later, Henry David Thoreau withdrew in solitude to Walden pond to reconstruct his life from the ground up. Although neither left much of a mark on the popular political rhetoric of the age, they proved tremendously influential over the long arc of individualist ideas in America. Along with Fuller and Walt Whitman, they inspired generations of countercultural dissidents who rebelled against the conventionalism, materialism, and latent injustice of the American success narrative and moved to replace it with more authentic forms of self-creation. In their various iterations—ascetic and sensual, secular and spiritual—these rebellions have drawn on the Romantic idea that every individual is unique and that fulfillment can be found only by cultivating and expressing this uniqueness in the teeth of society's conformist pressures.[184]

PART IV

Aftermath

10

Industrialization

IN THE SECOND HALF of the nineteenth century, American society was transformed by a rising tide of industrialization, economic consolidation, and vast productivity growth that touched nearly every aspect of life. A new economy driven by coal, steam, and iron and organized by massive firms turned the United States into the world's leading manufacturer. Vibrant modern cities ringed with suburbs grew quickly and drew millions from the country's rural areas. Breakneck technological innovation brought mechanized production to the factory and farm alike, while the transatlantic telegraph and the transcontinental railroad altered Americans' relationship to space and time and seemed to knit the world itself more tightly together. These awe-inspiring changes coincided with a tripling of the U.S. population and the closure of the western frontier, which brought an end to the period of continental expansion that had shaped American consciousness since the earliest colonial settlements.

Industrialization also brought profound social and economic change to white society. At the top of the economic pyramid, it created a class of wealthy barons whose fortunes would have been unimaginable to most Americans in the Jacksonian Era. By 1910, the richest 1 percent of Americans owned almost half of the country's wealth.[1] At the same time, the landless white working class expanded dramatically, its ranks filled in part by millions of European immigrants who crowded into urban slums in search of economic opportunity. Concentrated poverty and illness brought by urbanization contributed to an overall deterioration in the average American height and lifespan.[2] In vast stretches of rural America, meanwhile, farmers suffered the joint effects of two consecutive economic depressions, falling agricultural prices, and escalating personal debt. To those who lost their land and became tenants or sharecroppers, the Jeffersonian dream of independent proprietorship began to seem like a distant mirage.

These transformations precipitated an ideological crisis, for they challenged one of the central tenets of Jacksonian political faith: that a politics centered on individual rights and liberties, structured by free markets and strictly limited government, would coincide with broad social and economic equality for white men.[3] This Jacksonian faith had also been tested by the expansion of federal power during and after the Civil War. Southern secessionism had led many northerners to revise their belief in state sovereignty and embrace a more active central government, which yielded the Homestead Act, the Morrill Land Grant Act, and the Freedman's Bureau. Meanwhile, the Thirteenth, Fourteenth, and Fifteenth Amendments had reshaped the nation's constitutional order: before then, the federal government had very little say in determining or protecting individual rights and freedoms—these were left, by and large, to the states. With these Reconstruction amendments, the federal government became the self-appointed protector of individual rights against state and local governments alike.[4] In doing so, it inserted itself more insistently into the fabric of everyday life. For the first time, writes historian Eric Foner, many Americans came to identify a muscular national state "with the expansion of freedom and human rights."[5]

America's individualistic myths proved resilient in the face of these new challenges, and they shifted and adapted in different ways to meet them. For some, rising economic inequality represented a betrayal of the American promise of equal freedom. The antimonopoly movement that took shape in the later decades of the nineteenth century argued that the concentrated power of railroads and banks enabled them to steal the fruits of farmers' labor and strip them of their cherished independence. They claimed that the spread of regimented factory labor, with little hope of upward mobility, was creating an unfree class of white "wage slaves" who existed to produce wealth and luxury for the rich. Meanwhile, activists pressing for greater racial and gender equality continued to harness the individualistic myths to condemn white male supremacy as a form of unmerited caste privilege. More than their predecessors in the Jacksonian Era, these reformers called for federal intervention in the economy and society, including new forms of regulation and taxation, antitrust enforcement, and ambitious federal reconstruction of the South after the Civil War.

In the Gilded Age, however, these egalitarian perspectives struggled against the prevailing ideological currents. In both parties, elites were busy reinterpreting the three foundational myths to accommodate greater disparities in income and wealth, to buttress racial and gender hierarchies, and to present

egalitarian movements as dangerous, un-American encroachments on the prerogatives of the free individual. These changes unfolded in several different
ways. Editors and politicians moved, for example, to replace personal independence with freedom of contract as the foundation of economic liberty. They
invoked property rights as shields against public regulation, union activism,
and movements for racial justice. Drawing on Whig ideas, they substituted,
for the promise of a broad economic parity, the tantalizing prospect of upward
mobility in an increasingly stratified economy. These arguments were unified
by the powerful conviction, nurtured in the antebellum period and reaffirmed
after the war, that the deliberate redistribution of wealth was a violation of
American liberty and a brazen assault on the order of nature itself.

These justifications of growing inequality were reinforced by racial animus
and by the political legacy of slavery. The most ambitious projections of federal
power during and after the Civil War had involved the emancipation of Black
slaves and the subsequent enfranchisement of freedmen. In the South and
North alike, many whites recoiled from these disruptions of racial hierarchy
and used the rhetoric of small government and individual rights to shield
white supremacy from further interference. Meanwhile, widespread racism
and intense sectional antagonisms born of war and deliberately stoked by economic elites made the possibility of an inclusive working-class coalition remote.[6] In a political landscape defined by sectional grievance, politicians could
win working-class support without making credible commitments to egalitarian reform.[7] The push to reassert and broaden the economic egalitarianism of
the Jacksonian Democrats was fractured and often relegated to the political
margins.

The Erosion of Independence

The disintegration of the Whig Party in the early 1850s had ushered in a period
of chaotic realignment. Increasingly acrimonious standoffs over the future of
American slavery, which had come to dominate national politics after the
Mexican-American War (1846–48), had finally made it impossible for northern and southern Whigs to find common ground. Many northern Democrats,
meanwhile, had come to see their party as a southern-dominated, proslavery
institution, and they too went looking for another political home. When the
Republican Party consolidated in the 1850s, it was largely a northern coalition
unified by its opposition to slavery's expansion. As they tried to bind together
former Whigs and former Democrats, along with sundry other northern

activists and reformers, Republicans had turned to the ideal of *free labor* as the centerpiece of their political ideology.

In the broadest sense, free labor stood for a society without slavery—a society in which work was dignified and uncoerced, and in which workers owned the fruits of their own labor. It conjured visions of prosperity and progress, driven by the hard work and discipline of so many autonomous individuals. It served as a rallying cry against the expansion of slave society, which in the northern mind stood for coercion rather than freedom, idleness rather than discipline, and widespread poverty and blight rather than progressive "civilization." Because it was designed to unify men of various political persuasions, free labor remained a broad and amorphous ideal. It encompassed both the independent proprietor and the wage earner, both the small producer and the aspiring capitalist. Its advocates borrowed widely from all three foundational myths. For many northerners—including many Republicans—free labor was also deeply entangled with white supremacy: the free laborer was imagined as a white man, and "free labor civilization" as a civilization purged not just of slaves but of free Blacks, Native Americans, and Chinese immigrants.[8]

These latent tensions, which were temporarily suppressed by the Civil War, resurfaced sharply in the ensuing decades, and the myth of the independent proprietor emerged as one of the flashpoints in these controversies. With the advent of industrialization, many workers felt that the American promise of independence—and with it the prospect of meaningful economic freedom— had slipped from their grasp. This deep current of discontent coursed through the broad antimonopoly upheavals of the late nineteenth century. The Knights of Labor, for example, which became the largest and most powerful labor organization in America in the 1880s, still harnessed the myth of the independent proprietor to condemn the new industrial order. Wage labor, they argued, reduced working men to a condition of abject dependence on the will of their bosses. It inspired "sycophancy" and "servility," and effectively stripped working men of their freedom.[9] Meanwhile, rural Populists argued that the merchants who profited from the crop-lien system, the railroads that charged exorbitant fees to transport agricultural goods, and the banks that extracted high rates of interest and pursued deflationary monetary policies were using special political privileges to squeeze small farmers and destroy their independence.[10] Both struggled to imagine conditions under which the small producer's independence might be maintained in the face of changing economic conditions.

The myth of the independent proprietor was also invoked by freedmen who fought to restructure the southern economy in ways that would grant them meaningful autonomy. As they tried to free themselves from white supervision and control, many freedmen staked their hopes to the promise of "forty acres and a mule" and the dream of smallholder independence. Without access to land, they argued, free Blacks would remain but slaves by another name, working for a pittance at the beck of their former masters. Real freedom meant controlling the conditions of their own work, and this in turn meant owning their own small plot of land. Meanwhile, white plantation owners understood that thwarting this ambition was the key to retaining control over the southern labor force. They were joined by northern investors eager to restore the productivity and commercial value of southern lands, who promoted an alternative view of personal liberty centered on freedom of contract: Black laborers were free, they insisted, so long as they could bargain and compete for wages without formal impediment.[11]

Many Republicans agreed: as they oversaw America's transformation into an industrial powerhouse, they came to see the ideal of the independent proprietor as a relic of a bygone era.[12] Like the Whigs before them, they argued that America's future belonged less to the independent yeoman than to the self-made man. Or they tried to refashion the myth of independence from within to make it more compatible with the emerging industrial economy. As more and more Americans worked for wages, some began to insist that even long-term wage work was compatible with personal independence, as long as workers could sell their labor without interference and earn a decent wage.[13] This revisionism was already emerging in the antebellum Republican Party as its defenders answered the southern charge that northern wage labor was white slavery under another name. "You say he is a slave because he is poor, because he is obliged to labor," said New Hampshire senator Daniel Clark of the northern wage worker in 1858. "Yes, sir; but he can labor where he pleases, where he can find work, and when he pleases; and he can buy what food he pleases, what clothing he pleases; and is, in every sense, a freeman." In Clark's view, such workers had all they needed to lay claim to the proud mantle of independence.[14]

Among the postwar revisionists were influential defenders of laissez-faire for whom freedom of contract alone seemed sufficient proof of personal independence.[15] By 1883, for example, the Social Darwinist William Graham Sumner could affirm that "a society based on contract is a society of free and independent men, who form ties without favor or obligation, and cooperate without cringing or intrigue."[16] In his eyes, all workers were independent— even those without property or skill—as long as they were free to make labor contracts without undue interference from government. Following this logic, the Pennsylvania Supreme Court in 1886 struck down a law prohibiting businesses from paying their employees in "scrip" that could be redeemed only at company stores. The court ruled that the law prevented "persons who are *sui juris* from making their own contracts." From the Court's perspective, the law seemed "an insulting attempt to put the laborer under legislative tutelage, which is not only degrading to his manhood, but subversive to his rights as a citizen."[17] The real danger here, in other words, was that the law threatened to make the American worker a ward of the state, dependent on its sheltering embrace.

In some ways, this logic represents an extension of the reasoning of Jacksonian Democrats. For them, as we have seen, government was always the focal threat to liberty, the main source of domination and dependence. The Democratic posture of defensive vigilance was often directed at government and its power to elevate some people, through special privileges, over others. As we saw in chapter 7, this mistrust of government was strengthened by the rising conviction that market relations were *natural* and therefore free, whereas government interference was coercive and "artificial." Still, even as they railed against government interference in the economy, Jacksonian Democrats were acutely aware of the reality and danger of economic power: the power of banks over creditors and over everyone who used paper currency; the power of industrial employers over their increasingly dependent workforces; the power of speculators over the very integrity of the nation's economy. These forms of power may have originated in legislative privilege, but they were exercised in and through everyday economic transactions.

More fundamentally, then, the laissez-faire redefinition of independence amounted to a rejection of one of the egalitarian legacies of Jacksonian political thought. The Jacksonian ideal of economic independence celebrated the individual's control—his *dominion*—over his own work life and ownership of the resources necessary to sustain it. Unless it was a temporary means to independence, wage labor itself seemed to them a form of subservience: laborers worked in someone else's shop or factory, on someone else's terms, and typically at someone else's discretion. Unusually skilled or educated workers might enjoy substantial bargaining leverage over the terms of their employment, but most had very little. They may not have been forced, by law, into subjection, but what they *experienced*, as workingmen's advocates throughout the nineteenth century tirelessly pointed out, felt to them like a form of slavery.[18] To describe such workers as independent merely in virtue of their capacity to sell or withhold their labor voluntarily was to eviscerate the ethical content of the Jacksonian Democratic ideal.

Some liberal Republicans in the early postwar period recognized this evisceration for what it was. None other than E. L. Godkin, who would become a leading defender of laissez-faire and a scathing critic of union organizing, argued in 1867 that the wage earner's freedom of contract was but a pale shadow of the "moral and social independence" to which American workers had long felt entitled. "What I agree to do in order to escape from starvation," wrote Godkin, "or to save my wife and children from starvation, or ignorance of my ability to do anything else, I agree to do under compulsion, just as much as if I agreed to do it with a pistol at my head." In reality, impoverished wage workers were deeply dependent on their employers: they were "legally free while socially bound."[19] Day after day, they sold their labor out of desperation, and workdays of twelve or more hours left them precious little time for anything else. Nowhere was this bondage more acute than in the South, where freedmen were not only denied the opportunity to acquire their own land but found themselves working as hired laborers under the thumb of their former plantation masters, who had risen, phoenix-like, from the ashes of war and refashioned themselves as capitalist employers.

By the 1890s and into the Progressive Era, the erosion of personal independence was widely seen as a national crisis, and reformers strove either to restore it or to find some modern facsimile. For many Progressives, the answer lay in empowering workers to have a say in the management of economic affairs, through empowered unions or other forms of economic democracy. For others, the answer lay instead in the promise of economic security and a living wage. Still others emphasized the broader material rewards of rising prosperity and the expanding personal choices available in a modern consumer society.[20] These latter perspectives, too, represented a substantial retreat from the expansive ideal of personal autonomy embedded in the dream of independence. This retreat is reflected, for example, in the hopes of Progressive economist John Bates Clark: "By processes that others control," he argued, "and by wealth that others own, the laborer will get, in the end, the most valuable personal gains."[21] This perspective, which is entirely heedless of the distribution of *power* in society and its vast implications for personal freedom, is typical of academic economists to this day; through them, it has profoundly influenced American policymaking, from the Progressive Era to the present.

On the other hand, one of the dark legacies of Jacksonian independence continued unabated in the Gilded Age: the ideal and the myth were still routinely invoked to justify both the coercive assimilation and the forced expulsion of

Native Americans. As the country continued its headlong expansion to the Pacific coast, it encroached constantly on tribal lands. The federal government subsidized and encouraged this expansion at every turn, and in doing so it officially embraced a program of assimilation and Christianization focused on converting Native American men into virtuous yeomen who owned their own farms and adopted "civilized," Americanized lifestyles. In fact, these policies served the interests of white Americans: they contracted the size of Native American holdings and made it easier for whites to buy them. The Dawes Act of 1887, which parceled out Native American lands into private holdings, resulted in the seizure of tens of millions of acres for white settlers and corporations.[22] Meanwhile, throughout the prior two decades, Native Americans who still lived on their ancestral homelands and refused to conform to the ideal of the property-owning farmer—those who continued to hold land communally, for example—were condemned as "savages" and marked for removal and dispossession. They were forced from their homes at gunpoint, herded into boxcars, and taken to distant reservations, where they were assigned to harsh territories that no one else wanted.[23]

Native Americans found diverse ways of resisting these settler-colonialist incursions. Some tribes, famously, fought daring battles against the superior technologies of the U.S. military and waged guerilla warfare against the encroaching white population. Some hindered federal policymakers by peacefully refusing, en masse, to register as citizens and accept their allotments of private land.[24] Native American leaders and activists drafted pamphlets, manifestos, and petitions, sent lobbyists to Washington, and filed lawsuits defending their people's territorial rights and indicting white expansionism as a violation of U.S. treaty obligations. Others resorted to less confrontational strategies: taking advantage of weak and intermittent enforcement, for example, the Ho-Chunks of Wisconsin and Minnesota routinely left reservations after the U.S. military had withdrawn and returned to their ancestral homes. They also bought small plots of land there and used them to present themselves as "civilized" small proprietors even as they held onto their tribal identity and culture. These strategies sometimes met with limited success: in Wisconsin, for example, hundreds were able to secure exemptions from forced expulsion.[25]

Many whites, meanwhile, denounced such exceptions as perversions of the law: invoking a racialized image of the small proprietor and rejecting the official policy of assimilation, they argued that the virtues born of land ownership and citizenship were confined to whites alone, and they pressed for a more aggressive expulsion and confinement—if not outright "extermination"—of native peoples. Thus did the myth of the independent proprietor remain central to a settler-colonial project that continued to define the United States throughout the nineteenth century.[26]

Equal Rights and Laissez-Faire

Like the myth of the independent proprietor, the myth of the rights-bearer was appropriated for many different purposes between the Civil War and the end of the century. After the war, women and African Americans continued to invoke the Lockean idea of natural rights to press for egalitarian reform. The Fourteenth and Fifteenth Amendments strengthened their hands: the Fourteenth Amendment guaranteed citizenship to all *persons* born or naturalized in the United States; it also asserted that no state shall "deprive any person of life, liberty, or property, without due process of law," nor deny to "any person within its jurisdiction the equal protection of the laws." The Fifteenth Amendment extended the vote to all men, regardless of "race, color, or previous condition of servitude." For the first time, federal law declared unambiguously that the American rights-bearer was not strictly a white man. Birthright citizenship alone, writes Foner, "represented a dramatic repudiation of the powerful tradition of equating citizenship with whiteness."[27]

Of course, these abstract declarations, issued by a distant federal authority, did not make equal rights a reality, for the federal government lacked the capacity—and in many cases the willingness—to enforce them. In practice, legal judgments remained in the hands of local officials, who exercised broad discretion and typically used the law to reinforce existing social hierarchies.[28] Activists understood this and labored to make rights real. The key challenge, wrote the Black-owned *New Orleans Tribune* in 1867, was simply "the extension of equal rights and privileges to all men, irrespective of color and race." The "mere declaration" of these rights was insufficient; the real work lay in bringing them "into effect," to make them something more than "glittering generalit[ies]."[29] Across the South, freedmen worked to achieve this by throwing themselves into electoral politics, winning political power, and pressing legislative changes that would strengthen the rule of law, expand their access to public services, and outlaw discrimination.[30] Meanwhile African Americans in the North formed equal rights leagues to combat public and private discrimination and assert their rights to testify in court, to send their children to public schools, to ride public transit, and to frequent restaurants and hotels. Over and over, they demanded that whites honor and live up to the spirit of their own constitutions, declarations, and national myths.[31]

Meanwhile, advocates for "equality of the sexes," like the abolitionists before them, worked continually to universalize the natural rights of the Declaration of Independence.[32] "The declaration that 'All men [which means all human beings irrespective of sex] have an equal right to life, liberty, and the pursuit of happiness,' is enough for woman as for man," wrote suffragist Ernestine Rose in a letter to Susan B. Anthony. She asked only that Americans "carry that declaration to its logical consistency" and extend it fully to women.[33] In its 1876 Declaration of Rights, the National Woman Suffrage Association proclaimed that women were as yet a subordinate caste, subject to an "aristocracy of sex" that exposed women to despotic male power. Its authors demanded "our full equality with man in natural rights." "Woman was made first for her own happiness," the Declaration continued, "with the absolute right to herself—to all the opportunities and advantages life affords, for her complete development."[34] Demanding equal rights for women of color in 1867, Sojourner Truth reasoned from a different premise: "if I have to answer for the deeds done in my body just as much as a man," she argued, "I have a right to have just as much as a man."[35]

As these last two quotations suggest, the idea of equal rights could have expansive implications. Calling for "equal rights" for women, the former abolitionist Alonzo Grover included "rights of person, rights of labor, rights of property, rights of culture, rights of leisure, rights to participate in the making and administering of the laws."[36] Part of the radicalism of rights-talk lay precisely in this slipperiness: talk of equal rights could easily shade from "natural rights"—which were themselves indeterminate and often broadly construed—to civil rights, to social and political rights. In fact, the abolitionists themselves had often used the idea of equal rights to express an ambitious vision of human flourishing centered on what we might call *effective* freedom (as opposed to merely formal freedom).[37] Drawing on the tenets of natural religion, abolitionists had argued that God evidently intended human beings to be happy. To this end, he had endowed them with a range of capacities whose unfolding and cultivation would bring them pleasure and fulfillment. These included not just moral agency and meaningful autonomy but also the capacity for knowledge and understanding, for productive work, for friendship and love. Natural rights, they argued, corresponded to these fundamental capabilities that God had implanted in human nature; rights were "the scythe," writes legal historian

Elizabeth Clark, "that cleared the path for the individual . . . to grow and develop."[38]

This more expansive view of rights found expression, for example, in Black activists' denunciations of racial prejudice, both before and after emancipation. Black abolitionists had spoken constantly of its oppressive effects on the mind and spirit. In barring free Blacks from colleges, seminaries, trade schools, and skilled professions, wrote Rev. Hosea Easton, prejudice had the effect of "withering every incentive to improvement—rendering passive all the faculties of the intellect—subjecting the soul to a morbid state of insensibility." It denied free Blacks the power to shape their lives as they saw fit, to unfold their abilities, to formulate and pursue meaningful goals. It thus conspired to "wreck . . . the best work of nature's God."[39] Black leaders often presented such prejudice—whether it was expressed informally or encoded in law—as an affront to equal rights. More than just guarantees of immunity against interference, then, rights could also connote *inclusion* on equal terms in social life and access to its economic and political opportunities. During and after the Civil War, for example, egalitarian activists linked the idea of equal rights to public provision of resources and opportunities. They argued that equal access to public education was owed to Black children as a matter of right, to give them "a fair chance to develop their faculties and powers."[40] Arguing that they possessed a right to the fruits of their labor, some freedmen also claimed a right to some portion of their former masters' estates.[41]

For both women and Black men, voting rights were absolutely central to these struggles. Women's suffrage activists presented their demands as a matter of extending *political* rights equally and giving women "free avenue to a complete development of all [their] powers."[42] They also consistently linked suffrage to a broader slate of natural or human rights: the 1877 annual convention of the National Woman Suffrage Association observed that because women were disenfranchised, "one-half of the citizens of the republic . . . are everywhere subjects of legislative caprice, and may anywhere be robbed of their most sacred rights."[43] Its members therefore called for a Sixteenth Amendment to the Constitution guaranteeing women equal suffrage. Elizabeth Cady Stanton concurred: voting rights, she insisted, were "the only sure protection for our rights of person and property."[44] Both demanded that women be recognized as rights-bearers who stood on equal terms with men; both also argued that no one could be a full-fledged rights-bearer without the vote, for without it their basic human rights stood at the mercy of others. Like other suffrage activists, they presented universal suffrage as the full realization of the American ideal of freedom enshrined in its founding documents; in this sense, they laid claim self-consciously to the foundational myth of the rights-bearer.[45]

For the most part, these efforts to expand the ambit of equal rights in the Gilded Age ended in failure. The collapse of Reconstruction and the rise of Jim Crow, combined with the Supreme Court's full retreat from the egalitarian implications of the Reconstruction amendments, meant the wholesale destruction of the rights of African Americans in the South. Women won greater control over their property and income, but they achieved neither national suffrage nor the equality in marriage that many reformers sought. Meanwhile, in the broader economic debates that headlined Gilded Age politics, the myth of the rights-bearer was used to justify inequality: it was repurposed to defend an increasingly corporate economy marked by vast disparities of wealth, and it was merged with the myth of the self-made man, expressed in the rags-to-respectability narratives of Horatio Alger and the ubiquitous Darwinian language of competition and struggle.[46] This ideological realignment was driven largely by industrial elites and their allies in the media, the judiciary, and in American universities, who drew increasingly on the free-market ideal—and the rights of property and contract embedded in it—as a weapon against government regulation. It was buttressed by repeated warnings that America was being infected by dangerous currents of European radicalism that threatened to vitiate its exceptional freedoms.

By the late nineteenth century, a host of political groups—from agrarian Populists to trade unionists to socialists—had begun looking to the state to help them combat rising inequality and contain the collateral damages of industrialization. The idea that the state should not interfere with economic affairs lest it disrupt their benign natural order served the purposes of corporate leaders trying to stave off these challenges.[47] "Non-interference," wrote Progressive intellectual Charles Merriam, "became the slogan of many interests obviously anxious to avoid governmental regulations," including "railroads threatened with regulation, corporations held in check by public measures, [and] certain industries resisting sanitary and social regulation."[48] And so the free-market ideal, which in Jacksonian America was deployed in large part to defend small producers against the policy agendas of modernizing elites, was reinvented as a shield for America's leading corporations and the "captains of industry" at their heads.[49] It was their rights of property and contract, now, that were asserted with special vigor.

The very idea of government "interference" in the economy, of course, supposes that there exists a separate economic domain that can be cleanly separated from politics and shielded from unwelcome political intrusions. In post–Civil War America, the language of nature continued to facilitate this distinction: the economy was natural, government regulation artificial. Liberal intellectuals such as Godkin, Clark, Horace White, and David Ames Wells defended the "natural" economic laws against legislative interference.[50] Arthur Latham Perry, whose *Elements of Political Economy* was the most popular American-authored textbook in the field, declared that "the laws of exchange are based on nothing less solid than the will of God." "It is a high-handed infringement of natural rights," he continued, "a blow aimed at the life and source of property, when any authority whatever interferes to restrict or prohibit the freedom of exchange."[51] Perry's view was deeply entrenched in American universities, where wealthy donors oversaw the content of the academic curriculum.[52] Businessmen and their spokesmen, meanwhile, commonly invoked the beneficent order of natural economic laws, which would work their magic "if human legislators would only let them alone!"[53]

The idea of a natural, competitive economic order drew further support from Social Darwinism, a philosophy that was widely popularized in the United States. William Graham Sumner, its leading American exponent, marshaled the authority of nature in defense of a stern doctrine of economic laissez-faire: "The truth is," he insisted, "that the social order is fixed by laws of nature precisely analogous to those of the physical order." These laws had ordained a harsh, competitive social world; socialism was therefore as futile and quixotic as "a plan for changing the physical order" of the world.[54] Steel magnate Andrew Carnegie was among Sumner's devotees. The "law of competition," he wrote, however harsh it might seem, was "essential for the future progress of the race," for it guaranteed the "survival of the fittest."[55] In fact, Social Darwinism was the perfect vehicle for marrying the Whig ideal of freedom as mobility with the Jacksonian standard of natural economic order: the "fit" would rise to positions of leadership, power, and wealth in this new natural order, which promised unbounded opportunity for the talented and industrious. The Darwinian revolution had introduced a harsher, more hierarchical idea of nature to rival the more benign and harmonious Newtonian idea invoked by the Jacksonian Democrats.[56]

It is highly significant that these ideas of natural economic order, drawn in varying combinations from liberal political economy and popularized Darwinian biology, were not confined to the academic and business elites: instead, they circulated widely among American readers and worshippers in the Gilded Age. A phalanx of journalists and editors promoted them enthusiastically, and success manuals and popular economic treatises sung the praises of unhampered competition in language drawn partly from Social Darwinist texts.[57] "Competition in economics," wrote Richard R. Bowker in his popular *Economics for the People*, "is the same as the law of the 'survival of the fittest,' or 'natural selection,' in nature. It is the natural order of affairs by which each man is required to work at his best, and under which each man works to his best advantage." He urged that American society be brought "more into line with natural law," which would deliver freedom and prosperity for future generations.[58] In many optimistic popularizations, however, *fitness* was not mainly a natural or inborn quality but rather the fruit of assiduous effort and discipline; it was therefore accessible, in principle, to everyone.[59]

At the same time, many Protestant churches embraced laissez-faire ideology. Prominent ministers continued to identify economic laws with the providential order and to preach a gospel of individual discipline, virtue, and hard work in the face of economic hardship even as they excoriated unions as "conspiracies against the laws of God." Workers who sought to limit competition from non-union labor, in particular, were attacked for violating the "fundamental rights of man—the right to labor and to support himself by labor."[60] Sumner was himself an ordained Episcopalian priest, and his teachings were warmly received by a mainstream Protestant press eager for a new, scientific foundation for its free-market orthodoxies.[61] In these ways, the fundamental Jacksonian narrative of a pristine natural order under assault from unnatural government was deepened and preserved, even as its content was adjusted to fit new economic circumstances. Nowhere else in the world were these ideas so deeply ensconced in popular culture.

Of course, the elites who profited most from the ideology of natural competition rarely applied it consistently. While Sumner and other economists followed their Jacksonian predecessors in denouncing protective tariffs, for example, as another instance of government meddling with natural law, the industrial elites who appropriated their ideas did not. American protectionists argued that international trade was an exception to the norms of laissez-faire; like the Whigs had before the Civil War, they suggested that free-trade ideology was a tool of British imperialism designed to keep America "dependent on British markets and cheap wages."[62] State support was needed, they insisted, to shore up American industry. Behind closed doors, industrial elites also sought other exceptions: they lobbied for vast grants of free land and guaranteed bonds to subsidize railroad development; they resisted anti-trust enforcement while successfully demanding state-sponsored violence against organized labor.[63] All the while, they celebrated individual competition and free enterprise and issued dire warnings about the increasing meddling of government in economic affairs. What they wanted, in short, was government support and subsidy for their own economic interests and none for the farmers and factory workers who mobilized against them.[64] To normalize this asymmetry, moreover, they sought either to conceal the extent of their own government aid or to redescribe it as natural. So while corporations were assimilated to the category of "natural persons," and endowed with constitutional rights, unions were routinely castigated as "unnatural" combinations, their strikes treated as criminal offenses, their leaders imprisoned.[65]

These oligarchic tendencies were further reinforced by the ascendant language of contract, which penetrated the myth of the rights-bearer just as it did the myth of the independent proprietor. As we explored in chapters 6 and 7, Jacksonian Democrats had asserted producers' rights to the fruits of their labor, which they had linked to an idealized vision of the free and natural market. At the same time, they had often denounced wage labor as a form of subordination incompatible with personal autonomy. In so doing, they had denied that freedom of contract alone was enough to secure labor's fruits.[66] This view had unsettling implications, however, in a society in which more and more of the labor force worked for wages, in which labor unrest was growing palpably, and in which millions of newly freed, restive Black workers were dreaming of independence and social equality. Postwar Republicans—including many former abolitionists—therefore moved to reposition freedom of contract as the centerpiece of economic freedom and indeed of the individual's economic *rights*.[67] For them, the worker's "right to sell his labor" without interference, along with the employer's property right in his own business, became the defining economic entitlements of the rights-bearing individual.[68] In this view, the freely contracting wage worker, guided by the beneficent laws of the natural, competitive economy, was the paragon of personal freedom.[69]

Over the course of the Gilded Age, these laissez-faire ideas were subject to a rising chorus of challenges. Critics of various backgrounds and persuasions argued that industrial transformation called for a renewed emphasis on the common good, on social solidarity, on collective organization. Protestant theologians and evangelists preaching the social gospel argued that biblical ideals of human equality and mutuality demanded ambitious egalitarian reforms. Populist reformers asserted the need for democratic control of the economy as they called for vast expansions of federal power over railroads and banks and for farmers' cooperatives to restore dignity and independence to American yeomen. Labor unions challenged free-market orthodoxies and staged dramatic actions to press for shorter workdays, safer workplaces, and higher wages. Popular books such as Henry George's *Progress and Poverty* and Edward Bellamy's *Looking Backward* called for dramatic redistributions of wealth.

A close look at many of these critical perspectives, however, reveals how powerfully they too were drawn by the gravitational pull of America's individualist myths. Henry George is a case in point. First published in 1879, *Progress and Poverty* was one of the most widely read books in the second half of the nineteenth century and a touchstone for countless reformers.[70] At its core lies a Lockean account of property rights: all legitimate property, George argued, came from a single source: "the natural right of the man to himself," which conferred on every individual a right "to the enjoyment of the fruits of his own exertions."[71] George's radicalism lay in his claim that *land*, since it was not itself the fruit of anyone's labor (except God's), could not legitimately be owned. In fact, he argued that the individual's right to the fruits of his labor was meaningless without common access to the land: as long as American producers were compelled to work as laborers on another's land and pay escalating rents, the proceeds of their labor would be siphoned away by an unproductive rentier class. Land ownership itself was the "monopoly" he denounced.

George's vision of common ownership was grounded partly in the romance of the American West. For most of American history, he wrote, Americans were conscious of the immense "public domain" of western lands that they could access cheaply. "This public domain," he insisted, "has been the transmuting force which has turned the thriftless, unambitious European peasant into the self-reliant Western farmer." He linked the economic crisis of the Gilded Age to the closing of the frontier and the rising value of land, which drove up rents and enriched the land-owning class at everyone else's expense. America would soon come to resemble Europe, George warned, where white men were born into a world already owned by others and found "all the best seats at the banquet of life marked 'taken.'"[72] His solution—a "single tax" on land, which would turn it into a shared national resource—aimed to re-create an exceptional America founded on "equal rights" and natural law, a thriving, market society in which "the riches of any individual" arose strictly from their own labor. It was his attempt to eliminate, once and for all, the parasitic aristocracy that had haunted the Jacksonian imagination.[73]

Agrarian Populists, too, drew constantly on the rhetorical tropes of Jacksonian social criticism. Speaking on behalf of "the yeomanry of the country, the small landed proprietors," they argued that America's humble producing classes were being victimized by unproductive elites who siphoned away the fruits of their labor.[74] They condemned bankers, financiers, and speculators for distorting markets and wielding corrupt political influence for their own personal gain, and they demanded equal rights for small producers. They lamented the erosion of personal independence and the rise of widespread tenancy, and denounced monopolistic corporations as "artificial creations, controlling almost boundless wealth, whose influence is vast enough to shape the laws of the government which created them."[75] They were for small property ownership, thriving commodity markets undistorted by special privileges, orderly progress and widely shared prosperity driven by the autonomous effort and discipline of so many small farmers.[76] Like the Jacksonian Democrats before them, many white Populists joined these ideas with a virulent strain of white supremacy that treated people of color—including Chinese laborers, whose presence provoked a rising hysteria in western states—as a degraded and dependent underclass incapable of personal autonomy.[77] On the other hand, a minority of white Populists pressed for a racially integrated alliance of small farmers, and an independent Black Populist movement married its agrarian agenda to a broader fight against racial discrimination and violence.[78]

As we saw in chapter 7, Jacksonian Democrats had called for government intervention to disrupt "monopolies," which for them was a very broad category. To this end, they had demanded that the government destroy the Bank of the United States, prevent speculators from buying up vast tracts of land, and stabilize the currency against wealthy manipulators. The controversies over money and banks had led some Democrats to call for public banking, and it had led to the creation of an independent treasury under Martin Van Buren. As they confronted far greater threats to their way of life, late nineteenth-century Populists broadened this call for antimonopolistic action in ways Jacksonian Democrats would never have accepted: they called for the nationalization of railroads and banking, along with an eight-hour workday and a graduated income tax. But many continued to believe that federal action would serve a *defensive* function: it was designed to curtail the corrupt privileges of bankers and railroad magnates and restore the natural link between productive labor and economic success.[79] Their political rhetoric also remained mostly hostile to what Populists perceived as "socialistic schemes" and "vicious class legislation."[80] Populism was a broad ideological umbrella, but it bore the unmistakable imprint of egalitarian producerism, centered on the property rights of the small farmer and expressed in the mythologized language of the rights-bearer. Were all monopolies destroyed, and equal rights vindicated for small producers, wrote Populist firebrand James "Cyclone" Davis in 1894, "then the man who produced the most would be the most prosperous, and each individual would have to depend on his own industry or energy to make or secure his comforts and blessings."[81]

The fate of the Populist movement illustrates two very significant facts about the course of economic egalitarianism in the United States. First, across the entire nineteenth century—from Jefferson through William Jennings Bryan—its leading exponents tended to present themselves as spokesmen for small farmers. As such, they embraced individualistic narratives centered on ownership, independence, and access to markets. They also mistrusted socialist ideas that reflected the consciousness, above all, of the propertyless, urban working classes of Europe.[82] Second—and tragically—economic egalitarians in the United States have consistently found themselves allied to a political party that also stood for southern white supremacy. From the antebellum period onward, slavery and the sectional antagonisms that arose from it created a broad southern constituency that stood opposed to northern, state-driven capitalism. As they fought to win elections, economic egalitarians continually forged alliances with this constituency, which tended to wield individualistic ideas to protect racial hierarchy from federal intrusion.[83] The Populist "fusion" with the Democratic Party in 1896 epitomized this link, which would later distort New Deal policies (as Franklin Roosevelt courted the votes of southern senators) and thwart the achievement of egalitarian reform through the end of the twentieth century and into the twenty-first.[84]

Self-Made Men

If the myth of the independent proprietor began to fade in the Gilded Age, the myth of the self-made man grew more prominent. It suffused not only the political rhetoric of the period but also its popular literature and its success and etiquette manuals. It resonated not only with a new capitalist elite eager to justify its wealth and influence but also with the middle and working classes in America's growing towns and cities searching for a sense of control over their own lives and a way of making sense of the dizzying changes unfolding around them. As it had in the Jacksonian Era, the myth of the self-made man appealed to the American electorate by channeling both a widely felt conservative impulse and a deep vein of utopian religious hope.

In the Gilded Age, as in the Jacksonian Era, the myth of the self-made man served to justify growing economic inequality. It reassured Americans that the new, corporate millionaires of the Gilded Age were not privileged aristocrats in the European style; they were plain men who had risen to wealth and power through tireless effort, perseverance, and old-fashioned ingenuity. What they had achieved was none other than the American dream of success, which lay open to anyone willing to work hard enough to seize it. Their vast wealth, moreover, would soon dissipate after their death, for their pampered sons were unlikely to acquire the grit and determination of their fathers. According to the myth, self-made men flashed across the American firmament with Promethean energy and then disappeared into the night—"as bright meteors vanish from the blue overhanging sky"—delivering progress and opportunity but leaving behind no residue of heritable inequality.[85]

On the other hand, those who mobilized to raise workers' wages or increase their bargaining power violated the meritocratic order of society—and indeed, of the cosmos itself—by using coercion to dole out "unearned" advantages.[86] In his popular 1903 book, *Young Man Entering Business*, essayist Orison Marden implored his young readers to reject the view that structural obstacles had unfairly denied them opportunities. In his view, this was simply a rationalization for personal failure. In America, he taught, *everyone* was blessed with opportunities to succeed. Those who failed had let fortune slip through their fingers: "as boys they did not look upon every errand as a chance to be polite, prompt, energetic; on every lesson in school as a foundation stone in their success-structure." "They did not think," he continued, "that the demoralizing hours of indolence and shiftlessness which they were weaving into the web of their lives would mar the fabric forever, and reproach them through all time."[87] They had no one to blame, in short, but themselves, and certainly no legitimate claim to the hard-earned wealth of others.

In the Gilded Age, as in the Jacksonian Era, this myth was often linked to the idea of American exceptionalism, which American orators constantly reinforced through a contrast with the hardened hierarchies of the Old World. Speaking to the students of Spencerian Business College in 1869, future president James Garfield argued that in Europe, "wealth and society are built up like the strata of rock which compose the crust of the earth." No poor boy could hope to penetrate them, no matter how hard he worked. In America, by contrast, the strata "resemble rather the ocean, where every drop, even the lowest, is free to mingle with all the others, and may shine at last on the crest of the highest wave." In a society marked by both fluidity and limitless abundance, he continued, no obstacle could "prove too great for any brave heart":

through industry, frugality, and dogged perseverance, determined young men could become anything they wanted.[88]

It is easy to see why economic elites have seized on this myth—from the Jacksonian Era to the present—to justify their power and wealth, for it suits this purpose to perfection.[89] It takes more work to understand why it has resonated so deeply with the American electorate. First, white men *have* enjoyed considerable economic mobility throughout much of the country's history. Economic historians have shown that even in the Gilded Age, opportunities were relatively plentiful.[90] In this sense, the myth has corresponded loosely to many Americans' lived experience: even those who did not "advance" themselves often knew of others who did. Another key lies, however, in the myth's congruence with the older Protestant narratives that we explored in earlier chapters. From Ben Franklin onward, Americans have embraced a story of upward mobility centered on the Protestant virtues of industry, frugality, honesty, and moderation. In its eighteenth-century version, these virtues served the twin functions of warding off moral vice and dissipation and also earning social respectability and economic independence. Like its later incarnations, this agrarian and artisanal articulation of the myth was premised on an exceptionalist image of America as a relatively classless society marked by opportunity and abundance. More fundamentally, it rested on the faith in America as a New Eden that offered humanity itself a chance for liberation and rebirth under the watchful eyes of a benevolent God.

This "moderate" incarnation, which has long shaped the attitudes of the American middle class, embodies one of the few existing strains of genuine conservatism in the United States. It celebrates a way of life defined by productive labor and property ownership, "personal accountability and neighborly self-help," the traditional family, broad private freedom, and—all too often—racial entitlement.[91] It envisions a hard-earned, moderate prosperity against a background of social and institutional stability. It mistrusts both the centralized state and the big corporation because both are agents of sweeping disruption and change. The success literature of the Gilded Age often reflects this conservative frame of mind. In Horatio Alger's stories, for example, readers find themselves transported to a world that looks much like Ben Franklin's Philadelphia: a world of merchants and apprentices where self-reliant and unpretentious young men are rewarded for their moral virtue.[92] Faced with the dizzying dislocations of the industrial era, Alger and other success writers often depicted an uncomplicated society of small businessmen and craftsmen, in which individuals still controlled their own economic fates.[93]

More fundamentally, Alger's stories, like so much of the success literature of the age, express an almost desperate yearning for moral order. Virtue is rewarded and vice punished. Greedy and duplicitous strivers may find temporary success, but a cosmic karma reasserts itself in the end and cuts them down to size. The influential *McGuffey's Readers*, which were widely used as schoolbooks from the 1840s into the twentieth century, reinforced this message at every opportunity. The hardworking and honest boy becomes "a rich and useful man," his indolent and supercilious companion joins "a party of tramps" before he turns thirty.[94] Acts of cruelty, dishonesty, or negligence are soon met with a swift and unforeseen comeuppance. Everyone gets what they deserve, and moral virtue—most of all the cardinal, Protestant virtues of old—earns material rewards. The "rags-to-riches" literature, writes historian Richard Weiss, rested on the assumption that "justice must reign in a universe governed by moral law and that in such a universe man's freedom to sin or not to sin gave him power to govern his own destiny."[95]

It is hard not to read such stories as secularized reenactments of the cosmic Christian drama of sin and salvation. Just as faith and virtue brought eternal reward, so too did they earn success, salvation's secular counterpart. Just as salvation lay, in the evangelical creed that saturated nineteenth-century America, within the individual's control, so too did its earthly analogue. The capitalist ideology of success resonates with American voters—especially Protestant conservatives—partly because it affirms this redemptive view of American society. In his 1867 "Address on Success in Business," Horace Greeley reassured his audience that "success in life is within the reach of every one who will truly and nobly seek it—that there is scope for all—that the universe is not bankrupt—that there is abundance of work for those who are wise enough to look for it." With hard work, "sound morality," and "a careful adaptation of means to ends," he continued, "there is in this land of our larger opportunities, more just and well grounded hopes, than in any other land whereon the sun ever shone."[96] The exceptional fairness and openness of the nation's economy is revealed here as an unshakable article of faith, for it validates the moral goodness and harmony of God's creation.[97]

In the Jacksonian Era, leading Whigs had described America's exceptional, meritocratic economy as the result of both fortuitous natural abundance and deliberate political engineering: they taught that protective tariffs, government-backed credit, and sustained public investment in education and economic development could sustain both progress and opportunity indefinitely. After the Civil War, as economic elites moved to defend themselves against the rising threat of government regulation, they tended to suppress this political component. In their revised, laissez-faire articulation of the myth, America was a natural economic utopia, powered by rugged and enterprising individuals, whose productivity needed shielding from the hubris of regulators and the envy of the undeserving poor. Again, this reformulation married the Jacksonian Democrats' faith in a just and natural order with the Whig view of freedom as mobility and self-creation under conditions of material abundance.[98]

Of course, the globalized, corporate capitalism that has since wrapped itself in this mythology is anything but conservative. Since the Civil War, nothing has been more destructive of the traditional lifeways of middle-class Americans than the radical economic dreams of the business elite. With their relentless quest for efficiency and wealth came, in the words of W. E. B. Du Bois, a "ruthless indifference toward waste, death, ugliness and disaster."[99] The eclipse of the family farm and the advent of state-subsidized, corporate agriculture, with its vast centralization, top-down control, and efficient, chemical-saturated monocultures offer just one example of this upheaval. "The American capitalist," wrote historian Clinton Rossiter, "however 'conservative' his views on government, family, property, school, and church, has been the most marvelous agent of social change the world has ever known."[100] In America, the capitalist ideology of success sits like a parasite on the older, Protestant dreams of respectability and independence, absorbing their political energy and leading them to self-destruction.

Like the other two myths, the myth of the self-made man remained deeply interwoven with racial hierarchy. Over the course of the Gilded Age, white Americans asserted their rights and opportunities through a maelstrom of racial violence. Federal troops pushed further and further into Native American lands and committed widespread atrocities to satiate white land hunger and pave the way for Anglo-Saxon freedoms. Chinese workers in the West were attacked and murdered by white mobs and denounced as a rising threat to free white labor. African Americans in the South were brutalized and killed with impunity as "redeemers" reasserted white supremacy and white property rights against the Reconstruction agenda. Meanwhile, in Cuba and the Philippines, the United States launched colonial ventures whose justifications were deeply racialized. In the North and South alike, Americans tried to salve the wounds of the Civil War and rediscover national unity by affirming the solidarity and superiority of the white race.[101]

As they had been in the Jacksonian Era, racial violence and subordination were underwritten by a pervasive racial essentialism that inscribed individualistic traits into the white or Anglo-Saxon race while stripping them from people of color. Although the Civil War had temporarily shifted racial attitudes among many northerners, the 1870s witnessed the recrudescence of old racial stereotypes. Increasingly worried about labor unrest and union power in their own states—and alarmed by reports of the radical socialism of the Paris Commune in 1870–71—northern Republicans became unsettled by Black activism in the South. The northern press grew increasingly receptive, specifically, to the racist portrayal of African Americans as shiftless and improvident, incapable of hard work, and determined to use their newfound political power to confiscate white wealth and extract patronage from the state. Black workers and voters pressing for civil rights and basic economic opportunities were thus described as an alien and radical element that used big government to promote widespread dependence and subvert the ideal of the self-made man. The restoration of white supremacist rule in the South following the withdrawal of federal troops in 1877, meanwhile, could be presented as a vindication of America's individualistic ideals.[102]

This discourse of Black dependence was complemented by parallel celebrations of white self-reliance and freedom. In his popular 1885 treatise *Our Country*, for example, Reverend Josiah Strong argued that every race embodied "some great idea—one or more." In his view, Anglo-Saxons embodied both pure Christianity and individual *liberty*. "It was left for the Anglo-Saxon branch" of humanity, he wrote, "fully to recognize the right of the individual to himself, and formally to declare it the foundation stone of government." Strong believed that the Anglo-Saxon aptitude for liberty included a superior "money-making power" as well as a "genius for colonizing": "his unequaled energy, his indomitable perseverance, and his personal independence, made him a pioneer. He excels all others in pushing his way into new countries," just as he excelled in pushing his way up from poverty to wealth. Of course, he thought that the United States stood at the vanguard of Anglo-Saxon power. Weaving together Darwinian language with millennial Protestantism, he argued that America was destined to spread Anglo-Saxon liberty to the world. Other races would be left to choose between "ready and pliant assimilation" and gradual disappearance.[103]

Racial minorities in the United States quickly learned that even this offer of assimilation was usually a lie. In his 1903 allegory, "Of the Coming of John," Du Bois reflected on Black men's tortured relationship to the American ideal of the self-made man. A bright and compliant Black boy from a village in southeastern Georgia, John Jones is sent off to school in the city, despite the grumbling of local whites that "it'll spoil him,—ruin him." Through years of work and struggle, overcoming his own indiscipline and the inadequacy of his rural education, John finishes high school and college. "All the world toward which he strove," writes Du Bois, "was of his own building, and he builded slow and hard." John's labored self-improvement, which brings him not only intellectual cultivation but the skills and resolve to apply himself to a productive philanthropic career, epitomizes the upward trajectory detailed in the success literature of the age.[104]

Except that John, unlike his white counterparts, discovers that there is no place for him. His new self-awareness helps him see, more clearly than ever, the "Veil that lay between him and the white world." Even in cosmopolitan New York, he finds himself unwelcome in educated, white society. Back in his hometown, he is hired at the Black school on the condition that he "teach the darkies to be faithful servants and laborers as [their] fathers were," rather than filling their heads with subversive notions of self-improvement. John's profound sense of alienation is deepened by the rift that has opened between him and the local Black townspeople, including his own family. After his years away in college and in the city, he is overwhelmed by the "sordidness and narrowness" of their lives. Their religious enthusiasm seems like crude, superstitious fanaticism. To them, meanwhile, John seems "cold and preoccupied," disrespectful, and almost unrecognizable.[105] A self-made man, John finds himself isolated, indignant, and powerless, for he has trespassed onto terrain that remains "the privilege of white men."[106] In the end, he pays for this unseemly hubris with his life.

Frederick Douglass was somewhat more sanguine. His lecture "Self-Made Men," which he delivered over fifty times in the decades following the Civil War, exhorted all Americans, white and Black, to discover the "marvelous power" of their own will to improve. Outside of the South, Douglass insisted, America was indeed "the home and patron of self-made men": "here, all doors fly open to them. They may aspire to any position." Douglass, of all people, had no illusions about the discriminatory barriers that still confronted Black men in the postwar northern economy, but he also believed that disillusionment and resignation were toxic. To meet racism with redoubled effort, to reach continually for self-improvement through "well directed, honest toil," was the only path to self-respect. In his eyes, the ideal of the self-made man, which he deployed fully conscious of its mythic proportions, became a source of resistance to the humiliations inflicted by racial prejudice.[107] He also used it to subtly mock his white listeners' meritocratic self-image, which was belied by their unearned racial privilege.[108]

Crucially, both he and Du Bois invoked the myth to denounce racism and structural injustice in America. "Give the Negro fair play," said Douglass, "and let him alone" to rise or fall on the strength of his own efforts. In his eyes, "fair play" was a substantial requirement: "it is not fair play to start the Negro out in life, from nothing and with nothing, while others start with the advantage of a thousand years behind them."[109] Douglass called for a universal, federally funded educational system; he argued for a vast federal initiative to facilitate Black land ownership (and later, to help southern Blacks move west to claim land under the Homestead Act); and he remained an implacable critic of racial prejudice.[110] Du Bois, meanwhile, embraced a more far-reaching, socialist vision of economic equality and shared governance. In his view, industrialization had undermined the great "American Assumption" that wealth came to whoever worked hard enough. It had never been true for Blacks; now even white men found it out of reach.[111] For both Douglass and Du Bois, the myth became a standard against which to measure the scope of American injustice; it also served as a call to reform American society and create the material preconditions—as each saw them—for equal freedom.

Between the Civil War and the dawn of the twentieth century, all three foundational myths were used for diverse political ends. For just over a decade right after the war, the Reconstruction period saw them deployed in service of ambitious egalitarian goals, including broad civil rights reforms and universal male suffrage. The astonishing successes achieved in the 1860s and early 1870s marked the culmination of decades of reformist agitation begun by the abolitionists in the 1830s. In the 1880s and 1890s, the Knights of Labor and the Populist movement also harnessed the myths to revive and deepen the egalitarian thrust of Jacksonian Democratic politics. Taken together, however, these decades brought more reversals than gains. As the war's egalitarian legacy faded and Reconstruction collapsed, white Americans reaffirmed the fusion of individualism and racial hierarchy. Escalating, state-sponsored violence against unions and strikers, along with the decline of the Knights of Labor, dealt heavy blows to the cause of producers' rights. At the same time, the Populist movement's political defeat helped render the rural economy more intensely unequal and exploitative. All the while, as both major parties and their media organs successfully repurposed the foundational myths to justify growing inequality, the idea of economic freedom they carried grew thin and brittle. These developments left long-term legacies: for much of the twentieth century, egalitarians in the United States would feel that they were working against the grain of their country's ideological inheritance.

11

Conclusions

THE TWENTIETH CENTURY brought tremendous changes to American political thought. The Progressive Era and then the New Deal successfully challenged free-market orthodoxies and vastly expanded Americans' view of government's proper role in the economy. The United States' transformation into a militarized superpower in the wake of World War II gave rise to a dramatically revised view of its appropriate role in global politics, and the ensuing Cold War reshaped and revitalized American conservatism. The civil rights movement challenged decades of white complacency about racial injustice and made it a significant fault line again in partisan politics. Critics of the Vietnam War joined civil rights activists and feminists in popularizing powerful new languages of social criticism and countercultural dissent, which attacked the reigning mythologies of American exceptionalism. The 1930s and 1940s, which were defined by the herculean collective projects of world war and economic recovery from the Great Depression, brought especially sharp challenges to the individualist rhetoric that had shaped American political culture since the Jacksonian Era.

It is therefore remarkable that the three foundational myths explored in this book should remain so familiar to us in the twenty-first century. To this day, they continue to supply the basic storylines that so many Americans use to make sense of their politics. Their influence is especially pronounced on the American right: even after the Trump insurgency muddied its ideological message, the right continues to speak a language of free markets, individual rights, and personal responsibility that would have been plainly recognizable in the Gilded Age. It continues to sing the song of exceptional American liberty, menaced by the timeless specter of socialism. Its popular discourse is anchored by assertions of personal freedom: gun rights, property rights, religious liberty. Moreover, this discourse is routinely enveloped in thinly veiled racist tropes that portray both African Americans and immigrants of color as irresponsible dependents feeding at the public trough, bereft of the individualistic virtues of independence and industriousness.[1]

This right-leaning individualism was revitalized in the 1970s and 1980s, buoyed by a resurgent free-market ideology. The "Reagan revolution" restored what historian Daniel Rodgers calls a "rhetoric of populist market optimism" centered on a faith in the free market as a natural and harmonious system calibrated to deliver both freedom and prosperity.[2] Business elites fiercely opposed to the New Deal had worked feverishly to keep this rhetoric alive and restore its popularity in the middle decades of the twentieth century. They drew support from the strident anti-communism of the 1950s, which further rejuvenated the idea of America as an individualist haven, defined by "free enterprise" and expansive individual rights, standing against the ungodly collectivist menace of the Soviet Union.[3] The ideological shifts of the 1980s were also driven, finally, by a resurgent evangelical movement that embraced free-market ideas in its struggle against the influence of liberal elites in government.

Meanwhile, since the 1960s and the eclipse of Lyndon Johnson's Great Society initiatives, the American left has accentuated its own competing narratives of personal liberation. The struggle for women's equality and reproductive rights, for marriage equality and LGBTQ rights, and even for racial inclusion has often been couched in the language of personal autonomy and opportunity: activists in these areas have aimed to liberate individuals from oppressive and arbitrary constraint that prevent people from living lives of their own. In the landmark 2003 *Goodridge* decision, for example, which legalized same-sex marriage in the state of Massachusetts, the majority appealed to the state's long-standing constitutional protection of "personal liberty against government incursion." It affirmed its "respect for individual autonomy," and for the "dignity and equality of all individuals," and forbade the "creation of second class citizens."[4] This very language of individual autonomy and equal rights has underwritten most of the egalitarian accomplishments of the post-1960s left.

In the economic sphere, however, the Democratic Party has used individualist rhetoric to retreat from the egalitarianism of the New Deal years. From Bill Clinton's attacks on welfare dependency to Barack Obama's discourse of personal achievement, Democrats have found themselves operating in a rhetorical landscape defined largely by Reagan. In a well-publicized 2013 address, for example, Obama restated the fundamental economic promise of American life as he saw it: "the idea that success doesn't depend on being born into wealth or privilege, it depends on effort and merit." Lamenting the decline of economic mobility in the United States, he quoted Abraham Lincoln: "while we do not propose any war upon capital, we do wish to allow the humblest man an equal chance to get rich with everybody else." These words were broadly representative of the party's redistributive aims from the 1980s through the Obama years: to expand economic opportunities for poorer Americans and restore the sacred link between success and "effort and merit," so that hardworking Americans of all backgrounds could escape dependency and pull themselves up the economic ladder. For Obama as for Clinton, this was nothing less than the age-old "American Dream."[5]

The last few years have seen the emergence of a more emboldened economic left. From the Occupy movement through Bernie Sanders's popular presidential campaigns and the early ambitions of the Biden presidency, progressive activists and their allies in the Democratic Party have begun to revive the midcentury belief that "freedom from want" should be a fundamental political goal. It remains too early to predict whether this is a temporary response to the stresses of economic recession and a global pandemic or whether it signals a longer-term commitment to use the power of government to attack both oligarchy and white supremacy. Either way, it seems unlikely that America's individualist myths will be easily displaced. For the foreseeable future, they will continue to define the imagined political landscape for millions upon millions of Americans and pay political dividends to those who can successfully harness them.

In exploring the roots of these individualistic ideas, this book has tried to correct some of the mistakes that distorted earlier treatments of the subject. Since the mid-twentieth century, scholarly discussions of American individualism have unfolded in the shadow of the "consensus" interpretation of American history, which presented individualism as a primordial feature of the country's ideological landscape dating back to the colonial period. This book argues instead that American individualism rose to dominance in the Jacksonian Era. It attributes this ideological shift to a set of powerful changes that unsettled American society in the first half of the nineteenth century and led many Americans to pivot away from the political thought of the founding generation: the advent of mass democracy, the vast expansion of the market, and the anti-institutional revivalism of the Second Great Awakening. This book explores how Jacksonian Democrats, in particular, crafted and popularized individualist narratives that helped Americans find their bearings in this changing political, economic, and religious landscape.

More than the consensus historians, this book also emphasizes the complexity and multiplicity of both American individualism and the broader political culture that has encased it. It shows how individualist assumptions embedded themselves in contrasting political narratives and perspectives that, although they shared certain fundamental assumptions, nonetheless embodied widely divergent visions of American society. It shows, for example, how they underwrote both sharp critiques and impassioned defenses of industrializing capitalism, and more broadly how they informed both genuinely radical perspectives and nostalgic, conservative yearnings. It argues, furthermore, that individualist myths and ideas competed and interacted, over time, with collectivist alternatives centered, for example, on white male solidarity and supremacy or Christian community. In these ways, this book resists describing American individualism as a source of political consensus.

Finally, these midcentury historians often identified individualism as a fundamentally practical outlook. To them, it represented the triumph of petit-bourgeois values, of the unhampered pursuit of material success, or of a commonsense aversion to grand political ambition: for better or worse, they maintained, Americans rejected the idealism and "crusading spirit" that energized so many political movements across the Atlantic and led them to demand bold collective action.[6] By contrast, this book emphasizes the utopian impulse that has so often animated American individualism. In their mythologized visions of agrarian virtue, of natural markets, and of classless meritocracy, Americans have consistently linked individual freedom to a story of divine justice and human redemption. Rather than forgoing the utopian impulse altogether, they displaced its locus from the state to American *society*—or the American economy—with far-reaching consequences. In fact, the preceding chapters have suggested that this utopian impulse has strengthened American individualism considerably by turning it into a potent source of collective meaning.

Drawing on this revised view of American individualism, this final chapter offers some critical reflections on its implications for American politics in the twenty-first century. It dwells particularly on the themes of equality and inequality that still lie at the center of so many of the ongoing controversies over the meaning and scope of individual freedom in the United States.

Vectors of Inequality

The great scars of injustice that stretch across American history have arisen, overwhelmingly, from profound inequality and the vulnerability it creates. Native Americans were dismissed as racial inferiors, denied the protections of American statute and treaty, and serially victimized by white settlers, speculators, and vigilantes. African Americans were dehumanized, brutally enslaved, and for more than a century after emancipation consigned to the lowest rung of a violent and distinctively American caste hierarchy whose invidious distinctions distort American politics and society to this day. Women were denied the privileges of citizenship, legally subsumed into their husbands' personalities, and subjected to pervasive domination and surveillance. And millions of poor Americans were—and still are—consigned to privation, indignity, and hopelessness even as their labor helped produce fantastic wealth for a privileged elite.

There can be no doubt that the foundational myths explored in this book have contributed to these inequalities. Time and again, Americans blocked egalitarian reforms through appeals to an antigovernmental ideal of personal freedom. Time and again, they concealed or ignored their nation's structural injustices by invoking the idealized self-images conveyed by their foundational myths. These tendencies were exacerbated by three powerful ideological forces that have intermingled with and shaped individualist ideas over the last two centuries: white male supremacy, utopian visions of apolitical order, and a strident belief in national exceptionalism. All three have consistently blunted the egalitarian potentials that have also inhered, from the very beginning, in American individualism. In doing so, all three have contributed to profound injustices.

The first source of injustice lies in the complex relationship between American individualism and white male supremacy. There are many disparate threads to untangle here. First, in projecting laziness, servility, and groupthink onto people of color and constructing whiteness as their inverse, white Americans have continually inscribed individualist ideals into their own racial identity.[7] A similar dynamic has shaped the construction of American masculinity across the centuries: women have been portrayed as dependent and irrational, men as self-reliant, self-disciplined, and well suited for the rugged, competitive world that prevails outside of the nurturing confines of the home. These pervasive tropes have reinforced the belief that America's distinctive values and institutions belong mainly—if not exclusively—to white or Anglo-Saxon men, and that both women and people of color should in various ways be marginalized, excluded, or held in subjection. They have encased American individualism, in other words, in a collectivist story of both racial and gender hierarchy.

White racism has also shaped America's individualistic discourses in more specific ways. From the Jacksonian Era onward, racial animus not only impeded the formation of inclusive working-class coalitions in American politics but also weakened class identity altogether by persuading poor whites that they shared common cause with their wealthy employers and ringleaders.[8] It thus reinforced a mythology of America classlessness that has long inhibited egalitarian reform. Moreover, racial resentment over federal action to end slavery and enforce civil rights, accented by a persistent fear that redistributive policies would upend racial hierarchies, has weakened white Americans' support for the welfare state and mobilized antigovernmental individualism for patently inegalitarian ends.[9] The intense aversion to welfare assistance felt by so many poor whites in America to this day bears unmistakable traces of this racist legacy.[10] In all of these ways, racism has helped turn America's individualist myths into instruments of inequality and injustice.

These tendencies have then been supercharged by a persistent rhetoric of invasive threat. From the Jacksonian Era through today, white Americans have often felt menaced by a non-white other who threatens to enervate them, either genetically or culturally, and to destroy their freedom at its source. The recurrent fantasy of a violent, libidinous, or indolent Black "mass" besieging white society, or an alien "horde" of non-European immigrants threatening to destroy American values, has served as a long-standing foil for America's virtuous and enterprising white hero. Through these narratives of jeopardy, American individualism is continually transmuted into a powerful shared identity and cause, crying out for defense against invasive contaminants. Donald Trump's toxic politics of aggrieved whiteness has lately reenergized this vicious strain in American political discourse.

At the same time, it is remarkable how hard so many white Americans have labored to ignore or deny white supremacy's influence. Over the last two hundred years, American political rhetoric reveals a catalog of denials and evasions designed to protect the country's individualist self-image. Rather than seeing themselves as the agents of a colonial power asserting the prerogatives of whiteness, white Americans fantasized about the industrious settler taming a vast and virgin wilderness.[11] Rather than seeing themselves as members of an apartheid society premised on racial subjugation, they presented slavery as a foreign anomaly originally foisted on them by the British, which would be unwound at last through the voluntary emigration of freed slaves to Africa. When that dream faded, they replaced it with the fantasy that African Americans remained poor and marginalized because of their own lack of effort and discipline in a society that always rewarded both.[12] Finally, rather than addressing the cumulative effects of racial injustice, they built a sprawling and vastly punitive prison system premised instead on the criminal responsibility of the individual. Through denial, falsification, and flagrant inconsistency, white Americans have strained to reaffirm the universalism of their individualist myths. Here too is a measure of the enduring power of individualist ideas.

In our own day, the rhetoric of race-blind individualism deployed by conservative pundits and intellectuals continues to serve the same purpose: it is fundamentally a rhetoric of denial. To suggest that we should now, on the heels of centuries of oppression, marginalization, and exploitation, simply treat African Americans as equal contestants in the "race" of life is to suggest that this legacy of injustice has left no lasting mark. This profoundly distorted view ignores the massive, structural wealth gap, created by centuries of racial violence and discrimination and exacerbated by federally sponsored racial segregation, in both neighborhoods and schools, and by a criminal justice system that continues to deepen and reinforce racial hierarchy.[13] It also denies the overwhelming evidence of persistent racial prejudice across American society, which still limits and demeans countless young men and women of color.

The main problem here lies not with individualistic *ideals* but rather with white Americans' self-serving tendency to believe that their society already epitomizes them. We saw in chapter 2 that American individualism functions in two different ways, both as a moral ideal and as a description of social and political reality.[14] In this latter guise, it continues to cloud Americans' perception of their society and its history. But individualistic ideals are not blameless, either. In a country where self-respect is so deeply linked to personal autonomy and independence, many bridle instinctively at the suggestion that their achievements rest on any measure of inherited advantage. They are thus predisposed to overlook the effects of structural injustice. Determined to see themselves as "masters of their own fate," writes political theorist Jack Turner, individualists commonly deny the significance and even the reality of "social structure."[15]

The second source of injustice arises from the fact that wealthy elites have so often succeeded, from the Civil War to the present, in defining the content of personal freedom in ways that serve their interests. The idea that freedom means little more than *being left alone by government* benefits no one more than wealthy businessmen eager to shield their own economic empires and labor practices from regulation and their vast property holdings from taxation. It has proven disastrous, on the other hand, to those who have found themselves constrained by economic necessity to labor in unsafe workplaces; to suffer the pollution of their land, air, and water; to subsist on indecent wages; or to rely on chronically underfunded schools and public defenders. The outsized influence of money in American politics helps explain the dominance of business interests in American policymaking; corporate control of mass media also helps explain the broad dissemination of this cynically anemic idea of freedom. But these facts tell only part of the story, for they fail to explain why the American public has so often proven receptive to this elite-driven rhetoric.

The answer lies partly in the utopian impulse that has embedded itself in American individualism since the Age of Jackson. When they imagine *what life will be like* without the government's interference, Americans are all too often drawn to a mythologized vision of an emergent meritocratic order that is at once abundant, free, and broadly fair—and also uniquely and providentially *American*. These utopian assumptions, more than a bare aversion to government power, have supplied the content and the enduring appeal of this "negative" conception of freedom. We have explored several related expressions of these utopian assumptions in the preceding chapters: the agrarian myth of a peaceful, industrious, and civically virtuous society of yeomen who needed little governance; the dream of a fair and prosperous society harmonized by natural markets that embodied God's own benevolent will; the abiding faith in a classless meritocracy that rewards virtue and punishes vice. All posit a source of harmonious social order that lies mostly outside of politics. From the Jacksonian Era through today, American elites have successfully used these utopian visions to present government regulation and redistribution as unseemly distortions of the natural or providential way of things.[16]

Although the agrarian idyll of the Jeffersonian yeoman has mostly faded from view, the other two utopian visions continue to distort Americans' political perceptions today in ways that warrant further discussion here. First of all, it should go without saying that the idea of a natural market is pure fantasy. Markets are human creations; in the modern world, they are creatures of law and government. While the particular outcomes of market interactions are largely unplanned, the modern market is structured by a set of political rules—including the laws that regulate property and inheritance, contracts, monopolies, and bankruptcies—that are written and coercively enforced by public officials.[17] These rules have no *natural* configuration; instead, they reflect moral and political choices grounded in competing interests and values.[18] Crucially, these choices can and do "tilt" the economic playing field decisively toward one or another set of contestants—they shape the market, with vast distributive implications for those who compete in it.[19] In this sense, the market offers no escape from political power or from the political distribution of wealth and opportunity.[20] As we saw in chapter 9, Whigs understood this far more clearly than their Democratic rivals. But their view was overwhelmed by the tide of libertarian optimism that buoyed American political economy, in both its academic and popular forms, in the nineteenth century and beyond.[21]

Sociologist Karl Polanyi famously argued that free-market ideology, no less than Marxist communism, is commonly animated by powerful utopian assumptions. Chief among them is the assumption that the economy is a strictly voluntary domain, unblemished by the exercise of power.[22] It follows that the project of creating and sustaining a free society is largely a project of limiting the power and scope of government and allowing the "self-regulating market" to function unimpaired. Nowhere have these assumptions been more influential—among both intellectuals and the broader public—than in the United States. And nowhere have they been so deeply imbued with religious meaning. "The secret imaginative background," writes historian John William Ward, "that made it possible for Jacksonian political philosophy to come to the astonishing conclusion that America had no need for politics was a fervent belief in a fundamental law in the universe, a cosmic constitutionalism, which made it unnecessary for man to plan for, create, and achieve the good society."[23] To this day, this latent religious optimism, stoked now and again by the economic elites who profit from it, continues to nourish and renew a profound mistrust of government.

It is clearly manifest, for example, in the widely held conviction that expanding government investments in childcare, health care, and other vital services will create an "entitlement society" that rewards the undeserving and subverts American values. At its core, this conviction depends on an imagined "free market" baseline in which people get what they earn and deserve. Government spending is then presented as a *subversion* of this baseline and a shift from the logic of meritocracy and freedom to the logic of entitlement and coercion. Once we recognize that this baseline is itself fictitious, and that business elites have deployed it for well over a century to justify an economy profoundly structured by their own power and privilege, this whole way of thinking is revealed to be fraudulent. This does not mean, of course, that we must disavow the value of self-reliance itself or the aim of empowering citizens to exert meaningful control over their own lives; instead, it means that we must strive to disentangle these values from the utopian economic fictions that have long served the interests of American oligarchs.

As we began to explore in chapter 7, one of the most enduring legacies of this American utopianism has been an unduly narrow view of the dangers that threaten human freedom. In America, more than in any other advanced, post-industrial democracy, it remains difficult to *see* the harms perpetrated by private economic actors—including economic exploitation and dislocation and environmental degradation—as assaults on the personal freedoms of ordinary people perpetrated by the powerful. They often appear, instead, to be no more than the regrettable but unavoidable side effects of free markets, whose ultimately benign agency it would be perverse or futile to obstruct.[24]

The fiction of the self-regulating market has often overlapped with the other enduring strain of American utopianism: the fantasy of America as a pure meritocracy. Since the Jacksonian Era, the market has frequently been imagined as a meritocratic system that ensures individual mobility, while government has been seen as a source of cronyism, stasis, and undeserved privilege. As we explored in chapters 9 and 10, however, the idea of pure meritocracy has also been promulgated by those who resist at least some of the dogmas of laissez-faire. For antebellum Whigs, for example, mobility and meritocracy in America were created partly by the prudent and impartial oversight of government, which insulated American workers and manufacturers from predatory foreign competition, guaranteed a steady flow of credit, and invested in schools and infrastructure. But Whigs believed that this meritocratic order had already been largely achieved, and that it required no deliberate redistribution of wealth. These beliefs rested, in turn, on the conviction that American society was unique and different: it was classless, fluid, and essentially harmonious. In their eyes, it was fundamentally unlike European society, and it could therefore be governed with a light and impartial touch.

There were of course kernels of truth in these convictions at the time: throughout the nineteenth century, white American men *did* experience higher levels of economic mobility than their peers did in Europe.[25] But the idea of pure meritocracy has always been false. As historians have exhaustively documented, elites throughout American history have benefited from both inherited advantages and sustained government favoritism. The poor, meanwhile, have often found themselves struggling against structural impediments calculated to protect their employers and landlords. Moreover, brute luck has always profoundly shaped the fortunes of Americans across the economic spectrum. In denying or downplaying these realities, the merito-cratic vision of America has infused national politics with both arrogance and cruelty. It reflects the arrogance of affluent Americans eager to convince them-selves that their fortunes are entirely of their own making, that they owe no debt of gratitude to society at large, and that anything more than the most minimal taxation is an unjustified *taking* of the fruits of their labor. It also en-courages public cruelty toward the poor, who are presumed to be responsible for their own failures, and who are seen to be clamoring for "handouts" that rend the very fabric of moral desert.[26]

This gap between myth and reality is especially pronounced today, and its effects are therefore especially destructive. Several recent studies have shown that the rates of economic mobility in the United States are now relatively low—lower than in Canada and many Western European countries.[27] While the precise reasons for this divergence are still debated, they almost certainly include not only vast economic inequality itself but also the lack of public sup-port given to poor American families and their children. Poorer children in the United States are less likely to have access to pre-K education; their public schools are more likely to be underfunded and lower-performing; their parents are more likely to be in poor health and to have to work longer hours (for lower wages), leaving less time for parenting.[28] Robust public investment in health care, education, and antipoverty measures are especially critical in creating op-portunities for people born into poverty, and the fantasy of America as an es-sentially and effortlessly meritocratic society continues to inhibit it.[29]

This book has suggested two sources of the enduring utopian bent in Amer-ican political thought: the unprecedented economic conditions of the antebel-lum years, and Americans' longing for order in a fluid and unsettled world. First, in an economy of small producers, with abundant access to cheap land and wages held high by the high ratio of land to labor, it was still plausible for white men to imagine that expansive personal freedom and broad economic equality could be theirs without much help from government. The populariza-tion of free-market ideas during this period, infused with a resurgent religious nationalism born of evangelical revival, captured this rising optimism and made many Americans—in both major parties—receptive to utopian eco-nomic dreams. At the same time, the rise of mass political parties and the democratization of American political rhetoric helped transmute these dreams into popular myths that became part of the country's folklore.[30] It is hardly unusual, as historian John Murrin wrote, "for a people to think of their society in terms drawn from the objective conditions of a simpler but outdated age."[31] Nowhere is this residual influence clearer than in the utopian economic fictions that still encase American individualism in the twenty-first century.

Second, as Alexis de Tocqueville observed long ago, the fluidity of American society has often brought with it a persistent eddy of anxiety. Even as they welcomed a freewheeling openness about their lives, even as they celebrated the absence of government's heavy hand, Americans have also felt the need to reassure themselves that their society would not dissolve into a ruthless and anarchic free-for-all.[32] Their fascination with the speculator or dishonest broker, the huckster, and the desperado—all men who circumvent the honest order of things and get *something for nothing*—speaks to this persistent uneasiness. Time and again, they have tried to banish it by positing a providential order that guides so many disparate individuals toward virtue and progress.[33] As we explored in chapter 2, myths are powerful sources of collective meaning. They help dispel the world's apparent indifference to human travails. The utopian fictions explored here, variously embedded in all three foundational myths, have served the particular psychological needs of a people who, in a society largely unmoored from traditional ties and institutions, have identified so deeply with narratives of personal liberation.

The final source of injustice lies in the potent idea of national exceptionalism that continues to adhere to the country's individualist mythology. For two centuries now, the American ideal of individual freedom in a meritocratic order has drawn strength from an idealized vision of national purpose and identity. The free and enterprising individual appears as an archetype of American uniqueness that is continually threatened by alien forces.[34] Nineteenth-century Americans felt themselves haunted by aristocratic ghosts of the Old World or by the atheistic radicalism of the French Revolution and the Paris Commune; twentieth-century Americans felt the menace of Soviet communism. These antagonists were defined by collectivist features— impenetrable social classes, powerful and authoritarian states, tyrannical visions of radical equality—against which Americans learned to measure and define themselves.

Against this background, all three myths reassured Americans that individual freedom *inheres* in the United States and always has. When Americans— especially white Americans—have felt a growing disillusionment with their government or economy, they have therefore been drawn instinctively to a project of restoration and purification, not revolution or emulation. They have gone searching for their lost freedoms in the clauses of their constitutions and founding declarations and the timeless principles enshrined there. As a number of historians have observed, this yearning for a pristine and uncorrupted essence, which already exists somewhere in the nation's DNA if not in its literal past, has been an integral feature of American social criticism from the Puritans onward.[35] Its effect has been to turn many Americans inward and to bind their political imaginations with the specters of betrayal and heresy. Critics and reformers who have challenged the central tenets of America's individualist mythology have time and again been hounded and marginalized by the accusation that they harbored *un-American* proclivities.

In the Jacksonian Era, such accusations could still cut both ways: even as Democrats and abolitionists were denounced as Jacobins importing radical European ideas to a society where they had no place, Whigs were condemned for harboring aristocratic pretensions that were alien to America's tradition of equal rights. From the Gilded Age onward, however, such charges have served mainly as a cudgel aimed at egalitarian reformers, who have been denounced as anarchists, socialists, or communists intent on destroying the American way of life. In these conservative tales of national exceptionalism, individualism has been fused ever more tightly to the celebration of free enterprise and to a deregulatory agenda that caters above all to the interests of big business while exacerbating the vulnerability of the poor.

Equal Freedom

As we have explored throughout this book, all three foundational myths were flexible and indeterminate, and all three were used for many different political purposes. Although they often helped rationalize or occlude inequality, they were also continually mobilized to condemn it. These egalitarian countercurrents were no outliers: from the Age of Jackson onward, all three myths routinely channeled a set of egalitarian impulses that pervaded Americans' thinking about their politics and economics alike. Implicitly or explicitly, white men situated their dreams of personal freedom in a landscape of broad political and economic parity. But they were not alone: in the antebellum period and beyond, women, African Americans, abolitionists, Catholic immigrants, Native Americans, and other marginalized groups channeled the very same myths to press for inclusion.

The economic egalitarianism of the Jacksonian Era was most explicit in the myth of the independent proprietor, which expressed a complex and ambitiously anti-aristocratic conception of economic freedom. As we have explored at length, independence meant control over one's own time and workday, secured by ownership of critical productive resources: land, tools, a shop or small business. But that was not all. In a burgeoning economy, it also connoted a modest prosperity, which would itself open up a range of personal choices, including access to consumer goods and comforts and wealth enough to make old age comfortable. At the same time, for the small farmers who were routinely held up as its paragons, personal independence brought economic security against the vicissitudes of the market: if prices fell or demand dried up, they could still live off the land they cultivated. Such security was part of what distinguished them, in their own eyes, from wage workers whose livelihood was always radically vulnerable to economic downturns and to the whims of others. Finally, the proprietor's self-control and non-subservience ramified outward from workplaces into civic spaces, where independent men could look their fellow citizens in the eye as equals instead of having to genuflect before their economic betters. Thus did economic freedom underwrite a vision of civic equality and democracy.

In the Jacksonian Era, white men's independence was unquestionably entangled with colonial expansionism, gender domination, and racism. So was the ideal of democracy itself. But like democracy, independence was also a rhetorical weapon in the fight for greater and more meaningful equality, wielded first by white men and then by others clamoring for comparable status and dignity. During Reconstruction, for example, freedmen were powerfully drawn to personal independence because it offered them an expansive vision of personal liberty and a foundation for resistance to white domination. With access to their own land, they could afford to refuse the exploitative labor contracts—and the invasive surveillance and control—preferred by white land owners. The struggle over the meaning of free labor in the Reconstruction South was a struggle to define slavery's antipode. For freedmen, as for millions of white northern workers who bridled against what they called "wage slavery," the ideal of personal independence offered the most compelling answer.[36]

This egalitarian legacy lived on in the first half of the twentieth century. In the eyes of the labor unionists who called for "industrial democracy" and Progressive intellectuals such as John Dewey, Herbert Croly, and Louis Brandeis, an economy controlled by corporate elites would, despite its tremendous productivity and wealth, always remain a precarious and diminishing place for labor.[37] "Instead of independence," wrote Dewey, "there exists parasitical dependence on a wide scale." The modern workplace was a site of "servility and regimentation," which cramped the individual mind, confined workers to a narrow range of rote tasks, and subjected them to authoritarian discipline.[38] In this system, even the worker's material well-being was vulnerable to mercurial corporate imperatives. Croly, meanwhile, argued that workers were entitled to a substantial stake in the management of private enterprises. In his eyes, the roots of workplace democracy lay not in European socialism but in the ideal of independent proprietorship that animated so much of nineteenth-century American political thought. "How can the wage-earners," he asked, "obtain an amount or a degree of economic independence analogous to that upon which the pioneer democrat could count?"[39] More recently, egalitarians have suggested a universal basic income as an answer to this quandary.[40]

For the most part, however, the question is scarcely asked. What lives on in its place bears only a weak resemblance to the dream of Jacksonian independence. It is manifest, for example, in the American fascination with gun rights and suburban home ownership. It is also manifest in their persistent idealization of small business owners and small farmers, whose prominence in American political rhetoric belies their diminishing role in the national economy. Most importantly, it is evident in the pervasive disdain for welfare dependency, which continues to shape American politics. To rely on the state for "handouts" is to suffer an indignity, to forfeit one's standing as an independent citizen—to become a mere dependent.[41] In this widely shared view, the welfare state stands out as the most powerful source of dependency in American life. Here the triumph of laissez-faire revisionism is plainly manifest: to depend on the state is an insidious and degrading form of dependence; on the other hand, to depend on a corporate employer for one's livelihood (and one's health care, family leave, and leisure time) is fully compatible with being a proud and self-reliant earner.[42] This view seems plausible only because elites have successfully concealed the vision of economic freedom embraced by so many Americans in the antebellum years.

The myth of the rights-bearer, too, has sometimes carried explosively egalitarian implications. As we explored in chapter 8, abolitionists fought not only to universalize the Declaration's promise of equal rights but also to broaden its meaning and scope. For many of them, equal rights referred not just to basic protections for person and property, not just to a range of civil rights guaranteeing free expression and association, but also to social and political rights. It connoted non-discrimination, equal opportunity, and democratic inclusion. For some it also included "positive" provisions of public resources: guaranteed or subsidized land for freedmen, for example, and decent public schools. For all of them, it also meant protection from arbitrary or despotic uses of state power. In abolitionists' writings, rights became a way of imagining the preconditions of human flourishing: they mapped out the protections and opportunities individuals needed to develop themselves, to make meaningful choices, to live with dignity and self-respect. These tendencies lie at the heart of twentieth-century human rights activism and of the expansive ideal of freedom encoded in the 1948 Universal Declaration of Human Rights.

Moreover, many abolitionists insisted that equal rights could be realized only as part of a culture of inclusive moral solidarity and sustained collective action. In this sense, their view of rights stands as a challenge to the depoliticized vision of liberal society promoted by American intellectuals—on the left and right alike—for the past half century. This orthodox view holds that rights are enshrined in constitutions and curated by enlightened judges, who use them to enforce salutary moral limits on political power. So conceived, rights contract the *scope* of democratic politics: with essential liberties "locked in" by constitutions and their impartial guardians, politics becomes a relatively innocuous contest over resources and opportunities, carried out by competing interest and advocacy groups. With the stakes thus diminished, sustained political participation comes to seem less like an obligation and more like a lifestyle choice.[43]

Writing at a time when wealthy slaveholders controlled many of the country's high offices, and when most American elites favored the deportation of Blacks to Africa, abolitionists could not possibly have embraced this wishful view. Absent organized popular mobilization to protect and expand rights, they argued, the elites entrusted to protect them would either promote their own class's oligarchic interests or absorb the white supremacist currents that bubbled up insistently from the electorate. The infamous *Dred Scott* decision of 1857, in which the Supreme Court declared that Black Americans could never be considered citizens of the United States and had no claim to its constitutional rights, reflected this reality all too clearly. For many abolitionists, the pursuit of equal freedom in a broadly meritocratic society was therefore inseparable from a certain ideal of civic character, grounded in inclusive empathy and an aversion to complicity in injustice, and sustained through participation in civic and religious communities.

Whether such moral and civic habits can set down deep roots in our highly individualistic, post-industrial society remains an unanswered question. From Alexis de Tocqueville onward, critics of American individualism have worried that it would eventually sap the very sources of solidarity on which the country's moral successes were premised. They have warned that Americans' steady withdrawal into private life, fueled by the acquisitiveness, insecurity, and compulsive overwork of the modern capitalist economy, would leave them fractured and easily manipulated, with neither the moral character nor the political organization necessary to defend their free institutions, let alone realize a more just and inclusive social order.[44] The long-term decline of organized labor, the increasing co-optation of evangelical Christianity by capitalist ideologues and hucksters, and the rise of social media as a technique of mass manipulation masquerading as community have lately added fuel to these anxieties.[45]

On the other hand, the egalitarian tradition that extends from abolitionism through the Black Lives Matter movement reminds us that a politics focused on securing equal rights can go hand in hand with a culture of political engagement and movement-building. It also reminds us that individualism alone has never been enough to sustain a just and inclusive politics. Successful egalitarian movements in American history have always drawn on other, complementary moral resources. They have been animated by an ethic of solidarity arising from Christian community, working-class identity, civic nationality, and other sources.[46] They have been strengthened by civic habits nurtured through shared participation in local self-governance—in towns, unions, churches, and local social justice movements. America's individualist myths have consistently underemphasized these other, centripetal aspects of American political culture, which have encouraged citizens to nurture and protect other people's freedoms, not just their own. In our own time, the environmental movement, leavened by the consciousness of impending climate catastrophe, has emerged as another promising source of such solidarity and participatory community, especially for younger Americans.

To achieve equal freedom in the twenty-first century, then, Americans must find ways of marrying individualistic ends with robustly democratic means. They must also reject utopian fiction and exceptionalist fantasy and recognize American society for what it is: a fragile human construction deeply scarred by historical injustice and buffeted by the untamable vicissitudes of the global economy. Such recognition should, finally, chasten the meritocratic ideal that has long defined the individualist perspective in the United States. A just political community, under these conditions, works deliberately to expand opportunities and reduce barriers to social mobility, so that all citizens can realistically hope to be rewarded for their effort and talent. But it also acknowledges the unavoidable influence of bad luck and unearned disadvantage and offsets them with ample safeguards and second chances. It promotes a civic ethics grounded in gratitude rather than hubris, and egalitarian compassion rather than cruelty. Perhaps most fundamentally, it views freedom itself as a delicate human creation that stands in need of constant reinforcement, not an effusion of God or nature.[47]

Some egalitarians will, of course, find this ideal of equal freedom insufficient. They will argue that social justice in America requires a thoroughgoing rejection of individualism, or they will maintain that American individualism is irredeemably tainted by its associations with inequality and domination. Since this is not the place to meet these objections fully, a more modest answer will have to suffice.[48] Over the last two centuries, America's individualist myths have proven powerful and resilient. They have survived profound economic changes and political realignments, and they have continually buoyed the political fortunes of those who have channeled them skillfully. Many of the most effective egalitarian reformers—from Susan B. Anthony to Martin Luther King Jr.—understood as much and worked self-consciously to bend their arc toward greater justice and inclusion. They appreciated the internal diversity, complexity, and malleability of America's individualist inheritance and located, within it, the seeds of egalitarian renewal. Perhaps most importantly, they understood that such potent myths cannot simply be dispelled, and that ceding them to racists and oligarchs would portend disaster for their political hopes. These facts alone should give egalitarians today reason to study and master the idioms of American individualism.[49]

Seen through the lens of its foundational myths, the United States now stands at a crossroads. The end of the Cold War and the rising generations of citizens who scarcely remember it have shifted long-standing discourses of personal freedom. Many no longer define their politics—consciously or unconsciously—with reference to the socialist *other*. Many have also been drawn into political awareness by the global climate crisis, whose fault lines are new and different. Meanwhile, decades of wage stagnation and rising inequality have unraveled the Reagan-era consensus and its deregulatory, business-first agenda. These shifts have created a palpable instability in the American self-conception, and with it a possibility of renegotiation and change. Now as ever, the winners in this struggle will likely be those who construct, out of the raw materials of America's individualist mythology, the most compelling story of what this country can and should be.

On The Meaning(s) of Individualism

THE TERM "INDIVIDUALISM," as it relates to American political ideas, has many different meanings.[1] Although they seldom define the term carefully, historians acknowledge this multiplicity in the range of adjectives they deploy. Readers find the conceptual field littered with alternatives, including economic individualism, entrepreneurial individualism, possessive individualism, Jeffersonian individualism, atomistic individualism, liberal individualism, rugged individualism, competitive individualism, expressive individualism, Romantic individualism, spiritual individualism, and more. This appendix distinguishes between five distinct meanings of the term, each of which historians sometimes apply to American political ideas, and each of which has in fact shaped them in important ways. Each entry is sketched in broad brushstrokes, and each also includes a brief example of one prominent historian's usage.[2] The final entry speaks to the relationship between individualism and liberalism, understood as a tradition of political thought.

Moral Individualism

Moral individualism asserts the "*supreme and intrinsic value, or dignity, of the individual human being.*"[3] It stands opposed to moral collectivism, which locates the ultimate source of moral value in collective entities: institutions, cultures, kinship groups, societies, nations. The moral individualist holds that the moral value of such entities stems entirely from the individuals who comprise or are touched by them. In Western thought, moral individualism has typically carried egalitarian connotations: its advocates have argued that *ordinary persons*, not just kings and nobles, possess morally significant characteristics that entitle them to equal moral respect.[4] This egalitarian strain of moral individualism lies at the heart of both Christian and Enlightenment ethics.

In *Making the American Self*, Daniel Walker Howe sets out to explore the widening acceptance of moral individualism in eighteenth- and nineteenth-century America. "This book tells part of the story," he writes, "of the acceptance of what can be called 'individualism,' that is, the belief that ordinary men and women have a dignity and value in their own right, and that they are sufficiently trustworthy to be allowed a measure of autonomy in their lives."[5] In fact, his definition contains two different ideas. To the essential content of moral individualism, Howe adds the conviction that human dignity is best respected by allowing each individual some control over his or her own life. Although this second idea does not necessarily follow from the first, the two grew almost inseparable by the end of the nineteenth century.[6]

Epistemic (or Intellectual) Individualism

Epistemic individualism holds that (adult) individuals ought to seek knowledge through the use of their own faculties—their own reason, intuition, or powers of observation. It applies focally to religious, moral, and political knowledge. In these areas in particular, it urges individuals to make up their own minds rather than deferring to the authority of others. It stands opposed, for instance, to the view that parishioners should defer to the moral and spiritual authority of the clergy, or that political subjects should defer to the moral and political authority of virtuous elites. Historians often highlight epistemic individualism in the context of the Protestant Reformation and its diverse intellectual legacies. In his two-volume history of dissenting religion in New England, for example, William McLoughlin argues that "the radical Reformation doctrine of the supremacy of private judgment in religion became united, after 1775, to the democratic concept of a higher law than that of any church or state constitution." "Together," he continues, "they eventually produced the anti-institutional individualism which dominated American life in the nineteenth century."[7] "Higher law" here refers to the idea that legitimate governments should adhere to certain universal moral principles or natural laws, which are accessible to all individuals through reason or conscience. It invites citizens to judge for themselves whether their government is just or even legitimate. In politics as in matters of the soul, writes McLoughlin, nineteenth-century Americans came to believe that individuals should judge for themselves.

Political Individualism

The term "political individualism" could be used to mean two different things: first, that the highest *purpose* of politics is to protect or enhance individual liberty; second, that all legitimate political authority derives from individual consent. Both find succinct expression in the Declaration of Independence, with its assertion that governments are instituted to secure individual rights, and that such governments derive their "just powers from the consent of the governed." We focus here on the first of these meanings: political individualists believe that government exists largely to protect individuals from harm and to enhance the range of meaningful choices available to them, so that they can pursue lives that reflect their own convictions and desires. Historians of American political thought have often used the term "individualism" in this sense. Reflecting in broad brushstrokes on the tenor of American political ideas, for example, Clinton Rossiter wrote that "the core of our faith is individualism. 'The state was made for man, not man for the state' is the magic formula with which Americans bid the evil spirits of authoritarianism be gone."[8] For Rossiter, this faith was expressed in the conviction that the state existed, above all, to preserve individual freedom.

Social Individualism

As we explored in chapters 3 and 7, the idea of society as an organic whole composed of unequal but interdependent parts persisted well into the nineteenth century. Many Federalist elites, for example, believed in a fundamentally hierarchical social order in which individuals played their appointed roles. Social individualism, by contrast, holds that social cohesion can and should arise through the voluntary cooperation of autonomous individuals. There are two separate ideas here. The first is that society *is* a collection of autonomous individuals rather than an organic whole or a hierarchy of complementary orders or castes. The second is that society *should be* bound together, as much as possible, by free and voluntary cooperation, not by coercion. When Joyce Appleby used the term "individualism," she referred broadly to the emergence of the "autonomous individual . . . as an ideal" over the course of the eighteenth and early nineteenth centuries. Social individualism was integral to this development. The ascendant Jeffersonian ideology of the 1790s, she writes, envisioned "the natural harmony of autonomous individuals freely exerting themselves to take care of their own interests while expanding the range of free exchange and free inquiry."[9]

Economic Individualism

Although economic individualism is a subset of social individualism, its powerful influence on the shape of modern life makes it worth discussing separately. Economic individualism holds that economic decisions—mainly decisions about what and how much to produce—should by and large be made by private individuals pursuing their own interests. Economic individualists also believe that competition, not coercion, is the best way of disciplining and organizing economic life. The economic doctrine of laissez-faire, with its insistence that the state refrain, as much as possible, from interfering in market transactions, is an especially uncompromising expression of economic individualism. When historians apply the term "individualism" to American history, they commonly refer to some or all of these economic values and beliefs. Some use it simply as shorthand for the glorification of acquisitive self-interest. Others, such as Richard Hofstadter, have offered somewhat narrower definitions. Summarizing the American "philosophy of economic individualism," Hofstadter offered the following list of commitments: "the sanctity of private property, the right of the individual to dispose of and invest it, the value of opportunity, and the natural evolution of self-interest and self-assertion, within broad legal limits, into a beneficent social order." He called these the "staple tenets of the central faith" that ran through all (mainstream) political ideologies in the United States.[10]

Although this book touches on all five of these forms of individualism, it accords primary importance to two of them. In chapter 2, individualism was defined as the belief that America *is and ought to be (a) a polity devoted to the expansion of private liberty and (b) a meritocratic society in which individuals are responsible for their own fates.* We can see now that this definition combines political individualism with a meritocratic strain of social individualism. These two fundamental ideas laced through all three foundational myths and bent the arc of American political thought in a persistently individualistic direction.

We have also seen, however, that these two forms of individualism often belonged to clusters of ideas that included some or all of the other three. Americans have typically believed, for example, that political individualism *presupposes* moral individualism. This connection is affirmed by Locke and by the Declaration of Independence, and we seldom find it challenged in the American political tradition. Meanwhile, all three foundational myths explored here conjoined political and social individualism with epistemic individualism: all variously mythologized the individual's capacity to make his own judgments, both publicly and privately, as part of the meaning of individual freedom. Finally, social individualism in America has often appeared in the form of economic individualism: since the Jacksonian Era, the idea of a meritocratic society of autonomous individuals has typically been rendered in the language of free and competitive markets. All five forms have shaped the variegated landscape of American individualism.

Liberalism and Individualism

Some readers will wonder whether the term "liberalism" could have been used, throughout this book, in place of "individualism." I have resisted this substitution for two reasons. First, liberalism as a concept is no clearer or less contested than individualism, and its association with the American center-left leaves it even more prone to misunderstanding. Second and more importantly, liberalism does not necessarily entail the meritocratic form of social individualism that has long flourished in the United States. Liberalism is a broad and diverse political tradition, and it encompasses some political perspectives that stand at odds with American individualism (in the sense defined above).

What then is liberalism? However else historians may use the term, liberalism certainly refers to a long-standing tradition[11] in the history of political ideas. Understood as a political doctrine, writes political theorist Judith Shklar, liberalism "has only one overriding aim: to secure the political conditions that are necessary for the exercise of personal freedom."[12] It also suggests a particular *idea* of freedom: liberals have always located the most important freedoms in private life. Above all, they have defended the freedom to worship, to speak and associate, to work and form meaningful relationships, to own property, and to do these things securely, without the constant threat of arbitrary intrusion. They have insisted, in other words, that individuals be free to make their own choices about those matters that are most important to them, so long as they can do so without injuring others.[13] Liberals believe that such freedom is the highest aim of government.

If these are the most fundamental liberal aims, liberal philosophers and politicians have also advocated a characteristic set of strategies to achieve them. These include, most importantly, the rule of law, governed by a standard of impartiality and overseen by an independent judiciary; the limitation of state power by constitutional restraints, including specifically enumerated individual rights; the accountability of public officials to their constituents; and the privatization of economic decision making. Together, these strategies reveal a central feature of the liberal imagination: liberals have always seen the modern state as uniquely threatening to individual freedom, for it commands "unique resources of physical might and persuasion."[14] Their political strategies have sought to tame and constrain the government's power, to render it less menacing to the individual.[15]

This does not mean, however, that liberals have worried *only* about state power. Most liberal thinkers have understood that individuals are vulnerable to diverse forms of oppression and harm, not all of which originate in the state. From the abolitionist movement onward, for example, some American liberals have turned to government to disrupt persistent patterns of racism, misogyny, and intolerance deeply lodged in traditional ways of life. With the advent of industrialization, moreover, many liberals began to see the corporate economy as a source of oppression and exploitation, and the welfare state as a way of shielding individuals from these dangers. These left-liberals diverged, increasingly, from the right-leaning liberals who saw, in such expansions of state power, the oppressive specter of big government. In the United States, both sides of this disagreement have remained broadly liberal, for both have held fast to the commitments outlined in the previous two paragraphs.[16]

What, then, is the relationship between liberalism and individualism? Briefly put: both political and moral individualism are defining features of the liberal tradition. There is simply no plausible way to define the liberal tradition without encompassing political individualism. The liberal commitment to individual rights and liberties has always rested, moreover, on an affirmation of the fundamental moral dignity or value of the individual. Of course, *which* individuals possessed this moral dignity—and *which* were therefore owed equal rights and equal political consideration—has been a deeply fraught question throughout the history of modern liberalism. Indeed, the history of liberalism can be told as an ongoing struggle between more and less exclusive visions of the rights-bearing individual. On the exclusive end of the spectrum, Western liberals have repeatedly invoked the "equal rights" of white men to justify the systematic oppression and exploitation of women and people of color, both domestically and abroad. On the inclusive end, they have pressed for a politics of universal human rights that cuts across both domains.[17]

The extent of liberalism's commitment to social, epistemic, and economic individualism, on the other hand, has varied considerably across time and across different liberal thinkers and persuasions. Liberalism's relationship to social individualism is complicated. The idea of human society as a collection of individuals bound together by contract runs strong in liberal thought from John Locke and Adam Smith onward. At the same time, many have been drawn to liberal politics out of a desire to protect group identity—especially the identities of persecuted minorities. Modern liberalism originated in the European wars of religion, and it was initially associated with a politics of toleration designed to depoliticize religious identity and allow it to flourish privately. In fact, many liberal intellectuals have imagined society as a collection of overlapping groups, some more like voluntary associations or interest groups, others more like inherited cultures or ascriptive identities. And while they have always insisted that individuals should be free to critically examine their group identities and to resist or leave them, reflective liberals have seldom urged people to divest themselves of their collective identities and reconstitute themselves as maximally autonomous "atoms." On the contrary, many liberals have affirmed the fundamental importance of group identity in rendering the world meaningful.[18]

What is more, many liberals have also maintained that group identity and association serve important *political* purposes. Some have argued, for example, that local associations and identity groups serve as critical "buffers" between the individual and the state. In their view, towns, churches, guilds, subnational cultures, and other groups offer competing sources of authority and affiliation and ensure that individuals do not stand alone before the all-encompassing power of the state. These liberals maintain that individual freedom tends to flourish in human communities that remain substantially "local, customary, unplanned, diverse, and decentralized."[19] Other liberals have argued that strong patterns of group affiliation and identification are essential in holding democratic officials accountable and compelling them to protect the rights and liberties of ordinary people. They argue that even liberal democracies drift toward oligarchy and tyranny unless they are called to account by groups of organized citizens bound together by mutual trust and by shared values and purposes. In their view, unaffiliated (or loosely affiliated) individuals are relatively powerless and ripe for political manipulation and domination.[20]

Liberalism's relationship to epistemic and economic individualism, too, is complex and varied. For our purposes here, we need only note, first, that many liberals have believed that personal freedom is best protected by delegating important political and economic decisions—including public health measures, for example—to experts rather than inviting everyone to make up their own minds. This deference to expertise, which has created recurrent tensions between liberalism and democracy, has been much discussed in the recent literature on the rise of authoritarian populism.[21] Second, although all liberals have embraced markets as a strategy for organizing economic life and shielding it from state control, they have disagreed deeply about how these markets should be constructed and regulated and how thoroughly they should be allowed to shape the distribution of wealth and opportunity. Under the influence of such towering liberal figures as Franklin Roosevelt, John Dewey, and John Rawls, many left-liberals in America have favored comprehensive economic regulation and redistribution designed to render market economies more egalitarian, more inclusive, and more accountable to democratic constituencies.

As a tradition, then, liberalism reflects varying levels of commitment to individualism. There can be no doubt, however, that popular liberal ideas in America have, by and large, been sharply individualistic: Americans have tended to embrace not only moral and political individualism but also epistemic, social, and economic individualism more deeply and unreservedly than liberals have elsewhere. Social individualism has been especially pronounced in the United States: as we have seen throughout this book, Americans have tended to see—and to celebrate—their own society as a meritocratic association of individuals, each responsible for their own fates. While this book should not be read as a study of liberalism *in general*, it certainly can be read as a study of the particular evolution of liberal ideas in America. In the Jacksonian Era, all three myths studied here were already being used to justify a fundamentally liberal politics; all three have shaped the tenor of American liberalism ever since.

NOTES

Chapter 1

1. Andrew Kohut et al., "The American-Western European Values Gap: American Exceptionalism Subsides" (Washington, DC: Pew Research Center, 2011), 7–8. See also Stefanie Stantcheva, "Prisoners of the American Dream," https://www.project-syndicate.org /commentary/social-mobility-american-and-european-views-by-stefanie-stantcheva-2018-02.

2. George Barna, *Growing True Disciples: New Strategies for Producing Genuine Followers of Christ* (Colorado Springs: Waterbrook, 2001), 67.

3. These changes had begun as early as the 1790s, and they came unevenly to different parts of the country. See Reeve Huston, "Rethinking the Origins of Partisan Democracy in the United States, 1795–1840," in *Practicing Democracy: Popular Politics in the United States from the Constitution to the Civil War*, ed. Daniel Peart and Adam I. P. Smith (Charlottesville: University of Virginia Press, 2015).

4. For a useful overview of these transformations, see John Lauritz Larson, *The Market Revolution in America: Liberty, Ambition, and the Eclipse of the Common Good* (Cambridge: Cambridge University Press, 2010).

5. For further discussion of slavery's relationship to the burgeoning market economy, see Sven Beckert and Seth Rockman, eds., *Slavery's Capitalism: A New History of American Economic Development* (Philadelphia: University of Pennsylvania Press, 2016).

6. This fact was appreciated by a number of twentieth-century historians and intellectuals, including Arthur Schlesinger Jr., who treated Jacksonian Democratic ideology as the purest expression of what he called the "Jeffersonian myth," which in his view still held Americans captive as late as the 1940s. Arthur Schlesinger Jr., *The Age of Jackson* (Boston: Little, Brown, 1945), 510–23. See also Judith Shklar, *American Citizenship: The Quest for Inclusion* (Cambridge, MA: Harvard University Press, 1991), 63–101; Marvin Meyers, *The Jacksonian Persuasion: Politics and Belief*, 2nd ed. (New York: Vintage Books, 1960 [1957]), 3–32; John William Ward, *Andrew Jackson: Symbol for an Age* (London: Oxford University Press, 1955).

7. Joyce Appleby, "New Cultural Heroes in the Early National Period," in *The Culture of the Market: Historical Essays*, ed. Thomas L. Haskell and Richard F. Teichgraeber III (Cambridge: Cambridge University Press, 1993), 168.

8. In its approach to the Jacksonian Democrats, this book is particularly indebted to two earlier studies: Rush Welter's 1975 volume, *The Mind of America: 1820–1860*, and John Ashworth's 1983 book, *"Agrarians" and "Aristocrats": Party Political Ideology in the United States, 1837–1846*.

9. For a definition of intellectual "tradition" as this term is used throughout this book, see the appendix, note 11.

10. For a definition of liberalism and a discussion of its relationship to individualism, see the appendix.

11. See, for instance, Louis Hartz, *The Liberal Tradition in America: An Interpretation of American Political Thought since the Revolution* (New York: Harcourt, Brace & World, 1955); Richard Hofstadter, *The American Political Tradition and the Men Who Made It* (New York: Vintage Books, 1989 [1948]); Daniel J. Boorstin, *The Genius of American Politics* (Chicago: University of Chicago Press, 1953). For more recent iterations of this view, see Samuel Huntington, *American Politics: The Promise of Disharmony* (Cambridge, MA: Harvard University Press, 1981); Seymour Martin Lipset, *American Exceptionalism: A Double-Edged Sword* (New York: W. W. Norton, 1996); J. David Greenstone, "Political Culture and American Political Development: Liberty, Union, and the Liberal Bipolarity," *Studies in American Political Development* 1 (1986): 1–49.

12. See, for example, Bernard Bailyn, *The Ideological Origins of the American Revolution*, enlarged ed. (Cambridge, MA: Harvard University Press, 1992 [1967]); Gordon Wood, *The Creation of the American Republic: 1776–1787* (Chapel Hill: University of North Carolina Press, 1998 [1969]); Drew R. McCoy, *The Elusive Republic: Political Economy in Jeffersonian America* (Chapel Hill: University of North Carolina Press, 1980); Barry Alan Shain, *The Myth of American Individualism: The Protestant Origins of American Political Thought* (Princeton: Princeton University Press, 1994). For the role of state and local governments, see William J. Novak, *The People's Welfare: Law and Regulation in Nineteenth-Century America* (Chapel Hill: University of North Carolina Press, 1996).

13. James A. Morone, *Hellfire Nation: The Politics of Sin in American History* (New Haven: Yale University Press, 2003). See also Wilson Carey McWilliams, *Redeeming Democracy in America*, ed. Patrick J. Deneen and Susan J. McWilliams (Lawrence: University Press of Kansas, 2011); John P. Diggins, *The Lost Soul of American Politics: Virtue, Self-Interest, and the Foundations of Liberalism* (Chicago: University of Chicago Press, 1984); Leo Ribuffo, *Right, Center, Left: Essays in American History* (New Brunswick, NJ: Rutgers University Press, 1992).

14. For critical assessments of the consensus view, see James A. Morone, "Storybook Truths about America," *Studies in American Political Development* 19 (2005): 216–26; James T. Kloppenberg, "In Retrospect: Louis Hartz's *The Liberal Tradition in America*," *Reviews in American History* 29, no. 3 (2001): 460–78; Rogers M. Smith, *Civic Ideals: Conflicting Visions of Citizenship in U.S. History* (New Haven: Yale University Press, 1997), 13–39; James P. Young, *Reconsidering American Liberalism: The Troubled Odyssey of the Liberal Idea* (Boulder, CO: Westview Press, 1996), esp. 1–12; Daniel Joseph Singal, "Beyond Consensus: Richard Hofstadter and American Historiography," *American Historical Review* 89, no. 4 (1984): 976–1004; Marvin Meyers, "Louis Hartz, *The Liberal Tradition in America*: An Appraisal," *Comparative Studies in Society and History* 5, no. 3 (1963): 261–68; John Higham, "The Cult of the 'American Consensus': Homogenizing Our History," *Commentary* 27, no. 2 (1959): 93–100.

15. Although this book also cites and considers longer, more academic works, it treats these as salient to the extent that they reflect or help illuminate popular currents of thought.

16. For explorations of these alternative myths, see, for instance, Edmund Morgan, *Inventing the People: The Rise of Popular Sovereignty in England and America* (New York: W. W. Norton, 1988); James A. Morone, *The Democratic Wish: Popular Participation and the Limits of American*

Government, rev. ed. (New Haven: Yale University Press, 1998); Jason Frank, *Constituent Moments: Enacting the People in Postrevolutionary America* (Durham: Duke University Press, 2010); Abram Van Engen, *City on a Hill: A History of American Exceptionalism* (New Haven: Yale University Press, 2020); Ernest Lee Tuveson, *Redeemer Nation: The Idea of America's Millennial Role* (Chicago: University of Chicago Press, 1968); Jacqueline Jones, *A Dreadful Deceit: The Myth of Race from the Colonial Era to Obama's America* (New York: Basic Books, 2013); Ibram X. Kendi, *Stamped from the Beginning: The Definitive History of Racist Ideas in America* (New York: Bold Type Books, 2016). The mythology of the frontier has also played a formative role in American political thought; see Henry Nash Smith, *Virgin Land: The American West as Symbol and Myth* (Cambridge, MA: Harvard University Press, 1970 [1950]); Greg Grandin, *The End of the Myth: From the Frontier to the Border Wall in the Mind of America* (New York: Metropolitan Books, 2019).

17. In the Jacksonian Era, these myths were circulated widely by political parties determined to create and hold together truly national constituencies. Even as they exaggerated national uniformity, these myths therefore helped *produce* a national political consciousness that is worth studying in its own right.

18. For one sophisticated discussion of these relationships, see Rogers M. Smith, *Political Peoplehood: The Role of Values, Interest, and Identities* (Chicago: University of Chicago Press, 2015).

Chapter 2

1. Alasdair MacIntyre, *After Virtue: A Study in Moral Theory*, 3rd ed. (Notre Dame: University of Notre Dame Press, 2007 [1981]), 216.

2. The definition of "myth" remains a matter of considerable scholarly controversy, which cannot be canvassed here. In keeping with Christopher Flood's usage, I exclude stories that "are publicly acknowledged to be fictional" from the category of myth. Christopher Flood, *Political Myth: A Theoretical Introduction* (London: Routledge, 2002), 67. On the other hand, those who accept myths as true often engage in some willing suspension of disbelief.

3. Ibid., 71–99; Chiara Bottici, *A Philosophy of Political Myth* (Cambridge: Cambrige University Press, 2007), 213–26.

4. Bottici, *A Philosophy of Political Myth*, 178–79.

5. For further discussion, see Rogers M. Smith, *Political Peoplehood: The Role of Values, Interest, and Identities* (Chicago: University of Chicago Press, 2015), 37–66; Rogers M. Smith, *Civic Ideals: Conflicting Visions of Citizenship in U.S. History* (New Haven: Yale University Press, 1997), 30–39. Smith argues that religious sanctification and ethnic or racial superiority are the two most common elements in these idealized constructions of national peoples.

6. Smith, *Political Peoplehood*, 19–91.

7. Bottici, *A Philosophy of Political Myth*, 200. Bottici describes human beings as incomplete animals: for us, the opacity and indifference of the world produces an anguish that can only be extinguished through art, and more precisely, through stories that render it both intelligible and meaningful. The human being is thus "an animal suspended in webs of significance" of which myths have always formed an integral part. Ibid., 124.

8. Flood, *Political Myth: A Theoretical Introduction*, 71–99; Bottici, *A Philosophy of Political Myth*, 116–33, 177–202. As we will see, foundational myths are often infused with elements of the sacred, so they are rarely wholly separate from religious mythology.

9. This relationship is explored in depth in, for example, Ernst Cassirer, *The Myth of the State* (New Haven: Yale University Press, 1946); Murray Edelman, *The Symbolic Uses of Politics* (Urbana: University of Illinois Press, 1964); Henry Tudor, *Political Myth* (London: Macmillan, 1972); Flood, *Political Myth: A Theoretical Introduction*; Bottici, *A Philosophy of Political Myth*.

10. John M. Murrin, "A Roof without Walls: The Dilemma of American National Identity," in *Rethinking America: From Empire to Republic*, ed. John M. Murrin (Oxford: Oxford University Press, 2018 [1987]), 191.

11. David Hackett Fischer, *Albion's Seed: Four British Folkways in America* (New York: Oxford University Press, 1989), 821–34; Benjamin Park, *American Nationalisms: Imagining Union in the Age of Revolutions, 1783–1833* (Cambridge: Cambridge University Press, 2018), 27–68; Jack P. Greene, *The Intellectual Construction of America: Exceptionalism and Identity from 1492 to 1800* (Chapel Hill: University of North Carolina Press, 1993), 162–99.

12. Alan Taylor, *American Republics: A Continental History of the United States, 1783–1850* (New York: W. W. Norton, 2021), 5–62. By the 1840s, elites in both of the dominant political parties—the Democrats and the Whigs—were heavily invested in this nationalist project. As they struggled to maintain a broad, cross-regional voting base, both parties worked hard to suppress sharp regional antagonisms and to present themselves as embodiments of the will of a sovereign and free national people. In doing so, both appropriated and refashioned America's national myths and used them to project an idealized image of the American people and of themselves as its natural leaders.

13. William Ellery Channing, *The Importance and Means of a National Literature* (London: Edward Rainford, 1830), 35.

14. "To be American meant to be free," writes Major Wilson of the national myths that circulated between 1815 and 1862, "and in the contours of the national debate Americans searched for the meanings of their freedom." Major L. Wilson, *Space, Time, and Freedom: The Quest for Nationality and the Irrepressible Conflict, 1815–1861* (Westport, CT: Greenwood Press, 1974), ix. See also Eric Foner, *The Story of American Freedom* (New York: W. W. Norton, 1998), 47–94; Greene, *The Intellectual Construction of America*, 162–209.

15. I use the term "mythology" to describe a set of myths, unified by certain common themes or purposes, that circulate in a given society.

16. This openness and flexibility has led me to resist the term "ideology," which is often used to describe top-down systems of cultural control. On the malleability and the subversive potential of national myths, see Sacvan Bercovitch, *The American Jeremiad* (Madison: University of Wisconsin Press, 1978), 180, 111, 158–60; Smith, *Political Peoplehood: The Role of Values, Interest, and Identities*, 42–43.

17. On the simultaneously generative and limiting effects of political myth, see Flood, *Political Myth: A Theoretical Introduction*, 82–83. Although he is not writing about myth in particular, Daniel Rodgers captures these qualities too in *Contested Truths: Keywords in American Politics since Independence* (New York: Basic Books, 1987), 3–16.

18. An excellent discussion of these several conceptions of freedom can be found in Foner, *The Story of American Freedom*, xiii–28, 47–68.

19. For a seminal discussion of this myth, see Richard Hofstadter, *The Age of Reform* (New York: Vintage, 1955), 23–59. See also Henry Nash Smith, *Virgin Land: The American West as Symbol and Myth* (Cambridge, MA: Harvard University Press, 1970 [1950]), 123–203; Leo Marx,

The Machine in the Garden: Technology and the Pastoral Ideal in America (Oxford: Oxford University Press, 2000 [1964]), 97–144.

20. For the seminal discussion of this Lockean mythology in America, see Louis Hartz, *The Liberal Tradition in America: An Interpretation of American Political Thought since the Revolution* (New York: Harcourt, Brace & World, 1955), 3–32, 59–64.

21. For discussions of the pervasiveness and complexity of this myth in American culture, see Irvin Wyllie, *The Self-Made Man in America: The Myth of Rags to Riches* (New Brunswick, NJ: Rutgers University Press, 1954); John G. Cawelti, *Apostles of the Self-Made Man* (Chicago: University of Chicago Press, 1965).

22. An overview of these competing connotations can be found in Fischer, *Albion's Seed*.

23. As many scholars have shown, this privatization of freedom was already well underway at the American founding. The Constitution itself can be understood as an attempt to secure greater political stability by *depoliticizing* the American public and refocusing its energies—and its conception of free agency—into economic life. See, for instance, Michael Lienesch, *New Order of the Ages: Time, the Constitution, and the Making of Modern American Political Thought* (Princeton: Princeton University Press, 1988), 170–74; Stephanie Walls, *Individualism in the United States: A Transformation in American Political Thought* (New York: Bloomsbury, 2015).

24. See, for instance, Alexis de Tocqueville, *Democracy in America*, trans. Arthur Goldhammer, vol. 2 (New York: Library of America, 2004 [1840]), 585–87, 625–28; Michel Chevalier, *Society, Manners and Politics in the United States; Being a Series of Letters on North America* (Boston: Weeks, Jordan, and Co., 1839), 283–90, 405–22.

25. Tocqueville, *Democracy in America*, 2:587.

26. "Private liberty," in this context, simply means the absence of constraints and the profusion of options in private life. A "meritocracy," meanwhile, is a society in which rewards flow to individuals in strict proportion to their merit. Americans have typically understood *merit* to involve some combination of effort and talent. Thus those who achieve the highest rungs of success are thought to be those who work tirelessly *and* who were blessed with "God-given ability."

27. See, for instance, Yehoshua Arieli, *Individualism and Nationalism in American Ideology* (Baltimore: Penguin Books, 1964); Hartz, *The Liberal Tradition in America*, 3–32; Michael Kazin and Joseph A. McCartin, eds., *Americanism: New Perspectives on the History of an Ideal* (Chapel Hill: University of North Carolina Press, 2006), 1–21; Liah Greenfeld, *Nationalism: Five Roads to Modernity* (Cambridge, MA: Harvard University Press, 1992), 397–484; Hans Kohn, *American Nationalism: An Interpretive Essay* (Westport, CT: Greenwood Press, 1957), 7–19.

28. For further discussion of the prominence of the "Old World" in Americans' idea of their own national identity, see Rush Welter, *The Mind of America: 1820–1860* (New York: Columbia University Press, 1975), 26–44.

29. In the late eighteenth and early nineteenth centuries, moreover, many Americans also believed that Black and Native American men could achieve propertied independence and its attendant virtues.

30. Smith, *Civic Ideals*, 206–12.

31. Ibid., 197–242. The idea of Protestant Americanism was more complicated, because Protestantism was a richer and more diverse reservoir of shared meaning and value. Still, when Americans used their Protestant heritage to project a unified national identity, we typically find

them assimilating it to their freedom-myths. The invidious contrast with Catholicism encouraged this fusion: whereas Catholicism was widely described as a slavish faith that rewarded unthinking obedience and abject submission, Protestantism was widely associated with individual freedom: it ostensibly taught people to think for themselves, to cherish their rights and liberties, to define the course of their own lives.

32. David Brion Davis, *The Problem of Slavery in the Age of Emancipation* (New York: Knopf, 2014), 42.

33. Robert P. Forbes, *The Missouri Compromise and Its Aftermath: Slavery and the Meaning of America* (Chapel Hill: University of North Carolina Press, 2007), 30.

34. See Matthew Frye Jacobson, *Whiteness of a Different Color: European Immigrants and the Alchemy of Race* (Cambridge, MA: Harvard University Press, 1998); Noel Ignatiev, *How the Irish Became White* (New York: Routledge, 1995).

35. For a perceptive discussion of this defining contrast, see Daniel T. Rodgers, *Atlantic Crossings: Social Politics in a Progressive Age* (Cambridge, MA: Harvard University Press, 1998), 33–39.

36. The anti-communist hysteria that erupted periodically in the twentieth century shows that even this inclusive version of American national identity could yield harsh consequences for those who did not to assimilate to its norms. Gary Gerstle, *American Crucible: Race and Nation in the Twentieth Century* (Princeton: Princeton University Press, 2001), 238–67.

37. Lloyd Kramer has noted the importance of these dual contrasts in constructing American national identity; see Lloyd Kramer, *Nationalism in Europe and America: Politics, Cultures, and Identities since 1775* (Chapel Hill: University of North Carolina Press, 2011), 127–30. For an incisive discussion of the inclusive and exclusive dimensions of the American idea of citizenship and national identity, see Judith Shklar, *American Citizenship: The Quest for Inclusion* (Cambridge, MA: Harvard University Press, 1991).

38. Gerstle, *American Crucible*, 3–13. For another sustained reflection on this tension, see Patrice Higonnet, *Attendant Cruelties: Nation and Nationalism in American History* (New York: Other Press, 2007).

39. Gerstle, *American Crucible*; Smith, *Civic Ideals*; Shklar, *American Citizenship*; Foner, *The Story of American Freedom*.

40. This point is crucial in appreciating the power of America's individualist myths. It casts doubt on Rogers Smith's argument that individualist ideals, because they take the form of universal values or principles, "have offered few reasons why Americans should see themselves as a distinct people, apart from others" (*Civic Ideals*, 38).

41. E. P. Thompson summarizes these liberties as follows: "freedom from absolutism (the constitutional Monarchy), freedom from arbitrary arrest, trial by jury, equality before the law, the freedom of the home from arbitrary entrance and search, some limited liberty of thought, of speech, and of conscience, the vicarious participation in liberty (or in its semblance) afforded by the right of parliamentary opposition and by elections and election tumults (although the people had no vote they had the right to parade, huzza and cheer on the hustings), as well as freedom to travel, trade, and sell one's own labor." E. P. Thompson, *The Making of the English Working Class* (New York: Vintage Books, 1963), 79. See also Foner, *The Story of American Freedom*, 3–14.

42. For detailed exploration of these contrasting cultures of freedom in eighteenth-century America, see Fischer, *Albion's Seed*.

43. Joyce Appleby, *Inheriting the Revolution: The First Generation of Americans* (Cambridge, MA: Belknap Press, 2000), 56–89; Jeremy Atack and Fred Bateman, *To Their Own Soil: Agriculture in the Antebellum North* (Ames: Iowa State University Press, 1987), 3–14, 86–101, 201–66; Daniel Feller, *The Jacksonian Promise: America, 1815–1840* (Baltimore: Johns Hopkins University Press, 1995), 1–32; Robert H. Wiebe, *The Opening of American Society: From the Adoption of the Constitution to the Eve of Disunion* (New York: Alfred A. Knopf, 1984), 146–56, 257–64.

44. John Ashworth, *Slavery, Capitalism, and Politics in the Antebellum Republic*, vol. 1: *Commerce and Compromise, 1820–1850* (Cambridge: Cambridge University Press, 1995), 304–5; Eric Foner, "Free Labor and Nineteenth-Century Political Ideology," in *The Market Revolution in America: Social, Political, and Religious Expressions, 1800–1880*, ed. Melvyn Stokes and Stephen Conway (Charlottesville: University Press of Virginia, 1996), 103. For more detail, see Christopher Clark, *The Roots of Rural Capitalism: Western Massachusetts, 1780–1860* (Ithaca: Cornell University Press, 1990), 152–55, 273–313; Alan Kulikoff, *The Agrarian Origins of American Capitalism* (Charlottesville: University Press of Virginia, 1992), 34–59; Gavin Wright and Howard Kunreuther, "Cotton, Corn and Risk in the Nineteenth Century," *Journal of Economic History* 35, no. 3 (1975): 526–51.

45. James L. Huston, *The British Gentry, the Southern Planter, and the Northern Family Farmer: Agriculture and Sectional Antagonism in North America* (Baton Rouge: Louisiana State University Press, 2015), 193–204; Joyce Appleby, *The Relentless Revolution: A History of Capitalism* (New York: W. W. Norton, 2010), 178.

46. James L. Huston, *Securing the Fruits of Labor: The American Concept of Wealth Distribution, 1765–1900* (Baton Rouge: Louisiana State University Press, 1998), 105–6. To make note of the many-layered privileges that white Americans enjoyed compared to their European counterparts is not to deny, of course, that many white Americans were poor; that opportunities were unequally distributed among white families; or that the "market revolution" brought significant economic dislocation and anxiety in both the cities and the countryside. Over the last half century, an abundance of scholarly research has explored the economic hardships experienced, for example, by poor tenant farmers, immigrant rail workers, and urban wage workers. See, for instance, Jonathan A. Glickstein, *American Exceptionalism, American Anxiety: Wages, Competition, and Degraded Labor in the Antebellum United States* (Charlottesville: University of Virginia Press, 2002); Seth Rockman, *Scraping By: Wage Labor, Slavery, and Survival in Early Baltimore* (Baltimore: Johns Hopkins University Press, 2009); David Montgomery, *Citizen Worker: The Experience of Workers in the United States with Democracy and the Free Market during the Nineteenth Century* (New York: Cambridge University Press, 1993); Sean Wilentz, *Chants Democratic: New York City and the Rise of the American Working Class, 1788–1850* (New York: Oxford University Press, 1984).

47. Appleby, *Inheriting the Revolution*, 89; Feller, *The Jacksonian Promise*, 1–13.

48. Appleby, *Inheriting the Revolution*, 88.

49. John Mack Faragher, *Sugar Creek: Life on the Illinois Prairie* (New Haven: Yale University Press, 1986), 50; Wiebe, *The Opening of American Society*, 132.

50. Quoted in Rowland Berthoff, *An Unsettled People: Social Order and Disorder in American History* (New York: Harper & Row, 1971), 218.

51. George Pierson, "The M-Factor in American History," *American Quarterly* 14, no. 2 (1962): 286. "Once across the mountains," writes Robert Wiebe, "the migrants lived in a fluid society of strangers" (*The Opening of American Society*, 132).

52. Quoted in Faragher, *Sugar Creek*, 51–52.

53. Pierson, "The M-Factor in American History," 284. See also Rowland Berthoff, "The American Social Order: A Conservative Hypothesis," *American Historical Review* 65, no. 3 (1960): 501.

54. Appleby, *Inheriting the Revolution*, 20; Clayne Pope, "Inequality in the Nineteenth Century," in *The Cambridge Economic History of the United States*, vol. 2, ed. Stanley L. Engerman and Robert E. Gallman (Cambridge: Cambridge University Press, 2000).

55. Clayne Pope finds, for example, that the frontier was a source of considerable upward mobility for white farmworkers, regardless of their ethnic background: "Farm laborers systematically moved into farm ownership, and poor farmers usually increased their wealth" ("Inequality in the Nineteenth Century," 2:130).

56. Berthoff, *An Unsettled People*, 177–203.

57. "Most entrepreneurs failed at least once in their careers," writes Appleby, "and all were exposed to the consequences of the bankruptcy of the bosses or associates" (*Inheriting the Revolution*, 87–88). Andrew Jackson himself felt the effects of this volatility: as a young man, he almost ended up in debtor's prison after an ill-advised economic transaction left him responsible for a friend's escalating debts.

58. Ibid., 21.

59. Harriet Martineau, *Society in America*, vol. 1 (New York: Saunders and Olney, 1837), 22, 12. Such observations were commonplace in the works of European visitors. The German transplant Francis Lieber, for instance, wrote that "in America there is no peasant." The farmer, he observed, did not form a separate underclass; "He is a citizen to all intents and purposes, not only as to political rights, but as to his whole standing and social connexion." Francis Lieber, *The Stranger in America: Comprising Sketches of the Manners, Society, and National Peculiarities of the United States . . .*, vol. 2 (London: Richard Bentley, 1835), 157.

60. Chevalier, *Society, Manners and Politics in the United States*, 283. Such observations are best understood as illuminating *relative* differences between European and American societies. There were of course social classes in America, as antebellum historians have exhaustively documented, just as there were populations of poor whites who saw little opportunity for economic advancement. See note 46 in this chapter.

61. Appleby, *Inheriting the Revolution*, 138.

62. Curtis D. Johnson, *Redeeming America: Evangelicals and the Road to Civil War*, American Way Series (Chicago: Ivan R. Dee, 1993), 86–114; Randolph Roth, *The Democratic Dilemma: Religion, Reform, and the Social Order in the Connecticut River Valley of Vermont, 1791–1850* (Cambridge: Cambridge University Press, 1987), 187–219.

63. Richard J. Carwardine, *Evangelicals and Politics in Antebellum America* (Knoxville: University of Tennessee Press, 1997 [1993]), 2.

64. John H. Wigger, *Taking Heaven by Storm: Methodism and the Rise of Popular Christianity in America* (Urbana: University of Illinois Press, 1998), 80–103.

65. Nathan O. Hatch, *The Democratization of American Christianity* (New Haven: Yale University Press, 1989), 17–46. "These movements," writes Hatch, "empowered ordinary people to take their deepest spiritual impulses at face value rather than subjecting them to the scrutiny of orthodox doctrine and the frowns of respectable clergymen" (10). See also Mark A. Noll, *America's God: From Jonathan Edwards to Abraham Lincoln* (Oxford: Oxford University Press, 2002), 367–85.

66. Arminians rejected the Calvinist idea of predestination and argued that human beings could exercise some agency in securing their own salvation.

67. For examples, see Lorenzo Dow, *Perambulations of a Cosmopolite, or, Travels & Labors of Lorenzo Dow, in Europe and America* (New York: R. C. Valentine, 1855 [1816]); John Taylor, *A History of Ten Baptist Churches ...* (Cincinnati: Art Guild Reprints, 1986 [1823]); Barton Stone and John Rogers, *The Biography of Eld. Barton Warren Stone, Written by Himself* (Cincinnati: J. A. & U. P. James, 1847); William Burke, "Autobiography of Rev. William Burke," in *Sketches of Western Methodism: Biographical, Historical, and Miscellaneous, Illustrative of Pioneer Life*, ed. James Finley and W. P. Strickland (Cincinnati: R. P. Thompson, 1855); Peter Cartwright, *Autobiography of Peter Cartwright, the Backwoods Preacher* (New York: Carlton & Porter, 1857); James Finley, *Autobiography of James Finley, or, Pioneer Life in the West*, ed. W. P. Strickland (Cincinnati: Cranston and Curtis, 1853); Jacob Young, *Autobiography of a Pioneer, or, The Nativity, Experience, Travels, and Ministerial Labors of Rev. Jacob Young; with Incidents, Observations, and Reflections* (Cincinnati: Poe & Hitchcock, 1860 [1859]); Heman Bangs, *The Autobiography and Journal of Rev. Heman Bangs; with an Introduction by Rev. Bishop Janes ...* (New York: N. Tibbals & Son, 1872). This emphasis on individual agency is also reflected, paradigmatically, in the tremendously influential sermons of evangelist Charles Finney. See especially Charles Grandison Finney, *Sermons on Important Subjects* (New York: John S. Taylor, 1836).

68. Noll, *America's God*, 214.

69. Sidney Mead, "Denominationalism: The Shape of Protestantism in America," *Church History* 23, no. 4 (1954): 291–320; Richard Hofstadter, *Anti-Intellectualism in American Life* (New York: Knopf, 1963), 82–86; Sydney Ahlstrom, *A Religious History of the American People*, 2nd ed. (New Haven: Yale University Press, 1972), 381–82; Jon Butler, *Awash in a Sea of Faith: Christianizing the American People* (Cambridge, MA: Harvard University Press, 1990), 273–75; Roger Finke and Rodney Stark, *The Churching of America, 1776–1990: Winners and Losers in Our Religious Economy* (New Brunswick, NJ: Rutgers University Press, 1992), 55–116.

70. Many of the influential European socialist thinkers of the first half of the nineteenth century, including Henri de Saint-Simon, Auguste Comte, Pierre Leroux, and others, believed that socialist society would be held in place partly by a unified church that would buttress the new society's socialist ethics and solidarity.

71. One of the seminal explorations of this weakness is still Hartz, *The Liberal Tradition in America*.

Part I

1. Jack P. Greene, *Pursuits of Happiness: The Social Development of Early Modern British Colonies and the Formation of American Culture* (Chapel Hill: University of North Carolina Press, 1988), 195.

2. This point should not be exaggerated, however: even seventeenth-century English republicanism had shown individualistic features. Personal independence, in particular, had long connoted autonomy and self-assertion, resistance to tyranny, and freedom of mind and judgment.

3. See, for instance, Gordon Wood, *The Radicalism of the American Revolution* (New York: Random House, 1992); Drew R. McCoy, *The Elusive Republic: Political Economy in Jeffersonian America* (Chapel Hill: University of North Carolina Press, 1980); Barry Alan Shain, *The Myth*

of American Individualism: The Protestant Origins of American Political Thought (Princeton: Princeton University Press, 1994); Michael J. Sandel, *Democracy's Discontent: America in Search of a Public Philosophy* (Cambridge, MA: Harvard University Press, 1996).

Chapter 3

1. Thomas Jefferson, "Notes on the State of Virginia," in *The Writings of Thomas Jefferson*, vol. 2, ed. Albert Ellery Bergh (Washington, DC: Thomas Jefferson Memorial Association, 1907 [1785]), 229.

2. Ibid.

3. Quoted in Rowland Berthoff, "Independence and Attachment, Virtue and Interest: From Republican Citizen to Free Enterpriser, 1787–1837," in *Uprooted Americans: Essays to Honor Oscar Handlin*, ed. Richard Bushman et al. (Boston: Little, Brown, 1979), 109.

4. Richard L. Bushman, "'This New Man': Dependence and Independence, 1776," in *Uprooted Americans*, ed. Bushman et al., 90.

5. Reviewing hundreds of letters written by English and Scottish emigrants to America in the first half of the nineteenth century, historian Charlotte Erickson found that "no other goal was mentioned so frequently as that of independence." Charlotte Erickson, *Invisible Immigrants: The Adaptation of English and Scottish Immigrants in Nineteenth-Century America* (Coral Gables: University of Miami Press, 1972), 27.

6. The erosion, in America, of the patrician ideal of leisured independence has been well-documented. See, for instance, Gordon Wood, *The Radicalism of the American Revolution* (New York: Random House, 1992), 271–86. The internal complexity of independence, which shaped its evolution over time, has received considerably less attention.

7. Gregory Claeys, *Citizens and Saints: Politics and Anti-Politics in Early British Socialism* (Cambridge: Cambridge University Press, 1989), 27. See also Eric MacGilvray, *The Invention of Market Freedom* (Cambridge: Cambridge University Press, 2011), 20–22; James T. Kloppenberg, "Premature Requiem: Republicanism in American History," in *The Virtues of Liberalism* (New York: Oxford University Press, 1998). Many defenders of limited or constitutional monarchy, for example, laid claim to republican ideas and values.

8. Drew R. McCoy, *The Elusive Republic: Political Economy in Jeffersonian America* (Chapel Hill: University of North Carolina Press, 1980), 77.

9. Gordon Wood, *The Creation of the American Republic: 1776–1787* (Chapel Hill: University of North Carolina Press, 1998 [1969]), 66–67.

10. The precise meaning of this central republican idea—virtue—was always contested. As we will see, it evolved over time, and it acquired different content as it was mobilized in different political context and controversies. For an extended discussion of the evolution of the concept in eighteenth-century America, see Richard Vetterli and Gary Bryner, *In Search of the Republic: Public Virtue and the Roots of American Government* (Lanham, MD: Rowman and Littlefield, 1996).

11. Writers and politicians influenced by republican ideas disagreed widely about which of these dangers was most significant, and these disagreements lent variety and flexibility to the republican perspective.

12. Independent proprietorship on the land was less important to the earlier, Florentine articulations of republicanism. As republican ideas were transposed from the commercial

republics of Florence and Venice to a largely agrarian England, and as they were read back into the myth of medieval Saxon freedom before the Norman conquest, they were grafted onto a pastoral tradition and an essentially agrarian vision of property and liberty. James Harrington was a key figure in this transposition, which also had foundations in classical Roman agrarianism. See J. G. A. Pocock, "Historical Introduction," in *The Political Works of James Harrington* (Cambridge: Cambridge University Press, 1977); J. G. A. Pocock, *The Machiavellian Moment: Florentine Political Thought and the Atlantic Republican Tradition* (Princeton: Princeton University Press, 1975), 386–91.

13. J. G. A. Pocock, "Virtue and Commerce in the Eighteenth Century," *Journal of Interdisciplinary History* 3, no. 1 (1972): 129.

14. "The man that cannot live upon his own," writes James Harrington, "must be a servant, but he that can live upon his own may be a freeman." James Harrington, "A System of Politics, Delineated in Short and East Aphorisms," in *The Oceana and Other Works of James Harrington, with an Account of His Life by John Toland* (London: T. Becket and T. Cadell, 1771 [1700]), 465.

15. Matthew McCormack, *The Independent Man: Citizenship and Gender Politics in Georgian England* (Manchester: Manchester University Press, 2005), 5–19; Daniel Vickers, *Farmers and Fishermen: Two Centuries of Work in Essex County, Massachusetts, 1630–1850* (Chapel Hill: University of North Carolina Press, 1994), 15–19; MacGilvray, *The Invention of Market Freedom*, 28.

16. Pocock, *The Machiavellian Moment*, 450. It was a truism of republican thought, moreover, that "power follows property": whoever controlled the balance of a country's property would, in effect, wield political power. Caroline Robbins, *The Eighteenth-Century Commonwealthman: Studies in the Transmission, Development, and Circumstance of English Liberal Thought from the Restoration of Charles II until the War with the Thirteen Colonies* (Indianapolis: Liberty Fund, 2004 [1959]), 34–35, 102.

17. John Trenchard and Thomas Gordon, "No. 68," in *Cato's Letters*, vol. 2 (London: Witkins, Woodward, Walthoe, and Peele, 1737 [1721]), 319.

18. Edmund Morgan, *American Slavery, American Freedom: The Ordeal of Colonial Virginia* (New York: W. W. Norton, 1975), 377.

19. McCormack, *The Independent Man*, 19. See also Alan Kulikoff, "The Transition to Capitalism in Rural America," *William and Mary Quarterly* 46, no. 1 (1989): 137–40, 143–44.

20. For further discussion of independence and gender, see chapter 4.

21. McCormack, *The Independent Man*, 2; Vickers, *Farmers and Fishermen*, 15–16.

22. In this high form, it was associated with a distinctive ideal of character, which represented "the epitome of political virtue." McCormack, *The Independent Man*, 2.

23. Ibid., 24; J. G. A. Pocock, "Virtue and Commerce in the Eighteenth Century," 121.

24. McCormack, *The Independent Man*, 67–69; H. T. Dickinson, *Liberty and Property: Political Ideology in Eighteenth-Century Britain* (New York: Holmes and Meier, 1977), 85–89; Samuel Dennis Glover, "The Putney Debates: Popular versus Elitist Republicanism," *Past & Present*, no. 164 (1999): 51–52; Robbins, *The Eighteenth-Century Commonwealthman*, 13.

25. McCormack, *The Independent Man*; Glover, "The Putney Debates."

26. Vickers, *Farmers and Fishermen*, 17.

27. McCormack, *The Independent Man*, 16–17; Ronald Schultz, *The Republic of Labor: Philadelphia Artisans and the Politics of Class, 1720–1830* (New York: Oxford University Press, 1993), 5–7. In these contexts, independence was often linked to an ethnic vision of English manliness,

reaching back to the idealized Saxon past, that emphasized such virtues as honesty, self-assertion, and military valor. Later reformers pushing for expansions of the franchise would appeal to these more plebian conceptions of independence to justify their reforms.

28. Quoted in Wood, *The Creation of the American Republic*, 168.

29. John Adams, "John Adams to James Sullivan, May 26, 1776," in *The Works of John Adams*, vol. 9, ed. Charles F. Adams (Boston: Little, Brown, 1856 [1776]), 376. Adams shared this view with Sir William Blackstone, whose *Commentaries on the Laws of England* was deeply influential in colonial America. Sean Wilentz, *The Rise of American Democracy: Jefferson to Lincoln* (New York: Norton, 2005), 8; Dennis R. Nolan, "Sir William Blackstone and the New American Republic: A Study of Intellectual Impact," *NYU Law Review* 51 (1976): 731–68.

30. Wood, *The Creation of the American Republic*, 168.

31. Morgan, *American Slavery, American Freedom*, 338–44.

32. Ibid., 377; Robert E. Shalhope, *John Taylor of Caroline: Pastoral Republican* (Columbia: University of South Carolina Press, 1980), 44; Jack P. Greene, *Pursuits of Happiness: The Social Development of Early Modern British Colonies and the Formation of American Culture* (Chapel Hill: University of North Carolina Press, 1988), 196.

33. Pocock, *The Machiavellian Moment*, 515.

34. Henry St. John Bolingbroke, "A Letter on the Spirit of Patriotism," in *The Works of the Late Right Honourable Henry St. John, Lord Viscount Bolingbroke*, vol. 3 (London: D. Mallet, 1754 [1736]), 14.

35. McCormack, *The Independent Man*, 89, 32–44.

36. T. H. Breen, *Tobacco Culture: The Mentality of the Great Tidewater Planters on the Eve of Revolution* (Princeton: Princeton University Press, 1985), 84–106; Bushman, "'This New Man': Dependence and Independence, 1776," 84.

37. Wood, *The Radicalism of the American Revolution*, 33. See also Enrico Dal Lago, "Patriarchs and Republicans: Eighteenth-Century Virginian Planters and Classical Politics," *Historical Research* 76, no. 194 (2003): 499–504.

38. Richard Beeman, "Deference, Republicanism, and the Emergence of Popular Politics in Eighteenth-Century America," *William and Mary Quarterly* 49, no. 3 (1992): 407. For further discussion, see also Gary B. Nash, "Artisans and Politics in Eighteenth-Century Philadelphia," in *The Origins of Anglo-American Radicalism*, ed. Margaret C. Jacob and James R. Jacob (London: George Allen & Unwin, 1984); Edmund Morgan, *Inventing the People: The Rise of Popular Sovereignty in England and America* (New York: W. W. Norton, 1988), 160–208; Pocock, *The Machiavellian Moment*, 515.

39. Pocock, *The Machiavellian Moment*, 515, 414.

40. On the crucial political role of the class of independent, land-owning elites in English republican ideology, see Dickinson, *Liberty and Property*, 165–84, 102–3; Morgan, *Inventing the People*, 166–73.

41. Breen, *Tobacco Culture*, 89. Breen shows, however, that this exalted ideal was often a fiction: the great Tidewater tobacco planters chronically ran up debts to cover their expenses between crops.

42. McCormack, *The Independent Man*, 51. The secret ballot did not become widespread in England and America until the nineteenth century.

43. As one might expect, the practice of elections in colonial America did not often live up to this republican ideal: votes were bought, coalitions organized, campaigns strategized. In fact, historian Richard Beeman suggests that it was often the losers who invoked the lofty republican ideal of independence to chastise their rivals for resorting to the sordid business of popular electioneering. Beeman, "Deference, Republicanism, and the Emergence of Popular Politics in Eighteenth-Century America," 427–30. See also Morgan, *Inventing the People*, 174–208.

44. Constant Truman, "Advice to the Free-Holders and Electors of Pennsylvania" (Philadelphia: Andrew Bradford, 1735), 6, 2.

45. Christopher Michael Curtis, *Jefferson's Freeholders and the Politics of Ownership in the Old Dominion* (Cambridge: Cambridge University Press, 2012), 168.

46. Wood, *The Creation of the American Republic*, 78.

47. Morgan, *American Slavery, American Freedom*, 383.

48. Pocock, *The Machiavellian Moment*, 407.

49. See ibid., chaps. 13 and 14; MacGilvray, *The Invention of Market Freedom*, chap. 3.

50. Henry St. John Bolingbroke, "Some Reflections on the Present State of the Nation," in *The Works of the Late Right Honourable Henry St. John, Lord Viscount Bolingbroke*, vol. 3 (London: D. Mallet, 1754 [1753]), 174. See also Wood, *The Radicalism of the American Revolution*, 105–09.

51. Breen, *Tobacco Culture*, 84–159.

52. Pocock, *The Machiavellian Moment*, 447–49; MacGilvray, *The Invention of Market Freedom*, 106.

53. MacGilvray, *The Invention of Market Freedom*, 103. See also Vetterli and Bryner, *In Search of the Republic*, 200–234.

54. Charles de Montesquieu, *The Spirit of the Laws*, trans. Anne Cohler, Basia Miller, and Harold Stone (New York: Cambridge University Press, 1989 [1748]), 48. See also Andreas Kalyvas and Ira Katznelson, *Liberal Beginnings: Making a Republic for the Moderns* (Cambridge: Cambridge University Press, 2008), 18–87; MacGilvray, *The Invention of Market Freedom*, 96, 104–5.

55. MacGilvray, *The Invention of Market Freedom*, 94–95; Albert Hirschman, *The Passions and the Interests: Political Arguments for Capitalism before Its Triumph* (Princeton: Princeton University Press, 1977), 70–93.

56. See MacGilvray, *The Invention of Market Freedom*, chap. 4; Kalyvas and Katznelson, *Liberal Beginnings*. As late as 1846, we can find this debate playing out in the halls of Congress; see Congressman Edwin Ewing of Tennessee, *Cong. Globe*, 29th Cong., 1st sess., Appendix 500–505 (March 1846).

57. John M. Murrin, "Feudalism, Communalism, and the Yeoman Freeholder: The American Revolution Considered as a Social Accident," in *Rethinking America: From Empire to Republic*, ed. John M. Murrin (New York: Oxford University Press, 2018 [1973]), 144.

58. Richard Price, *Observations on the Importance of the American Revolution and the Means of Making It a Benefit to the World* ([London], 1784), 69, 4.

59. Wood, *The Radicalism of the American Revolution*, 123; Greene, *Pursuits of Happiness*, 188, 195. This fact stood out to Scottish traveler John Melish, who published his observations about America in 1812: "The inhabitants of the country are generally proprietors of the farms they cultivate, and, having no landlord to make their *boo* to, nor rent to pay, they must be

independent." John Melish, *Travels in the United States of America . . .*, vol. 1 (Philadelphia: Printed for the author, 1812), 78.

60. Joyce Appleby, "Commercial Farming and the 'Agrarian Myth' in the Early Republic," *Journal of American History* 68, no. 4 (1982): 847.

61. Bushman, "'This New Man': Dependence and Independence, 1776," 85–88.

62. Wood, *The Radicalism of the American Revolution*, 114; Bushman, "'This New Man': Dependence and Independence, 1776," 86–89.

63. Jefferson, "Notes on the State of Virginia," 2:229.

64. See also Benjamin Franklin, "To Mrs. Catherine Greene," in *The Works of Benjamin Franklin*, vol. 10, ed. Jared Sparks (London: 1882 [1789]), 386.

65. Drew R. McCoy, "Jefferson and Madison on Malthus: Population Growth in Jeffersonian Political Economy," *Virginia Magazine of History and Biography* 88, no. 3 (1980): 259–76; Stephen Watts, *The Republic Reborn: War and the Making of Liberal America, 1790–1820* (Baltimore: Johns Hopkins University Press, 1987), 71–81, 219–20.

66. "Self-dependence," he argued, was the very foundation of human equality: it was only in the absence of hierarchical bonds of dependence that "all mankind appear equal." Alan Magruder, *Political, Commercial, and Moral Reflections on the Late Cession of Louisiana* (Lexington, KY: D. Bradford, 1803), 77, 78.

67. George Logan, *Five Letters Addressed to the Yeomanry of the United States* (Philadelphia: Eleazer Oswald, 1792), 4, 11–12, 28. Others concurred with this judgment; see Magruder, *Political, Commercial, and Moral Reflections on the Late Cession of Louisiana*, 77; John Taylor, *Arator, Being a Series of Agricultural Essays, Practical and Political*, 5th ed. (Petersburg, VA: Whitworth and Yancey, 1818 [1813]), 24, 22.

68. "Stockjobber" was a derogatory term used to refer to people who made their money buying and selling equities and government debt.

69. "Cultivators," wrote Jefferson to John Jay in 1785, "are the most vigorous, the most independent, the most virtuous and they are tied to their country, and wedded to its liberty and interests, by the most lasting bonds." Thomas Jefferson, "To John Jay. Paris, August 23, 1785," in *Memoir, Correspondence, and Miscellanies, from the Papers of Thomas Jefferson*, vol. 1, ed. Thomas Jefferson Randolph (Boston: Gray and Bowen, 1830 [1785]), 291.

70. As late as the Virginia Constitution Convention of 1829, conservative planters appealed to propertied independence as a way of justifying a substantial property qualification for the franchise. See Curtis, *Jefferson's Freeholders and the Politics of Ownership in the Old Dominion*, 113; Merrill D. Peterson, *The Jefferson Image in the American Mind* (New York: Oxford University Press, 1960), 43–44; Alexander Keyssar, *The Right to Vote: The Contested History of Democracy in the United States*, rev. ed. (New York: Basic Books, 2009), 39.

71. Hector St. John de Crevecoeur, *Letters from an American Farmer* (New York: E. P. Dutton & Co., 1957 [1782]), 28, 16.

72. Peterson, *The Jefferson Image in the American Mind*, 85. See also Louis Hartz, *The Liberal Tradition in America: An Interpretation of American Political Thought since the Revolution* (New York: Harcourt, Brace & World, 1955), 119–20. Peterson's view is incomplete; it neglects the more radical strains of democratic thought that thrived among urban artisans and laborers—see, for instance, Seth Cotlar, *Tom Paine's America: The Rise and Fall of Transatlantic Radicalism in the Early Republic* (Charlottesville: University of Virginia Press, 2011).

73. Aziz Rana, *The Two Faces of American Freedom* (Cambridge, MA: Harvard University Press, 2010); Paul Frymer, *Building an American Empire: The Era of Territorial and Political Expansion* (Princeton: Princeton University Press, 2017).

74. For the British roots of this tendency, see John Brewer, "English Radicalism in the Age of George III," in *Three British Revolutions: 1641, 1688, 1776*, ed. J. G. A. Pocock (Princeton: Princeton University Press, 1980), 345; Dickinson, *Liberty and Property*, 226.

75. Brewer, "English Radicalism in the Age of George III," 346, 355–57. See also Gary J. Kornblith, "Self-Made Men: The Development of Middling-Class Consciousness in New England," *Massachusetts Review* 26, no. 2/3 (1985): 467–69. Interestingly, Adam Smith made this very argument in the *Wealth of Nations*; see Adam Smith, *An Inquiry into the Nature and Causes of the Wealth of Nations*, vol. 1 (London: Methuen & Co., 1904 [1776]), 387.

76. Sean Wilentz, *Chants Democratic: New York City and the Rise of the American Working Class, 1788–1850* (New York: Oxford University Press, 1984), 27–32, 90, 92–95. See also McCoy, *The Elusive Republic*, 65.

77. Tristam Burges, "The Spirit of Independence: An Oration Delivered before the Providence Association of Mechanics and Manufacturers" (Providence: B. Wheeler, 1800), 12, 13, 15. See also Wilentz, *Chants Democratic*, 94–95; William R. Sutton, "'To Extract Poison from the Blessings of God's Providence': Producerist Respectability and Methodist Suspicions of Capitalist Change in the Early Republic," in *Methodism and the Shaping of American Culture*, ed. Nathan O. Hatch and John H. Wigger (Nashville: Kingswood Books, 2001).

78. For a discussion of these contrasting ideas of virtue in eighteenth-century America, see Jack P. Greene, "The Concept of Virtue in Late Colonial British America," in *Virtue, Corruption, and Self-Interest: Political Values in the Eighteenth Century*, ed. Richard K. Matthews (Bethlehem, PA: Lehigh University Press, 1994); Vetterli and Bryner, *In Search of the Republic*.

79. McCoy, *The Elusive Republic*, 81–82.

80. Joyce Appleby, *Capitalism and a New Social Order: The Republican Vision of the 1790s* (New York: New York University Press, 1984), 90.

81. Magruder, *Political, Commercial, and Moral Reflections on the Late Cession of Louisiana*, 50.

82. Jean M. Yarbrough, *American Virtues: Thomas Jefferson on the Character of a Free People* (Lawrence: University Press of Kansas, 1998), 64; John Ashworth, "The Jeffersonians: Classical Republicans or Liberal Capitalists?" *Journal of American Studies* 18, no. 3 (1984): 431–32; Charles Sellers, *The Market Revolution: Jacksonian America, 1815–1848* (New York: Oxford University Press, 1991), 39. This broad incentive formed part of the mythology of American exceptionalism: the wide diffusion of land ownership in America gave rise to an agricultural population imbued with the virtues of industry and ingenuity, unlike the European peasant who "feels no ambition to make improvements." Nathaniel Gage, "Address before the Essex Agricultural Society, at Topsfield, September 27, 1837, at Their Annual Cattle Show" (Salem: Essex Agricultural Society, 1837), 10.

83. Thomas Jefferson, "Jefferson to George Washington, 14 August 1787," in *The Writings of Thomas Jefferson*, vol. 2, ed. Albert Ellery Bergh (Boston: Gray and Bowen, 1830 [1787]), 223.

84. Taylor, *Arator, Being a Series of Agricultural Essays, Practical and Political*, 37.

85. Wood, *The Radicalism of the American Revolution*, 197–212; Garrett Ward Sheldon, *The Political Philosophy of Thomas Jefferson* (Baltimore: Johns Hopkins University Press, 1991), 121–22; Breen, *Tobacco Culture*, 84–106.

86. Charles Sydnor, *Gentlemen Freeholders: Political Practices in Washington's Virginia* (Chapel Hill: University of North Carolina Press, 1952), 46; Gordon Wood, *Empire of Liberty: A History of the Early Republic, 1789–1815* (Oxford: Oxford University Press, 2009), 160.

87. Wood, *The Creation of the American Republic*, 71. See also Dal Lago, "Patriarchs and Republicans: Eighteenth-Century Virginian Planters and Classical Politics," 500–501; Kenneth S. Greenberg, *Masters and Statesmen: The Political Culture of American Slavery* (Baltimore: Johns Hopkins University Press, 1985), 3–22. For an excellent discussion of the polarity between plebian and patrician independence in the antebellum South, see Stephanie McCurry, *Masters of Small Worlds: Yeoman Households, Gender Relations, and the Political Culture of the Antebellum South Carolina Low Country* (New York: Oxford University Press, 1995), 37–91.

88. Dal Lago, "Patriarchs and Republicans: Eighteenth-Century Virginian Planters and Classical Politics"; David Hackett Fischer, *Albion's Seed: Four British Folkways in America* (New York: Oxford University Press, 1989), 411–18.

89. *Proceedings and Debates of the Virginia State Convention, of 1829–30*, vol. 1 (Richmond: Samuel Shepherd & Co., 1830), 158.

90. After this speech, in which he also compared the "peasantry" of the West to the slaves of the East, Leigh was burned in effigy by the farmers of Harrisonburg. Merrill D. Peterson, ed., *Democracy, Liberty, and Property: The State Constitutional Conventions of the 1820s* (Indianapolis: Bobbs-Merrill, 1966), 337. In fact, this quote would become infamous: it was used throughout the 1830s to illustrate the South's animosity to free labor.

91. *Proceedings and Debates of the Virginia State Convention, of 1829–30*, vol. 1, 158.

92. *Thomas Jefferson and the New Nation: A Biography* (New York: Oxford University Press, 1970), 113; Thomas Jefferson, "To John Adams," in *Thomas Jefferson: Political Writings*, ed. Joyce Appleby and Terence Ball (Cambridge: Cambridge University Press, 1999 [1813]), 187.

93. "Bill for the More General Diffusion of Knowledge," in *Thomas Jefferson: Political Writings*, ed. Joyce Appleby and Terence Ball (Cambridge: Cambridge University Press, 1999 [1779]), 236.

94. Taylor, *Arator, Being a Series of Agricultural Essays, Practical and Political*, 42.

95. Bernard Bailyn, *The Ideological Origins of the American Revolution*, enlarged ed. (Cambridge, MA: Harvard University Press, 1992 [1967]), 55–93.

96. Dickinson, *Liberty and Property*, 103–10, 170–85.

97. Morgan, *Inventing the People*, 167–68.

98. Quoted in Ralph Ketcham, *James Madison: A Biography* (Charlottesville: University Press of Virginia, 1990 [1971]), 262.

99. Yarbrough, *American Virtues: Thomas Jefferson on the Character of a Free People*, 114; Forrest McDonald, *Novus Ordo Seclorum: The Intellectual Origins of the Constitution* (Lawrence: University Press of Kansas, 1985), 76.

100. Morgan, *Inventing the People*, 169. Morgan is generalizing here about the seventeenth and eighteenth centuries, but he pointedly includes the agrarian ideology of Jefferson, Madison, and their rising political coalition in the 1790s and beyond. Other historians have argued that it was this deferential culture, which insulated southern elites such as Jefferson and Madison from democratic challenges, that bolstered their confidence in the political acumen of the mass electorate and helped make them standard-bearers for democratic reforms. See Richard Buel Jr.,

Securing the Revolution: Ideology in American Politics, 1789–1815 (Ithaca: Cornell University Press, 1972), 81; Wood, *Empire of Liberty*, 167.

101. Gordon Wood, *The Radicalism of the American Revolution*, 229–369.

102. Saul Cornell, "Aristocracy Assailed: The Ideology of Backcountry Anti-Federalism," *Journal of American History* 76, no. 4 (1990): 1156–68.

103. Brutus, "Essay III, 15 November 1787," in *The Anti-Federalist: Writings by Opponents of the Constitution*, ed. Herbert J. Storing (Chicago: University of Chicago Press, 1985 [1787]), 125.

104. Cornell, "Aristocracy Assailed: The Ideology of Backcountry Anti-Federalism."

105. William Duane, *Politics for American Farmers . . .* (Washington, DC: R. C. Weightman, 1807), 3, 14, 19, 21, 30, 66. In fact, Duane reprinted sections of John Taylor's tract, *Construction Construed and Constitutions Vindicated* in 1819, emphasizing the arguments against banking and speculation and leaving out Taylor's defense of slavery. Wilentz, *The Rise of American Democracy: Jefferson to Lincoln*, 214.

106. Duane was especially sensitive to the ways in which "energetic government" stripped farmers and artisans of their independence. Duane, *Politics for American Farmers*, 65, 14, 62, 57.

107. Ibid., 3.

108. For a helpful discussion of the producerist ethic that flourished among urban artisans, see Sutton, "'To Extract Poison from the Blessings of God's Providence.'"

109. Emphasis in original. Duane, *Politics for American Farmers*, 83, 95. Even so, he worried that these mechanics were making themselves "dependent" for economic reasons: "Is there a man who knows these things, and has not observed many a worthy mechanic and tradesman pin his political opinion on the sleeve of [men of wealth] through fear of losing a customer." Here Duane reproduces Jefferson's worry precisely, except that Duane believes that these mechanics and tradesmen can choose to resist such dependence. William Duane, "Local Politics," *Aurora General Advertiser*, September 21, 1810, p. 2.

110. Duane, *Politics for American Farmers*, 83.

Chapter 4

1. A freeholder was someone who possessed full, private ownership of his land.

2. *Cong. Globe*, 25th Cong., 2nd sess., Appendix 393 (June 1838).

3. A number of historians have drawn attention to the enduring importance of republican thought in Jacksonian America; see, for instance, Harry L. Watson, *Liberty and Power: The Politics of Jacksonian America* (New York: Hill and Wang, 1990), 42–72; James L. Huston, "Virtue Besieged: Virtue, Equality, and the General Welfare in the Tariff Debates of the 1820s," *Journal of the Early Republic* 14, no. 4 (1994): 523–47; J. William Harris, "Last of the Classical Republicans: An Interpretation of John C. Calhoun," *Civil War History* 30, no. 3 (1984): 255–67; Kenneth S. Greenberg, *Masters and Statesmen: The Political Culture of American Slavery* (Baltimore: Johns Hopkins University Press, 1985), 4–22; Donald K. Pickens, "The Republican Synthesis and Thaddeus Stevens," *Civil War History* 31, no. 1 (1985): 57–73; Jean H. Baker, *Affairs of Party: The Political Culture of Northern Democrats in the Mid-Nineteenth Century* (Ithaca: Cornell University Press, 1983), 143–76; Major L. Wilson, *The Presidency of Martin Van Buren* (Lawrence: University Press of Kansas, 1984), 87–90.

4. Douglas T. Miller, *Jacksonian Aristocracy: Class and Democracy in New York, 1830–1860* (New York: Oxford University Press, 1967), 32–35; Henry Nash Smith, *Virgin Land: The American West as Symbol and Myth* (Cambridge, MA: Harvard University Press, 1970 [1950]), 159; Steven Hahn, *The Roots of Southern Populism: Yeoman Farmers and the Transformation of the Georgia Upcountry, 1850–1890* (New York: Oxford University Press, 1983), 36; Jeremy Atack and Fred Bateman, *To Their Own Soil: Agriculture in the Antebellum North* (Ames: Iowa State University Press, 1987), 225; J. Mills Thornton III, *Politics and Power in a Slave Society: Alabama, 1800–1860* (Baton Rouge: Louisiana State University Press, 1978), 310–11.

5. James Oakes, "From Republicanism to Liberalism: Ideological Change and the Crisis of the Old South," *American Quarterly* 37, no. 4 (1985): 561; Thornton, *Politics and Power in a Slave Society: Alabama, 1800–1860*, 310.

6. This insight was famously developed by Louis Hartz; see Louis Hartz, *The Liberal Tradition in America: An Interpretation of American Political Thought since the Revolution* (New York: Harcourt, Brace & World, 1955), 5–24, 114–42. For further discussion of the Democrats' embrace of the market economy, see chapters 6 and 7.

7. Like many other aspects of Jackson's carefully cultivated public persona, this was only partly true. Jackson had been involved in politics for much of his life.

8. For an illuminating discussion of the "corrupt bargain" as a galvanizing event in the rising Jacksonian coalition and for Jackson's own political beliefs, see Robert V. Remini, *The Legacy of Andrew Jackson: Essays on Democracy, Indian Removal, and Slavery* (Baton Rouge: Louisiana State University Press, 1988), 13–20.

9. Sean Wilentz, *The Rise of American Democracy: Jefferson to Lincoln* (New York: Norton, 2005), 183–202. For a slightly different perspective, see also Donald Ratcliffe, "The Right to Vote and the Rise of Democracy, 1787–1828," *Journal of the Early Republic* 33, no. 2 (2013): 219–54; Andrew W. Robertson, "Jeffersonian Parties, Politics, and Participation: the Tortuous Trajectory of American Democracy," in *Practicing Democracy: Popular Politics in the United States from the Constitution to the Civil War*, ed. Daniel Peart and Adam I. P. Smith (Charlottesville: University of Virginia Press, 2015).

10. Michael F. Holt, *The Rise and Fall of the American Whig Party: Jacksonian Politics and the Onset of the Civil War* (New York: Oxford University Press, 1999), 8.

11. Mark R. Cheathem, *The Coming of Democracy: Presidential Campaigning in the Age of Jackson* (Baltimore: Johns Hopkins University Press, 2018), 1–63; David S. Heidler and Jeanne T. Heidler, *The Rise of Andrew Jackson: Myth, Manipulation, and the Making of Modern Politics* (New York: Basic Books, 2018), 264–363. For instructive discussions of the expansion of the franchise and of popular political participation in the early republic, see Alexander Keyssar, *The Right to Vote: The Contested History of Democracy in the United States*, rev. ed. (New York: Basic Books, 2009); Ratcliffe, "The Right to Vote and the Rise of Democracy"; Robertson, "Jeffersonian Parties, Politics, and Participation"; Reeve Huston, "Rethinking the Origins of Partisan Democracy in the United States, 1795–1840," in *Practicing Democracy: Popular Politics in the United States from the Constitution to the Civil War*, ed. Daniel Peart and Adam I. P. Smith (Charlottesville: University of Virginia Press, 2015).

12. In fact, Jackson had himself been an avid land speculator and had long belonged to a class of slaveholding elites whose interests (and political views) sometimes clashed with those of poorer farmers. See, for instance, J. M. Opal, "General Jackson's Passports: Natural Rights and

Sovereign Citizens in the Political Thought of Andrew Jackson, 1780s–1820s," *Studies in American Political Development* 27 (2013): 69–85. Even as he took office in 1829, it was unclear where exactly Jackson stood on many of the pressing economic questions of his day.

13. Amos Kendall, "Democratic Celebration," *Globe*, December 13, 1832, p. 2; Samuel Clesson Allen, "Address Delivered at Northampton, before the Hampshire, Franklin, and Hampden Agricultural Society, October 27th, 1830" (Northampton: T. Watson Shepard, 1830), 27.

14. For an excellent discussion of the Americans' view of the arc(s) of history in the Jacksonian Era, see Rush Welter, *The Mind of America: 1820–1860* (New York: Columbia University Press, 1975), 3–74. For American anxieties about the fragility of their exceptionalist project, see Jonathan A. Glickstein, *American Exceptionalism, American Anxiety: Wages, Competition, and Degraded Labor in the Antebellum United States.* (Charlottesville: University of Virginia Press, 2002).

15. Andrew H. Browning, *The Panic of 1819: The First Great Depression* (Columbia: University of Missouri Press, 2019), 217–250; Charles Sellers, *The Market Revolution: Jacksonian America, 1815–1848* (New York: Oxford University Press, 1991), 149–164.

16. Quoted in Sellers, *The Market Revolution*, 162.

17. William Allen, "Great Democratic Festival," *Globe* (reprinted from the *Lancaster Eagle*), September 9, 1837, p. 2.

18. Reprinted as "The Farmers," *Extra Globe*, November 3, 1834, p. 296.

19. "Address to the Democratic Republican Electors of the State of New York" (Washington, DC: Globe, 1840), 19.

20. For a thorough investigation of the Second Bank of the United States' role and influence in the American economy, see Jane Ellen Knodell, *The Second Bank of the United States: "Central" Banker in an Era of Nation Building, 1816–1836* (Abingdon, UK: Routledge, 2017).

21. For an excellent discussion of the political contest over the Bank, see Watson, *Liberty and Power*, 132–71.

22. "A Patriot," *Extra Globe*, August 23, 1834, p. 135.

23. Along similar lines, the editor of the *Louisville Public Advertiser* worried that the vast financial power of the "Mammoth Bank" would render "my offspring the mere serfs of a monied aristocracy." "From the Editor," *Louisville Public Advertiser*, reprinted in the *Indiana Democrat*, May 31, 1834, p. 3.

24. Thomas Hart Benton, "Speech of Mr. Benton, of Missouri, on Introducing a Resolution against the Renewal of the Charter of the Bank of the United States" (Washington, DC: Duff Green, 1831), 13. See also "Bank Reform," *Ohio Statesman*, September 5, 1837, pp. 1–2.

25. Miller, *Jacksonian Aristocracy*, 30–34; Bruce Laurie, *Artisans into Workers: Labor in Nineteenth-Century America* (New York: Hill and Wang, 1989), 38–39, 83.

26. Sellers, *The Market Revolution*, 18–27; John Lauritz Larson, *The Market Revolution in America: Liberty, Ambition, and the Eclipse of the Common Good* (Cambridge: Cambridge University Press, 2010), 104–12.

27. Richard Stott, "Artisans and Capitalist Development," *Journal of the Early Republic* 16, no. 2 (1996): 262–65. Historians disagree about how quickly this change was unfolding. See, for instance, Laurie, *Artisans into Workers*, 15–112; Robert H. Babcock, "The Decline of Artisan Republicanism in Portland, Maine, 1825–1850," *New England Quarterly* 63, no. 1 (1990): 3–34; James L. Huston, *Securing the Fruits of Labor: The American Concept of Wealth Distribution, 1765–1900* (Baton Rouge: Louisiana State University Press, 1998), 126–29.

28. Seth Luther, "An Address to the Working Men of New England on the State of Education and on the Condition of the Producing Classes in Europe and America" (New York: George H. Evans, 1833), 24–26.

29. Quoted in Ransom Gillet, *The Life and Times of Silas Wright*, 2 vols. (Albany: Argus Company, 1874), 2:1487–88.

30. The *Globe* had long served as the chief organ of the Jacksonian Democratic Party.

31. "Domestic Industry," *Globe*, January 11, 1842, p. 3. See also Richard Latner, "Preserving 'the Natural Equality of Rank and Influence': Liberalism, Republicanism, and Equality of Condition in Jacksonian Politics," in *The Culture of the Market: Historical Essays*, ed. Thomas L. Haskell and Richard F. Teichgraeber III (Cambridge: Cambridge University Press, 1993), 222.

32. "Address to the Workingmen of Massachusetts, by the Committee Appointed for That Purpose by the Northampton Convention," *New England Artisan*, October 25, 1834, p. 1.

33. "The manufactory," writes Wilentz, "may be thought of as a machineless factory—defined here as a concentration of more than twenty workers, each of whom performed the old handicraft tasks in a strictly subdivided routine." Sean Wilentz, *Chants Democratic: New York City and the Rise of the American Working Class, 1788–1850* (New York: Oxford University Press, 1984), 115.

34. Jonathan A. Glickstein, *Concepts of Free Labor in Antebellum America* (New Haven: Yale University Press, 1991), 10–11, 53–92.

35. Wilentz, *Chants Democratic*, 115.

36. William West, "Chattel and Wages Slavery," *Liberator*, September 25, 1846, p. 156.

37. Both sides agreed that a modest tariff was necessary to fund the federal government; it was the additional, *protective* tariffs designed specifically to shield certain American manufacturing sectors from competition that typically drew the ire of Democrats.

38. "Art. I.—Report of the Secretary of the Treasury," *Western Review* 1, no. 1 (1846): 5.

39. "Domestic Industry," 3.

40. For an excellent overview of these debates and their political context, see John R. Van Atta, "'A Lawless Rabble': Henry Clay and the Cultural Politics of Squatters' Rights, 1832–1841," *Journal of the Early Republic* 28, no. 3 (2008): 337–78.

41. *Cong. Globe*, 25th Cong., 2nd sess., Appendix 137 (January 1838).

42. *Cong. Globe*, 25th Cong., 2nd sess., Appendix 140 (January 1838).

43. *Cong. Globe*, 24th Cong., 2nd sess., Appendix 168 (January 1837).

44. *Cong. Globe*, 25th Cong., 2nd sess., Appendix 139 (January 1838).

45. *Cong. Globe*, 24th Cong., 2nd sess., Appendix 169 (January 1837).

46. "Address to the Workingmen of the United States," *Extra Globe*, September 26, 1840, p. 294. In the 1840s, this argument was also taken up by the influential labor leader George Henry Evans and tirelessly promulgated in his newspaper, the *Working Man's Advocate*. For further discussion, see Paul K. Conkin, *Prophets of Prosperity: America's First Political Economists* (Bloomington: Indiana University Press, 1980), 222–58.

47. Benjamin Faneuil Hunt, "Speech of Col. Benjamin Faneuil Hunt, of Charleston, South Carolina, Delivered at the Request of the Democratic Republican General Committee" (New York: James Rees, 1840), 6.

48. Ibid. Jefferson had made the same observation thirty-five years earlier; see Thomas Jefferson, "Letter to Mr. Lithson, Jan. 4, 1805," in *The Writings of Thomas Jefferson*, vol. 11, ed. Albert

Ellery Bergh and Andrew Adgate Lipscomb (Washington, DC: Thomas Jefferson Memorial Association, 1905 [1805]), 55–56. Economic historians have cast serious doubt on the validity of his line of argument; see Clayne Pope, "Inequality in the Nineteenth Century," in *The Cambridge Economic History of the United States*, vol. 2, ed. Stanley L. Engerman and Robert E. Gallman (Cambridge: Cambridge University Press, 2000), 111.

49. Sellers, *The Market Revolution*, 8–33; Lawrence Frederick Kohl, *The Politics of Individualism: Parties and the American Character in the Jacksonian Era* (New York: Oxford University Press, 1989), 21–62. Sellers also argues, however, that the ethic of personal independence was premised on an essentially capitalist conception of property as absolute dominion (which contrasted with the "use-value communalism" of pre-capitalist culture), and so contained the seeds of its own demise. Sellers, *The Market Revolution*, 10.

50. For the "dual economy" of the American South, see Harry L. Watson, "Slavery and Development in a Dual Economy: The South and the Market Revolution," in *The Market Revolution in America: Social, Political, and Religious Expressions, 1800–1880*, ed. Melvyn Stokes and Stephen Conway (Charlottesville: University Press of Virginia, 1996).

51. Robert Rantoul Jr., "An Oration Delivered before the Inhabitants of the Town of South Reading . . . on the Fourth of July, 1832" (Salem: Foote & Brown, 1832), 29.

52. For further discussion of the widespread, bipartisan belief in American progress, see Daniel Feller, *The Jacksonian Promise: America, 1815–1840* (Baltimore: Johns Hopkins University Press, 1995), 1–13; Welter, *The Mind of America: 1820–1860*, 3–25.

53. C. B. MacPherson, *The Political Theory of Possessive Individualism: Hobbes to Locke* (Oxford: Clarendon Press, 1962), 51, 52. See also Alan Kulikoff, "The Transition to Capitalism in Rural America," *William and Mary Quarterly* 46, no. 1 (1989): 136–41. One Democratic pamphlet, for example, attacked the Whig Party by attributing this statement to one of its leaders: "labor is a commodity, bought and sold like merchandise in the market." "The Democrat's Almanac and People's Register for 1841" (Boston: E. Littlefield, 1841), 10.

54. As Christopher Clark points out, historians have too often conflated the advent of market society with the advent of capitalism. Christopher Clark, "The Consequences of the Market Revolution in the American North," in *The Market Revolution in America: Social, Political, and Religious Expressions, 1800–1880*, ed. Melvyn Stokes and Stephen Conway (Charlottesville: University Press of Virginia, 1996), 30. Democratic writers occasionally captured this distinction themselves, as for instance in an 1848 article in the *Chicago Democrat* that praised the onset of the "Commercial Era" but warned of its corruption by "Capital," which threatened to turn a commercial economy of small proprietors into a world of capitalists and destitute wage workers stripped of their independence. "Land Reform. From the *Chicago Democrat*," *North Star*, February 25, 1848. See also Elizabeth Anderson, "When the Market Was 'Left,'" in *Private Government: How Employers Rule Our Lives (and Why We Don't Talk about It)* (Princeton: Princeton University Press, 2017), 22–33.

55. John Ashworth, *Slavery, Capitalism, and Politics in the Antebellum Republic*, vol. 1: *Commerce and Compromise, 1820–1850* (Cambridge: Cambridge University Press, 1995), 307; Paul Goodman, "Moral Purpose and Republican Politics in Antebellum America, 1830–1860," *Maryland Historian* 20 (1989): 10.

56. J. G. A. Pocock, *The Machiavellian Moment: Florentine Political Thought and the Atlantic Republican Tradition* (Princeton: Princeton University Press, 1975), 390; John Phillip Reid, *The*

Concept of Liberty in the Age of the American Revolution (Chicago: University of Chicago Press, 1988), 5; Gordon Wood, *The Radicalism of the American Revolution* (New York: Random House, 1992), 178–79.

57. Pocock, *The Machiavellian Moment*, 390–91, 450; Richard L. Bushman, "'This New Man': Dependence and Independence, 1776," in *Uprooted Americans: Essays to Honor Oscar Handlin*, ed. Richard L. Bushman et al. (Boston: Little, Brown, 1979), 90.

58. Rowland Berthoff, quoting Benjamin Watkins Leigh, "Independence and Attachment, Virtue and Interest: From Republican Citizen to Free Enterpriser, 1787–1837," in *Uprooted Americans: Essays to Honor Oscar Handlin*, ed. Richard L. Bushman et al. (Boston: Little, Brown, 1979), 111; Wood, *The Radicalism of the American Revolution*, 269–70.

59. Pocock, *The Machiavellian Moment*, 391.

60. Holly Brewer, "Entailing Aristocracy in Colonial Virginia: 'Ancient Feudal Restraints' and Revolutionary Reform," *William and Mary Quarterly* 54, no. 2 (1997): 307–11. See also Forrest McDonald, *Novus Ordo Seclorum: The Intellectual Origins of the Constitution* (Lawrence: University Press of Kansas, 1985), 13–36; Gregory S. Alexander, *Commodity and Propriety: Competing Visions of Property in American Legal Thought, 1776–1970* (Chicago: University of Chicago Press, 1997); Christopher Michael Curtis, *Jefferson's Freeholders and the Politics of Ownership in the Old Dominion* (Cambridge: Cambridge University Press, 2012).

61. Thomas Jefferson, "To John Adams," in *Thomas Jefferson: Political Writings*, ed. Joyce Appleby and Terence Ball (Cambridge: Cambridge University Press, 1999 [1813]). Primogeniture refers to an inheritance rule which grants the family's entire estate to its eldest son. Legal scholars have argued that these attacks were largely symbolic, since primogeniture and entail were not used very often in America; see Alexander, *Commodity and Propriety*, 40. Nonetheless, they entered the popular lore about Jefferson.

62. Alexander, *Commodity and Propriety*, 53, 45.

63. Quoted in Bushman, "'This New Man': Dependence and Independence, 1776," 90.

64. Alexander, *Commodity and Propriety*, 120; Sellers, *The Market Revolution*, 45–50.

65. Looking back at the Kentucky he grew up in, Henry Clay claimed to be unable to "recollect a single individual, or the descendants of any individual, who had remained on the lands which they had originally settled." Quoted in Berthoff, "Independence and Attachment, Virtue and Interest," 112. See also Daniel Feller, *The Public Lands in Jacksonian Politics* (Madison: University of Wisconsin Press, 1984), 195–97; Marvin Meyers, *The Jacksonian Persuasion: Politics and Belief*, 2nd ed. (New York: Vintage Books, 1960 [1957]), 135.

66. Curtis, *Jefferson's Freeholders and the Politics of Ownership in the Old Dominion*, 97–125.

67. Isaac Kramnick, "The 'Great National Discussion': The Discourse of Politics in 1787," *William and Mary Quarterly* 45, no. 1 (1988): 17. See also Rowland Berthoff, "Peasants and Artisans, Puritans and Republicans: Personal Liberty and Communal Equality in American History," *Journal of American History* 69, no. 3 (1982): 579–98; Judith Shklar, *American Citizenship: The Quest for Inclusion* (Cambridge, MA: Harvard University Press, 1991), 63–73.

68. Quoted in Kramnick, "The 'Great National Discussion,'" 17.

69. Ibid., 16. See also Drew R. McCoy, *The Elusive Republic: Political Economy in Jeffersonian America* (Chapel Hill: University of North Carolina Press, 1980), 77–85; Jack P. Greene, "The Concept of Virtue in Late Colonial British America," in *Virtue, Corruption, and Self-Interest: Political Values in the Eighteenth Century*, ed. Richard K. Matthews (Bethlehem, PA: Lehigh

University Press, 1994); Joyce Appleby, *Capitalism and a New Social Order: The Republican Vision of the 1790s* (New York: New York University Press, 1984), 96; Wood, *The Radicalism of the American Revolution*, 216–18.

70. Benjamin Franklin, *Autobiography* (New York: Norton, 2012 [1791]), 90, 80.

71. Eric MacGilvray, *The Invention of Market Freedom* (Cambridge: Cambridge University Press, 2011), 104.

72. "[I]t is hard for an empty sack to stand upright," he wrote, quoting a contemporary proverb. Franklin, *Autobiography*, 91.

73. Kramnick, "The 'Great National Discussion,'" 17.

74. Daniel Walker Howe, *Making the American Self: Jonathan Edwards to Abraham Lincoln* (Oxford: Oxford University Press, 2009 [1997]), 28. See also Richard L. Bushman, *From Puritan to Yankee: Character and the Social Order in Connecticut, 1690–1765* (Cambridge, MA: Harvard University Press, 1967), 276–88.

75. Howe, *Making the American Self*, 29.

76. Alexis de Tocqueville famously commented on this widely held view in Jacksonian America: "Americans," he wrote, "are pleased to explain nearly all their actions in terms of self-interest properly understood. They will obligingly demonstrate how enlightened love of themselves regularly leads them to help one another out and makes them ready and willing to sacrifice a portion of their time and wealth for the good of the state." Alexis de Tocqueville, *Democracy in America*, trans. Arthur Goldhammer, vol. 2 (New York: Library of America, 2004 [1840]), 611.

77. Berthoff, "Independence and Attachment, Virtue and Interest," 117–18. See also Shklar, *American Citizenship*, 63–73.

78. Robert Rantoul Jr., "Remarks on Education," in *Memoirs, Speeches, and Writings of Robert Rantoul, Jr.*, ed. Luther Hamilton (Boston: John P. Jewett and Co., 1854 [1838]), 85. See also McCoy, *The Elusive Republic*, 77–79.

79. Gordon S. Wood, "Classical Republicanism and the American Revolution," *Chicago-Kent Law Review* 66 (1990): 32.

80. For a succinct overview of these shifts, see Rowland Berthoff, "Conventional Mentality: Free Blacks, Women, and Business Corporations as Unequal Persons, 1820–1870," *Journal of American History* 76, no. 3 (1989): 753–84.

81. MacGilvray, *The Invention of Market Freedom*, 165. See also Berthoff, "Peasants and Artisans, Puritans and Republicans."

82. Lois E. Horton, "From Class to Race in Early America: Northern Post-Emancipation Racial Reconstruction," *Journal of the Early Republic* 19, no. 4 (1999): 2, 28–33; Joshua A. Lynn, *Preserving the White Man's Republic: Jacksonian Democracy, Race, and the Transformation of American Conservatism* (Charlottesville: University of Virginia Press, 2019). For Democrats, race was the decisive marker of otherness and inferiority. They threw open their arms to European immigrants, including Irish and German immigrants, whose virtues they trumpeted on the Senate floor even as their Whig opponents worried aloud about the "knaves and paupers of the old world . . . flocking in most pernicious herds to this country." William Merrick, *Cong. Globe*, 25th Cong., 2nd sess., Appendix 130 (January 1838).

83. Thomas Roderick Dew, "Review of the Debate in the Virginia Legislature of 1831 and 1832" (Richmond: T. W. White, 1832), 113. See also J. K. Paulding, *Slavery in the United States*

(New York: Harper & Bros., 1836), 73. "However scornful of such claims in private," writes historian Lacy Ford Jr., "the slaveholding elite had to accept white equality, the spirit of *herrenvolk* democracy, in the public realm to ensure white solidarity in the coming stand against antislavery." Lacy K. Ford Jr., "Making the 'White Man's Country' White: Race, Slavery, and State-Building in the Jacksonian South," *Journal of the Early Republic* 19, no. 4 (1999): 736.

84. Alexander, *Commodity and Propriety*, 219; David R. Roediger, *The Wages of Whiteness: Race and the Making of the American Working Class* (London: Verso, 1991), 46–47, 72–73, 144–45; Edmund Morgan, *American Slavery, American Freedom: The Ordeal of Colonial Virginia* (New York: W. W. Norton, 1975), 381. For an extended discussion of race and slavery in the construction of American citizenship and civic status, see also Shklar, *American Citizenship*.

85. Lewis Cass, "Removal of the Indians," *North American Review* 30 (1830): 74.

86. Richard H. Colfax, "Evidence against the Views of the Abolitionists, Consisting of Physical and Moral Proofs, of the Natural Inferiority of the Negroes" (New York: James T. M. Bleakley, 1833), 26.

87. Cass, "Removal of the Indians," 69, 71.

88. Reginald Horsman, *Race and Manifest Destiny: The Origins of American Racial Anglo-Saxonism* (Cambridge, MA: Harvard University Press, 1981), 116–57; Deborah A. Rosen, *American Indians and State Law: Sovereignty, Race, and Citizenship, 1790–1880* (Lincoln: University of Nebraska Press, 2007), 102–52.

89. Samuel George Morton, "An Inquiry into the Distinctive Characteristics of the Aboriginal Race of America" (Philadelphia: John Penington, 1844), 12.

90. Speech of Rep. Duncan of Ohio on the Oregon Bill, *Cong. Globe*, 28th Cong., 2nd sess., Appendix 178 (January 1845). Imperial expansion was one of the contexts in which the content of whiteness was being negotiated and contested. Who exactly counted as white (or Anglo-Saxon), and therefore "fit" for American freedom, was of great consequence in these debates. Matthew Frye Jacobson, *Whiteness of a Different Color: European Immigrants and the Alchemy of Race* (Cambridge, MA: Harvard University Press, 1998), 203–22; Paul Frymer, *Building an American Empire: The Era of Territorial and Political Expansion* (Princeton: Princeton University Press, 2017), 128–71.

91. Ken Mueller, *Senator Benton and the People: Master Race Democracy on the Early American Frontiers* (DeKalb: Northern Illinois University Press, 2014), 133–76.

92. Land unlocked the "impulsive aspiration of the spirit of progress," wrote the *Democratic Review*, which lay latent in the "European stocks" of humanity. It did no such thing for the Native Americans, however, who "have ever existed indeed, like a vacuum in the system of nature, which is at every moment in peril." "Our Indian Policy," *United States Magazine and Democratic Review* 14 (1844): 170, 169.

93. Some scholars have used the term *Herrenvolk* democracy—or "master race" democracy—to describe this particular political configuration. See, originally, Pierre van den Berghe, *Race and Racism: A Comparative Perspective* (New York: Wiley, 1967).

94. Rogers M. Smith, *Civic Ideals: Conflicting Visions of Citizenship in U.S. History* (New Haven: Yale University Press, 1997), 197–242.

95. Daniel Vickers, "Competency and Competition: Economic Culture in Early America," *William and Mary Quarterly* 47, no. 1 (1990): 28. Of course, these facts belied one of the central

elements of the mythology of the yeoman farmer: that he was essentially *peaceful*. For an excellent illustration, see John A. Dix, "Rural Life and Embellishment," in *Speeches and Occasional Addresses*, vol. 2 (New York: D. Appleton, 1864 [1851]), 336.

96. For extensive discussion of the U.S. government's use of land policy as a tool of imperial expansion, see Frymer, *Building an American Empire*. For further discussion of land hunger among southern farmers, see Keri Leigh Merritt, *Masterless Men: Poor Whites and Slavery in the Antebellum South* (Cambridge: Cambridge University Press, 2017), 38–61.

97. Ashworth, *Slavery, Capitalism, and Politics in the Antebellum Republic*, vol. 1: *Commerce and Compromise, 1820–1850*, 371–72.

98. Speech of Rep. Duncan of Ohio on the Oregon Bill, *Cong. Globe*, 28th Cong., 2nd sess., Appendix 178 (January 1845).

99. See, for instance, Reynolds, speech to Congress on the Oregon Bill, *Cong. Globe*, 27th Cong., 3rd sess., Appendix 111 (January 1843); Daniel S. Dickinson, speech to the Senate on the Oregon question, *Cong. Globe*, 29th Cong., 1st sess., Appendix 327 (February 1846).

100. Aziz Rana, *The Two Faces of American Freedom* (Cambridge, MA: Harvard University Press, 2010), 12–13.

101. Ibid., 9.

102. See, for instance, Daniel S. Dickinson, Speech to the Senate on the Oregon question, *Cong. Globe*, 29th Cong., 1st sess., Appendix 321–327 (February 1846).

103. See, for instance, John Ross et al., "Memorial and Protest of the Cherokee Nation," in *Letter from John Ross ... Followed by a Copy of the Protest of the Cherokee Delegation* ([Washington, DC], 1836); "The Following Memorial ... ," *Cherokee Phoenix*, March 5, 1831.

104. John Ridge, "Strictures," *Cherokee Phoenix*, March 13, 1828. He responds, for example, to the accusation that the Cherokee were "naturally or constitutionally incapable of making treaties, or *contracts*." See also Kelly Wisecup, "Practicing Sovereignty: Colonial Temporalities, Cherokee Justice, and the 'Socrates' Writings of John Ridge," *Native American and Indigenous Studies* 4, no. 1 (2017): 30–60.

105. *Report of the Proceedings and Debates in the Convention to Revise the Constitution of the State of Michigan* (Lansing: R. W. Ingals, 1850), 295, 293. "The black race has been marked and condemned to servility," proclaimed an Indiana delegate, "by the decree of Omnipotence; and should feeble man claim to erase from them the leprosy which God has placed upon them?" *Report of the Debates and Proceedings of the Convention for the Revision of the Constitution of the State of Indiana, 1850*, vol. 1 (Indianapolis: A. H. Brown, 1850), 251.

106. L. H. Clarke, ed., *Report of the Debates and Proceedings of the Convention of the State of New York ...* (New York: J. Seymour, 1821), 105. See also Philip S. Foner, *A History of Black Americans*, vol. 2 (Westport, CT: Greenwood Press, 1983), 206–7.

107. Scott Malcomson, *One Drop of Blood: The American Misadventure of Race* (New York: Farrar, Straus and Giroux, 2000), 323–29.

108. Keyssar, *The Right to Vote*, 44–49. The political rights of Native Americans were also narrowed, though less dramatically, between 1790 and 1850.

109. Roediger, *The Wages of Whiteness*, 49. See also David Brion Davis, *The Problem of Slavery in the Age of Emancipation* (New York: Knopf, 2014), 15–44; Shklar, *American Citizenship*, 63–101; Jacqueline Jones, *A Dreadful Deceit: The Myth of Race from the Colonial Era to Obama's America* (New York: Basic Books, 2013), 97–144.

110. James Collins et al., quoted in Philip Foner and Ronald Lewis, eds., *The Black Worker: A Documentary History from Colonial Times to the Present*, vol. 1 (Philadelphia: Temple University Press, 1978), 176.

111. Ford, "Making the 'White Man's Country' White," 737. See also Cheryl I. Harris, "Whiteness as Property," *Harvard Law Review* 106, no. 8 (1993): 1707–91.

112. See Edward E. Baptist, *The Half Has Never Been Told: Slavery and the Making of American Capitalism* (New York: Basic Books, 2014); Sven Beckert and Seth Rockman, eds., *Slavery's Capitalism: A New History of American Economic Development* (Philadelphia: University of Pennsylvania Press, 2016).

113. http://webstersdictionary1828.com.

114. Roediger, *The Wages of Whiteness*, 49–50.

115. Berthoff, "Conventional Mentality," 773. See also Linda K. Kerber, "The Paradox of Women's Citizenship in the Early Republic: The Case of Martin vs. Massachusetts, 1805," *American Historical Review* 97, no. 2 (1992): 351, 354.

116. See Matthew McCormack, *The Independent Man: Citizenship and Gender Politics in Georgian England* (Manchester: Manchester University Press, 2005), 12–30.

117. There were some exceptions to this rule; see Jane H. Pease and William H. Pease, *Ladies, Women, and Wenches: Choice and Constraint in Antebellum Charleston and Boston* (Chapel Hill: University of North Carolina Press, 1990), 90–114.

118. Quoted in Norma Basch, *In the Eyes of the Law: Women, Marriage, and Property in Nineteenth-Century New York* (Ithaca: Cornell University Press, 1982), 48–49. Blackstone's formulation was widely used in nineteenth-century America. Ibid., 42–69.

119. For an overview of antebellum debates over gender roles, see Michael D. Pierson, *Free Hearts and Free Homes: Gender and American Antislavery Politics* (Chapel Hill: University of North Carolina Press, 2003), 6–20.

120. *Official Report of the Debates and Proceedings in the State Convention, Assembled May 4th, 1853, to Revise and Amend the Constitution of the Commonwealth of Massachusetts*, vol. 1 (Boston: White & Potter, 1853), 210.

121. Judith Wellman, "Women's Rights, Republicanism, and Revolutionary Rhetoric in Antebellum New York State," *New York History* 69, no. 3 (1988): 356, 375.

122. Kerber, "The Paradox of Women's Citizenship in the Early Republic," 370.

123. Nancy Isenberg, *Sex and Citizenship in Antebellum America* (Chapel Hill: University of North Carolina Press, 1998), 15–74; Berthoff, "Conventional Mentality," 757–58; Wellman, "Women's Rights, Republicanism, and Revolutionary Rhetoric in Antebellum New York State," 353.

124. These reforms had begun earlier in some New England states; see Silvana R. Siddali, *Frontier Democracy: Constitutional Conventions in the Old Northwest* (Cambridge: Cambridge University Press, 2016), 314.

125. *Report of the Debates and Proceedings of the Convention for the Revision of the Constitution of the State of Indiana, 1850*, vol. 1, 466. Like Owen, many early feminists appealed to republican values, notably the ideal of personal independence, in pressing their claims for greater freedom. See Jean Matthews, "Race, Sex, and the Dimensions of Liberty in Antebellum America," *Journal of the Early Republic* 6, no. 3 (1986): 275–91.

126. *Report of the Debates and Proceedings of the Convention for the Revision of the Constitution of the State of Indiana, 1850*, vol. 1, 475.

127. Ibid., 470. Interestingly, Haddon is here restating verbatim the argument made four years earlier at the New York constitutional convention of 1846 by a Mr. O'Conor. *Report of the Debates and Proceedings of the Convention for the Revision of the Constitution of the State of New York, 1846* (Albany: Evening Atlas, 1846), 1057.

128. *Report of the Debates of the Convention of California on the Formation of the State Constitution, in September and October, 1849* (Washington, DC: John T. Towers, 1850 [1849]), 260; *Report of the Debates and Proceedings of the Convention for the Revision of the Constitution of the State of Indiana, 1850,* vol. 1, 477, 475, 485, 486, 806, 818; Berthoff, "Conventional Mentality."

129. "Were they to encourage a knifelike individualism to invade and divide the family itself," asks Basch, "the remaining haven in a brutally competitive society?" Basch, *In the Eyes of the Law,* 141.

130. Even Owen, for example, argued that property rights would only enhance women's domestic virtues by freeing them from fear and abuse, so that their selfless natures could unfold more completely. *Report of the Debates and Proceedings of the Convention for the Revision of the Constitution of the State of Indiana, 1850,* vol. 1, 465–67.

131. Ibid., 486. Another telling articulation of this view was offered by Mr. Preston of Louisiana; see *Proceedings and Debates of the Convention of Louisiana: Which Assembled at the City of New Orleans January 14, 1844* (New Orleans: Besancon, Ferguson & Co., 1845 [1844]), 150.

132. *Report of the Debates and Proceedings of the Convention for the Revision of the Constitution of the State of Indiana, 1850,* vol. 1, 476, 475. The domestic sphere was not, however, entirely cordoned off from political life. As mothers and wives, for example, women were expected to help shape their sons and husbands into virtuous citizens. See Linda K. Kerber, *Women of the Republic: Intellect and Ideology in Revolutionary America* (Chapel Hill: University of North Carolina Press, 1980), 269–88; Jan Lewis, "The Republican Wife: Virtue and Seduction in the Early Republic," *William and Mary Quarterly* 44, no. 4 (1987): 689–721. Certain forms of public influence were also seen as compatible with female domesticity: antebellum women, writes Mary Kelley, could "claim a female citizenship as educators, writers, editors, and reformers who were shaping the character of civil society." Mary Kelley, *Learning to Stand and Speak* (Chapel Hill: University of North Carolina Press, 2006), 246.

133. Lydia Sigourney, *Letters to Young Ladies,* 2nd ed. (Hartford: W. Watson, 1835 [1833]), 37–38. See also Basch, *In the Eyes of the Law,* 140.

134. Catharine Beecher was Harriet Beecher Stowe's sister and a distinguished writer and educator in her own right. Catharine Beecher, *An Essay on Slavery and Abolitionism, with Reference to the Duty of American Females* (Philadelphia: Henry Perkins, 1837), 101–2.

135. This was a very common rhetorical pattern: arguments for women's subordination (and for the importance of shielding them from the harsh world of power and interest) were couched in celebrations of their superior moral purity. They were to be the source of men's moral salvation.

136. Beecher, *An Essay on Slavery and Abolitionism, with Reference to the Duty of American Females,* 110–37.

137. For further reflections on this duality in the stereotypical perception of women, see Pease and Pease, *Ladies, Women, and Wenches;* Lewis, "The Republican Wife: Virtue and Seduction in the Early Republic."

138. *Report of the Debates and Proceedings of the Convention for the Revision of the Constitution of the State of Indiana, 1850*, vol. 1, 485. See also p. 473. The supposed fact of French women's promiscuity was often invoked in these debates. Basch, *In the Eyes of the Law*, 146–47.

139. See Isenberg, *Sex and Citizenship in Antebellum America*, 41–74. For an excellent discussion of the gendered boundaries of the public sphere in Jacksonian America, see Mary P. Ryan, *Women in Public: Between Banners and Ballots, 1825–1880* (Baltimore: Johns Hopkins University Press, 1990), 130–41. For an enlightening discussion of the political thought of these three early feminists, see Lisa Pace Vetter, *The Political Thought of America's Founding Feminists* (New York: New York University Press, 2017).

140. *Report of the Debates and Proceedings of the Convention for the Revision of the Constitution of the State of Indiana, 1850*, vol. 1, 815, 817. See also Basch, *In the Eyes of the Law*, 56–57.

141. *Report of the Debates and Proceedings of the Convention for the Revision of the Constitution of the State of Indiana, 1850*, vol. 1, 472–73.

142. *Report of the Debates of the Convention of California on the Formation of the State Constitution, in September and October, 1849*, 260.

143. Elizabeth Cady Stanton, "Address to the Legislature of New York" (Albany: Weed, Parsons, and Co., 1854), 16–17.

Chapter 5

1. Felix Grundy, *Register of Debates*, 22nd Cong., 1st sess. 407 (February 1832).

2. Jefferson's influence on the Jacksonian Democrats is well-documented. For evidence of Taylor's influence on Jacksonian thinkers, see, for example, "Democracy," *Globe*, July 5, 1837, p. 3; Stephen Simpson, *The Working Man's Manual* (Philadelphia: Thomas L. Bonsal, 1831), 18; "Radicalism," *United States Magazine and Democratic Review* 3, no. 10 (1838): 107. See also John Ashworth, *Slavery, Capitalism, and Politics in the Antebellum Republic*, vol. 1: *Commerce and Compromise, 1820–1850* (Cambridge: Cambridge University Press, 1995), 35, 381; Rush Welter, *The Mind of America: 1820–1860* (New York: Columbia University Press, 1975), 407; Arthur Schlesinger Jr., *The Age of Jackson* (Boston: Little, Brown, 1945), 155, 119.

3. This view is clearly and consistently expressed, for example, in the *Federalist Papers*.

4. On the other hand, many Jacksonians lauded the *defensive* uses of federal power, to break up monopolies, curb the excesses of the financial "aristocracy," rein in land speculators, and more—and these defensive aims inspired considerable political activism. See chapter 7 for further discussion.

5. Governor Marcus Morton of Massachusetts, quoted in the *Wisconsin Democrat*, February 21, 1843, p. 3.

6. Emphasis in original; George Camp, *Democracy* (New York: Harper and Brothers, 1841), 13. See also John William Ward, "Jacksonian Democratic Thought: 'A Natural Charter of Privilege,'" in *The Development of an American Culture*, ed. Stanley Coben and Lorman Ratner (New York: St. Martin's Press, 1983 [1970]), 58.

7. "The Great Nation of Futurity," *United States Magazine and Democratic Review* 6, no. 23 (1839): 427. See also Welter, *The Mind of America: 1820–1860*, 6; John Ashworth, *"Agrarians" & "Aristocrats": Party Political Ideology in the United States, 1837–1846* (Cambridge: Cambridge University Press, 1983), 7–20.

8. Robert Rantoul Jr., "An Oration Delivered before the Inhabitants of the Town of South Reading . . . on the Fourth of July, 1832" (Salem: Foote & Brown, 1832), 8.

9. Benjamin Butler, "Representative Democracy in the United States: An Address Delivered before the Senate of Union College" (Albany: C. Van Benthuysen, 1841), 17.

10. Robert Rantoul Jr., "An Oration Delivered before the Gloucester Mechanic Association on the Fourth of July, 1833" (Salem: Foote & Chisholm, 1833), 39. The Federalist-turned-Democrat Francis Baylies made a similar point: "We have but few of that class, which in Europe constitute 'the rabble;' and there is a high degree of independent and manly feeling among our poorest citizens, which will long preserve them from the influence of bribery, corruption, and intimidation." "Reply," *Globe*, May 29, 1833, 2.

11. "Democracy," *Globe*, July 5, 1837, p. 3.

12. Seth Luther, "An Address to the Working Men of New England on the State of Education and on the Condition of the Producing Classes in Europe and America" (New York: George H. Evans, 1833), 13, 14.

13. "The Factory System," *Working Man's Advocate*, March 24, 1832, p. 3.

14. Anon., "The Condition of Labor: An Address to the Members of the Labor Reform League of New England, by One of the Members" (Boston: Published by the author, 1847), 11.

15. *Canaille* is a derogatory term for "the masses."

16. Thomas Jefferson, "To John Adams," in *Thomas Jefferson: Political Writings*, ed. Joyce Appleby and Terence Ball (Cambridge: Cambridge University Press, 1999 [1813]), 190.

17. Gordon Wood, *The Creation of the American Republic: 1776–1787* (Chapel Hill: University of North Carolina Press, 1998 [1969]), 30.

18. William Allen, quoting Italian jurist and philosopher Cesare Beccaria, "Great Democratic Festival," *Globe* (reprinted from the *Lancaster Eagle*), September 9, 1837, p. 2.

19. Amos Kendall, "Democratic Celebration," *Globe*, December 13, 1832, p. 2.

20. See, for example, Theodore Sedgwick Jr., *Public and Private Economy, Part First* (New York: Harper & Brothers, 1836), 198; William Balch, "Popular Liberty and Equal Rights: An Oration Delivered before the Mass Convention of the R.I. Suffrage Association" (Providence: B. F. Moore, 1841), 7; "Art. I.—Report of the Secretary of the Treasury," *Western Review* 1, no. 1 (1846): 2–3.

21. See, for example, Rantoul, "An Oration Delivered before the Inhabitants of the Town of South Reading . . . on the Fourth of July, 1832," 3–15; Edwin Forrest, Esq., "Oration Delivered at the Democratic Republican Celebration of the Sixty-Second Anniversary of the Independence of the United States" (New York: J. W. Bell, 1838).

22. See, for instance, Kendall, "Democratic Celebration," 2; Samuel Clesson Allen, "Address Delivered at Northampton, before the Hampshire, Franklin, and Hampden Agricultural Society, October 27th, 1830" (Northampton: T. Watson Shepard, 1830).

23. "Address to the Workingmen of Massachusetts, by the Committee Appointed for That Purpose by the Northampton Convention," *New England Artisan*, October 25, 1834, p. 1.

24. Harry L. Watson, "Andrew Jackson's Populism," *Tennessee Historical Quarterly* 76 (2017): 225.

25. For an excellent discussion of this tendency in Democratic thought, see Welter, *The Mind of America: 1820–1860*, 165–79, 219–49; Ashworth, *"Agrarians" & "Aristocrats,"* 17–20.

26. Harry L. Watson, *Liberty and Power: The Politics of Jacksonian America* (New York: Hill and Wang, 1990), 47. For an overview of the way republican ideals informed the Jacksonian Democrats' political theory, see ibid., 42–72.

27. In this view, they followed John Taylor of Caroline, who asserted that "*a transfer of property by law, is aristocracy, and that aristocracy is a transfer of property by law.*" John Taylor, *An Inquiry into the Principles and Policy of the Government of the United States* (Fredericksburg: Green and Cady, 1814), 397. See also Ashworth, *"Agrarians" & "Aristocrats,"* 127–29; Welter, *The Mind of America: 1820–1860*, 78; Yehoshua Arieli, *Individualism and Nationalism in American Ideology* (Baltimore: Penguin Books, 1964), 160.

28. Quoted in William Leggett, "American Nobility," in *A Collection of the Political Writings of William Leggett*, vol. 2, ed. Theodore Sedgwick Jr. (New York: Taylor & Dodd, 1840 [1836]), 158.

29. This story of corruption by enterprising elites tapped a deep vein of republican populism running back to Machiavelli, which held, for example, that the decline and fall of the Roman republic was caused by "the concentration of land and wealth in the hands of an untrustworthy and unpatriotic aristocracy, as well as by the attendant decline of the class of sturdy freeholders." Samuel Dennis Glover, "The Putney Debates: Popular versus Elitist Republicanism," *Past & Present*, no. 164 (1999): 52.

30. Balch, "Popular Liberty and Equal Rights," 13. The same held true, others argued, for beneficiaries of public largesse: "A thousand facts in the history of the past . . . show that when men get chartered privileges they demand more and more at the public expense." William G. Boggs, "The Crisis Met: A Reply to Junius" (New York: Office of the Evening Post, 1840), 4.

31. George Bancroft, "Letter to the Workingmen of Northampton," *Boston Courier*, October 22, 1834, p. 3.

32. See chapter 3, pp. 50–51.

33. Bernard Bailyn, *The Ideological Origins of the American Revolution*, enlarged ed. (Cambridge, MA: Harvard University Press, 1992 [1967]), 55–93.

34. Daniel Walker Howe, *The Political Culture of the American Whigs* (Chicago: University of Chicago Press, 1979), 29. This Democratic view found precedent in the broad assaults on American aristocracy that had blossomed in the 1780s and 1790s; see Gordon Wood, *The Radicalism of the American Revolution* (New York: Random House, 1992), 271–86; Herbert J. Storing, *What the Anti-Federalists Were For: The Political Thought of the Opponents of the Constitution* (Chicago: University of Chicago Press, 1981), 18.

35. Allen, "Great Democratic Festival," 2.

36. William Leggett, "Rich and Poor," in *A Collection of the Political Writings of William Leggett*, vol. 1, ed. Theodore Sedgwick Jr. (New York: Taylor & Dodd, 1840 [1834]), 109, 110. See also "Danger of Aristocracy," *Mechanic's Advocate*, February 12, 1848, p. 76.

37. Welter, *The Mind of America: 1820–1860*, 178–79. Here too, the Democrats inherited elements of the Country tradition, which conceived of popular assemblies mainly as defenses against the crown's overreach. Wood, *The Creation of the American Republic*, 24; Ashworth, *"Agrarians" & "Aristocrats,"* 18–19; J. G. A. Pocock, "Machiavelli, Harrington, and English Political Ideologies in the Eighteenth Century," *William and Mary Quarterly* 22, no. 4 (1965): 565.

38. That is, constituents' right to instruct representatives as to how they should vote on particular policy questions.

39. Welter, *The Mind of America: 1820–1860*, 174–75.

40. "There exists in every government," wrote the *Democratic Review*, "no matter how constituted, whether representative or not, a difference of interests between the *governing* and the *governed.*" The author presents this as *the most important divide* in any government. "True Theory and Philosophy of Our System of Government," *United States Magazine and Democratic Review* 15, no. 75 (1844): 231. See also L. Ray Gunn, *The Decline of Authority: Public Economic Policy and Political Development in New York, 1800–1860* (Ithaca: Cornell University Press, 1988), 154–68.

41. Samuel Young, "Oration Delivered at the Democratic Republican Celebration of the Sixty-Fourth Anniversary of the Independence of the United States" (New York: Jared W. Bell, 1840), 13–14.

42. Bancroft, "Letter to the Workingmen of Northampton," 3.

43. "Nathaniel Macon," *United States Magazine and Democratic Review* 1, no. 1 (1837): 26.

44. It is significant that Andrew Jackson's signal accomplishment in office was a veto—the Bank veto. In fact, Jackson vetoed more legislation than all previous presidents combined.

45. Orestes A. Brownson, "Art. IV: The American Democrat," *Boston Quarterly Review* 1, no. 3 (1838): 375. At the time, Brownson was still an avid Democrat.

46. Rantoul, "An Oration Delivered before the Inhabitants of the Town of South Reading . . . on the Fourth of July, 1832," 25.

47. Andrew Jackson, "Farewell Address," in *A Compilation of the Messages and Papers of the Presidents, 1789–1902*, vol. 3, ed. James D. Richardson (New York: Bureau of National Literature, 1903 [1837]), 306.

48. William Gouge, "A Short History of Banking in the United States of America," in *A Short History of Paper Money and Banking, . . . to Which Is Prefixed an Inquiry into the Principles of the System* (Philadelphia: T. W. Ustick, 1833), 232. See also "The Moral of the Crisis," *United States Magazine and Democratic Review* 1, no. 1 (1837): 112, 111. For Gouge's influence, see Sean Wilentz, *The Rise of American Democracy: Jefferson to Lincoln* (New York: Norton, 2005), 510.

49. Anon., "An Address to the Farmers of Rhode Island, on the Subject of the General Election of Officers, in April, 1828," (Providence: H. H. Brown, 1828), 8.

50. Allen, "Great Democratic Festival," 2.

51. Thomas Hart Benton, "Speech of Mr. Benton, of Missouri, on Introducing a Resolution against the Renewal of the Charter of the Bank of the United States" (Washington, DC: Duff Green, 1831), 13.

52. Kendall, "Democratic Celebration," 2; Samuel Tilden, "Divorce of Bank and State: An Address to the Farmers, Mechanics, and Workingmen of the State of New York," in *The Writings and Speeches of Samuel J. Tilden*, vol. 1, ed. John Bigelow (New York: Harper and Bros., 1885 [1838]), 86–87. See also Andrew J. Donelson, "Draft by Andrew J. Donelson on Public Lands, the Tariff, and Nullification," in *The Papers of Andrew Jackson*, vol. 10, ed. Thomas Coens Daniel Feller, and Laura-Eve Moss (Knoxville: University of Tennessee Press, 2016 [1832]), 644.

53. Luther, "An Address to the Working Men of New England on the State of Education and on the Condition of the Producing Classes in Europe and America," 24.

54. Felix Grundy, *Register of Debates*, 22nd Cong., 1st sess. 407 (February 1832). See also Sedgwick, *Public and Private Economy, Part First*, 222; State Rights and Free Trade Association, "Political Tract No. 8: Free Trade and the American System; a Dialogue between a Merchant and a Planter" (Columbia: Times and Telescope, 1832), 11.

55. Anon., "The Condition of Labor: An Address to the Members of the Labor Reform League of New England, by One of the Members" (Boston: Published by the author, 1847), 10.

56. "New York City vs. New York State," *United States Magazine and Democratic Review 6*, no. 23 (1839): 500, 501. See also John A. Dix, "Rural Life and Embellishment," in *Speeches and Occasional Addresses*, vol. 2 (New York: D. Appleton & Co., 1864 [1851]), 335.

57. Henry Nash Smith, *Virgin Land: The American West as Symbol and Myth* (Cambridge, MA: Harvard University Press, 1970 [1950]), 171.

58. Nathaniel Gage, "Address before the Essex Agricultural Society, at Topsfield, September 27, 1837, at Their Annual Cattle Show" (Salem: Essex Agricultural Society, 1837), 12, 14. See also "American Society," *Knickerbocker Magazine 8* (1836): 210.

59. "I was more independent than any farmer in Concord," wrote Thoreau, "for I was not anchored to a house or farm, but could follow the bent of my genius, which is a very crooked one, every moment." Henry David Thoreau, *Walden* (Boston: Beacon Press, 1997 [1854]), 51.

60. Mark A. Noll, *America's God: From Jonathan Edwards to Abraham Lincoln* (Oxford: Oxford University Press, 2002), 203–6. Partly because they believed in a firm separation of church and state, the Democrats did not stress this point as often as their political opponents did. For an excellent example of the way Democrats drew on religious principles in articulating their faith in the democratic public, see Anon., "On the Intelligence of the People," *United States Magazine and Democratic Review 8*, no. 34 (1840). For further discussion of the Protestant assumptions widely shared by Democrats, see chapter 7.

61. John William Ward, *Andrew Jackson: Symbol for an Age* (London: Oxford University Press, 1955), 27–29.

62. "New York City vs. New York State," 501.

63. William F. Otis, "An Oration Delivered before the 'Young Men of Boston,' on the Fourth of July, 1831" (Boston: Carter, Hendee, and Babcock, 1831), 33.

64. Jackson himself was commonly hailed by his promoters as one of "Nature's great men," "educated in Nature's school," and "artificial in nothing," in sharp contrast to the haughty, urbane refinement of his opponent, John Quincy Adams. Quoted in Ward, *Andrew Jackson: Symbol for an Age*, 51–53.

65. On this pastoral theme in American thought, which linked virtue to nature, see Leo Marx, *The Machine in the Garden: Technology and the Pastoral Ideal in America* (Oxford: Oxford University Press, 2000 [1964]).

66. Gregory S. Alexander, *Commodity and Propriety: Competing Visions of Property in American Legal Thought, 1776–1970* (Chicago: University of Chicago Press, 1997), 45–55; Bailyn, *The Ideological Origins of the American Revolution*, 79–84.

67. George Bancroft, "An Oration Delivered before the Democracy of Springfield . . . , July 4th, 1836" (Springfield, MA: George and Charles Merriam, 1836), 18.

68. "New York City vs. New York State," 501.

69. Ashworth, *Slavery, Capitalism, and Politics in the Antebellum Republic*, vol. 1: *Commerce and Compromise, 1820–1850*, 311; Ashworth, *"Agrarians" & "Aristocrats,"* 16–20.

70. Taylor, *An Inquiry into the Principles and Policy of the Government of the United States*, 530–31.

71. Camp, *Democracy*, 96–103. See also Ashworth, *"Agrarians" & "Aristocrats,"* 15–19. Democrats had little doubt, moreover, that the people would *know* enough to protect themselves.

"Every man knows whether he enjoys more or less liberty," said one participant in the Louisiana constitutional convention of 1845, "or is exposed to few or greater burthens. It is unnecessary to be profoundly versed in government to appreciate all this." *Proceedings and Debates of the Convention of Louisiana . . . Jan. 14, 1844* (New Orleans: Besancon, Ferguson, & Co., 1845), 175.

72. Jackson, "Farewell Address," 296, 305. See also Watson, "Andrew Jackson's Populism," 223–24; Ward, "Jacksonian Democratic Thought," 68.

73. Anon., "On the Intelligence of the People," 364, 363, 366.

74. Welter, *The Mind of America: 1820–1860*, 179–85.

75. John O'Sullivan, "Introduction: The Democratic Principle—the Importance of Its Assertion, and Application to Our Political System and Literature," *United States Magazine and Democratic Review* 1, no. 1 (1837): 7. In fact, many Democrats saw broad conceptual affinities between democracy and the market. Like the market, they argued, democracy was a system of equal rights and free competition (for office) premised on the eradication of special privileges. Like the market, they also saw it as a strategy for limiting government power. See, for instance, James Fenimore Cooper, *The American Democrat* (New York: A. Knopf, 1931 [1838]), 117–20.

76. James Madison, "Federalist No. 10," in *The Federalist*, ed. George W. Carey and James McClellan (Indianapolis: Liberty Fund, 2003 [1787]), 43–44, 47.

77. Although they invoked Jefferson constantly, the Jacksonian Democrats hardly ever mentioned Madison (or indeed any of the debates surrounding the ratification of the Constitution); there is little evidence that they were engaging his ideas explicitly.

78. In this sense, though they would never have acknowledged it, they followed Adams more closely than Jefferson; see Judith Shklar, "The American Idea of Aristocracy," in *Redeeming American Political Thought*, ed. Stanley Hoffmann and Dennis Thompson (Chicago: University of Chicago Press, 1998), 152.

79. See Jonathan H. Earle, *Jacksonian Antislavery and the Politics of Free Soil, 1824–1854* (Chapel Hill: University of North Carolina Press, 2004), 1–48.

80. Jean M. Yarbrough, *American Virtues: Thomas Jefferson on the Character of a Free People* (Lawrence: University Press of Kansas, 1998), 110.

81. Robert E. Shalhope, *John Taylor of Caroline: Pastoral Republican* (Columbia: University of South Carolina Press, 1980), 64–65.

82. Thomas Jefferson, "To Joseph C. Cabell," in *Thomas Jefferson: Political Writings*, ed. Joyce Appleby and Terence Ball (Cambridge: Cambridge University Press, 1999 [1816]), 205.

83. Gordon Wood, *Empire of Liberty: A History of the Early Republic, 1789–1815* (Oxford: Oxford University Press, 2009), 287.

84. Thomas Jefferson, "A Bill for Amending the Constitution of the College of William and Mary," in *The Papers of Thomas Jefferson*, vol. 2, ed. Julian P. Boyd (Princeton: Princeton University Press, 1950 [1779]), 538–39.

85. Shalhope, *John Taylor of Caroline: Pastoral Republican*, 105.

86. Jefferson, "To John Adams," 187.

87. Wood, *The Creation of the American Republic*, 492–518.

88. "Centinel, Letter I," in *The Anti-Federalist: Writings by the Opponents of the Constitution*, ed. Murray Dry (Chicago: University of Chicago Press, 1985 [1787]), 14. See also "Essays of Brutus, I," in *The Anti-Federalist: Writings by the Opponents of the Constitution*, ed. Dry. In this

area—in his faith in an aristocracy of talent and virtue—Jefferson's sympathies lay, arguably, closer to the Federalists. Shklar, "The American Idea of Aristocracy," 152.

89. Merrill D. Peterson, *The Jefferson Image in the American Mind* (New York: Oxford University Press, 1960), 82–83; Ashworth, *Slavery, Capitalism, and Politics in the Antebellum Republic*, vol. 1: *Commerce and Compromise, 1820–1850*, 296–97. This flattening had begun earlier, as can be seen in the political rhetoric of the Democratic-Republican societies of the 1790s. But it won the field decisively in the Jacksonian Era.

90. Welter, *The Mind of America: 1820–1860*, 81–82; Ashworth, *"Agrarians" & "Aristocrats,"* 11–15.

91. Quoted in Ashworth, *"Agrarians" & "Aristocrats,"* 13.

92. Andrew Jackson, "First Annual Message," in *A Compilation of the Messages and Papers of the Presidents, 1789–1902*, vol. 2, ed. James D. Richardson (New York: Bureau of National Literature, 1903 [1829]), 449. For a discussion of Jackson's own fervent belief in majoritarian democracy, see Robert V. Remini, *The Legacy of Andrew Jackson: Essays on Democracy, Indian Removal, and Slavery* (Baton Rouge: Louisiana State University Press, 1988), 7–44.

93. Ward, *Andrew Jackson: Symbol for an Age*, 52, 71; Ward, "Jacksonian Democratic Thought." See also John Henry Eaton, *The Letters of Wyoming, to the People of the United States, on the Presidential Election* (Philadelphia: S. Simpson & J. Conrad, 1824), 88. The explicit anti-intellectualism of Jacksonian rhetoric marks another key difference between the Jacksonians and their Jeffersonian precursors; see Ward, *Andrew Jackson: Symbol for an Age*, 49–50; Richard Hofstadter, *Anti-Intellectualism in American Life* (New York: Knopf, 1963), 154.

94. Forrest, "Oration Delivered at the Democratic Republican Celebration of the Sixty-Second Anniversary of the Independence of the United States," 8–10.

95. Orestes Brownson, "Art. IV: Address of the Democratic State Convention of Massachusetts," *Boston Quarterly Review* 1, no. 1 (1838): 57. See also Welter, *The Mind of America: 1820–1860*, 171; Silvana R. Siddali, *Frontier Democracy: Constitutional Conventions in the Old Northwest* (Cambridge: Cambridge University Press, 2016), 129–31, 145.

96. Forrest, "Oration Delivered at the Democratic Republican Celebration of the Sixty-Second Anniversary of the Independence of the United States," 7. One Jackson eulogist put it this way in his 1845 "Funeral Address": the statesmen of the American West "imbibed together the healthy air of the forest and the pure principles of liberty, as they trod the pathless wood. In their own free hearts, they found the latent feelings which carried them straight forward in the path of building up their social institutions." Quoted in Ward, *Andrew Jackson: Symbol for an Age*, 73.

97. None of this is meant to imply that voters in the Jacksonian Era were apathetic or disengaged from politics, or that the prevailing ideologies encouraged them to be so. This unlikely view has been defended by Glenn Altschuler and Stuart Blumin. See Glenn C. Altschuler and Stuart M. Blumin, *Rude Republic: Americans and Their Politics in the Nineteenth Century* (Princeton: Princeton University Press, 2000).

98. Brian Balogh, *A Government out of Sight: The Mystery of National Authority in Nineteenth-Century America* (Cambridge: Cambridge University Press, 2009), 18–31, 117–21. Balogh argues that this shift had already taken place in Jeffersonian ideology; my own view locates it later.

99. Eaton, *The Letters of Wyoming, to the People of the United States, on the Presidential Election*, 51, 53, 62. This Democratic posture was an electoral winner, and candidates on both sides quickly

learned not to promote their superior educations or social backgrounds under any circumstances; all were *plain farmers* or *plain republicans* now; see Harry L. Watson, *Jacksonian Politics and Community Conflict: The Emergence of the Second American Party System in Cumberland County, North Carolina* (Baton Rouge: Louisiana State University Press, 1981), 172–73.

100. Edward Pessen, *Jacksonian America: Society, Personality, and Politics* (Homewood, IL: Dorsey Press, 1969), 183.

101. Ibid., 56, 160, 182–95; Charles Sellers, "Capitalism and Democracy in American Historical Mythology," in *The Market Revolution in America: Social, Political, and Religious Expressions, 1800–1880*, ed. Melvyn Stokes and Stephen Conway (Charlottesville: University Press of Virginia, 1996), 322; Charles Sellers, *The Market Revolution: Jacksonian America, 1815–1848* (New York: Oxford University Press, 1991), 345–62.

102. Ashworth, *Slavery, Capitalism, and Politics in the Antebellum Republic*, vol. 1: *Commerce and Compromise, 1820–1850*, 340. Ashworth argues, in fact, that the reason agrarian egalitarianism was so strong in America was precisely that it had the support of this powerful class. "What had happened, in effect," he writes, "was that a pre-capitalist radical tradition had come to prominence in the United States because it was quite compatible with the maintenance of the rights of an extraordinarily powerful and determined social group: the slaveholders of the South. In other countries that radicalism remained outside politics in normal times; it required war, social revolution, or both. In the United States, however, this radicalism, at the center of which lay a demand for a society of equalized, atomized power, was admirably suited to the needs of slaveholders" (347).

103. John Taylor, *Arator, Being a Series of Agricultural Essays, Practical and Political*, 5th ed. (Petersburg, VA: Whitworth and Yancey, 1818 [1813]), 14, vi.

104. Richard J. Carwardine, "'Antinomians' and 'Arminians': Methodists and the Market Revolution," in *The Market Revolution in America: Social, Political, and Religious Expressions, 1800–1880*, ed. Melvyn Stokes and Stephen Conway (Charlottesville: University Press of Virginia, 1996), 298; Nathan O. Hatch, *The Democratization of American Christianity* (New Haven: Yale University Press, 1989), 170.

105. Francis Asbury, the visionary leader of the American Methodist movement, quoted in Hatch, *The Democratization of American Christianity*, 83.

106. Ibid., 45.

107. Noll, *America's God*, 382.

108. See Richard Hofstadter, *Anti-Intellectualism in American Life* (New York: Vintage Books, 1962), 154–55; Curtis D. Johnson, *Redeeming America: Evangelicals and the Road to Civil War*, American Way Series (Chicago: Ivan R. Dee, 1993), 15.

109. William G. McLoughlin, *New England Dissent, 1630–1833: The Baptists and the Separation of Church and State*, vol. 2 (Cambridge, MA: Harvard University Press, 1971), 1282.

110. Wilentz, *The Rise of American Democracy: Jefferson to Lincoln*, 516; Richard P. McCormick, *The Second American Party System* (Chapel Hill: University of North Carolina Press, 1966), 349.

111. Wilentz, *The Rise of American Democracy: Jefferson to Lincoln*, 516.

112. For an excellent discussion of the unevenness of party formation across the United States, see McCormick, *The Second American Party System*. The following discussion of party formation draws heavily on Gerald Leonard's illuminating study of Jacksonian Illinois: Gerald

Leonard, *The Invention of Party Politics: Federalism, Popular Sovereignty, and Constitutional Development in Jacksonian Illinois* (Chapel Hill: University of North Carolina Press, 2002).

113. *Illinois Intelligencer*, June 9, 1819, quoted in Leonard, *The Invention of Party Politics*, 59–60.

114. *Sangamo Journal*, February 20, 1836, quoted in Leonard, *The Invention of Party Politics*, 58.

115. *Sangamo Journal*, October 29, 1836, quoted in Leonard, *The Invention of Party Politics*, 153–54. See also Thomas Brown, *Politics and Statesmanship: Essays on the American Whig Party* (New York: Columbia University Press, 1985), 32.

116. "From the Savannah Republican. Van Buren Opposed to the South and West," *Richmond Whig*, May 1, 1835, 4.

117. "Why Are Not the Whigs United?" reprinted in the *National Intelligencer*, May 21, 1835, p. 3. See also "New Constitution of Tennessee," reprinted in the *National Intelligencer*, May 11, 1835, p. 2.

118. See, for instance, John Pendleton Kennedy, *Defence of the Whigs. By a Member of the Twenty-Seventh Congress* (New York: Harper & Brothers, 1844); Anon., "The Andover Husking; a Political Tale Suited to the Circumstances of the Present Time, and Dedicated to the Whigs of Massachusetts" (Boston: J. H. Eastburn, 1842).

119. Anon., *The Political Mirror, or, Review of Jacksonism* (New York: J. P. Peaslee, 1835), 204.

120. "It may be truly said," wrote the author of the *Political Mirror*, "that there is no placeman nor expectant of place, whether in a high or low class, priest or layman, who is his own master." Ibid., 2.

121. Calvin Colton, "Junius Tracts No. VI. Democracy" (New York: Greeley & McElrath, 1844), 10. See also James Barbour, "Proceedings of the Democratic Whig National Convention" (Harrisburg, PA: R. S. Elliott & Co., 1839); Anon., "An Address to the Freemen of Rhode Island, by a Republican Farmer" ([Providence, RI], 1829).

122. See, for instance, John Whipple, "Address of John Whipple, to the People of Rhode Island, on the Approaching Election" (Providence, RI: Knowles and Vose, 1843); Nicholas Biddle, "An Address Delivered before the Alumni Association of Nassau-Hall, on the Day of the Annual Commencement of the College, September 30, 1835" (Princeton: Robert E. Hornor, 1835); Samuel L. Southard, "Mr. Southard's Speech, Continued," *National Intelligencer*, March 31, 1835.

123. Colton, "Junius Tracts No. VI. Democracy," 10.

124. The *Albany Daily Advertiser*, for example, lampooned the Democratic Jackson-worshippers for abandoning their "republican independence" and prostrating themselves before their political "Deity"; "Politics of the Day. From the *Albany Daily Advertiser*. Royal Democracy," *National Intelligencer*, April 21, 1835, p. 3.

125. For further discussion, see Brown, *Politics and Statesmanship: Essays on the American Whig Party*, 27–34; Joshua A. Lynn, "Popular Sovereignty as Populism in the Early American Republic," in *People Power: Popular Sovereignty from Machiavelli to Modernity*, ed. Christopher Barker and Robert G. Ingram (Manchester: Manchester University Press, 2022), 144–59.

126. Stephen Douglas, "To the Democratic Republicans of Illinois, Dec. 1835," in *The Letters of Stephen A. Douglas*, ed. Robert W. Johannsen (Urbana: University of Illinois Press, 1961 [1835]), 27, 25.

127. *Chicago Democrat*, July 8, 1835, quoted in Leonard, *The Invention of Party Politics*, 132.

128. Stephen Douglas, "To the Democratic Republicans of Illinois, Nov. 1837," in *The Letters of Stephen A. Douglas*, ed. Robert W. Johannsen (Urbana: University of Illinois Press, 1961 [1837]), 47.

129. Martin Van Buren, *Inquiry into the Origins and Course of Political Parties in the United States* (New York: Hurd & Houghton, 1867), 4.

130. Leonard, *The Invention of Party Politics*, 46. Van Buren cited Jean-Jacques Rousseau's principle that "the right to exercise sovereignty belongs inalienably to the people." Van Buren, *Inquiry into the Origins and Course of Political Parties in the United States*, 11.

131. Van Buren, *Inquiry into the Origins and Course of Political Parties in the United States*, 5. He did, however, acknowledge a single exception to this political rule.

132. Leonard, *The Invention of Party Politics*, 135–37, 129.

133. "Statement by the Democratic Republicans of the United States, Washington, July 31, 1835," in *History of American Presidential Elections, 1789–1968*, vol. 1, ed. Arthur Schlesinger Jr. (New York: Chelsea House, 1971 [1835]), 621, 622–23.

134. For further discussion, see Seth Cotlar, *Tom Paine's America: The Rise and Fall of Transatlantic Radicalism in the Early Republic* (Charlottesville: University of Virginia Press, 2011).

135. For further reflection on this transposition, see Smith, *Virgin Land: The American West as Symbol and Myth*, 133–44, 165–73.

136. For an astute discussion of this utopian impulse in connection with the American frontier, see Greg Grandin, *The End of the Myth: From the Frontier to the Border Wall in the Mind of America* (New York: Metropolitan Books, 2019), 113–31, esp. 123–24.

Part II

1. *The Constitutions of the United States and of the State of Ohio with Amendments, Annotations, and Indexes . . .* (Cincinnati: Robert Clarke & Co., 1886), 63.

2. Rush Welter, *The Mind of America: 1820–1860* (New York: Columbia University Press, 1975), 416.

3. In practice, rights were not nearly this absolute; their enforcement was also highly uneven and depended on the discretion of local officials. See, for instance, Laura Edwards, "The Reconstruction of Rights: The Fourteenth Amendment and Popular Conceptions of Governance," *Journal of Supreme Court History* 41, no. 3 (2016): 310–28.

4. Daniel T. Rodgers, *Contested Truths: Keywords in American Politics since Independence* (New York: Basic Books, 1987), 46, 45–79. See also Hendrik Hartog, "The Constitution of Aspiration and 'The Rights That Belong to Us All,'" *Journal of American History* 74, no. 3 (1987): 1013–34.

Chapter 6

1. John Taylor, *Arator, Being a Series of Agricultural Essays, Practical and Political*, 5th ed. (Petersburg, VA: Whitworth and Yancey, 1818 [1813]), 193.

2. As Daniel Rodgers explains, this entitlement was never considered absolute: "As for property," he writes, "no one doubted that a person's goods were alienable, taxable, condemnable, 'subservient to public uses' . . . 'when necessity requires it.' What the bills of right designated as

inalienable was not every last farthing a person owned but a set of verbs—acquiring, possessing, and defending—surrounding the word 'property,' porous enough to allow public necessity and public weal their legitimate shares." Daniel T. Rodgers, *Contested Truths: Keywords in American Politics since Independence* (New York: Basic Books, 1987), 63.

3. For Locke's influence in America, see Michael P. Zuckert, *The Natural Rights Republic: Studies in the Foundation of the American Political Tradition* (Notre Dame: University of Notre Dame Press, 1996); Michael P. Zuckert, *Natural Rights and the New Republicanism* (Princeton: Princeton University Press, 1994), 289–320; Steven M. Dworetz, *The Unvarnished Doctrine: Locke, Liberalism, and the American Revolution* (Durham: Duke University Press, 1990); Jerome Huyler, *Locke in America: The Moral Philosophy of the Founding Era* (Lawrence: University Press of Kansas, 1995); Donald Lutz, "The Relative Influence of European Writers on Late Eighteenth-Century American Political Thought," *American Political Science Review* 78, no. 1 (1984): 189–97.

4. This chapter's analysis of the labor theory of property is indebted, especially, to James L. Huston, *Securing the Fruits of Labor: The American Concept of Wealth Distribution, 1765–1900* (Baton Rouge: Louisiana State University Press, 1998).

5. "Whatsoever then he removes out of the State that Nature hath provided, and left it in, he hath mixed his *Labour* with, and joined to it something that is his own, and thereby makes it his *Property*." John Locke, *Two Treatises of Government* (Cambridge: Cambridge University Press, 2000 [1690]), 288.

6. Locke did attach certain conditions to this theory, however. Individuals could not, for example, rightly appropriate more than they could use; they also had to leave "enough, and as good" for others. This latter requirement is the famous Lockean "proviso" whose precise meaning has been a matter of long-standing controversy.

7. Judith Shklar, *American Citizenship: The Quest for Inclusion* (Cambridge, MA: Harvard University Press, 1991), 68. See also Gordon Wood, *The Radicalism of the American Revolution* (New York: Random House, 1992), 33–36.

8. Captain Basil Hall, *Travels in North America in the Years 1827 and 1828*, vol. 1 (Philadelphia: Carey, Lea & Carey, 1829), 258.

9. Joyce Appleby, *Capitalism and a New Social Order: The Republican Vision of the 1790s* (New York: New York University Press, 1984), 27–35; Drew R. McCoy, *The Elusive Republic: Political Economy in Jeffersonian America* (Chapel Hill: University of North Carolina Press, 1980), 17–47.

10. Adam Smith, *An Inquiry into the Nature and Causes of the Wealth of Nations*, vol. 1 (London: Methuen & Co., 1904 [1776]), 2.

11. Appleby, *Capitalism and a New Social Order*, 35; Jeffrey Sklansky, *The Soul's Economy: Market Society and Selfhood in American Thought, 1820–1920* (Chapel Hill: University of North Carolina Press, 2002), 18–19. The young Democrat Walt Whitman, writing for the *New-York Democrat* in 1844, captures this new attitude toward human labor and productivity perfectly: "It is to labor," he wrote, "that man owes every thing possessed of changeable value. Labor is the talisman that has raised him from the condition of the savage; that has changed the desert and the forest into cultivated fields; that has covered the earth with cities and the ocean with ships; that has given us plenty, comfort and elegance, instead of want, misery and barbarism." Walt Whitman, "True Democratic Logic," in *The Collected Writings of Walt Whitman, the Journalism*, vol. 1, ed. Herbert Bergman (New York: Peter Lang, 1998 [1844]), 197.

12. Michael Walzer, *The Revolution of the Saints: A Study in the Origins of Radical Politics* (Cambridge, MA: Harvard University Press, 1965), 210–11; Max Weber, *The Protestant Ethic and the Spirit of Capitalism*, trans. Stephen Kalberg (Los Angeles: Roxbury, 2002 [1905]), 105–6.

13. McCoy, *The Elusive Republic*, 78–79. The links between this Puritan theme and Locke's theory of property were quite explicit: in fact, Locke's *Second Treatise* can be read as "the classical text of radical Calvinist politics." See Isaac Kramnick, "The 'Great National Discussion': The Discourse of Politics in 1787," *William and Mary Quarterly* 45, no. 1 (1988): 3–32.

14. J. E. Crowley, *This Sheba, Self: The Conceptualization of Economic Life in Eighteenth-Century America* (Baltimore: Johns Hopkins University Press, 1974), 3, 17, 53–56.

15. Ronald Schultz, "God and Workingmen: Popular Religion and the Formation of Philadelphia's Working Class, 1790–1830," in *Religion in a Revolutionary Age*, ed. Ronald Hoffman and Peter J. Albert (Charlottesville: University Press of Virginia, 1994), 139.

16. Isaac Kramnick, *Republicanism and Bourgeois Radicalism: Political Ideology in Late Eighteenth-Century England and America* (Ithaca: Cornell University Press, 1990), 7–8. Kramnick is writing here about the emergence of a distinctly liberal worldview in the Anglo-American eighteenth century. For a discussion of this worldview in the early American republic specifically, see Gordon Wood, "The Enemy Is Us: Democratic Capitalism in the Early Republic," *Journal of the Early Republic* 16, no. 2 (1996): 293–308; Daniel T. Rodgers, *The Work Ethic in Industrial America, 1850–1920*, 2nd ed. (Chicago: University of Chicago Press, 2014 [1978]), 1–29.

17. Wood, *The Radicalism of the American Revolution*, 276–86. For a wonderful and brief encapsulation of this view in Jacksonian America, see Orville Dewey, "The Nobility of Labor," *Emancipator*, April 8, 1841.

18. Michael Merrill and Sean Wilentz, introduction to *The Key of Liberty* by William Manning, ed. Merrill and Wilentz (Cambridge, MA: Harvard University Press, 1993), 60. See also Huston, *Securing the Fruits of Labor*, 13–28; Sklansky, *The Soul's Economy*, 19–31; Huyler, *Locke in America*, 219–23, 237–46. The labor theory of value, which is conceptually distinct from the labor theory of property, holds that all economic value, or *wealth*, is created by labor alone. For a discussion of the labor theory of value in the early republic, see Alex Gourevitch, *From Slavery to the Cooperative Commonwealth: Labor and Republican Liberty in the Nineteenth Century* (New York: Cambridge University Press, 2014), 82–86; Sean Wilentz, *Chants Democratic: New York City and the Rise of the American Working Class, 1788–1850* (New York: Oxford University Press, 1984), 157–68.

19. Ezra Stiles, "The United States Elevated to Glory and Honor. A Sermon, Preached before His Excellency Jonathan Trumbull, Esq. . . ." (New Haven: Thomas & Samuel Green, 1783), 35.

20. Hector St. John de Crevecoeur, *Letters from an American Farmer* (New York: E. P. Dutton & Co., 1957 [1782]), 40.

21. Michel Chevalier, *Society, Manners and Politics in the United States, Being a Series of Letters on North America* (Boston: Weeks, Jordan, and Co., 1839), 437. See also pp. 206–7, 209. "The doctrine that all property is derived from human labor," writes Wilentz, "claimed an enormous array of supporters in early national and antebellum America." Sean Wilentz, "America's Lost Egalitarian Tradition," *Daedalus* 131, no. 1 (2002): 67; Huston, *Securing the Fruits of Labor*, 186.

22. Huston uses this term to describe societies in which "aristocrats used their social position to obtain political power to draw away the fruits of labor from the laborer and bestow those fruits upon themselves" (*Securing the Fruits of Labor*, 31).

23. Theodore Sedgwick Jr., *Public and Private Economy, Part First* (New York: Harper & Brothers, 1836), 180.

24. Anon., "Address to Working Men, on the Low Price of Wages, by a Mechanic" (New York, 1840), 4.

25. He also argued that banking, which "enables a few to acquire wealth without labor," was, in this sense, fundamentally European in character and must have originated in "Russia or Spain," where the degradation of the working man was most acute. Ibid.

26. Nathan Appleton, "Labor, Its Relations in Europe and the United States Compared" (Boston: Eastburn's Press, 1844), 9–10.

27. Brian Manning, *The English People and the English Revolution, 1640–1649* (London: Heinemann, 1976), 279. See also Ronald Schultz, *The Republic of Labor: Philadelphia Artisans and the Politics of Class, 1720–1830* (New York: Oxford University Press, 1993), 10–13. The Levellers were themselves channeling older Puritan currents of thought; see Walzer, *The Revolution of the Saints*, 211.

28. John Lilburne, "The Mournful Cries of Many Thousand Poor Tradesmen" (London: Humphrey Harward, 1648), 53.

29. "When a man hath got bread, *viz.* necessaries by his labor," the author continues, "it is his bread; now the other that sweats not at all, yet makes this man to pay him tribute out of his labor, by Rates, Taxes, Rents, &c. it is theft." Gerrard Winstanley, "More Light Shining in Buckingham-Shire . . ." (London, 1649), 10. This remarkable little pamphlet defends equal liberty for all men, free trade, and a natural right to the land, "for if man shall eat bread by his sweat, then he must needs have ground to sow corn" (ibid.). These words would carry subversive power for over 250 years. See, for instance, Theophilus Fisk, "An Oration on Banking, Education, &C. Delivered at the Queen-Street Theater, in the City of Charleston, S.C., July 4th, 1837" (Charleston, SC: Office of the Examiner, 1837), 4; Eric Foner, *The Fiery Trial: Abraham Lincoln and American Slavery* (New York: Norton, 2010), 113; Bruce Palmer, *"Man over Money": The Southern Populist Critique of American Capitalism* (Chapel Hill: University of North Carolina Press, 1980), 11.

30. For the legacies of Leveller thought in America, see Schultz, *The Republic of Labor*, 3–139; James L. Huston, *The British Gentry, the Southern Planter, and the Northern Family Farmer: Agriculture and Sectional Antagonism in North America* (Baton Rouge: Louisiana State University Press, 2015), 3–28; Alfred F. Young, "English Plebian Culture and Eighteenth-Century American Radicalism," in *The Origins of Anglo-American Radicalism*, ed. Margaret C. Jacob and James R. Jacob (New Jersey: Humanities Press International, 1984).

31. William Manning, *The Key of Liberty* (Cambridge, MA: Harvard University Press, 1993 [1799]), 125–39.

32. Ibid., 136. The most dogged opposition to all free government, Manning maintained, had always come from "those that live without Labor" (138).

33. William R. Sutton, *Journeymen for Jesus: Evangelical Artisans Confront Capitalism in Jacksonian Baltimore* (University Park: Pennsylvania State University Press, 1998), 30–33; Eric Foner, *Tom Paine and Revolutionary America* (New York: Oxford University Press, 1976), 38–45.

34. C. F. Volney, a French historian whose writing circulated in "cheap pocket-book form" among the urban working classes in Britain and America, was one such source. E. P. Thompson, *The Making of the English Working Class* (New York: Vintage Books, 1963), 98–99. See

Constantin François de Chasseboeuf Volney, comte de, *The Ruins, or, A Survey of the Revolutions of Empires* (Albany: S. Shaw, 1822 [1791]), 48–51. A group of French political economists called the Physiocrats, who had influenced Jefferson, Franklin, and John Taylor of Caroline, were another relevant source. They too had embraced the labor theory of property as a fundamental principle of natural law and used it to condemn the system of legalized "depredations" that enabled the French nobility to appropriate property without labor. See Ronald L. Meek, *The Economics of Physiocracy* (London: Ruskin House, 1962), 15–36.

35. Thomas Paine, *Rights of Man* (Mineola, NY: Dover Publications, 1999 [1791–92]), 112, 146.

36. Ibid., 147. "Every man wishes to pursue his occupation, and to enjoy the fruits of his labours, and the produce of his property in peace and safety, and with the least possible expence. When these things are accomplished," Paine asserted, "all the objects for which government ought to be established are answered" (136).

37. Thomas Jefferson, "To Joseph Milligan, April 6, 1816," in *The Writings of Thomas Jefferson*, vol. 13, ed. Albert Ellery Bergh (Washington, DC: Thomas Jefferson Memorial Association 1907 [1816]), 466.

38. William Duane, *Politics for American Farmers* ... (Washington, DC: R. C. Weightman, 1807), 94. For further discussion of these ideas, see Huston, *Securing the Fruits of Labor*, 29–58; Richard J. Twomey, *Jacobins and Jeffersonians: Anglo-American Radicalism in the United States, 1790–1820* (New York: Garland, 1989), 138–70; Stephen Watts, *The Republic Reborn: War and the Making of Liberal America, 1790–1820* (Baltimore: Johns Hopkins University Press, 1987), 224–32; Arthur Schlesinger Jr., *The Age of Jackson* (Boston: Little, Brown, 1945), 21–26.

39. This was true of both Volney and the Physiocrats; see note 34 in this chapter.

40. Manning, *The Key of Liberty*, 127; see also pp. 135–43.

41. Foner, *Tom Paine and Revolutionary America*, 145–82.

42. Ibid., 40.

43. "Political Mechanics," *Indiana Democrat*, September 4, 1830, p. 3. Speaking to fellow partisans in New Hampshire, Democratic leaders described their Whig opponents as men who, "reversing the Scriptural injunction, would live not 'by the sweat of their own brows,' but *by the sweat of the brows of others*." Harry Hibbard et al., "Address of the State Convention to the Democratic Republicans of New Hampshire," *New Hampshire Patriot and State Gazette*, August 3, 1840, p. 1. See also Frederick Robinson, "An Oration Delivered before the Trades Union of Boston and Vicinity, on Fort Hill, Boston, on the Fifty-Eighth Anniversary of American Independence" (Boston, 1834), 6.

44. See, for instance, Samuel Tilden, "Divorce of Bank and State: An Address to the Farmers, Mechanics, and Workingmen of the State of New York," in *The Writings and Speeches of Samuel J. Tilden*, vol. 1, ed. John Bigelow (New York: Harper and Bros., 1885 [1838]), 82–83; Sedgwick, *Public and Private Economy, Part First*, 72, 207, 209; Amos Kendall, "Democratic Celebration," *Globe*, December 13, 1832, p. 2.

45. To be more precise, Democrats also treated popular ratification as a necessary condition of the Constitution's legitimacy, but it was not a *sufficient* condition: had the people agreed to "artificial" principles, the resulting Constitution would, in their view, have been illegitimate.

46. See, for instance, B. F. Bailey, Esq., "An Oration, Delivered at Burlington, VT, on the Fourth of July, 1828, Being the Fifty-Second Anniversary of American Independence"

(Burlington, VT: E. & T. Mills, 1828), 4; George Bancroft, "Mr. Bancroft's Address," *Franklin Mercury*, February 24, 1835, pp. 2–3; George Camp, *Democracy* (New York: Harper and Brothers, 1841), 48.

47. Stephen Simpson, *The Working Man's Manual* (Philadelphia: Thomas L. Bonsal, 1831), 9. The Democrats were here largely repeating arguments that Paine had leveled at Edmund Burke in his *Rights of Man*.

48. Robert Rantoul Jr., "An Address to the Workingmen of the United States of America," in *Memoirs, Speeches, and Writings of Robert Rantoul, Jr.*, ed. Luther Hamilton (Boston: John P. Jewett & Co., 1854 [1833]), 224, 229.

49. "What Is the Reason? 'How Much Land and Property, and I Have None!'" *United States Magazine and Democratic Review* 16, no. 79 (1845): 20. The different political conclusions reached by Rantoul and by this author (whose politics veered toward utopian socialism) illustrate the labor theory of value's flexibility.

50. William G. Boggs, "The Working Man Defended, by the Author of the 'Crisis Met'" (New York: Office of the Evening Post, 1840), 4.

51. Tilden, "Divorce of Bank and State," 1:83.

52. Virginia Democrat Hugh Garland summed up the difference between the two parties this way: "Shall man, the workmanship of [God's] hands, endowed with faculties divine, and made heir of immortality, live according to the laws of his nature, enjoy the birth-rights of his creation, tread the green earth, breathe the limpid air untrammelled, live by the sweat of his own brow, enjoy the fruits of his own toil, and as free of limb, so be free of heart; free to choose his mode of happiness, and to follow the impulses of that divine, ever-active principle pervading all things, existing in all natures, and strongest in his own bosom to subvert its noxious qualities, to sweep away infection, and suppress all evil? Or shall he live in servitude to his fellow man— till the earth, and bear its fruits an offering to a fellow worm; walk prone and cowering like a brute, employed as a tool, an implement or passive thing, without acknowledgment of right or interest in the end; his soul made abject, to be abused as selfishness may prompt, made weak in all good, and strong alone in evil?" Hugh Garland, "The Second War of Revolution; or the Great Principles Involved in the Present Controversy between Parties" (Washington, DC: Democratic Review, 1839), 19–20.

53. John Ashworth, *"Agrarians" & "Aristocrats": Party Political Ideology in the United States, 1837–1846* (Cambridge: Cambridge University Press, 1983), 23–24; Lawrence Frederick Kohl, *The Politics of Individualism: Parties and the American Character in the Jacksonian Era* (New York: Oxford University Press, 1989), 186–227.

54. William Fulton, *Cong. Globe,* 25th Cong., 2nd sess., Appendix 136 (January 1838).

55. James Buchanan, *Cong. Globe,* 25th Cong., 2nd sess., Appendix 132 (January 1838). See also Henry Nash Smith, *Virgin Land: The American West as Symbol and Myth* (Cambridge, MA: Harvard University Press, 1970 [1950]), 169–70.

56. John Galbraith, *Register of Debates,* 24th Cong., 2nd sess., Appendix 153 (March 1837).

57. "Freedom of the Public Lands," *Northampton Democrat,* January 26, 1847, p. 2.

58. Willie Mangum, *Register of Debates,* 22nd Cong., 1st sess. 314 (February 1832).

59. This argument was commonly heard among Democrats. See also State Rights and Free Trade Association, "Political Tract No. 8: Free Trade and the American System; a Dialogue between a Merchant and a Planter" (Columbia: Times and Telescope, 1832), 4.

60. John Taylor, *Tyranny Unmasked* (Indianapolis: Liberty Fund, 1992 [1821]), 152. This became a common refrain among southern planters. See, for instance, *Proceedings and Debates of the Virginia State Convention, of 1829–30*, vol. 1 (Richmond: Samuel Shepherd & Co., 1830), 250–51.

61. John Claiborne, *Cong. Globe*, 24th Cong., 2nd sess., Appendix 89 (January 1837). Claiborne also indicted banks and "stockjobbers" in these same terms.

62. Amos Kendall, "Free Trade," *Kendall's Expositor* 3, no. 4 (1843): 60–61.

63. William Gouge, "An Inquiry into the Principles of the System," in *A Short History of Paper Money and Banking, . . . to Which Is Prefixed an Inquiry into the Principles of the System . . .* (Philadelphia: T. W. Ustick, 1833), 91.

64. Galbraith, *Register of Debates*, 24th Cong., 2nd sess., Appendix 150, 151 (March 1837). See also "Convention of the Democratic Party of Mississippi," *Extra Globe*, July 12, 1834; "The Farmers," *Extra Globe*, November 3, 1834, pp. 295–96; Rush Welter, *The Mind of America: 1820–1860* (New York: Columbia University Press, 1975), 84–86.

65. There was a good deal of truth in this charge, as workers were commonly paid in depreciated banknotes, which they were forced to accept at face value. Charles Sellers, *The Market Revolution: Jacksonian America, 1815–1848* (New York: Oxford University Press, 1991), 160. See also Schlesinger, *The Age of Jackson*, 115–31.

66. "The Democracy," *New York Evening Post*, October 2, 1834, p. 2. Interestingly, the author also praised gold and silver because, unlike paper currency, their value was a function of the *labor* it took to find and extract them.

67. See Robert Richard, "The 'Great Depression,' the People's Bank, and Jacksonian Fiscal Populism in North Carolina, 1819–1833," *Tennessee Historical Quarterly* 76, no. 3 (2017): 240–57.

68. "The Tax Law—Capital against Labor," *Tri-Weekly Ohio Statesman*, August 18, 1845, p. 3.

69. Pessen, *Jacksonian America*, 182–83, 187, 195.

70. Randolph Roth, *The Democratic Dilemma: Religion, Reform, and the Social Order in the Connecticut River Valley of Vermont, 1791–1850* (Cambridge: Cambridge University Press, 1987), 251.

71. Ibid., 254. See also Sellers, *The Market Revolution*, 345–63; Daniel Peart, "An 'Era of No Feelings'? Rethinking the Relationship between Political Parties and Popular Participation in the Early United States," in *Practicing Democracy: Popular Politics in the United States from the Constitution to the Civil War*, ed. Daniel Peart and Adam I. P. Smith (Charlottesville: University of Virginia Press, 2015). Historians disagree as to how well political parties in Jacksonian America represented the interests and demands of their constituents; see Reeve Huston, "The Parties and 'the People': The New York Anti-Rent Wars and the Contours of Jacksonian Politics," *Journal of the Early Republic* 20, no. 2 (2000): 243–44.

72. See, for instance, Sutton, *Journeymen for Jesus*, 167–211; Wilentz, *Chants Democratic*, 172–216. Political compromise is required, of course, in every functional democratic system. Two-party dynamics made it difficult, however, for urban workers to establish their own political parties, which might have given their more robustly egalitarian ideas a firmer institutional foundation, and their own leaders a seat at the political table.

73. Huston, *Securing the Fruits of Labor*, 8, 130–31, 219–58.

74. Jonathan A. Glickstein, *American Exceptionalism, American Anxiety: Wages, Competition, and Degraded Labor in the Antebellum United States* (Charlottesville: University of Virginia Press, 2002), 119–36.

75. Theophilus Fisk, "Capital against Labor: An Address Delivered at Julien Hall, before the Mechanics of Boston" (Boston: Daily Reformer, 1835), 7.

76. Maurice Neufeld, "Realms of Thought and Organized Labor in the Age of Jackson," *Labor History* 10, no. 1 (1969): 7; Wilentz, *Chants Democratic*, 158; Huston, *Securing the Fruits of Labor*, 75–76; Rantoul, "An Address to the Workingmen of the United States of America." See also Congressman Franklin Plummer's remarks on the floor of the House, *Register of Debates*, 23rd Cong., 1st sess. 4834–35 (May 1834).

77. Wilentz, "America's Lost Egalitarian Tradition," 72.

78. This is too simple, of course: farm goods were produced by families, sometimes with the help of slaves, and their productive contributions were owned and controlled by the white male head of household.

79. Huston, *Securing the Fruits of Labor*, 73, 192–93; Glickstein, *American Exceptionalism, American Anxiety*, 128; Schlesinger, *The Age of Jackson*, 311.

80. See, for instance, "Political Economy. No. II," *Extra Globe*, November 17, 1834, p. 325.

81. Tom Paine had also acknowledged this growing difficulty in 1797; see Thomas Paine, *Agrarian Justice*, 2nd ed. (Paris: W. Adlard, 1797), 30.

82. William R. Sutton, "'To Extract Poison from the Blessings of God's Providence': Producerist Respectability and Methodist Suspicions of Capitalist Change in the Early Republic," in *Methodism and the Shaping of American Culture*, ed. Nathan O. Hatch and John H. Wigger (Nashville: Kingswood Books, 2001), 228.

83. Noel Thompson, *The People's Science: The Popular Political Economy of Exploitation and Crisis, 1816–1834* (Cambridge: Cambridge University Press, 1984), 111–57. See also Esther Lowenthal, *The Ricardian Socialists* (New York: Columbia University, 1911).

84. Wilentz, *Chants Democratic*, 157–68; Schultz, *The Republic of Labor*, 181–233; Sutton, *Journeymen for Jesus*, 131–211; Gourevitch, *From Slavery to the Cooperative Commonwealth*, 82–96; Bruce Laurie, *Artisans into Workers: Labor in Nineteenth-Century America* (New York: Hill and Wang, 1989); Edward Pessen, *Most Uncommon Jacksonians: The Radical Leaders of the Early Labor Movement* (Albany: State University of New York Press, 1967), 173–96.

85. "Art. I.—Report of the Secretary of the Treasury," *Western Review* 1, no. 1 (1846): 37.

86. "The Reciprocal Influence of the Physical Sciences and of Free Political Institutions," *United States Magazine and Democratic Review* 18, no. 91 (1846): 13. For further discussion, see Huston, *Securing the Fruits of Labor*, 69–75. See also Condy Raguet, *The Principles of Free Trade, Illustrated in a Series of Short and Familiar Essays. Originally Published in the Banner of the Constitution* (Philadelphia: Carey, Lee, and Blanchard, 1835 [1829–32]), 274–75, 270.

87. Kendall, "Free Trade," 60.

88. "The Tariff Question," *Southern Literary Messenger* 8, no. 7 (1842): 425.

89. Of course, any tax on goods, services, or income can be understood as preventing people from obtaining market rate for their labor. But certain taxes are required to preserve the institutional framework within which the market can function. Jacksonians tended to argue that so long as taxes were modest and equitably distributed, they did not impinge on anyone's rights.

90. Amos Kendall, "Warring on Mankind," *Kendall's Expositor* 1, no. 25 (1841): 390.

91. "Principles of Taxation," *New York Evening Post*, reprinted in the *Wisconsin Democrat*, October 25, 1842, p. 2. Elsewhere, the *Post* described market prices as "natural," and tariffs as

means of depriving American farmers and artisans of the "proceeds of their labor." "Operation of the Tariff," reprinted in the *Wisconsin Democrat*, May 4, 1843, p. 3.

92. Welter, *The Mind of America: 1820–1860*, 85.

93. "Free Trade Convention," *New York Evening Post* (reprinted from the *Philadelphia Gazette*), October 8, 1831, p. 2. Others simply asserted a fundamental natural right of "entering into those . . . species of honest business from which they think they may derive emolument." A New Yorker, "For the Evening Post," *New York Evening Post*, September 15, 1835, p. 2. "Address to the People of the United States, by the Convention of South Carolina," *New York Evening Post*, December 1, 1832, p. 2.

94. State Rights and Free Trade Association, "Political Tract No. 8: Free Trade and the American System; a Dialogue between a Merchant and a Planter," 8.

95. Clement Comer Clay (Alabama), *Cong. Globe*, 25th Cong., 2nd sess. 143 (January 1838); Samuel Cartwright, "Convention of the Democratic Party of Mississippi," *Extra Globe*, July 1, 2, 1834, p. 44.

96. John Ashworth, "The Jacksonian as Leveller," *Journal of American Studies* 14, no. 3 (1980): 413.

97. Andrew Jackson, "Farewell Address," in *A Compilation of the Messages and Papers of the Presidents, 1789–1902*, vol. 3, ed. James D. Richardson (New York: Bureau of National Literature, 1903 [1837]), 305.

98. John Bell, *Register of Debates*, 22nd Cong., 1st sess. 3361 (June 1832).

99. "Morton's Message—Equal Distribution of Intestate Property," *Providence Daily Journal*, January 25, 1843, p. 2. See also William Allen, *Cong. Globe*, 25th Cong, 2nd sess., Appendix 251 (February 1838).

100. Harry L. Watson, "Andrew Jackson's Populism," *Tennessee Historical Quarterly* 76 (2017): 232; Richard Latner, "Preserving 'the Natural Equality of Rank and Influence': Liberalism, Republicanism, and Equality of Condition in Jacksonian Politics," in *The Culture of the Market: Historical Essays*, ed. Thomas L. Haskell and Richard F. Teichgraeber III (Cambridge: Cambridge University Press, 1993), 208; Ashworth, "The Jacksonian as Leveller," 412; Welter, *The Mind of America: 1820–1860*, 86.

101. Of course, many Native Americans did practice agriculture, and many in the Southwest, which was the epicenter of the conflict in the Jacksonian Era, had thoroughly assimilated to the intensive farming practiced by their American counterparts. Moreover, early white settlers had learned many farming techniques from the Native Americans themselves.

102. Lewis Cass, "Removal of the Indians," *North American Review* 30 (1830): 77.

103. James Wayne, *Register of Debates*, 21st Cong., 1st sess. 1125 (May 1830). Vattel was cited repeatedly in justifying violence against Native Americans; he was also a key source in shaping Andrew Jackson's own idea of the prerogatives of "civilized nations." J. M. Opal, *Avenging the People: Andrew Jackson, the Rule of Law, and the American Nation* (New York: Oxford University Press, 2017), 3, 5–8, 95, 168, 170.

104. Wayne, *Register of Debates*, 1124–26. See also Claudio Saunt, *Unworthy Republic: The Dispossession of Native Americans and the Road to Indian Territory* (New York: W. W. Norton, 2020), 27–83; Paul Frymer, *Building an American Empire: The Era of Territorial and Political Expansion* (Princeton: Princeton University Press, 2017), 104–13.

105. Locke's innovation marked a "crucial turning-point in the history of the idea of property," writes Barbara Arneil, and it was eagerly adopted in America. Barbara Arneil, *John Locke and America: The Defence of English Colonialism* (Oxford: Clarendon Press, 1996), 170, 171–76.

106. Locke, *Two Treatises of Government*, 290–91.

107. For a discussion of Locke's involvement with the Carolina constitution, see David Armitage, *Foundations of Modern International Thought* (Cambridge: Cambridge University Pres, 2013), 90–113.

108. Locke, *Two Treatises of Government*, 294.

109. Hugh Henry Brackenridge, *Law Miscellanies: Containing an Introduction to the Study of the Law; Notes on Blackstone's Commentaries* (Philadelphia: P. Byrne, 1814), 124. He too argued that the Native American way of life was "abhorrent" in the eyes of God.

110. Cited in Arneil, *John Locke and America: The Defence of English Colonialism*, 191; this line appears in Jefferson's notes on a border dispute between Pennsylvania and Connecticut.

111. Thomas Jefferson, "Draft of the 5th Annual Message to Senate and House of Representatives," in *State of the Union Messages of the Presidents of the United States*, vol. 1, ed. Fred Israel (New York: Chelsea House, 1967 [1805]), 82.

112. Lewis Cass, "Removal of the Indians," *North American Review* 30 (1830): 75. See also Michael Paul Rogin, *Fathers and Children: Andrew Jackson and the Subjugation of the American Indian* (New York: Knopf, 1975), 114–25.

113. Horace Greeley, *An Overland Journey from New York to San Francisco in the Summer of 1859* (New York: C. M. Saxton, Barker, and Co., 1860), 151. See also Michael Paul Rogin, "Liberal Society and the Indian Question," in *"Ronald Reagan," the Movie, and Other Episodes in Political Demonology* (Berkeley: University of California Press, 1987); Saunt, *Unworthy Republic*, 231–81.

114. Richard Wilde, *Register of Debates*, 21st Cong., 1st sess. 1093, 1096 (May 1830).

115. See Reginald Horsman, *Race and Manifest Destiny: The Origins of American Racial Anglo-Saxonism* (Cambridge, MA: Harvard University Press, 1981), 116–38, 189–207.

116. For the Enlightenment view, see Nicholas Guyatt, *Bind Us Apart: How Enlightened Americans Invented Racial Segregation* (New York: Basic Books, 2016), 1–132. For its eclipse, see James Brewer Stewart, "The Emergence of Racial Modernity and the Rise of the White North, 1790–1840," *Journal of the Early Republic* 18, no. 2 (1998): 181–217.

117. Francis Parkman, *The Conspiracy of Pontiac* (New York: Collier Books, 1962 [1851]), 63. See also Daniel Dickinson, "Address Delivered at the Fair of the Queens County Agricultural Society, October 17th, 1843," in *Speeches, Correspondence, Etc. of the Late Daniel Dickinson of New York*, vol. 1, ed. John R. Dickinson (New York: G. P. Putnam & Sons, 1867 [1843]), 114–15; Deborah A. Rosen, *American Indians and State Law: Sovereignty, Race, and Citizenship, 1790–1880* (Lincoln: University of Nebraska Press, 2007), 104–8.

118. Cheryl I. Harris, "Whiteness as Property," *Harvard Law Review* 106, no. 8 (1993): 1721–24.

119. John Ross et al., "Memorial and Protest of the Cherokee Nation," in *Letter from John Ross . . . Followed by a Copy of the Protest of the Cherokee Delegation* ([Washington, DC], 1836), 17, 22–23, 29–30. See also "New Echota," *Cherokee Phoenix*, November 18, 1829.

120. Ross, "Memorial and Protest of the Cherokee Nation," 30, 29. See also "New Echota," *Cherokee Phoenix*, May 18, 1833.

121. Langton Byllesby, "Observations on the Sources and Effects of Unequal Wealth" (New York: Lewis J. Nichols, 1826), 33. See also Simpson, *The Working Man's Manual*, 49.

122. Gourevitch, *From Slavery to the Cooperative Commonwealth*, 69, 80; Ashworth, "Agrarians" & "Aristocrats," 31.

123. "Address to the Workingmen of the United States," *Extra Globe*, September 26, 1840, p. 293.

124. Edward E. Baptist, *The Half Has Never Been Told: Slavery and the Making of American Capitalism* (New York: Basic Books, 2014), 141.

125. Ibid., 117, 111–44.

126. Huston, *Securing the Fruits of Labor*, 61–63. See also Shklar, *American Citizenship*, 79.

127. Crevecoeur, *Letters from an American Farmer*, 155, 156.

128. Rogers M. Smith, *Civic Ideals: Conflicting Visions of Citizenship in U.S. History* (New Haven: Yale University Press, 1997), 203–6; Harris, "Whiteness as Property."

129. J. K. Paulding, *Slavery in the United States* (New York: Harper & Bros., 1836), 58, 70, 72, 59. For comparable examples, see William Drayton, *The South Vindicated from the Treason and Fanaticism of the Northern Abolitionists* (Philadelphia: H. Manly, 1836); Richard H. Colfax, "Evidence against the Views of the Abolitionists, Consisting of Physical and Moral Proofs, of the Natural Inferiority of the Negroes" (New York: James T. M. Bleakley, 1833). See also Gerald S. Henig, "The Jacksonian Attitude toward Abolitionism in the 1830's," *Tennessee Historical Quarterly* 28, no. 1 (Spring 1969): 50–52.

130. *Providence Gazette*, quoted in Jacqueline Jones, *A Dreadful Deceit: The Myth of Race from the Colonial Era to Obama's America* (New York: Basic Books, 2013), 100. Or they insisted, more broadly, that because Blacks were incapable of living responsibly on their own, their freedom would unleash an "inundation of vice and crime" that would endanger white rights. James Whitcomb, "Mr. Whitcomb's Report," *Indiana Democrat*, February 18, 1832, p. 3.

131. John Claiborne, *Cong. Globe*, 24th Cong., 2nd sess., Appendix 92 (January 1837).

132. David R. Roediger, *The Wages of Whiteness: Race and the Making of the American Working Class* (London: Verso, 1991), 68–71.

133. Ibid., 72–74. See also Noel Ignatiev, *How the Irish Became White* (New York: Routledge, 1995), 62–121; Joel Olson, *The Abolition of White Democracy* (Minneapolis: University of Minnesota Press, 2004), 31–63.

134. See Jonathan H. Earle, *Jacksonian Antislavery and the Politics of Free Soil, 1824–1854* (Chapel Hill: University of North Carolina Press, 2004); Sean Wilentz, "Slavery, Antislavery, and Jacksonian Democracy," in *The Market Revolution in America: Social, Political, and Religious Expressions, 1800–1880*, ed. Melvyn Stokes and Stephen Conway (Charlottesville: University Press of Virginia, 1996).

135. Thomas Morris, *Cong. Globe*, 25th Cong., 3rd sess., Appendix 168 (February 1839). In fact, the term "slave power," which Whigs and Republicans used to describe the organized, corrupting political influence of slavery, was simply a modification of the Jacksonian concept of "money power"—and it was originally coined by Morris himself.

136. Sedgwick, *Public and Private Economy, Part First*, 246–55. See also Eric Foner, *Free Soil, Free Labor, Free Men: The Ideology of the Republican Party before the Civil War* (London: Oxford University Press, 1970), 65, 68; John Ashworth, *Slavery, Capitalism, and Politics in the Antebellum*

Republic, vol. 2: *The Coming of the Civil War, 1850–1861* (New York: Cambridge University Press, 2007), 187–92.

137. "Freedom of the Public Lands," 2.

138. Such unfavorable comparisons to southern slavery were commonly drawn; Roediger, *The Wages of Whiteness*, 76–77.

139. Frederick Douglass, "Lecture on Slavery, No. 1," in *Antislavery Political Writings, 1833–1860*, ed. C. Bradley Thompson (Armonk, NY: M. E. Sharpe, 2004 [1850]), 26.

140. Reprinted as "Objections Glanced At," *Friend of Man*, August 11, 1836, p. 1.

141. John Mack Faragher, *Sugar Creek: Life on the Illinois Prairie* (New Haven: Yale University Press, 1986), 101. See also Nancy Grey Osterud, "Gender and the Transition to Capitalism in Rural America," *Agricultural History* 67, no. 2 (1993): 14–29.

142. Thomas Nichols, *Forty Years of American Life*, 2 vols. (London: John Maxwell & Co., 1864), 1:23; Jeanne Boydston, *Home and Work: Housework, Wages, and the Ideology of Labor in the Early Republic* (New York: Oxford University Press, 1990), 93.

143. Faragher, *Sugar Creek*, 101. See also Nancy F. Cott, *The Bonds of Womanhood: "Woman's Sphere" in New England, 1780–1835* (New Haven: Yale University Press, 1977), 19–62.

144. Boydston, *Home and Work*, 89, 91.

145. Ibid., 135.

146. Jesse T. Peck, *The True Woman; or, Life and Happiness at Home and Abroad* (New York: Carlton & Porter, 1857), 243.

147. Ibid., 145. See also Cott, *The Bonds of Womanhood*, 63–100.

148. Boydston, *Home and Work*, 149, 142–63. See also Frances E. Olsen, "The Family and the Market: A Study of Ideology and Legal Reform," *Harvard Law Review* 96, no. 7 (1983): 1497–1578.

149. Sarah Grimke, *Letters on the Equality of the Sexes and the Condition of Woman* (Boston: Isaac Knapp, 1838 [1837]), 30, 50.

150. "Men have always in some way," she wrote, "regarded women as mere instruments of selfish gratifications." Ibid., 31.

151. *Report of the Debates and Proceedings of the Convention for the Revision of the Constitution of the State of Indiana, 1850*, vol. 1 (Indianapolis: A. H. Brown, 1850), 465.

152. Wilentz, "America's Lost Egalitarian Tradition," 68; Huston, *Securing the Fruits of Labor*, 192–93.

153. Glickstein, *American Exceptionalism, American Anxiety*, 122–23.

Chapter 7

1. George Camp, *Democracy* (New York: Harper and Brothers, 1841), 177.

2. "The market," as it appears in this chapter, refers to what Charles Lindblom calls the "market system." He defines this as a "system of societywide coordination of human activities not by central command but by mutual interactions in the form of transactions." Charles E. Lindblom, *The Market System: What It Is, How It Works, and What to Make of It* (New Haven: Yale University Press, 2002), 4. These transactions link buyers and sellers of goods and services; of loans, securities, and other financial instruments; and in increasingly "mature" capitalist economy, they also link buyers and sellers of labor. This chapter explores how the market, so

conceived, was conceptualized in the Jacksonian Era. In some cases, this can be inferred from explicit contemporary discussions of "markets" or "the market." Jacksonians wrote, for example, about "market value," "market price," and "market exchange"; they contrasted "natural" to "artificial" markets. They wrote about the "home market" as opposed to the international market. They sometimes referred to "the market" in general (as in: "when the market is not over-supplied," or "the greater the quantity of such articles which is thrown into the market, the more their price will lessen"). Frederick Robinson, "An Oration Delivered before the Trades Union of Boston and Vicinity, on Fort Hill, Boston, on the Fifty-Eighth Anniversary of American Independence" (Boston, 1834), 28; Anti-Slavery Convention of American Women, "An Address to Free Colored Americans" (New York: William S. Dorr, 1837), 18. In most of these instances, however, they were referring to particular markets (for certain goods or services) rather than the market system as a whole. To understand how they imagined the economy as a *system of society-wide coordination*, therefore, we must often try to unearth the assumptions that framed and informed these discussions. This chapter seeks to reconstruct these assumptions mainly using the Democrats' defenses of free trade against protectionism and competition against "monopoly."

3. Isaac Newton had conceived of nature as a harmonious system governed by rational laws that could be discovered through empirical study.

4. "At the formation of our government," wrote Jefferson of the Federalist view, "many had formed their political opinions on European writings and practices, believing . . . that men in numerous associations cannot be restrained within the limits of order and justice, but by forces physical and moral, wielded over them by authorities independent of their will." Thomas Jefferson, "To William Johnson," in *Thomas Jefferson: Political Writings*, ed. Joyce Appleby and Terence Ball (Cambridge: Cambridge University Press, 1999 [1823]), 450.

5. John Adams, "To Thomas Jefferson from John Adams, 9 October 1787," in *The Papers of Thomas Jefferson*, vol. 12, ed. Julian P. Boyd (Princeton: Princeton University Press, 1955 [1787]), 220–21.

6. Quoted in Gordon Wood, *Empire of Liberty: A History of the Early Republic, 1789–1815* (Oxford: Oxford University Press, 2009), 111. For this reason, Hamilton later expressed anxiety about the Louisiana Purchase: it would threaten social order by removing so many Americans from proximity to the strong arm of the state; Joyce Appleby, "Commercial Farming and the 'Agrarian Myth' in the Early Republic," *Journal of American History* 68, no. 4 (1982): 848.

7. Charles Maurice Wiltse, *The Jeffersonian Tradition in American Democracy* (New York: Hill and Wang, 1960 [1935]), 101.

8. This pessimistic view had been reinforced, for example, by Shays' Rebellion, in which a group of Massachusetts farmers in 1786 had raised a militia and taken up arms against the state.

9. William Symmes, quoted in Nathan O. Hatch, *The Sacred Cause of Liberty: Republican Thought and the Millennium in Revolutionary New England* (New Haven: Yale University Press, 1977), 115. See also Joyce Appleby, *Capitalism and a New Social Order: The Republican Vision of the 1790s* (New York: New York University Press, 1984), 27.

10. This latter goal was reflected, for example, in the infamous Alien and Sedition Acts.

11. Hatch, *The Sacred Cause of Liberty*, 93.

12. "Jay to General Washington, Philadelphia, June 27, 1786," *The Correspondence and Public Papers of John Jay*, vol. 3: 1782–1793 (New York: G. P. Putnam's Sons, 1891 [1786]), 204–5.

13. Appleby has traced the origins of these ideas back to the nascent debates over trade and manufacturing in late seventeenth-century Britain and the writings of early political economists Thomas Mun, Josiah Child, Nicholas Barbon, and Charles Davenant; see Joyce Appleby, *Economic Thought and Ideology in Seventeenth Century England* (Princeton: Princeton University Press, 1978). John Locke's vastly influential work, *An Essay Concerning Human Understanding* (1690), is another key source; in it, Locke argued that "a desire of happiness and an aversion to misery . . . do continue constantly to operate and influence all our actions without ceasing: these may be observed in all persons and all ages, steady and universal." John Locke, "An Essay Concerning Human Understanding," in *The Works of John Locke, in Nine Volumes*, vol. 1 (London: C. Baldwin, 1824 [1690]), 35.

14. Adam Smith, *An Inquiry into the Nature and Causes of the Wealth of Nations*, vol. 1 (London: Methuen & Co., 1904 [1776]), 323. See also Appleby, *Capitalism and a New Social Order*, 25; Gordon Wood, *The Radicalism of the American Revolution* (New York: Random House, 1992), 218–20; Drew R. McCoy, *The Elusive Republic: Political Economy in Jeffersonian America* (Chapel Hill: University of North Carolina Press, 1980), 13–47. For further background, see Istvan Hont, *Jealousy of Trade: International Competition and the Nation-State in Historical Perspective* (Cambridge, MA: Belknap Press, 2005), 159–322.

15. Appleby, *Capitalism and a New Social Order*, 31.

16. Ibid., 33. The French Physiocrats too had imagined society in these terms, and their ideas had influenced Jefferson among other Americans. For an illuminating discussion of the Physiocrats and the birth of the idea of natural economic order, see Bernard Harcourt, *The Illusion of Free Markets: Punishment and the Myth of Natural Order* (Cambridge, MA: Harvard University Press, 2011), 78–91.

17. Yehoshua Arieli, *Individualism and Nationalism in American Ideology* (Baltimore: Penguin Books, 1964), 106. Arieli traces the origins of this idea of natural society to the philosophy of Lord Shaftesbury, one of Locke's distinguished students. See ibid., 88–120.

18. Jonathan Mayhew, "The Love of Our Neighbor," in *Seven Sermons Upon the Following Subjects . . .* (Boston: Rogers and Fowle, 1749), 126.

19. Appleby, *Capitalism and a New Social Order*, 23.

20. Joyce Appleby, *Liberalism and Republicanism in the Historical Imagination* (Cambridge, MA: Harvard University Press, 1992), 169.

21. For a discussion of the influence of Scottish Enlightenment ideas on Jefferson, see Gary Wills, *Inventing America: Jefferson's Declaration of Independence* (Garden City, NY: Doubleday, 1978), 200ff.

22. Thomas Paine, *Rights of Man* (Mineola, NY: Dover Publications, 1999 [1791–92]), 107, 109. Paine's own thinking was deeply influenced by Newtonian science; see Eric Foner, *Tom Paine and Revolutionary America* (New York: Oxford University Press, 1976), 6.

23. John O'Sullivan, "Introduction: The Democratic Principle—the Importance of Its Assertion, and Application to Our Political System and Literature," *United States Magazine and Democratic Review* 1, no. 1 (1837): 7.

24. Samuel Young, "Oration Delivered at the Democratic Republican Celebration of the Sixty-Fourth Anniversary of the Independence of the United States" (New York: Jared W. Bell, 1840), 10.

25. William Rives, "Speech of Mr. Rives, of Virginia, on the Currency of the United States, and the Collection of the Public Revenue. Delivered in the Senate U.S. January 10, 1837"

(Washington, DC: Globe, 1837), 6. Theodore Sedgwick Jr., too, wrote that Adam Smith's "discoveries on the earth were like those of Newton in the heavens." Theodore Sedgwick Jr., *Public and Private Economy, Part Second* (New York: Harper & Brothers, 1838), 119.

26. Appleby, *Capitalism and a New Social Order*, 95.

27. Ibid., 34; Appleby, *Liberalism and Republicanism in the Historical Imagination*, 171; Arieli, *Individualism and Nationalism in American Ideology*, 90–91; Isaac Kramnick, *Republicanism and Bourgeois Radicalism: Political Ideology in Late Eighteenth-Century England and America* (Ithaca: Cornell University Press, 1990), 86–97.

28. Paine, *Rights of Man*, 109, 108.

29. John Witte Jr., *The Reformation of Rights: Law, Religion, and Human Rights in Early Modern Calvinism* (Cambridge: Cambridge University Press, 2007), 281, 229–30, 128–29.

30. Paine, *Rights of Man*, 30.

31. For an instructive discussion of Jefferson's understanding of natural rights and the intellectual chasm that separated it from the Puritan view, see Michael P. Zuckert, *The Natural Rights Republic: Studies in the Foundation of the American Political Tradition* (Notre Dame: University of Notre Dame Press, 1996).

32. Jedidiah Morse, "A Discourse Delivered at the African Meeting House in Boston . . ." (Boston: Lincoln & Emands, 1808), 6.

33. David Hackett Fischer, *The Revolution of American Conservatism: The Federalist Party in the Era of Jeffersonian Democracy* (New York: Harper & Row, 1965), 4.

34. For the origins of this conception of social order in seventeenth- and eighteenth-century American thought, see Barry Alan Shain, *The Myth of American Individualism: The Protestant Origins of American Political Thought* (Princeton: Princeton University Press, 1994), 48–83.

35. For further discussion of this view as it was expressed in the debates held at state constitutional conventions throughout the Jacksonian period, see Silvana R. Siddali, *Frontier Democracy: Constitutional Conventions in the Old Northwest* (Cambridge: Cambridge University Press, 2016), 87–112.

36. Walt Whitman, "Some Plain Paragraphs, for Plain People," in *The Collected Writings of Walt Whitman, the Journalism*, vol. 1, ed. Herbert Bergman (New York: Peter Lang, 1998 [1846]), 295.

37. Brian Balogh, *A Government out of Sight: The Mystery of National Authority in Nineteenth-Century America* (Cambridge: Cambridge University Press, 2009), 277–81; John Lauritz Larson, *The Market Revolution in America: Liberty, Ambition, and the Eclipse of the Common Good* (Cambridge: Cambridge University Press, 2010), 148.

38. See, for instance, Alex Zakaras, "Individuality, Radical Politics, and the Metaphor of the Machine," in *The Edinburgh Critical History of Nineteenth-Century Philosophy*, ed. Alison Stone (Edinburgh: Edinburgh University Press, 2011); Koenraad W. Swart, "'Individualism' in the Mid-Nineteenth Century (1826–1860)," *Journal of the History of Ideas* 23, no. 1 (1962): 77–90.

39. A number of historians have drawn attention to the Democrats' use of the concept of nature in political and economic thought; this chapter builds on their work. See, for instance, John William Ward, "Jacksonian Democratic Thought: 'A Natural Charter of Privilege,'" in *The Development of an American Culture*, ed. Stanley Coben and Lorman Ratner (New York: St. Martin's Press, 1983 [1970]); John William Ward, *Andrew Jackson: Symbol for an Age* (London: Oxford University Press, 1955), 13–97; Rush Welter, *The Mind of America: 1820–1860* (New York:

Columbia University Press, 1975), 85–90; John Ashworth, *"Agrarians" & "Aristocrats": Party Political Ideology in the United States, 1837–1846* (Cambridge: Cambridge University Press, 1983), 21–34, 92–111; Marvin Meyers, *The Jacksonian Persuasion: Politics and Belief*, 2nd ed. (New York: Vintage Books, 1960 [1957]), 26, 10; Jean H. Baker, *Affairs of Party: The Political Culture of Northern Democrats in the Mid-Nineteenth Century* (Ithaca: Cornell University Press, 1983), 143–48, 177–211.

40. Another distinction is relevant here too: this idea of natural order, derived from natural law, is importantly different from and more abstract than the more literal ideas of nature associated either with the pastoral ideal or with the vast American "wilderness."

41. Paine, *Rights of Man*, 109.

42. John Bell, *Register of Debates*, 22nd Cong., 1st sess. 3360 (June 1832). At the time, Bell was still in the Jacksonian fold; he became a Whig in the mid-1830s.

43. John Galbraith, *Register of Debates*, 24th Cong., 2nd sess., Appendix 153 (March 1837).

44. See, for instance, Condy Raguet, *The Principles of Free Trade, Illustrated in a Series of Short and Familiar Essays. Originally Published in the Banner of the Constitution* (Philadelphia: Carey, Lee, and Blanchard, 1835 [1829–32]), 330.

45. Sean Wilentz, "America's Lost Egalitarian Tradition," *Daedalus* 131, no. 1 (2002): 71; Meyers, *The Jacksonian Persuasion*, 10, 26.

46. John Taylor, *Tyranny Unmasked* (Indianapolis: Liberty Fund, 1992 [1821]), 236.

47. Andrew Jackson, "Veto Message," in *A Compilation of the Messages and Papers of the Presidents, 1789–1902*, vol. 2, ed. James D. Richardson (New York: Bureau of National Literature, 1903 [1832]), 590.

48. Jeffrey Sklansky, "William Leggett and the Melodrama of the Market," in *Capitalism Takes Command: The Social Transformation of Nineteenth-Century America*, ed. Michael Zakim and Gary J. Kornblith (Chicago: University of Chicago Press, 2012), 211–12.

49. Mark A. Noll, *America's God: From Jonathan Edwards to Abraham Lincoln* (Oxford: Oxford University Press, 2002), 236–37. For further discussion of the influence of Scottish common sense philosophy on American theology, see pp. 93–113, 233–38; D. H. Meyer, *The Instructed Conscience: The Shaping of the American National Ethic* (Philadelphia: University of Pennsylvania Press, 1972); Henry F. May, *The Enlightenment in America* (New York: Oxford University Press, 1976), 307–62.

50. Natural religion was seldom presented as a complete alternative to revealed religion: without the complementary insights of revelation, natural religion would only ever supply a partial impression of God and of human duty. See, for instance, Francis Wayland, *The Elements of Moral Science* (New York: Cooke and Co., 1835), 135–37.

51. Meyer, *The Instructed Conscience*, 24, 19. For further instructive discussion of the content and influence of natural religion in antebellum America, see Daniel Walker Howe, *The Unitarian Conscience: Harvard Moral Philosophy, 1805–1861* (Cambridge, MA: Harvard University Press, 1970), 69–120; Mark A. Noll, *Princeton and the Republic, 1768–1822: The Search for a Christian Enlightenment in the Era of Samuel Stanhope Smith* (Princeton: Princeton University Press, 1989).

52. Meyer, *The Instructed Conscience*, 27. This view should not be confused with Deism, which posited a distant, "watchmaker" God who was uninvolved in the day-to-day oversight of his creation, and which enjoyed only a brief heyday in America around the turn of the nineteenth century. The "governmental" idea of God as the ruler of a law-governed universe was fully

compatible with the notion that divine exertion was constantly needed, every second of every minute, just to keep matter in motion. Whig political economist Francis Bowen argued, for example, that since "spirit alone" was capable of moving matter, "God's spirit must be ever active—guiding each trajectory, pushing the planets around in their orbits, giving each living cell its energy, directing each molecule of boiling water." God's creation was not, he insisted, left to itself, "like a deserted child." Quoted in ibid., 96. For a more popular exposition of the same view, see, for instance, "On the Physical Agency of the Deity," *Christian Advocate and Journal*, July 12, 1833, p. 1. For a discussion of Deism's limited hold on the American mind, see Noll, *America's God*, 143–45.

53. See Theodore Dwight Bozeman, *Protestants in an Age of Science: The Baconian Ideal and Antebellum American Religious Thought* (Chapel Hill: University of North Carolina Press, 1977); Benjamin M. Friedman, *Religion and the Rise of Capitalism* (New York: Alfred A. Knopf, 2021), 131–96.

54. John Witherspoon, *Lectures on Moral Philosophy*, ed. Varnum Lansing Collins (Princeton: Princeton University Press, 1912 [1772]), 4. Witherspoon was president of the College of New Jersey (now Princeton) and an influential purveyor of Scottish philosophy in America.

55. Wayland, *The Elements of Moral Science*, 94, 95. See also Elisha P. Hurlbut, *Essays on Human Rights and Their Political Guaranties* (New York: Fowlers and Wells, 1848), 15–16.

56. Meyer, *The Instructed Conscience*, 46. See also James H. Moorhead, "Between Progress and Apocalypse: A Reassessment of Millennialism in American Religious Thought, 1800–1880," *Journal of American History* 71, no. 3 (1984): 528.

57. The renowned itinerant Methodist preacher and Democratic partisan "Crazy" Lorenzo Dow declared, for instance, that "man was designed by his Maker to be happy, and the pursuit of happiness is enjoined upon him, and it is his duty to promote the same in others." Lorenzo Dow, *Perambulations of a Cosmopolite, or, Travels & Labors of Lorenzo Dow, in Europe and America* (New York: R. C. Valentine, 1855 [1816]), 333.

58. See Stewart Davenport, *Friends of the Unrighteous Mammon: Northern Christians and Market Capitalism, 1815–1860* (Chicago: University of Chicago Press, 2008), 19–83; Henry F. May, *Protestant Churches and Industrial America* (New York: Harper & Brothers, 1949), 15–16, 44–45.

59. John McVickar, "Concluding Remarks," in *Outlines of Political Economy . . .* (New York: Wilder & Campbell, 1825), 187. The Democratic political economist Theodore Sedgwick Jr. argued in a similar vein that "the laws of nature, which make men labour, are the laws of happiness"; Theodore Sedgwick Jr., *Public and Private Economy, Part First* (New York: Harper & Brothers, 1836), 162.

60. As William Sutton notes, this view was increasingly sanctified by evangelical thought leaders; see William R. Sutton, *Journeymen for Jesus: Evangelical Artisans Confront Capitalism in Jacksonian Baltimore* (University Park: Pennsylvania State University Press, 1998), 6. For a detailed discussion of the relationship between religion and academic political economy, see Davenport, *Friends of the Unrighteous Mammon*.

61. For Smith's sparse references to "natural liberty," see Smith, *An Inquiry into the Nature and Causes of the Wealth of Nations*, 1:435; Adam Smith, *An Inquiry into the Nature and Causes of the Wealth of Nations*, vol. 2 (London: Methuen & Co., 1904 [1776]), 184.

62. Davenport, *Friends of the Unrighteous Mammon*, 53.

63. Ibid., 30–33; Nancy Cohen, *The Reconstruction of American Liberalism, 1865–1914* (Chapel Hill: University of North Carolina Press, 2002), 40.

64. T. E. C. Leslie, quoted in May, *Protestant Churches and Industrial America*, 136.

65. They also argued that human beings were designed by God to find happiness in the exercise of moral virtue. For these reasons, prudent self-interest and moral virtue could never be at odds. Meyer, *The Instructed Conscience*, 99–102.

66. For a revealing example of this style of reasoning, see "The Reciprocal Influence of the Physical Sciences and Free Political Institutions," *United States Magazine and Democratic Review* 18, no. 91 (1846).

67. "Address to the Workingmen of the United States," *Extra Globe*, September 26, 1840, pp. 289, 291.

68. Thomas Cooper, "Distribution of Wealth," *Southern Review* 8 (1831): 180. The Whig political economist Francis Bowen agreed; see Francis Bowen, "French Ideas of Democracy and a Community of Goods," *North American Review* 69, no. 145 (1849): 312. See also James Fenimore Cooper, "To Sir Edward Waller, Bart.," in *The Travelling Bachelor, or, Notions of the Americans* (New York: Stringer and Townsend, 1856 [1828]), 671.

69. "Free Trade Convention," *New York Evening Post* (reprinted from the *Philadelphia Gazette*), October 8, 1831, p. 2.

70. Free trade would, according to the *Democratic Review*, spread "everywhere whatever the Deity has made for the fruition of his creatures"—such was the "intention of nature." Anon., "Free Trade," *United States Magazine and Democratic Review* 9, no. 40 (1841): 342, 341. For a discussion of the intellectual roots of this providential view of commerce, see Jacob Viner, *The Role of Providence in the Social Order: An Essay in Intellectual History* (Philadelphia: American Philosophical Society, 1972 [1966]), 32–54.

71. Robert Hayne, *Register of Debates*, 22nd Cong., 1st sess. 94 (January 1832). This providential vision of free trade would, within a few years, be enshrined in the most influential economics textbooks in the United States. Friedman, *Religion and the Rise of Capitalism*, 255–62.

72. Ibid., 95.

73. "Report of the Secretary of the Treasury," *New York Evening Post*, December 12, 1848, p. 1.

74. This argument can be found in America as early as the 1790s, when Philadelphia merchants deployed it to condemn price controls for grain and other staples in times of economic hardship. See Ronald Schultz, *The Republic of Labor: Philadelphia Artisans and the Politics of Class, 1720–1830* (New York: Oxford University Press, 1993), 63–64.

75. "To Merchants," *New York Evening Post*, October 20, 1840, p. 2. See also Thomas Roderick Dew, *Lectures on the Restrictive System: Delivered to the Senior Political Class of William and Mary College* (Richmond: S. Shepherd & Co., 1829), 23.

76. "Address of the Frailty Club to Whomever It May Concern," *Jeffersonian*, May 30, 1842, p. 90.

77. In the eyes of the *Western Review*, economic protectionists were "presuming to act as if they were wiser than their Creator." "Art. I.—Report of the Secretary of the Treasury," *Western Review* 1, no. 1 (1846): 34.

78. Cobden was one of the leading lights of the so-called Manchester School. For a discussion of his influence in Jacksonian America, see Marc-William Palen, *The "Conspiracy" of Free Trade: The Anglo-American Struggle over Empire and Economic Globalization, 1846–1896* (Cambridge: Cambridge University Press, 2016), 12–32.

79. Richard Cobden, "Free Trade," in *Speeches on Free Trade* (London: Macmillan, 1903 [1843]), 35.

80. For the seminal discussion of the free labor ideology of the 1850s and its reliance on the labor theory of property, see the first chapter of Eric Foner, *Free Soil, Free Labor, Free Men: The Ideology of the Republican Party before the Civil War* (London: Oxford University Press, 1970).

81. William Leggett, "The Natural System," in *A Collection of the Political Writings of William Leggett*, vol. 2, ed. Theodore Sedgwick Jr. (New York: Taylor & Dodd, 1840 [1837]), 332–33. See also Sklansky, "William Leggett and the Melodrama of the Market."

82. Over the course of the twentieth century, the utilitarian logic of the marketplace, whose goal was an aggregate maximization of human well-being, was increasingly seen to stand in tension with the protection of individual rights. Generally speaking, Jacksonian Democrats saw no such tension.

83. See, for instance, Arthur Schlesinger Jr., *The Age of Jackson* (Boston: Little, Brown, 1945), 350–60; Ashworth, *"Agrarians" & "Aristocrats,"* 200.

84. For further discussion and evidence, see Ward, "Jacksonian Democratic Thought"; Siddali, *Frontier Democracy*, 84–112.

85. On the "people's bank," see Robert Richard, "The 'Great Depression,' the People's Bank, and Jacksonian Fiscal Populism in North Carolina, 1819–1833," *Tennessee Historical Quarterly* 76, no. 3 (2017): 240–57. On the Democrats' willingness to use state power to shape the economy, see Sean Wilentz, *The Rise of American Democracy: Jefferson to Lincoln* (New York: Norton, 2005), 438; Michael F. Holt, *The Rise and Fall of the American Whig Party: Jacksonian Politics and the Onset of the Civil War* (New York: Oxford University Press, 1999), 66; Schlesinger, *The Age of Jackson*, 512–18.

86. Calvin Colton, *The Crisis of the Country*, 2nd ed. (Philadelphia: T. K. and P. G. Collins, 1840), 6; Anon., "The Credit System," *National Magazine and Republican Review* 1, no. 1 (1839).

87. John O'Sullivan, "Note," *United States Magazine and Democratic Review* 12, no. 59 (1843): 538.

88. "Meeting of Mechanics and Workingmen," *Bay State Democrat*, September 15, 1840, p. 1–2.

89. Daniel T. Rodgers, *Atlantic Crossings: Social Politics in a Progressive Age* (Cambridge, MA: Harvard University Press, 1998), 81.

90. Emphasis added. Such coercion, he continued, was sustained by "a most complicated, unnatural, and costly machinery of government." Robert Rantoul Jr., "An Address to the Workingmen of the United States of America," in *Memoirs, Speeches, and Writings of Robert Rantoul, Jr.*, ed. Luther Hamilton (Boston: John P. Jewett & Co., 1854 [1833]), 237.

91. Emphasis added. Condy Raguet, "The Free Trade Advocate," *New York Evening Post*, April 10, 1829, p. 2. See also Dew, *Lectures on the Restrictive System: Delivered to the Senior Political Class of William and Mary College*, 39; "White Slavery," *United States Magazine and Democratic Review* 11, no. 51 (1842): 271; "Art. I.—Report of the Secretary of the Treasury," 24.

92. Of course, the Democrats did not deny the need for government coercion altogether; rather, they insisted that it was legitimate only when used to protect the natural rights of individuals. When so used, it reinforced the natural order of society.

93. "Free Trade Meeting in Portland," *New York Evening Post* (reprinted from the *Eastern Argus*), August 30, 1831, p. 1.

94. Dew, *Lectures on the Restrictive System: Delivered to the Senior Political Class of William and Mary College*, 46.

95. "Free Trade Meeting in Portland," 1.

96. O'Sullivan, "Introduction: The Democratic Principle—the Importance of Its Assertion, and Application to Our Political System and Literature," 7.

97. Friedrich List, *National System of Political Economy*, trans. G. A. Matile (Philadelphia: J. B. Lippincott & Co., 1856 [1841]), 249.

98. Even as they celebrate the aggregate benefits of free trade, Raguet's essays, for example, constantly acknowledge the constraints and disruptions imposed by foreign competition on domestic production across a wide range of economic sectors. He conceived of such constraints as *natural*. See Raguet, *The Principles of Free Trade, Illustrated in a Series of Short and Familiar Essays*.

99. It might be argued that legal constraints are backed by the threat of state coercion, whereas market constraints are not. But this is not true. Markets are created and enforced by states, through a wide range of laws regulating private property and contracts, for example. Violations of these laws will occasion state coercion just as surely as the refusal to pay a tariff on imported goods.

100. See, for instance, "Free Trade Convention," 2.

101. John C. Larue, "Lecture Delivered before the Louisiana Democratic Association . . . ," *Jeffersonian*, December 1, 1846, p. 2.

102. Ibid.

103. The natural law tradition had long held that no genuine freedom could be obtained by violating natural law. Brownson channeled this tradition when he wrote, for example, that "freedom to do that which is unjust according to the laws of God or,—which is the same thing,—the law of nature, is license, not liberty, and is as much opposed to liberty, as lust is to love." Orestes Brownson, "Art. IV: Address of the Democratic State Convention of Massachusetts," *Boston Quarterly Review* 1, no. 1 (1838): 56.

104. "Report of the Secretary of the Treasury," 1.

105. O'Sullivan, "Introduction: The Democratic Principle—the Importance of Its Assertion, and Application to Our Political System and Literature," 7.

106. "Art. I.—Report of the Secretary of the Treasury," 36–37.

107. For an interesting discussion of these same tendencies in the economic thought of the French Physiocrats, see Harcourt, *The Illusion of Free Markets*, 78–91.

108. The market's complexity might, for example, make its patterns difficult to anticipate, even for prudent businessmen—and this difficulty might occasionally bring economic loss.

109. See Rodgers, *Atlantic Crossings*, 79–80.

110. William Leggett, "The Functions of Government," in *A Collection of the Political Writings of William Leggett*, vol. 1, ed. Theodore Sedgwick Jr. (New York: Taylor & Dodd, 1840 [1834]), 163.

111. See Eric MacGilvray, *The Invention of Market Freedom* (Cambridge: Cambridge University Press, 2011), 170–73. There were some, of course, who argued that market forces were themselves coercive and arbitrary. Philadelphia shoemaker, activist, and editor William Heighton, for instance, argued that economic competition was the source of the laborer's bondage: "Necessity compels us to work for such prices as are offered, and pay such prices as are

demanded for every thing; we must either do this, resort to fraud or theft, or perish by hunger and nakedness." The language of compulsion is significant here: in his view, economic competition *forced* wages down, *forced* workingmen to labor for a pittance, and deprived them of the fruits of their labor. William Heighton, "William Heighton, an Address Delivered before the Mechanics and Working Classes Generally, of the City and County of Philadelphia" (Philadelphia: Mechanics' Gazette, 1828), 8–9. See also "Freedom of the Public Lands," *Northampton Democrat*, January 26, 1847, p. 2; Alex Gourevitch, *From Slavery to the Cooperative Commonwealth: Labor and Republican Liberty in the Nineteenth Century* (New York: Cambridge University Press, 2014), 77–81.

112. "Blessings of a National Bank," *Wisconsin Democrat* (reprinted from the *Boston Post*), January 31, 1843, p. 6.

113. As early as the Revolutionary period, Americans attributed the rise of inequality in their own society to "artificial political manipulations by the British"; Wilentz, "America's Lost Egalitarian Tradition," 69.

114. Martin Van Buren, "Letter from Mr. Van Buren on the Wages of Labor," *Bay State Democrat*, September 26, 1840, p. 3. For a similar argument, see also "White Slavery," 261.

115. Rantoul, "An Address to the Workingmen of the United States of America," 237, 238. Lawrence Frederick Kohl, *The Politics of Individualism: Parties and the American Character in the Jacksonian Era* (New York: Oxford University Press, 1989), 186–90.

116. William Allen, *Cong. Globe*, 25th Cong., 2nd sess., Appendix 251 (February 1838).

117. Charles Sellers, *The Market Revolution: Jacksonian America, 1815–1848* (New York: Oxford University Press, 1991), 325; Jonathan A. Glickstein, *American Exceptionalism, American Anxiety: Wages, Competition, and Degraded Labor in the Antebellum United States* (Charlottesville: University of Virginia Press, 2002), 132–33.

118. Sklansky, "William Leggett and the Melodrama of the Market," 200–203.

119. Levi Slamm, "Workingmen's Meeting," *New York Evening Post*, November 5, 1838, p. 1. See also Theophilus Fisk, "An Oration on Banking, Education, &C. Delivered at the Queen-Street Theater, in the City of Charleston, S.C., July 4th, 1837" (Charleston, SC: Office of the Examiner, 1837), 2, 3. The view that inequality *as such* was objectionable and should be mitigated by state redistribution was typically condemned—even by egalitarians such as Slamm and Fisk—as "agrarianism" (referring to the ancient Roman agrarian law), which was widely thought to be at odds with the American commitment to equal rights.

120. Ely Moore, "Oration Delivered before the Mechanics and Workingmen of the City of New York . . ." (New York: John Windt, 1843), 22.

121. Edward Pessen, *Most Uncommon Jacksonians: The Radical Leaders of the Early Labor Movement* (Albany: State University of New York Press, 1967), 103. See also Eric Foner, "Radical Individualism in America," *Literature of Liberty: A Review of Contemporary Liberal Thought* 1, no. 3 (1978): 15.

122. This is what they meant when they insisted that they were not "levellers."

123. "Probably few men in America," wrote historian Richard Hofstadter of Leggett, "preached the bourgeois ideals of personal and property rights, freedom of contract, laissez faire, individualism, and private enterprise with as fine a sense for the needs and desires of the common man." Richard Hofstadter, "William Leggett, Spokesman of Jacksonian Democracy," *Political Science Quarterly* 58, no. 4 (December 1843): 594.

124. William Leggett, "The Inequality of Human Condition," in *A Collection of the Political Writings of William Leggett*, vol. 2, ed. Theodore Sedgwick Jr. (New York: Taylor & Dodd, 1840 [1836]), 164.

125. William Leggett, "The Crisis," in *A Collection of the Political Writings of William Leggett*, vol. 2, ed. Theodore Sedgwick Jr. (New York: Taylor & Dodd, 1840 [1837]), 312.

126. Leggett, "The Natural System," 2:332. Further evidence of this faith in an individualistic yet egalitarian natural order can be found in the early debates over unionization. We find defenders of labor unions, for example, almost apologizing for their willingness to join these "combinations" that seemed to inhibit free competition. See, for instance, Ely Moore, "Address Delivered before the General Trades' Union of the City of New-York . . ." (New York: J. Ormond, 1833), 12–13; "A Democrat," "Democracy—Trade Union," *New England Artisan*, June 21, 1834, p. 1.

127. Stephen Simpson, *The Working Man's Manual* (Philadelphia: Thomas L. Bonsal, 1831), 225, 223. See also Pessen, *Most Uncommon Jacksonians*, 129–44.

128. For an extended discussion of the meaning of "equal rights" in Jacksonian rhetoric, see Welter, *The Mind of America: 1820–1860*, 77–104.

129. State Rights and Free Trade Association, "Political Tract No. 8: Free Trade and the American System; a Dialogue between a Merchant and a Planter" (Columbia: Times and Telescope, 1832), 8.

130. See, for example, Young, "Oration Delivered at the Democratic Republican Celebration of the Sixty-Fourth Anniversary of the Independence of the United States," 6–7; George Bancroft, "An Oration Delivered before the Democracy of Springfield . . . , July 4th, 1836" (Springfield, MA: George and Charles Merriam, 1836), 12.

131. L. Ray Gunn, *The Decline of Authority: Public Economic Policy and Political Development in New York, 1800–1860* (Ithaca: Cornell University Press, 1988), 254.

132. Ibid., 187–201. See also Naomi R. Lamoreaux and John Joseph Wallis, "Economic Crisis, General Laws, and the Mid-Nineteenth-Century Transformation of American Political Economy," *Journal of the Early Republic* 41, no. 3 (2021): 403–33.

133. "Address to the Workingmen of the United States," 292. See also Thomas Hart Benton, *Thirty Years' View, or, A History of the Working of the American Government for Thirty Years, from 1820 to 1850*, vol. 1 (New York: D. Appleton & Co., 1854), 249–50.

134. "True Theory and Philosophy of Our System of Government," *United States Magazine and Democratic Review* 15, no. 75 (1844): 231.

135. "Political Tolerance," *United States Magazine and Democratic Review* 3, no. 9 (1838): 64. See also Theodore Sedgwick Jr., "What Is a Monopoly? Or Some Considerations on the Subject of Corporations and Currency" (New York: George P. Scott & Co., 1835).

136. "True Theory and Philosophy of Our System of Government," 231.

137. George Bancroft, "Address at Hartford before the Delegates to the Democratic Convention of the Young Men of Connecticut" (Hartford, 1840), 7. See also Robinson, "An Oration Delivered before the Trades Union of Boston and Vicinity," 5; Hugh Garland, "An Oration Pronounced in Castle Garden, July 27, 1840" (New York: William G. Boggs, 1840), 24.

138. Theodore Sedgwick Jr., who was somewhat more precise, explained it in these terms: "every grant of exclusive privilege, strictly speaking, creates a monopoly; it carries on its face that the grantee has received facilities for making pecuniary or other gains, from which the mass

of his fellow citizens are excluded. This is the very substance of a monopoly." "Every such grant," he continued, "is directly in the teeth of the doctrine of equal rights" and "equally adverse to the fundamental maxim of free trade." Sedgwick, "What Is a Monopoly? Or Some Considerations upon the Subject of Corporations and Currency," 12, 13.

139. Jackson, "Veto Message," 2, 576, 590. See also Senator John Milton Niles, "Speech on the Bill Imposing Additional Duties, as Depositaries in Certain Cases, on Public Officers &C." (Washington, DC: Globe, 1838), 21.

140. Kohl, *The Politics of Individualism*, 31.

141. Wilentz, "America's Lost Egalitarian Tradition," 71.

142. See, for instance, "Free Trade Meeting," *New York Evening Post*, October 8, 1831; John Bell, *Register of Debates*, 22nd Cong., 1st sess. 3357 (June 1832); Edwin Forrest, Esq., "Oration Delivered at the Democratic Republican Celebration of the Sixty-Second Anniversary of the Independence of the United States" (New York: J. W. Bell, 1838), 21, 19.

143. "Political Tolerance," 64. See also Rantoul, "An Address to the Workingmen of the United States of America," 228–36.

144. Edward D. Barber, "An Oration, Delivered before the Democrats of Washington County, at Montpelier, on the 4th of July, 1839" (Monpelier, VT: Patriot Office, 1839), 14, 16.

145. Benjamin Faneuil Hunt, "Speech of Col. Benjamin Faneuil Hunt, of Charleston, South Carolina, Delivered at the Request of the Democratic Republican General Committee . . ." (New York: James Rees, 1840), 6. Hunt cited Adam Smith as an authority. See also William Gouge, "An Inquiry into the Principles of the System," in *A Short History of Paper Money and Banking, . . . to Which Is Prefixed an Inquiry into the Principles of the System . . .* (Philadelphia: T. W. Ustick, 1833), 91 92; "The Moral of the Crisis," *United States Magazine and Democratic Review* 1, no. 1 (1837): 111; Ashworth, *"Agrarians" & "Aristocrats,"* 39–40.

146. Trenchard and Gordon, "No. 85," in *Cato's Letters*, vol. 3 (London: Witkins, Woodward, Walthoe, and Peele, 1737 [1722]), 162; John Trenchard and Thomas Gordon, "No. 66," in *Cato's Letters*, vol. 2 (London: Witkins, Woodward, Walthoe, and Peele, 1737 [1721]), 294.

147. Trenchard and Gordon, "No. 64," in *Cato's Letters*, 2:268–69.

148. Trenchard and Gordon, "No. 91," in *Cato's Letters*, 3:213.

149. For a discussion of the "bourgeois" radicalism of Price, Priestley, and Burgh, see Kramnick, *Republicanism and Bourgeois Radicalism*. For an analysis of the liberal and republican elements in *Cato's Letters*, see Michael P. Zuckert, *Natural Rights and the New Republicanism* (Princeton: Princeton University Press, 1994), 297–319.

150. The distinction between moderate, prudent self-interest and its excessive manifestations in the vices of avarice and pride was crucial to the gradual embrace of self-interest as a respectable human motive over the course of the eighteenth century. See, for instance, Daniel Walker Howe, *Making the American Self: Jonathan Edwards to Abraham Lincoln* (Oxford: Oxford University Press, 2009 [1997]), 28–29.

151. Christopher Tomlins, *Law, Labor, and Ideology in the Early American Republic* (Cambridge: Cambridge University Press, 1993), 25.

152. This view can be found in the producerist and mercantilist traditions well before it blossomed in the economic thinking of the Scottish Enlightenment. See J. E. Crowley, *This Sheba, Self: The Conceptualization of Economic Life in Eighteenth-Century America* (Baltimore: Johns Hopkins University Press, 1974), 34–94. For a discussion of this shift among (mostly Whig)

354 NOTES TO PAGES 158–162

American political economists, see Davenport, *Friends of the Unrighteous Mammon*, 88–92. See also J. G. A. Pocock, "Virtue and Commerce in the Eighteenth Century," *Journal of Interdisciplinary History* 3, no. 1 (1972): 119–34.

153. Here, too, the Jacksonians were carrying forward a tradition that extends back through *Cato's Letters*; see Trenchard and Gordon, "No. 64," "No. 91."

154. Meyers, *The Jacksonian Persuasion*, 12. See also Ward, "Jacksonian Democratic Thought," 76–77.

155. William G. Boggs, "The Crisis Met: A Reply to Junius" (New York: Office of the Evening Post, 1840), 12.

156. James L. Huston, *Securing the Fruits of Labor: The American Concept of Wealth Distribution, 1765–1900* (Baton Rouge: Louisiana State University Press, 1998), 74. See also Jonathan A. Glickstein, *Concepts of Free Labor in Antebellum America* (New Haven: Yale University Press, 1991), 13.

Chapter 8

1. "Free Discussion. Voice of the North," *Philanthropist*, May 6, 1836, p. 4.

2. African Americans often chose to celebrate on July 5, rather than the fourth, both as an expression of alienation from America's vaunted liberty and to avoid violence at the hands of inebriated white mobs.

3. Theodore Parker, "The Aspect of Freedom in America. A Speech at the Mass Anti-Slavery Celebration of Independence, at Abington, July 5, 1852," in *Additional Speeches, Addresses, and Occasional Sermons*, vol. 1 (Boston: Little, Brown, 1855 [1852]), 110.

4. Ibid., 113.

5. I use the term "abolitionist" to describe those who publicly argued that "slaves should be freed immediately, unconditionally, and without expatriation or compensation to the owners." Aileen S. Kraditor, *Means and Ends in American Abolitionism: Garrison and His Critics on Strategy and Tactics, 1834–1850* (New York: Pantheon Books, 1967), 8.

6. This chapter devotes very little attention to the more secular, Enlightenment strains of abolitionism that flourished among some urban workingmen. It focuses instead on the overtly religious strains that comprised the vast majority of the movement. For the cultural and ideological affinities between abolitionists and Whigs, see, for instance, James Brewer Stewart, "Reconsidering the Abolitionists in an Age of Fundamentalist Politics," *Journal of the Early Republic* 26, no. 1 (2006): 1–23.

7. The term "human rights" was not new: it had been used occasionally in the late eighteenth century, though less frequently than the alternative "rights of man." The term became much more widespread in the 1830s, however, driven in large part by abolitionists, who adopted it as a fundamental moral concept. The *Liberator*, for example, used the term eight times in 1831, twelve times in 1832, forty-five times in 1835, and over seventy times in each of the following three years (1836, 1837, and 1838).

8. On the participation of working-class whites, see, for instance, Bruce Laurie, *Beyond Garrison: Antislavery and Social Reform* (Cambridge: Cambridge University Press, 2005); Paul Goodman, *Of One Blood: Abolitionism and the Origins of Racial Equality* (Berkeley: University of California Press, 1998), xvii, 161–72.

9. See, for instance, Kraditor, *Means and Ends in American Abolitionism*; Manisha Sinha, *The Slave's Cause: A History of Abolition* (New Haven: Yale University Press, 2016), 256–65.

10. For an excellent discussion of Black abolitionists in the context of the movement as a whole, see Sinha, *The Slave's Cause*, 195–227, 299–338, 381–460.

11. This aim fits with historians' recent interest in the ideological bonds that unified not just abolitionists but the broader antislavery movement. See W. Caleb McDaniel, "The Bonds and Boundaries of Antislavery," *Journal of the Civil War Era* 4, no. 1 (2014): 84–105.

12. R. G. Williams, "Testimony from the Slave States," *Human Rights*, September 1835, p. 2.

13. "Our nation," exclaimed a contributor to the *Quarterly Anti-Slavery Magazine*, "the cradle of freedom—the foster parent of oppression! The guardian angel of every people who struggle to be free—the endorser of all despots! The asylum of the oppressed—the last retreat of the monster of despotism! The land of the *free*—the home of the *slave!*" A Kentuckian, "American Slavery vs. Liberty," *Quarterly Anti-Slavery Magazine* 2, no. 5 (1836): 28. See also William Lloyd Garrison, "Ought We Not to Blush?" *Liberator*, January 15, 1831, p. 9.

14. Frederick Douglass, "What to the Slave Is the Fourth of July?" in *The Oxford Frederick Douglass Reader*, ed. William L. Andrews (New York: Oxford University Press, 1996 [1852]), 119. See also Edward D. Barber, "An Oration Delivered before the Addison County Anti-Slavery Society, on the Fourth of July, 1836" (Middlebury, VT: Knapp and Jewett, 1836), 9; Alfred Haswell, "America," *Friend of Man* (1841): 4; "The Foregoing Altered by G.," *Friend of Man*, January 26, 1841.

15. Abolitionists frequently contrasted American slavery unfavorably, for example, with both Roman slavery and the slavery practiced in the Old Testament. The oppression borne by American slaves, they argued, was far more invasive, brutal, and complete.

16. David Lee Child, "The Despotism of Freedom; or the Tyranny and Cruelty of American Republican Slave-Masters, Shown to Be the Worst in the World . . ." (Boston: Boston Young Men's Anti-Slavery Association, 1833), 11–12.

17. Nathaniel Rogers, "An Address Delivered before the Concord Female Anti-Slavery Society" (Concord, NH: William White, 1838 [1837]), 7; Daniel J. McInerney, *The Fortunate Heirs of Freedom: Abolition and Republican Thought* (Lincoln: University of Nebraska Press, 1994), 7–25.

18. See, for instance, George Bourne, *Slavery Illustrated in Its Effects Upon Woman and Domestic Society* (Boston: Isaac Knapp, 1837), 28–38; Angelina Grimke, "Letters to Catherine [*sic*] E. Beecher. No. II," *National Enquirer*, July 15, 1837, p. 72; Anti-Slavery Convention of American Women, "An Address to Free Colored Americans" (New York: W. S. Dorr, 1837), 6. For the particular significance of the Exodus narrative in the antebellum African American community, see Eddie S. Glaude Jr., *Exodus! Religion, Race, and Nation in Early Nineteenth-Century Black America* (Chicago: University of Chicago Press, 2000).

19. See, for instance, "How the Example of the Freest Nation on Earth Makes Republicans," *Emancipator*, July 21, 1836, p. 47.

20. William Wells Brown, *Narrative of William W. Brown, a Fugitive Slave. Written by Himself* (Boston: Anti-Slavery Office, 1847), 84, 105. This contrast was further driven home by such headlines as "JOHN BULL'S MONARCHY A REFUGE FROM BROTHER JONATHAN'S SLAVERY," which was illustrated with an image of a Black man escaping to Canada (Brother Jonathan was a personification of New England). *American Anti-Slavery Almanac for 1839* 1, no. 4 (1839): 9.

21. Elizur Wright, "The Sin of Slavery, and Its Remedy" (New York, 1833), 3. See also "The Anti-Slavery Enterprise—Its Aspects," *National Anti-Slavery Standard*, July 9, 1840, p. 1.

22. Reprinted as "Christianity and the Rights of Man," *North Star*, July 7, 1848, p. 1.

23. William Ellery Channing, *The Duty of the Free States, or, Remarks Suggested by the Case of the Creole* (Boston: William Crosby & Co., 1842), 44. Channing held himself at a distance from what he saw as the more radical tendencies within the abolitionist movement, but by the end of his life he had undeniably joined the abolitionist ranks.

24. Abolitionists often cited the passage in Jefferson's *Notes on the State of Virginia* in which he had observed that "the whole commerce between master and slave, is a perpetual exercise of the most boisterous passions, the most unremitting despotism on one part, and degrading submission on the other." See, for instance, J. C. H., "American Slavery—Its Effects Upon Its Immediate Victims. Letter No. II," *North Star*, February 18, 1848, p. 3. In fact, they commonly downplayed the proslavery convictions of many American founders and exaggerated the founding generation's antislavery credentials. None other than John Quincy Adams went so far as to declare that "George Washington was . . . in the broadest and most comprehensive sense of the term, an ABOLITIONIST. So was Thomas Jefferson." John Quincy Adams, "Untitled," *Pennsylvania Freeman*, December 27, 1838, p. 1.

25. "Extracts from the Second Annual Report of the Monroe County Anti-Slavery Society," *Friend of Man*, July 14, 1836, p. 3. "We shall ultimately triumph," he continued, "and our happy land become what it so loudly but falsely boasts to be, an asylum for the oppressed and a home for the free; and the colored man be restored, to the rights of man."

26. Rev. David Nickens, "An Address to the People of Color in Chillicothe," *Liberator*, August 11, 1832, p. 126.

27. "Address by William Whipper, Alfred Niger, and Augustus Price," in *The Black Abolitionist Papers*, vol. 3, ed. C. Peter Ripley (Chapel Hill: University of North Carolina Press, 1991 [1835]), 148–49.

28. Glaude, *Exodus! Religion, Race, and Nation in Early Nineteenth-Century Black America*, 34–43, 96, 82–104.

29. David Brion Davis, *The Problem of Slavery in the Age of Emancipation* (New York: Knopf, 2014), 177.

30. Barber, "An Oration Delivered before the Addison County Anti-Slavery Society, on the Fourth of July, 1836," 4.

31. Enoch Mack, "Fourth of July Oration, 1838," in *Trumpets of Glory: Fourth of July Orations, 1786–1861*, ed. Henry A. Hawken (Granby, CT: Salmon Brook Historical Society, 1976 [1838]), 174. See also Douglass, "What to the Slave Is the Fourth of July?" 112.

32. Black slaves, wrote James K. Paulding in his 1836 defense of slavery, clearly "did not come within the scope and meaning of the declaration of independence," nor of any constitutional provision. "They are neither comprehended in the phrase 'man,' nor 'citizen,' and constitute exceptions under the denomination of '*all other persons*.'" J. K. Paulding, *Slavery in the United States* (New York: Harper & Bros., 1836), 44.

33. For a discussion of the slaveholders' repudiation of the doctrine of natural rights, see Eugene D. Genovese, *The Slaveholders' Dilemma: Freedom and Progress in Southern Conservative Thought, 1820–1860* (Columbia: University of South Carolina Press, 1992), 49–52.

34. Some proslavery evangelicals rejected Jefferson's legacy entirely, deriding him as "a noted old infidel" whose assertion of equal rights for all men was "manifestly erroneous." Richard J.

Carwardine, *Evangelicals and Politics in Antebellum America* (New Haven: Yale University Press, 1993), 155.

35. Abolitionist newspapers often recounted the details of such daily discrimination. Black candidates were barred from most seminaries; Black congregants were segregated and consigned to "negro seats" in the back of the church and subjected to a variety of other insults and indignities. See, for example, "Prejudice against Color," *Human Rights*, June 1837, p. 2.

36. John R. McKivigan, *The War against Proslavery Religion: Abolitionism and the Northern Churches, 1830–1865* (Ithaca: Cornell University Press, 1984); Ronald G. Walters, *The Antislavery Appeal: American Abolitionism after 1830* (Baltimore: Johns Hopkins University Press, 1976), 37–53. "We are called upon," wrote Garrison, "to prove that which is self-evident." It was the Bible they turned to for proof. William Lloyd Garrison, *Thoughts on African Colonization* (New York: Arno Press, 1968 [1832]), 70.

37. Samuel Langdon, D.D., "Government Corrupted by Vice, and Recovered by Righteousness," in *The Pulpit of the American Revolution: or, The Political Sermons of the Period of 1776*, 2nd ed., ed. John Wingate Thornton (Boston: D. Lothrop & Co., 1876 [1775]), 250.

38. Steven M. Dworetz, *The Unvarnished Doctrine: Locke, Liberalism, and the American Revolution* (Durham: Duke University Press, 1990), 65–134. See also Jerome Huyler, *Locke in America: The Moral Philosophy of the Founding Era* (Lawrence: University Press of Kansas, 1995), 219–23, 237–46; Michael P. Zuckert, *The Natural Rights Republic: Studies in the Foundation of the American Political Tradition* (Notre Dame: University of Notre Dame Press, 1996).

39. Henry F. May, *The Enlightenment in America* (New York: Oxford University Press, 1976), 252–304.

40. As late as the 1770s, Baptist preachers were being whipped in Virginia for preaching without official state licenses and criticizing the Anglican establishment. Thomas S. Kidd, *God of Liberty: A Religious History of the American Revolution* (New York: Basic Books, 2010), 37–40.

41. Ibid., 37–55, 75–95.

42. By 1850, these two churches accounted for more than half of all religious adherents in America. The meteoric rise of the Methodist Church is especially striking: whereas they could claim only 2.5 percent of churchgoers in 1776, their share had risen to an astonishing 34.2 percent by 1850. John H. Wigger, *Taking Heaven by Storm: Methodism and the Rise of Popular Christianity in America* (Urbana: University of Illinois Press, 1998), 60. Meanwhile, the two churches that dominated the religious landscape on the eve of the Revolution—the Congregationalist Church in New England and the Anglican Church in the South—had declined substantially. Whereas the Congregationalists had been the most numerous denomination in 1776, the Methodists alone were *ten times* larger by 1850.

43. Both the Puritan (in the North) and Anglican (in the South) establishments originally strove for religious uniformity in the colonies over which they presided, and this led both to persecute and discriminate against religious dissenters.

44. Matthew 22:21.

45. Roger Williams, *The Bloody Tenant of Persecution* (Providence, RI: Narragansett Club, 1867 [1644]), 36. For an excellent discussion of the political significance of this idea of dual jurisdictions, see Steven D. Smith, *The Rise and Decline of American Religious Freedom* (Cambridge, MA: Harvard University Press, 2014). For the origins of these radical ideas in the Protestants' early struggles for toleration in Europe, see John Witte Jr., *The Reformation of Rights:*

Law, Religion, and Human Rights in Early Modern Calvinism (Cambridge: Cambridge University Press, 2007).

46. See, for instance, Isaac Backus, "An Appeal to the Public for Religious Liberty," in *Isaac Backus on Church, State, and Calvinism: Pamphlets, 1754–1789*, ed. William G. McLoughlin (Cambridge, MA: Harvard University Press, 1968 [1773]), 313.

47. For evidence of Locke's influence, see, for instance, William G. McLoughlin, *New England Dissent, 1630–1833: The Baptists and the Separation of Church and State*, vol. 1 (Cambridge, MA: Harvard University Press, 1971), 388–412.

48. Ebenezer Frothingham, "A Key to Unlock the Door, That Leads in, to Take a Fair View of the Religious Constitution, Established by Law, in the Colony of Connecticut" (New Haven: Benjamin Mecom, 1767), 45–46. For another compelling example, see Elisha Williams, "The Essential Rights and Liberties of Protestants" (Boston: S. Kneeland, 1744).

49. McLoughlin, *New England Dissent, 1630–1833*, 1:388. See also Daniel T. Rodgers, *Contested Truths: Keywords in American Politics since Independence* (New York: Basic Books, 1987), 53–56.

50. Popular religion, writes historian Nathan Hatch, was "laced with Jeffersonian political thought, even heavy doses of Jefferson's prose." Nathan O. Hatch, *The Democratization of American Christianity* (New Haven: Yale University Press, 1989), 36.

51. John Leland, "Short Essays on Government, and the Proposed Revision of the Constitution of Government for the Commonwealth of Massachusetts," in *The Writings of the Late Elder John Leland, Including Some Events in His Life, Written by Himself, with Additional Sketches, &C.*, ed. L. F. Greene (New York: G. W. Wood, 1845 [1820]), 474. Leland, who was himself an outspoken critic of slavery, appealed to these rights as part of a broadly liberal, individualist view of government and its purposes: "government is the formation of an association of individuals," he argued, "by mutual agreement, for mutual defence and advantage" (476).

52. Lorenzo Dow, "Analects upon Natural, Social, and Moral Philosophy," in *Perambulations of a Cosmopolite, or, Travels and Labors of Lorenzo Dow, in Europe and America* (New York: Richard C. Valentine, 1855 [1816]), 317.

53. Ibid., 300. Dow ultimately grounded the rights of conscience in the moral teaching of the gospel. Ibid., 299, 303, 314. Another telling illustration of this confluence of Lockean and evangelical perspectives can be found in the struggle for religious toleration in Virginia in the mid-1780s. Many of the evangelical petitioners to the Virginia legislature adopted Madison's language of natural rights even as they argued that religious disestablishment was necessary to halt the corruption of Christianity and the spread of Deism and "irreligion." These unpublished legislative petitions can be found at https://www.virginiamemory.com/collections/petitions.

54. Thomas Buckley, *Establishing Religious Freedom: Jefferson's Statute in Virginia* (Charlottesville: University of Virginia Press, 2013), 148. They often argued, specifically, that disestablishment would return Christianity to the pure form that it enjoyed in its earliest incarnation, before Emperor Constantine had corrupted it by officially joining it with the Roman state.

55. For helpful discussions of abolitionism's roots in the religious reform movements of the Second Great Awakening, see James Brewer Stewart, *Holy Warriors: The Abolitionists and American Slavery*, rev. ed. (New York: Hill and Wang, 1996); James Brewer Stewart, "Abolitionists, the Bible, and the Challenge of Slavery," in *The Bible and Social Reform*, ed. Ernest R. Sandeen (Philadelphia: Fortress Press, 1982); Lawrence J. Friedman, *Gregarious Saints: Self and Community in American Abolitionism, 1830–1870* (Cambridge: Cambridge University Press, 1982);

John R. McKivigan, ed., *Abolitionism and American Religion* (New York: Garland, 1999); Walters, *The Antislavery Appeal*; Goodman, *Of One Blood*; Whitney R. Cross, *The Burned-over District: The Social and Intellectual History of Enthusiastic Religion in Western New York, 1800–1850* (New York: Harper & Row, 1950).

56. Samuel Crothers, "The Harmony of Moses and the Apostles," *Quarterly Anti-Slavery Magazine* 1, no. 1 (1835): 76–77. See also Beriah Green, "The Church Carried Along; or, the Opinions of a D.D. On Slavery," *Quarterly Anti-Slavery Magazine* 2, no. 5 (1836): 43; "Objections Glanced At," *Friend of Man*, August 11, 1836, p. 1. "[God] said, 'let us make man in our own image,'" argued abolitionist Henry B. Stanton. "This, then, is the foundation of the inalienable rights of man: because he was made in the image of God." Henry B. Stanton, "Speech of Henry B. Stanton," *Pennsylvania Freeman*, August 16, 1838, p. 1.

57. "Address by William Whipper, Alfred Niger, and Augustus Price," 3:147, 149.

58. Amos Phelps, *Lectures on Slavery, and Its Remedy* (Boston: New England Anti-Slavery Society, 1834), 39–40. See also "Anti-Slavery," *Friend of Man*, June 23, 1836, p. 1; Channing, *The Duty of the Free States*, 39–42.

59. Gerrit Smith, "Gerrit Smith's Letter to the Rev. Lyman Beecher, D. D.," *Friend of Man*, July 14, 1836, p. 1. See also Garrison, *Thoughts on African Colonization*, 71; Lewis Perry, *Radical Abolitionism: Anarchy and the Government of God in Antislavery Thought* (Ithaca: Cornell University Press, 1973), 48–54. This view of slavery was also shared by the tremendously influential antislavery evangelist Charles Grandison Finney. James David Essig, "The Lord's Free Man: Charles G. Finney and His Abolitionism," *Civil War History* 24, no. 1 (1978): 34–35.

60. Perry, *Radical Abolitionism*, 48–54. A few abolitionists, notably Garrison, eventually took the further step of denouncing all human government as a usurpation of divine sovereignty and became anarchists. With this final step, Luther's (and Roger Williams's) spiritual jurisdiction finally swallowed up its secular counterpart altogether. Ibid., 55–91.

61. "Anti-Slavery," *Friend of Man*, June 23, 1836, p. 1.

62. William Henry Brisbane, *Slaveholding Examined in the Light of the Holy Bible* (New York: American Anti-Slavery Society, 1849), 170. See also James Brown, *American Slavery in Its Moral and Political Aspects* . . . (Oswego, NY: G. Henry, 1840), 34, 51–52; Arnold Buffum, "Constitution of the New-England Anti-Slavery Society: With an Address to the Public" (Boston: Garrison and Knapp, 1832), 7–8.

63. "Influence of Slavery on Slaveholders," *Quarterly Anti-Slavery Magazine* 1, no. 4 (1836): 322. See also Buffum, "Constitution of the New-England Anti-Slavery Society," 7–8.

64. William Goodell, "Prospectus," *Friend of Man*, June 23, 1836, p. 1. Goodell, who was himself a Calvinist, read natural rights back into key passages of Genesis. Describing the human sinfulness that precipitated the great flood, he wrote that "this period of the world, so remarkable for its universal and extreme wickedness, was equally remarkable it seems for its universal and extreme contempt and reckless invasion of inalienable human rights." He also described Cain's murder of Abel as an outrage against "inalienable rights." William Goodell, *The Democracy of Christianity, or An Analysis of the Bible and Its Doctrines in Their Relation to the Principle of Democracy*, vol. 1 (New York: Cady & Burgess, 1849), 28, 27. For similar arguments, see also Brisbane, *Slaveholding Examined in the Light of the Holy Bible*, 158; H. F. T., "Slavery as It Is," *Human Rights*, June 1837, p. 3; Crothers, "The Harmony of Moses and the Apostles," 75–78.

65. Robert Stewart et al., "Declaration of Sentiment," *Liberator*, May 16, 1835, p. 78.

66. These various biblical arguments, among others, had informed the earliest, Quaker antislavery writers in the seventeenth and early eighteenth centuries. See David Brion Davis, *The Problem of Slavery in Western Culture* (Ithaca: Cornell University Press, 1966), 316–26; Sinha, *The Slave's Cause*, 9–24. Antebellum abolitionists fused them with the natural rights tradition.

67. John G. Whittier, "John G. Whittier's Letter to Edward Everett," *Liberator*, February 20, 1836, p. 30.

68. Some abolitionists went so far as to declare rights protection the *only* legitimate business of government; see "Anti-Slavery," *Friend of Man*, June 23, 1836, p. 1; Elisha P. Hurlbut, *Essays on Human Rights and Their Political Guaranties* (New York: Fowlers and Wells, 1848), 36.

69. Theodore Weld, *American Slavery as It Is: Testimony of a Thousand Witnesses* (New York: American Anti-Slavery Society, 1839), 151. See also "Mobs—Free Discussion—Right of the People Peaceably to Assemble—Things to Be Thought Of," *American Anti-Slavery Almanac for 1840* 1, no. 5 (1840): 4.

70. For the most radical abolitionists, such as Garrison, this charge extended to the U.S. Constitution itself.

71. Third Annual Report of the American Anti-Slavery Society, cited in McInerney, *The Fortunate Heirs of Freedom*, 19. See also "Proceedings of a Convention of Delegates, Assembled from the Various Parts of the State of Pennsylvania," *National Enquirer*, February 11, 1837, p. 86; Channing, *The Duty of the Free States*, 16–19.

72. Some historians have argued that abolitionists saw slavery as a form of private domination "exercised by one individual over another." Eric Foner, "Abolitionism and the Labor Movement in Antebellum America," in *Politics and Ideology in the Age of the Civil War* (New York: Oxford University Press, 1980), 65. This is a mistake: if slaveholders were the "proximate" agents of domination, abolitionists almost always described their power as enabled and mediated by government. In fact, they relied heavily on this view in arguing—as they often did—that northern citizens were complicit in slavery. "Slavery is created by law," said A. H. Freeman, arguing that the citizens of New Jersey shared responsibility for it, "and is countenanced and upheld by the national government as well as by the authorities of our own State." A. H. Freeman, "To the People of New Jersey," *Emancipator*, January 28, 1841, p. 1.

73. Brisbane, *Slaveholding Examined in the Light of the Holy Bible*, 157. See also "Liberty," *Friend of Man*, July 21, 1836, p. 2. Such passages abound in abolitionist writing; in them, one hears strong echoes of the long-standing Protestant fight for religious toleration and freedom.

74. For a good example, see Freeman, "To the People of New Jersey," 1.

75. It is worth emphasizing that this chapter makes no attempt to offer a full overview of the political thought of American abolitionism. It focuses specifically and disproportionately on the first of these languages, which, although quite central to abolitionist rhetoric, was hardly exhaustive. It is also worth noting, however, that these three languages often combined and overlapped. Abolitionists sometimes presented human rights, for example, as a strategy for mitigating domination; they also invoked rights—and rights violations—in explaining why slavery was sinful. For a good example of this final tendency, see Mrs. M. B. Davis, "Scenes of Oppression in the Refined Circles of the South, Addressed to the Women of Illinois" (Peoria, IL: Peoria County Anti-Slavery Society, 1846), 11, 16.

76. See, for instance, James A. Morone, *Hellfire Nation: The Politics of Sin in American History* (New Haven: Yale University Press, 2003), 144–68.

77. For an example of this style of criticism, see Bourne, *Slavery Illustrated in Its Effects Upon Woman and Domestic Society*. See also Ronald G. Walters, "The Erotic South: Civilization and Sexuality in American Abolitionism," *American Quarterly* 25, no. 2 (1973): 177–201.

78. Hugh Davis, *Joshua Leavitt: Evangelical Abolitionist* (Baton Rouge: Louisiana State University Press, 1990), 99–101; Goodman, *Of One Blood*, 69–80; Stewart, "Abolitionists, the Bible, and the Challenge of Slavery."

79. See, for instance, Clifford S. Griffin, *Their Brothers' Keepers: Moral Stewardship in the United States, 1800–1865* (New Brunswick, NJ: Rutgers University Press, 1960).

80. They also believed that government could do this without taking sides in any of the controversial debates, over theology and church governance, that divided different Protestant denominations. Enlisting the government's support in policing private morals was therefore was fully compatible, in their view, with the separation of church and state.

81. For an exploration of the long-standing polarity in American political thought between liberal individualism and biblical Protestantism, see Wilson Carey McWilliams, *Redeeming Democracy in America*, ed. Patrick J. Deneen and Susan J. McWilliams (Lawrence: University Press of Kansas, 2011).

82. They were sometimes quite explicit about this lineage. The *Reflector and Watchman*, for example, drew a straight line from the Reformation through Roger Williams's fight for freedom of conscience to the Declaration of Independence and the abolitionist movement. See "Christianity and the Rights of Man," 1.

83. See Witte, *The Reformation of Rights*; Robert P. Forbes, "Slavery and the Evangelical Enlightenment," in *Religion and the Antebellum Debate over Slavery*, ed. John R. McKivigan and Mitchell Snay (Athens: University of Georgia Press, 1998).

84. Carwardine, *Evangelicals and Politics in Antebellum America*, 141; Donald G. Mathews, "The Methodist Schism of 1844 and the Popularization of Antislavery Sentiment," *Mid-America: An Historical Review* 51, no. 1 (1968): 19–20. For further discussion of a broader antislavery ideology, see McDaniel, "The Bonds and Boundaries of Antislavery."

85. Cozzens was pastor of the First Evangelical Church in Milton, Massachusetts, and a critic of what he perceived to be the uncompromising radicalism of the abolitionist movement. Samuel W. Cozzens, "The Prominent Sins of the Times. A Sermon, Delivered in Milton and Dorchester, on the Day of the Annual State Fast" (Boston: T. R. Marvin, 1844), 8. See also Leonard Bacon, *Slavery Discussed in Occasional Essays, from 1833 to 1846* (New York: Baker and Scribner, 1846), 75–77; George Duffield, "A Sermon on American Slavery: Its Nature, and the Duties of Christians in Relation to It" (Detroit: J. S. and S. A. Bragg, 1840).

86. Carwardine, *Evangelicals and Politics in Antebellum America*, 147–52.

87. Angelina Grimke, "Appeal to the Christian Women of the South" (New York: American Anti-Slavery Society, 1836), 16. For further discussion of Grimke's appeal to human rights, see Lisa Pace Vetter, *The Political Thought of America's Founding Feminists* (New York: New York University Press, 2017), 114–23.

88. Frederick Douglass, "Lecture on Slavery, No. 1," in *Antislavery Political Writings, 1833–1860*, ed. C. Bradley Thompson (Armonk, NY: M. E. Sharpe, 2004 [1850]), 26. See also Brown, *American Slavery in Its Moral and Political Aspects*, 34, 90; Phelps, *Lectures on Slavery, and Its Remedy*, 38–39.

89. Brown, *American Slavery in Its Moral and Political Aspects*, 90.

90. Charles Follen et al., "Address to the People of the United States," *Liberator*, September 6, 1834, p. 141. See also Theodore Weld, *The Bible against Slavery: An Inquiry into the Patriarchal and Mosaic Systems on the Subject of Human Rights* (New York: American Anti-Slavery Society, 1838), 10.

91. Elizabeth B. Clark, "'The Sacred Rights of the Weak': Pain, Sympathy, and the Culture of Individual Rights in Antebellum America," *Journal of American History* 82, no. 2 (1995): 487–88.

92. Weld, *American Slavery as It Is*, 7. "The thought that I should one day be free, and call my body my own," wrote William Wells Brown, as he pondered the "whips," "chains," and "bloodhounds" of America slavery, "buoyed me up, and made my heart leap for joy." Brown, *Narrative of William W. Brown*, 71, 70.

93. For further discussion, see James Oakes, *The Scorpion's Sting: Antislavery and the Coming of the Civil War* (New York: W. W. Norton, 2014), 57–70.

94. "Declaration of Sentiments of the American Anti-Slavery Society. Adopted at the Formation of Said Society, in Philadelphia on the 4th Day of December, 1833" (New York: American Anti-Slavery Society, 1833), 1.

95. Lydia Maria Child, "An Appeal to the Women of the Nominally Free States" (New York: William S. Dorr, 1837), 7.

96. Goodell, "Prospectus," *Friend of Man*, June 23, 1836, p. 1.

97. Slaves "are denied the rights and privileges of men," said one Quaker abolitionist. "In almost all the slave states, they are forbidden under the most severe penalties to read even the inspired volume." "An Address. From Farmington, [NY] Quarterly Meeting of Orthodox Friends, to Its Members on Slavery," *National Enquirer*, January 28, 1837, p. 81.

98. Brisbane, *Slaveholding Examined in the Light of the Holy Bible*, 167. See also "Lay Preacher," "From Our Washington Correspondent," *Emancipator*, March 5, 1840, p. 178.

99. McInerney, *The Fortunate Heirs of Freedom*, 67–68. Even when slaves were given access to religious instruction, abolitionists argued that they were indoctrinated into a corrupt and oppressive faith that served slaveholders' interests—"a religion of superstition and idolatry,— that teaches the victim of oppression to look up to his oppressor as God's own agent." J. C. H., "American Slavery—Its Effects Upon Its Immediate Victims. Letter No. II," 3.

100. Lydia Maria Child, "Anti-Slavery Catechism," 2nd ed. (Newburyport: Charles Whipple, 1839), 18. See also Buffum, "Constitution of the New-England Anti-Slavery Society," 12.

101. The entire ad ran as follows: "*Valuable Negroes*. An excellent female servant, thirty-four years of age, with her two children, the one *four years old*, and the other turned of *twelve months*, will be *sold low for cash*. The whole will be sold together, or SEPARATELY, to suit *purchasers*." Elizabeth Chandler, "A Specimen," *Genius of Universal Emancipation*, May 1831, p. 9.

102. Kentuckian, "American Slavery vs. Liberty," 24. See also Barber, "An Oration Delivered before the Addison County Anti-Slavery Society, on the Fourth of July, 1836," 5. Abolitionists often presented marriage rights in the liberal language of contract; see Amy Dru Stanley, *From Bondage to Contract: Wage Labor, Marriage, and the Market in the Age of Slave Emancipation* (Cambridge: Cambridge University Press, 1998), 1–59.

103. Charles Olcott, "Two Lectures on the Subjects of Slavery and Abolition, Compiled for the Special Use of the Anti-Slavery Lecturers and Debaters, and Intended for Public Reading" (Massillon, OH, 1838), 8.

104. Theodore Parker, *Letter to the People of the United States Touching the Matter of Slavery* (Boston: James Munroe & Co., 1848), 86, 87. See also Child, "Anti-Slavery Catechism," 5; Daniel Foster, "An Address on Slavery, Delivered in Danvers, Mass" (Boston: Bela Marsh, 1849), 25.

105. See, for example, Grimke, "Appeal to the Christian Women of the South," 4–12.

106. Clark, "'The Sacred Rights of the Weak,'" 463. See also Stanley, *From Bondage to Contract*, 26–29.

107. Clark, "'The Sacred Rights of the Weak.'" See also Stewart, *Holy Warriors*, 38–39; Ellen Carol DuBois, "Outgrowing the Compact of the Fathers: Equal Rights, Woman Suffrage, and the United States Constitution, 1820–1878," *Journal of American History* 74, no. 3 (1987): 836–62.

108. James Forten Jr., "Speech by James Forten, Jr. Delivered before the Philadelphia Female Anti-Slavery Society," in *The Black Abolitionist Papers*, vol. 3, ed. C. Peter Ripley (Chapel Hill: University of North Carolina Press, 1992 [1836]), 157.

109. "Anti-Colonization," *Genius of Universal Emancipation* (June 1831): 18. See also "The State Governments," *Anti-Slavery Almanac for 1839* 1, no. 4 (1839): 11. Free Blacks in the southern states faced even more draconian restrictions; see Alejandro de la Fuente and Ariela J. Gross, *Becoming Free, Becoming Black: Race, Freedom, and Law in Cuba, Virginia, and Louisiana* (Cambridge: Cambridge University Press, 2020), 132–218.

110. George M. Fredrickson, *The Black Image in the White Mind: The Debate on Afro-American Character and Destiny, 1817–1914* (New York: Harper & Row, 1971), 12–21. See also Davis, *The Problem of Slavery in the Age of Emancipation*, 105–25.

111. For an excellent discussion of colonization and its seminal importance in shaping the American abolitionist movement, see Davis, *The Problem of Slavery in the Age of Emancipation*, 81–192.

112. Wright, "The Sin of Slavery, and Its Remedy," 25–26.

113. David Ruggles, "Important Meeting," *Colored American*, October 28, 1837, p. 3; "Important Meeting of People of Color in the City of New York," *Weekly Advocate*, February 22, 1837, p. 1. See also David Ruggles, "Beware of Kidnappers," *Weekly Advocate*, January 14, 1837, p. 3.

114. "Trial by Jury," *Emancipator*, February 9, 1837, p. 164. These fears were only amplified by the 1850 fugitive slave law and the slew of well-publicized kidnappings—both successful and unsuccessful—that unfolded under its aegis. The law's ratification in 1850 caused a wave of Black emigration to Canada from northern cities. Benjamin Quarles, *Black Abolitionists* (New York: Oxford University Press, 1969), 199–200.

115. Forten, "Speech by James Forten, Jr. Delivered before the Philadelphia Female Anti-Slavery Society," 3:157.

116. See "Kidnapping—Jury Trial," *Human Rights*, February 1837, p. 2. Abolitionist newspapers were full of stories about kidnappings of northern Blacks—many of them successful.

117. For a discussion of Black activism on this issue, see Quarles, *Black Abolitionists*, 169–95.

118. "Important Meeting," *Colored American*, September 2, 1837, p. 1.

119. "Free Suffrage," *Liberator*, December 10, 1841, p. 199.

120. "Should Colored Men Vote?" *Emancipator*, January 14, 1841, p. 1.

121. "The First Martyr Has Fallen, in the Holy Cause of Abolition!" *Emancipator*, November 23, 1837, p. 117.

122. "Horrid Tragedy," *Philanthropist*, November 21, 1837, p. 3.

123. "With Whom Are We in Union?" *Colored American*, May 6, 1837, p. 3.

124. Davis, "Scenes of Oppression in the Refined Circles of the South, Addressed to the Women of Illinois," 8.

125. Sinha, *The Slave's Cause*, 229–39; Stewart, *Holy Warriors*, 77–78.

126. "It is impossible," wrote the *Philanthropist*, "that any set of men should live in the habitual and utter violation of the rights of others, a violation springing from the most unworthy motives, without gradually losing not only their veneration for human rights, but a just conception of their nature." "Effects of Southern Slavery on Northern Principles," *Philanthropist*, June 2, 1837, p. 2.

127. "Extracts from the Second Annual Report of the Monroe County Anti-Slavery Society," 3. As such passages should make clear, Lincoln's famous image of a country divided against itself had its roots in abolitionist rhetoric.

128. Although their views of racial difference were strikingly egalitarian for their time, most white abolitionists stopped short of believing in full social equality. Even as they pushed for equal civil rights for free Blacks, many doubted that Blacks would ever achieve social or intellectual parity with whites. They often made the paternalistic assumption, moreover, that Blacks would need white instruction and edification to assimilate to the middle class—and they took it upon themselves to provide it. It is worth noting, however, that a number of abolitionists recognized these failings and worked deliberately to counteract them. Friedman, *Gregarious Saints*, 160–95; Laurie, *Beyond Garrison*, 87–124; Quarles, *Black Abolitionists*, 49, 72.

129. Grimke, "Appeal to the Christian Women of the South," 30.

130. "An Appeal to Abolitionists on the Duty of Abstaining from the Purchase and Use of the Products of Unrequited Toil," *Pennsylvania Freeman*, June 14, 1838, p. 2. See also "On Selfishness," *Colored American*, August 19, 1837, p. 3.

131. "Schools, Etc.," *Anti-Slavery Almanac for 1839* 1, no. 4 (1839): 13; Brown, *American Slavery in Its Moral and Political Aspects*, 32; "Slavery," *Emancipator*, June 1, 1833, p. 17.

132. Quoting the poet Oliver Goldsmith, "Slavery Party," *Philanthropist*, June 2, 1837, p. 3.

133. Elizabeth Chandler, "From Elizabeth Margaret Chandler's Works. Consumers of Slave Products," *Colored American*, April 22, 1837, p. 1. See also "First of August, 1840," *National Anti-Slavery Standard*, August 6, 1840, p. 3; "An Appeal to Abolitionists on the Duty of Abstaining from the Purchase and Use of the Products of Unrequited Toil," 2.

134. See also "The Verdict of a Healthful Moral Sense," *National Anti-Slavery Standard*, July 2, 1840, p. 1.

135. Child, "The Despotism of Freedom; or the Tyranny and Cruelty of American Republican Slave-Masters," 50.

136. See Elizabeth Fox-Genovese and Eugene D. Genovese, *The Mind of the Master Class: History and Faith in the Southern Slaveholder's Worldview* (Cambridge: Cambridge University Press, 2005); Sven Beckert and Seth Rockman, eds., *Slavery's Capitalism: A New History of American Economic Development* (Philadelphia: University of Pennsylvania Press, 2016); Edward E. Baptist, *The Half Has Never Been Told: Slavery and the Making of American Capitalism* (New York: Basic Books, 2014).

137. "The Domestic Slave Trade," *Human Rights*, July 1837, p. 1. Abolitionists commonly used "business language" to convey the casual, transactional, profit-driven quality of the slaveholder's decision making, especially as concerned the sale and "breeding" of slaves.

138. McInerney, *The Fortunate Heirs of Freedom*, 108–19.

139. Phelps, *Lectures on Slavery, and Its Remedy*, 56.

140. Bourne, *Slavery Illustrated in Its Effects Upon Woman and Domestic Society*, 62. "The bills of sale were made out in the usual horse-jockeying slang," Bourne continued, "with the additional guarantee of maidenhood [virginity] and other moral accomplishments. When he saw his correspondent the next morning, the Georgia merchant informed him that he had already defiled his new purchase, and that he was delighted with his *female bargain*" (63).

141. "Anti-Slavery," *Friend of Man*, June 23, 1836, p. 1.

142. J. D., "The Way to Wealth in the Model Republic," *North Star*, February 18, 1848, p. 3. See also "Spirit of the Age," *Colored American*, May 6, 1837, p. 3.

143. "Now, what shall keep things as they are?" asked Elizur Wright. "What shall eternize the hammer of the man-auctioneer, and the lash of the man driver, and work without pay? THE ENLARGEMENT OF THE MARKET! Aye, that is the policy, which, but for the 'fanatics,' would sow slave-raising establishments on every hill of New England! For who shall say that the men of even New England are proof against good markets?" Elizur Wright, "Untitled," *Quarterly Anti-Slavery Magazine* 1, no. 4 (1836): 314.

144. Twenty dollars a year was a sum they sometimes cited. See, for instance, Theodore Parker, "A Letter on Slavery," in *The Slave Power*, ed. James K. Hosmer (Boston: American Unitarian Association, 1916 [1847]), 30; "Liberation," *Liberator*, April 24, 1846, p. 65.

145. Parker, "A Letter on Slavery," 30.

146. See, for instance, Foster, "An Address on Slavery, Delivered in Danvers, Mass," 31; "Slavocracy," *Emancipator*, June 17, 1841.

147. Henry David Thoreau, "Civil Disobedience," in *Henry David Thoreau: Collected Essays and Poems*, ed. Elizabeth Hall Witherell (New York: Library of America, 2001 [1848]), 207.

148. This brief summary does not do justice to the complexity and subtlety of these historians' arguments. See Stanley, *From Bondage to Contract*, 1–98; John Ashworth, *Slavery, Capitalism, and Politics in the Antebellum Republic*, vol. 1: *Commerce and Compromise, 1820–1850* (Cambridge: Cambridge University Press, 1995), 125–91; Foner, "Abolitionism and the Labor Movement in Antebellum America." Although he was writing mainly about eighteenth-century Quakers, David Brion Davis's penetrating analysis of abolitionism and capitalism did a great deal to establish this view. See David Brion Davis, *The Problem of Slavery in the Age of Revolution, 1770–1823* (Oxford: Oxford University Press, 1999 [1975]), 213–54.

149. This reinterpretation of abolitionism as a movement grounded, at least partly, in a critique of the market economy and its excesses has been developed by a number of historians over the last several decades. See Goodman, *Of One Blood*, xvi, 69–80, 139–60; McInerney, *The Fortunate Heirs of Freedom*, 107–25; Sinha, *The Slave's Cause*, 12–20, 347–58. To their insights, one further observation should be added: the idea that abolitionists played a key role, historically, in justifying wage labor is peculiar in light of the fact that the Whig Party was doing so more explicitly and deliberately (see chapter 9). In their time, Whigs were far more influential than abolitionists, who after all comprised a small and often despised minority of the northern population.

150. See, for instance, "David Nelson's Address," *Philanthropist*, May 6, 1836, p. 1; "Loudon County, Virginia," *Genius of Universal Emancipation*, January 1832, pp. 125–26; Parker, "A Letter on Slavery," 43–64. Eric Foner has detailed how prevalent this argument had become in the

Republican Party of the 1850s. See Eric Foner, *Free Soil, Free Labor, Free Men: The Ideology of the Republican Party before the Civil War* (London: Oxford University Press, 1970), 40–72.

151. When abolitionists denounced mob violence, they sometimes described it in similar terms, as an affront to democracy: here were groups of rabid citizens usurping the legitimate authority of democratic institutions and meting out an irregular and unlawful "justice."

152. "What Have the Free States to Do with Slavery?" *Anti-Slavery Almanac for 1839* 1, no. 4 (1839): 5, 9.

153. Weld, *American Slavery as It Is*, 143.

154. Hon. William Claggett, "An Address, Delivered before the Portsmouth Anti-Slavery Society, on the Fourth of July, A.D. 1839" (Portsmouth, NH: C. W. Brewster, 1839), 10.

155. Many abolitionists described such pathologies, however, as *corruptions* of democracy: true democracy, they insisted, was premised on equal rights. See, for instance, Goodell, *The Democracy of Christianity*, vol. 1–2, 30ff.

156. Such arguments reflected the Whigs' anxieties more than the Democrats'. Weld, *American Slavery as It Is*, 144. See also Hosea Easton, *A Treatise on the Intellectual Character, and Civil and Political Condition, of the Coloured People of the U. States . . .* (Boston: Isaac Knapp, 1837), 39.

157. Child, "Anti-Slavery Catechism," 35.

158. "Prejudice against Color," *Liberator*, November 25, 1842, p. 188.

159. The immense popularity of blackface minstrelsy (which Douglass reviled) as a form of popular entertainment in the northern states spoke to this dynamic. See, for instance, Eric Lott, *Love and Theft: Blackface Minstrelsy and the American Working Class* (New York: Oxford University Press, 1993).

160. Frederick Douglass, "Prejudice against Color," *North Star*, June 13, 1850, p. 2; James Oliver Horton and Lois E. Horton, *In Hope of Liberty: Culture, Community, and Protest among Northern Free Blacks, 1700–1860* (New York: Oxford University Press, 1997), 204–5. For similar analysis, see, for instance, Gerrit Smith, "Gerrit Smith's Speech," *Emancipator*, May 17, 1838, p. 10; "Clinton Seminary," *National Anti-Slavery Standard*, May 20, 1841; Frederick Douglass, "The Skin Aristocracy in America: An Address Delivered in Coventry, England, February 2, 1847," *Coventry Herald and Observer*, February 5, 1847. In fact, abolitionists commonly described racism as an expression of racial "pride" or the "spirit of caste," arguing in effect that the belief in Black inferiority shaped white racial identity.

161. Easton, *A Treatise on the Intellectual Character, and Civil and Political Condition, of the Coloured People of the U. States*, 39.

162. "Answer of D. L. Child to James Fulton, Jr.," *National Anti-Slavery Standard*, August 22, 1844, p. 2. The original quotation is from Emerson's "Address . . . on the Anniversary of the Emancipation of the Negroes in the British West Indies."

163. Reprinted as "Blue and Black Laws," *North Star*, December 3, 1847, p. 1.

164. Cheryl Harris has argued that this prerogative was an essential part of the liberty that whites claimed as their birthright. See Cheryl I. Harris, "Whiteness as Property," *Harvard Law Review* 106, no. 8 (1993): 1707–91.

165. "Doings in Iowa," *Emancipator*, April 8, 1841, p. 3.

166. William Lloyd Garrison, "The American Union," *Liberator*, January 10, 1845, p. 5.

167. In their emphasis on moral culture, the abolitionists shared more with the Whigs than the Democrats. Whigs strove deliberately to promote a culture of Christian virtue and

self-discipline, through schooling, moral reform movements and missionary work, economic development, and the coercive force of the law.

168. For a discussion of this tendency in Frederick Douglass's thought, see Nicholas Buccola, *The Political Thought of Frederick Douglass: In Pursuit of American Liberty* (New York: New York University Press, 2012), 101–27.

169. "No Mistake," *Liberator*, April 2, 1831, p. 54. See also Grimke, "Appeal to the Christian Women of the South," 30.

170. Hebrews 13:3.

171. Elizabeth Chandler, "A Specimen," *Genius of Universal Emancipation*, May 1831, p. 10. See also "A Simple Fact," *National Anti-Slavery Standard*, September 5, 1844, p. 4.

172. Mack, "Fourth of July Oration, 1838," 181. See also Grimke, "Appeal to the Christian Women of the South," 13.

173. "Appeal of Forty Thousand Citizens Threatened with Disenfranchisement, to the People of Pennsylvania," *Pennsylvania Freeman*, March 29, 1838, p. 1.

174. Isabel Wilkerson has called this work "radical empathy": "radical empathy," she writes, "means putting in the work to educate oneself and listen with a humble heart to understand another's experience from their perspective, not as we imagine we would feel." Isabel Wilkerson, *Caste: The Origins of Our Discontents* (New York: Random House, 2020), 386.

175. Theodore Wright, "Prejudice against the Colored Man," *Colored American*, July 8, 1837, p. 1. In fact, Black abolitionists had long embraced such direct emotional appeals as core elements of their antislavery rhetoric; see Richard S. Newman, *The Transformation of American Abolitionism: Fighting Slavery in the Early Republic* (Chapel Hill: University of North Carolina Press, 2002), 90–96.

176. "You are a slave," wrote James Pennington to his white readers, "a being in whom another owns property. You may rise with his pride, but remember the day is at hand when you must also fall with his folly. To-day you may be pampered by his meekness; but to-morrow you will suffer in the storm of his passion." Pennington was trying to help his readers understand that even supposedly "mild" forms of domestic slavery subjected their victims to radical insecurity and soul-crushing domination. James W. C. Pennington, *The Fugitive Blacksmith; or, Events in the History of James W. C. Pennington, . . . Formerly a Slave in the State of Maryland, United States,* 2nd ed. (London: C. Gilpin, 1849), vii–viii. See also Harriet Jacobs, *Incidents in the Life of a Slave Girl*, ed. L. Maria Child (Boston, 1861), 6, 68.

177. See, for instance, Karen Halttunen, "Humanitarianism and the Pornography of Pain in Anglo-American Culture," *American Historical Review* 100, no. 2 (1995): 303–34; Marianne Noble, *The Masochistic Pleasures of Sentimental Literature* (Princeton: Princeton University Press, 2000); Karen Sanchez-Eppler, *Touching Liberty: Abolition, Feminism, and the Politics of the Body* (Berkeley: University of California Press, 1993), 14–48.

178. It is undeniably true, moreover, that the duty to sympathize with slaves and treat them kindly was often invoked as part of the racist discourse of natural inferiority. Cruelty to one's inferiors was widely seen as a moral failure. Margaret Abruzzo, *Polemical Pain: Slavery, Cruelty, and the Rise of Humanitarianism* (Baltimore: Johns Hopkins University Press, 2011), 8–9, 135–46.

179. See Clark, "'The Sacred Rights of the Weak.'" Clark rightly emphasizes that abolitionists saw empathy as a capacity that had to be actively cultivated and disciplined in service of

egalitarian ends. And some abolitionists, of course, believed that these egalitarian ends included equal rights for women.

180. "If and But," *Genius of Universal Emancipation*, May 1831, pp. 13–14.

181. Embedded in Elizabeth Chandler's dramatic appeal to motherly love (quoted earlier) was a call to act: "breathe a high resolve," she insisted, "that you will, from this time hencefor-ward, aid to the utmost of your power, in abolishing a system which gives birth to such atroci-ties." "A Specimen," 10. For reflections on the growing tendency to link empathy and action, see Abruzzo, *Polemical Pain*, 122–24; Anne C. Loveland, "Evangelicalism and 'Immediate Emancipa-tion' in American Antislavery Thought," *Journal of Southern History* 32, no. 2 (1966): 177–78, 180–83; Essig, "The Lord's Free Man," 27.

182. For enlightening discussions of the varied forms of activism that abolitionists pursued, see Laurie, *Beyond Garrison*; Quarles, *Black Abolitionists*.

183. "Justice and Expediency," *Emancipator*, June 1, 1833, p. 18.

184. "We entered into the crime together," Follen continued, "when tempted by the British government in our infancy. At years of discretion, when we became free, we deliberately pre-ferred power to righteousness, and *made the crime our own*." Follen et al., "Address to the People of the United States," 142.

185. Robert P. Forbes, *The Missouri Compromise and Its Aftermath: Slavery and the Meaning of America* (Chapel Hill: University of North Carolina Press, 2007), 106–7.

186. "To the Baptist Branch of Christ's Church in the Northern States," *Pennsylvania Free-man*, August 30, 1838, p. 3.

187. "'Abolition Insolence,'" *National Enquirer*, August 17, 1837, p. 90.

188. See Loveland, "Evangelicalism and 'Immediate Emancipation' in American Antislavery Thought."

189. Kraditor, *Means and Ends in American Abolitionism*, 79.

190. Carwardine, *Evangelicals and Politics in Antebellum America*, 134. In this commitment, they were influenced by a rising current of Christian perfectionism, which taught that people could achieve entire sanctification (freedom from sin) in this life. For some abolitionists (in-cluding Garrison), such doctrines held anarchist implications, which are ably explored in Perry, *Radical Abolitionism*.

191. They did, however, seek to withdraw from particular, corrupt institutions. The "come-outers" withdrew from churches that they saw as corrupted by slavery and formed their own antislavery churches; many abolitionists refused to identify with either political party for the same reasons; and of course many Garrisonians eventually endorsed "disunion" as a way of severing ties with the slaveholding South. But they typically understood these withdrawals as part of a concerted campaigns to reform American society as a whole, and they were driven in part by a desire to retain the moral high ground and with it their credibility as antislavery advo-cates. For an instructive discussion of the come-outers, for example, and the range of abolition-ist activities they undertook, see McKivigan, *The War against Proslavery Religion*, 93–110; Friedman, *Gregarious Saints*, 96–126.

192. To be specific (and restate points already made above): abolitionists argued that slavery was sustained by economic incentives that enriched a privileged class and ramified through the economy; by racist prejudices that offered collective psychological benefits to whites; and by political and constitutional structures that gave disproportionate power to the slaveholding

elite. The language of personal sin and redemption did not prevent them from acknowledging slavery's structural roots. It would be more accurate to say that these two perspectives complemented each other in abolitionist rhetoric (though of course different writers often emphasized one of these perspectives more than the other).

193. Vote scattering was the practice of writing in an abolitionist candidate who was not on the ballot. In states such as Massachusetts, in which the winner had to command a majority of the votes cast, this strategy could deny either official candidate a majority and force a runoff, during which abolitionists could offer their votes to the candidate who embraced an explicitly antislavery position. See Laurie, *Beyond Garrison*, 41–44.

194. For an excellent discussion of the Garrisonians' self-conscious moral and political strategies, see Kraditor, *Means and Ends in American Abolitionism*.

195. "Awake, Thou That Sleepest," *Pennsylvania Freeman*, April 12, 1838, p. 2.

196. For a discussion of the abolitionists' organizing and mass action strategies, see Newman, *The Transformation of American Abolitionism*, 131–75.

197. For excellent examples, see, for instance, T. B. Hudson, "Anti-Slavery Petitions," *North Star*, February 4, 1848, p. 1; "Incidents in the Life of an Anti-Slavery Agent," *North Star*, March 31, 1848. See also Laurie, *Beyond Garrison*.

198. Kraditor, *Means and Ends in American Abolitionism*, 119–23. Garrison's inclusion of women began in the late 1830s.

199. Sinha, *The Slave's Cause*, 267–78; Julie Roy Jeffrey, *The Great Silent Army of Abolitionism: Ordinary Women in the Antislavery Movement* (Chapel Hill: University of North Carolina Press, 1998). For detailed discussion of abolitionists' work in helping free slaves and harboring fugitives in the border states, see Stanley Harrold, *Border War: Fighting over Slavery before the Civil War* (Chapel Hill: University of North Carolina Press, 2010).

200. See Stewart, "Reconsidering the Abolitionists in an Age of Fundamentalist Politics"; Matt Karp, "The Mass Politics of Antislavery," *Catalyst* 3, no. 2 (2019): 131–78.

201. "Awake, Thou That Sleepest," *Pennsylvania Freeman*, April 12, 1838, p. 2.

202. "Moral Courage," *Weekly Advocate*, February 4, 1837, p. 2. See also Stewart, *Holy Warriors*, 46–47.

203. See, for instance, Andrew Delbanco, *The Abolitionist Imagination* (Cambridge, MA: Harvard University Press, 2012), 1–55.

204. For excellent discussions of these features of evangelical culture, see Hatch, *The Democratization of American Christianity*; Wigger, *Taking Heaven by Storm*, 104–24.

205. See also Richard Hofstadter, *Anti-Intellectualism in American Life* (New York: Knopf, 1963), 55–116.

206. David Walker, *Appeal . . . to the Colored Citizens of the World, but in Particular, and Very Expressly, to Those of the United States of America*, 2nd ed. (Boston: David Walker, 1830 [1829]), 77.

207. See James M. McPherson, *The Struggle for Equality: Abolitionists and the Negro in the Civil War and Reconstruction* (Princeton: Princeton University Press, 1964).

208. For further discussion of universalism and equality in the Declaration of Independence, see Danielle Allen, *Our Declaration: A Reading of the Declaration of Independence in Defense of Equality* (New York: Liveright Publishing, 2014).

209. Louis Hartz, *The Liberal Tradition in America: An Interpretation of American Political Thought since the Revolution* (New York: Harcourt, Brace & World, 1955), 60.

210. For further discussion of the meaning of liberalism, and of its relationship to individualism, see the appendix.

211. Hartz argued that Americans came to accept the Lockean myth, which Europeans understood merely as a useful fiction, as "a sober description of [historical] fact." Ibid.; Rodgers, *Contested Truths*, 55–56.

212. "Women's Rights Convention," *National Anti-Slavery Standard*, August 10, 1848, p. 4. The convention's Declaration of Sentiments was drafted by Elizabeth Cady Stanton.

213. Joshua A. Lynn, *Preserving the White Man's Republic: Jacksonian Democracy, Race, and the Transformation of American Conservatism* (Charlottesville: University of Virginia Press, 2019), 1–10.

214. Ibid., 12, 10, 34–67. See also Adam I. P. Smith, "The Emergence of Conservatism as a Political Concept in the United States before the Civil War," *Civil War History* 66, no. 3 (2020): 244–45, 250–51.

Part III

1. Benjamin Franklin, "Information to Those Who Would Remove to America," in *The Papers of Benjamin Franklin*, vol. 41, ed. Ellen R. Cohn (New Haven: Yale University Press, 2014 [1783–84]), 604.

2. See Jack P. Greene, *The Intellectual Construction of America: Exceptionalism and Identity from 1492 to 1800* (Chapel Hill: University of North Carolina Press, 1993), 95–129.

3. James L. Huston, *Securing the Fruits of Labor: The American Concept of Wealth Distribution, 1765–1900* (Baton Rouge: Louisiana State University Press, 1998), 66–69.

4. Rowland Berthoff, *An Unsettled People: Social Order and Disorder in American History* (New York: Harper & Row, 1971), 179.

5. Robert H. Wiebe, *The Opening of American Society: From the Adoption of the Constitution to the Eve of Disunion* (New York: Alfred A. Knopf, 1984), 271.

6. J. K. Paulding, *The Backwoodsman. A Poem* (Philadelphia: M. Thomas, 1818), 11, 19. See also Henry Nash Smith, *Virgin Land: The American West as Symbol and Myth* (Cambridge, MA: Harvard University Press, 1970 [1950]), 135–39. It is worth noting that Basil, the protagonist of Paulding's poem, eventually attains to greater heights: he becomes "Judge, general, congressman" and lives "like a prince" (174) in his old age. These lavish rewards are not, however, part of his original ambition.

7. In one sense, of course, it was not moderate at all, for many of its advocates believed it to be premised on an expanding supply of cheap land, which underwrote an expansionist colonial agenda.

8. Joyce Appleby, "New Cultural Heroes in the Early National Period," in *The Culture of the Market: Historical Essays*, ed. Thomas L. Haskell and Richard F. Teichgraeber III (Cambridge: Cambridge University Press, 1993), 176, 180. See also Richard Hofstadter, *The Age of Reform* (New York: Vintage, 1955), 39–44.

9. See also Gary J. Kornblith, "Self-Made Men: The Development of Middling-Class Consciousness in New England," *Massachusetts Review* 26, no. 2/3 (1985): 461–74; Daniel Walker Howe, *Making the American Self: Jonathan Edwards to Abraham Lincoln* (Oxford: Oxford University Press, 2009 [1997]).

10. In fact, Whig avatar Henry Clay has often been credited with popularizing the term "self-made man." Howe, *Making the American Self*, 136. A search of contemporary newspapers shows that the term itself came into circulation in the 1820s.

11. John Ashworth calls this cardinal Whig value "individuality." See John Ashworth, *"Agrarians" & "Aristocrats": Party Political Ideology in the United States, 1837–1846* (Cambridge: Cambridge University Press, 1983), 52, 62, 64.

12. This idea of occupational mobility contradicted the long-standing ideal of artisanal self-making, in which the artisan rose from apprentice to master, honing his skill and developing new and better techniques over a lifetime of work in the same craft. See, for instance, Tristam Burges, "The Spirit of Independence: An Oration Delivered before the Providence Association of Mechanics and Manufacturers" (Providence: B. Wheeler, 1800), 11.

13. "What distinguished the self-made man," writes Daniel Walker Howe, "was that his identity was a voluntarily chosen, conscious construction" (*Making the American Self*, 136).

Chapter 9

1. Calvin Colton, "Junius Tracts No. VII. Labor and Capital" (New York: Greeley & McElrath, 1844), 7.

2. For further discussion of this version of the exceptionalist story, see Jonathan A. Glickstein, *Concepts of Free Labor in Antebellum America* (New Haven: Yale University Press, 1991), 38–52.

3. For an excellent treatment of this diversity, see Daniel Walker Howe, *The Political Culture of the American Whigs* (Chicago: University of Chicago Press, 1979).

4. David Francis Bacon, *Progressive Democracy: A Discourse, on the History, Philosophy, and Tendency of American Politics . . .* (New York: Central Clay Committee, 1844), 15. See also Thomas Brown, *Politics and Statesmanship: Essays on the American Whig Party* (New York: Columbia University Press, 1985), 181–82.

5. *Cong. Globe*, 28th Cong., 1st sess., Appendix, 286 (March 1844).

6. Alonzo Potter, "Trades' Unions," *New-York Review* 2, no. 3 (1838): 11. See, for instance, William Brownlow, "A Political Register, Setting Forth the Principles of the Whig and Locofoco Parties in the United States . . ." (Jonesborough, TN: Jonesborough Whig, 1844), 123; Alonzo Potter, *Political Economy: Its Objects, Uses, and Principles: Considered with Reference to the Condition of the American People* (New York: Harper & Brothers, 1840), 243; Caleb Cushing, "Speeches Delivered in the House of Representatives of Massachusetts, on the Subject of the Currency and Public Deposits" (Salem: Register Press, 1834), 27–28.

7. "Harry and John," *Daily Ohio State Journal*, August 9, 1842, p. 2.

8. Alonzo Potter, "Carey's Principles of Political Economy," *New-York Review* 3, no. 5 (1838): 2.

9. Daniel D. Barnard, "The Social System. An Address Pronounced before the House of Convocation of Trinity College" (Hartford, CT: Calendar Press, 1848), 27. See also Potter, *Political Economy: Its Objects, Uses, and Principles*, 243.

10. "Introductory," *American Review: A Whig Journal* 1, no. 1 (1845): 3. The name "Loco-Foco," which the Whigs attached to the Democratic Party, was also intended to highlight its economic radicalism.

11. Ibid., 1; "The Elections," *National Intelligencer*, October 17, 1844, p. 2. Such language was typical of Whig writers presenting an overview of fundamental Whig commitments; see also William Watson, "The Whig Party; Its Objects—Its Principles—Its Candidates—Its Duties—and Its Prospects. An Address to the People of Rhode Island" (Providence, RI: Knowles and Vose, 1844), 5; Adam I. P. Smith, "The Emergence of Conservatism as a Political Concept in the United States before the Civil War," *Civil War History* 66, no. 3 (2020): 231–55.

12. Anon., "Civilization: American and European," *American Review: A Whig Journal* 4, no. 1 (1846): 42. See also Watson, "The Whig Party; Its Objects—Its Principles—Its Candidates—Its Duties—and Its Prospects," 4.

13. Pennsylvania Whig Party, "Proceedings of the Whigs of Chester County, Favorable to a Distinct Organization of the Whig Party" (West Chester, PA, 1838), 5, 9; Howe, *The Political Culture of the American Whigs*, 73. See also Henry Clay, "Speech on the Sub-Treasury Bill" (Washington, DC, 1840), 5–6.

14. Howe, *The Political Culture of the American Whigs*, 20.

15. See ibid., 70–71.

16. Francis Bowen, "The Recent Contest in Rhode Island: An Article from the North American Review, for April, 1844" (Boston: Otis, Broaders, & Co., 1844), 59.

17. "From the Lynchburg Virginian of August 9," *National Intelligencer*, August 13, 1847, p. 3. Americans in 1776, the author added, wanted only "to preserve the franchises they *then* and ALWAYS HAD enjoyed, not to extort new ones."

18. "To the Editors," *National Intelligencer*, August 16, 1847, p. 2.

19. "From the Lynchburg Virginian of August 9," 3.

20. Bowen, "The Recent Contest in Rhode Island," 8.

21. For an extended discussion of this feature of Whig thought, see Howe, *The Political Culture of the American Whigs*, 69–95.

22. "Human Rights According to Modern Philosophy," *American Review: A Whig Journal* 2, no. 4 (1845): 329.

23. Howe goes so far as to describe a "cult of Edmund Burke," which was "widespread within the Whig party." Howe, *The Political Culture of the American Whigs*, 235. See also Drew Maciag, *Edmund Burke in America: The Contested Career of the Father of Modern Conservatism* (Ithaca: Cornell University Press, 2013), 73–104.

24. For Whigs, this view had important implications for popular sovereignty: the people's legitimate authority, they insisted, could be exercised only through established constitutional channels. Democrats, on the other hand, tended to believe that *the people* retained the authority to act directly, through extraconstitutional means, especially if their constitutions were unjust. For an excellent discussion of this disagreement, see, for instance, Robert E. Shalhope, *The Baltimore Bank Riot: Political Upheaval in Antebellum Maryland* (Urbana: University of Illinois Press, 2009), 106–63.

25. Barnard, "The Social System. An Address Pronounced before the House of Convocation of Trinity College," 11–12.

26. They spoke of society, for example, as a "creature, like a body whose breathing, pulsing, digesting, assimilative, and a hundred other, processes, all play into each other, in that wonderful reciprocity that makes a full-toned vital order." Horace Bushnell, "The True Wealth or Weal of

Nations," in *Representative Phi Beta Kappa Orations*, ed. Clark S. Northup et al. (Boston: Houghton Mifflin, 1915 [1837]), 6. See also Howe, *The Political Culture of the American Whigs*, 29–30.

27. Calvin Colton, "Junius Tracts No. V. Political Abolition" (New York: Greeley & McElrath, 1844), 12–13. See also Hubbard Winslow, "The Means of the Perpetuity and Prosperity of Our Republic. An Oration, Delivered by Request of the Municipal Authorities, of the City of Boston, July 4, 1838" (Boston: John H. Eastburn, 1838), 13; John Whipple, "Address of John Whipple, to the People of Rhode Island, on the Approaching Election" (Providence: Knowles and Vose, 1843), 5.

28. Colton, "Junius Tracts No. V. Political Abolition," 13. Rush Welter has pointed out that, "despite evident efforts to avoid appealing to natural rights," conservative Whigs did sometimes appeal to property as a natural right. Rush Welter, *The Mind of America: 1820–1860* (New York: Columbia University Press, 1975), 111.

29. *Cong. Globe*, 28th Cong., 1st sess., Appendix 463 (March 1844). See also Henry Clay, *Cong. Globe*, 31st Cong., 1st sess., Appendix 572 (May 1850).

30. For a detailed discussion of this shift, see Major L. Wilson, *Space, Time, and Freedom: The Quest for Nationality and the Irrepressible Conflict, 1815–1861* (Westport, CT: Greenwood Press, 1974). Wilson locates its origins as far back as the Missouri Compromise and the emergence of a northern free soil position that rested its argument explicitly on the foundation of equal natural rights for individuals. Ibid., 35–37.

31. William Seward, "Freedom in the New Territories," in *The Works of William H. Seward*, vol. 1, ed. George Baker (New York: Redfield, 1853 [1850]), 76, 74.

32. To Clay, Seward's argument seemed to partake of "wild, reckless, and abominable theories, which strike at the foundations of all property, and threaten to crush in ruins the fabric of civilized society." *Cong. Globe*, 31st Cong., 1st sess., Appendix 572 (May 1850).

33. Abraham Lincoln, "Speech on the Dred Scott Decision at Springfield, Illinois," in *Abraham Lincoln: Speeches and Writings, 1832–1858*, ed. Don E. Fehrenbacher (Washington, DC: Library of America, 1989 [1857]), 398. For further discussion of Lincoln's appeal to natural rights, see Eric Foner, *The Fiery Trial: Abraham Lincoln and American Slavery* (New York: Norton, 2010), 92–131. In the immensely controversial *Dred Scott* decision, the Court had ruled that Blacks—free or slave—could not be U.S. citizens and had no standing to sue in federal court; it had also ruled that the federal government had no power to ban slavery in the U.S. territories.

34. For an insightful discussion of this transformation in Whig thought as it absorbed or "rediscovered" Lockean natural rights, see Howe, *The Political Culture of the American Whigs*, 263–98. Howe argues that Lincoln and other antislavery Whigs had absorbed "what was best in Jacksonian Democracy: the commitment to the rights of the common man" (290).

35. "Capital and Labor," *Salem Register* (reprinted from the *Lawrence Courier*), January 1, 1849, p. 1. The author cites Adam Smith as his authority here, who "shows conclusively that where capital is increasing, wages must be, and are, good and rising; and where capital is at a stand still, wages are falling" (2).

36. Cushing, "Speeches Delivered in the House of Representatives of Massachusetts," 27.

37. Henry Carey, *Principles of Political Economy*, vol. 1 (Philadelphia: Carey, Lea & Blanchard, 1837), 382–83; Winslow, "The Means of the Perpetuity and Prosperity of Our Republic," 28.

38. Daniel Webster, "Lecture before the Society for the Diffusion of Useful Knowledge," in *The Writings and Speeches of Daniel Webster*, vol. 13 (Boston: Little, Brown 1903 [1836]), 74–75.

39. Edward Everett, "A Lecture on the Working Men's Party, First Delivered October Sixth, before the Charlestown Lyceum" (Boston: Gray and Bowen, 1830), 16, 17, 25.

40. Potter, *Political Economy: Its Objects, Uses, and Principles*, 228. Whigs also argued that the very distinction between labor and capital was untenable in America, because so many laborers owned their own capital. See Nathan Appleton, "Labor, Its Relations in Europe and the United States Compared" (Boston: Eastburn's Press, 1844), 14; Daniel Webster, "Mr. Webster at Andover," *Spectator*, November 15, 1843. My reading of Whig thought in this section closely follows John Ashworth's; see Ashworth, *"Agrarians" & "Aristocrats,"* 62–73.

41. Edward Everett, "Address Delivered before the Mercantile Library Association" (Boston: William D. Ticknor, 1838), 12, 13.

42. Appleton, "Labor, Its Relations in Europe and the United States Compared," 5.

43. Anon., "A Few Plain Facts, Addressed to the People of Pennsylvania" (Philadelphia: J. Crissy, 1844), 5.

44. Winslow, "The Means of the Perpetuity and Prosperity of Our Republic," 30. Many Whigs worried, however, that the social conditions of Europe would eventually come to America, and some argued that Americans should go to great lengths to avoid them; see, for instance, William Ellery Channing, *Lectures on the Elevation of the Laboring Portion of the Community* (Boston: Crosby and Nichols, 1863 [1840]), 116–17.

45. H. G. O. Colby, "The Relations of Wealth and Labor: Annual Address before the American Institute, Delivered Thursday Evening, October 20, 1842," *American Laborer* 1, no. 8 (1842): 239.

46. Anon., "A Word in Season; or Review of the Political Life and Opinions of Martin Van Buren, Addressed to the Entire Democracy of the American People" (Washington, DC: W. M. Morrison, 1840), 7. See also Jonathan Wainwright, "Inequality of Individual Wealth the Ordinance of Providence, and Essential to Civilization" (Boston: Dutton and Wentworth, 1835), 50.

47. Appleton, "Labor, Its Relations in Europe and the United States Compared," 8.

48. Everett, "Address Delivered before the Mercantile Library Association," 34–35.

49. Henry Clay, "Speech in Defence of the American System, against the British Colonial System . . . Delivered in the Senate of the United States, February 2d, 3d, and 6th, 1832" (Washington, DC: Gales and Seaton, 1832), 20. See also Anon., "The Credit System," *National Magazine and Republican Review* 1, no. 1 (1839): 58; Welter, *The Mind of America: 1820–1860*, 118–19.

50. Cushing, "Speeches Delivered in the House of Representatives of Massachusetts," 26; Anon., "The Credit System," *National Magazine and Republican Review* 1, no. 1 (1839): 66. See also Herbert Ershkowitz and William G. Shade, "Consensus or Conflict? Political Behavior in the State Legislatures during the Jacksonian Era," *Journal of American History* 58, no. 3 (1971): 615.

51. If anyone was trying "to enjoy the fruits of other men's labor," thundered Daniel Webster, it was those who clamored enviously against any "accumulated wealth." Quoted in John Calvin Adams, "An Appeal to the Whig National Convention, in Favor of the Nomination of Daniel Webster to the Presidency" (New York: R. Craighead, 1848), 10–11. See also Potter, *Political Economy: Its Objects, Uses, and Principles*, 237–38.

52. Winslow, "The Means of the Perpetuity and Prosperity of Our Republic," 30.

53. For an instructive discussion of the ideal of economic mobility in the political thought of Jacksonian America (among both Whigs and Democrats), see Welter, *The Mind of America: 1820–1860*, 118–22, 141–56. For a discussion of mobility in Whig thought, see Ashworth, *"Agrarians" & "Aristocrats,"* 65–69; Jonathan A. Glickstein, *American Exceptionalism, American Anxiety: Wages, Competition, and Degraded Labor in the Antebellum United States* (Charlottesville: University of Virginia Press, 2002), 41–44, 129–30.

54. Richard H. Bayard, "Speech of Richard H. Bayard of Delaware, on Mr. Benton's Motion to Expunge from the Journal of the Senate the Resolution of March 28th, 1834" (Wilmington: R. and J. B. Porter, 1837), 12.

55. Anon., "A Word in Season," 4. Girard was a French-born merchant and banker who rose from obscurity to become the richest man in America.

56. Anon., "The Andover Husking; a Political Tale Suited to the Circumstances of the Present Time, and Dedicated to the Whigs of Massachusetts" (Boston: J. H. Eastburn, 1842), 6.

57. Winslow, "The Means of the Perpetuity and Prosperity of Our Republic," 30. "At almost every second or third generation," he continued, Americans "become alternate master and servants to each other."

58. Colton, "Junius Tracts No. VII. Labor and Capital," 6.

59. Anon., "A Few Plain Facts, Addressed to the People of Pennsylvania," 5. See also Alexander Stuart, "Rights, Duties and Responsibilities of the Workingmen of America," *Richmond Whig*, November 29, 1844, p. 4; Bayard, "Speech of Richard H. Bayard of Delaware," 12.

60. Alonzo Potter, "Trades' Unions," *New-York Review* 2, no. 3 (1838): 9–10.

61. Colby, "The Relations of Wealth and Labor," 236–37. Edmund Burke had famously lamented that political radicalism threatened to rupture the political bonds and heritable identities that linked generations together and to make men "little better than the flies of summer." Colby was using the same language, but to strikingly opposite effect, for he was *praising* the evanescence of family fortunes, which left individuals free and responsible for their own fates.

62. John Aiken, "Labor and Wages, at Home and Abroad: In a Series of Newspaper Articles" (Lowell, MA: D. Bixby & Co., 1849), 16.

63. Webster, "Lecture before the Society for the Diffusion of Useful Knowledge," 76.

64. This myth contained important elements of truth: recent research suggests that American society retained substantially higher levels of economic mobility than European societies through the early twentieth century. Jason Long and Joseph P. Ferrie, "Intergenerational Occupational Mobility in Great Britain and the United States since 1850," *American Economic Review* 103, no. 4 (2013): 1109–37; Joseph P. Ferrie, "History Lessons: The End of American Exceptionalism? Mobility in the United States since 1850," *Journal of Economic Perspectives* 19, no. 3 (2005): 199–215.

65. Nathan S. S. Beman, "The Intellectual Position of Our Country: An Introductory Lecture Delivered before the Young Men's Association for Mutual Improvement, . . ." (Troy: N. Tuttle, 1839), 12.

66. Colton, "Junius Tracts No. VII. Labor and Capital," 15.

67. Colby, "The Relations of Wealth and Labor," 236. See also Bacon, *Progressive Democracy*, 19. This common phrase—"the architect of their own fortune," which sometimes appeared in quotes—seems to have originated in the Roman historian Sallust's *First Letter to Caesar*, which was assigned in American universities at the time.

68. Louis Hartz, *The Liberal Tradition in America: An Interpretation of American Political Thought since the Revolution* (New York: Harcourt, Brace & World, 1955), 111–12.

69. Potter, "Trades' Unions," 34.

70. Carey, *Principles of Political Economy*, 3:96. This contractual conception of freedom led some Whigs to suggest a fundamental parity between employers and employees: both could contract their labor or capital as they pleased. See, for instance, "Capital and Labor," *Portland Weekly Advertiser*, April 13, 1841, p. 4.

71. Horace Greeley, "Life—the Ideal and the Actual," in *Hints toward Reforms* (New York: Harper & Brothers, 1850), 66, 67, 65, 72, 71.

72. Everett, "A Lecture on the Working Men's Party," 4. Francis Wayland argued that economic progress was achieved precisely by stimulating this profusion of desires, which "remain dormant, until they are awakened into exercise by the presence, or by the knowledge, of their appropriate objects." Francis Wayland, *The Elements of Political Economy* (New York: Leavitt, Lord & Co., 1837), 199.

73. Potter, *Political Economy: Its Objects, Uses, and Principles*, 227.

74. Wainwright, "Inequality of Individual Wealth the Ordinance of Providence, and Essential to Civilization," 29.

75. Some Whigs were decidedly ambivalent, however, about this American restlessness, which they described as a "feverish anxiety to get on" and a source of rampant materialism and dissatisfaction. Francis Bowen, "Mill's Political Economy," *North American Review* 67, no. 141 (1848): 412. See also Henry W. Bellows, "The Influence of the Trading Spirit Upon the Social and Moral Life of America," *American Review: A Whig Journal* 1, no. 1 (1845): 95.

76. Samuel Foot, quoted in Joyce Appleby, *Inheriting the Revolution: The First Generation of Americans* (Cambridge, MA: Belknap Press, 2000), 109. See also pp. 122–26.

77. Howe, *The Political Culture of the American Whigs*, 266. See also John Ashworth, *Slavery, Capitalism, and Politics in the Antebellum Republic*, vol. 2: *The Coming of the Civil War, 1850–1861* (New York: Cambridge University Press, 2007), 276–77.

78. Abraham Lincoln, "Speech to the 148th Ohio Infantry Regiment," in *Collected Works of Abraham Lincoln*, vol. 7, ed. Roy P. Basler (New Brunswick, NJ: Rutgers University Press, 1953 [1864]), 528. Upward mobility was a regular theme of Lincoln's speeches; see Ashworth, *Slavery, Capitalism, and Politics in the Antebellum Republic*, vol. 2: *The Coming of the Civil War, 1850–1861*, 277–78.

79. For an iconic treatment of Lincoln and the myth of the self-made man, see Richard Hofstadter, *The American Political Tradition and the Men Who Made It* (New York: Vintage Books, 1989 [1948]), 121–73.

80. Richard L. Bushman, *The Refinement of America: Persons, Houses, Cities* (New York: Alfred A. Knopf, 1992), 238–79, 404.

81. Ibid., xv–xvi. See also Welter, *The Mind of America: 1820–1860*, 113–17.

82. Colton, "Junius Tracts No. VII. Labor and Capital," 6. See also Potter, "Trades' Unions," 27.

83. Channing, *Lectures on the Elevation of the Laboring Portion of the Community*, 99, 92, 93. Although Whigs tended to see consumer spending as a source of civilizational growth and progress, many simultaneously disapproved of lavish or *immodest* expenditures.

84. Ibid., 91, 99.

85. "Editorial Correspondence," *Philadelphia North American*, July 29, 1843, p. 2. See also Francis Bowen, "The Distribution of Property," *North American Review* 67, no. 140 (1848): 127. It was Lincoln himself who later gave the most famous articulation of this view: speaking at the Wisconsin State Fair in 1859, he declared that "if any continue through life in the condition of the hired laborer, it is not the fault of the system, but because of either a dependent nature which prefers it, or improvidence, folly, or singular misfortune." Abraham Lincoln, "Address before the Wisconsin State Agricultural Society, Milwaukee, Wisconsin," in *Collected Works of Abraham Lincoln*, vol. 3, ed. Roy P. Basler (New Brunswick, NJ: Rutgers University Press, 1953 [1859]), 479.

86. "Editorial Correspondence."

87. Quoted in John Ashworth, *Slavery, Capitalism, and Politics in the Antebellum Republic*, vol. 1: *Commerce and Compromise, 1820–1850* (Cambridge: Cambridge University Press, 1995), 322–23.

88. Aiken, "Labor and Wages, at Home and Abroad," 22. See also James Alexander, *The American Mechanic and Working-Man, in Two Volumes*, vol.1 (Philadelphia: William S. Martien, c. 1847), 130–31; Bowen, "Mill's Political Economy," 411.

89. Quoted in "Untitled," *Kennebec Journal*, August 25, 1843, p. 1.

90. Potter, "Trades' Unions," 24–25. See also James Alexander's *The American Mechanic and Working-Man*, in which he argues that union activism is "disorganizing and ruinous" and represents "*the beginning of the end!*" for American social order. American workers, he insists, should concentrate instead on individual self-improvement. Among the strategies he recommends is reading volumes of theology during scattered work breaks (if possible, he counsels that the volumes be read aloud to coworkers!). James Alexander, *The American Mechanic and Working-Man*, vol. 1, 123, 122, 178–84.

91. Thomas R. Hazard, "Facts for the Laboring Man" (Newport, RI: James Atkinson, 1840), 30.

92. See, for instance, Wayland, *The Elements of Political Economy*, 122–23.

93. Lyman Beecher, *Lectures on Political Atheism and Kindred Subjects; Together with Six Lectures on Intemperance* (Boston: John P. Jewett & Co., 1852), 118, 93, 94.

94. See, for instance, Lyman Atwater, "Judgments in the House of God; Considered Particularly with Reference to the Sins and Temptations Connected with Prevailing Pecuniary Disasters" (New York: E. B. Clayton & Sons, 1842); Orville Dewey, "On the Uses of Labour, and the Passion for a Fortune," in *Works of Orville Dewey, D.D., vol. 2* (New York: C. S. Francis & Co., 1847).

95. "Labor and Capital," *Commercial Advertiser*, August 1, 1845, p. 2.

96. The Congregationalist reverend Edward Payson explained this responsibility as follows in 1846: "My friends, whether you think it just or not . . . you will hereafter be called to an account for all the violations of the Sabbath, all the profanity, all the intemperance, all the vice of every kind of which you have made yourselves partakers by neglecting to employ those means for their prevention, which God and the laws of your country have put into your hands." Quoted in Clifford S. Griffin, *Their Brothers' Keepers: Moral Stewardship in the United States, 1800–1865* (New Brunswick, NJ: Rutgers University Press, 1960), 7.

97. Ashworth, *"Agrarians" & "Aristocrats,"* 138. For further discussion of the political ideas of conservative Democrats, see pp. 132–46.

98. Anon., "The Essays of Camillus, Addressed to the Hon. Joel Holleman" (Norfolk, VA: T. G. Broughton & Son, 1841), 70.

99. Calvin Colton, *The Crisis of the Country*, 2nd ed. (Philadelphia: T. K. and P. G. Collins, 1840), 1, 2. The Mississippi Whig orator S. S. Prentiss celebrated credit as "the poor man's capital." Michael F. Holt, *The Rise and Fall of the American Whig Party: Jacksonian Politics and the Onset of the Civil War* (New York: Oxford University Press, 1999), 108; Ashworth, *"Agrarians" & "Aristocrats,"* 80–81. See also Ershkowitz, "Consensus or Conflict?" 615.

100. "From the Albany Evening Journal. Address," *Morning Courier and New-York Enquirer*, October 2, 1838, p. 1. See also James Brooks, "Whig Meeting at Masonic Hall," *Morning Courier and New-York Enquirer*, October 13, 1838, p. 2.

101. Anon., "The Essays of Camillus," 70. Brooks, meanwhile, called credit "this American faith of man in man," and linked it to the ideals of the Declaration of Independence. Brooks, "Whig Meeting at Masonic Hall," 2.

102. "A. for example is satisfied of the integrity of B., and becomes his endorser at bank, whereby B. gets a start that finally places him at the top of fortune's wheel." Anon., "The Essays of Camillus," 70. See also John Davis, "Speech of Mr. Davis, of Massachusetts, on the Sub-Treasury Bill," *Albany Evening Journal—Extra*, August 25, 1840, p. 27.

103. Colton, *The Crisis of the Country*, 2.

104. Brown, *Politics and Statesmanship: Essays on the American Whig Party*, 39–40.

105. Whig moralists did denounce excessive speculation, indebtedness, and economic recklessness of all kinds. In fact, such criticisms were one of the commonplaces of Whig jeremiads; see, for instance, Atwater, "Judgments in the House of God"; Orville Dewey, "On the Moral End of Business," in *Works of Orville Dewey, D.D.*, vol. 2 (New York: C. S. Francis & Co., 1847), 195–200. But Whig criticisms of these vices were ultimately more measured than Democratic appraisals. Whigs almost always presented these excesses as *abuses* of the American economic system, which was itself fundamentally sound.

106. Quoted in Ashworth, *Slavery, Capitalism, and Politics in the Antebellum Republic*, vol. 1: *Commerce and Compromise, 1820–1850*, 321. For a fuller discussion of Whig attitudes toward wage labor, see pp. 315–23.

107. John Davis, "Gov. Davis' Inaugural Address," *Hampden Whig*, January 29, 1834, p. 1, "The poor," he goes on to say, "are able to enter even handed with the rich into the field of competition." See also Appleton, "Labor, Its Relations in Europe and the United States Compared," 13.

108. Stanley Lebergott, "The Pattern of Employment since 1800," in *American Economic History*, ed. Seymour Harris (New York: McGraw-Hill, 1961), 291–92.

109. Stewart Davenport, *Friends of the Unrighteous Mammon: Northern Christians and Market Capitalism, 1815–1860* (Chicago: University of Chicago Press, 2008), 3.

110. Like the Democrats, some Whigs also attributed America's relatively high wages to the availability of western lands, which reduced labor competition in the East. Welter, *The Mind of America: 1820–1860*, 315–16.

111. Anon., "A Few Plain Facts, Addressed to the People of Pennsylvania," 6; "Address of the Home League to the People of the United States," *American Laborer* 1, no. 11 (1843): 331. See also Horace Greeley, "Protection and Free Trade: The Question Stated and Considered" (New York: Greeley & McElrath, 1844), 13; Anon., "The Andover Husking," 8.

112. John Clayton, "Speech of Hon. John M. Clayton, at the Delaware Whig Mass Convention, Held at Wilmington, June 15, 1844" (New York: Greeley & McElrath, 1844), 10.

113. Brownlow, "A Political Register, Setting Forth the Principles of the Whig and Locofoco Parties in the United States," 65.

114. "Address of the Home League to the People of the United States," 331. See also Anon., "Tariff Doctrine," *Whig Banner*, July 6, 1844, p. 68.

115. Clay, "Speech in Defence of the American System, against the British Colonial System," 11, 15.

116. Anon., *The Political Mirror: or Review of Jacksonism* (New York: J. P. Peaslee, 1835), 170.

117. Edward Everett, "American Manufactures," in *Orations and Speeches on Various Occasions* (Boston: Little, Brown, 1878–79 [1831]), 83. See also Horace Greeley, "Liberty," *New York Tribune* 1842, p. 1.

118. Brownlow, "A Political Register, Setting Forth the Principles of the Whig and Locofoco Parties in the United States," 66. The most influential defenders of this position were Friedrich List and Henry Carey, who developed it into a full-blown critique of British colonial power.

119. Anon., "Facts for the Laboring Man: By a Laboring Man" (Newport, RI: James Atkinson, 1840), 21. Whigs commonly used military metaphors to describe international trade—something the Democrats almost never did.

120. *Cong. Globe*, 27th Cong, 3rd sess., Appendix 255 (July 1842). See also Bacon, *Progressive Democracy*, 14; "Free Traders and the German Illuminati," *Albany Evening Journal*, May 14, 1842, p. 2.

121. Colton, *The Crisis of the Country*, 12.

122. Calvin Colton, "Junius Tracts No. I. The Test; or, Parties Tried by Their Acts" (New York: Greeley & McElrath, 1844), 3.

123. Potter, "Trades' Unions," 36. Carey too used such language: see Carey, *Principles of Political Economy*, 1:xvi.

124. Greeley, "Protection and Free Trade: The Question Stated and Considered," 15.

125. Anon., "The Protective Policy," *Southern Literary Messenger* 8 (1842): 277. See also Daniel D. Barnard, "Man and the State, Social and Political. An Address before the Phi Beta Kappa Society of Yale College" (New Haven, CT: B. L. Hamlen, 1846), 16.

126. Howe, *The Political Culture of the American Whigs*, 34.

127. Clay, "Speech in Defence of the American System, against the British Colonial System," 4.

128. Colton, "Junius Tracts No. VII. Labor and Capital," 8, 14.

129. Holt, *The Rise and Fall of the American Whig Party*, 69.

130. Richard Fletcher, "Speech of Richard Fletcher to His Constituents: Delivered in Faneuil Hall, Monday, Nov., 6, 1837" (Boston: J. H. Eastburn, 1837), 7.

131. Robert Charles Winthrop, "Speech of Hon. R. C. Winthrop," in *The True Whig Sentiment of Massachusetts* ([Boston, 1846]), 20.

132. Bacon, *Progressive Democracy*, 12; "Capital and Labor"; Elliott R. Barkan, "The Emergence of a Whig Persuasion: Conservatism, Democratism, and the New York State Whigs," *New York History* 52, no. 4 (1971): 367–95.

133. Willard Phillips, *Propositions Concerning Protection and Free Trade* (Boston: C. C. Little and J. Brown, 1850), 11, 10, 38, 20.

134. Support for public education was not, however, a strictly partisan matter. Many Democrats also supported public education as a way of expanding opportunity and democratizing access to knowledge.

135. Appleton, "Labor, Its Relations in Europe and the United States Compared," 8.

136. William Seward, "Speech at a Whig Mass Meeting," in *The Works of William H. Seward*, ed. George Baker (New York: Redfield, 1853 [1844]), 263.

137. "If the doctrines taught in the English school are right," wrote Henry Carey of the writings of Thomas Malthus and David Ricardo, "then has the Creator made a serious blunder." Quoted in Howe, *The Political Culture of the American Whigs*, 114.

138. Charles Grandison Finney, *Sermons on Various Subjects* (New York: S. W. Benedict & Co., 1834), 7, 19. See also William G. McLoughlin, *Revivals, Awakenings, and Reform: An Essay on Religion and Social Change in America, 1607–1977* (Chicago: University of Chicago Press, 1978), 119; William Warren Sweet, *Religion in the Development of American Culture, 1765–1840* (New York: Scribner, 1952), 190–233.

139. Charles Grandison Finney, "Means to Be Used with Sinners," in *Lectures on Revivals of Religion*, ed. William G. McLoughlin (Cambridge, MA: Harvard University Press, 1960 [1835]), 146.

140. McLoughlin, *Revivals, Awakenings, and Reform*, 114.

141. Daniel D. Barnard, "An Address Delivered at Amherst, before the Literary Societies of Amherst College, August 27, 1839" (Albany, NY: Hoffman & White, 1839), 6. See also Anon., "The Progress of Society," *North American Review* 63, no. 133 (1846): 356.

142. Barnard, "Man and the State, Social and Political," 45.

143. Barnard, "An Address Delivered at Amherst, before the Literary Societies of Amherst College," 8–9.

144. This thousand-year peace is prophesied in Revelation 20:1–6.

145. James H. Moorhead, "Between Progress and Apocalypse: A Reassessment of Millennialism in American Religious Thought, 1800–1880," *Journal of American History* 71, no. 3 (1984): 525. For an excellent discussion of the development of post-millennialism from the seventeenth century onward and its relationship to the idea of historical progress, see Ernest Lee Tuveson, *Redeemer Nation: The Idea of America's Millennial Role* (Chicago: University of Chicago Press, 1968), 1–51. The alternative, pre-millennial view held that "Christ's visible return would occur *before* the millennium and that Jesus would be physically present during the saints' thousand-year reign." Pre-millennialists (also known as millenarians) tended to be much more pessimistic about the possibility of human progress; they believed that the world would have to be rescued from chaos by Christ's supernatural intervention. Curtis D. Johnson, *Redeeming America: Evangelicals and the Road to Civil War*, American Way Series (Chicago: Ivan R. Dee, 1993), 156.

146. Beecher, *Lectures on Political Atheism and Kindred Subjects*, 343.

147. Howe, *The Political Culture of the American Whigs*, 152–55. For a detailed discussion of the differences between these two nineteenth-century conceptions of progress, see Tuveson, *Redeemer Nation*, 51–90. For useful discussions of the prevalence of post-millennial faith in America, see ibid., 53–55; Richard J. Carwardine, *Evangelicals and Politics in Antebellum America* (New Haven: Yale University Press, 1993), 3, 19–22.

148. For insight into the sharp contrast between human nature before and after religious conversion, see, for instance, Heman Bangs, *The Autobiography and Journal of Rev. Heman Bangs;*

with an Introduction by Rev. Bishop Janes ... (New York: N. Tibbals & Son, 1872), 149–56; John Littlejohn, "Conscience," in *Selected Sermons by Reverend John Littlejohn*, ed. John. P. Glover (unpublished manuscript, United Methodist Heritage Center, Kentucky Wesleyan College), as well as "In Spirit and in Truth."

149. See, for instance, Gardiner Spring, "The Danger and Hope of the American People: A Discourse on the Day of the Annual Thanksgiving, in the State of New-York" (New York: John F. Trow, 1843), 25. For a discussion of anti-Catholicism among American evangelicals in the 1840s and 1850s, see Carwardine, *Evangelicals and Politics in Antebellum America*, 129, 199–234.

150. Thomas Skinner, "Religion and Liberty. A Discourse Delivered Dec. 17, 1840, ..." (New York: Wiley and Putnam, 1841), iii.

151. Moorhead, "Between Progress and Apocalypse," 535. Moorhead describes post-millennialism as a "compromise between a progressive, evolutionary view of history and the apocalyptic outlook of the book of Revelation" (541).

152. Anon., "The Progress of Society," *North American Review* 63, no. 133 (1846), 352, 351.

153. Welter, *The Mind of America: 1820–1860*, 20.

154. Beecher, *Lectures on Political Atheism and Kindred Subjects*, 316–17, 319, 325. These lectures were originally delivered in 1829 and subsequently revised in 1835 and 1852; see Howe, *The Political Culture of the American Whigs*, 156.

155. Beecher, *Lectures on Political Atheism and Kindred Subjects*, 99. See also "The Necessity of Revivals of Religion to the Perpetuity of Our Civil and Religious Institutions," *Spirit of the Pilgrims* 4, no. 9 (1831): 473.

156. Moorhead, "Between Progress and Apocalypse," 533–34.

157. Perry Miller, *The Life of the Mind in America: From the Revolution to the Civil War, Books One through Three* (San Diego: Harvest/HJB, 1965), 57.

158. Lucien Berry, "An Address Delivered by the Rev. L. W. Berry, D.D., Upon His Installation as President of the Indiana Asbury University" (Indianapolis: John D. Defrees, 1850), 29. Berry was a Methodist and a committed Whig.

159. Howe, *The Political Culture of the American Whigs*, 152. See also Miller, *The Life of the Mind in America*, 12–13, 69–70.

160. Spring, "The Danger and Hope of the American People," 45, 46.

161. Ibid., 17, 18, 44.

162. Beecher, *Lectures on Political Atheism and Kindred Subjects*, 328, 127–131, For an excellent discussion of this paradoxical evangelical conservatism, see Miller, *The Life of the Mind in America*, 69–71. For more on the conservative embrace of progress, see Welter, *The Mind of America: 1820–1860*, 7–18.

163. Robert Baird, *Religion in America; or, An Account of the Origin, Relation to the State, and Present Condition of the Evangelical Churches in the United States* (New York: Harper & Bros., 1856), 386. See also William Williams, "The Conservative Principle in Our Literature" (Philadelphia: American Baptist Publication Society, 1897 [1844]).

164. Johnson, *Redeeming America*, 162.

165. Ibid., 160.

166. Carey, *Principles of Political Economy*, 3:99–100.

167. William Ellery Channing, "Self-Culture" (Boston: James Munroe & Co., 1843 [1838]), 20–21.

168. Howe, *Making the American Self*, 113–14.

169. John F. Kasson, *Rudeness and Civility: Manners in Nineteenth-Century Urban America* (New York: Hill and Wang, 1990), 43. See also Karen Halttunen, *Confidence Men and Painted Women: A Study of Middle-Class Culture in America, 1830–1870* (New Haven: Yale University Press, 1982), 92; Welter, *The Mind of America: 1820–1860*, 143–50, 159–62.

170. Kasson, *Rudeness and Civility*, 43; Bushman, *The Refinement of America*.

171. Wigger is describing the appeal of Methodism in particular. John H. Wigger, *Taking Heaven by Storm: Methodism and the Rise of Popular Christianity in America* (Urbana: University of Illinois Press, 1998), 17. See also Johnson, *Redeeming America*, 58.

172. Finney, *Sermons on Various Subjects*, 9, 11.

173. Alexis de Tocqueville, *Democracy in America*, trans. Arthur Goldhammer, vol. 2 (New York: Library of America, 2004 [1840]), 586.

174. Tocqueville called social class in Europe a kind of "homeland within a homeland, more visible and more cherished than the country at large." Ibid.

175. Ibid., 515.

176. Ibid., 626, 625.

177. Smith, "The Emergence of Conservatism as a Political Concept in the United States before the Civil War."

178. See Richard Hofstadter, *Social Darwinism in American Thought*, rev. ed. (New York: George Braziller, 1959 [1944]), 9; Hartz, *The Liberal Tradition in America*, 89–113; Bernard Crick, "The Strange Quest for an American Conservatism," *Review of Politics* 17, no. 3 (1955): 359–76; Clinton Rossiter, *Conservatism in America: The Thankless Persuasion*, 2nd ed. (New York: Knopf, 1962), 67–84.

179. Margaret Fuller, *Woman in the Nineteenth Century, and Kindred Papers Relating to the Sphere, Condition and Duties, of Women* (Boston: John P. Jewett & Co., 1855 [1845]), 40–41. See also David M. Robinson, "Margaret Fuller and the Transcendental Ethos: *Woman in the Nineteenth Century*," *PMLA* 97, no. 1 (1982): 83–98.

180. Fuller, *Woman in the Nineteenth Century*, 159, 103–5.

181. Ibid., 107–8.

182. Ibid., 168–72.

183. For more sustained reflections on the nature and political content of Emerson's idea of self-reliance, see George Kateb, *Emerson and Self-Reliance* (Lanham, MD: Rowman & Littlefield, 2002 [1995]).

184. The Protestant counterpart to this Romantic ideal lies in the exhortations of revivalist preachers such as Charles Finney, who urged his audiences to renounce the sinful materialism of American life and the formulaic dogmas of institutional religion and find—and choose—Christ for themselves. This strain of Protestant anti-materialism has functioned as another, parallel American counterculture.

Chapter 10

1. Thomas Piketty, *Capital in the Twenty-First Century*, trans. Arthur Goldhammer (Cambridge, MA: Harvard University Press, 2014 [2013]), 348. In 1810, the richest 1 percent had owned around a quarter of the nation's wealth.

2. Richard White, *The Republic for Which It Stands: The United States during Reconstruction and the Gilded Age, 1865–1896* (New York: Oxford University Press, 2017), 477–517.

3. James L. Huston, *Securing the Fruits of Labor: The American Concept of Wealth Distribution, 1765–1900* (Baton Rouge: Louisiana State University Press, 1998), 339–78.

4. Historians now describe this as the "rights revolution." "This dramatic intrusion of central-ized power into the local and 'domestic' affairs of states," writes William Novak, "would have been unimaginable" to the American founders, who understood the Bill of Rights strictly as a table of protections against the federal government (not state and local governments). See William J. Novak, *The People's Welfare: Law and Regulation in Nineteenth-Century America* (Chapel Hill: University of North Carolina Press, 1996), 242, 235–48; Gary Gerstle, *Liberty and Coercion: The Paradox of American Government from the Founding to the Present* (Princeton: Princeton University Press, 2015), 74–86.

5. Eric Foner, *The Second Founding: How the Civil War and Reconstruction Remade the Con-stitution* (New York: W. W. Norton, 2019), 15, 11–20.

6. Heather Cox Richardson, *To Make Men Free: A History of the Republican Party* (New York: Basic Books, 2014), xv, 69–70; Jackson Lears, *Rebirth of a Nation: The Making of Modern Amer-ica, 1877–1920* (New York: HarperCollins, 2009), 153, 159–61.

7. Alan Dawley, *Class and Community: The Industrial Revolution in Lynn* (Cambridge, MA: Harvard University Press, 1976), 239. This dynamic was already evident in the late antebellum period; see, for instance, Jonathan A. Glickstein, *American Exceptionalism, American Anxiety: Wages, Competition, and Degraded Labor in the Antebellum United States* (Charlottesville: Uni-versity of Virginia Press, 2002), 142.

8. For the ambiguities of free labor, see Eric Foner, "Free Labor and Nineteenth-Century Political Ideology," in *The Market Revolution in America: Social, Political, and Religious Expressions, 1800–1880*, ed. Melvyn Stokes and Stephen Conway (Charlottesville: University Press of Virginia, 1996), 11–16; Nancy Cohen, *The Reconstruction of American Liberalism, 1865–1914* (Chapel Hill: University of North Carolina Press, 2002), 28–33; James L. Huston, *The British Gentry, the South-ern Planter, and the Northern Family Farmer: Agriculture and Sectional Antagonism in North Amer-ica* (Baton Rouge: Louisiana State University Press, 2015), 188–92; Jonathan A. Glickstein, *Con-cepts of Free Labor in Antebellum America* (New Haven: Yale University Press, 1991). The seminal treatment of free labor ideology is still Eric Foner, *Free Soil, Free Labor, Free Men: The Ideology of the Republican Party before the Civil War* (London: Oxford University Press, 1970).

9. Alex Gourevitch, *From Slavery to the Cooperative Commonwealth: Labor and Republican Liberty in the Nineteenth Century* (New York: Cambridge University Press, 2014), 97–173; Law-rence B. Glickman, *A Living Wage: American Workers and the Making of Consumer Society* (Ithaca: Cornell University Press, 1997), 11–34; Leon Fink, "Class Conflict American-Style," in *In Search of the Working Class: Essays in American Labor History and Political Culture* (Urbana: University of Illinois Press, 1994).

10. Thomas Goebel, "The Political Economy of American Populism from Jackson to the New Deal," *Studies in American Political Development* 11, no. 1 (1997): 109–48; Bruce Palmer, *"Man over Money": The Southern Populist Critique of American Capitalism* (Chapel Hill: University of North Carolina Press, 1980), 9–38, 111–25. See also Tamara Venit Shelton, *A Squatter's Republic: Land and the Politics of Monopoly in California, 1850–1900* (Berkeley: University of California Press, 2013).

11. Eric Foner, *Reconstruction: America's Unfinished Revolution, 1863–1877*, updated ed. (New York: HarperPerennial, 2014 [1988]), 102–10, 128–42; Omar H. Ali, *In the Lion's Mouth: Black Populism in the New South, 1886–1900* (Jackson: University Press of Mississippi, 2010), 13–20.

12. For a discussion of the Republican Party's retreat from the egalitarianism of the Reconstruction period, see Richardson, *To Make Men Free*, 79–138.

13. As Lawrence Glickman has shown, this change was driven partly by (some) labor advocates themselves as they tried to accommodate their ideas to new economic realities. Glickman, *A Living Wage*.

14. Daniel Clark, *Cong. Globe*, 35th Cong., 1st sess., Appendix 92 (March 1858). Another response came from Hannibal Hamlin of Maine, who also rejected the claim that manual labor necessarily implied "servitude": "Far from it. I affirm that the great portion of our laborers at the North own their own homes and they labor to adorn them." *Cong. Globe*, 35th Cong., 1st sess. 1025 (March 1858). These two responses—from Clark and Hamlin—anticipate the trajectory of American freedom over the next 150 years, as the ideal of economic independence was steadily replaced by the composite of freedom of contract, the consumer's freedom to purchase, and the home owner's dominion over his own private lair.

15. Gourevitch, *From Slavery to the Cooperative Commonwealth*, 47–66. For an excellent discussion of the rising ideological significance of freedom of contract, see Amy Dru Stanley, *From Bondage to Contract: Wage Labor, Marriage, and the Market in the Age of Slave Emancipation* (Cambridge: Cambridge University Press, 1998).

16. William Graham Sumner, *What Social Classes Owe to Each Other* (New York: Harper and Brothers, 1883), 26. This transformation had already begun in the Jacksonian Era. It was evident in the rhetoric of certain Whigs, notably Calvin Colton, who argued that American labor was free because it "does not *accept* a price imposed, but *commands* its own price. At least, it is always an *independent* party in the compact." Calvin Colton, "Junius Tracts No. VII. Labor and Capital" (New York: Greeley & McElrath, 1844), 9. See also Stanley, *From Bondage to Contract*, 75–76.

17. *Godcharles v. Wigeman*, quoted in Gourevitch, *From Slavery to the Cooperative Commonwealth*, 56–57.

18. "The landless man is compelled," wrote the *Northampton Democrat*, "—in spite of all laws against slavery and involuntary servitude—to labor for what his more fortunate neighbor chooses to give, or die of starvation. Is this right?" "Freedom of the Public Lands," *Northampton Democrat*, January 26, 1847, p. 2. For a seminal discussion of this shift, see Stanley, *From Bondage to Contract*, 60–97.

19. E. L. Godkin, "The Labor Crisis," *North American Review* 105, no. 216 (1867): 186, 188.

20. Eric Foner, *The Story of American Freedom* (New York: W. W. Norton, 1998), 140–51; Cohen, *The Reconstruction of American Liberalism, 1865–1914*, 209–56; Glickman, *A Living Wage*.

21. Quoted in Cohen, *The Reconstruction of American Liberalism, 1865–1914*, 211. See also Lears, *Rebirth of a Nation*, 262.

22. Paul Frymer, *Building an American Empire: The Era of Territorial and Political Expansion* (Princeton: Princeton University Press, 2017), 155–67; C. Joseph Genetin-Pilawa, *Crooked Paths to Allotment: The Fight over Federal Indian Policy after the Civil War* (Chapel Hill: University of North Carolina Press, 2012), 134–55. On the individualistic assumptions encoded in the concept of *civilization*, see David Wallace Adams, *Education for Extinction: American Indians and the Boarding School Experience, 1875–1928* (Lawrence: University Press of Kansas, 1995), 12–21.

23. Stephen Kantrowitz, "'Not Quite Constitutionalized': The Meanings of 'Civilization' and the Limits of Native American Citizenship," in *The World the Civil War Made*, ed. Gregory P. Downs and Kate Masur (Chapel Hill: University of North Carolina Press, 2015); Frederick E. Hoxie, *This Indian Country: American Indian Activists and the Place They Made* (New York: Penguin Books, 2012), 99–223; White, *The Republic for Which It Stands*, 151–54.

24. Frymer, *Building an American Empire*, 163–64.

25. Kantrowitz, "'Not Quite Constitutionalized,'" 91–94.

26. Ibid.

27. Foner, *The Second Founding*, 71.

28. Laura F. Edwards, "The Reconstruction of Rights: The Fourteenth Amendment and Popular Conceptions of Governance," *Journal of Supreme Court History* 41, no. 3 (2016): 310–28; Foner, *The Second Founding*.

29. "What Is the Test?" *New Orleans Tribune*, November 28, 1867, p. 4. The Fourteenth Amendment was not ratified until 1868, but the Civil Rights Act of 1866 had affirmed a broad slate of equal rights to "persons . . . of every race and color"; the wartime Louisiana Constitution of 1864 had also extended rights of citizenship to many Black men.

30. Eric Foner, "Rights and the Constitution in Black Life during the Civil War and Reconstruction," *Journal of American History* 74, no. 3 (1987): 874–79.

31. Hugh Davis, *"We Will Be Satisfied with Nothing Less": The African American Struggle for Equal Rights in the North during Reconstruction* (Ithaca: Cornell University Press, 2011), 72–132; Tera W. Hunter, *To 'Joy My Freedom: Southern Black Women's Lives and Labors after the Civil War* (Cambridge, MA: Harvard University Press, 1997), 21–43, 74–97.

32. For an excellent discussion of women's rights activism and its fraught relationship to Republican Party politics and ideology, see Melanie Susan Gustafson, *Women and the Republican Party, 1854–1924* (Urbana: University of Illinois Press, 2001).

33. Brackets in original. Elizabeth Cady Stanton, Susan B. Anthony, and Matilda Joslyn Gage, eds., *History of Woman Suffrage*, vol. 3 (Salem, NH: Ayer Company, 1985 [1881–1922]), 51.

34. National Woman Suffrage Association, "Declaration of Rights of the Women of the United States," in *The Selected Papers of Elizabeth Cady Stanton and Susan B. Anthony*, vol. 3, ed. Ann D. Gordon (New Brunswick, NJ: Rutgers University Press, 2003 [1876]), 238, 239.

35. Sojourner Truth, "Address to the First Annual Meeting of the American Equal Rights Association," in *The Concise History of Woman Suffrage: Selections from the Classic Work of Stanton, Anthony, Gage, and Harper*, ed. Mari Jo Buhle and Paul Buhle (Urbana: University of Illinois Press, 1978 [1867]), 235.

36. Stanton, Anthony, and Gage, *History of Woman Suffrage*, 3:592.

37. Effective freedom means being *able* to do what you want to do. It connotes both the absence of interference by others and the *power* to choose among a range of options. Such power typically requires, for example, access to resources.

38. Elizabeth B. Clark, "Anticlericalism and Antistatism," in *Women, Church, and State: Religion and the Culture of Individual Rights in Nineteenth-Century America* (unpublished manuscript, 1999), 66, https://scholarship.law.bu.edu/clark_book/. This view of rights, too, could be grounded in the Declaration of Independence, which after all asserted an equal right to the "pursuit of happiness."

39. Hosea Easton, *A Treatise on the Intellectual Character, and Civil and Political Condition, of the Coloured People of the U. States . . .* (Boston: Isaac Knapp, 1837), 39.

40. Resolutions of the Massachusetts and New York Anti-Slavery Societies (1863), quoted in James M. McPherson, *The Struggle for Equality: Abolitionists and the Negro in the Civil War and Reconstruction* (Princeton: Princeton University Press, 1964), 179. See also Foner, *The Second Founding*, 13–15.

41. Heather Cox Richardson, *The Death of Reconstruction: Race, Labor, and Politics in the Post–Civil War North, 1865–1901* (Cambridge, MA: Harvard University Press, 2001), 53–55; Foner, "Rights and the Constitution in Black Life during the Civil War and Reconstruction," 871.

42. Stanton, Anthony, and Gage, *History of Woman Suffrage*, 3:829.

43. Ibid., 3:61.

44. Ibid., 3:85.

45. Women's suffragists sometimes buttressed their arguments, however, by contrasting the wholesome political influence of American women with some corrupting *other*: Stanton herself defended an "educational qualification," for example, as "our most effective defence against the ignorant foreign vote." Elizabeth Cady Stanton, "E.C.S. to Matilda Joslyn Gage and the National Woman Suffrage Association," in *The Selected Papers of Elizabeth Cady Stanton and Susan B. Anthony*, vol. 3, ed. Ann D. Gordon (New Brunswick, NJ: Rutgers University Press, 2003 [1877]), 310, 311.

46. Even before the Civil War, the emerging Republican Party played a key role in this realignment; see Foner, *Free Soil, Free Labor, Free Men*; John Ashworth, *Slavery, Capitalism, and Politics in the Antebellum Republic*, vol. 2: *The Coming of the Civil War, 1850–1861* (New York: Cambridge University Press, 2007), 287–94.

47. Richard Hofstadter, *Social Darwinism in American Thought*, rev. ed. (New York: George Braziller, 1959 [1944]), 46.

48. Charles Edward Merriam, *American Political Ideas: Studies in the Development of American Political Thought, 1865–1917* (New York: Macmillan, 1920), 315.

49. Harry L. Watson, "Andrew Jackson's Populism," *Tennessee Historical Quarterly* 76 (2017): 237. See also Arthur Schlesinger Jr., *The Age of Jackson* (Boston: Little, Brown, 1945), 518.

50. See, for instance, Horace White, "Freedom of Labor," *Chicago Tribune*, May 8, 1867, p. 2; "The Agrarian Philosophers," *Chicago Tribune*, May 25, 1867; E. L. Godkin, "The Tyranny of the Majority," *North American Review* 104, no. 214 (1867): 224–25; Cohen, *The Reconstruction of American Liberalism, 1865–1914*, 38–39, 47–48, 60, 91–92, 103, 210.

51. Arthur Latham Perry, *Elements of Political Economy*, 2nd ed. (New York: Charles Scribner, 1867), 79, 84. He then clarified that such interference was acceptable only when it protected other rights "which are as well based as the right of exchange."

52. Daniel T. Rodgers, *Atlantic Crossings: Social Politics in a Progressive Age* (Cambridge, MA: Harvard University Press, 1998), 97–111. "The 1890s were littered with . . . academic heresy cases" involving economists, writes Rodgers, which typically ended in their dismissal by wealthy trustees (105).

53. Andrew Carnegie, *Triumphant Democracy: Sixty Years' March of the Republic*, revised ed. (New York: Charles Scribner's Sons, 1912), 52. See also Sidney Fine, *Laissez Faire and the General-Welfare State: A Study of Conflict in American Thought, 1865–1901* (Ann Arbor: University of Michigan Press, 1956), 102–6; Daniel R. Ernst, *Lawyers against Labor: From Individual Rights to Corporate Liberalism* (Urbana: University of Illinois Press, 1995), 31–37.

54. William Graham Sumner, *The Challenge of Facts and Other Essays* (New Haven: Yale University Press, 1914 [1889]), 37, 38. Sumner rejected the idea of natural rights because he worried that, on certain interpretations, they seemed to give idle or profligate people legitimate claim to a share of other people's property. Nonetheless, he argued that his natural, competitive vision of social order was the one that best protected individual rights, properly understood. Sumner, *What Social Classes Owe to Each Other*, 134–38, 163.

55. Andrew Carnegie, "Wealth," *North American Review* 148, no. 391 (1889): 655.

56. For a seminal discussion, see Hofstadter, *Social Darwinism in American Thought*.

57. Fine, *Laissez Faire and the General-Welfare State*, 41–46; Judy Hilkey, *Character Is Capital: Success Manuals and Manhood in Gilded Age America* (Chapel Hill: University of North Carolina Press, 1997), 78–85; Clinton Rossiter, *Conservatism in America: The Thankless Persuasion*, 2nd ed. (New York: Knopf, 1962), 146–53.

58. After likening the laws of competition to the laws of gravity, he noted that "all natural laws have their ill side: gravitation, which keeps us firm on our feet so long as we are on solid ground, knocks us to pieces if we attempt to walk off a house-top or over the opening of a pit. It is not the law, but the attempt to ignore it, that gives us trouble." R. R. Bowker, *Economics for the People: Being Plain Talks on Economics Especially for Use in Business, in Schools and in Women's Reading Classes*, 4th ed. (New York: Harper Bros., 1893 [1886]), 60, 269, 62.

59. John G. Cawelti, *Apostles of the Self-Made Man* (Chicago: University of Chicago Press, 1965), 173.

60. Lyman Atwater, "The Labor Question in Its Economic and Christian Aspects," *Presbyterian Quarterly and Princeton Review* 1, no. 3 (1872): 485, 482. See also Henry Ward Beecher, "Plymouth Pulpit: The Strike and Its Lessons," *Christian Union* 16, no. 6 (1877): 112–14; Henry F. May, *Protestant Churches and Industrial America* (New York: Harper & Brothers, 1949). Of course, American Protestantism was hardly monolithic: the last two decades of the nineteenth century also witnessed the rise of the social gospel movement, which rejected economic laissez-faire and sought deliberate remedies for the poverty and inequality brought about by the industrial revolution.

61. May, *Protestant Churches and Industrial America*, 143–44.

62. Marc-William Palen, *The "Conspiracy" of Free Trade: The Anglo-American Struggle over Empire and Economic Globalization, 1846–1896* (Cambridge: Cambridge University Press, 2016), 123.

63. Merriam, *American Political Ideas*, 325–26; Fine, *Laissez Faire and the General-Welfare State*, 30, 112–13; Rowland Berthoff, *An Unsettled People: Social Order and Disorder in American History* (New York: Harper & Row, 1971), 332–61.

64. David F. Prindle, *The Paradox of Democratic Capitalism: Politics and Economics in American Thought* (Baltimore: Johns Hopkins University Press, 2006), 112–13; Lears, *Rebirth of a Nation*, 82–86, 127–28.

65. Fine, *Laissez Faire and the General-Welfare State*, 104–5; Brian Balogh, *A Government out of Sight: The Mystery of National Authority in Nineteenth-Century America* (Cambridge: Cambridge University Press, 2009), 315–22, 329–39; Leon Fink, "Labor, Liberty, and the Law: Trade Unionism and the Problem of the American Constitutional Order," *Journal of American History* 74, no. 3 (1987): 904–25; White, *The Republic for Which It Stands*, 314. The redescription of the corporation in the mythic language of American rights-bearer remains one of the great conceptual sleights of hand in American political history.

66. This denial can be seen, for example, in the Democrats' argument that cheap land in the West served as a critical *safety valve* for eastern labor. So long as this alternative existed, they had argued, wage labor could honestly be described as a choice, a meaningful exercise of freedom of contract. See chapter 4, pages 61–63.

67. Cohen, *The Reconstruction of American Liberalism, 1865–1914*, 31–40; Stanley, *From Bondage to Contract*, 35–55. Horace White, for example, the influential anti-union editor of the *Chicago Tribune*, saw violations of contract freedom as violations of the "inalienable rights of man." Cohen, *The Reconstruction of American Liberalism, 1865–1914*, 39. Stanley offers a different account of this retrenchment: she argues that freedom of contract was a linchpin of the abolitionist conception of freedom dating back well before the Civil War, and that it migrated from their rhetoric into wider circulation after emancipation. For reasons explored in both chapters 8 and 9, I am skeptical of this interpretation; see chapter 8, pages 180–184 and note 149.

68. Alfred B. Mason and John J. Lalor, *The Primer of Political Economy: In Sixteen Definitions and Forty Propositions* (Chicago: A. C. McClurg, 1891 [1875]), 37.

69. Stanley, *From Bondage to Contract*, 60–97. For evidence of this rhetorical tendency even among critics of laissez-faire orthodoxies, see, for instance, Francis Amasa Walker, *Political Economy* (New York: Henry Holt, 1885 [1883]), 228, 223–24.

70. None other than John Dewey thought that George's writing circulated more widely "than almost all other books on political economy put together." Quoted in White, *The Republic for Which It Stands*, 453.

71. Henry George, *Progress and Poverty* (London: Aziloth Books, 2016 [1879]), 205, 204.

72. Ibid., 238.

73. Ibid., 175–83, 266–74, 337–40. George believed, however, that this meritocracy would be enhanced by a broad range of public goods, administered by the state, designed not just to widen and equalize opportunities but also to add to the comforts of life. Rising land values would produce a windfall of tax revenue whose benefits, he thought, should be widely shared.

74. The Populist newspaper, the *Wool Hat*, quoted in Palmer, "Man over Money," 12. Eric Foner describes the Populist movement as "the last great political manifestation of the nineteenth-century vision of America as a commonwealth of small producers" (*The Story of American Freedom*, 127).

75. James "Cyclone" Davis, quoted in Goebel, "The Political Economy of American Populism from Jackson to the New Deal," 128.

76. This interpretation of the Populists is indebted mainly to Bruce Palmer, Lawrence Goodwyn, and Thomas Goebel. For a contrasting interpretation, see Charles Postel, *The Populist Vision* (Oxford: Oxford University Press, 2007). Postel severs the Populists almost entirely from their intellectual and political antecedents. Mostly ignoring the powerful, producerist language of grievance that courses through Populist writings and speeches and places them in a century-long tradition of egalitarian protest, he turns them into proto-Progressive modernizers and state-builders.

77. Ibid., 173–203.

78. See Ali, *In the Lion's Mouth*.

79. See, for instance, L. L. Polk, "Agricultural Depression: Its Causes, the Remedy" (Raleigh: Edwards & Broughton, 1890), 10–11, 24–32.

80. Palmer, "Man over Money," 28–49. See also Lawrence Goodwyn, *Democratic Promise: The Populist Moment in America* (New York: Oxford University Press, 1976), 351–86.

81. James "Cyclone" Davis, *A Political Revelation* (Dallas: Advance Publishing, 1894), 100–101.

82. "Not the *absence* of non-liberal ideas," writes Eric Foner, "but the *persistence* of a radical vision resting on small property inhibited the rise of socialist ideologies" in the United States. Eric Foner, "Why Is There No Socialism in the United States?" *History Workshop*, no. 17 (1984): 63. See also Huston, *The British Gentry, the Southern Planter, and the Northern Family Farmer*, 188–89.

83. Of course, many economic egalitarians have *also* been white supremacists whose vision of equality ended at the boundary of the Anglo-Saxon race.

84. For the decisive influence of southern white supremacy on the New Deal, see Ira Katznelson, *Fear Itself: The New Deal and the Origins of Our Time* (New York: W. W. Norton, 2013).

85. Frederick Douglass, "Self-Made Men," in *The Essential Douglass: Selected Writings and Speeches*, ed. Nicholas Buccola (Indianapolis: Hackett, 2016 [1893]), 348; Irvin G. Wyllie, *The Self-Made Man in America: The Myth of Rags to Riches* (New Brunswick, NJ: Rutgers University Press, 1954), 90, 55–93; Cawelti, *Apostles of the Self-Made Man*, 167–99.

86. Wyllie, *The Self-Made Man in America*, 65–66.

87. Orison Swett Marden, *The Young Man Entering Business* (New York: Thomas Y. Crowell and Co., 1903), 210.

88. James Garfield, "Elements of Success: Address before the Students of the Spencerian Business College, Washington, D.C., June 29, 1869," in *President Garfield and Education: Hiram College Memorial*, ed. B. A. Hinsdale (Boston: James R. Osgood & Co., 1882 [1869]), 332. See also Richardson, *The Death of Reconstruction*, 61–72.

89. For a discussion of the persistence of this meritocratic myth in American politics today, see Michael J. Sandel, *The Tyranny of Merit: What's Become of the Common Good?* (New York: Farrar, Straus and Giroux, 2020); Daniel Markovits, *The Meritocracy Trap: How America's Foundational Myth Feeds Inequality, Dismantles the Middle Class, and Devours the Elite* (New York: Penguin Books, 2019).

90. Clayne Pope, "Inequality in the Nineteenth Century," in *The Cambridge Economic History of the United States*, vol. 2, ed. Stanley L. Engerman and Robert E. Gallman (Cambridge: Cambridge University Press, 2000).

91. Christopher Lasch, *The True and Only Heaven: Progress and Its Critics*, 1st ed. (New York: Norton, 1991), 486. Lasch underemphasizes the extent to which the nineteenth-century version of this ideal depended on territorial conquest and expansion.

92. Richard Weiss, *The American Myth of Success: From Horatio Alger to Norman Vincent Peale* (Urbana: University of Illinois Press, 1988 [1969]), 48–63.

93. Cawelti, *Apostles of the Self-Made Man*, 121–22; Weiss, *The American Myth of Success*, 116.

94. William Holmes McGuffey, "Charlie and Rob," in *McGuffey's Third Eclectic Reader*, rev. ed. (New York: American Book Co., 1920 [1879]), 107; Stanley W. Lindberg, "Institutionalizing a Myth: The Mcguffey Readers and the Self-Made Man," *Journal of American Culture* 2, no. 1 (1979). "The road to wealth, to honor, to usefulness, and happiness," says the 1843 edition of *McGuffey's Third Eclectic Reader*, "is open to all, and all who will, may enter upon it with the almost certain prospect of success"—provided of course that they applied themselves diligently and virtuously. Quoted in Weiss, *The American Myth of Success*, 33.

95. Weiss, *The American Myth of Success*, 6; see also pp. 116–17. For women, meanwhile, virtue was typically defined by "respectability": women embodied their respectability by marrying respectable men and assisting their upward trajectory with their own habits of thrift and industry, and by raising virtuous children.

96. Horace Greeley, "An Address on Success in Business . . ." (New York: S. S. Packard, 1867), 38.

97. Weiss, *The American Myth of Success*, 115; Wyllie, *The Self-Made Man in America*, 54.

98. For a perfect expression of this refashioned faith, see Beecher, "Plymouth Pulpit: The Strike and Its Lessons."

99. W. E. B. Du Bois, *Black Reconstruction: An Essay toward a History of the Part Which Black Folk Played in the Attempt to Reconstruct Democracy in America, 1860–1880* (New York: Harcourt, Brace & Co., 1935), 182.

100. Rossiter, *Conservatism in America: The Thankless Persuasion*, 203. On the scale of radicalism alone, Rossiter goes so far as to class the Fords and Rockefellers of the world alongside the Lenins and Maos. Ibid., 205–6.

101. White, *The Republic for Which It Stands*, 275–86, 290–305, 379–84, 635–49, 739–46; Lears, *Rebirth of a Nation*, 12–50; Foner, *Reconstruction: America's Unfinished Revolution*, 425–44; Gary Gerstle, *American Crucible: Race and Nation in the Twentieth Century* (Princeton: Princeton University Press, 2001), 14–80; Jean Pfaelzer, *Driven Out: The Forgotten War against Chinese Americans* (New York: Random House, 2007).

102. For a seminal discussion, see Richardson, *The Death of Reconstruction*, 83–121, 183–224.

103. Josiah Strong, *Our Country: Its Possible Future and Its Present Crisis* (New York: Baker & Taylor, 1885), 159, 173, 175.

104. W. E. B. Du Bois, "Of the Coming of John," in *The Souls of Black Folk* (Chicago: A. C. McClurg & Co., 1903), 230, 233.

105. Ibid., 234, 243, 239, 240.

106. "We daily hear," writes Du Bois, "that an education that encourages aspiration, that sets the loftiest of ideals and seeks as an end culture and character rather than bread-winning, is the privilege of white men and the danger and delusion of black" ("Of the Training of Black Men," in *The Souls of Black Folk*, 94).

107. Douglass, "Self-Made Men," 340, 347, 346. Jack Turner emphasizes this "practical" utility of the myth for Douglass. Jack Turner, *Awakening to Race: Individualism and Social Consciousness in America* (Chicago: University of Chicago Press, 2012), 50–55.

108. Self-made men, he argued, are men "who owe little or nothing to birth, relationship, friendly surroundings," men who rose "without the aid of any of the favoring conditions by which other men usually rise in the world." Douglass was well aware that, as a successful Black man, he exemplified this ideal in a way that white counterparts never could. Douglass, "Self-Made Men," 335.

109. Ibid., 341.

110. Turner, *Awakening to Race*, 55–62; Nicholas Buccola, *The Political Thought of Frederick Douglass: In Pursuit of American Liberty* (New York: New York University Press, 2012), 114–25.

111. Du Bois, *Black Reconstruction*, 182–83.

Chapter 11

1. See, for instance, Martin Gilens, *Why Americans Hate Welfare: Race, Media, and the Politics of Antipoverty Policy* (Chicago: University of Chicago Press, 1999); Jessica Autumn Brown, "The New 'Southern Strategy': Immigration, Race, and 'Welfare Dependency' in Contemporary U.S. Republican Discourse," *Geopolitics, History, and International Relations* 8, no. 2 (2016): 22–41.

2. Daniel T. Rodgers, *Age of Fracture* (Cambridge, MA: Harvard University Press, 2011), 72.

3. For an illuminating study of the mythology of free enterprise in twentieth-century America, see Lawrence B. Glickman, *Free Enterprise: An American History* (New Haven: Yale University Press, 2019).

4. *Goodridge v. Department of Public Health,* 440 Mass. 309, pp. 328, 313, 312.

5. https://obamawhitehouse.archives.gov/the-press-office/2013/12/04/remarks-president-economic-mobility. "The American dream that we were all raised on," Bill Clinton proclaimed in 1993, "is a simple but powerful one: If you work hard and play by the rules, you should be given a chance to go as far as your God-given ability will take you." Cited in Michael J. Sandel, *The Tyranny of Merit: What's Become of the Common Good?* (New York: Farrar, Straus and Giroux, 2020), 67. For another prominent example, see Hillary Clinton's speech on July 13, 2015; https://www.vox.com/2015/7/13/8953349/Clinton-economic-speech-transcript.

6. See, for instance, Louis Hartz, *The Liberal Tradition in America: An Interpretation of American Political Thought since the Revolution* (New York: Harcourt, Brace & World, 1955), 3–23, 35–66; Richard Hofstadter, *The American Political Tradition and the Men Who Made It* (New York: Vintage Books, 1989 [1948]), xxxiii–xl; Daniel J. Boorstin, *The Genius of American Politics* (Chicago: University of Chicago Press, 1953), 1–7, 22–29, 170–89. "There have been dreamers enough in American history," wrote Hartz, ". . . but the central course of our political thought has betrayed an unconquerable pragmatism" (*The Liberal Tradition in America*, 43). Some of the more recent defenders of the consensus view—such as J. David Greenstone and Samuel Huntington—have allowed more room for moralistic zeal.

7. There is no denying that white supremacy is a form of collectivism. The point here is that it has also formed a symbiotic relationship with America's dominant, individualist myths.

8. This argument was forcefully articulated by W. E. B. Du Bois in 1935; see W. E. B. Du Bois, *Black Reconstruction: An Essay toward a History of the Part Which Black Folk Played in the Attempt to Reconstruct Democracy in America, 1860–1880* (New York: Harcourt, Brace & Co., 1935), 700–701. See also James Brewer Stewart, "The Emergence of Racial Modernity and the Rise of the White North, 1790–1840," *Journal of the Early Republic* 18, no. 2 (1998): 181–217.

9. For different approaches to this insight, see, for instance, Heather Cox Richardson, *How the South Won the Civil War: Oligarchy, Democracy, and the Continuing Fight for the Soul of America* (New York: Oxford University Press, 2020); Arlie Russell Hochschild, *Strangers in Their Own Land: Anger and Mourning on the American Right* (New York: The New Press, 2016).

10. Gilens, *Why Americans Hate Welfare*; Jonathan Metzl, *Dying of Whiteness: How the Politics of Racial Resentment Is Killing America's Heartland* (New York: Basic Books, 2019).

11. Or they fantasized about a peaceful, contractual expansion, which was periodically betrayed by the irrational violence of "savages."

12. For further evidence, see Donald R. Kinder and Tali Mendelberg, "Individualism Reconsidered: Principles and Prejudice in Contemporary American Opinion," in *Racialized Politics: The Debate about Racism in America*, ed. David O. Sears, Jim Sidanius, and Lawrence Bobo (Chicago: University of Chicago Press, 2000).

13. As of 2019, the average white family owned nearly *eight times* as much wealth as the average Black family. Neil Bhutta et al., "Disparities in Wealth by Race and Ethnicity in the 2019 Survey of Consumer Finances," *FEDS Notes* (2020), https://doi.org/10.17016/2380-7172.2797. For a penetrating discussion of race and the American dream, see Jennifer Hochschild, *Facing Up to the American Dream: Race, Class, and the Soul of the Nation* (Princeton: Princeton University Press, 1995).

14. Indeed, one of the key functions of foundational myth is to transmute moral and political ideals into glorified *descriptions* of the nation and its history (which can then serve as the basis of national identity).

15. Jack Turner, "American Individualism and Structural Injustice: Tocqueville, Gender, and Race," *Polity* 40, no. 2 (2008): 215. See also Charles W. Mills, "White Ignorance," in *Black Rights/ White Wrongs: The Critique of Racial Liberalism* (New York: Oxford University Press, 2017 [2007]).

16. For an excellent discussion of free enterprise as a "language of naturalization" among twentieth-century conservatives, see Glickman, *Free Enterprise: An American History*, 4, 167–97. Glickman explores how these conservatives labored to present the New Deal as an "artificial" distortion of the "natural laws of economics" (173).

17. For an illustration of this point, see Bernard Harcourt's description of the litany of rules and regulations that govern modern stock and commodity exchanges, beginning with the Chicago Board of Trade in the late nineteenth century. Bernard Harcourt, *The Illusion of Free Markets: Punishment and the Myth of Natural Order* (Cambridge, MA: Harvard University Press, 2011), 188, 190.

18. One of the lasting residues of market utopianism is the notion that utility maximization is a value-free premise that is somehow given or revealed to us by the nature of things; this fiction continues to animate a great deal of neoclassical economics. In fact, the conviction that economic and political rules should be calibrated to maximize utility, regardless of their distributive effects, is a controversial moral position rejected by most moral and political philosophers today.

19. For further discussion of this point, see Liam Murphy and Thomas Nagel, *The Myth of Ownership: Taxes and Justice* (Oxford: Oxford University Press, 2002), 31–37; Robert B. Reich, *Saving Capitalism: For the Many, Not the Few* (New York: Knopf, 2015). For a more global point of view, see Joseph Stiglitz, *Making Globalization Work: The Next Steps to Global Justice* (New York: Norton, 2006).

20. The market is better understood as a form of political *indirectness*, which carries both great potential for human freedom and considerable danger to it.

21. Friedrich Hayek, for example, whose work had been immensely influential on the American right, imagined market society as "a spontaneous order or cosmos" akin to an "order of nature." F. A. Hayek, "The Confusion of Language in Political Thought" (London: Institute of Economic Affairs, 1968), 15, 28, 11. See also Glickman, *Free Enterprise: An American History*, 167–97.

22. Karl Polanyi, *The Great Transformation: The Political and Economic Origins of Our Time* (Boston: Beacon Press, 1957 [1944]), 178–91. This fantasy has more than a little in common with the Marxist hope that the politics will be entirely superseded, in communist utopia, by an apolitical "administration of things." Both reflect an aspiration to transcend politics itself, which is one of the defining characteristics of modern utopian thought.

23. John William Ward, "Jacksonian Democratic Thought: 'A Natural Charter of Privilege,'" in *The Development of an American Culture*, ed. Stanley Coben and Lorman Ratner (New York: St. Martin's Press, 1983 [1970]), 72. See also John Dewey, *Liberalism and Social Action* (Amherst, NY: Prometheus Books, 2000 [1935]), 19–20, 41–60.

24. The notion, explored in chapter 7, that freedom is wholly unimpaired by submission to the market's natural constraints has been defended by several of the libertarian thinkers whose ideas have deeply shaped the ideology of the American right, from Herbert Spencer to Ludwig von Mises and Friedrich Hayek. For a helpful discussion, see Eric MacGilvray, *The Invention of Market Freedom* (Cambridge: Cambridge University Press, 2011), 166–73.

25. Clayne Pope, "Inequality in the Nineteenth Century," in *The Cambridge Economic History of the United States*, vol. 2, ed. Stanley L. Engerman and Robert E. Gallman (Cambridge: Cambridge University Press, 2000).

26. Sandel, *The Tyranny of Merit*, 44–45.

27. Miles Corak, "Income Inequality, Equality of Opportunity, and Intergenerational Mobility," *Journal of Economic Perspectives* 27, no. 3 (2013): 79–102; Espen Bratberg et al., "A Comparison of Intergenerational Mobility Curves in Germany, Norway, Sweden, and the U.S.," *Scandinavian Journal of Economics* 119, no. 1 (2017): 72–101; Pablo A. Mitnik and David B. Grusky, "Economic Mobility in the United States" (Pew Charitable Trusts and the Russell Sage Foundation, 2015); Raj Chetty et al., "The Fading American Dream: Trends in Absolute Income Mobility since 1940," *Science* 356, no. 6336 (2017): 398–406; Joseph P. Ferrie, "History Lessons: The End of American Exceptionalism? Mobility in the United States since 1850," *Journal of Economic Perspectives* 19, no. 3 (2005): 199–215.

28. Miles Corak, "Economic Mobility," in *State of the Union: The Poverty and Inequality Report*, special issue of *Pathways: A Magazine on Poverty, Inequality, and Social Policy* (2016): 51–57.

29. "A Broken Social Elevator? How to Promote Social Mobility" (Paris: OECD, 2018), 287–333; Greg J. Duncan and Richard Murnane, eds., *Whither Opportunity? Rising Inequality, Schools, and Children's Life Chances* (New York: Russell Sage Foundation, 2011).

30. It is significant that the very moment that arguably marked the high tide of antiaristocratic popular sentiment in America was simultaneously a moment in which Americans in both major parties proclaimed that the world—and especially the economy—was "governed too much."

31. John M. Murrin, "Feudalism, Communalism, and the Yeoman Freeholder: The American Revolution Considered as a Social Accident," in *Rethinking America: From Empire to Republic*, ed. John M. Murrin (New York: Oxford University Press, 2018 [1973]), 149. For further discussion, see Elizabeth Anderson, "When the Market Was 'Left,'" in *Private Government: How Employers Rule Our Lives (and Why We Don't Talk about It)* (Princeton: Princeton University Press, 2017), 1–36.

32. For an excellent discussion of this anxiety and its sources in the early republic, see Gordon Wood, *The Radicalism of the American Revolution* (New York: Random House, 1992), 305–25.

33. Jackson Lears, *Something for Nothing: Luck in America* (New York: Penguin Books, 2003), 3–4, 97–145.

34. "In virtually every one of the countless biographies of American heroes," writes Sacvan Bercovitch, "the author insists that 'true individualism' is not something unique—not a Byronic or Nietzschean assertion of superiority—but an exemplum of American enterprise: a model of progress and control that typifies the society as a whole." Sacvan Bercovitch, *The American Jeremiad* (Madison: University of Wisconsin Press, 1978), 156.

35. See ibid., 132–75; Hartz, *The Liberal Tradition in America*, 47–54.

36. Eric Foner, *Reconstruction: America's Unfinished Revolution, 1863–1877*, updated ed. (New York: HarperPerennial, 2014 [1988]), 124–75; Jonathan A. Glickstein, *American Exceptionalism, American Anxiety: Wages, Competition, and Degraded Labor in the Antebellum United States* (Charlottesville: University of Virginia Press, 2002), 79–87.

37. Daniel T. Rodgers, *The Work Ethic in Industrial America, 1850–1920*, 2nd ed. (Chicago: University of Chicago Press, 2014 [1978]), 30–64.

38. Dewey, *Liberalism and Social Action*, 45–46. See also Herbert Croly, *Progressive Democracy* (New York: Macmillan, 1914), 382–83.

39. Croly, *Progressive Democracy*, 380. See also Christopher Lasch, *The True and Only Heaven: Progress and Its Critics*, 1st ed. (New York: Norton, 1991), 206–8, 340–42.

40. For a philosophically sophisticated version of this idea, see Philippe Van Parijs, *Basic Income: A Radical Proposal for a Free Society and a Sane Economy* (Cambridge, MA: Harvard University Press, 2017).

41. "Welfare dependence," wrote Judith Shklar in 1991, "has become the new focus of Jacksonian fears." Judith Shklar, *American Citizenship: The Quest for Inclusion* (Cambridge, MA: Harvard University Press, 1991), 96.

42. Ibid., 94, 96. For an alternative way of imagining state benefits, one need only consider the Alaska Permanent Fund, which conservative Alaskans have come to see as their rightful share of the state's natural resource wealth.

43. Examples of this view abound. Richard Posner offers an influential example of its right-leaning versions, Ronald Dworkin of its left-leaning counterparts. In fact, this liberal constitutionalist vision was already strongly implicit in the *Federalist Papers*, which imagined politics as a competition between rival, self-interested factions, unfolding within the bounds of a just constitutional order and supervised by virtuous elites.

44. For a recent version of this critique, see Patrick J. Deneen, *Why Liberalism Failed* (New Haven: Yale University Presss, 2018).

45. One of the clear results of this co-optation has been the redirection of reformist evangelical zeal toward a set of political objectives—such as the criminalization of abortion—that are entirely unthreatening to the concentrated economic power of American plutocrats.

46. On the egalitarian potentials of civic nationalism, see, for instance, Eric Foner, *The Story of American Freedom* (New York: W. W. Norton, 1998), 219–47.

47. This posture reflects what political theorist Susan McWilliams has called "tragic awareness," which stands opposed to both utopian fancy and exceptionalist conceit. Susan McWilliams, "The Tragedy in American Political Thought," *American Political Thought* 3 (2014): 137–45; Susan McWilliams Barndt, *The American Road Trip and American Political Thought* (Lanham, MD: Lexington Books, 2018), 91–92.

48. A fuller response would, among other things, explore the many ways in which modern collectivist ideologies—ethnocultural, communitarian, and socialist—have also been weaponized and turned into ideologies of oppression. In fact, there exists no sustained tradition of political thought that has escaped the last two centuries without being harnessed for moral evil.

49. For a compelling elaboration of this argument, see Charles W. Mills, "Occupy Liberalism!" in *Black Rights/White Wrongs: The Critique of Racial Liberalism* (New York: Oxford University Press, 2017 [2012]).

Appendix

1. "Individualism" is also used to describe a wide range of phenomena that lie beyond the scope of intellectual history. It is sometimes used, for example, to describe *sociological* patterns that have arisen with the disintegration of traditional or premodern societies. See, for instance, Lawrence Frederick Kohl, *The Politics of Individualism: Parties and the American Character in the Jacksonian Era* (New York: Oxford University Press, 1989), 6–18.

2. For a more detailed exposition of these categories, see Alex Zakaras, "Individualism," in *Encyclopedia of Political Thought*, vol. 5, ed. Michael Gibbons et al. (New York: Wiley-Blackwell, 2014); Steven Lukes, *Individualism* (New York: Harper & Row, 1973).

3. Emphasis in original. Lukes, *Individualism*, 45.

4. Ibid., 45–51; Georg Simmel, "Freedom and the Individual," in *On Individuality and Social Forms*, ed. D. N. Levine (Chicago: University of Chicago Press, 1971), 218–22. There have of course been exceptions: Friedrich Nietzsche, for example, was a moral individualist.

5. Daniel Walker Howe, *Making the American Self: Jonathan Edwards to Abraham Lincoln* (Oxford: Oxford University Press, 2009 [1997]), 9.

6. Defenders of American patriarchy, for example, have long argued that the best way to honor women's *equal dignity* (before God) was to subject them to male control and protect them from their own irrational proclivities.

7. William G. McLoughlin, *New England Dissent, 1630–1833: The Baptists and the Separation of Church and State*, vol. 2 (Cambridge, MA: Harvard University Press, 1971), 1282. For seminal discussions, see Nathan O. Hatch, *The Democratization of American Christianity* (New Haven: Yale University Press, 1989); Richard Hofstadter, *Anti-Intellectualism in American Life* (New York: Knopf, 1963).

8. Clinton Rossiter, *Conservatism in America: The Thankless Persuasion*, 2nd ed. (New York: Knopf, 1962), 72–73.

9. Joyce Appleby, *Inheriting the Revolution: The First Generation of Americans* (Cambridge, MA: Belknap Press, 2000), 7; Joyce Appleby, *Capitalism and a New Social Order: The Republican Vision of the 1790s* (New York: New York University Press, 1984), 94. Alexis de Tocqueville's *Democracy in America* remains one of the most penetrating analyses of social individualism in the United States. Unfortunately, his explicit definition of individualism is misleading. He famously defined individualism as "a reflective and tranquil sentiment that disposes each citizen to cut himself off from the mass of his fellow men and withdraw into the circle of family and friends, so that, having created a little society for his own use, he gladly leaves the larger society to take care of itself." Using this definition—which does not do justice to Tocqueville's own analysis—we would have to describe the utopian socialists who retreated into small communes

in Jacksonian America as individualists. Alexis de Tocqueville, *Democracy in America*, trans. Arthur Goldhammer, vol. 2 (New York: Library of America, 2004 [1840]), 585.

10. Richard Hofstadter, *The American Political Tradition and the Men Who Made It* (New York: Vintage Books, 1989 [1948]), xxxvii.

11. By "tradition," I mean two things: (a) the existence of similar patterns of thought that persist over time, and (b) a measure of self-referential awareness, so that at least *some* of those who express these ideas understand themselves to be drawing on, interpreting, or elaborating the arguments of like-minded people who came before them. Such awareness is obviously not available to any tradition's earliest practitioners. Note that on this view, the semantic question of whether people used the term "liberal" to describe themselves is not central.

12. Judith Shklar, "The Liberalism of Fear," in *Liberalism and the Moral Life*, ed. Nancy L. Rosenblum (Cambridge, MA: Harvard University Press, 1989), 21.

13. There is an important assumption here: liberals suppose that most of the time, people care most deeply about their private lives and relationships; these are the things that, in their own eyes, make their lives go well or poorly.

14. Shklar, "The Liberalism of Fear," 21.

15. Although this usage has been fairly well established among political theorists for over a century, historians today often resist it. Historians of the United States often use the term "liberalism" to refer to what I have described as economic individualism, joined to various other historically specific commitments. See, for instance, Richard White, *The Republic for Which It Stands: The United States during Reconstruction and the Gilded Age, 1865–1896* (New York: Oxford University Press, 2017), 172–76. Or they define it polemically in ways that already incorporate leading anti-liberal criticisms. See, for instance, Nancy Cohen, *The Reconstruction of American Liberalism, 1865–1914* (Chapel Hill: University of North Carolina Press, 2002), 6–9.

16. For seminal discussions, see, for instance, John Dewey, *Liberalism and Social Action* (Amherst, NY: Prometheus Books, 2000 [1935]); Milton Friedman, *Capitalism and Freedom* (Chicago: University of Chicago Press, 2002 [1962]).

17. It is perhaps worth clarifying that *all* liberals—on both the inclusive and exclusive ends of the spectrum—argue that equal rights are owed *only* to members of a certain group, and all offer explanations as to what makes this group uniquely worthy of moral and political consideration. For inclusive liberals, this group is typically the human species; members of other (known) species are excluded. In this sense, liberal ideals are always linked to both collective identity and moral hierarchy.

18. For further elaboration of these alternative tendencies within liberalism, see, for instance, Will Kymlicka, *Liberalism, Community, and Culture* (Oxford: Clarendon Press, 1989); Jacob T. Levy, "Liberalism's Divide, After Socialism and Before," *Social Philosophy and Policy* 20, no. 1 (2003): 278–97; William A. Galston, "Two Concepts of Liberalism," *Ethics* 105, no. 3 (1995): 516–34; Stephen Macedo, *Liberal Virtues: Citizenship, Virtue, and Community in Liberal Constitutionalism* (Oxford: Clarendon Press, 1990).

19. Levy, "Liberalism's Divide, After Socialism and Before," 282.

20. See, for instance, Jeffrey Stout, *Blessed Are the Organized: Grassroots Democracy in America* (Princeton: Princeton University Press, 2010). The last two paragraphs contain three separate points: the first is about social ontology, or how liberals tend to imagine the basic "building blocks" of human societies; the second is about ethics, or how liberals imagine the good or

happy life; the third is about politics, and how liberals imagine the political preconditions of personal freedom. In all three areas, many liberals have treated group identity as fundamental.

21. See, for instance, Yascha Mounk, *The People vs. Democracy: Why Our Freedom Is in Danger and How to Save It* (Cambridge, MA: Harvard University Press, 2018); Michael J. Sandel, *The Tyranny of Merit: What's Become of the Common Good?* (New York: Farrar, Straus and Giroux, 2020).

INDEX

abolitionists: activism of, 190, 193, 369n193; American ideals of, 160–61, 162–65, 169–70, 172; appeals to empathy by, 161, 187, 188, 189–90, 194, 283, 367–68n179; Black, 110, 129, 162, 164, 189, 193, 253, 367nn175–76; Christian principles of, 161, 188–92, 194, 234; egalitarianism of, 190, 367–68n179; emotional appeals of, 188–90, 194, 367–68n179; factions of, 162, 172, 192, 193, 368n191; on government responsibility for slavery, 172, 360n72; individualism of, 192–94; legacy of, 161, 177; moral arguments of, 172–73, 188–92, 194, 234; on natural rights, 160, 161, 166, 169–72, 174–80, 209, 252–53, 373n30; newspapers of, 179, 180, 182, 188, 193, 357n35; objectives of, 187–88; Protestantism and, 161, 162, 166–71, 173–74, 188–92, 194, 361n82; on racial equality, 23, 24, 181, 364n128; radical, 15, 21, 359n60, 360n70; in Reconstruction era, 194–95; rights-bearer myth and, 6, 107, 129, 160, 282–83; rights language used by, 162, 165, 169–72, 174–80, 190, 196, 360n75; self-made man myth and, 238; on sources of racial injustice, 180–84, 185–86; on structural roots of slavery, 192–93, 368–69n192; use of term, 354n5; violence against, 179–80, 181, 185; women, 193. *See also* slavery
ACS. *See* American Colonization Society
Adams, John, 40, 134
Adams, John Quincy, 56, 57, 95, 356n24

African Americans: abolitionists, 110, 129, 162, 164, 189, 193, 253, 367nn175–76; citizenship of, 21, 24, 251, 283, 373n33, 385n29; civil rights of, 178–79, 196; dependence seen, 55, 73, 265, 319n105; deportation proposals for, 165, 178; education of, 265–66, 267, 390n106; escaped slaves, 127, 163, 188, 189, 191, 238; free laborers, 247, 249, 257; independent proprietor myth and, 246–47, 281; kidnappings of, 178–79, 189, 363n114, 363n116; land ownership by, 267, 281; Populists, 259; racist stereotypes of, 22, 55, 73, 127–28, 185–86, 265, 273, 274, 341n130, 366n160, 367n178; rights of, 129, 174, 177–79, 184, 251–53, 254, 265, 363n109, 385n29; self-made man myth and, 238, 265–67, 390n108; views of July Fourth, 194, 354n2; voting rights of, 73, 179, 187, 245, 251, 253; women, 252. *See also* racial discrimination; racial hierarchy; racial injustice; slavery
agrarian populism, 259, 260
agrarian republic: elites in, 50; independent proprietor myth and, 16, 44, 45–47, 52; Jefferson's vision of, 35, 45–46, 81, 275
agriculture: corporate, 264; markets, 45–46, 48, 211; slave labor in, 3, 26, 74, 127, 191; technology in, 217, 243; women's labor in, 130. *See also* farmers; Southern planters
Aiken, John, 215, 220
Alger, Horatio, 254, 262–63
Allen, William, 58–59, 85, 87, 88, 152

industrialization in, 74, 225; inequality in, 39–42, 44–45, 116, 166, 220, 225; laborers in, 71, 116, 121, 220, 225; landowners in, 38–39, 41, 45, 64–65; Levellers in, 114, 129, 334n27, 334n29; neoclassical republicanism in, 34, 37–40, 50–51, 64–65, 137, 303n2, 304–5n12; Parliament of, 41; political economy in, 26, 142, 145, 153; socialism in, 121; traditions of freedom in, 24–25, 207, 300n41; voting rights in, 39–40. *See also* Scottish Enlightenment

Brown, William Wells, 163, 362n92

Brownson, Orestes A., 88, 350n103

Burges, Tristan, 48, 371n12

Burgh, James, 157

Burke, Edmund, 208, 209, 372n23, 375n61

Bushman, Richard L., 218

businesses. *See* corporations; market economy; small proprietors

Calvinist theology: criticism from evangelicals, 98; Locke and, 333n13; pessimism of, 134, 140, 230; predestination in, 229; on sin, 204, 230; on value of labor, 112. *See also* Protestantism; Puritans

Camp, George, 82–83, 91, 132

capitalism: corporate, 237–38; distinction from market economy, 315n54; self-made man myth and, 263; slavery and, 183–84; Whig defense of, 203–4, 210–12. *See also* market economy

capitalists, 60, 61, 89, 129, 315n54. *See also* elites

Carey, Henry, 216, 234, 379n118, 380n137

Carnegie, Andrew, 255

Cass, Lewis, 69–70, 124

Catholicism. *See* Roman Catholicism

Chandler, Elizabeth, 181, 188, 368n181

Channing, William Ellery, 15, 164, 219, 235, 356n23

Cherokees, 24, 71, 73, 126, 319n104

Chevalier, Michel, 28, 113

Child, David Lee, 162–63, 181

Child, Lydia Maria, 176, 185

Christianity: civic virtue and, 90; disestablishment of church, 168, 358nn53–54; egalitarianism of, 161, 188; golden rule of, 170, 171; mission efforts among Native Americans, 250; perfectionism, 204, 229–30, 368n190; religious instruction of slaves, 176, 362n99; Roman Catholicism, 21, 231, 299–300n31. *See also* Protestantism

cities: growth of, 243; inhabitants of, 89–90; manufacturing in, 35, 60–61, 314n33

citizenship: of African Americans, 21, 24, 251, 283, 373n33, 385n29; Fourteenth Amendment and, 194, 244, 251, 385n29; gender and, 76; independence and, 39–40, 54, 72; republican, 67, 72

civic virtue, 37–38, 64, 65, 66–68, 88, 90, 91–92, 154–59, 223

civil rights, 177, 178–79, 196, 282, 385n29. *See also* rights; voting rights

Civil War, aftermath of, 194–95, 244, 245, 246–47, 264, 267

Claiborne, John, 117, 128

Clark, Christopher, 315n54

Clark, Daniel, 247, 255

Clark, Elizabeth B., 177, 252–53, 367–68n179

class hierarchy: absence of in America, 17, 27–28, 36, 203, 277; among whites, 301n46; in Britain, 103, 114; in colonial America, 41, 42; in Europe, 19, 20–21, 36, 113, 115, 261, 382n174; independence and, 39–42. *See also* egalitarianism; elites; inequality; middle class; social and economic mobility; working class

classical republicanism, 36–37, 83, 94, 304–5n12. *See also* neoclassical republicanism

Clay, Henry: American Colonization Society and, 178; American System of, 227; on corporations, 213; on free trade, 225; on land policy, 61; on mobility of settlers, 316n65; presidential campaign of (1824), 56; self-made man myth and, 371n10 (Part III); supporters of, 100; as Whig leader, 57, 209, 373n32

A NOTE ON THE TYPE

This book has been composed in Arno, an Old-style serif typeface in the classic Venetian tradition, designed by Robert Slimbach at Adobe.